# 'wrinkles' in Practical Navigation

Squire Thornton S. Lecky

REVISED AND ENLARGED EDITION.

# "WRINKLES"

IN

# PRACTICAL NAVIGATION.

BY

S. T. S. LECKY, MASTER MARINER.

LIEUT. R.N.R.

*Fellow of the Royal Astronomical Society,*
*Fellow of the Royal Geographical Society,*
*Associate of the Literary and Philosophical Society,*
*Member of the Science and Arts Association of Liverpool,*
*Extra Master. Passed in Steam, Compass Adjustment, &c.*
*Younger Brother of the Trinity House.*

*Author of "The Danger Angle and Off-Shore Distance Tables."*

WITH 80 ILLUSTRATIONS.

LONDON:
GEORGE PHILIP & SON, 32 FLEET STREET, E.C.
LIVERPOOL: CAXTON BUILDINGS, SOUTH JOHN STREET, AND ATLAS BUILDINGS,
49 & 51, SOUTH CASTLE STREET.
1884.

TO

SIR THOMAS BRASSEY, K.C.B., M.P.,

CIVIL LORD OF THE ADMIRALTY,

WHOSE WELL-KNOWN INTEREST IN THE SCIENCE OF NAVIGATION,
AS WELL AS PERSONAL COURAGE AND NAUTICAL SKILL,
WERE SO WELL ILLUSTRATED BY HIS

CIRCUMNAVIGATION OF THE GLOBE

IN COMMAND OF HIS OWN YACHT,

THIS VOLUME,

BY ONE WHO HAD THE PRIVILEGE OF A PLACE IN THE FAMOUS

"SUNBEAM,"

DURING A PORTION OF HER ADVENTUROUS VOYAGE,
IS RESPECTFULLY AND GRATEFULLY INSCRIBED.

# PREFACE.

THE particular aim of this treatise is to furnish seamen with thoroughly *practical* hints, such as are not found in the ordinary works on Navigation; or, if they do exist, are scattered through so many pages, and so smothered by their surroundings, as to require too much digging out—too many shells to be cracked before arriving at the kernel—a tedious process, which the practical mind recoils from: further, to indicate the shortest and most reliable methods, as well as the instruments and books necessary to enable the Navigator (amateur or professional) to conduct his vessel safely and expeditiously from port to port.

The various nautical instruments are treated of separately, their peculiarities explained, and the errors to which they are liable pointed out, with the best means of remedying them, or of compensating their effects.

The volume contains but little that is claimed as strictly original: it is based upon life-long observation, matter gleaned from the works of men of repute, and information derived from intercourse with shipmates and the cloth generally.

The mass of material at one's disposal renders its clear presentment within a moderate compass somewhat difficult, but great pains have been taken to select only the really essential problems, and, in view of those to whom the work is addressed, to choose the simplest possible language. If the style is thus more familiar than dignified, it is hoped that it may with greater success attract the ear, and rivet the understanding of the nautical reader, thereby awakening and sustaining such an interest in the subject as will be most likely to create mental impressions of a lasting kind. Diagrams accompany many of the examples by way of illustrating and giving prominence to some of the more "important simplicities" of navigation, which are unhappily too often disregarded by reason of their true significance not being understood and appreciated. To this end, also, a free use has been made of capitals, and certain words and sentences are rendered conspicuous by a change of type when it appears advantageous to do so.

If occasionally the reader of quick apprehension is irritated by too great minuteness, he must remember that as far as possible every imaginable question has to be anticipated, and that a single point left unexplained may render useless an otherwise careful description.

Every sailor knows what is meant by a "Wrinkle"; some possess more than others, and in penning the following pages the writer has endeavoured to display his to the best advantage, and place them "cut and dried" at the disposal of such members of the profession as have had a less varied experience than himself, and fewer facilities of acquiring an intimate knowledge of this branch of their business.

Methods have been selected which offer peculiar advantages in the matter of *brevity of solution.* To seamen this is very important, as all know; at the same time *accuracy of the results* has been kept in view, and care taken that the latter quality is not unduly sacrificed to the former.

Rigorous exactness of working—so necessary in the schoolroom—is but seldom required on board ship; it is, therefore, only introduced in the process of rating chronometers, and one or two other instances, where, from the nature of the question, one is absolutely *forced* to deal with minute arithmetical quantities. Very many problems of interest to the scientific Navigator, as well as the discussion of many refinements of correction and reduction—which, neat as they may be in theory, are of little practical value—have been purposely omitted. On the other hand, an endeavour has been made to avoid the slovenly "Rule of thumb," "Rough and ready" principle which has given rise to the saying—somewhat unjust to a good class of seamen—"it is near enough for a collier."

These and other characteristics, it is hoped, may commend the work to the notice and approval of the profession.

It must not be imagined that this book is written in any respect as a *direct* help to the Local Marine Board Examinations; there are plenty of excellent ones published for that express purpose. This has entirely to do, as its name indicates, with every-day navigation on board ship: the reader is supposed, indeed, to be in proud possession of his Master's certificate—if with blue seal so much the better; to have overcome the moonshine terrors of Decimal Arithmetic, and to have some slight knowledge of Plane Trigonometry. If, however, these pages should be read by one who has yet to undergo the ordeal of examination, the writer trusts that the introduction behind the scenes, and the knowledge of first principles thereby acquired, will teach him *to think for himself,* and be of service generally in enabling him to gain the coveted parchment.

To the daring yachtsman, ambitious of personally undertaking the conduct of his white-winged craft to distant parts of the world, and who has already acquired a certain groundwork of navigation, it is hoped that this Manual will present not a few advantages: it will be a sort of nautical finger-post at the junction of many devious paths, which will point out to him the safest way to his destination; and, whilst providing him with sound advice on most of the necessary points, will not distract his attention and waste his time on what, even to the professional, may be regarded as superfluous, or of questionable importance.

Under this last heading comes Marine Surveying—which is, consequently, excluded *in toto* as constituting a distinct study, and one which, in these exact days, can scarcely be said to come within the province of merchant seamen, whatever it may have done in times gone by. If, however, Marine Surveying should be taken up by anyone who has a natural taste for that sort of thing, with leisure and opportunity for indulging it, he should study such books as are devoted *exclusively* to it, since it is a subject more difficult than many at first would suppose. *

In one matter, more especially, the Author would crave the gracious forbearance of the Critic. He wishes it thoroughly understood that not in the least degree does he claim for his present venture what is known as "literary merit." A lad who, at twelve or thirteen, adopts the rough career of a sailor, when more fortunate ones of the same age are only just commencing their education, cannot reasonably be expected in after life to shine as a brilliant star in the literary firmament. It is scarcely consistent with the "eternal fitness of things" that he should. Our Gallic neighbours have a proverb which is in every way applicable—"Chacun son metier, et les vaches sont bien gardées;" which, when freely translated into the nautical language of Britain, reads thus—"The Gunner to his linstock, the Steersman to the wheel, and the Cook to the foresheet."

The book, therefore, is merely a friendly offer of help from one sailor to another—nothing more. Some readers, no doubt, will make it their proud boast that they "clambered in through the hawse-pipes," whilst others will have "entered by the cabin windows." To both the Author is not without hope his "Wrinkles" may prove acceptable, and that, like a "Handy-Billy" clapped

---

* About the most complete work is "Hydrographical Surveying," by Capt W Wharton, R.N. It was published by John Murray in 1882

on to the fall of a "Luff-tackle Purchase," the present book may assist the more powerful ones in pulling the Shipmaster through many of the navigational troubles by which he is often beset.

In conclusion, should Experts complain that they do not find anything novel in this volume, the writer would merely remind them that it was not his intention that they should. The book has been prepared for comparatively young members of the profession; and one of the leading objects has been to elucidate in plain English some of those important elementary principles which the *Savants* have enveloped in such a haze of mystery as to render pursuit hopeless to any but a skilled mathematician.

Comparatively few sailors are good mathematicians, and, in the writer's opinion, it is fortunate that such is the case; for Nature rarely combines the mathematical talent of a Cambridge wrangler with that practical tact, observation of outward things, and readiness on an emergency, so essential to a successful sea Captain, who, curiously enough, is always expected to be as many-sided as the "Admirable Crichton"—at once Sailor, Navigator, Parson, Lawyer, Doctor, and a host of things besides.

The Author has only to add that he has done his best to secure accuracy in the printing of the book, and trusts that few errors of moment will be found to have crept in. He will at all times be thankful to receive corrections and suggestions for the improvement of future editions.

SQUIRE THORNTON STRATFORD LECKY.

LIVERPOOL, *November 1881.*

# PREFACE TO THE SECOND EDITION.

---

SINCE launching "Wrinkles" with fear and trembling on the uncertain sea of public criticism, there has been quite a tropical deluge of approving letters, which could not but reassure even the most timid.

Coming as they have done from brother "Shells," both of the Navy and Merchant Service, and from eminent scientific men in both hemispheres, these tokens of appreciation carried with them the convincing assurance that in this, my first serious effort at authorship, the right nail had been successfully struck on the head. Nor has the Press, both at home and abroad, been backward in saying kindly things, so that in nearly every quarter I have reason to be grateful for the friendly reception accorded to my "first-born."

It is not to be wondered at, therefore, if I have felt impelled to put best foot foremost, and try if the work could not be brought still nearer the mark.

Wading laboriously through an unwieldy manuscript, and reading it afterwards in print, are two widely different things, and I must admit that an inspection of "Wrinkles" in its finished form did not bring with it the amount of satisfaction I had been looking forward to. It was impossible to ignore the fact that in not a few instances the cart had been placed before the horse, and what with this and other little shortcomings I was conscious of a somewhat lubberly "Lash-up." (This, dear reader, is in confidence).

Thus it comes about that although the critics—by way of encouragement, I suppose—have good-naturedly shut their eyes to the indifferent cooking of my literary "Sea pie," I personally felt dissatisfied, and, with a determination to reprint the book from start to finish, made a clean sweep by throwing the stereotype plates—not overboard exactly—but into the melting pot, which nearly amounts to the same thing.

This wholesale and very costly "clearing of the decks" enabled me—whilst leaving the plan of the work unchanged in its main features—to effect many desirable minor alterations, and to introduce nearly 100 pages of new matter. The regenerating process admitted also of the various subjects being brought up to date in accordance with our present knowledge; and the Nautical Almanac elements, necessary to work out the examples, have been added in the appendix.

The list of Time-signals for rating chronometers has been considerably enlarged, so as to embrace all those now in operation. The longitudes upon which the Signals depend are from the very latest determinations—principally telegraphic.

These improvements explain the bulkier appearance of "Wrinkles," and it is hoped will win for the book increased popularity and so recompense me for much "midnight oil."

The fortunate individuals who have not tried their hands at book-making can have but a faint idea of what such an undertaking involves, to say nothing of the pecuniary risk which attaches to it. For myself, I do not mind confessing that if I could have foreseen that "Wrinkles" would have cost even one tithe of the labour expended upon it, I never would have been so bold as to attempt its production; but in a weak moment the promise was made, and once fairly committed to the task there was nothing for it but to "wire in."

Encouraged by the support given to its predecessor, Edition No. 2 now goes forth asking well-wishers to "pass the word along," and so help to swell the lists of "The Faithful."

S. T. S. L.

NEYLAND HOUSE,
NEW MILFORD,
*January, 1884.*

# CONTENTS.

## PART I.

### CHAPTER I.

### NAUTICAL LIBRARY, AND INSTRUMENTS OF NAVIGATION.



### CHAPTER II.

### THE MARINER'S COMPASS, AND IMPORTANT FACTS CONNECTED WITH IT.

## Chapter III.

## THE MARINE CHRONOMETER.



## Chapter IV.

## THE SEXTANT.



## Chapter V.

## THE ARTIFICIAL AND SEA HORIZONS.

CHAPTER V.—*(continued).*



CHAPTER VI.

CHARTS.



CHAPTER VII.

THE PARALLEL RULER.



CHAPTER VIII.

DIVIDERS.



CHAPTER IX.

THE PELORUS, WITH REMARKS ON AZIMUTHS.

## CHAPTER XII.

### THE MARINE BINOCULAR AND TELESCOPE.



## CHAPTER XIII.

### SIR W. THOMSON'S NAVIGATIONAL INSTRUMENTS.



## CHAPTER XIV.

### THE MERCURIAL AND ANEROID BAROMETERS.



## CHAPTER XV.

### WEATHEROLOGY.

CHAPTER XV.—(*continued*).



CHAPTER XVI.

TIDES, CURRENTS, WAVES, AND BREAKERS.

## CHAPTER VI.

### TIME.



## CHAPTER VII.

### LATITUDE BY EX-MERIDIAN ALTITUDE OF A STAR.



## CHAPTER VIII.

### LONGITUDE BY CHRONOMETER.

CHAPTER VIII.—(*continued*).



CHAPTER IX.

"SUMNER LINES."

## CHAPTER X.

## DOUBLE ALTITUDES.

Pre-eminence given to Double Altitudes—Chartlet No. 3—Example of Double Altitudes—Astronomical cross bearings—How to manage when ship shifts her position between the first and second observation—Calculation better than Plotting—Calculation by Sumner's original method too tedious—Johnson's Double Altitude Problem the best—Johnson's Rules—Similarity of principle between Rosser's and Johnson's methods—Preference given to Johnson—Winter better than summer for Double Altitudes—Double Altitudes applicable to all heavenly bodies—Simultaneous Altitudes of stars preferable to Double Altitudes ... ... ... ... Page 318—327.

## CHAPTER XI.

## SIMULTANEOUS ALTITUDES.

How to ascertain position of a star at any given instant—Advantages of simultaneous star altitudes—Star Azimuths—Example of simultaneous altitudes of Sirius and Benetnasch—How to find Hour Angle when the regular table is not available—How to select stars for simultaneous altitudes—Examples for practice—"Cooking" ... ... ... Page 328—334.

## CHAPTER XII.

## COMPASS ADJUSTMENT.

The Earth a Magnet—Position of its Magnetic Poles—Magnetic Polarity distinguished by colour—First law in Magnetism—Variation of the Compass—Deviation of the Compass—Effect of Deviation on ship's course—Local Attraction—Compass useless when in the vicinity of Magnetic Pole—Magnetic Equator—Action of a freely suspended needle on the Magnetic Equator—Distinction between hard steel and soft iron—Experiments with a common kitchen poker and a boat's compass—"Line of Force"—"Dip"—Induced Magnetism—Percussion, its effect—Magnetic change produced in soft iron by geographical change of place—Effect of vertical iron on the compass—Action of vertical iron not dependent on direction of ship's head—Behaviour of horizontal iron—Action of horizontal iron dependent upon the angle it makes with the Magnetic Meridian—Horizontal iron produces same Deviation in all Latitudes—By one magnet an indefinite number can be made—"Saturation Point"—Permanent Magnets—Neutral Point—Interesting experiment—Sub-permanent Magnetism—Direction of ship's Sub-permanent Magnetic Poles—Diagrams—Stability of Sub-permanent Magnetism—Varying effect of Sub-permanent Magnetism—Duty of steel magnets when used for compass adjustment—Duty of vertical wrought-iron rods or pillars—Quadrantal Deviation—Necessity for magnetic analysis of an iron ship previous to adjustment—Tracing Semicircular Deviation to its true source—Cause of Deviation when ship's head is on the North or South points—Cause of Deviation when ship's head is on the East or West points—Knowledge conveyed by being acquainted with direction of ship's head when building—Quadrantal Correctors—How and where to place

CHAPTER XII.—(*continued*).

Magnets—Size of Magnets, and their proper distance from the card—How to place Quadrantal Correctors—How to place iron pillar—Preparations for adjusting—Draw chalk lines on deck—Set hack watch to Apparent Time at Ship—Make list of Sun's correct Magnetic Bearing for every four minutes, extending over a period of say three hours—See that Compass Lubber lines are truly fore-and-aft—How to use Friend's Pelorus—To adjust on North—Diagram—To adjust on East—Diagram—To adjust on N.E.—Rule as to placing Quadrantal Correctors—Magnetic effect of hollow iron—Semicircular and Quandrantal Deviation, why thus named—Variable effect on Compass Needle of Compensating Magnets—Variable effect of Quadrantal Correctors—Final corrections—Sea adjustment preferable to Dock adjustment—Caution as to steam-tenders and tug-boats—How to arrive at amount of Deviation to be. corrected by iron pillar—Effect of ship built head North—Effect of ship built head East—Diminished directive force, cause of sluggish Compasses—Practical example of difficult Compass adjustment—Iron mainmast a Magnet—Separating Inductive from Sub-permanent Magnetism—Diagram—Heeling error—Retentive Magnetism—Duration of Retentive Magnetism—Effect of Retentive Magnetism when course is changed—Tendency of ship to deviate towards last course—Effect of Retentive Magnetism on Compasses of vessels entering New York Bay or the River Delaware—Effect of Retentive Magnetism in Irish Channel—How to eliminate the effect of Retentive Magnetism when adjusting—Over compensation of Quadrantal Deviation occasionally an advantage—Facilities for adjustment of Eastern-going steamers—How to arrive at amount of Deviation due to vertical iron—Experiment with iron pillar—Magnetic effect of iron pillar, according to its distance from the Compass—Adjusting on North and South in the Suez Canal—Port Said—Compensation of Quadrantal Deviation not interfered with by Retentive Magnetism—How to determine amount of Quadrantal Deviation—Quadrantal more embarrassing to the navigator than Semi-circular Deviation—Heeling Error—Compensation effected by means of "Dipping Needle"—Adjustment of Heeling Error only good for the Magnetic latitude in which it is made—Advantages accruing from compensation of the Heeling Error—Heeling Diagrams—Result of improper and imperfect Compensation—How to keep spare Magnets—Advisability of determining the natural errors before adjusting—Comparative uselessness of Deviation Cards—Names of Ports on or near the Magnetic Equator—Adjusting by bearing of a distant object—How to obtain the Astronomical true bearing of a distant object—Simple rule, easy to remember—Facilities for Compass Adjustment at Arica and Peru—List of Correct Magnetic Bearings of mountain peaks visible from the anchorage—Plymouth, special buoys provided for swinging Government ships—Correct Magnetic Bearing of Sheepstor—Observations unreliable when ship swings rapidly—River Mersey, Vauxhall Chimney—Deviation of wooden vessels sometimes marked on the points of the Compass Card itself—Transit bearings of shore marks—How to name the Deviation—List of useful Transit marks—Adjustment by bearing of one distant object—Transit Bearings in Belfast Lough—Compasses unaccountably jumping a point or two—Supposed causes—Probable causes—Wheelhouse lockers—

CHAPTER XII.—(*continued*).

Deviation Cards unreliable—Useful form of Compass Record—"Total Error"—Modes of finding Deviation from an Azimuth—Explanation of Compass Record here suggested—Valuable Paper on the Earth's Magnetism—Barrett's Deviation Diagram—Sir George Airey, late Astronomer-Royal, on the advantages of having the Compasses of an Iron Ship Adjusted.
Page 335—382.

CHAPTER XIII.

TO FIND THE ERROR AND RATE OF A CHRONOMETER.

Equal Altitudes not recommended for this purpose—Their disadvantages enumerated—Personal Equation—How to eliminate errors of observation—Reversal of Artificial Horizon—Chronometer Rating in Suez Canal—Principle of getting the correct Greenwich Mean Time by Astronomical observations on shore—List of positions in the Suez Canal—Original error, and accumulated rate—Rating Chronometers by sights at sea—Latitude and Longitude of St. Paul's Rocks, and Cape Agulhas Lighthouse—Interval between observations necessary to get rate—Rating by Transit of Star—Example of Rating by Transit of Star—To find the error of a Chronometer by observations of Stars East and West of the Meridian—When a number of observations are taken, they should be worked out separately—Time-signals—Flash and report of Time-gun—Velocity of sound in air—List of places where Time-signals are made ... ... ... Page 383—400

CHAPTER XIV.

SHAPING THE COURSE.

Course now usually set in degrees, instead of the nearest quarter point—The True Course—The Correct Magnetic Course—The Compass Course—Plus and Minus Signs, when prefixed to Variation or Deviation, used to express their name—Magnetic Chart of the World—Annual change in the Variation—Liability to change of Correct Magnetic bearings—Tables of Channel Courses, require revision from time to time—Periodical change of course, to allow for Geographical change of Variation—Retentive Magnetism the possible cause of Wreck—"Critical Points"—Difficulty of steering by a badly placed Compass—Great Circle Sailing—The only straight lines on a Mercator's Chart which represents Arcs of Great Circles—How to depict a Great Circle on the Globe—To prove that the Arc of a Great Circle is the shortest distance between the places which it joins—The true Course on a Great Circle is constantly changing—True Course on Mercator's Chart is the same throughout—Windward Great Circle Sailing—Example taken from Bergen's Epitome shewing the advantages of Great Circle Sailing—Certain occasional advantages—Bergen's Great Circle Charts—Track on Polar side of Great Circle—Why the initial courses of the Great Circle track are dissimilar—Mercator's Charts do not shew objects in their true relative positions—Current Sailing—Leeway and Heave of the Sea—Expediency of keeping a Steamer away in strong head-wind—Duncan's Triangular Sailing—Diagram and Example ... ... .. ... ... Page 401—418.

## CHAPTER XV.

## THE DANGER ANGLE, AND CORRECT DETERMINATION OF DISTANCE FROM LAND.

Acquaintance with height of the eye useful in estimating distance—Distance of the Visible Horizon—Distance from Beacon Lights—Table of Distances by Alan Stevenson—Elevation of Beacon Lights measured from High-water Level—Necessity for checking Light Ranges by the Distance Table—Visibility of Lights unduly increased by Abnormal refraction—One Bearing and a Horizontal Angle give a better "fix" than Cross Bearings—On first seeing a light, to know distance ship will pass from it—Utility of Sir W. Thomson's Azimuth Mirror—Distance by Four-point Bearing—Diagrams—Method used when light is not seen till nearly abeam—"Rake of the eye"—"Fix" by Vertical Angle and Compass Bearing—Arc of Excess—"On and off" measurements—Becher's Tables of Masthead Angles—Lecky's Off-shore Distance Tables—Precautions to be observed in the measurement of Vertical Angles—Diagrams—Distinction between Water-line and Horizon—"Fix" by two Vertical Angles—Diagram—The Danger Angle—Vertical Danger Angle—Horizontal Danger Angle—Ease with which, by means of Danger Angle, the River Tagus can be entered—Diagrams shewing that a circle can be drawn to pass through any three given points not situated in the same straight line—Best way to take accurate Cross Bearings.
Page 419—437.

## CHAPTER XVI.

## THE COMPOSITION AND RESOLUTION OF FORCES AND MOTIONS.

Knowledge of this subject very important to seamen—Motion and Force—A single Force, how represented on paper—Parallelogram of Forces and Velocities—Given one angle in a Parallelogram, to find the remaining three—Example of Composition of Motions—Diagram shewing true and apparent direction of the Wind—Resolution of forces—Diagram shewing how the strain on a mast or span can be calculated—Calculation of strains in any direction ... ... ... ... ... ... ... Page 438—444

## CHAPTER XVII.

## ALGEBRA.

Algebraic Addition—Subtraction—Multiplication—Division...Page 445—446

## APPENDIX A.



## APPENDIX B.



## APPENDIX C.



## APPENDIX D.



## NAUTICAL ALMANAC ELEMENTS.

# PART I.

## CHAPTER I.

### NAUTICAL LIBRARY, AND INSTRUMENTS OF NAVIGATION.

THERE are so many works on Navigation that any one so disposed might easily convert his cabin into a book closet, leaving no room to stow away himself and wardrobe. As such a wholesale procedure would be neither convenient nor profitable, one is constrained to make a selection. The following list is confidently recommended as embracing all that are necessary; and the purchaser should make sure that he gets the *latest editions*. They can be readily procured from or through any publisher of nautical works:—

Necessary books.

1. The Epitome the reader is most accustomed to use—generally Norie's or Bergen's.
2. Raper's Practice of Navigation.
3. Towson's Ex-meridian Tables.
*4. Merrifield's Magnetism and Deviation of the Compass.
*5. Towson's Deviation of the Compass, for Masters and Mates.
*6. Evan's Elementary Manual for Deviations of the Compass.
7. Burdwood's Azimuth Tables, from 60° to 30° of latitude in both Hemispheres ("Red Book").
8. Davis's Azimuth Tables, from 30° of latitude to the Equator in both Hemispheres ("Red Book").
9. Johnson on Finding the Latitude and Longitude in Cloudy Weather.
10. Galbraith and Haughton's Manual of the Tides.
11. Weather Warnings for Watchers, by the "Clerk" himself.
12. Aids to the Study and Forecast of Weather. By W. Clement Ley, M.A.
13. Admiralty Tide Tables for current year.

A

14. Imray's Lights and Tides of the World, or Findlay's Lighthouses and Fog Signals.
15. Gray's Rule of the Road.
16. Nautical Almanac for current and following year.

The Wind and Current Charts emanating from the Meteorological Office, and Sailing Directories for the parts intended to be navigated. Among these may be mentioned as worthy of special commendation:—

Findlay's North and South Atlantic.
" " " Pacific.
" Indian Ocean.
Imray's North Pacific.
" Indian Ocean.

The above list only comprises books which may be considered absolutely essential to safe navigation in the present day, when the question of speed enters so largely into the calculation. Their cost would amount to about £10—no very great expenditure when considered in connection with a shipmaster's responsibilities; indeed, the addition of a few other interesting volumes may suggest itself to some, who should then procure—

Cost of books.

Extra books.

1. The Admiralty Manual of Scientific Enquiry.
2. Buchan's Introductory Text Book of Meteorology.
3. Bedford's Sailor's Pocket Book.
4. Ansted's Physical Geography.
5. Astronomy, by Sir John Herschel.
6. The 10 volumes of Chambers' Encyclopedia.
7. The Geography of the Oceans. By. J. F. Williams.
8. Tinmouth on Points of Seamanship.

Nautical Magazine.

To complete his stock-in-trade, every navigator should take the monthly numbers of the *Nautical Magazine*. Not only do they afford light and agreeable reading for leisure moments, but they contain important notices relating to alterations and additions in buoyage and lights, discovery of new dangers, fresh laws affecting shipping, alterations in those now existing, publication of latest Admiralty Charts, and other items interesting to the intelligent seaman.

## NAUTICAL INSTRUMENTS.

List of instruments.

To the master of any vessel, other than a mere coaster, the following nautical instruments are indispensable:—Compasses, chronometers, sextant, artificial horizon, night glasses, telescope, common or patent log, hand and deep-sea leads, parallel rulers, dividers and charts, pelorus, barometer or aneroid—the latter for preference. In addition to these, there is one valuable instrument called a STATION POINTER, which is seldom or never met with on board a merchant ship, and is particularly useful in vessels frequenting narrow waters and intricate channels. Steamers trading to the Baltic, Black Sea, East Indies and China, should certainly be furnished with it.

**Station Pointer.**

It is proposed to treat of the above instruments separately, devoting a chapter to each.

---

## CHAPTER II.

### THE MARINER'S COMPASS, AND IMPORTANT FACTS CONNECTED WITH IT.

Apathy of builders

Curiously enough, until quite recently ship-builders and owners did not bestow on the compass the amount of consideration which it undoubtedly merits. It is *pre-eminently* the instrument upon which the safety of the vessel depends, and it justly ranks *first* in importance. It would be easier to dispense with the Chronometer, or even the Sextant, than with this invaluable guide. With a faulty compass a straight course cannot be made. Formerly, when time was less an object than it is now, a bad landfall, or distance lost on the voyage through zigzagging over the ocean, was of no particular moment; but in these days of keen competition, when the public look for the arrival of Trans-Atlantic and other mail steamers almost to the very hour, and the rival companies wage paper wars over the splitting of minutes in the passages of their respective vessels, it is necessary that *good navigating appliances* should back up *good ships*.

Rivalry in making passages.

Standard Compass.

Compasses for use on board ship are of two classes—the Standard and the Steering Compass. Taking them in this order, the Standard first claims the reader's attention.

Placing of Standard Compass.

To begin then, it is of the *greatest importance* that a spot should be selected for the Standard compass where it would only be acted upon *by the general magnetic character of the ship, and not by particular masses of iron in its immediate vicinity.* To this some builders pay considerable attention, whilst others, unfortunately, seem unaware of the necessity for such a precaution, taking it for granted that the compass adjuster can effect his object, quite irrespective of how the compass may be fenced in with iron.

Position important.

The Standard may not inaptly be termed the "Navigating compass." By it the course should be set, and all bearings taken for ascertaining the ship's position. To this end, it must be placed where an *all-round* view of the horizon can be had, excepting, of course, when the masts or funnel intervene. In some few vessels of the larger class a special platform is erected, and in such cases the handrails and supports are of wood or brass. Unless, however, the whole structure is firmly and securely bolted down to the hull of the ship, it will be certain to vibrate in strong winds, or with much motion, and so destroy the steadiness of the card, rendering almost useless what may otherwise be a good compass.

**Box Binnacle.** The binnacle should be large enough and of such a shape as would permit of the adjusting magnets being placed *inside* it, instead of on the deck. This is a neat and compact arrangement, and access to the interior can be had through a small door provided with *a good patent lock and key.* To prevent tampering with the magnets, or the inside being made use of by quarter-masters as a handy stow-hole for odds and ends, this door should be religiously kept locked, and the key in the possession of the captain.

**Sir W. Thomson's Binnacle.** Sir W. Thomson's Binnacle is so arranged, and one of the great advantages of his plan is that when it becomes necessary to remove the binnacle for any purpose—such as calking decks, &c., there is no occasion to disturb the magnets; whereas when they are nailed to the deck round about the binnacle, it will sometimes happen that they are taken up by calkers ignorant of the mischief they are doing; and when replaced—as likely as not the magnets are shifted end for end, and put down at a greater or less distance from the compass than they occupied previously.

**Danger from proximity of iron.** When the Standard compass is improperly situated—as, for example, on a narrow bridge, hemmed in by iron hand-rails, flanked by boats' davits, awning stanchions, ridge chains, stokehole ventilators of large size with *moveable cowls,* and probably not two feet from the iron stand of the engine-room telegraph, or twice that distance from the donkey boiler,—it is rather too much to expect that its behaviour will be satisfactory. No adjuster in the world could even *pretend* to compensate the errors of such a compass. He might certainly manage, by a liberal use of magnets, to lick it into something like shape for the time being; but such an adjustment could not be depended upon for twelve hours after it was effected, and on a voyage to the southward the deviations would soon become so large as to be unmanageable.

**Large errors before compensation.**

Compasses are not unfrequently so badly placed that the adjuster has to compensate errors amounting to eleven or twelve points.

The reader may imagine that the foregoing is an overdrawn picture, but if he will take the trouble to look around, he will not be long in finding how true its description is. Sometimes, too, it occurs in steamers that the end of a trysail-boom, when guyed amidships, comes within 18 inches or less of the compass. In this case, if the foot of the sail should be made to haul out with a traveller, on a massive iron jackstay—a very common mode of fitting now-a-days—it is clear the effect on the needle will entirely depend on the position of the boom, whether eased off to port or starboard, topped-up, or in the crutch.

The writer was in one vessel where the *wire* toppinglifts of the main-boom came down within six feet or so of the standard compass, and were proved to produce an effect of 5° when the boom was guyed over from one side to the other. Precaution, then, should be taken, that no iron *subject to temporary removal*, be within ten or twelve feet of the compass; and the latter should stand at least 4 feet 6 inches above the deck, not only on account of the beams, but to avoid the possibility of being influenced by any moveable article of iron *on the deck next below it*.

**Height of compass above deck.**

It is common enough, where the vessel is steered forward, to find a compass placed on the bridge just above the one in the wheelhouse.* In such cases it is imperative that the upper or bridge binnacle should be raised above the deck as much as possible, or the compensating magnets contained within it will affect the other compass in the wheelhouse, and *vice versâ*. If raising the binnacle on a wooden stool or solid block should render it inconveniently high, it is not a killing matter to build a suitable step—or even a couple of them—round about its base. The reciprocal action of one compass and its magnets upon another—more particularly in the position here referred to—is a thing very likely to be overlooked from the mere fact of the compasses not both being seen at one and the same time.

**One compass affecting another.**

**Fitting out new ship.**

When fitting out a new ship, it is not uncommon for the builder to consult the wishes of the future captain in the matter of compasses, &c.; if, however, the latter does not join the vessel till she is nearly finished and ready for delivery, it will be too late to expect much in the way of alteration, as builders, at all times

* See diagram facing page 20.

averse to it, are particularly so when they are just about to make the vessel over to her owners. But there is no reason why the captain, if dissatisfied with the existing arrangements, should not *himself* endeavour to remedy them in the course of some subsequent voyage. It is an easy matter with a spare compass to make trial of various places about the decks, until one is hit upon comparatively free from the influence of the ship's iron, and *there* the standard should be rigged up, even if other less important matters have to give way for it.

**Alterations in position.**

It is well to know also that in every vessel there is a "neutral spot" where a compass would have little or no deviation; but, unfortunately, it may be found to exist in an impracticable position. Nevertheless it is worth looking for. There is only one caution necessary—before finally screwing down the binnacle in the newly found neutral spot, be sure that it is *really* so by testing the deviation on two adjacent cardinal points, such as north and east, as it may happen that a place has been hit upon where the compass will be tolerably correct on one point and very much out on another. It is questionable, however, whether this neutral spot would deserve the name in all latitudes.

**Neutral spot of ship.**

The writer is led to the above remarks by having noticed that the Standard compass of ships several years old had been allowed to remain from the commencement in most unsuitable positions, as if their captains considered, that once placed, there they should for ever remain.

The following is a description of a Standard or Navigating compass—honest and simple—which has stood the test of several years' trial, and been found to fulfil all the desirable conditions in a fair degree :—

In point of size it is a compromise between the justly lauded Admiralty Standard compass and the gigantic ones which, until recently, were in use on board of some of the Atlantic Mail Steamers. In the attempt to gain steadiness, and secure large marginal divisions to steer by, the cards of these last-mentioned compasses sometimes attained the amazing diameter of 18 in. and 20 in. The card about to be described has a diameter of 11 in., and is mounted similarly to the Admiralty one, on two pairs of needles, respectively $8\frac{1}{4}$ and 6 inches in length, by half an inch in depth, and $\frac{1}{16}$ of an inch in thickness. The longer pair occupy the central position, the ends of each being 15° from the north and south line, whilst the outer, or short needles, are each 45°

**Lecky's Radial Line Card.**

from the same point, after the manner represented in Diagram No. 1. The needles, as will be seen, are secured to the card on

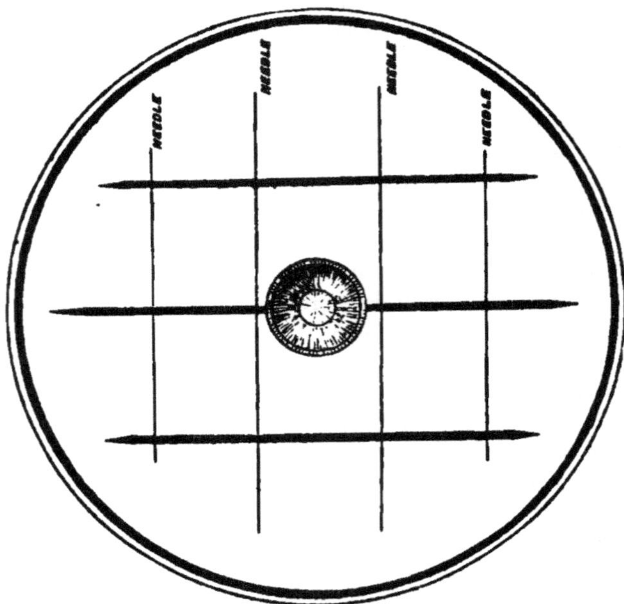


*Diagram 1.*

their edges in the usual way, are parallel to each other, and equidistant. By this arrangement *the advantages of a large card* are secured without *the drawback of long needles*, which are objectionable for many reasons: the principal being that they are opposed to a perfect compensation of the compass by magnets, and that there is no practical gain of directive power, the latter being more than counterbalanced by the friction on the point of support, resulting from the increased weight. It follows from this last, that in all compasses the needles should be very thin, and the brass or aluminium carriers as light as possible.

**Short needles and large card.**

It may be laid down as a fundamental principle that *the smaller the needles, the more correctly they point; and the larger a card the more accurately it is read.* When very large needles are used, *sluggishness* results, which the unwary navigator is too apt to mistake for *steadiness*.

Who has not seen a piece of marline or spun-yarn made fast to the compass bowl, and occasionally twitched by the man at the wheel to "keep the card alive," or, as it is sometimes termed in Jack's phraseology, "to keep the compass afloat." Independent of long needles, there are many causes to which this state of affairs can be traced, and they will be referred to further on.

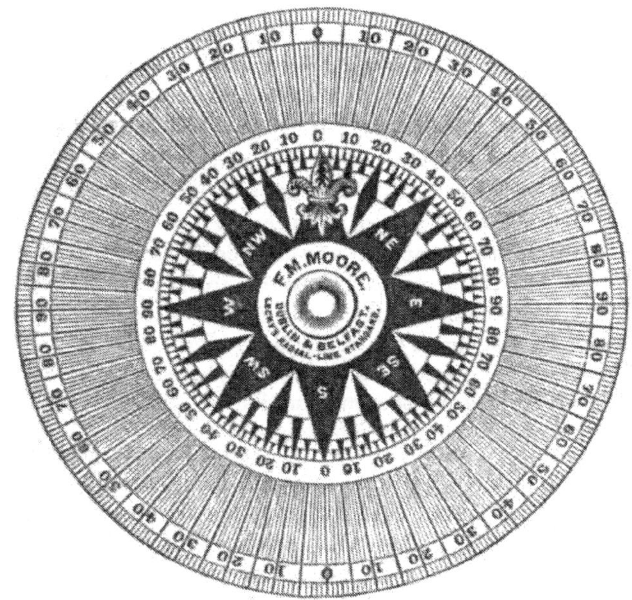


*Diagram 2.*

It will be noticed, by reference to above diagram, that the upper surface of the card is of novel pattern. The outer rim is divided by radial lines into single degrees, every fifth and tenth being, for sake of clearness, marked stronger than the others. Now that the course—on board steamships at least—is very commonly set in degrees, this, which might otherwise be considered an objection, is no longer one. Each quadrant is numbered by tens, from zero at north and south, up to 90° at east and west. The diameter of the central space, representing the usual points and half points, is 6·35 inches, and the length of the Stile or Shadow-pin mounted on the centre of the card is so proportioned (3·75 inches), that when the sun attains a greater elevation than 50°, its shadow will fall *within* the before-mentioned radial lines —showing at once, without reference to anything else, that the altitude is no longer favourable for observing azimuths. In this respect the compass is self-indicating.

**In steamships the course should be set in degrees.**

**Lecky's card self-indicating.**

It is true that bearings of the heavenly bodies may be taken with other instruments up to altitudes of even 60° or upwards; but to get a *correct* azimuth, when the body observed is so near the zenith, necessitates a much more refined instrument than the ordinary ship's compass.

As a rule, *except under great pressure*, azimuths should not be taken at a higher altitude than 30°; in fact, the nearer to the horizon the better.

To continue the description of this form of Standard compass,—the glass cover of the bowl is of a curved form, struck with a radius of 6·5 inches, to allow room underneath for the play of the Shadow-pin; and the bowl, of stout copper, is suspended by six strong india rubber supporters to an additional or inner brass ring. This last arrangement, now in tolerably common use, diminishes the shocks which would otherwise be communicated to the card by the jar of the engines and propeller, and by the pitching of the vessel in a heavy head-sea. These may be lessened still further by the introduction of a small spiral spring into the socket for the pivot which sustains the card.

**Essentials of a good compass**

In a *well made* compass, let the particular form be what it may, the *essentials* are—that the pivot should be accurately centred in the bowl; that is to say, that its point should be exactly in the intersection of the two diameters, passing through the centres of the gimbals, and in the same horizontal plane; the *upper* edges of the needles should also lie in the same horizontal plane, or, *if anything*, an eighth of an inch lower. To avoid distortion from shrinking, the card should be mounted on its mica base *before printing*, otherwise the graduation of the marginal divisions is likely to be in error. The shadow-pin should not only be straight, but accurately centred on the card, and the general balance of the instrument so well preserved that the shadow-pin will stand truly vertical under all circumstances.

The compass should be *sensitive* in *smooth*, and *steady* in *rough* water.

The bowl, if inclined to list one way or the other, can be made to hang horizontally by neatly serving the gimbal-ring with lead wire; and in case the card itself should be a little out, some melted sealing wax sparingly dropped on the under side will speedily restore its balance. The card, when poised on its support, should not be more than ¾ of an inch below the upper edge of the bowl where the latter meets the glass cover, otherwise the sun would require to have considerable elevation before its shadow could strike down on it. Moreover, the higher the level of the card, the easier it is to take bearings directly by the eye. The pivot should have a fine point of hard steel or iridium, ground to fit the sapphire cap, and the magnetic axes of the needles must be strictly parallel to the north and south points of the card.

**Reasons for mounting needles on edge.**

Before going further, it may be as well briefly to explain one of the reasons why in modern compasses the needles are secured to the card on their edges, instead of on their flats, as formerly. As just stated, it is necessary, for obvious reasons, that the *magnetic* axes of the needles should be parallel to the meridian line of the card. Now, when needles or steel bars are magnetized, it sometimes happens that the poles do not lie exactly in the *axis of the figure*, but obliquely to it, *vide* diagram; in which case, if mounted on their flats, the above condition could not be

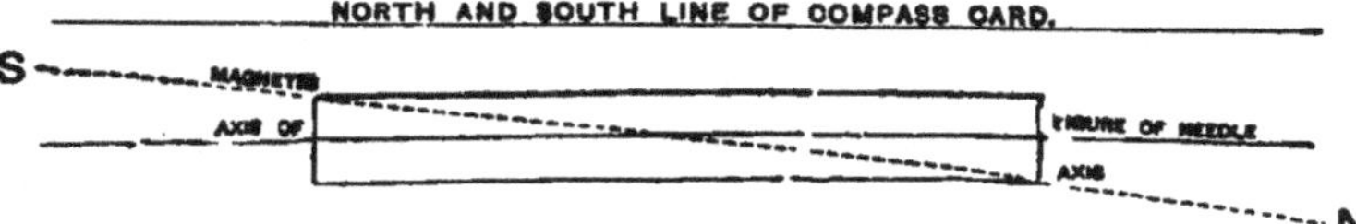


conveniently fulfilled, but by mounting the needles on their edges it can.

If the foregoing points are conscientiously attended to in the manufacture of the instrument, it will be found to give good results, and prove itself steady in a seaway. This latter quality may be still further ensured by attaching a flat circular band of brass to the *margin* of the card, on its under side, something after the fashion of the fly-wheel; its effect is to reduce the vibrational period of the needles by throwing the weight to the outer edge, and in this manner it is a most valuable auxiliary in conferring steadiness on the card. The dimensions of the brass ring are, $\frac{3}{16}$ of an inch in width on the flat, and $\frac{1}{16}$ of an inch in thickness. Sir William Thomson has ingeniously availed himself of this principle in his patent Standard compass, which has proved such a wonderful success.

**Use of brass rim to card.**

With the compass described above, azimuths of the sun or moon can readily be taken by simply watching where the shadow falls on the radial lines of the card. If partially veiled by clouds, so as to cast no shadow, a little practice will enable anyone to take a direct eye-bearing of the sun (if not too high) with a probable error of less than a degree. Bearings of objects on the horizon, such as ships, land, or lights, can be obtained with the utmost accuracy, by getting the Shadow-pin, margin of the card, and object in the same straight line. The writer and his officers have over and over again observed azimuths of stars —taking 3 or 4 on widely different bearings as a check. When worked out, the results generally corresponded within a degree, and never exceeded two degrees, even when the vessel had considerable motion.

**Taking azimuths and bearings.**

See that the compass has not lateral end-play in the gimbals, which would jar the card, and cause it to oscillate every time the ship rolled. If the gimbals do not fit close up to the sides, insert a small piece of soft wood, but do not jam them or impede their action.

See also that the freedom of the card is not interfered with by its edges touching the bowl; this sometimes happens with a too-neat-fitting card when expanded by damp. Test it by spinning the card on its supporting pivot.

**Stile or Shadow-pin.**

In taking azimuths by the shadow of the sun or moon, the extreme convenience of the Stile is at once demonstrated. The reading on the card can easily be made to half a degree, even less. There is no stooping or manipulating of a refractory azimuth-ring and speculum, the use of which, when the bearing happens to be on the beam, is rendered additionally awkward in compasses fitted with chain boxes; nor does one's nose get smeared with any oil and brickdust that may be left on the brasswork by a careless quartermaster or lamp-trimmer.

In swinging ship for a deviation table, there is nothing to do but stand still, with book and pencil in hand, and, as the ship is steadied on the required point, note the reading of the shadow simultaneously with the hour and minute by watch, previously set to Apparent Time at Ship. In fact the observer is master of the situation without an effort. With this compass, swinging the ship completely round, steadying her on every other point, should not occupy more than 20 or 25 minutes.

**Best arrangement of Shadow-pin.**

Many compasses are fitted with a Shadow-pin, to ship in a socket on the glass cover; but there are several serious objections to this arrangement. The pin, from its exposed position, is continually getting bent; if removable, it gets lost; if left on, and the binnacle top be hurriedly shipped or unshipped, it is apt to get a knock, which will probably break the glass, and cause no end of inconvenience.

Again, it is seldom that the Shadow-pin is stepped exactly in the same vertical line as the centre of the card, which ought *strictly* to be the case if a correct result is looked for; the sun has to attain quite a considerable altitude before the shadow can possibly fall on the card; and finally, from the motion of the bowl and the card not being always coincident, the shadow on the latter ranges about much more than it need do.

On the other hand, when the Shadow-pin is mounted on the card itself, it does not suffer by handling; if made straight, it will remain so; it is protected from injury; it is more easily centred; and from its curved shape the glass cover is stronger.

The correctness of *all* the various instruments used for taking azimuths depends, in the first place, upon their parts preserving either a true horizontal or vertical position, so that, if the objection be made to a Shadow-pin on the card that it may not always stand truly vertical, it must not be forgotten that it applies with equal, if not greater, force to all the other modes of observing: and it is this liability of instruments to deviate from their proper position, whether vertical or horizontal, that makes it advisable to take azimuths at low altitudes, whereby any errors due to this cause are reduced to a minimum.

Balance of card.

To test the balance of the card is a simple matter. First of all unship it and assure yourself that the shadow-pin stands exactly at right angles to its surface; this can be done with an ordinary set-square. Next, replace the card and put on the glass cover; then, standing at a convenient distance from the binnacle, and the helmet or top being removed, stoop sufficiently to make the shadow-pin appear to grow out of the sea horizon beyond. A good eye will now have no difficulty in judging whether or not the pin is at right angles to the true horizontal line.

But this is only half of the test, since, though the pin may be all right when looked at from one point of view, it may be very much out from another: therefore examine it a second time in a direction eight points to the right or left of the former one, and if the pin still continues upright, its verticality on all other points is definitely established. Thus if the ship should be steering west, and you make the first trial along the N.W. point of the compass, the second trial should be made either along the N.E. or S.W. point.

Sealing-wax as a counterpoise.

If, however, the pin should be found inclined to one side or the other, note carefully the direction of its inclination, and having unshipped the card, drop a little melted sealing-wax on the under and opposite side, close out to the edge. Replace the card, examine it afresh, and repeat the dose until the result is satisfactory. It is best to do this on a smooth day, when the ship is upright and steady.

If the card should get overloaded with sealing-wax, it is easy to chip it off when hard.

The compass just described was contrived by the writer, and is a comparatively cheap and thoroughly useful form of Standard. It is unpatented, and can therefore be made by any optician, and, to avoid the expense of a fresh plate, mounted impressions of the card can be had through the post for a few pence from F. M. Moore, 102, High Street, Belfast, who has constructed compasses on this pattern.

**Sir W. Thomson's Patent Compass.**

When the owner's pocket can afford it, however, there is no Standard compass which in any way can rival the one invented and patented by Sir Wm. Thomson, of Glasgow. Its mechanical construction is as near perfection as may be; and looking at it either theoretically or practically, it has advantages which no other known compass possesses.

Unfortunately there is considerable misapprehension abroad as to this compass; the writer has heard men, who ought to have known better, say, "Oh! it is too complicated for ordinary folks." Now there could not be a greater mistake than this. The entire arrangement is beautiful in its extreme simplicity, and there is absolutely nothing to get out of order.

"The proof of the pudding is in the eating of it," and five years' experience of Sir William's compass in all weathers and climates has convinced the writer that it is no more liable to a mishap than any other kind—perhaps not so much, whilst the facilities for adjusting it stand unrivalled. We next come to

## THE STEERING COMPASS.

**Spirit Compass.**

Among the best is one in which the *card* is *almost* floated in diluted spirits of wine.* The bowl is, of course, hermetically sealed, to prevent the escape of the spirit; and in the better descriptions there is a compensatory arrangement, which permits, without injury to the several parts, the expansion and contraction consequent on change of temperature.

**Advantages of Spirit Compass.**

The objects of this form of compass are, first, to diminish the friction due to the weight of the card on the pivot, thereby

* Pure alcohol—familiarly known as spirits of wine—is preferable to water, or any other liquid, on account of its not freezing even at very low temperatures.

materially increasing its sensitiveness, and secondly, to render the compass steady in heavy weather, or when placed in positions where there is much tremor arising from machinery or otherwise. The flotation power of the card is so adjusted that, though the latter is several ounces in weight, its pressure on the point of support does not exceed 15 or 20 grains. The bowl should be so completely filled by the spirit as to leave no air-bubble. If one should at any time appear, the bowl must be unshipped and turned upside down, to permit of the deficiency being made good through the proper filling hole, which is then closed by a screw-cap and washer. *On no account must the glass cover ever be started.*

**Flotation power.**

There is only one other caution necessary in the use of liquid compasses. In tropical climates they should be carefully shielded from the rays of the sun, which, if permitted to beat upon them, would turn the card a dirty yellow, and eventually, a brown color; besides risking the breakage of the glass top, owing to excessive expansion of the spirit. From neglect of this simple precaution the writer has seen several liquid compasses come to grief most unexpectedly, causing much annoyance during the rest of the passage, and expense at the end of it. This is the only kind of compass which is suitable for boat work; in all other descriptions the card swings so much as to be useless.*

**Protection from strong sun.**

**Boat compass.**

An erroneous idea sometimes prevails, that, in an iron vessel such a compass is less affected than those of the common pattern. This is really not the case, nor do the makers wish to convey such an idea. As explained above, a card, when *nearly* afloat, is much more sensitive and obedient to the earth's directive force than the same one would be if suffered to rest its whole weight on the sustaining pivot, and that is all. The writer cannot here do better than quote Mr. Towson's remarks on this subject. He says, on page 122, in his work entitled "Practical Information on the Deviation of the Compass for the use of Masters and Mates":—

"In connexion with compass deviations, many practical men have vainly attempted to discover some substance or medium that would insulate the needle from the influence of the magnetism of the ship's iron. Many imagined discoveries of this character have been patented, and have served both to waste the time and money of the patentees, and to distract the attention of the mariner from

**Impossible to intercept magnetism.**

* In the best liquid compasses the card is of hard enamel, which permits of pure spirits of wine being used without discoloration, and renders freezing impossible. These points can never be gained in the ordinary painted card.

that class of study which alone can promote his safety in navigating an iron ship. It may be stated with confidence that there is no available medium that can intercept magnetic influence. For two centuries, at least, every class of bodies has been submitted to experiment, in order to discover a material capable of intercepting the influence of one magnet on another, not for the purpose of preventing deviation, but because the mechanic clearly perceives that if such a material were discovered, a motive power could be produced by various arrangements of permanent magnets and insulating bodies. But no one has succeeded in making this discovery. Should, however, the efforts, which for centuries have been unsuccessful, be realized, although a new motive power would thereby be available, it would be altogether valueless in connexion with the compasses of iron ships. The magnetism of the earth generally, the loadstone, soft iron, hard steel, or the electro-magnet, is all of the same nature. If we shut off one, we shut off all.

"If, therefore, we could succeed in insulating the needle from the magnetism of the ship, we should by the same means intercept the magnetism of the earth, and thus the compass would be rendered absolutely useless. In the first place, then, the object sought for is not available; and, secondly, if such a medium did exist, it would be entirely valueless in connexion with the compasses of iron ships."

**Popular errors as to causes of deviation.**

There is an ill-founded opinion prevalent among certain pilots and seamen that the compass is affected by fog; by certain strong winds of long duration; by the proximity of the vessel's keel to the bottom, in the shallow waters of rivers and estuaries, such as the Rio de la Plata; and by the phenomenon known as the *Aurora Borealis* and *Australis*. The sooner such notions are abandoned the better for the navigator, as they divert his mind from the *true* source of error. The first three causes do not affect the compass in the *slightest* degree, and any disturbance due to the latter can only be detected by the delicately suspended needles in an observatory ashore, where an unusual deflection of the sixth of a degree is considered a big thing.

If, therefore, under conditions such as those just alluded to, an unexpected amount of deviation should be found, the navigator must unhesitatingly reject the fog theory, &c., and endeavour to trace the error of his compass to its *real* cause.

Again, it can confidently be asserted that thunderstorms produce no effect whatever on the compass, unless, indeed, the ship's hull should actually be damaged by lightning—which, common though it be in the case of *wooden* vessels, appears to be impossible with *iron* ones, as there is no instance on record of such a thing having happened, though there are numerous instances of their masts—when not of iron—having been rent and shattered like match-wood. Iron is a good conductor, but water is still better; the iron ship, therefore, when struck by lightning, gives the electric fluid a free and speedy passage to the water, where it is at once harmlessly dissipated. Wood, on the contrary, is a non-conductor, and suffers accordingly. **Lightning damage.**

The proximity of the vessel to land of volcanic origin is supposed by some seamen to influence the compass. It is true that many masses of rock are intensely magnetic, and affect the compass most powerfully *if placed sufficiently near to them;* but it has been ascertained, beyond a doubt, that such land causes no disturbance of the compasses aboard ship, as they are entirely beyond its influence at the distance vessels are usually navigated from the shore. **Magnetic Land.**

From time to time one hears extremely foolish accounts of vessels being wrecked through the attraction of land. The writer recollects one in particular—the loss, some few years ago, of a steamer, near Cape Santa Maria, in the River Plate—which was attributed by some sage newspaper correspondent to the effect of a supposed magnetic hill in the vicinity of the wreck. As a matter of fact, the vessel was lost through ignorance of the North-Easterly current, which invariably runs on that coast with great strength during a Pampero. **Sinbad the Sailor revived.**

Anyone can test these points for himself. In thick fogs it is often beautifully clear above, so that "time azimuths" can readily be taken of sun, moon, or stars, which can be repeated after the fog has cleared off; and these observations can again be compared with those *taken on the same course* a short time *previous* to the fog setting in. In like manner, when passing close to islands known to be magnetic—such as St. Helena, or the Salvages—a series of azimuths would do more to convince the sceptic than any amount of writing on the subject. **Observations during fog.**

It may be stated therefore—in the most positive manner—that neither *mechanically* nor *magnetically* does fog affect the compass.

The writer would wish it understood that the foregoing remarks are based entirely on his own experience, quite irrespective of similar statements made by well-known authorities; and in every instance most careful experiments were instituted to confirm or disprove all such theories.

Position of Steering Compass.

In a large vessel where, to gain power, the wheel is of considerable diameter—say 7 feet or upwards—*two* steering compasses are absolutely necessary, each so placed, to starboard and port, that the helmsman may have the compass directly in front of him, no matter at which side of the wheel he may be standing. If there should happen to be but *one* compass, an error, due to parallax, will be introduced in the course. Looking at the compass in an oblique direction causes an apparent change in the relative positions of the lubber-line and the marginal divisions of the card—the greater the clearance between the edge of the card and the compass bowl, the greater the error. Unless the helmsman can get the centre of the card and the lubber-point in one with his course, he is sure to steer to one side of it. Where, from the inconvenient closeness of a skylight, stanchion, or other deck fixture, a single midship compass is unavoidably placed very near to the wheel, or is so placed because the steersman's sight will not define the degrees at a greater distance, this error or parallactic displacement of the lubber-line is aggravated, amounting frequently to a quarter of a point. Now, in a moderate day's run of say 300 miles, in thick weather, this becomes a serious consideration, as it affects the ship's position at the end of it to the tune of 15 miles. Hence the necessity for a compass directly facing the steersman, which should be as far distant from him as may be compatible with distinct vision; and to this end its diameter ought not, in the case of a spirit compass, to be less than eleven inches. If constructed, however, on the principle patented by Sir William Thomson, there would be a great advantage in increasing the size to fifteen or even sixteen inches.*

Parallax a source of error.

By placing the compass as far forward of the wheel as possible, it is less within the influence of the iron spindle, tiller, rudderhead, and stern-post, all of which in an iron vessel are powerfully magnetic. If, however, as is frequently the case now, the afterwheelhouse should be constructed wholly of iron, with possibly an iron deck in addition, and steam steering gear, it seems certain that *trustworthy* compensation by magnets must be extremely difficult, and only to be accomplished after a lengthened investigation of the nature of the many forces acting on the compass.

In sailing vessels it is not uncommon to find an attempt made

* Quite recently Sir William Thomson has constructed 15-inch steering compasses which have been found by the writer and others to give excellent results.

to remedy this liability to error, when steering with a single compass in the midship line, by having the binnacle containing it made to slide over from side to side as required; but it is easy to see that, even in a wooden ship, such an arrangement is far from advisable, as the iron spindle of the wheel must affect the compass in a different direction every time the latter is moved across. However, there is nothing like *trial*, and when the ship is in the graving dock, or at sea in a calm, with perfectly smooth water, the sliding binnacle can be tried in both positions; but the result cannot be considered satisfactory *unless the experiment is tried with the ship's head in different directions.* **Sliding Binnacles.**

Now-a-days many large steamers are steered by steam; one man, with a miniature wheel about 30 inches in diameter, sufficing to control the movements of the vessel's head. In this case one compass is all that is necessary, as the helmsman stands *directly behind* the wheel, the spindle and pedestal containing the connections being immediately on the fore side.* **Steam Steering Gear.**

It is necessary here to say a few words touching the fittings, as, unless particularly specified, they are not always made of *brass.* In one large mail steamer commanded by the writer, the spindle of the wheel and vertical shafting communicating with the steam-steering engine were actually made of *iron*, though their ends came within *seven inches* of the compass. How the maker had the hardihood to venture on such a petty economy, involving such serious consequences, it is difficult to say. The iron work alluded to was enclosed in a brass pedestal, which would have concealed it most effectually; but fortunately, before the ship was delivered to her owners, the matter was discovered and reported to the builders, who insisted upon the maker substituting a brass spindle and 8 feet of brass shafting for the iron. One cannot therefore be too wide-awake in these things when looking after the finish of a new ship. **Concealed iron.**

In the same vessel there was a large teak skylight, almost touching the wheelhouse on the foreside; and to prevent the leaves of the skylight warping with the heat of the sun, one of the foremen caused three iron brackets, or stiffeners, to be screwed firmly on the under side of each leaf, and was very much astonished when told that every time the skylight might be opened or shut, that the compass in the wheelhouse would be affected to the extent of several degrees. Nothing short of actual trial would

* *Vide Diagrams* 12 *and* 13, *page* 354.

convince him that such would be the case—his argument being, that as the wooden bulkhead of the wheelhouse intervened, the iron brackets could not possibly disturb the compass. However, the question was set at rest soon after, when the compasses came down from the maker. The disturbance caused by opening and shutting the skylight amounted nearly to half a point, so the after iron brackets were removed, and brass ones substituted.

**Iron in ambush.** In another large steamer, also commanded by the writer, the heels of the main hatch cargo derricks were fitted into substantial iron shoes, shaped something after the fashion of a tuning fork, and connected by a pin to the lugs of the goose-neck in the usual manner.

Each shoe was four feet long, and firmly secured to its derrick by a couple of stout iron bands driven tightly on over-all. This mode of fitting is good and strong, and every way superior to the common rag-bolt. Reference to the diagram facing this page will show that the derricks were stepped on the forward break of the saloon deck-house in such a manner, that when raised to plumb the hatchway the upper ends of the shoes came within three feet six inches of the wheelhouse compass, and on about the same level as the card.

Now, as the iron shoes were neatly let in flush with the surface of the wood, and as moreover the derricks—from head to heel—were plenteously smothered in mast-color paint, after the manner of steamboats in general, it was not likely that any one would readily suspect the presence of so dangerous and well-ambushed an enemy.

**Instructive experiment.** On the 25th of October, 188—, when going round from Portsmouth to Liverpool, it was decided to try what effect would be produced on the wheelhouse compass by placing the derricks in their usual working position. The ship at the time was some ten miles to the westward of the Bill of Portland, and the course steered was West (corr. mag.). Azimuths were taken with the derricks in the two positions shewn in the diagram, and the difference in the compass between "derricks up" and "derricks down" *amounted to no less than* 18°!!! The Bridge compass being well elevated, proved to be beyond the influence of the iron shoes, as it was not affected in the slightest degree. Can it be wondered, then, that vessels are lost without those in charge being able to account for it. Regular comparisons, at short intervals, between the Standard and Steering compass should be a standing

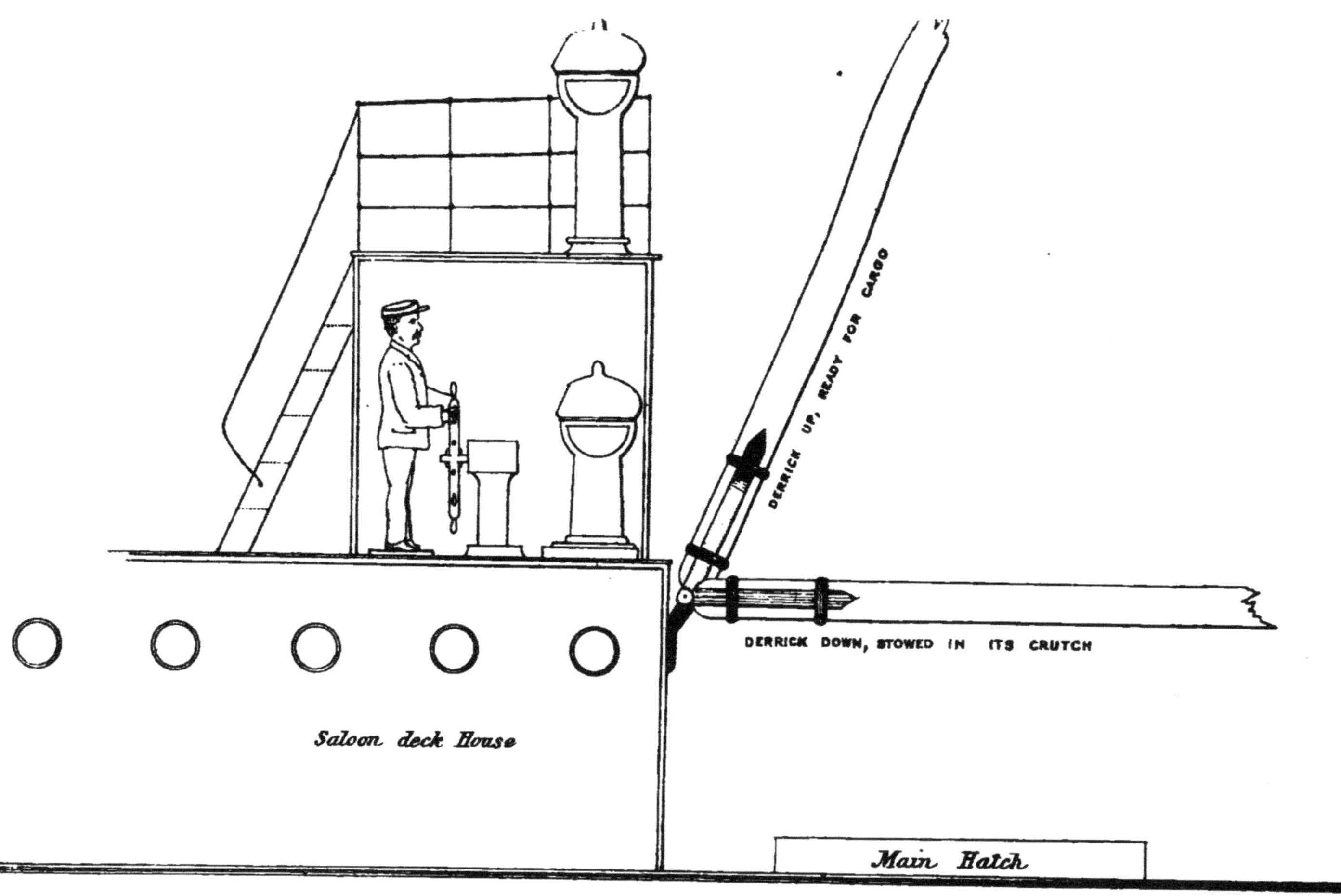
DERRICK UP, READY FOR CARGO
DERRICK DOWN, STOWED IN ITS CRUTCH
Saloon deck House
Main Hatch

rule on board ship, and would materially assist in the detection of "foggy" cases like the above.*

When a rag-bolt is buried in the heart of the spar, it is even less likely to attract attention than the shoe is.

Many men fancy that by covering an iron stanchion with canvass, and then painting it, or by sheathing it with brass or Muntz's metal, they can destroy, or rather shut off, its magnetic influence on a compass; but unfortunately this is *totally impossible*. As already stated in these pages, no substance has ever been discovered which will accomplish this.

It cannot be too strongly impressed on the sailor's mind that if a given piece of iron produces, say ten degrees of effect, on a compass at a distance of three feet, it will produce precisely the same effect if the space between them should be built up *solid* with any non-magnetic material he chooses to name. In "Evans's Elementary Manual" we are told:—"Magnetism exerts its influence through all bodies, even the most dense. This is a remarkable property which is not possessed by light, heat, or electricity." **Magnetism penetrates all bodies.**

There appears to be a diversity of opinion among shipbuilders as to the proper place for locating the steam-steering engine. Some have it amidship, on the main deck, just under the fore-wheelhouse; whilst others prefer to place it in the after-wheelhouse, where it is controlled from forward by means of very simple shafting, leading aft under the deck. Allusion is here made to this only in so far as it has to do with the compass. Where the engine is placed aft, it is possible at all events, to have the steering compass in the *fore*-wheelhouse tolerably free from iron in its vicinity, and on this account, if on no other, it should be so placed. Fortunately this plan possesses mechanical as well as other advantages which renders its ultimate adoption a matter of certainty. **Proper position for Steam Steering Engine.**

Before quitting the subject of compasses, there are a few more points to be noted in connection with it. In a ship fitted with a mast, tripod, or pole compass, it would be an excellent plan to consider *it* as the "Standard compass," and the one on deck otherwise known by that name to be called the "Navigating compass." Mast compasses, when properly constructed by experienced makers, and well placed, are often very reliable. Their deviation is very small in amount, *and much more constant* than compasses nearer the hull. Nevertheless they are apt to defeat their object **Masthead and Pole Compasses.**

* The reader need not worry over the blue and red shading just at present. It will be fully explained in the chapter on Compass Adjustment.

and abuse the confidence reposed in them, if stupidly placed near wire rigging, iron caps or bands, iron stropped blocks, chain tyes, or haulyards, &c.

If, therefore, in a steamer, it should be decided to have a Mast compass (and in the writer's opinion no iron steam vessel should be without one), proper provision must be made for it—the mast, of course, must be of wood, the rigging of rope, and the above precautions followed out to the letter.

The ship's course should always be *set* by the "Navigating compass," *checked* by the "Standard compass," and *referred* to the "Steering compass" by a signal agreed upon, such as the whistle in general use among officers.

All observations should be made by the *Navigating* compass.

It is clearly impracticable to ascertain the deviation of the Standard (mast) compass by *direct* observations, although it can be done very easily by a method described further on, under the heading of Friend's Pelorus, or still more easily by comparison with another compass, the error of which has already been determined. The same applies to the steering compass when inside a wheelhouse.

**Elevated Compasses wear more rapidly.** Mast or pole compasses require more looking after than others. For example, the increased motion aloft causes extra wear and tear of the pivot point and jewelled cap. These should be examined at frequent intervals, *especially if the ship should be in a rough weather trade.* The magnifying glass found in all sextant cases, and a fine sewing needle, serve to scrutinize the cap. If the stone is found to be flawed, it should be at once replaced with a spare one, of which several are generally supplied in a first outfit. If the pivot point is broken or dulled, it can be touched up on the carpenter's oilstone.

**Displaced Lubber Line.** In case the elevated compass should be mounted North Country fashion—on a single pole, it is open to a special error. What seaman is there who has not seen a spruce topgallant-mast warp with a tropical sun, until the sheavehole looked over one bow or other, instead of right ahead? In the case of the pole compass, this twisting of the supporting spar has frequently occurred, and without doubt will occur again; and, as an inevitable consequence, the lubber-line is slewed to the right or left of its proper place, perhaps to a serious extent. Against this latter source of error it is specially important to warn the navigator. To some it may appear needless to do so, but experience shows that misplaced lubber-lines have escaped detection for months, and in some cases years. The supporting spar of the Pole compass should therefore be fashioned out of wood not liable to twist (red pine and teak appear to be suitable), and, as an additional preventative, it should be well coated with *white* paint mixed with raw oil, and all rents carefully puttied up.

**General caution as to lubber-lines.**

In one steamer, the brass band carrying the masthead compass had been slewed out of position by the span of the after-hatch cargo derrick, and had remained so for several voyages. The error in the place of the lubber-line due to this cause was 7°. It has come under the writer's observation that numerous vessels have been nearly lost through want of attention to this highly important matter.

On taking command of a vessel about to proceed to sea, it should be one of the first duties of the captain to ascertain if the lubber point of his "Navigating compass" be exactly in a true fore-and-aft line. In one instance, where the error from this cause amounted to 6°, a steamer was all but run ashore on the Arklow Bank during misty weather; and the vessel actually completed her voyage to the Brazils and back without the master discovering what was the matter, though his courses, day after day, *must* have conveyed to his mind that there was a screw loose somewhere. In another instance a line-of-battle ship, after shaping a course from Milford Haven to the Sevenstones, was found, at daybreak, to be miles outside the Scilly Islands. On investigation, the lubber-line of the "Navigating Compass" was discovered to be 5° to port of the midship-line.

**Co-efficient A.**

Like a snake in the grass, this kind of error lies concealed, and cannot be dragged to light by azimuths or amplitudes, as these observations, unless treated in a mathematical manner, reveal only the errors of the *card*, and not those of the *bowl.** Pay strict

* When the compass is so situated as to make it difficult to refer the lubber-line directly to the ship's head, and it is suspected to be badly placed, its error may be very closely determined :—*Carefully* ascertain the deviation on the four cardinal points, by comparison with the Standard or by the Pelorus, marking it + when easterly, and − when westerly. Add together those of a similar name. Take the difference between the two amounts thus found, retaining the sign of the greater, and divide it by 4. This remainder is known as the coefficient A, and, in a well made compass, is due for the most part to a misplaced lubber-line. When the sign is +, the lubber-line should be moved to the right.

| | | | |
|---|---|---|---|
| Deviation ship's head north | − 12° | Head south | + 2° |
| ,, ,, east | − 24° | ,, west | + 18° |
| | − 36° | | + 20° |
| | + 20° | | |
| | 4) − 16° | | |
| Coefficient A | − 4° | | |

attention, then, to this matter, as it is one of the "*important simplicities*" of navigation. When compass bowls are being painted inside, see therefore, that the lubber-lines are not obliterated, and afterwards put in almost at random by some one ignorant of the mischief which may accrue from their carelessness. It is surely an easy task to paint close up to the lubber-line with a small camel-hair brush; and, to avoid mistakes in reshipping the bowl, when temporarily removed from the binnacle for any purpose, there should be only *one* lubber-line. This will prevent the possibility of reversal in the gimbals. Compass bowls are not unfrequently marked with *four* lubber-lines, but what service three of them render is not manifest. The useless ones should be painted over at the earliest possible moment.

**More than one Lubber Line not advisable.**

The reader must not imagine that "Pole Compasses" are the only ones liable to this defect, which has been known to exist in "Standard Compasses," "Steering Compasses," and even "Navigating Compasses." When detected, cover over the faulty line with two coats of thick white paint, and, with a black lead pencil, rule it carefully in again, in its proper place. Avoid making the line gouty, or too thick.

It should be borne in mind by owners and others that a perfect compass is not the *only* want of the navigator. In fact, too much cannot be done by adopting improved nautical instruments of all kinds, so as to lessen the constant risk incidental to such an arduous, responsible, and hazardous profession.

---

## CHAPTER III.

### THE MARINE CHRONOMETER.

The days of navigating by a carpenter's two-foot rule have gone by, and accurate time-keeping chronometers are a necessity of the "lightning age" in which we live. Without them the rapid ocean voyages, which are now of every-day occurrence, could not possibly be made, although the writer has heard it stated, in all seriousness, by non-nautical men, that the quick transit, from port to port, of the present ocean-express steamers, obviates the necessity for carrying chronometers!!! Such an idea, of course, could only be entertained by men entirely ignorant of the principles and requirements of navigation, and is scarcely in accordance with the steady increase in the establishment, all over the world, of Time-signals for the special use of shipping.

**Chronometers versus Lunars**

It may be truly said that when chronometers came in, lunars went out—concerning the latter, something will appear in subsequent pages. Of late years not only has the chronometer been perfected in a high degree, as a reliable timekeeper, but its price has been reduced so low, by excessive and unhealthy competition, that to be without one, on any over-sea voyage, would be considered almost criminal negligence.

**Time Signals**

In the principal ports, both at home and abroad, the process of rating is rendered quite simple by means of public time-signals. In some places the exact time is given by gun-fire, and at others by the dropping of a ball, or the instantaneous collapse of a cone. No matter what may be the method employed, the result is the same, and he who is now ignorant of the error and performance of his chronometers, cannot plead want of facilities for determining them.*

The almost universal introduction, both by land and sea, of the electric telegraph, has lately been much used for the better deter-

---

* See Table of Standard Time-signals on pages 395-400.

mination of meridian distances. Observations of the Transit of Venus in 1874 and 1882 conduced also to this end, as certain of them necessitated a knowledge of the exact longitude of selected stations which, until that time, had been known only approximately. In fact, it may be broadly asserted, that there are now but few habitable spots on the globe of which the longitude is not known with sufficient accuracy for purposes of navigation.

**Three Chronometers a necessity.** Vessels destined for long voyages should carry not fewer than three chronometers. If there are only two, and one becomes inaccurate, it is impossible to decide which is in error, whereas, with the former number, *and regular daily comparisons*, a tolerably correct judgment may be formed as to the going of each. The only advantage, therefore, in carrying a second chronometer lies in the fact of having a stand-by in the case of accident to one of them—such as the breaking of the mainspring, or other part of the delicate mechanism.

**Much vibration injurious.** Chronometers should, if possible, be kept in a part of the vessel free from jars or much continuous vibration; not in the after-end of a screw-steamer, nor in proximity to a steam-winch; neither should it be permitted to roll heavy bales or cases along the deck in their vicinity. If, however, this last cannot be avoided, it would be well to remove the chronometers from their outer cases for the time being, and bed them on soft feather pillows. On no account should they be slung in hammocks or cots whilst at sea, as it has been found to cause great irregularity in their performance.

In most steamers of modern build there is a chart-room on the upper deck, about the midships of the vessel, and this, for many reasons, is a good place. In the absence of a chart-room the Captain's own cabin is, of course, the next best place; and in this case it is well (in steamers) to have a fourth chronometer in the

**Hack Watch.** second officer's room, as a hack-watch for general use among the officers. If knocked about (so to speak), it will probably not go so well as the others, but this is immaterial, as a comparison can be made at convenience with the standard instrument; indeed it should be made every third or fourth day, and entered in a small book kept in the outer case of the hack-watch.

**How to stow Chronometers** Chronometers are sometimes improperly stowed in one of the drawers of an ordinary set intended originally for clothing, &c. This is a very bad practice. To give them fair play, they should have a special mahogany box (as nearly air-tight as possible), fitted with a strong glass top, and divided by partitions, according to the number carried—each compartment being lined with green baize, and stuffed with best curled hair.

The chronometers should be removed from their own outer boxes, and the upper part of the double lid of the inner case dispensed with by taking the screws out of the hinges, so that the face of the instrument may be seen through the glass where the rate paper is usually kept. Being duly deposited in their several receptacles, all three can be seen through the double glass, and, as the opening of the lids for time-taking is rendered unnecessary, sudden fluctuations of temperature are thereby avoided. **Details of fitting.**

The only occasion upon which the case requires to be touched is in the morning, to wind and compare, which should be done with closed doors.

In some first-class vessels, to protect the plate-glass top from the possibility of accidents, a substantial outer mahogany case is fitted over all. If this wise precaution be taken, the reader will understand that the chronometers are then in three distinct cases—first, their own, with upper portion of the double top removed; the second, with stuffed compartments and glass top; and the third, a strong outer shell entirely of hard wood. The steamships of the Pacific Steam Navigation Co., for example, have their time-keepers cared for in this way, and it is a plan well worthy of being generally adopted.

To those not accustomed to this arrangement, it may be considered cumbersome, and likely to occupy more space than can usually be afforded; but such is not really the fact, and too much pains cannot be taken to guard these valuable instruments from *draughts*, *damp*, and *dust*. In port, the chronometers having first been removed, the inner case should be well dried in the sun, and means taken to prevent cockroaches from making it their home—rent free. A little camphor will do this.

Experience has fully demonstrated that any sudden alteration in the rate of a chronometer, which is otherwise fairly treated, *is more due to change of temperature* than any other cause. The great aim, therefore, of chronometer makers is so to adjust the relationship of the several parts of the balance, that their expansion and contraction may counteract the change of elasticity in the hairspring caused by change of temperature. Nevertheless, there are very few instruments so perfectly compensated, that they may be depended upon to preserve exactly the same rate, with a change of even 10° of temperature. How, then, can it be expected that a chronometer will continue its "shop rate" on a **Change of rate principally due to change of temperature.** **Shop rate unreliable.**

voyage extending over, say four months, during which the temperature has ranged between 40° and 85° Fahrenheit?

**Paper by Arthur E. Nevins.**

Mr. Arthur E. Nevins, in a paper read before the Literary and Philosophical Society of Liverpool, says:—

"At present, chronometer makers allow no corrections upon the rate given for changes of temperature—and the universal practice at sea is to allow one rate for the voyage, whatever the temperature may be—apparently under the impression that an acknowledgment that such a correction is necessary, would be equivalent to acknowledging that the instrument was a defective one. The present method of compensating a marine chronometer is not absolutely perfect, but still leaves the rate of the watch subject to variations, owing to changes of temperature; and it is the infinite variety in amount and direction of these changes of rate in different watches, which causes the instruments on board a ship to differ from each other in the way they so frequently do.

"Every good watch is, however, always affected in the same way, and to the same amount, every time that it is exposed to the same temperature, and the changes in watches follow a fixed law; and knowing, from observation, how they perform in certain temperatures, it is possible to calculate in what way they will perform in any other temperature to which they may be exposed.

**Hartnup's Laws.**

This law was discovered by Mr. Hartnup, the Astronomer to the Mersey Docks and Harbour Board, as the result of testing upwards of two thousand watches which passed through his hands at the Liverpool Observatory—having been sent there by the makers to be tested and supplied with accurate rates.

"Mr. Hartnup's laws are the following:—

1st. Every chronometer goes fastest (*i.e.*, gains most or loses least) in some certain temperature, which has to be calculated for each chronometer from the rates that it makes in three fixed temperatures; the temperatures used at the Bidston Observatory for testing watches being 55°, 70°, and 85° Fahrenheit.

2nd. As the temperature varies, either increasing or decreasing from that in which the watch goes fastest, the watch goes slower; and its rate varies in the ratio of the square of the distance in degrees of temperature, from its maximum gaining temperature. For example—if a watch goes fastest in temperature 75°, it will go slower as the temperature either rises above or falls below 75°; and it will go slower by the same amount in any two temperatures that are the same distance from 75°, one being above and the other below, as in 65° and 85°—one being 10° below and the other 10° above 75°.

"The importance of a knowledge of these facts in using

chronometers is easily seen.* Supposing a ship bound to the southward has three chronometers, *A*, *B*, and *C*, and they are all sent to the same chronometer maker to be rated. He gives the rate which these chronometers have kept while in his shop at a mean temperature of, say 60°. We will further suppose that *A* goes fastest in 60°, *B* in 70°, and *C* in 80°. As the ship gets into warmer weather in approaching the tropics, until she gets into a temperature of 80° or more, *A* gradually goes slower and slower all the time; *B* goes faster until the temperature rises to 70°, and then commences to lose, going slower and slower as the temperature increases more and more; and *C* goes faster all the time until it reaches 80°, which is about as high a steady temperature as will be attained for any length of time out at sea.

**Chronometers may agree in misleading.**

"Now, for these three chronometers to agree in showing the same longitude, it would be necessary for them all to keep steadily to the rates given them in England, or wherever they have been rated; but if they do not keep to these rates, the longitudes indicated by them will differ continually, and, by so doing, cause uncertainty and anxiety to the person using them.

"There is another case which may also occur, and which is really more important than the one above mentioned. It may happen, especially if all the chronometers on board are by the same maker, that they all go fastest in about the same temperature. Now, supposing that all these went fastest in, say 80°, and as in the above mentioned instance the rates of all of them were obtained in about 60° by the maker, they would all go steadily faster than the rates given as the weather got warmer, and would therefore all continue to indicate nearly, or exactly, corresponding longitudes, and these longitudes *would all be wrong;* but in this case the person using them would feel confidence in his position, and perhaps come to harm unexpectedly."

Sir William Thomson, in his "Lecture on Navigation," published by William Collins, Sons & Co., London and Glasgow, gives the following example, illustrative of the great value of Hartnup's method:—

**Advantage of temperature rates.**

"A certain chronometer, J. Bassnett & Son, No. 713, after being rated by Mr. Hartnup, was put on board the ship 'Tenasserim,' in Liverpool, December 1873, for a voyage to Calcutta. . . . . The ship sailed from Liverpool on the 21st of January, 1874, and

* Seamen, as a rule, entertain the erroneous idea that a chronometer will always gain in cold and lose in hot weather.—*Lecky.*

on her voyage the chronometer was subjected to variations of temperature, ranging from 50° to 90°. The chronometer was tested by the Calcutta time-gun on the 26th of May. The time reckoned by it, with correction for temperature on Hartnup's plan, was found wrong by 8½ seconds. Another chronometer, similarly corrected by Mr. Hartnup's method, and from his rating, gave an error of only 3½ seconds. . . . . The reckonings of Greenwich time from the two chronometers, according to the ordinary method, differed actually by 4 minutes 35 seconds, corresponding to 68¾ geographical miles* of error for the ship's place."

**Tendency of new Chronometers to gain on their rate.**

Apart from considerations of temperature, most new chronometers, however good, have a tendency to gain gradually on their rate; that is to say, if the mean gaining rate for two months be five-tenths of a second per day, it will probably be seven-tenths or upwards in the next two months, and so on. The cause of this is involved in some mystery. It is supposed to be due to some molecular change in the material of the spring, which appears at first to strengthen it. It is also probably produced by a thickening of the lubricating oil, which tends to diminish the amplitude of vibration of the balance, and thus cause an acceleration of the rate. A good chronometer, after its newness has worn off, will settle down to a steady rate, depending upon temperature.

For the convenience of the navigator, rules have been formulated and tables compiled in connection with this subject of rating for temperature. The author has availed himself of Mr. Hartnup's kind permission to insert them in the Appendix.

When it is intended to take account of change of rate from changes of temperature, a maximum and minimum thermometer should be kept in the chronometer case, and the reading of their indices taken daily, and recorded in the chronometer journal at the time of comparing.

**Mode of winding Chronometers**

In winding chronometers, care should be exercised to perform the operation *steadily*, without any jerky action which might endanger the chain. Most two-day watches require seven and a half turns of the key, the motion is always left-handed, and the last turn should be made slowly, but steadily, and *continued until the mechanism is felt to butt*, or, in other words, the chronometer should always be wound as far as it will go. A catch, acting at the proper moment, prevents undue stress being put upon the chain.

Cases have occurred where, through fear of causing injury, the

* If reckoned on the equator.—*Lecky*.

officer having charge of the chronometers has neglected to take the *full* number of turns, and the consequence has been that, after a time, the chronometer has run down just before the usual time of winding. The winding index on the face should prevent such a mishap, nevertheless it has occurred.

A chronometer has to be turned "face down" to wind, and it must be eased back handsomely when the operation is completed, and not allowed to swing back with a jerk. This daily reversing of the watch is said to be a good thing, as it distributes the oil in the bearings.

Furthermore, chronometers should be wound punctually *at the same hour every day*, otherwise an unused part of the mainspring comes into action, which, if badly adjusted, is almost certain to produce an irregularity in the rate. For a similar reason it has been found that eight-day chronometers do not preserve altogether the same rate throughout the entire week; that is to say, that (though other conditions may be the same) their daily rate towards the end of the week will not agree with their daily rate at the commencement of it; notwithstanding which, the *mean* rates of two consecutive weeks may agree exactly. On account also of the lightness of the balance, eight-day chronometers do not go so well on board steamers which suffer much vibration from their machinery.

**Eight-day inferior to Two-day Chronometers**

If a chronometer should run down through neglect or other cause, on being wound up again it will probably not start till it has been quickly, *but not violently*, slued half round and back again. This is easily done by placing the instrument on the table and turning it horizontally between the hands.

**When run down, what to do.**

When a chronometer has run down, do not immediately wind it up and move the hands to the proper time, but wait till the Greenwich Mean Time by some other chronometer corresponds nearly with what the hands of the stopped one point to, *then* wind it up, and start it at the right instant. If this is neatly done, it is possible to set it going within a second or two of G.M.T.

Altering the hands of a chronometer does not necessarily hurt the instrument, but it is not *advisable* for any but a skilled person to do it; nor does it inevitably follow that, because a chronometer has been allowed to run down for a few hours, its rate will alter. The writer's experience of half a dozen instances goes to show that it will remain much as before.

**Effect on after performance.**

In such a delicate piece of mechanism, small and totally unlooked for causes will sometimes operate to derange the rate very

**Side play in gimbals.** considerably; for example, too much side-play in the gimbals will have this effect. A chronometer loosely hung may go with beautiful regularity *in port*, and astonish its owner by its after performance *at sea*; therefore, when the vessel is rolling considerably, the chronometers should be watched to see that they do not go over in the gimbals with a jerk; if they do, the gimbals must be tightened up until the jerk is no longer perceptible. On the other hand, do not jam the free movement of the instrument. Too little play is almost as bad as too much.

The writer on one occasion found his favourite time-keeper very wild in its rate, and for a long time he was at a loss to account for it. However, one day, when the vessel was going along in a heavy beam sea, he noticed the lateral play in the gimbals, and at once concluded that therein lay the cause of the trouble, which proved to be the case. When this was remedied (a very simple matter for a man whose fingers are not all thumbs), the chronometer resumed its former good behaviour.

**Magnetisation of Balance.** On another occasion, whilst loading in the tiers at Pernambuco, the master of an iron barque, lying alongside, asked the writer to step on board, and look at a chronometer which he complained of as going in a most erratic manner ever since the vessel's arrival in port. After due examination of the works with the magnifying glass out of the sextant case, nothing could be discovered to account for the vagaries of the instrument. It was only when leaving the cabin that it occurred to the writer to ask what was in the square wooden box lying close against the chronometer complained of. The cat was let out of the bag when the master of the barque innocently explained that it was his Standard compass, which he had unshipped and placed below for greater security whilst in port. The powerful compass needles had by induction magnetized the steel portion of the balance, and ruined the going of the chronometer.

**Care in selecting place for Chronometers** For similar reasons great care should be taken not to stow the chronometers either close against an iron bulkhead, an iron ship's side, the upper or lower end of a vertical iron stanchion, or within 8 feet of compass compensating magnets. Nor should the chronometer case be screwed down to a table containing drawers which *might* be used to hold spare compass cards, or even, in exceptional cases, a horse-shoe magnet. Such things are often done unwittingly, and the ill-used chronometer condemned as a worthless instrument, when *in fact the blame rested entirely with its owner.*

Beware also of compass and chronometer makers who mix these instruments together in their shops as if they were so many pots and pans.

In many steamers the chart-room or captain's cabin is immediately abaft the fore wheelhouse, with which it communicates by a door or window. Should the chronometers happen to be stowed on a shelf or in a case on the *fore side* of this chart-room, they will probably be too near to the adjusting magnets of the wheel-house compass.

As already stated, the mere fact of a bulkhead separating them won't stop the mischief in the slightest degree.

**Avoid hidden iron.**

Again, in many poop-decked steamers the Captain's cabin is at the fore-end of the poop, with windows looking out on the main deck, and most likely the Chief Officer occupies a similarly situated one on the opposite side. Now, it very often happens in steamers of the class alluded to, that to resist the effects of the sea, the transverse bulkhead forming the fore-end of the poop is constructed of iron, and sheathed with wood, to give it a finish. Of course it is lined inside also, and so the captain, unconscious of the mischief likely to ensue, may stow his chronometer close up against the concealed iron.

Chronometers should be kept away from iron almost as religiously as compasses.

In modern vessels, where iron is fast superseding wood in cabin as well as in deck fittings, it is sometimes exceedingly difficult to select a really good place for the time-keepers. Very often it is "Hobson's choice;" nevertheless these matters should receive full consideration, *if the vessel is to go safely*. From the foregoing causes alone, the "Shore-rate" and the "Sea-rate" will seldom agree. It is advisable, therefore, that when practicable, chronometers should be rated on board, in the positions they are intended to occupy during the voyage. As before remarked, there are many facilities, such as time-guns and time-balls, for effecting it.

**Necessity for comparison previous to sailing.**

Chronometers, when received on board previous to sailing, should be compared with each other, and the respective errors and rates applied to each, to note if they agree in their Greenwich Mean Time. This may seem a very needless precaution, but the propriety of it has twice been made apparent to the writer; and what has occurred to one may happen to others also.

Suppose that this matter of comparing be neglected, and that there should be only two chronometers on board; suppose further, that a wrong original error has been given with one of them (say, to the extent of one minute), and that the vessel proceeds to sea with dirty weather, and perhaps is several days out before getting sights ; then, when the comparison is made, the navigator finds to his dismay that his chronometers differ from each other to the extent of a quarter of a degree of longtitude. The Dead Reckoning cannot help him—indeed, if it were depended upon, it might just double the error. The only thing left to be done is to make some well-known point of land as soon as possible, take careful sights, and find out which chronometer is at fault.

If you intend passing close to an island for this purpose, do not go on the side which will bring the land between you and the sun, or *where will your horizon be?* Always think beforehand of the necessities of the case.

As few merchant vessels carry more than three chronometers, that number will be adopted in treating of the proper mode of making the daily comparisons. For brevity, the several instruments should be known by letters, instead of the maker's numbers. The letter should be marked on a small slip of paper, and gummed conspicuously on the outside of chronometer case. For example, when standing facing them, the left-hand chronometer might be called *A*, the middle one *B*, and the right-hand one *C*,—everything, when possible, being taken in its *natural order* or sequence.

**Chronometer Journal.**

An excellent form of chronometer journal is appended, and reference to it will shew that three chronometers enable three different comparisons to be made—the last being a check upon the others ; for example, *A* is compared with *B* ; *B* with *C* ; and *A* with *C*. These comparisons should not be made simultaneously by three different observers, which is the common method on board ship ; as it is *impossible* by it to attain the necessary accuracy. All the comparisons must be made by *one* individual, and a fortnight's practice, or at most a month's, will enable him to effect this to the *tenth* of a second. When we consider how small a portion of time is represented by such a minute division, it is not improbable that some may feel incredulous as to the practicability of estimating it correctly. But after the preliminary drill with the method about to be indicated, the doubters will be able to assure themselves that not only is it not impossible, but that with care it is sufficiently easy.

In all observatories on shore, the astronomer and his assistants are in the constant habit of splitting "tenths" with wonderful precision, and it may interest the reader to know that there are mechanical contrivances for dividing a second of time even into *one thousand parts.* As these do not enter into the practice of navigation, a description of them in these pages would be out of place.

**How to compare with precision.**

To compare accurately, the operator, being quite alone, should close both windows and doors, so as to exclude noise. Having opened the *outer* cases, he should make ready with book and pencil for the first comparison, by opening the *inner* case of *A*, which will allow its ticking to be distinctly heard, whilst *B* is regarded through its glass lid.

It will be perceived by the reader that the operation is performed by the delicate relationship or sympathy existing between the eye and ear. *A* will be heard, and *B* will be seen.

Now, look steadily at *A*, and mentally count *with it*, assisting by a quick motion of the hand corresponding to every half-second beat. Having got well into the swing or rhythm of the beats, and decided to "stop," say, at 60s (the even minute); remove the eye to *B* when *A*'s second-hand has got to 52s. or 53s., keeping the sound of each half-beat still in your ears, and the hand going with it. When you have arrived *by sound* at 60s. (your chosen "stopping" point) the eye will enable you to decide upon the number of seconds and parts of a second shewn by *B*.

The other two comparisons will be made in a precisely similar manner. Of course in actual practice you note down beforehand the hour and even minute, by the *open* chronometer, at which you intend to "stop," or compare with the *closed* one; also, note the *hour* of the latter, and when proficient, the minute can also be noted, leaving only the seconds and tenths for the comparison.

The beginner, after a few trials by himself, will soon drop into the way of comparing with accuracy, and will congratulate himself upon being independent of outside aid, whenever he may wish to do so.

Having in this manner compared all three chronometers, *A* with *B*, *B* with *C*, and *A* with *C*, accuracy of the result can, in a measure, be tested by comparing the interval between *A* and *C*, with the sum or difference, as the case may be, of the other two intervals, for example—(*vide Form of Chronometer Journal*) on ☉ May 18th we have

| | H. | M. | S. |
|---|---|---|---|
| Time by Chron. *A* | 2 | 31 | 00·0 |
| " " *B* | 2 | 12 | 39·4 |
| Interval | | 18 | 20·6 |

| | H. | M. | S. |
|---|---|---|---|
| Chr. *B* | 2 | 15 | 00·0 |
| " *C* | 2 | 14 | 5·4 |
| Interval | | 0 | 54·6 |

| | H. | M. | S. |
|---|---|---|---|
| Chr. *A* | 2 | 36 | 00·0 |
| " *C* | 2 | 16 | 44·8 |
| Interval | | 19 | 15·2 |

## DAILY RATES AND ERRORS OF CHRONOMETERS ON BOARD S.S. "BRITISH EMPIRE."

NOTE.—The + sign means fast or gaining; the — sign means slow or losing.

| Date 1879. | | A Accumulated Error. | Daily Rate. Gaining. | Daily Rate. Losing. | B Accumulated Error. | Daily Rate. Gaining. | Daily Rate. Losing. | C Accumulated Error. | Daily Rate. Gaining. | Daily Rate. Losing. | Temperature. 8 a.m. | Temperature. 2 p.m. | Temperature. 8 p.m. | Mean Daily Temp. | Reference to remarks on opposite page. |
|---|---|---|---|---|---|---|---|---|---|---|---|---|---|---|---|
| | | m. s. | s. t. | | m. s. | | s. t. | m. s. | | s. t. | | | | | |
| ☉ May | 18 | + 6 31·8 | + 1·6 | | − 11 44·3 | | − 3·1 | − 12 43·5 | | − 2·0 | 65° | 73° | 70° | 69° | * |
| ☾ " | 19 | + 6 33·4 | + 1·6 | | − 11 47·4 | | − 3·1 | − 12 45·5 | | − 2·0 | 65° | 72° | 71° | 69° | † |
| ♂ " | 20 | + 6 35·0 | + 1·6 | | − 11 50·5 | | − 3·1 | − 12 47·5 | | − 2·0 | 60° | 69° | 67° | 65° | ‡ |
| ☿ " | 21 | + 6 36·6 | + 1·6 | | − 11 53·6 | | − 3·1 | − 12 49·5 | | − 2·0 | 59° | 67° | 63° | 62° | § |

## DAILY COMPARISONS OF CHRONOMETERS.

| Date 1879. | | A compared with B. A | A compared with B. B | 1st difference. | 2nd difference. | B compared with C. B | B compared with C. C | 1st difference. | 2nd difference. | A compared with C. A | A compared with C. C | 1st difference. | 2nd difference. |
|---|---|---|---|---|---|---|---|---|---|---|---|---|---|
| | | h. m. s. | h. m. s. | m. s. | s. t. | h. m. s. | h. m. s. | m. s. | s. t. | h. m. s. | h. m. s. | m. s. | s. t. |
| ☉ May | 18 | 2 31 00·0 | 2 12 39·4 | 18 20·6 | — | 2 15 00·0 | 2 14 5·4 | 0 54·6 | — | 2 36 00·0 | 2 16 44·8 | 19 15·2 | — |
| ☾ " | 19 | 2 34 00·0 | 2 15 34·6 | 18 25·4 | + 4·8 | 2 18 00·0 | 2 17 6·5 | 0 53·5 | − 1·1 | 2 39 00·0 | 2 19 41·2 | 19 18·8 | + 3·6 |
| ♂ " | 20 | 2 00 00·0 | 1 41 30·0 | 18 30·0 | + 4·6 | 1 45 00·0 | 1 44 7·5 | 0 52·5 | − 1·0 | 2 05 00·0 | 1 45 37·5 | 19 22·5 | + 3·7 |
| ☿ " | 21 | 1 31 00·0 | 1 12 25·6 | 18 34·4 | + 4·4 | 1 14 00·0 | 1 13 8·3 | 0 51·7 | − 0·8 | 1 35 00·0 | 1 15 33·8 | 19 26·2 | + 3·7 |

NOTE.—When *temperature rates* are used, the values in the daily rate columns will require to be altered as the temperature varies.

[In ordering this form the size must be increased to 14 in. × 8 in. over all. The divisional lines may be either red or black, according to purchaser's fancy. All the *left hand* pages are blank, to allow space for remarks.]

Here 18m. 20·6s. added to 0m. 54·6s. gives 19m. 15·2s., equal to the interval between *A* and *C*, from which it may be assumed the comparisons have been accurately made, although, strictly speaking, such is by no means a certainty.

Chauvenet, in his valuable work on Spherical and Practical Astronomy, says—

**Comparing Chronometers**

"When two chronometers are compared which keep the same kind of time, and both of which beat half-seconds, it will mostly happen that the beats of the two instruments are not synchronous, but one will fall after the other by a certain fraction of a beat, which will be pretty nearly constant, and must be estimated by the ear. This estimate may be made within half a beat, or a quarter of a second, without difficulty; but it requires much practice to estimate the fraction within 0·1s. with certainty. But if a mean time or *Solar* chronometer is compared with a *Sidereal* chronometer, their difference may be obtained with ease within *one-twentieth* of a second. Since 1s. sidereal time is less than 1s. mean time, the beats of the Sidereal chronometer will not remain at a constant fraction behind those of the Solar chronometer, but will gradually gain on them, so that at certain times they will be coincident.

**Solar and Sidereal Chronometers**

"Now, if the comparison be made at the time this coincidence occurs, there will be no fraction for the ear to estimate, and the difference of the two instruments *at this time* will be obtained exactly. The only error will be that which arises from judging the beats to be in coincidence when they are really separate by a small fraction, and it is found that the ear will easily distinguish the beats as not synchronous so long as they differ by as much as 0·05s. (half-a-tenth); consequently, the comparison is accurately obtained within that quantity. Indeed with practice it is obtained within 0·03s. or even 0·02s. Now, since 1s. sidereal time=0·99727s. mean time, the Sidereal chronometer gains 0·00273s. on the Solar chronometer in 1s.; and therefore it gains 0·5s. in 183s., or very nearly 3m.; hence, once every three minutes the two chronometers will beat together. When this is about to occur, the observer begins to count the seconds of one chronometer, while he directs his eye to the other; when he no longer perceives any difference in the beats, he notes the corresponding half-seconds of the two instruments."

It follows that when two Solar chronometers are to be compared, it will in general be most accurately done by comparing each with a Sidereal chronometer by coincident beats, and afterwards reducing the comparisons. It is not likely that the ordinary navigator will possess a Sidereal chronometer, but the method is introduced here as likely to prove interesting, and to shew what *can* be done.

**Chronometer Journal.** It has been already stated that chronometers should be compared daily, and with methodical regularity, and the proper entries made in a book known as the Chronometer Journal.* The writer has for many years used the form given at page 36, and it is so self explanatory that very little more is requisite. The "2nd difference" is merely the difference between the quantities for any two consecutive days in the column headed "1st difference." Thus, in the comparison of *A* with *B*, on May 18th the "1st difference" is 18m. 20·6s, and on May 19th is 18m. 25·4s.; the difference between these two is 4·8s., and, as the one chronometer is *gaining* and the other *losing*, it ought to be equal to the *sum* of their daily rates. As *A*'s rate is + 1·6s., and *B*'s − 3·1s., the sum 4·7s. shows a dissimilarity of only one-tenth of a second.

In the case of the "2nd difference" of *B* and *C* = 1·1s., as *both* these chronometers are *losing*, it ought to be equal to the *difference* of their daily rates, which happens exactly to be the case.

Of course, if two chronometers were *both gaining*, the "2nd difference" would in like manner be equal to the *difference* of their daily rates. But when their rates are going in *opposite* directions, the amount in the "2nd difference" column ought to be equal to their *sum*.

By scrutinizing the journal day by day, a fair judgment may be formed of how the chronometers are behaving. In the event of the "2nd difference" not agreeing with the daily rates, a careful analysis of the comparisons and record of temperatures, combined with a consideration of the respective merits of the instruments, may enable one to form a pretty just estimate of the value and direction of the change. For instance, if *A* does not agree with *B*, nor yet with *C*, but if *B* and *C* run well together, the inference that *A* has gone wrong would be a reasonable one, especially if *A* happened to be an old offender. In any case the navigator is put upon his guard, which is always something.

At the Bidston Observatory, near Liverpool, any master sailing

---

* It is not uncommon to see the error of a chronometer marked opposite each day, on the margin of the page for the month, in the Nautical Almanac. This, in the estimation of some people, may be "handy," and in a sense it is so; but on a long voyage a properly kept "Journal" would look more ship-shape and business-like, quite apart from the question of utility.

out of the port can have his chronometer rated for temperature. The time requisite is six weeks, and on leaving, a paper accompanies the chronometer shewing its performance for every 5° of temperature between 45° and 95°; so that if the recommendation be attended to concerning the advisability of keeping a maximum and minimum thermometer in the case with the chronometers, and the rate altered to suit as often as necessary, the navigator can make sure of his Greenwich time within a few seconds, after a lapse of some months.* The Observatory *temperature rates* can be copied out on any of the left-hand pages of the journal, all of which are headed "Remarks," and ruled in faint blue lines.

**Rating for temperature at Bidston Observatory.**

In the specimen page of the Journal just given, it will be noticed that for conciseness, it is only drawn up for four days; but in ordering one similar, the printer should be instructed to make the page deep enough to contain a week's work; also to leave an inch and a-half of space at the bottom for adding up and getting the *mean* of the "second differences" and temperatures, so as to adjust the rates in accordance with their indications.

Whenever the errors and rates have been ascertained afresh by observation, the proper entries corresponding to the given date should be made in *red* ink, so as to be easily found for reference.

**Red ink entries.**

The winding and comparing ought to be invariably done by one person. In large Mail Steamship Companies, the second officer is generally constituted the "Navigating officer," and, as such, has charge of the chronometers. It is his duty every morning to make *formal* report to the commander that they have been attended to. It would be easy to devise a plan suitable to any particular ship, whereby it would become impossible to neglect this important duty. In some men-of-war, the crew cannot be piped to their mid-day meal until the chronometers have been reported. In a merchant vessel it is usual to wind them in the morning. But whatever the time fixed upon, there should be a certain formality observed, which could not be omitted without sure and speedy detection.†

**Winding and Comparing done by Navigating Officer.**

These sensitive instruments cannot receive too much care, for it is perfectly wonderful what apparently insignificant causes will sometimes affect them. Many years ago the writer owned two very valuable chronometers, which he highly prized, as their performance had been most satisfactory. On a passage home

* See Appendix A.

† A card, with the words "Wind Chronometers" printed or written on it, might be laid on the captain's plate by the steward every morning at breakfast time.

from the River Plate they both came to grief quite unexpectedly. Comparisons with a third time-keeper, kept in the second officer's room, and observations on shore at St. Vincent, shewed that they had taken up a prodigious losing rate, which grew day by day until on arrival at Liverpool it amounted to 20 and 25 seconds. Examination by the maker disclosed the annoying fact, that the springs and other steel portions of the works were thickly pitted with rust. Now, the Captain's room was situated directly over the main hold, which on that particular passage happened to be stowed full of salted hides. The coat of the mast, which came up through one corner of the cabin, had worked adrift on the side which was hidden from view, and the only inference to be drawn was, that the salt steam from the hold had penetrated to the mechanism, with the unfortunate result already mentioned. Though thoroughly cleaned and "re-sprung" they never went so well again.

**Injury to Chronometers through springs rusting.**

**Causes likely to alter rate.**

Jolting in a railway train, or a conveyance of any description, is liable to alter the steady going of a chronometer. The quick jerk of a boat propelled by oars is still more likely to prove injurious. If, therefore, a chronometer has to be taken from one place to another in a pulling boat, it should be held free in the hand by the leather strap, taking care to avoid a circular motion. When travelling by train place it on a pile of overcoats or railway rugs, in such a position that it will not fall. The *principal* cause, however, of a chronometer altering its rate when reasonable care has been taken of it, *is change of temperature.*

**"Tripping."**

In connection with this subject of rough carriage, the reader should know that a chronometer is exposed to a variety of mishaps which are very little understood except by "the trade."—For example, when the locking-spring of the escapement is too weak, it is possible for two teeth of the "'scape-wheel" (instead of only one) to pass the locking-pallet during a single vibration of the balance. This is called "tripping," and it is evident that in this way a chronometer may gain several seconds in a very short space of time, to the complete mystification of whoever has to do with it, unless he happens to be posted in respect of this peculiarity.

Tripping may occur also through a worn "'scape-wheel," the pallet-stone being badly set, or the several parts not being relatively in good adjustment.

On the other hand, should the locking-spring be too strong, the pallet will not get back sufficiently to release the "'scape-wheel," and the chronometer will not go at all, or if it does condescend to do so, will only move by fits and starts. Of course the maker would never let an instrument leave his hands in such a plight, but it is mentioned to shew the refinement of skill which is necessary in the manufacture and adjustment of such delicate mechanism.

Again,—owing to the axis of the balance-wheel being but slender, a sudden jerk may bend it or break the extremely fine pivot-points, a misfortune which at once puts the chronometer "out of action" till the damage has been repaired.

**Necessity for staying Chronometers previous to removal.**

Before removing it from its outer case to carry it anywhere, a chronometer should be stayed, otherwise the instrument is apt to capsize in the gimbals, and when the inner case is next opened, to astonish the individual who has carried it by his finding the XII next to himself, instead of facing him on the far side as usual. Incredible as it may appear, the writer knew an officer, who, to his consternation, got a chronometer into this very same fix, and worse than all, neither knew how it happened, nor what to do to get it back into its original position.

**Poising a Chronometer in the Gimbals.**

The poising of a chronometer in the gimbals has a very great influence on its rate. This can be tested on shore by staying the chronometer and keeping the case on its side for three or four days with the XII up. Next try it with the III, VI, and IX up, and it will be found that the rate in each case will be different to what it was when the chronometer had a horizontal position. The more expensive pocket watches are adjusted for any position, but marine chronometers are intended always to be kept strictly horizontal, with the face up.

**Auxiliary Compensation**

Experience has proved that chronometers, with the words "Auxiliary compensation" engraved upon their face, are not one whit better than those fitted with the ordinary balance. Without this knowledge, a purchaser of one of these instruments might fancy he was getting something "very special."

**Cleaning Chronometers**

A caution will do no harm to those who, because an instrument is going pretty well, allow many years to pass without having it cleaned. It should be borne in mind that wear and tear is *constantly* going on; that the oil thickens, and eventually gets dried up; and that when this happens, the pivots of the moving parts must necessarily grind themselves away, and work differently to what is intended. Never allow a chronometer to run longer than four years, without giving it an overhauling at the hands of a first-rate workman. But if it is a new instrument, it should be looked at after a year or eighteen months.

**Chronometer Makers and Chronometer Sellers.**

Be *sure* that the man you give it to is a *chronometer*-maker, and not a *watch* or *clock*-maker. The latter may be very good as such, and yet understand very little about marine chronometers. Moreover, a large percentage of those who style themselves chronometer-*makers* are only chronometer-*sellers*, as the instruments are purchased by them at trade price from the wholesale manufacturers. If you know where to look for it, you can easily find the manufacturer's private mark.

**How to obtain good Chronometers.**

In concluding this chapter, it may not come amiss to those desirous of purchasing a reliable timekeeper to be told where to find it, and how to get it. Many of the best makers send instruments to the Greenwich and Liverpool Observatories to be tested. At both these institutions their performance is subjected to a rigorous cross-examination, and a careful record kept of their behaviour under various trying circumstances, and extending over several months. The Greenwich trial is exclusively for the Royal Navy; but at Bidston (Liverpool) the books are always courteously open for the inspection of those desirous of purchasing, and consequently, it should be an easy matter to select a good instrument from the many before you. When found, go at once to the maker, whoever he may be (even though his name should *not* be Poole or Dent), and drive as good a bargain with him as you can. Do not grudge an extra pound or two; you will save it in sleep on a voyage.

The two best chronometers the writer ever had the good fortune to meet with were obtained by him in this manner at the Liverpool Observatory, Bidston Hill. They were selected from a large number, and curiously enough, were by the *same* maker, and had *consecutive* numbers—a thing that might not happen again in one hundred years.*

* There is no longer a stock of chronometers for sale at Bidston Observatory; but before purchasing in Liverpool, it can always be stipulated that the instrument shall be sent to Bidston to be tested,—that is to say, if the intending purchaser can afford the time. For example, when a vessel is being built, the owner knows that she will require to be furnished with chronometers. If, then, he requests his chronometer-maker to send a certain number to the Bidston Observatory for trial, the necessary ones can be selected when the vessel is ready for sea, and he will enjoy the same privilege as the Admiralty have, for many years past, by means of their annual test of chronometers at the Greenwich Observatory. It by no means follows that, because a man has made a chronometer which has been purchased as a good one by the Admiralty, all subsequent chronometers made by him will be *equally* good. From an examination of the published "Rates of Chronometers on trial, for purchase by the Board of Admiralty, at the Royal Observatory, Greenwich," it will be seen that the maker who has a chronometer first or second on the list in the order of merit, also not unfrequently has another near the bottom of the same list. This shews the necessity of testing the chronometers themselves, irrespective of the names which they bear.

## CHAPTER IV.

### THE SEXTANT.

The Sextant, of all astronomical instruments,.is most especially adapted to the purpose of the navigator, and for this reason it is incumbent upon him to render himself in every way familiar with its principle and make.

The multitude are sometimes puzzled to know why a sextant (derived from the Latin word *sextans*, signifying the *sixth* of a circle) should be thus named, when it is capable of measuring angles up to 120°, or the *third* of a circle.

**Optical principle of construction.** If the possessor of one will but look at the arc, he will find out by his eye alone that, as a matter of fact, it consists only of the *sixth* part of a circle. The optical principle upon which the instrument is founded (that of double reflection), *permits of half a degree of the arc being numbered and considered as a whole degree.* Thus, in the sextant, what is really only an arc of 60°, is divided into 120 equal parts, *each of which does duty as a degree.*

**The Octant, better known as Quadrant.** The instrument commonly known as a Quadrant is improperly so called. Though it is capable of measuring angles up to 90°, the arc only consists of the *eighth* part of a circle, and, in accordance with the rule adopted in the former case, it should be termed an Octant. These terms, being at present opposed to each other, are a source of confusion, and should be rectified by abolishing the word Quadrant, and substituting Octant. Instruments capable of measuring angles up to 144° are in like manner termed Quintants. **Quintants.**

The optical principle upon which the Sextant is founded is thus announced :—

**Statement of Optical Law governing Sextant.** "If a ray of light suffers two successive reflections in the same plane by two plane mirrors, the angle between the first and last direction of the ray is twice the angle of the mirrors."

The following illustration is taken from Herschel's Astronomy, page 103.*

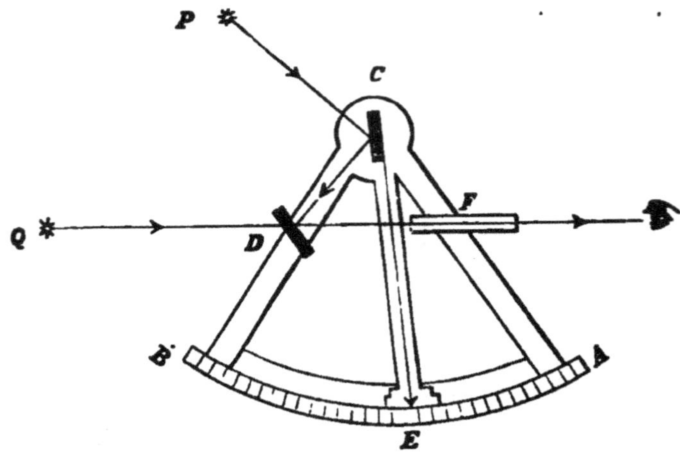


Demonstration of law of double reflection.

Let *AB* be the limb or graduated arc of a portion of a circle 60° in extent, but divided into 120 equal parts. On the radius *CB* let a silvered plane glass *D* be fixed at right angles to the plane of the circle, and on the moveable radius *CE* let another such silvered glass *C* be fixed.

The horizon glass *D* is permanently fixed parallel to *AC*, and only one-half of it is silvered, the other half allowing objects to be seen through it.

The Index glass *C* is wholly silvered, and its plane is parallel to the length of the moveable radius *CE*, at the extremity (*E*) of which a vernier is placed to read off the divisions of the limb.

On the radius *AC* is set a telescope *F*, through which any object *Q* may be seen by *direct* rays which pass through the unsilvered portion of the glass *D*, while another object *P* is seen through the same telescope by rays which, after reflection at *C*, have been thrown upon the silvered part of *D*, and are thence directed by a second reflection into the telescope.

The two images so formed will both be seen in the field of view at once, and by moving the radius *CE*, will (if the reflectors be truly perpendicular to the plane of the circle) meet and pass over without obliterating each other.

The motion, however, is arrested when they meet, and at this point the angle included between the direction *CP* of one object,

* Published by Longmans & Co.

and *FQ* of the other, is twice the angle *ECA*, included between the fixed and moveable radii *CA*, *CE*.

Now the graduations of the limb being purposely made only *half* as distant as would correspond to degrees, the arc *AE*, when read off as if the graduations were *whole* degrees, will in fact read *double* its *real* amount, and therefore the numbers so read off will express, *not* the angle *ECA*, but its *double*, which is the *actual* angle subtended by the objects.*

The navigator who takes a proper pride in his work should possess a *first-class* Sextant or Quintant, and a *good* Octant. The latter is fully equal to everyday work *in the broad ocean*,—for example, during the winter months in the North Atlantic. The delicate exactness of the other instrument is quite thrown away when one can only get flying shots at the horizon, from the crest of a 60-feet wave. Showers of salt spray, with the chance of an occasional knock, certainly seem less suited to the sextant than to its hardier and more humble relative.

On the other hand, for fine weather use, for stars, lunars, observations on shore with artificial horizon, and for fixing the ship's position in the neighbourhood of land by angles, the Quintant is undoubtedly the proper and only reliable instrument. A *good* Quintant or Sextant costs money—*and is worth it*. Unless you are a fair judge of one, it is as easy to be deceived in purchasing a sextant as in buying a horse. The market is glutted with sextants *made for sale*. Every pawnbroker's window in a seaport town is half full of them. Some vendors even hold out the inducement in large type that their instruments are "free from error." If indeed by accident such should happen to be the case at the moment of purchase, it need not be a matter of speculation how long they will remain so. The thing is absurd, and might with equal justice be said of a chronometer or a patent log.

**Care in purchasing Sextant.**

The intending purchaser should spend half-an-hour or so in satisfying himself as to the following points. Avoid a sextant of less than 8 inches radius. The divisions of a smaller instrument are difficult to read, especially at night, and are not likely to be near so accurately cut. A 6 or 7-inch sextant is of course somewhat lighter to handle, but sailors are not women.

**Points to be noted.**

Give the preference to a "pillar" sextant over one whose framework is cast all in one piece.

* It can be easily demonstrated that the angle *ECA*, between zero of the arc and zero of the Index vernier, is equal to the angle of the mirrors *CED*, which is all that is wanted to establish the truth of the theorem given above.

One of the eye-pieces of the inverting telescope should have a tolerably high magnifying power—say 14 or 15 diameters, as contacts of the sun's limbs in observations with the Artificial Horizon are easier made in proportion to the size of the suns.

Examine the vernier, in order to see that its feather edge lies perfectly flush with the face of the arc, otherwise, by a slight side movement of the eye to the right or left of a point exactly vertical to where the divisions "cut," a false reading is obtained. This is very likely to occur at night, when reading off by the light from a swinging lamp.

An extended vernier, by which is meant a vernier whose divisions are twice the distance apart of those on the arc, is now considered to be "the correct thing," and is a great help to accurate reading.

To test the arc, place the zero of the vernier very carefully at various divisions along the arc, and then note if the left hand division of the vernier coincides exactly with one on the arc. If the latter is correctly graduated, it should coincide in *every instance*. Cheap sextants won't stand this test.

A steel tangent-screw will not only last longer, but will work more evenly than a brass one.

**Color of Index and Horizon Screens.**

The index and horizon glass screens should be of neutral tint, instead of red, yellow, green, &c. The various depths of shade correspond to the *thickness* of the glass. The coloured screens which screw on to the eye end of the telescopes should also be neutral tint.

**Test for parallelism of back & front face of Mi.rors.**

The front and back faces of the index glass ought to be strictly parallel to each other. This can be tested by placing the sextants on a table or other steady support, and looking obliquely into the mirror at the reflection of some distant object. The image should have sharp and well defined edges. If they are at all blurred or indistinct, the glass is more or less prismatic.

Another method of determining this is to examine the reflected image of a star with the index set to a reading of 120° or thereabouts. The index glass reflects from its outer as well as from its silvered face, though in a less degree. If the faces are parallel, the rays from the star reflected from the two faces will be parallel after leaving the glass; they will therefore be converged to the same focus in the telescope, and produce but a single image. But if the glass is prismatic, there will be two images, a fainter image superimposed upon the stronger one, and not quite coincident with it. The star, therefore, will not shew as a well defined point without sensible magnitude, which it ought to do if the glass were perfect.

Want of parallelism of the *horizon-glass* is of less consequence. It affects all angles (the index correction included) by the same quantity, and therefore produces no error in the results.

Next, examine the coloured screens for the same defect. If their faces are not ground parallel, the sextant will have a different index error for each pair or combination of screens. Detection in this case is easy. Make an accurate contact of the sun's limbs, on or off the arc, as the case may be, using with the telescope one of the coloured screens belonging to it.* Then, after discarding this screen from the telescope, turn down suitable combinations of the index and horizon screens, and see if the contact still remains perfect. If not, make it so, and the difference between the first and last reading will be the error of that pair of screens, and so on for the remainder. **Test for Colored Screens.**

In sextants manufactured by Pistor and Martins, of Berlin, the screens are so arranged as to admit of being instantaneously reversed; therefore, to eliminate the errors of these glasses, it is only necessary to take one half of a set of observations with one position of the screens, and the other half with the reverse position. **Screens fitted to reverse.**

Imperfection in the coloured shade, just alluded to, which ships on to the eye-piece of the telescope, is of no particular importance, as the object and reflected image are affected alike, and the angle between them remains unchanged.

Finally, the arc in a good sextant should be of platinum or gold, and the divisions both on it and the vernier should look fine and clean cut when viewed under the microscope. To *ensure* these requisites, purchase the instrument from a maker of repute.

The index error should be found before and after all important observations. At night it can be determined with great facility by means of a star of the 2nd or 3rd magnitude. Set the vernier a few minutes one side or other of zero, screw in the telescope and direct it to a suitable star, and by means of the slow-motion-screw bring the images exactly in one. The reading will be the index error, subtractive if *on* the arc, and additive if *off* the arc. As a star of the 3rd magnitude is a mere speck of light, the method admits of great accuracy, *and will be found much less* **Index Error.**

* Captain Wharton, in his *Hydrographical Surveying*, says :—"Several dark eye-pieces should be provided, with neutral tint glass in them of different intensities. These should be fitted, not to *screw* on to the eye-piece, but ground conical, to slip on to a similar conically ground surface on the telescope eye-piece.

*fatiguing to the eye than a similar observation of the sun.* The reflected image should pass exactly over the direct one; if it passes on either side of it, the horizon-glass is not perpendicular to the plane of the instrument, and wants attending to.

**Index error by Sea Horizon.**

It is a common practice to ascertain the index error by the sea horizon in a manner similar to the foregoing, and the method is a correct one; but it will not work on shore where the top of some straight and level object is employed to represent the horizon, unless the object so selected be *at least* half a mile distant. The index and horizon-glasses would subtend a sensible angle at the place of an object *within* that distance; and, though the glasses should be parallel to each other, coincidence would not be established between the reflected and true images.

Beware, therefore, of self-styled opticians who are occasionally to be seen at their shop doors adjusting sextants by the roof of the house opposite. In doing so they betray their own ignorance as well as their customer's confidence. Some one, with more humour than reverence, has suggested the word "Shoptician" as a fitting title for such men. Perhaps it is.

**Adjustments.**

The four adjustments, and the means of making them, are so lucidly explained in the various Epitomes of navigation, and they are so simple in themselves, that it is quite unnecessary to waste space in treating of them here; as a rule, a *good* instrument, if carefully nursed, will remain in sufficiently close adjustment for an indefinite time. Some officers are never satisfied unless they are tinkering at the adjustment of their sextants, and, as a consequence, the screws work slack, and the sextant does not remain correct for 24 hours on a stretch—in fact, the more it is meddled with, the worse it gets.

Raper is very emphatic on this matter. He says:—

**Raper's advice as to Adjustments.**

"The adjusting screws are *never to be touched except from necessity*, and then with the greatest possible caution. Particular attention is called to this point, because it is a common failing of 'over handy gentlemen,' (to use Troughton's language) to 'torment' their instruments. It is better that error should exist, provided it is allowed for nearly, than that mischief should ensue to the instrument from ignorant attempts at a perfect adjustment; and the skilful observer, instead of implicitly depending upon the supposed perfection of his instrument, will endeavour to avail himself of those cases in which errors, if they exist, will destroy each other."

If of a mechanical turn, however, and really anxious to learn the way a sextant is put together, first-rate practice can be had with a cheap second-hand one, which can be taken to pieces with impunity, put together again, and experimented upon in a variety of interesting ways: for instance, it would be instructive to determine by reversal, the error, if any, due to a prismatic form of the index and other glasses. The reflectors might also be resilvered according to Belcher's method, as described in the Sailors' Pocket Book.

In case your sextant is not already fitted with a good "star telescope," by all means get one. It will pick out the horizon on a dark night when the unassisted eye would be in error several minutes of arc. Some men, after getting the star roughly down near the horizon, hold their sextant in one hand, and a binocular close up to it with the other, and then endeavour to perfect the contact. This is a bad plan, and to convince any one that it is so, let them try it with the sun in broad day-light. It is true the horizon is rendered much more distinct, but with every motion of the binocular the object will dance about—sometimes above the horizon, and sometimes below it. **Star Telescope.** **Improper to use Binoculars.**

To ensure a correct altitude, the line of sight of the telescope used *must be parallel* to the plane of the instrument; this is termed "the line of collimation," and it is abundantly evident that one cannot guarantee to effect this by guess-work, in the dark, with a pair of night-glasses held loosely in the hand. In table 54 of Raper's Epitome will be found the amount of error corresponding to the altitude of the body observed, and the angle the telescope makes with the plane of the sextant.*

It is also well to know that the error, due to the optical axis of the binocular not being held strictly parallel to the plane of the instrument, *always* lies in the direction of making the altitude *too great*, so that those who incline to this mode of observing would do well to make allowance in accordance with the rule.

For convenience of reference in case of a suspected mistake in reading off, the lid of the sextant case should be fitted to close with the index clamped at any part of the arc.

Do not stow your sextant case in a drawer, or on an out-of-the-way shelf, from which a sudden jerk of the vessel might send it flying. Rather, get a brass band $\frac{3}{16}$ of an inch thick, and $\frac{3}{4}$ of an inch broad. Let it be bevelled to fit three sides of the box a little better than half way up. Cover this with coloured flannel or wash leather, and screw it to the bulkhead in such a manner **Mode of stowing Sextant Case.**

* Vide Appendix C

approaching the cushion, and again on rebounding from it. If the ball be propelled from the bottom *left*-hand pocket, so that it strikes the exact centre of the top cushion, it will return to the bottom *right*-hand pocket. All schoolboys are practically familiar with it in the common game of hand-ball, although some of the younger ones may possibly never have heard of the above rule relating to it.

**Artificial preferable to sea horizon.**

The Artificial Horizon, in conjunction with the all important sextant, is of service for astronomical observations on shore when the sea horizon is not obtainable. Even if the sea horizon were available, the artificial one possesses many advantages over it. For example, the accuracy of all observations taken with the sea horizon depends, in the first place, upon a correct knowledge of the estimated or measured height of the observer's eye above the sea level, whereas with the Artificial Horizon it is quite immaterial what the height of the eye may be, as it does not enter into the after calculation.

**Sea horizon not reliable.**

Secondly, owing to the uncertainty of the effects of refraction, the apparent position of the sea horizon can never be depended upon. It is found to be sometimes above its normal place, and at others below it. The rule seems to be, that when the sea is *warmer* than the air, the horizon appears *below* its mean place; and when the sea is *colder* than the air, the horizon appears *above* its mean place. The known capriciousness of terrestrial refraction has prevented the formation of a table of values in connection with this subject.

**Irregularity of refraction.**

Celestial refraction also varies much, so that the tabular amount applied to the altitudes of heavenly bodies may not at the time be the actual value. It is important to arrive as nearly as possible at the correct thing, by using the auxiliary Table III. of Norie's Epitome, to correct the *mean* refraction given in Table IV. An investigation of Table III. will shew that the refraction is greatest with a high barometer and low thermometer.

**Sea Horizon saw-edged when rough.**

Again, if the sea be at all rough, and the observer not much elevated above it, the waves will give a dancing appearance to the horizon, from which the mercurial one is of course exempt. That eminent authority the late Lieut. Raper* says,—

"The image of a celestial object reflected from the surface of a fluid at rest, appears as much *below* the true horizontal line as the object itself appears *above* it; the angular distance measured between the object and its image is therefore *double* the altitude.

* Page 170.

An advantage resulting from this is that in halving the angle shewn by the instrument, *we halve at the same time all the errors of observation.** The reflected image in the fluid is always less bright than the object, but, as it is perfectly formed, and as the surface is truly horizontal, the Artificial Horizon, when it can be employed, is always to be preferred to the sea horizon."

To the navigator, the Artificial Horizon is seldom of other value than to enable him to ascertain the error and rate of his chronometer at ports abroad, where there are no time signals for the purpose. In its use there are many points to be attended to, all of which conduce materially to the desired accuracy of the result. **Its use for rating Chronometers**

The trough should not be less than four inches inside length, because the convexity of the mercury at the edges renders that part unfit for reflecting truly. Moreover, the surface of the central portion is necessarily foreshortened to the observer, and becomes more so as the altitude of the object decreases. **Size of Trough**

The trough should stand sufficiently high inside the roof to admit of the surface of the mercury being on a level with the lower edges of the glasses, otherwise one is needlessly deprived of the full power of the instrument—that is to say, its range for measuring angles is lessened. For the same reason, and also to avoid all possibility of convexity of surface, do not be stingy with the quicksilver. Fill the trough as full as you conveniently can, and do not be content with merely covering the bottom of the dish. The quicksilver is usually contained in an iron bottle, the mouth of which is fitted with a screw plug or stopper. For additional safety, an iron cone (with a fine hole at its apex) screws on over all.

To fill the trough for observing, proceed as follows:—Carefully wipe clean the glasses of the roof, both inside and out; do this with soft chamois leather, breathing on the glasses to get off specks or stains. Next clean out the trough, and remove all dust from its inside with a hat brush. This is very important, since dust being specifically lighter than mercury, should any be left behind, it will infallibly rise to the surface and mar the observation; then place the trough in its selected position, ready for filling. Take the iron bottle, remove the cone and plug, and replace the cone, taking care to screw it on pretty tightly, as mercury is very searching. The cone is now intended to do duty as a filter, and to prevent scum from passing into the trough with the quicksilver. To facilitate this, cover the small hole with **Directions for use.** **Scum on Mercury.**

* Italics by the author.

the finger, and shake the bottle, *holding it upside down, so that the scum may rise to the surface inside.* Then placing it over the trough, and close down (the bottle being still held inverted), remove the finger, and allow the quicksilver to flow. When the trough is sufficiently full, cover the aperture with the finger *before reversing the bottle,* which may then be set down on one side.

It is necessary, when pouring the mercury into the trough, to stop while there yet remains a reasonable quantity in the bottle, otherwise, if it were *all* allowed to run out, the scum would pass with it, and by clouding the otherwise bright surface of the mercury, oblige you to perform the whole operation over again. To cleanse the mercury when it has become very dirty, run it all out of its own bottle, shake it well up in a soda water bottle with some lump sugar broken small, and then strain it through silk. The action of the sugar is purely mechanical.

**Dust to be avoided.**

Having sufficient mercury in the trough, *immediately* put on the roof to prevent dust getting on its surface, on which it would provokingly float, and impair its brilliancy and reflecting power. It is possible, however, to brush it off by sweeping the surface with the straight edge of a piece of clean blotting paper, cut to the full width of the trough.

**Careful handling.**

To put the mercury back again into the bottle is a more ticklish job, and requires a strong hand to lift the trough, and a steady one to preserve its balance without spilling the contents. To do this, the cone is unscrewed from the neck of the bottle, and inserted in its mouth to act like an ordinary funnel; the mercury is then poured *slowly* into it through a small hole for the purpose, at one corner of the iron trough. To avoid loss, it will be found a good plan to place the bottle in the centre of a wash-hand basin. If that is not convenient, the empty sextant case will do nearly as well; *but care should be taken that no globules of mercury are left in it,* for if these get into contact with the arc of the sextant, woe betide the owner of it.

It is advisable, also, to have a somewhat larger trough or stand upon which to place the inner one with its roof. This outer stand or stool should have sides about three-quarters of an inch in height, and should be lined at the bottom with thick cloth, into which the metal edges of the roof would sink, and so exclude the external air. Its inside measurement should be fully two inches greater than the outside measurement of the mercury trough, so as to admit of the latter being easily lifted out of it, and also to allow the inner one to be turned in azimuth (as the sun moves onward), without disturbing its level. It should be substantially made of cast iron, of good weight, and fitted with three short legs, something after the manner of a common kitchen pot.

The most essential requisite in an Artificial Horizon is, that the glasses forming the roof should be pure and free from flaws or veins, and that the faces of each pane should be ground perfectly parallel. The reason for this is the same as that given in the last chapter in connection with the index-mirror of the sextant. Should, however, the glasses be imperfect in this respect, the resulting error in the altitude can be eliminated by turning the roof end-for-end in the middle of each set of observations, and to effect this with certainty, one side of the roof should bear a conspicuous mark—a white cross or star painted on it would do very well. In taking stars on opposite sides of the meridian or zenith, always keep the marked side towards you.*

**Pure glass for roof, and faces parallel.**

**Elimination of errors.**

Intending to take sights with the Artificial Horizon, the first thing is to select a suitable and well sheltered spot, and firm ground should be obtained if possible.

**Shelter and firm ground.**

A beginner will be surprised to find how small a movement at a considerable distance will ruffle the surface of the quicksilver, so as to render observations impossible. On this account the *im mediate* vicinity of the shore is generally unsuitable. Though the spot of observation was fully one hundred yards from the water-line, a very moderate swell breaking on the shingly beach in Callao Bay was found to shake the quicksilver of the artificial horizon, when placed in the back yard of the Hospital belonging to the Pacific Steam Navigation Company, so that it was only during "the smooths" that sights could be obtained.

For the same reason, avoid the neighbourhood of waterfalls, mills, factories, foundries, and shops of workmen generally. The passing of vehicles on a road will also have a disturbing influence on the mercury. Fortunately this fluid, from its great weight, very quickly comes to rest after being shaken, therefore, so long as the tremor is not actually continuous, one can generally manage to secure good observations. Wind is a frequent source of quaking mercury, and care should be taken to have the horizon trough firmly placed, and the roof bedded on something soft, so that the wind cannot get under its lower edge.

**Surface of mercury soon placid after disturbance.**

A screen of canvass to windward is a good thing, as a rule, but on some ground this causes such vibration of the earth as to be worse than the free blast of the wind.

* See pages 384, 385.

For "Equal Altitudes," a spot free from disturbance is absolutely necessary, or, from inability to secure observations corresponding in altitude with those taken in the forenoon, the whole day's work may be lost—to say nothing of the annoyance of the thing.

Again, a place open to the public is objectionable, from the number of idle curiosity-mongers who are sure to surround the party, and, without intending it, make themselves very disagreeable by ignorantly getting in the way, &c.

Supposing a spot suitable in all these particulars has been found, there yet remains an important consideration.

If you are going to observe in the afternoon as well as the forenoon, due regard must be had to the sun's bearing at the first named time, so that when wanted in the afternoon it may not be rendered invisible by houses, trees, hills, or other obstructions. This being seen to, get ready for work by filling the trough as before mentioned, and place it nearly in a line with the object to be observed; *but slightly in the direction that the object is moving*, so as to avoid having to slue the trough in azimuth before the completion of the entire set.

**How to place trough for observing.**

To make delicate observations depending so much upon eye and nerve, *it is necessary to be comfortable in body*. About the easiest position for the observer is, to sit down on the ground at the proper distance from the horizon, and to have the back well supported by a rough box filled with sand or stones, or a chair steadied by some one else sitting on it.

**Position of observer.**

One cannot be comfortable, however, even on a bed of roses, if half stung to death by mosquitoes; so in countries where these plagues exist, and night observations are required, it will be necessary to give a wide berth to swampy localities which are sure to be infested by armies of them, especially if the air be still: indeed, for this reason it is preferable to court a breeze instead of shutting it out.

**Mosquitoes and Sandflies.**

Sandflies are yet worse, as *nothing* will get rid of them; even sailors, who are a long-suffering class, and learn to put up with most things, are not proof against their attacks, and many an otherwise favourable opportunity of getting stars has been spoilt by these diabolical insects.

Should it be intended to observe the sun, turn down *temporarily* the necessary horizon and index-screens; and, being placed so that his image can be seen reflected from the centre of the mercury in the trough, direct the sextant to the sun, and bring it down until it more or less covers the image in the mercury, then quickly turn back the hinged screens—they are no longer needed—in with the telescope, and screw on to its eye-piece a suitable screen, light enough to give a well-defined image of the sun, and yet not too bright to dazzle and fatigue the eye. Beginners are very apt to use too bright suns, and in consequence the effect known as "irradiation," spoils the sharpness of the limbs.* Look to your tangent-screw to see that it is not at the wrong end of its run, which of course would depend upon whether the sun might be rising or falling, otherwise you might find yourself "two blocks" in the middle of a set. By this time the images will be near the point of separation. Tell your assistant with the chronometer to "look out," and at the *actual* moment of contact of the limbs call out "stop."†

**Telescope screens preferable to index or horizon screens.**

In the morning for *lower* limbs the suns will separate, and for *upper* limbs will close. The contrary is the case in the afternoon, and this is irrespective of the kind of telescope employed, whether *direct* or *inverting*. Attention to this rule will prevent any confusion as to which limb was observed.

**Care as to *which* limb is observed.**

Observe upper and lower limbs alternately without unclamping the vernier: this neutralizes the effect of irradiation, and gives less work to do in reading off, besides being advantageous in giving practice with both opening and closing suns, and not having it all one way in the forenoon and another in the afternoon.

It is unwise to make the sets too long, as doing so wearies the eye and hand, and the observations suffer accordingly, especially in hot climates, where the necessity of observing in the full glare of the sun makes it a trying operation.

In "equal altitudes," take care that corresponding observations A.M. and P.M. are made of the *same* limbs. Ascertain index error immediately before and after sights, *using any of the eye-piece shades which were employed for the altitudes.*

In observing with the Artificial Horizon, it is preferable, for many reasons, to use the screens fitted to the eye-piece of the telescope instead of the hinged ones on the sextant. A couple, and sometimes three, of different degrees of shade are to be found in every decent sextant case, and their advantage over the others

**Eye-piece shades.**

* "Irradiation" is an optical illusion in virtue of which white objects, or those of a very brilliant colour, when seen on a dark ground, look larger than they really are.

† When observing, never "make contact" yourself by moving the tangent-screw, but overlap or open the images, as the case may be, clamp securely, and watch for the exact instant of contact. Use the telescope with greatest magnifying power, as it much facilitates correct contacts.

will be apparent to the reader who has studied attentively the chapter on the Sextant:—for example, the brilliancy of the sun varies as clouds pass over, and although to meet the contingency you have to change the shades, no inherent error is introduced by doing so, a happy circumstance, and very different to the result obtained by the use of the Index and Horizon Screens, which latter, however, must of necessity be used with the Sea Horizon.

**Correct position for telescope.**

Before commencing work, equalize the brightness of the two images by raising or lowering the telescope by the large milled headed screw for the purpose. This will bring the axis of the telescope almost in line with the edge of the silvered part of the horizon-glass, which is the best position for observing, and there it must remain all through the performance. No matter, then, what particular depth of shade you may afterwards be compelled to use for the eye-piece, the two images will preserve the same relative tint.

Refer to the example in Norie's Epitome, which shews the method of finding the *true* from the *observed* altitude. It is extremely simple, and need not baulk anyone.

**Observing power of Artificial Horizon.**

Recollect that as the Artificial Horizon gives *double* the actual altitude, you cannot with the ordinary Sextant observe higher altitudes than 60° or 62°; indeed so high an altitude is not to be recommended, for though a quintant will measure 140° or thereabouts, the image will not be sharply defined when reflected from the Index-mirror at such a large angle, unless the glass be more than usually good. To save disappointment, it is well to ascertain beforehand what is the lowest altitude your Artificial Horizon will permit you to take;—this is seldom under 18°, which gives you a range in altitude of about 40°.

**Requisites to take on shore**

When going on shore for sights, take with you a couple of chairs (unless you think you can borrow them), one for the chronometer, and the other for the time-keeper, and to support your own back as before mentioned. Take also pencil and note-book, chamois leather, a couple of towels to spread on the ground under the instruments, *and, in hot weather, an umbrella to keep the chronometer cool.* For night work, dispense with the umbrella, and substitute a couple of bull's-eye lamps—one for the chronometer, and the other for reading off by.

Don't forget the wash-basin or some substitute, unless you have a large reserve stock of quicksilver. Caution the lamp-men neither to flash the light in your eyes nor to throw it anywhere near the Artificial Horizon. A good arrangement is that in which the assistant is seated in the observer's back-supporting chair, with the chronometer immediately facing him on the other, so that the light necessary for taking the time need not interfere with anything else.

For these sort of expeditions, select handy men who have some *gumption*. Think over and make all your preparations well in advance, so as to avoid hurry-scurry and confusion when the time for action comes. Compare chronometers before leaving the ship, and again on your return on board.

**Artificial Horizons for sea use.** Many Artificial Horizons have been invented for use on board ship in times of fog, or for taking stars at night, when the natural horizon is very ill-defined, but only one of them can be considered fairly successful; and unless a man has plenty of money, and can afford to amuse himself with such toys, the others are just as well left alone.

**Davidson's Spirit Level Attachment.** The one referred to was exhibited at the Paris Exposition of 1867, by the inventor, Mr. George Davidson, of the United States Coast Survey, and is called "Davidson's Spirit Level Attachment."

It is stated that, in the hands of a practised observer, the mean of a series of seven sights will give a result within one minute of arc of the truth. The invention lies altogether in the observing telescope of the sextant, and is capable of easy adjustment.

Before placing too much faith in such an instrument, it would be the duty of every man to compare the results obtained by it with others got simultaneously from the sea horizon under *favourable* circumstances.

## THE SEA HORIZON.

**Observations in foggy weather.** Every seaman knows that by going aloft in clear weather his range of view is extended, and that on account of the earth's curvature the visible horizon recedes from him the higher he goes. In like manner, by descending towards the surface of the water his range of view is lessened, and the horizon approaches him. Advantage can be taken of this to get observations in foggy weather. By sitting in the bottom of a small boat in smooth water, or on the lowest step of the accommodation ladder, the eye will be about two feet above the sea level, at which height the horizon is little more than a mile and a quarter distant, so that unless the fog is very dense, serviceable observations are quite possible.

The writer, on three different occasions, when at anchor off the River Plate, during fog, has been enabled to ascertain the ship's position in the way described, and after verifying it by the lead, has proceeded up to Monte Video without seeing land. Of course the vessel was only allowed to go at slow speed, and the deep-sea and hand-leads were kept constantly going, as well as the ground-log,—the latter will be treated of by-and-by.

**Height of eye above sea level.** Every navigator ought to ascertain, before leaving dock, the height of his eye above the load water-line corresponding to his position on the bridge, upper, and main deck, and consequent distance of the visible horizon as seen from each of these places.

**Where to observe from in *clear* weather.** *In fine clear weather take your observations from the highest convenient place, say the bridge.* The reasons for this are that an error in the dip causes an error of the same amount in the altitude; and the dip changes most rapidly the less the elevation above the sea level. For a height of eye of 10 feet the dip is 3′, and for 40 feet it is only 6′ (*vide* Table V. of Norie's Epitome).

Raper says:—

"If the altitude be observed above the deck, as in the top for instance, the horizon will appear better defined, and the variations of the dip by the ship's motion will be less sensible; also the difference of temperature of the sea and air appear to affect the place of the visible horizon less as the observer is more elevated. Hence it would appear that altitudes should be taken from aloft when convenient."

**Where to observe from in *misty* weather.** *In thick or misty weather take your observations from as low a point as possible,* and in all cases apply the correction for height of the eye corresponding to what it is known to be at the spot where the observation was taken.

Reference has already been made to the uncertainty in the place of the sea horizon, due to the unequal temperature of the air and water. This displacement of the horizon sometimes occurs to a most serious extent, and unfortunately on board ship there are no means of detecting it *by observations of the sun,* unless, indeed, its altitude should happen to be above 60°, when, with a good Quintant, it can be taken *from opposite sides of the horizon,* by which means, *if the displacement should be equal all round,* the error due to this cause will be eliminated by taking the mean of the observations.

**Fore and back observations.**

This error in the place of the sea horizon is commonly found on the edge of soundings, and at the mouths of large rivers, and in the latter case is caused by the unequal temperature of the mingling currents of fresh and salt water. It exists in a marked degree in the Gulf Stream and its vicinity.

The writer once found the latitude by an excellent meridian altitude of the sun to be as much as 14′ in error. The time was mid-winter—the day a clear and cloudless one—the sea smooth, and the horizon clean-cut. Five observers at noon agreed within the usual minute or half-minute of arc; nevertheless, on making Long Island (U.S.A.) in less than two hours afterwards, the latitude was found wrong to the amount stated. Many such cases have come under the writer's notice, but this one alone is cited on account of the magnitude of the phenomenon.

**Sun below horizon whilst yet visible.**

As an instance of ignorance of some of the commonest truths in nature, the writer cannot refrain from introducing the following anecdote.

One evening he was pacing the deck with his Chief Officer, and seeing the sun's lower limb touching the horizon, told his subordinate that at that moment the *whole* of the sun's disc was really below it, although from the effects of refraction it was still visible. This the officer *could not* and *would not* believe. He was, however, convinced some few minutes later by a very familiar experiment. Being firmly seated in front of an empty wash-hand basin, so that the brass plug at the bottom was quite invisible, the basin was about half filled with water from a can, when, without moving his head, he at once, to his great astonishment, saw the plug. On letting the water run off, the plug again disappeared.

**Experiment with basin of water.**

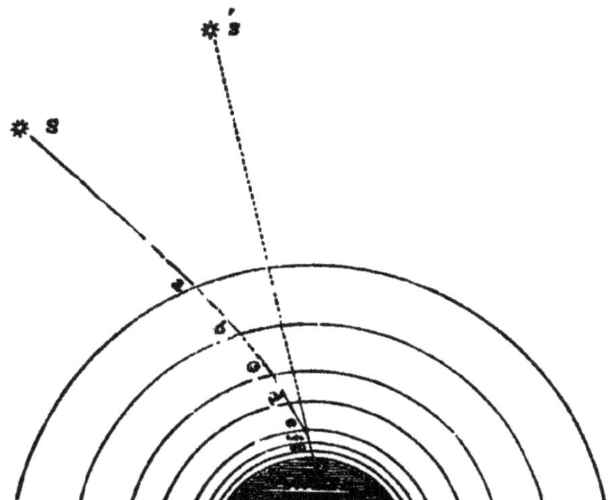


The figure represents a portion of the earth surrounded by the atmosphere, the density of which, as shewn by the increasing nearness of the circles, becomes greater as the surface is approached. The ray of light proceeding from the star $S$ is successively bent or refracted at the points $a\ b\ c\ d\ e\ f\ g$, and finally comes to the eye of the observer at $O$ in the direction $gO$, naturally causing him to imagine the star to be situated in the heavens at $S'$.

**Explanation of refraction.** It was then explained to him that air, in common with all transparent media, possesses the power of bending rays of light out of their straight course.

A ray of light from a celestial body, entering our atmosphere *obliquely*, is more and more bent down or curved as it approaches the earth, so that when it finally enters the eye, it does so in a direction different to what it had in traversing space.

The denser the air is, the greater the effect produced; consequently, there is more refraction near the surface of the earth than at several miles above it, where the air is thinner.

Water is a much better refracting medium than air. Every sailor is familiar with the bent appearance of an oar-blade in clear smooth water, though he may not know the cause. Literally speaking, then, refraction enables us "to see round corners."

See, then, how even the evidence of our own eyes, upon which we place such implicit faith, is liable to deceive us. As refraction causes a celestial body to appear higher than it really is, it must always be *subtracted* from the observed altitude. Reference to Table IV. of Norie will shew that refraction is greatest near the horizon, and vanishes when the object is in the zenith.

## DISAGREEMENT BETWEEN FORENOON AND AFTERNOON SIGHTS.

The question is constantly asked, Can you tell me why it is I can so seldom get my forenoon and afternoon sights to agree? The explanation is simple enough, and as the subject is worthy of being carefully gone into, an attempt will be made to render it clear.

To simplify matters, the reader will be good enough to suppose himself in a vessel at anchor, in the month of December, some few miles south-eastward of Monte Video, and that his chronometers are exactly correct, and his position known to a nicety by cross bearings of Flores Island and the Cerro.

**Elevation or depression of Sea horizon.** Next, let us suppose that, owing to abnormal refraction, the horizon is depressed, say three minutes of arc, and remains in that condition all day.

Let sights be taken at six o'clock in the morning, and again at six in the evening. From the horizon being unduly depressed, these altitudes will be too great by 3 minutes of arc, and when worked out will in each case give too small an hour angle, with the result that the A.M. sights will place the ship 4′ of longitude *eastward* of her true position, and the P.M. sights will place her an equal amount *westward* of her true position, introducing thereby a discrepancy of 8′ of longitude between the morning and afternoon sights—though the sights themselves have been most carefully taken, and the ship has not shifted her position in the least.

To pursue the matter yet further. If the sights were worked with the incorrect latitude obtained from the meridian altitude, still greater error would result. The latitude, from having been worked with an altitude too great by 3′, would itself be in error that amount.

Now by working the A.M. sights with too northerly a latitude, the resulting longitude is thrown 1½′ still further to the eastward—and in like manner, with the P.M. sights, the resulting longitude is thrown 1½′ still further to the westward. **Error due to incorrect latitude.**

It follows that an apparently trivial error of 3′ in the position of the sea horizon can *very easily* introduce a discrepancy of 11′ in the longitude as shown by A.M. and P.M. sights. Cases, sufficiently common, could be selected, depending upon latitude, declination and hour angle, where an error of 3′ in the place of the horizon would cause the A.M. and P.M. longitude to differ as much as 15′ or 16′.

From the foregoing we see that discrepancy between forenoon and afternoon sights can arise from the latitude used being slightly incorrect, also from abnormal refraction, from the course and distance in the interval not being altogether what it was supposed to be, and from badly graduated arcs, as well as other imperfections in cheap sextants. **Error in course and distance.**

When these causes all happen to conspire together (which must *sometimes* be the case), there may be a very great discrepancy between the A.M. and P.M. observations. Moreover, the navigator is apt to lose sight of the fact that he has carried on his longitude *by dead reckoning* for 6 hours, say from 9 o'clock in the morning till 3 o'clock in the afternoon. He is apt to think he had it exact *at noon*, whereas he only had his *latitude* correct at that time.

Again, to work his sights, he is obliged to use the latitude *by account* worked back from noon; so that, taking all these things into consideration, it cannot be wondered at if there should generally be a discrepancy of results.

Popular fallacy concerning afternoon sights.

The writer has known officers to look with great suspicion upon afternoon sights, and openly state that they never knew them to come out right, and were not worth taking. The well informed navigator will see that they are as much to be relied upon as similar ones in the forenoon.*

Abnormal refraction in Red Sea and Persian Gulf.

In the Red Sea and Persian Gulf, the horizon is very liable to displacement from the hot winds coming off the scorching deserts, and the refraction in the day time is generally in excess of the tabular value.

Zebayir and Hanish Islands.

The writer has been enabled to practically demonstrate this to the complete satisfaction of his brother officers, during a voyage to Calcutta and back. It was alleged by those on board, who had repeatedly passed certain islands in the Red Sea known as the Zebayir and Hanish groups, that they were not shewn *relatively* in their proper positions on the chart, and to determine the correctness of this statement the writer devoted some considerable time and labour.

The Zebayir Islands lie, roughly speaking, about 70 miles to the northward and westward of the Hanish group, and both of them directly in the track of steamers passing up and down. The distance between them is such, that if one group should be passed about sight time in the morning, the other group will be passed about sight time in the afternoon.†

Singular instance of seeming discrepancy in relative longitude.

It was found on the outward passage, when sights were taken in the morning off the Zebayir group, that they were apparently marked too far west on the chart; and when similar observations were made in the afternoon, the Hanish group appeared to be shewn too far east on the chart. This was a serious business, as the relative bearing of the two groups of islands was thereby materially altered. The question, moreover, was one independent of the correctness of the chronometers, as the islands were shewn *relatively* to be out of place some 7 or 8 miles.

After a very careful discussion of all the data in connection with the subject (including observations on previous voyages by

* To keep up the traditions of the sea, some few men are still in the habit of "making the sun over the foreyard" as soon as "one bell" is struck; which perhaps—according to the amount of "northing" in the grog—has a tendency to render them a little uncertain in their movements later on in the day. But there is absolutely no evidence to shew that steady "Old Sol" thinks he has earned the right to get upon "the loose," or take an afternoon nap, simply because he has done his duty to himself and the world by passing the meridian up to time.

† The course and distance from Centre Peak Island of the Zebayir group, to High Island off the north end of Jebel Zukur, is S. 30¼° E. (true) 65½ miles.

other observers), the writer came to the conclusion, that in all probability the altitudes of the sun had been vitiated by excessive refraction. To test this, on the passage home, sights were again taken off the Hanish Islands, *which this time happened to be passed in the morning*, and similar observations made off the Zebayir Islands, *which were passed in the afternoon*, thus reversing the conditions of the outward voyage. The result fully justified the writer's expectations, as the Hanish group were now shewn too far west on the chart, and the Zebayir Islands too far east, while on the outward passage just the opposite had been the case. So that all this bother and uncertainty as to the relative position of two important groups of islands was unmistakeably proved to be due to errors of observation, arising from excessive refraction.

**Great caution necessary in navigation.**

These things point strongly to the necessity for great caution in the navigation of a ship. Nothing "slapdash" should be allowed in connection with it, nor too much taken for granted. Who can tell how many wrecks might be traced to this cause, which at the time were ignorantly set down to some extraordinary "jump" of the compasses, or some unlooked for current? Seamen would do well to give this important subject the attention it merits.

---

## CHAPTER VI.

### CHARTS.

A few words concerning the nature of Charts, and the difficulty of their construction, will prove both interesting and instructive to the seaman; in any case, it is only right that he should know something about the tools he has to work with. To this end he should not fail to peruse Commander Hull's very able paper on "The Use of Admiralty Charts in the Practice of Common and Proper Piloting," to be found in the *British Merchant Service Journal* for December, 1880.*

**Difficulty of Chart construction.**

When we attempt to represent any considerable portion of the earth's surface on paper, we are at once met by the formidable difficulty caused by its curved form. A little reflection will convince anyone that it is impossible to make a spherical surface like that of our globe coincide exactly with a flat surface, such as a sheet of paper.

If an orange be cut in two, the inside scraped out of one of the halves, and an attempt then made to flatten the cup-shaped rind on the table, what would happen? It is certain that in so doing the edges would give way and tear up nearly to the centre, showing the impossibility of performing the feat with a non-elastic substance.

It is obvious, therefore, that *no* representation of the earth on a flat sheet of paper, such as a chart, can exhibit all its parts in their true magnitudes and relative positions.

In the construction of charts, it consequently becomes necessary to adopt such a method of laying down the places, which it is intended to depict, as will best fulfil the particular purpose for which they may be required. The various methods adopted for this purpose are called *projections*. Among them may be enume-

---

* London: Richardson & Best, 5, Queen's Head Passage, Paternoster Row, E.C. Price 6d.

rated the Orthographic, Stereographic, Polyconic, Gnomonic, and Mercator's. Of all these, the one commonly used by the seaman is Mercator's. It takes its name from the inventor, who originated the idea about the year 1556; but the *true* principles of the projection were not demonstrated till half a century later, by Mr. Edward Wright, of Caius College, Cambridge. **Chart projections.**

In Mercator's Chart the *meridians* are all drawn as *straight lines* perpendicular to the Equator, and at equal distances from each other. The *parallels of latitude*, also, are represented by *straight lines* parallel to the Equator, and also, like it, at right angles to the meridians. **Mercator's Chart.**

Now, on the *actual* globe, the degrees of latitude are (practically speaking) equal to each other, but the degrees of longitude diminish as they recede from the equator, and converge to a point at the Poles. For example: on the Equator a degree of longitude contains 60 nautical miles, in the latitude of London it contains 37½ miles, in the latitude of 65° North (say at Archangel, in Russia) it contains but 25½ miles, and so goes on lessening in the higher latitudes, until at the North Pole it has no value whatever—which is equal to saying, that *there* longitude has no existence. An observer at the North Pole, let him face round as he may, could only look true South. There is no direction of east or west, by which to convey the idea of longitude, and the sun when visible would always be on the meridian. **Varying lengths of degrees of longitude.**

Since in Mercator's projection the meridians, as already stated, are equidistant in every part, and the degrees of longitude are everywhere made equal to their dimensions on the Equator; it becomes necessary, in order to preserve a due proportion between them and the degrees of latitude, to increase the length of the latter in a corresponding ratio. From the true proportions being preserved throughout between the meridians and the parallels, the *shapes* of the objects delineated on the chart are in every part correct. But as the *lengths* of the degrees both of latitude and longitude, at a distance from the Equator, are enormously exaggerated, the *sizes* of the objects in those parts of the chart are increased accordingly: so that the whole map, if it comprises many degrees of latitude on one side of the Equator, gives a most inaccurate notion of the *relative magnitudes* of its northern and southern parts. **Earth's surface distorted in Mercator's projection.**

For instance, looking at the Admiralty General Chart of the North Atlantic, No. 2059, there will be found in Ungava Bay, on the north coast of Labrador, an island named Akpatok; and to the southward of Cuba, in the Caribbean Sea, will be found the well-known island of Jamaica. Anyone looking at the chart, and unacquainted with the facts detailed above, would undoubtedly think these two islands were exactly of the same length, and would be confirmed in this impression by actual measurement with dividers. But, following out the rule governing measurements on a Mercator's Chart, whereby it becomes necessary to measure the dimensions of each object *in its own parallel of latitude*, it will astonish the uninitiated to find that the island of Akpatok is 65 miles in length, while that of Jamaica is 130 miles, or exactly double. This example will put the wary navigator on his guard not to trust to appearances without first thoroughly understanding the *principles* which govern them.

This defect in the Mercator's Chart does not in any way detract from its utility for nautical purposes.

**Utility of Mercator's Chart for nautical purposes.**

Its great advantage to the sailor consists in the fact that—1st, the ship's course between any two places, however remote, is *represented by a straight line*; 2nd, *this line makes the same angle with each meridian.* Therefore, to find the true course (or rhumb line) on the chart from any one point to any other, it is only necessary to connect them by a straight pencil line, and measure its angle with any one of the meridians which it crosses. This may be accomplished with a common horn protractor; or, as is more usually done, by transferring with a pair of parallel rulers the direction of the aforesaid line to the nearest *true* compass diagram, and so at once read off the course or bearing in points and quarter points. If this course can be carefully preserved, the port bound to will in due time be reached.

In the chapter on Great Circle Sailing it will be demonstrated that, in following up this subject, there are other important matters to be taken into consideration by the man who wishes to subscribe himself "Yours truly, A Master Mariner."

**Mercator's Chart inexact in very high latitudes.**

This projection of Mercator's is not exact in very high latitudes, because cross-bearings of several distant visible objects, which are in fact the same as Great Circle courses, are projected on the chart as straight lines, when they are in reality curves; therefore their intersections will not agree; or, three objects seen in range will not, when projected in their true places on the chart, lie in a straight line. For this reason Mercator's Charts would not be suitable for Polar navigation. Indeed they could not be drawn by the draughtsman, since, according to the principles of the projection, the poles are at an infinite distance, and could not be shewn on paper.

From the foregoing it will be apparent that a Mercator's Chart gives a very incorrect representation of the earth's surface; but, of all the known projections, it is the one best adapted to the wants of the seaman, and has therefore, with the exception just given, been universally adopted for his guidance.

To treat of the other projections of the sphere—more especially the Gnomonic—would be to trench on the surveyor's ground, which is not the intention of this work. For harbour plans the earth is considered a plane, and no account whatever is taken of its curvature, which would be quite inappreciable within the confined limits of such a survey. **Harbour Plans.**

In providing his ship with charts, it will be a matter for the navigator's consideration as to whether he should procure Admiralty or Blue-backed Charts. On this point there is considerable diversity of opinion, though it would appear of late years as if the former were gaining favour, and becoming more popular with the public. **Admiralty Charts versus Blue-backs.**

It is the opinion of the writer that none can compare with those issued by the Hydrographic Office of our own Admiralty, that of the French Government, and the United States of America. In the first place, they are wonderfully cheap, which is ofttimes a consideration; in the next place, they are *official documents,* emanating from the highest authorities; and it would probably be safer to get your ship ashore through any omission or error in a Government Chart, than through a similar one in a "blue chart," especially as it will sometimes happen that the first-named possess the very latest information, which the others may not.

Some recent decisions at "*Board of Trade enquiries into the losses of ships,*" go to show that the authorities display a preference for the Admiralty Chart. No doubt the proprietors of the "Blue-backs" do all in their power to get the "latest corrections," and keep their works up to the mark; but it is difficult to see how they can successfully compete with a Government office, possessing a hundred times their resources. Though they do their best, they can only in many cases get their information second-hand. **Admiralty Charts preferred by Courts of Inquiry.**

By way of affording a standard of comparison, it may be stated that the Hydrographic Office, in London, issues and keeps up to date some 2,600 charts, against about 300 issued by the largest of the private publishers. These figures speak for themselves.

To the mind of the writer, the Admiralty publications offer

superior advantages. They are almost invariably on an appropriate scale; their delineation is remarkable for its clearness; a glance tells which is land and which is water; *correct magnetic* compass diagrams (except on General Ocean Charts) are inserted at convenient intervals, and the charts themselves are never cumbersome in point of size. They leave no wants unsupplied by showing too little, nor do they confuse by showing too much. The art of the draughtsman and engraver is exhibited in all the details, and not the least advantage is the uniformity of system which characterizes each one.*

**Compass-diagrams.**

The use of charts where true and magnetic compass-diagrams are superposed one on the other—that is to say—are drawn from the same centre, is fraught with danger. It is at best but a complicated arrangement, very apt to give rise to mistakes at critical times,—indeed the writer has known it to do so, and on one occasion the vessel got ashore in consequence.

Compass diagrams, except on Ocean Charts, should only shew the *correct magnetic* points. If the *true* bearing or course be

---

**Attempts to Boycott "Wrinkles."**

* A reviewer of the 1st Ed. of "Wrinkles," in a well-known periodical, for which the writer of these pages has not only much veneration, but likewise a loving regard, coolly suggested that the paragraphs having reference to "Blue-backs" should be re-written in a more favourable strain, as in his (the reviewer's) opinion, they bear unjustly upon the publications in question. The writer regrets that his convictions will not allow him to comply with this modest suggestion, and that in studying the sailor's interests he is obliged to run counter to those of other people. In this matter of charts—so long as present conditions exist—the writer's colours are "nailed to the mast," and whilst freely admitting the meritorious character of the work done by private firms long before the machinery of the Hydrographic Department of the Admiralty had attained its present excellence, he thinks the day of "Blue-backs" has departed, and that it is only a question of time as to when they will be completely snuffed out by the overwhelming resources at command of the Government, to say nothing of the boundless advantages afforded by an *unlimited exchequer*. It is not so very long since the Government, for the good of the Commonwealth, took over the telegraph lines from the private companies, and similarly for a few thousands they might buy up the chart publishers, who, as firms of long-standing reputation, must groan under the hardship of seeing their means of livelihood slowly but surely undermined by an all-powerful department, against which it is impossible, in the nature of things, they can hope to compete on anything like equal terms. Since in these pages the author has assumed the *rôle* of guide, he is constrained to express an honest opinion in all that concerns his brother seamen, notwithstanding that doing so means a pecuniary loss to himself, inasmuch as certain "Cheap Johns" in the "shoptician" way of business, who recognise their own portraits here and there throughout the book, have not only declined to sell "Wrinkles" themselves, but have endeavoured to prevent others doing so. The innate love of fair play—so strong a characteristic of Britons—will however, capsize any attempt to "Boycott" the book, and indeed the call for another edition in so short a time shews that the gentry in question may as well accept defeat and throw up the sponge, *bon gré mal gré*.

required, Field's parallel ruler, or a protractor of any kind, will give it with far greater accuracy than a diagram of the kind referred to, which is seldom divided to anything under quarter-points.

A great drawback to "Blue charts" is the absence, in many instances, of the heights of mountain ranges, peaks, hills, islands, and lighthouses. These are all of great assistance in navigation, and no chart is complete without them. Lighthouse heights, when not on the chart, can, it is true, be got from the lighthouse-book, but it is more convenient to have them on the chart.

**Holland backing unnecessary except in special cases.**

Admiralty charts can be backed with "brown holland," which, so far as the material is concerned, makes them last almost for ever; but it increases the expense, and, seeing that some sheets are continually having alterations made in them, according as the banks and channels shift about, it is not advisable to resort to backing.*

Except, perhaps, for the smaller class of vessels, where the Captain buys his own charts, the unwieldy "blue-back" has had its day, and it is only a question of "How long?" until it is superseded by the cheaper and handier productions of the Admiralty. As a result of trying to make them suit all purposes, the scale of the blue charts is, in general, *too large for ocean navigation.*

In case an Admiralty sheet should be destroyed by the capsizing of an ink bottle, the spilling of lamp oil, or any of the accidents which *do* happen, it is merely a loss of from one to five shillings; whereas, when its rival comes to grief, it cannot be replaced under from ten to fifteen shillings. Moreover, the extra cost of the latter offers temptation to keep it in use till completely out of date, and so marked and smudged as to be in many places illegible—a circumstance likely to lead to disaster, if indeed it has not already done so. The Board of Trade has lately become very

---

* In the case of Magnetic Charts of the World, which are only published about once in ten years, of course "backing" is advisable, and here is the way to do it:—Wring the brown holland well out in cold water, and then tack it round the edge of a drawing-board or small kitchen table: rub the paste on to the holland with a hard brush: damp the *back* of the chart with a sponge until the *face* looks dull, then roll it evenly up on a clean, smoothly-turned wooden roller: place this on the near side of the holland, and unroll carefully: leave it until all is quite dry.

The paste should be made with best flour, mixed very thick with cold water. To a dessert-spoonful of brown sugar add five drops of oil of lavender, and five drops of corrosive sublimate; mix this well up with the flour and water, and then add perfectly boiling water to the thickness of custard.

Board of Trade Notice requiring corrections to date of sailing.

particular on this point, and one of the official notices directs the attention of shipowners, and their servants and agents, to the necessity of seeing that the charts taken or sent on board their ships *are corrected down to the time of sailing.*

With the Admiralty chart the sailor can see at a glance if he has the latest information. The year and the month of the various corrections are engraved at the foot; should the correction be large, the notation is made against the imprint; if small, it is given in the left-hand bottom corner; thus an Admiralty chart tells its own history. Perhaps some day the private publishers may see the advantage of adopting the same system.

Charts should invariably be kept on their flats, ready for the rulers to slide over them, instead of being rolled up, and folding them should be avoided if possible. Rolled paper is an abomination at all times—

> "It will and it won't,
> It can't and it don't;"

and if you lose your temper, you tear it, and so make bad worse.

Chart drawers preferable to chart racks.

Every vessel, therefore, should be provided with shallow chart drawers, say 3 ft. 9 in. long, by 2 ft. wide and 4 in. deep. The sheets can then be numbered and classified, and so are ready for use at a moment's notice.

When the writer some years ago was in the habit of navigating Magellan Strait and the many hundred miles of intricate channels leading from it to the Gulf of Penas, and thence to Chiloe, it was necessary to keep the charts and plans on the bridge for constant reference; but seeing that the climate of that region is probably about the most rainy and tempestuous in the world, means had to be devised to protect the charts from the weather, or they would speedily have become so much pulp. This was accomplished as follows.

Wood backing for charts.

First of all, the sheets of the various channels were cut up into convenient lengths, and the carpenter was brought into requisition to make teak-wood backings for them of well seasoned half-inch stuff, dressed smooth. The backing was made an inch longer and broader than the chart or plan it was intended to receive.

Next, some 'size' was made by filling a breakfast cup with isinglass, and pouring on it as much boiling water as the cup would hold. After the 'size' had cooled, and was just beginning to thicken, *both* sides of the chart got several good coats, rubbed in with a soft brush as fast as the paper would take it. When the 'size' was well absorbed and had partially dried, the *back* was treated with flour paste free from lumps, and laid on smoothly, after which the chart was put down on the teak-wood: this had to be done very carefully to avoid creases.

To make the paper lie evenly and to prevent air-bubbles from remaining underneath, a wooden roller was run from top to bottom and back again. This rolling process must not be overdone, or it will cause distortion; and it is as well to place the roller on the middle of the sheet at starting, and roll from you, and then back again the whole way; this with a turn or two sideways ought to be sufficient.

When the chart had thoroughly dried on the board, both it and the teak-wood received three flowing coats of white varnish, made by mixing Canada balsam with twice its weight of best oil of turpentine. Each coat was laid on with a broad, flat, camel-hair brush, and allowed to get perfectly hard before the next was applied.

**Canada balsam.**

When treated in this manner the charts were completely weather-proof, and equal to any amount of rough usage. Should the "size" in the cup get hard like jelly, a few minutes on the stove will bring it back to a proper consistency.

Many vessels have been lost owing to their being economically (?) navigated near land by small scale charts, which cannot possibly shew coast dangers.

Wharton,* in alluding to the increasing necessity for large scale charts constructed from detailed surveys, says :—" A steamer works against time; her paying capabilities largely depend on her getting quickly from port to port, and captains will take every practicable short cut that offers, and shave round capes and corners in a manner to be deprecated, but which will continue as long as celerity is an object. A channel which a sailing vessel will work through in perfect safety, from the obvious necessity of keeping a certain distance off shore, for fear of failing wind, missing stays, &c., will be the scene of the wreck of many a steamer, from the inveterate love of shortening distances, and going too near to dangerous coasts only imperfectly surveyed. Better charts will not cure navigators of this propensity, but will save many disasters by revealing unknown dangers near the land."

**Cutting off corners in Navigation.**

Captain Wharton might have added that this "short cut navigation" is not only due to fierce competition in trade, but unfortunately to an unwise rivalry among seamen themselves, and an utter disregard on their part of the maxim "Let every man

* *Hydrographical Surveying*, page 52.

steer by his own compass." Because Mr. Brown and Mr. Jones do certain things which look very like putting their heads in the fire, Mr. Robinson—even against his better judgment—thinks he must do the same, and so the thing goes on till the weakest comes to the wall.

**Owners should provide Charts.** Charts and Sailing Directories are as much part of the ship's equipment as the *Compass* or the *Lead*, and should be provided by the owner. When the captain has no longer to pay for them, he will keep a better stock, and not take his ship all over the world by one or two general charts, to the manifest risk of life and property.

There is a small sheet published (price 6d.) shewing the signs and abbreviations adopted in the Admiralty charts. It is worth having.

## CHAPTER VII.

### THE PARALLEL RULER.

This, in its commonest form, is an instrument so very familiar to the seaman, and withal so simple in itself, that it may seem unnecessary to refer to it; nevertheless, there is *something* to be said even about the parallel ruler, and it *may* so happen that that *something*—or a portion of it—may be new to the reader.

**Field's Improved Parallel Ruler.**

The ordinary black ruler, with brass joints, is usually employed to *transfer the direction* of a bearing or course to the nearest compass diagram on the chart, whereby to ascertain its name and value. Now, in ocean charts, where compass diagrams are very properly few and far between, a great deal of slipping and sliding, and trying back, as well as "smudging" of the chart, may be saved, and much greater accuracy ensured, by the use of a kindred instrument, known as "*Captain Field's Improved Parallel Ruler.*"

Apparently, at first sight, it only differs from the other in being made of boxwood instead of ebony; but a closer inspection reveals that one of its edges is divided into degrees, similar to the 6-inch ivory protractor found in most small cases of mathematical instruments; the opposite edge is also divided, but in points, half-points, and quarter-points; these latter, however, are never likely to be used, as the degree marked side of the ruler is preferable.

**How to use it.**

The advantage derived from this instrument is, that by laying it down on the course you wish to determine, *so that its centre mark shall be on a meridian line*, you at once read off the true course on the divided edge, *where it is cut by the aforesaid meridian line.*

Few things can be neater or handier in practice, and it gives the course in degrees (and by estimation, to parts of a degree), with an accuracy but little short of that obtained by actual com-
**Size of Ruler.** putation. The ruler is to be had in three sizes; but the two smaller ones, from the minuteness of the angular divisions, are not to be recommended. The 24-inch ruler will be found very convenient, and the marking clear and well defined. After it has been in use a little time, get it cleaned and *French-polished.*

The ordinary parallel ruler, or indeed a straight-edge of any kind, when used in conjunction with a common semi-circular horn protractor, will give equal satisfaction. If you have not a
**The Horn Protractor.** horn protractor, it can be procured for three shillings or so at any optician's. Do not get one with a less radius than 3½ or 4 inches, which is a good serviceable size.

To use it, proceed as follows:—

Having the chart on the table, with its north side from you as usual, lay the straight-edge over the course you wish to steer or determine, and place close against it (edge to edge) the horn protractor, sliding the latter along (its straight side being always in contact with the ruler) *till its centre mark comes fair over any meridian line on the chart;* the exact true course in degrees and half degrees will be found at the circumference, where the latter is cut by the same meridian line, thus:—

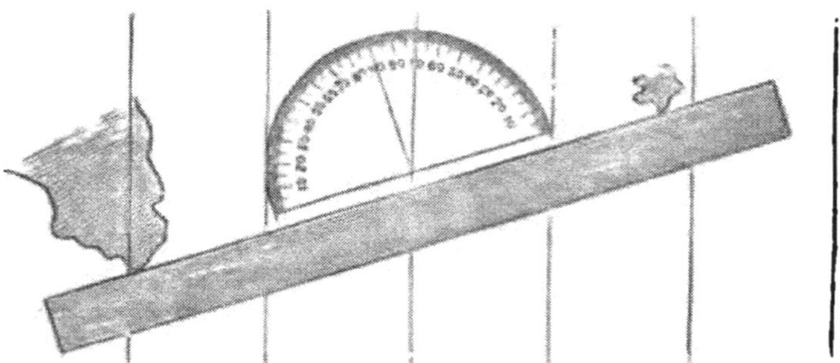

In this particular case it is N. 70° E. or S. 70° W (true).

Almost every one going to sea *abaft* the mast, has a gunter's scale, which would answer first-rate with the horn protractor in the manner just described; but if there should not be one, and the parallel ruler be broken or lost, any lath or piece of wood, dressed straight with the carpenter's trying-plane, would do just as well.

The horn protractor can, however, be rendered of equal service *without* any kind of straight-edge, by the simplest possible contrivance.

Bore a fine needle-hole at its centre mark, and another about a quarter of an inch or so below it; through these two holes reeve a couple of feet of sewing cotton (silk is better), and knot one end; keep the knot on the *top* side of the lower hole, so that it may not prevent the protractor from lying flat on the chart, and bring the other end up through the puncture at the *central point*, and haul it tight. **How to fit and use it.**

To ascertain a course or bearing, it is merely necessary to lay the horn protractor, with its zero line on any convenient *meridian*, sliding it towards the north or south, so that the thread when stretched may lie exactly over the two positions on the chart between which it is required to know the course, thus:—

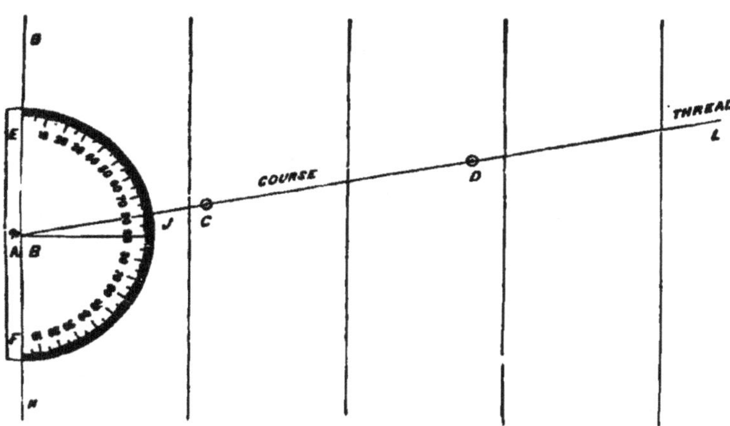


In the diagram, *A* represents the knotted end of the thread; *B*, the centre hole through which the thread comes up; *EF*, the zero line of the protractor, laid exactly over *GH*, a meridian line; *CD*, two positions on the chart between which it is required to know the course; the line *BJCDI* represents the thread. The true course (N. 80° E. or S. 80° W.) will be found at *J*, where the margin of the protractor is cut by the thread.

The oblong ivory protractor already mentioned could be used in a precisely similar manner, but the horn one has the advantages of transparency and larger marginal divisions. Both are divided **Oblong ivory protractor.**

from zero at $E$ and $F$ up to 90° at the middle line, and when using them in the manner indicated above, the course is in each case to be reckoned *from* North or South *towards* East or West, as the case may be.

As already explained in a previous chapter, the course between any two places on a Mercator's chart *is the angle which a straight line connecting them makes with the meridian.*

**True, correct magnetic, and compass courses.**

Here seems a good place to say a few words about COURSES. So far, reference has merely been made to the *true course;* when the Variation has been applied, it becomes the *correct magnetic course;* and when the Deviation has been applied to this last, it becomes the *compass course*, or the one which is to be actually steered by that particular compass for which the deviation has been allowed. The navigator will do well, then, to bear in mind that there is—1st, the *True Course;* 2nd, the *Correct Magnetic Course;* and 3rd, the *Compass Course.* Do not get confused, but keep these courses distinct in your mind, and avoid calling them by names other than those here given.

**Deviation and local attraction**

One word about Deviation. It is too often mixed up with Local Attraction, the two expressions being used indifferently to mean the same thing. This is wrong, as they are entirely distinct. The first named is due to causes *within* the ship herself; the latter, to *outside* influences. Remember this.

For laying off courses as above, the writer had made to order an ivory protractor, 10 inches by 3 inches. This size admits of good large divisions, but it is expensive. A similar one in boxwood would cost less, and probably be practically as good. The only thing that can be said against boxwood is its greater liability to chip at the edges.

Ebonite scales and protractors are found to answer well, and do not expand or contract *so* much as other sorts, but this extreme refinement is a thing apart from our subject, and need not be considered.

## CHAPTER VIII.

### DIVIDERS.

To give a "natty man" satisfaction in their use, dividers should be of good quality. The points must be fine, and formed of well tempered *steel* that cannot be bent or blunted. Above all, the *joint* should be good, for if not, it will be provokingly difficult to set the legs to any required distance, on account of the spring and want of uniformity in their motion. A pair of dividers with an indifferent joint, when being opened or closed, will move by fits and starts, and either go beyond the measurement required or stop short of it. The joint should also be stiff enough in its action to hold the legs in any required position without fear of alteration when handled with ordinary care. These are the things which require to be tested when making a purchase. Instrument cases always contain a key for tightening up the joints of the dividers when they work slack. What are known as Hair Dividers give *very* exact measurements, but for sea use they are *too* good, and too costly.

**Steel points and smooth working joints.**

**Hair Dividers.**

It is convenient to have a small bracket fastened on to the bulkhead over the chart table, to contain two pairs of dividers—large and small. Screw a piece of polished mahogany 8 inches long by 3 inches broad, and ¾ inch thick, flat against the bulkhead. About two-thirds of the distance from the bottom insert a couple of brass eyes side by side. The dividers may be shipped into these, and their points rest on a ¾-inch ledge or shelf, forming a foot to the bracket. This shelf should have a moderately thin piece of india-rubber let flush into its upper surface, as a bed to receive the points without injury when dropped hurriedly into their place. To a landsman all this may seem needless trouble, but the sailor knows the value of the maxim—"A place for everything, and everything in its place." Moreover, a ship rolls and tumbles about in all directions—a house does not; so that afloat

**Bracket for Dividers.**

it is absolutely necessary to have safe places of deposit for other things besides glass and crockery.

**Pen and pencil rack.** There is a very neat little American "dodge" for holding pens, which can be purchased in Liverpool for a few pence, and is very useful. It consists of a spiral spring secured to a thin back plate, and the whole is gilded, and looks quite ornamental. The pen is held between any two parts of the spring. One of these ingenious little contrivances will contain four or five pens or pencils. It is secured to the bulkhead by a small screw at top and bottom.

DIVIDERS FOR USE WITH ONE HAND.

When a ship is rolling violently, and it becomes necessary to consult a chart, every seaman is aware of the difficulty experienced in keeping the chart and parallel ruler on the table with one hand, whilst with the other he is trying to manipulate the dividers. Some clever fellow, who has evidently been pretty often in this fix, has invented a pair of dividers *for use with one hand*, which are worthy of coming into general use. They were first shown to the writer by the captain of a schooner-yacht on the Clyde, who claimed to be the inventor. The dividers are represented above, and it will be seen that they are opened by a pressure of the palm of the hand on the circular part, which causes the legs to overlap each other and the points to separate. The closing movement is readily controlled by the thumb and forefinger, which, for this purpose, act against the palm pressure. As they are unpatented, they can be ordered from any instrument maker, and can be made with any degree of finish "*to suit the pocket*" of the purchaser.

**Dividers for use with one hand.**

## CHAPTER IX.

### THE PELORUS, WITH REMARKS ON AZIMUTHS.

This valuable instrument, the invention of Lieutenant Friend, R.N., deserves more than a mere passing notice. Its utility is so great that every iron ship should be provided with one.

The Pelorus is a *dumb card*—that is to say, a compass card *without needles*—made of brass, entirely unmagnetic, and not partaking in any way of the character of a compass, except that its face shows the points and degrees in the usual manner. The card is something less than 7 inches in diameter, and is mounted on gimbals, which, in conjunction with a central balance-weight suspended from the under side of the instrument, enables it to preserve its horizontality, whatever the motion of the ship may be. **Dumb card**

The card revolves on an upright pivot like a "*teetotum*." This pivot also serves to carry the sight vanes, which can revolve upon it independently of the card, or can be secured to it at pleasure by a large milled-headed screw surmounting the pivot. One of the uprights of the sight vane is fitted with a thread, and has a hinged mirror or speculum at its base, and the other has a coloured eye-screen, which is made to slide up and down the bar at will. A fore-and-aft mark on the inner ring does duty as the lubber's point or ship's head, and another smaller milled-headed screw on the fore part enables the card to be clamped to this mark at any desired course without fear of shifting. The whole thing is so simple, that *anyone* looking at it can understand the arrangement in less than five minutes. The apparatus is enclosed in a mahogany box some eleven inches square, and from which it is inseparable.

The patent-right having long since expired, the instrument is now constructed to order by almost any compass maker at a cost of about £3 10s.

**Stands for Pelorus.**

Having a Pelorus, the first thing is to provide suitable stands for it in various parts of the ship, so that it may be moved from one to the other as may be found convenient. Sometimes at one position a sail, the funnel, a mast, *or an important passenger*, may be in the way of the body to be observed, in which case the Pelorus can be removed to another spot where the view is unobstructed. It will be found advantageous to fit at least four such stands—one on each side of the bridge, and a couple in the neighbourhood of the quarter-deck. A skylight, the top corner of a deck-house, or a meat safe, will answer the purpose very well. The stands on the bridge may be made in the form of a small table without legs, to bracket against the handrail. Some men go to the expense of a couple of turned teak-wood pedestals. The places selected need not be amidships—in fact, they are better when not so; but, wherever they may be, *it is absolutely necessary that great pains should be taken to ensure the fore-and-aft line of the instrument being strictly parallel with the ship's keel.*

**Care in placing Stands.**

**How to do it.**

To effect this with certainty (the instrument being in its intended position—say on the starboard or port side of the bridge), measure carefully the horizontal distance of its centre from the midship seam, and lay off this distance on the deck *both at the bow and stern end of the vessel.* At each such place erect a batten, and see that it stands perfectly plumb; the ship herself is, of course, supposed to be on an even beam; then set the North point of the card (though any other will do just as well) to the lubber line, and clamp it there by the small milled-headed screw at the fore side; release the sight vane, if clamped, and turn it so that the centre mark at the base of the upright holding the thread may also coincide with the North point; place the box by eye approximately square with the fore-and-aft line of the ship, taking care, of course, that the lubber's point is forward; now look from aft forward through the sight vanes, and slue the box slowly one way or the other till the batten at the bow is seen in one with the thread.

When exact coincidence is established, the result thus far is satisfactory; but to render it completely so, turn the sight vane half round on its axis without moving the box in any way, and set it to the South point of the card. If now, on looking at the after batten, it should be found to be exactly in one with the thread of the vane, all is well, and the fore-and-aft line of the Pelorus coincides truly with the fore-and-aft line of the ship.

Direction of lubber line to be parallel with keel.

The instrument must now be secured in this position by an all-round coaming about an inch high, forming a seat into which the box can at any time be shipped without further trouble. Bore a couple of holes through the coaming in each of the sides to act as scuppers. Do not take down the battens till the coaming is fitted and finished, when the line of the instrument should be *again* tested. If found to be slightly out, it can be remedied by a couple of milled-headed screws, at the side of the case, which act in opposite directions, on a sliding block carrying the trunnion of the gimbal. When this last adjustment is perfected, *the side screws must not again be touched;* and if on completing the remaining stands, their fore-and-aft lines be found not quite exact, it will be necessary to alter the *coamings* until they are so. In fixing the quarter-deck stands, the *after* battens can be dispensed with.

If at any time the ship should be in graving dock where some distant object can be seen, it will be very easy to test the relative accuracy of the stands by the following method:—Place the Pelorus in any one of its receptacles; clamp the North point of the card to the lubber line, and, looking through the sight vanes at the distant object, ascertain its bearing to the nearest quarter degree; remove the instrument to each of the other stands, and if the various bearings agree, it is evident that the fore-and-aft line of each station is also in agreement.

It must not be understood from this, that the Pelorus gives the *real* bearing of the distant object; it merely gives the horizontal angle between the object and the ship's head. The term "bearing" is in this case used merely for convenience.

Adjustment of compass lubber lines.

To ascertain if the lubber-points of your deck compasses agree with the Pelorus, unship the cards, put a small piece of cork on the point of the pivots, and replace the cards with their North points to the lubber line; put on the glass covers; ship the azimuth instrument, and take the bearing as before.

Each compass now becomes a dumb card in itself; should there be any discordance, put up the battens and test the fore-and-aft line of the Pelorus; if found correct, it *must* be the lubber-points of the *compasses* which are astray. These are easily painted out, and ruled in afresh in their proper places. A soft black lead pencil is the best thing to do it with.

The distant object used in this operation should not be nearer than six or seven miles, unless it bear nearly ahead or astern—say a couple of points on either bow or quarter, when four or five miles will suffice. If the sun be shining, you are of course independent of everything else, since you can, if you are smart, use *it* as the distant object. The sun's bearing will seldom alter so much in the minute or so required to shift the instrument quickly from one place to another, as to introduce any appreciable error; but if extreme accuracy be required, it is an easy matter to get the exact change of bearing corresponding to the Latitude, Declination, and Apparent Time from Burdwood's Tables.

The Pelorus is handy for many purposes which will be referred to hereafter, but its chief use is to ascertain the Deviation of the compass, or to set the course. Before going into the details of how this is to be done, it will perhaps be advisable to say something about Azimuths. The general practice on board ship is to observe an azimuth or bearing of the sun by compass, at the same time that the morning sights are taken: the sun's *altitude*, as found by these sights, is used to find the true azimuth. This is a round-about method, involving much needless labour, and should be abolished now that tables are published which give by simple inspection the required information.

**Alt. azimuths.**

It will be made clear further on, that in an iron vessel the Deviation requires to be determined pretty frequently; and to be constantly getting out one's sextant to "shoot the sun," and afterwards take the bearing, and then work up a lengthy problem, is not conducive to this end. Half the trouble and all the fuss may be avoided by using the method wherein the *time*, instead of the *altitude*, is employed. This is called the method of "Time Azimuths;" therefore, when, according to common custom, an azimuth is taken along with the morning sights, instead of laboriously figuring out the sun's true bearing by the *altitude-azimuth* problem, the hour angle (time from noon) found by the sights can be employed to take out the true bearing direct by inspection.

**Time azimuths.**

## AZIMUTH TABLES.

**Burdwood's Tables.**

Some sixteen or seventeen years ago, Staff-Commander Burdwood, R.N., published a book entitled: "Sun's True Bearing, or Azimuth Tables," in which is given the sun's true bearing at intervals of 4 minutes for each degree of latitude between 60° and 30° in both hemispheres. In 1875, Captain Davis, R.N., brought out an extension of these tables down to the Equator, so that at the present time the sun's true bearing can be taken out from these books for any latitude between 60° north and 60° south, and for

**Davis's Tables**

any time between sunrise and sunset *excepting when the altitude exceeds* 60°.

Time azimuths preferable to alt. azimuths.

There are, however, many men prejudiced enough to believe that the "old-fashioned plan," as they call it, is preferable to the tables, as the latter, in their estimation, are liable to error. These are the men who insist upon their officers working up azimuths according to the "Epitome method." They forget, or do not know, that in all calculations the greater the number of figures employed, the greater the liability to error; and surely trained computers are less likely to make mistakes than seamen, who, by nature of their calling, are not nearly so well versed in such work. The writer does not mean to say that the tables are infallible, but he will back them at odds against the figures of the 'antediluvians' who pooh-pooh them. By glancing the eye up and down the column, and across the page to the right and left, a mistake of any importance is detected in an instant by the want of harmony in the run of the leading figures. In working out any problem in navigation, one might just as well refuse to employ the ready-made tables of secants, sines, and tangents, and insist upon computing for one's self the necessary logarithms for each particular case.

Burdwood, in his preface, says :—

Reason for preference.

"Results exhibited in a tabular form have certain advantages. In these tables, for example, the value of an error in either of the three elements used in the computation is seen at once, and hence the most desirable time for making the observations, so that an error in either the Apparent Time, Latitude, or Declination, shall produce the least error in the true bearing."

To use these tables, it is necessary to know the Latitude and Declination each within half a degree, and the Apparent Time at Ship within, say, a couple of minutes; but this latter depends upon circumstances, as reference to the tables will show that, under certain conditions, the sun's bearing *will not alter one degree in an hour*, and at other times it will alter a degree in three minutes. Herein, as Burdwood justly says, lies one of the great advantages of the tables.

## APPARENT TIME AT SHIP.

Though the finding of the Apparent Time at Ship is a simple operation, yet few know the right way of doing it; therefore it is as well to give a couple of examples. It is premised that the longitude is known within a quarter of a degree or so.

**To find Apparent Time at Ship and set pocket watch.**

Write down the error of chronometer, prefixing the *plus* (+) sign if it is slow, or the *minus* (-) sign if it is fast.

Write down the Equation of Time taken from page II. of the Nautical Almanac, and correct it roughly for Greenwich Mean Time. If the precept at the head of the column says the Equation is to be subtracted from Mean Time, prefix the *minus* sign; but if to be added, prefix the *plus* sign.

Turn the longitude into time, and if it is westerly, prefix the *minus* sign; if it is easterly, prefix the *plus* sign.

If the three quantities should happen to have similar signs, add them together, and prefix the common sign; but if the quantities should happen to have *unlike* signs, add the two similar ones together, and take the *difference* between their sum and the unlike quantity, prefixing the sign of the greater. This remainder will be the amount, which (to find Apparent Time at Ship) is either to be added to or subtracted from the chronometer time, according to its sign.

*Example:* Jan. 16th, 1880, about 10 hours P.M. at Greenwich; required to know the Apparent time at Ship, the longitude being 64° 38′ West, and the error of the chronometer 4m. 22s. slow of Greenwich Mean Time.

| | | H. | M. | S. | |
|---|---|---|---|---|---|
| Longitude, 64° 38′ W..... | − | 4 | 18 | 32 | Having like signs, add them together. |
| Equation of time.......... | − | 0 | 10 | 3 | |
| | − | 4 | 28 | 35 | Having unlike signs, take the difference. |
| Error of chronometer | + | 0 | 4 | 22 | |
| Chr. fast of App. Time at Ship | − | 4 | 24 | 13 | |

Therefore, to find Apparent Time at Ship, it will merely be necessary to subtract 4h. 24m. 13s. from the time shown by chronometer.

To set your watch or clock, fix upon a given Time, a minute or so *in advance* of what the chronometer actually shows, to enable you to prepare; let the time by chronometer at which you intend to regulate your watch be 10h. 26m. 13s.; subtract from this 4h. 24m. 13s., and 6h. 2m. 0s. will be the Apparent Time at Ship when the hands of the chronometer arrive at 10h. 26m. 13s.

This matter of setting the wheelhouse and other clocks to Apparent Time at Ship is such an every-day necessity, that we will give one more example. In this case the longitude is East, and the Equation of Time and chronometer error are both additive.

*Exam.* 2: September 24th, 1880, *about* 4 P.M. at Greenwich; required to know the Apparent time at Ship, the longitude being 17° 40′ East, and the chronometer 8m. 25s. slow of Greenwich Mean Time.

| | | H. | M. | S. | |
|---|---|---|---|---|---|
| Longitude, 17° 40′ E........ | + | 1 | 10 | 40 | Having like signs, are all additive. |
| Equation of time........ | + | 0 | 8 | 16 | |
| Error of chronometer........ | + | 0 | 8 | 25 | |
| Chr. slow of App. Time at Ship | + | 1 | 27 | 21 | |

Here we have 1h. 27m. 21s. to be added to the chronometer time; *so, to make the even minute for the watch,* let us fix upon 3h. 54m. 39s. by chronometer; adding the above correction to this, we get 5h. 22m. 0s. as the Apparent Time at Ship when the hands of the chronometer arrive at 3h. 54m. 39s.

It will be noticed in both these examples that, in choosing the chronometer time at which to regulate the watch, the proper number of odd seconds has been allowed, so that the watch may be set to the even minute without the trouble of counting seconds, or of estimating them when there is no second-hand.

The following example shows the mode of ascertaining the deviation by using the azimuth tables:—

## TIME-AZIMUTHS OF THE SUN.

Saturday, January 17th, 1880, about 0·45 P.M., the sun was observed to bear by Standard compass S. 15° W., when a chronometer, which was 4m. 23s. slow of Greenwich Mean Time, showed 5h. 29m. 30s.; latitude by account, 40° 12′ North; longitude by account, 70° 50′ West; variation at place of ship, corrected for secular change, − 9½°. Here, be it understood, that Easterly variation or deviation is always represented by the plus (+) sign, and Westerly variation or deviation by the minus (−) sign. **Example of finding Apparent Time at Ship.**

| | | H. | M. | S. | |
|---|---|---|---|---|---|
| Time by chronometer .............. | | 5 | 29 | 30 | Declination corrected for Greenwich Mean Time, 20° 46′ South. |
| Chronometer slow of G. Mean Time .. | + | | 4 | 23 | |
| Greenwich Mean Time ............ | | 5 | 33 | 53 | |
| Corrected Equa. of Time, page II, N.A. | − | | 10 | 19 | |
| Apparent Time at Greenwich ...... | | 5 | 23 | 34 | |
| Longitude in time ................ | − | 4 | 43 | 20 | |
| Apparent Time at Ship ............ | | 0 | 40 | 14 P.M. | |

Open the tables at the nearest whole degree of latitude (40°) having the declination of the *contrary* name; this will be found at page 109. In the right-hand margin seek for 0h. 40m. P.M., and under 21°, the nearest whole degree of declination, will be **Example of Time-Azimuth.**

found the sun's true bearing 169½°, which, according to the precept at the foot of the left-hand page, is to be reckoned from North to West.

The work now takes this form:—

| | | |
|---|---|---|
| ☉'s *True* bearing at 0h. 40m. P.M. ... | N. 169½° W. | |
| | 180° | |
| ☉'s *True* bearing, with name changed for convenience............... | S. 10½° W. | |
| Variation by chart ............ | − 9½° | Applied to the right. |
| ☉'s Correct magnetic bearing...... | S. 20° W. | Or what it would be in a wooden ship uninfluenced by iron. |
| ☉'s Bearing by compass .......... | S. 15° W. | |
| Deviation ..... .............. | + 5° | Because the corr. mag. bearing is to the *right* of the compass bearing. |

**Interpretation of Algebraic signs.** It will be noticed that in applying the variation to the sun's true bearing, it is added (because Westerly), although the minus ( − ) sign is prefixed. The minus ( − ) sign in this case is only the *name* of the variation, and does not mean that the quantity following it is to be subtracted. The deviation is + 5°, which means, in like manner, that its *name* is Easterly. Similarly, astronomers distinguish North declination by the plus ( + ) sign, and South declination by the minus ( − ) sign. It is quicker than writing the word it expresses.

In finding the *correct magnetic* bearing from the *true* bearing, stand in imagination at the centre of your compass-card, looking outwards towards the margin, and apply Westerly variation to the right, and Easterly to the left. To find the *compass course* from the *correct magnetic course*, apply the *deviation* in exactly the same manner.

## TIME-AZIMUTHS OF THE STARS.

**Azimuth tables applicable also to Moon and Stars.** Although Burdwood and Davis's Tables are termed "Tables of the *Sun's* True Bearing or Azimuth," they may, notwithstanding, be made available for determining the true bearing of the moon, planets, and stars, when the declination of those bodies ranges between 23° N. and 23° S. The following is a table of the mean places of stars of the 1st and 2nd magnitude included within that range of declination for January 1st, 1881.

| Names of Stars. | Mag. | Right Ascension. | Annual Variation. | Declination. | Annual Variation. |
|---|---|---|---|---|---|
| | | H. M. S. | S. | ° ′ ″ | ″ |
| β Ceti ........................ | 2 | 0 37 36·9 | + 3·01 | 18 38 25 S | + 19·80 |
| α Arietis ........................ | 2 | 2 00 28·0 | + 3·37 | 22 53 56 N | + 17·20 |
| α Tauri. (*Aldebaran*) ..... | 1 | 4 29 5·6 | + 3·44 | 16 16 7 N | + 7·58 |
| β Orionis. (*Rigel*) ......... | 1 | 5 8 49·1 | + 2·88 | 8 20 26 S | + 4·42 |
| δ Orionis........................ | 2 | 5 25 55·6 | + 3·06 | 0 23 19 S | + 2·93 |
| ε Orionis........................ | 2 | 5 30 10·5 | + 3·04 | 1 16 46 S | + 2·59 |
| α Orionis. (*Betelguese*)..... | 1 | 5 48 43·8 | + 3·25 | 7 23 00 N | + 0·98 |
| α Canis Maj. (*Sirius*)...... | 1 | 6 39 54·2 | + 2·65 | 16 33 14 S | − 4·72 |
| α Canis Minoris (*Procyon*) | 1 | 7 33 4·4 | + 3·14 | 5 31 42 N | − 9·01 |
| α Hydræ. (*Alphard*) ..... | 2 | 9 21 44·3 | + 2·95 | 8 8 37 S | − 15·43 |
| α Leonis. (*Regulus*) ...... | 1.2 | 10 2 2·0 | + 3·20 | 12 32 54 N | − 17·45 |
| γ[1] Leonis ..................... | 2 | 10 13 24·6 | + 3·32 | 20 26 34 N | − 18·08 |
| β Leonis. (*Denebola*)...... | 2 | 11 42 59·3 | + 3·06 | 15 14 14 N | − 20 10 |
| α Virginis. (*Spica*) ...... | 1 | 13 18 55·4 | + 3·15 | 10 32 23 S | − 18·92 |
| α Bootis. (*Arcturus*) ...... | 1 | 14 10 14·0 | + 2·73 | 19 48 11 N | − 18·83 |
| β Libræ. (*Zubenelg*) ...... | 2 | 15 10 36·2 | + 3·22 | 8 56 34 S | − 13·52 |
| β[1] Scorpii................... | 2 | 15 58 31·1 | + 3·48 | 19 28 43 S | − 10·16 |
| α Ophiuchi. (*Ras Alhague*) | 2 | 17 29 24·6 | + 2·78 | 12 38 53 N | − 2·87 |
| α Aquilæ. (*Altair*) ......... | 1.2 | 19 44 58·6 | + 2·93 | 8 33 [illegible] N | − 9·25 |
| α Pegasi. (*Markab*) ...... | 2 | 22 58 50·0 | + 2·98 | 14 33 55 N | − 19·32 |

**Bright stars within 23° N. and 23° S.**

When there are two figures in the magnitude column, they signify that the star occupies an intermediate place. They are sometimes written in one order, and sometimes in the reverse. thus,—1·2 and 2·1 mean that the star is below the 1st and above the 2nd magnitude: in the former case, nearer the 1st than the 2nd; in the latter, nearer the 2nd than the 1st. The separating dots are not to be considered as decimal points.

**Star-Azimuths.**

It is perfectly wonderful how few men avail themselves of the stars on a fine night, to see how their compasses are behaving. This arises principally from an ill-defined idea, that any problem connected with the stars is much too difficult to be meddled with. How different are the actual facts !!

**Advantages of Star-Azimuths over Sun or Moon.**

*Azimuths of the stars, planets, and moon, are just as easily and as quickly worked up as azimuths of the sun.*

The former possess a decided advantage over the latter, inasmuch as a mistake in the working is at once detected if you observe a couple or three stars, since, having different elements, the computations are independent of each other. Whereas you may take 20 azimuths by the sun, and even though all agree, they may every one be greatly in error, through having been inadvertently worked in each case with the wrong Latitude, or Declination, or Time.

The greater the number of observations, the more the error would be confirmed, and though you might somewhat wonder at it, you would probably accept the result, and perhaps get led into danger. Now, with the stars the case is entirely different, as the one is a check upon the other.

To find the hour angle or meridian distance of a star, a planet, or the moon, you have merely, on taking the bearing, to note time by the chronometer, and proceed as follows:—

**To determine Hour Angle.**

*1st.* To the time shewn by chronometer, apply its error for the day—the result will be Greenwich Mean Time, to which apply the longitude in time, *adding* it if the longitude be *East*, and *subtracting* it if the longitude be ***West;*** the result will be Mean Time at Ship.

*2nd.* Take from the Nautical Almanac (page II. for the month) the Sidereal Time (last column), and add to it the acceleration on Greenwich Mean Time, found in the table for the purpose on page 480 of the Nautical Almanac for 1884, or Table 38 of Norie's Epitome.

*3rd.* Add together the Mean Time at Ship and the corrected Sidereal Time; from the sum, increased if necessary by 24 hours, subtract the right ascension of the star; the remainder will be the star's hour angle West of the meridian.

**To name Hour Angle East or West.**

If the remainder be greater than 12 hours, take it from 24 hours, and the result will be the hour angle East of the meridian. Should the remainder be more than 24 hours, reject 24 hours, and the result will be the hour angle West of the meridian.*

This last part will seem somewhat confusing to the beginner, but it is nothing like so difficult as it looks. Moreover, should there be any doubt as to the amount of the hour angle, or its name, the question is easily settled by reference to Norie's Table 44, where the apparent time is given on which the principal stars pass the meridian.

**Check against mistake in naming Hour Angle.**

Knowing more or less the time at ship when you made the observation, and by Table 44 the *approximate* time on which the star will pass the meridian, you at once see whether the star is East or West of it. But, independently of this, in actual practice the *observed* compass bearing of the star will nearly always tell you which side it is, provided you apply to it the variation and approximate deviation. The preceding rule for finding the star's hour angle applies also to the moon and other planets.

Burdwood has a caution near the end of his preface, to this effect:—

* To understand this, independent of any printed rule, refer to diagram on page 240.

"With reference to the note at the foot of each page of the azimuth tables, as the sun in the forenoon or A.M. is East of the meridian, and in the afternoon or P.M. West of the meridian, in applying the note to indicate the bearing of a star, substitute *East* of the meridian for A.M., and *West* of the meridian for P.M." **Left hand column of Azimuth Tables never to be used but with Sun.**

In taking from the tables the azimuth of a star, or the moon, its hour angle must *always* be taken from the *right-hand column* of the page, under the words, "Apparent Time, P.M." The subjoined examples will, it is hoped, show with what ease and certainty star, planet, and moon azimuths can be worked.

*Example* 1.—About 10 P.M., Saturday, January 17th, 1880, ship being in latitude 39° 20′ N., and longitude 73° 11′ W., the star Sirius was observed to bear, by Standard compass, S. 15½° E., when a chronometer which was 4m. 24s. slow of G.M.T. showed 14h. 42m. 05s. Variation at ship's place, – 7°.

| | H. | M. | S. | |
|---|---|---|---|---|
| Time by chron. | 14 | 42 | 5 | |
| Error | + | 4 | 24 | |
| G. M. time | 14 | 46 | 29 | |
| Longitude in time | –4 | 52 | 44 | |
| Mean Time at Ship | 9 | 53 | 45 | |
| Sidereal Time from N.A | 19 | 45 | 12 | |
| Acceleration for 14h. 46m. 29s. | + | 2 | 26 | |
| R.A. of the meridian | 29 | 41 | 23 | |
| R.A. of * Sirius | 6 | 39 | 54 | |
| *'s hour angle | 23 | 01 | 29 | W. |
| | 24 | 00 | 00 | |
| *'s hour angle | 0 | 58 | 31 | E. |

Declination of Sirius, 16½° S.

Open Burdwood's Tables at latitude 39°, *contrary name to the declination* (page 99), and with declination 16½° and hour angle 0h. 58m. *in the right-hand column*, look for the bearing by interpolation, which will be found to be 163¼°; this, according to the precept at the bottom of the left-hand page, is to be read from North to East. The remainder of the work is as follows:—

| | |
|---|---|
| *True* bearing of * Sirius at 0h. 58m. East of meridian | N. 163¼° E. |
| | 180° |
| " " " with name changed | S. 16¾° E. |
| Variation by chart | – 7° |
| Star's *correct magnetic* bearing | S. 9¾° E. |
| Star's *compass* bearing | S. 15½° E. |
| Deviation | + 5¾° |

**Example of Star-Azimuth**

## TIME-AZIMUTHS OF THE MOON.

As a check upon Sirius, the moon's bearing was observed a few minutes later; and the figures are given to show the similarity of the working.

*Ex.* 2.—Bearing of moon by compass N. 89° W. at 14h. 49m. 41s. by chronometer. Other conditions same as in *Ex.* 1.

**Example of Moon-Azimuth.**

| | H. | M. | S. |
|---|---|---|---|
| Time by chronometer | 14 | 49 | 41 |
| Error ... + | | 4 | 24 |
| Greenwich mean time | 14 | 54 | 05 |
| Longitude in time ... − | 4 | 52 | 44 |
| Mean time at ship | 10 | 01 | 21 |
| Sidereal time (page II, Naut. Alm.) | 19 | 45 | 12 |
| Acceleration for 14h. 54m. 05s. ... + | | 2 | 27 |
| Right Ascension of the meridian | 29 | 49 | 00 |
| Moon's Right Ascension (page x., N.A.) | 0 | 45 | 00 |
| | 29 | 04 | 00 |
| Reject | 24 | 00 | 00 |
| Moon's hour angle | 5 | 04 | 00 W. |

Moon's declin. for 15 hrs., G.M.T., from page x., Naut. Alm. = 10½° N.

Open Burdwood's Tables at page 94, latitude *same name* as the declination, and with declination 10½° and hour angle 5h. 4m. in *the right-hand column*, look for the bearing, which, by interpolation, will be found to be 90¼°; this, according to the precept at the bottom of the page, is to be reckoned from North to West. The remainder of the work is as follows:—

| | |
|---|---|
| *True* bearing of moon at 5h. 4m. West of the meridian | N. 90¼° W. |
| Variation by chart | − 7° |
| Moon's *correct magnetic* bearing | N. 83¼° W. |
| Moon's *compass* bearing | N. 89° W. |
| Deviation | + 5¾° |

This result only differs a quarter of a degree from that given by Sirius, and proves the observations were carefully taken. The instrument used for the purpose was Sir William Thomson's azimuth mirror, which enables bearings of sun, moon, or stars to be taken with the *utmost ease and precision.* The writer has frequently taken azimuths of five different stars by it within a minute or so of each other; and when worked up, the greatest difference between any two has not *exceeded* half a degree, and sometimes the results have all agreed to the same quarter of a degree. There is no other instrument for nautical use capable of such extreme accuracy.

**Sir W. Thomson's Azimuth Mirror.**

After the sun and moon, planets are most easily observed for azimuths, especially Venus and Jupiter, which are young moons in themselves. Among the fixed stars Sirius is first favourite, but if the silvering of the Azimuth Mirror is in good order, it is not impossible to get stars of the 3rd magnitude in cases which admit of their being picked out with certainty from among others near to them.

For night work a *special* Bull's-eye lamp of *copper* is the correct thing. This lamp should be used wholly and solely for navigating work, and when employed for azimuths ought to be held well behind and above the observer, in such a manner as to concentrate the light on the far side of the compass-card. The working out of planet azimuths differs in no respect from those of the moon or fixed stars. Their Right Ascensions and Declinations will be found between pages 226 and 265 of the N. A. for 1884.

In the first of the examples just given, both the times and the declinations unfortunately necessitated interpolation in taking out the true bearings. This is a little awkward when it happens, as a certain amount of mental calculation is required to hit off the *exact* value of the bearing. But, after all, it is not a killing matter, and "practice soon makes perfect."

## TOWSON'S AZIMUTH TABLES.

So far, allusion has only been made to those stars whose declinations range between 23° N. and 23° S.; but to confine the navigator to these alone would be to deprive him of the aid of some of the brightest stars in the heavens. To meet this difficulty Mr J. T. Towson has compiled a set of very useful tables, by the help of which, and a very trifling amount of computation, a few seconds suffice to find the true bearing of the conspicuous stars whose declinations exceed 23°. **Towson's Azimuth Tables.**

The table referred to is numbered VII. in Towson's "Practical Information on the Deviation of the Compass, for the use of masters and mates of iron ships." It will be unnecessary here to give Mr. Towson's rules, &c., as reference to his admirable book will satisfy the reader as to their utility. To show, however, the conciseness of the method, as well as its accuracy, the true bearing of Sirius (Example 1) is again worked out according to Towson—*vide* his Table VII., page 98. *Data* as before.

| | ° ′ | | |
|---|---|---|---|
| Arc I | 17 3 | | Log I......... 9.3930 |
| Latitude | 39 20 | | Log II......... 0.0794 |
| Arc II | 56 23 | True bearing of Sirius | S. 16½°.E.=9.4724 |

Surely this method is *simple* enough, and *concise* enough, to please anybody. In table III. of the same book, the sun's true bearing, or that of any of the heavenly bodies whose declinations do not exceed 26½° North or South, is found in precisely a similar manner, so that, next to *actual inspection* by Burdwood's and Davis's Tables, Towson's method may be looked upon as the most convenient mode of working azimuths.

The practical conclusion arrived at from the foregoing amounts to this—if the declination of the body observed is within 23° one side or the other of the Equator, it is preferable to take the azimuth out by inspection from Burdwood's and Davis's Tables; but if the declination exceeds 23°, then recourse should be had to Towson's Table VII. The Latitude, Declination, and Time being given, a man reasonably smart at figures can work the azimuth by Towson's book *in a few seconds under a minute.*

### DEVIATION BY THE PELORUS.

**How to use the Pelorus.**

To revert to the Pelorus. The following is the method to be pursued to find by it the deviation of the compass on any course which is being steered at the time:—Work up position by dead reckoning from last observation; prick this off on the *Variation chart*, and note corresponding variation; correct this for the annual change by the chartlet at the north side of the sheet; set your watch to Apparent Time at Ship as already instructed; suppose it to be about 2 P.M. Then open Burdwood's or Davis's Tables; and to allow yourself sufficient time, ascertain the sun's true bearing a quarter of an hour or so in advance, say for every four minutes between 2·16 and 2·24 P.M. Apply the variation taken from the chart in order to convert the *true* bearings into *correct magnetic* ones; write these latter with corresponding times down on a slip of paper, and you are ready to begin when the time comes.

We will suppose there are several compasses in the ship (5 is not an uncommon number), and that you wish to ascertain the deviation of each by simultaneous observations. Of course you are provided with a whistle. Station a 'hand' by each compass, with instructions to note the exact direction of the ship's head when he hears the whistle.*

The Pelorus being in its stand, unclamp the card, so that it may be free to revolve on its axis; set the sight vane to the sun's "correct magnetic" bearing, corresponding to the Apparent Time by watch, and secure it firmly to the card by the large milled-headed screw on top. Tell your assistants to "look out," and the ship being nicely steadied on her course, move the card, with sight vanes attached, to the right or left till you see the sun's image reflected in the speculum and bisected by the thread; then whistle, and continue to do so, say for half a minute—so long as the sun

* An officer without a whistle is like a sailor without a knife.

is cut by the thread (of course it is understood that the card is not to be again moved after the first whistle). Now note the reading of the card opposite the lubber-line, and this will be the actual "correct magnetic" direction of the ship's head at the time the signal was made. The compasses, if free from error, will indicate the same thing. Should they not do so, the difference between the ship's head by Pelorus and the ship's head by compass will be the *deviation* of that particular compass on that particular course. The rule to determine its name is this:—

**Rules for naming Deviation.**

If the "correct magnetic course" be to the left of the "compass course" (looking outwards from the centre of the card), the deviation is westerly, but should it be to the right of the "compass course" the deviation is easterly.

**Deviation and Variation—in what respects similar.**

Westerly deviation throws a ship to the left of her course, and Easterly deviation throws her to the right. Exactly the same effect is produced by *variation* of the compass, and in this respect the two are similar.

One of the first things done by a lad going to sea is to learn how to "box the compass;" but the old sailor's method of doing this in points, ½ points, and ¼ points, will soon be obsolete. The student of to-day, who takes a pride in his profession, will learn how to "box the compass" in *degrees*—that is to say, he will learn to tell off-hand how many degrees correspond to any given compass course reckoned in points or parts of a point. It should not take longer than an hour to master this important matter.

**Boxing the Compass in degrees.**

**Setting course by Pelorus.**

*To set a course by Pelorus*, the operation is very similar to that described above. Proceed as before, except that this time the card is to be clamped not only to the sight vanes, corresponding to the sun's bearing at the appointed time, but also to the lubber's point at the correct magnetic course you wish to steer; thus, both the card and the sight vanes will be immoveable. Under these circumstances you must starboard or port the helm until the thread bisects the sun's image in the speculum; when carefully steadied in this direction, whistle as a signal to the helmsman and those looking out for the other compasses, that the vessel is on her course, and to "keep her steady as she goes."

Among the many advantages this instrument possesses, it enables the deviation of *any number* of compasses to be found by one observation, and this deviation is quite independent of the error due to any possible displacement of the lubber-lines.

**Principle of the Pelorus.**

The principle of the Pelorus is merely this, *that it measures the horizontal angle between the sun (or other object) and the ship's head.*

Under certain simple conditions the unassisted eye can do the same thing, only somewhat less accurately. For example, at the instant of noon to an observer in the English Channel, the sun bears South (true). If now, the vessel is so manœuvred by her helm as to bring the sun on the port beam—say on a line with the bridge handrail, or the forward or after side of a deck-house, hatch-coaming, or skylight—it is certain that her head *must* be West (true): if the helm should be ported so as to bring the sun dead aft in a line with the masts, the ship's head must be North (true): if the helm be still ported so as to bring the sun on the starboard beam, the ship's head must be East (true): and lastly, if the sun be brought right ahead, the course must be South (true). In this way the errors of the compasses might be approximately determined on the four points named.

In a ship there are many things which give true fore-and-aft lines, as well as thwartship ones, but the *intermediate* angles are wanting. The Pelorus supplies this deficiency, as it enables us to measure *any* angle between the beam and the fore-and-aft line: and this is the view which must be taken of it. You must divest yourself of the inclination to consider it a *compass;* to repeat, it is merely an instrument for measuring the *horizontal* angle between any object and the ship's head. Dumb cards *without* gimbals give incorrect—sometimes *very incorrect*—results, and should on no account be employed.

**"Compass Correctors."**

There are a number of instruments now before the public which profess to be "Compass correctors." It is not proposed to discuss their relative merits; but presuming them to be right in principle, which in some cases is open to question, it would be better if they were termed "Compass *course* correctors," or "Deviation detectors," as the former name is quite inapplicable. These instruments are mostly complicated; and if by any chance they get a knock or a fall, it would be difficult to re-adjust them. Whereas the construction of the Pelorus, while correct in principle, is so extremely simple in detail, that any sea-going engineer, or a handy carpenter, could "put it to rights" without much trouble. The Pelorus must not, from the similarity of names, be

**Palinurus and Polaris.**

confounded with another invention, known as the Palinurus—so called after a famous old Greek pilot—nor with the Polaris, both of which are totally different instruments. The Pelorus will be again referred to when "Compass Adjustment" comes to be treated on.

# CHAPTER X.

## THE STATION POINTER.

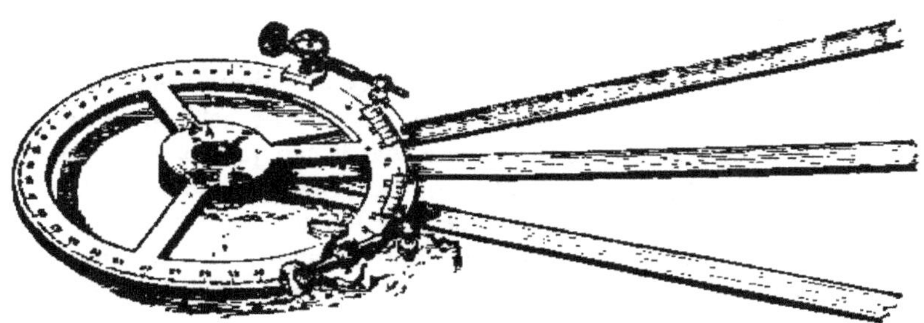

This is an instrument that very few men in the merchant service are acquainted with *even by name*, and in the Navy it is seldom used, except by officers of the surveying branch. When the great practical value of the instrument is considered, this statement seems almost inconceivable. Of the many methods for ascertaining a ship's position when in sight of a *properly* surveyed coast, none can in any way compare for ease and precision with that in which the Station Pointer figures as the chief assistant of the Sextant.

**An instrument comparatively unknown.**

The Station Pointer is composed of a graduated circle of brass, having one fixed and two moveable arms radiating from its centre. The moveable arms turn in one plane round this centre, which is common to both, and where they pass outward under the circle have verniers attached, so that the angle either of them makes with the fixed leg, which lies between them and constitutes the zero point of the circle, can be readily measured. They are made of different sizes, and more or less perfect in detail. All of them have clamping screws to set the moveable legs to any required angle, and some, like a sextant, are fitted with tangent

**Station Pointer described.**

screws and reading microscopes. It is an *exceedingly simple* instrument to understand, and has no special adjustments or delicate mechanism to get out of order.

Of course, like everything else, the Station Pointer must be used a few times before actual expertness can be hoped for. As before stated, its use when employed in connection with the sextant is to fix a ship's position on the chart by means of two horizontal angles subtended by three well-defined objects—such as towers, lighthouses, churches, windmills, islets, capes, points, mountain peaks, hills, or other marks which may be found on the chart and duly recognised.

**Practice in taking Sextant Angles.**

Every aspiring officer should be equally as quick with the sextant in observing *horizontal* angles as he generally is in observing vertical ones—the sun's altitude, for instance. Strange to say, this is not the case. The majority of officers seem to be under the impression that the sextant can only be held in an up-and-down position, and never dream that it can just as easily be used on its flat to take horizontal angles. Clearly such men have never taken a "lunar distance," or they would know better. A sextant is useful to measure *any* kind of angle, whether horizontal, oblique, or vertical. It should unquestionably be a part of an officer's education to learn to handle his sextant so as to observe as readily and as accurately one way as the other; and to this end, therefore, during spare half-hours in harbour, or when sailing along a coast, take the sextants out of their cases, and let a couple or more officers measure horizontal angles simultaneously, until by the agreement of results it is known that proficiency is attained.

**Rule for holding Sextant face down or face up.**

In taking a horizontal angle between two objects, stand erect and perfectly at ease, poise the sextant lightly in the right hand, with its face up, and level with the eye, do not cant the head to one side, nor bend forward—it looks awkward, and is unnecessary—and with the left hand advance the index-bar along the arc till contact is roughly established, then clamp and perfect the contact with the slow motion screw.

To secure distinct vision, it is advisable always to look *direct* at the fainter object of the two, and reflect the brighter one to it. Consequently, whenever it happens that the fainter object is to the right hand, it may be necessary to hold the sextant *face down*. There is absolutely no difficulty about this matter that cannot be overcome by a very moderate amount of practice, and, in after years, the knowledge may prove of incalculable value.

To exemplify the use of the Station Pointer, let us imagine a vessel sailing along a weather shore beset with off-lying dangers, and desirous of hugging the coast to keep in smooth water, and gain her port,—say Holyhead, coming from Liverpool.

Let the reader refer to Admiralty Chart 1170[B].

As soon as Point Lynas is passed, the captain will naturally get anxious about those bugbears to navigation, "the Coal" and "Ethel" rocks. It is true they are buoyed, but strong running tides, gales of wind and heavy seas, are apt to drag the buoys from their proper positions, and so lure to disaster, as in the case (not so long ago) of the S.S. "State of Louisiana" and the Hunter rock buoy, off Larne, on the Irish Coast. Besides, the compasses may be swinging so as to make bearings inaccurate. Possibly the vessel may be an iron one, and the deviation uncertain, or some obstacles may be in the way of the object of which you wish to get the bearing. Whatever difficulty may present itself in getting an accurate "fix" by the usual methods, none at all exists with the Sextant and Station Pointer.

**How to fix position by Station Pointer.**

Select three objects on shore which you know are laid down on the chart; for instance, Point Lynas Lighthouse, the East Mouse, and the Middle Mouse. Let an assistant measure with his sextant the horizontal angle between the first two, whilst you at the same moment measure the angle between the East and Middle Mouse, noting the time by watch for sake of reference. Having read off the sextants, take the Station Pointer, and holding the legs *from* you, open out the left-hand one and set it to the left-hand angle, between Point Lynas and the East Mouse. In like manner set the right-hand leg to the right-hand angle, between the East and Middle Mouse. Lay the instrument down on the chart, so that the feather-edge of the centre leg may pass over the East Mouse, whilst the others pass respectively over Lynas and the West Mouse; thus,

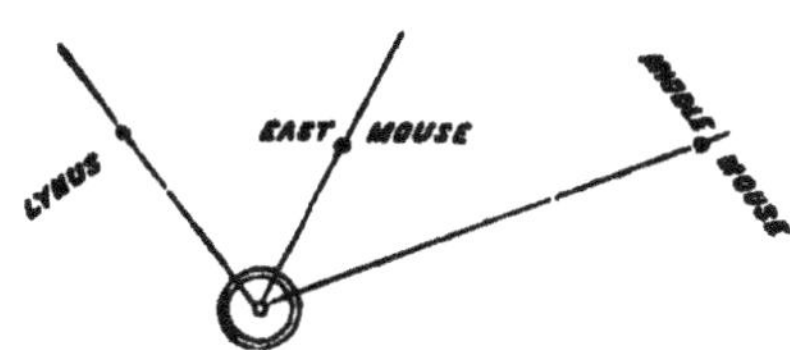


The centre of the instrument will then represent the *exact* position of the ship, and it may be pricked on the Chart through the small hole for the purpose.

As the vessel progresses Westward, fresh stations can be selected. For example, when abreast of the Middle Mouse, use it and Lynas for the left-hand angle, and the Skerries and Middle Mouse for the right-hand angle. As the "Coal" and "Ethel" rocks are approached, watch till the Middle Mouse is *in one* with Lynas Lighthouse. When in transit, *one* angle between them and the beacon on the West Mouse will fix the ship's position with great accuracy, and so on till the Skerries are rounded.

Any one who takes the trouble mentally to follow this operation as described above, will scarcely fail to see that it cannot be surpassed for *ease* and *dispatch*. Indeed, if there should be two assistants as angle-takers, whilst the 'chief' manipulates the Station Pointer in the chart-room, the vessel's position can be *accurately* laid down on the chart in from one to two minutes from the time the objects were pointed out between which the angles were to be taken. Any one doubtful has only to try to be convinced.

**The principle of the Station Pointer.**

To comprehend "the why and the wherefore" of this method, which by some is called "The three-point problem," and by others "The problem of the two circles," it is necessary to consult Euclid, but only in a very quiet way. The first thing to understand is, that *through any three points, not in a straight line, a complete circle can always be drawn, and but one;* (*vide* Euclid, IV. 5).

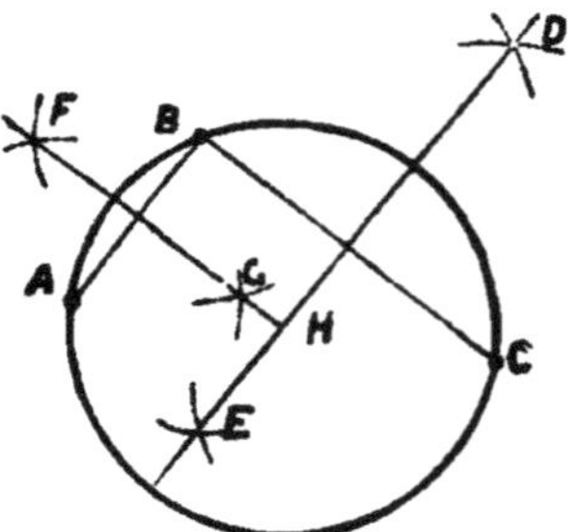


Let $A$, $B$, and $C$ represent the points through which the circle is to be traced. Draw lines joining $AB$ and $BC$.

Take any extent in the dividers greater than half the line $BC$, and with one foot in $C$ describe an arc: with the same radius, and one foot in $B$, describe another arc, cutting the former in $D$ and $E$; through $D$ and $E$ draw a straight line. In a similar manner from $A$ and $B$, describe two arcs, cutting each other at $F$ and $G$.

Through *F* and *G* draw a straight line, which produced will meet the one through *D* and *E* at the point *H*. Then from *H*, at the distance of any one of the given points, as *HB*, describe a circle, and it will pass through the other points *A* and *C* as required.

The student would do well to solve a few cases, until satisfied in his own mind that, no matter how the points may be placed with respect to each other, a circle can always be drawn that will pass through all three.

*2nd.* Another geometrical peculiarity has to be considered and understood.

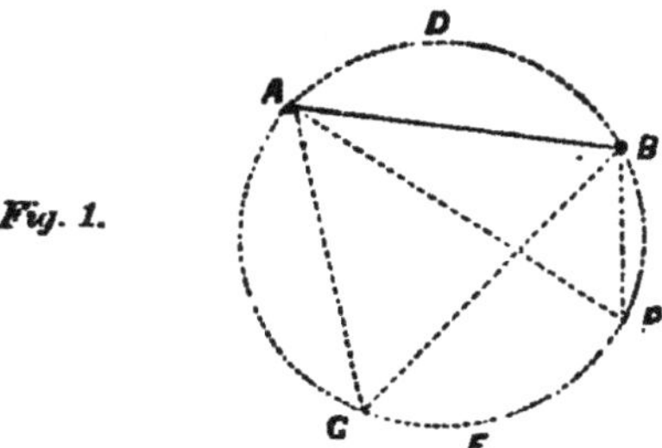

*Fig. 1.*

Anywhere on the circumference of a circle, select two points, as *A* and *B*, and connect them with a straight line; this line is termed the chord of the arc *ADB*. *ADB* is also one segment of the circle, and *AFB* is another. Euclid (III. 21) tells us that from *any* point in the circumference on the same side as *AFB*, *the points AB will subtend the same angle.* (Thus the angle *AGB* (Fig. 1) contains precisely the same number of degrees as the angle *APB*). This being the case, it is evident that the circumference *AFB* is the measure of a constant angle, which is termed "the angle in the segment *AFB*," and an observer getting this angle must be *somewhere* on the circumference *AFB*, the size of which depends upon the angle observed.

So far the work may not inaptly be compared to getting a "line of bearing;" but it is still necessary to fix the ship's place on this line,—or, in other words, to cross this bearing with another, just in the same way as you would do with compass bearings, or as you might cut the known parallel of latitude on the chart with the North and South line of longitude, in order to definitely lay off the ship's position. Latitude *alone* would not do so, nor would longitude; but the *intersection* of the one with the other indicates the precise position. For this purpose, therefore, let us imagine another circle somewhat similar to the foregoing.

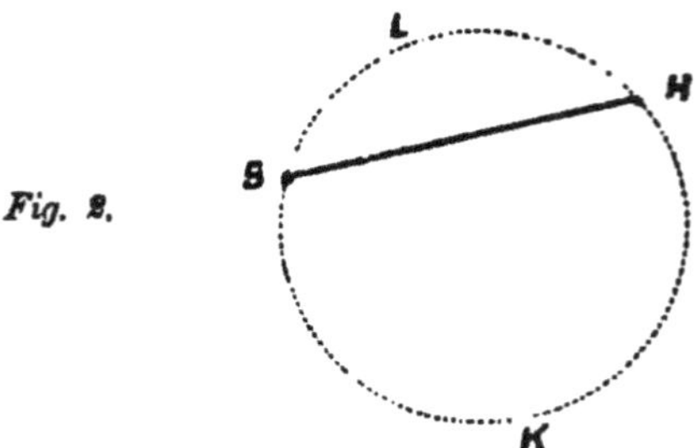

Fig. 2.

What has been said about the first, of course, holds good with this one also—namely, *that from any point in the circumference BKH, the points BH will subtend the same angle*, whatever that may happen to be, according to the size of the segment. Now, if the angle subtended by *AB* in Figure 1 were observed simultaneously with the angle subtended by *BH* in Figure 2, the two lines of bearing will intersect each other, and give the place of the ship.

To show this more clearly, let Figures 1 and 2 be joined together at the common point *B*.

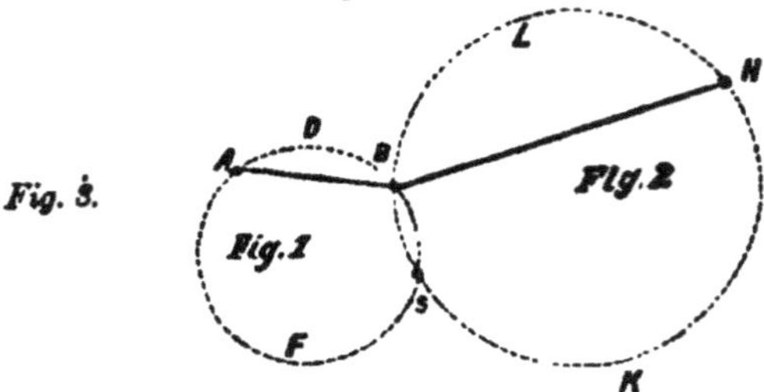

Fig. 3.

Let *A* represent Point Lynas, *B* the East Mouse, *H* the Middle Mouse, and *S* the ship. Let the angle observed between Lynas and the East Mouse be 40°, and the angle observed between the East and Middle Mouse 75°; draw the circles to suit these angles.

This is done by taking advantage of the fact that the angle at the centre of any segment is double the angle at the circumference.—(*Euclid*, III. 20.) We lay off, therefore, from both ends of the line whose subtended angle we have observed, the complement of that angle, or what it wants of 90°. The point where these lines meet is the centre of the circle, which is described with the distance from this centre to either end of the line, as radius. If the angle observed is more than 90°, the circle is described by laying off the number of degrees over 90°, on the *opposite side of the line* to that on which we know we are, and proceed as before.

Now, the angle between Lynas and the East Mouse having been observed as 40°, it follows from what has been said that the ship lies *somewhere* on the circumference of the one only segment (*AFB*) containing this angle which can possibly be drawn on the given base *AB*. The position of the ship, therefore, is known to this extent, and *half* the difficulty is disposed of; but that is not sufficient. Now, by similar reasoning it can be shewn that the ship lies *also* on the circumference of the one only segment *BKH*, which with the angle 75° can be drawn on the *other* given base *BH*. She must therefore be at *S*, *the only point which satisfies the double condition*, and the only one from which we could have obtained these two angles at the same instant.

In actual practice all this is done for us by the Station Pointer without the trouble of drawing the circles, but the explanation of the principle upon which it is based cannot fail but be interesting to the student.

In order, however, that dependence may be placed in the ship's position when ascertained by these means, *it is necessary to be familiar with the conditions under which the circles will make good cuts.* The nearer they intersect at right angles the better; just in the same way that we try to select objects for compass cross bearings which have a difference of bearing of from seven to nine points. If the difference of bearing is small—say only 20°—the point of intersection is so acute as to be very ill-defined, and any slight error in the bearings themselves may cause a very large one in the resulting position. If the following half-dozen rules are attended to, this need not be feared in 'fixes' with the Station Pointer.

**Half-dozen rules requiring attention.**

1. The three objects may lie in the same straight line.

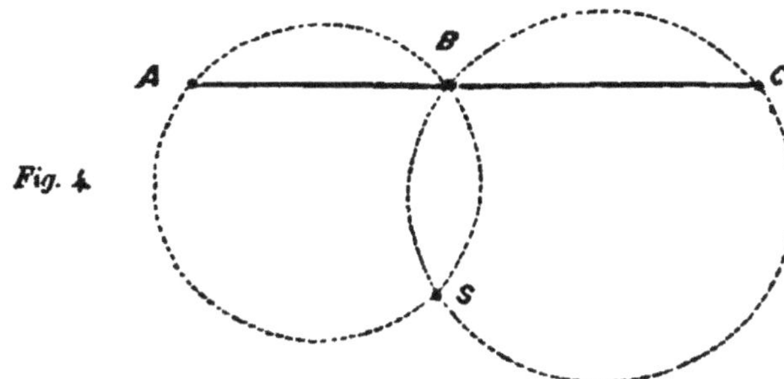

*Fig. 4.*

2. The three objects may lie in a curve, with the convexity towards the observer,—that is to say, the middle object is to be the nearest.

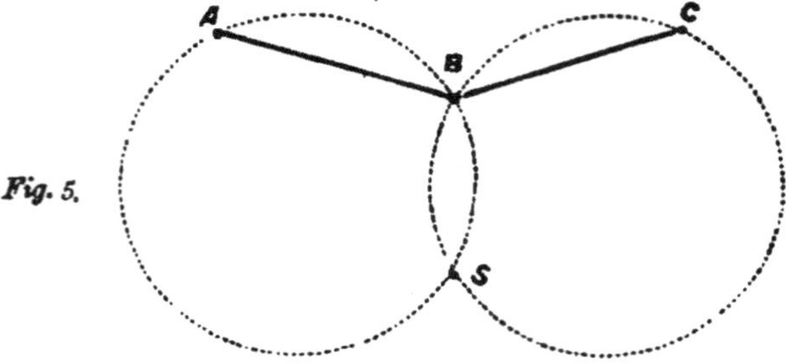

*Fig. 5.*

3. The three objects may be in a curve, concave to the observer, so long as the latter is either *on* or *within* a line joining the left and right hand objects.

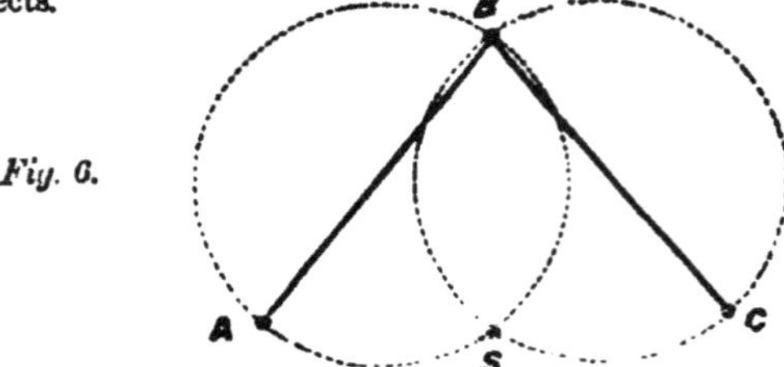

*Fig. 6.*

4. The three objects may lie in a curve, concave to the observer, so long as the latter is well *outside* the circle upon whose circumference the three objects are situated. In this case the 'fix' will be good, notwithstanding the small angles.

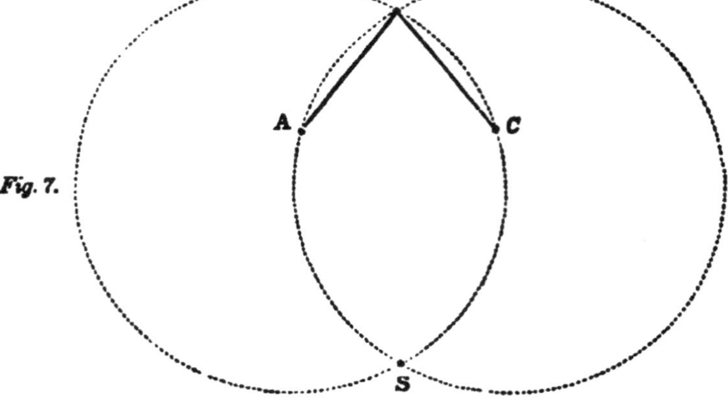

*Fig. 7.*

5. If two of the objects be much nearer to, as compared with the third, and seem, roughly speaking, about equidistant from, the observer, at whose position they subtend an angle ranging between 60° and 120°, whilst the angle between the third and middle point is comparatively small, the selection is a good one.

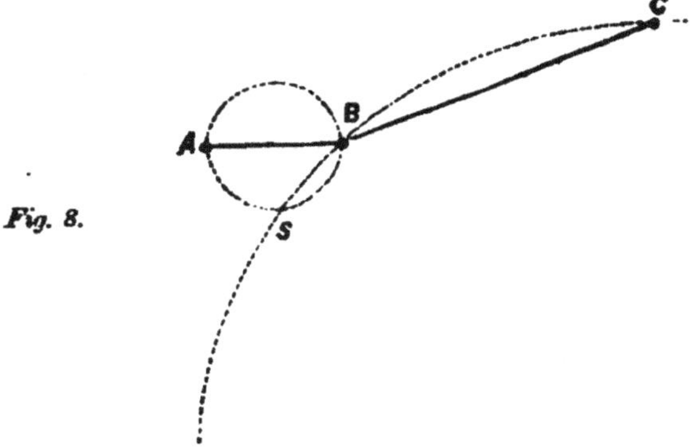


*Fig. 8.*

6. Two of the objects may be in transit with the observer. If this should be the case, *one* angle between them and the third is sufficient. This is the best and simplest 'fix' of all. The single angle should not be less than 30°.*

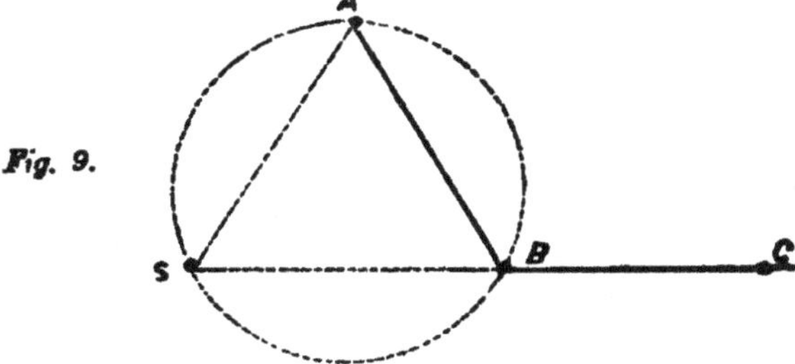


*Fig. 9.*

In this case the ship's position is fixed on the circumference of the segment *ASB*, by producing the line *BC* until it cuts it at *S*. If the observer were at any other part of the circumference, the points *B* and *C* would not be in transit; and if he kept them in transit, and advanced inside of the circumference, the angle *ASB* would at once increase. If, on the other hand, he receded from the circle, whilst keeping *B* and *C* in transit, the angle *ASB* would as quickly diminish. In this problem, the circle, as before, gives one line of bearing, so to speak, and the points in transit give the

**Two of the points in transit.**

* This can scarcely be included in the "problem of the two circles," but it is inserted here with the others for sake of convenience.

other; the intersection of these two lines of bearing of course fixes the observer's position.

In each of the six cases just given, the position of the observer will be fixed with greater accuracy than it possibly can be by compass bearings. On the other hand, it is necessary to guard against selecting objects lying in such relationship to each other, *that a circle joining all three would also pass through or near the place of the observer.* In such a case the position is indeterminate, as may easily be shewn by construction. For example:—

**Case to be guarded against.**

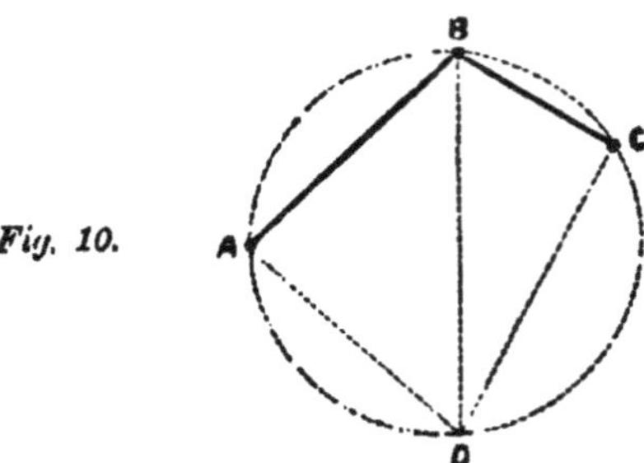


*Fig. 10.*

Let $D$ be the observer, and $AB$ and $BC$ the points subtending the angles $ADB$ and $BDC$. From what has been said in previous pages, it is clear that the angle $ADB$ will be found at *any* point in the segment $ADC$; and the same applies to the angle $BDC$. (Moreover, there is no second circle to make a cut with the first). Consequently, to fix the observer's position with the Station Pointer is impossible, though in this instance Compass cross-bearings of $A$ and $C$ would be splendid. The chances, however, are a thousand to one against the occurrence of such a case; but others may happen verging so closely upon it as practically to amount to the same thing.

**To tell value of "Fix."**

Where this sort of thing *does* happen, and the circles nearly coincide, it will be found that the centre of the Station Pointer may be moved about very considerably and the legs will still cover the three objects. On the other hand, the "fix" will be good in cases where a slight movement throws one or more of the points away from its own particular leg.

However, a little experience will soon enable anyone by the eye alone to judge if the objects are ill-conditioned, when, of course, one of the proposed points must be rejected, and another sought for in a better situation.

Another objectionable case is when the middle point is near, and the other points *both* far off. Constructing the figure will in this case shew that the two circles will so nearly touch *externally* as to make the cut a very indefinite one.

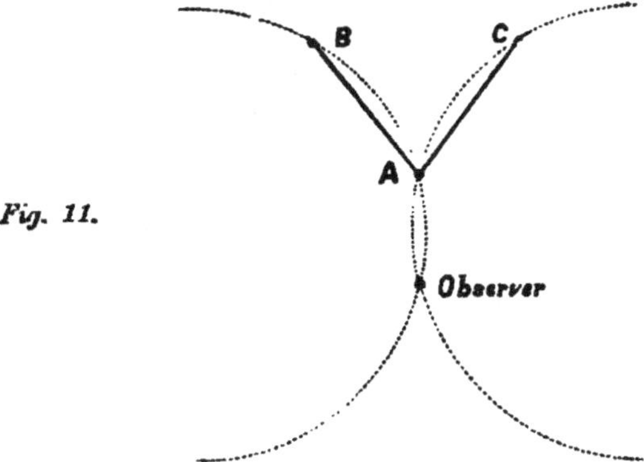


*Fig. 11.*

Were the observer in figure 11 to be as far from *A*, as *A* is from *B* or *C*, the fix would be a better one, as will be found on trial. The zealous student, anxious to master the subject, cannot do better than create imaginary cases, and by constructing the figures, will speedily acquire the knowledge which will guide him unerringly when the time comes to put it into practice.

**Station Pointer does not reveal ill-conditioned cases.**

It must constantly be remembered, that in using the Station Pointer, it does not follow that it will of itself reveal the objectionable cases here alluded to, in which the position is uncertain. For when a position is found on the chart by the legs of the instrument passing correctly over the three points, it may not occur to the operator that, by moving it about from place to place, several others may be found where the same effect will be produced.

Whether the position is laid down on the chart by the actual protraction of the angles and the circles, or, more readily, by the Station Pointer, any ambiguity which would be shewn by the one method, really exists also in the other, and in the case of the Station Pointer is all the more dangerous because it is not brought prominently into notice.

The writer does not by any means congratulate himself upon selecting the case of a vessel passing round the Skerries as a good illustration of the *value* of the Station Pointer. The north coast of Anglesea was chosen solely because that, while it sufficiently well served to shew how the instrument is used, it was probably also familiar ground to many of the readers of this book.

There are many parts of the world much better adapted to display the great *value* of the method wherein the Station Pointer saves so much time and labour—the eastern entrance to Magellan Straits may be quoted as a good example. Before passing the First Narrows, the tide has a velocity of 8 to 9 knots at springs, and a rise and fall of 44 feet. Low and distant marks, the absence of buoys, a wide expanse of water, with intricate channels amid vast banks of sand, necessitate most careful navigation and cool judgment. Should the vessel be going *with* the tide, there is not much time for consideration, and the most expeditious, as well as accurate method, is the one which finds favour with the man upon whose shoulders rests the responsibility. Under these circumstances the Station Pointer comes well to the front.

**Advantage of Station Pointer over Compass.**

Just notice the difference between it and the Compass. An angle is taken much more quickly, and very much more accurately, than a bearing. If the objects are distant, a trifling error in the bearing will materially affect the resulting position; while an error in the angle can scarcely amount to the tenth part of a degree. Again, when the courses are being altered pretty rapidly, to suit the windings of a channel, *the deviation is continually changing with each fresh direction of the ship's head;* and here, then, arises another element of uncertainty, to which may be added the possibility of applying the deviation the wrong way—a thing which may happen to the most clear-headed in moments of excitement and hurry.

**Varying Deviation.**

**Its wrong application.**

Further, at a most critical juncture, some obstacle may intervene between the Standard Compass and the object of which the bearing is required. Now, the Compass cannot be moved to any part of the ship, but the Sextant can—another very decided advantage. Moreover, as before stated, the Compass may be swinging one or more points with the motion of the ship, and this is *sure* to be the case crossing bars when there is any "run."

**Compass a fixture.**

A compass cross-bearing cannot very well be taken by two men at the same time. It is one man's work only, and whilst taking the second bearing he has to recollect the first, and afterwards both of them, till they are finally laid-off on the chart. In the meantime the ship is speeding on. With the Station Pointer method, three men (captain and two officers) can work together, and the angles are taken simultaneously. Let the officers take the angles, whilst the captain stands—Station Pointer in hand—with the chart spread out on the table before him. As the angles are read off, they are put upon the Station Pointer, popped down on the chart, and in an instant the ship's position is found to a nicety.

Where two objects can be got in transit, only one angle is necessary, and, consequently, only one assistant. These cases should be specially looked for and utilized.

**Relative position of Angle-takers.**

To avoid bungling, get into the habit of always working on an established system. There is nothing like method. For example, one officer should be told off for left-hand angles, and another for right-hand angles, and no chopping or changing permitted. Let them also stand side by side in their proper relative positions, so that they need not observe across each other, and that the mind may be trained to a sense of order.

When giving in the figures for the Station Pointer, they should speak briefly, distinctly, and one at a time, thus:—"Left-hand angle 64° 15′," and when the instrument is set to this—and not before—"Right-hand angle 43° 22′." This saves confusion.

**Both angles taken by one observer.**

It may, however, sometimes happen that the Navigator will have no assistants, and so be compelled to do the whole thing himself. In this case it is a first-rate dodge to have two flat pieces of brass fitted to slide along the arc of the sextant and clamp to it at any given part. Place one in front of, and the other in rear of the vernier, so that the latter can be made to butt against either, according to circumstances. We may give these two brass outriders the name of 'stops.'

**Special fitting to sextant.**

To use them, proceed after this fashion:—We will suppose a case where one angle is markedly larger than the other, and getting larger all the time as the vessel sails on, and that you resolve to take it first. Dispense altogether, therefore, with the 'stop' in rear of the vernier, by clamping it at the extreme zero end of the arc, where it will be out of the way. Then, unclamping the leading 'stop,' bring it into contact with the vernier, and with the two pressed together between the left thumb and forefinger, and the sextant at the eye—slide them along the arc until the observed objects *overlap* just a trifle, then quickly clamp the 'stop,' keep the vernier firmly pressed against it, and when exact coincidence is established between the marks selected by the angle getting larger, immediately release the vernier, take the smaller angle and clamp securely—you need not lose ten seconds in doing it, unless you are very buttery-fingered indeed.

Now read off the *last* angle, and at once transfer it to the Station Pointer, then unclamp the vernier and slide it forward against the 'stop,' which until now has been keeping guard over the *first* angle until you were at liberty to read it off. By this little stratagem it is possible for an adroit observer to measure two angles *almost* simultaneously.

Of course, if it were desirable to get the smaller angle first, you would have to employ the rear stop belonging to the zero end of the arc, and consign the other to the far end of the instrument. Very little practice is required to handle the 'stops' with expertness, and the Navigator will soon find out for himself that they are uncommonly handy not only for this, but for various other observations.*

**Chart table on bridge.**

In going through intricate channels, it is usual in steamers to have a chart table on the bridge, well sheltered under the weather-cloth. This impromptu chart-room is used at such times in preference to the regular one, which perhaps is inconveniently situated, and would necessitate constant running up and down the bridge ladder.

The Bosphorus, Dardanelles, Grecian Archipelago, Gulf of Suez, Red Sea, Gulf of Aden, and a thousand other places, might be mentioned where the Station Pointer would be found extremely useful. Those who have tried it, within the knowledge of the writer, have invariably spoken in its praise, and wondered how they were ever able to get along without it.

It may be noted here that if the points used to fix by are not correctly placed on the chart, the Station Pointer will not indicate anything wrong unless a third or "check angle" be taken and plotted. In case of non-agreement, it is certain that something is adrift. Be careful, therefore, not to use the Station Pointer unless your chart is the outcome of a regular trigonometrical survey by competent persons. On an Admiralty sheet this information is always given.

*Where the accuracy of the chart is doubtful, it is better to stick to the compass.*

**Tracing paper a substitute for Station Pointer.**

Tracing paper, on which a graduated circle has been printed, is at times an excellent substitute for the Station Pointer, and in some cases preferable to the instrument itself. When, for example, the objects used for the angles are very near the observer, they will come *within* the brass circle of the Station Pointer, and be more or less hidden by it. Plain tracing paper may also be

---

* Potter, of the Poultry, London, fits sextants in this manner. It is a patent of the late Capt. Davis, R.N. In connection with it there is a micrometer tangent-screw which is used for a totally different purpose, but doubtless Mr. Potter would supply either or both as might be required.

placed over a circle graduated on card-board, and the required pair of angles ruled in. These card-board circles can be procured from or through any optician. They are 10 inches in diameter, and divided to quarter degrees. This admits of angles being laid off by estimation to the eighth part of a degree, or even less. Windy days, however, do not suit tracing paper when used on the bridge.

**Graduated circles on card-board.**

A Station Pointer with a circle six inches in diameter, and 12-inch legs in the clear, is a handy size for navigating use on board ship. Lengthening bars 9 inches long ought to be supplied in the case. By attaching these to the extremity of the legs, an increased range is obtainable when necessary. It is sufficient that the vernier reads to single minutes. The divisions on the circle should be strongly marked on brass, for convenience of rapid setting in bad lights. When the arc is not too finely cut, a man with fairly good eyes can set his instrument quite correctly without the aid of the small magnifying glass which is always to be found in the case. This is an advantage not to be sneezed at, and is not to be had with a silver arc. Such an instrument, fitted with tangent screws, in mahogany case complete, costs £8, perhaps less.

**Convenient size for Station Pointer.**

To acquire the knack of getting the Station Pointer legs to cover their respective points quickly, is not difficult. First place the bevelled edge of the central leg on the middle object of the three, keeping it on this point as a sort of pivot; then move the body of the instrument to the right or left, and slide it to and fro on the paper till the other two points are also in contact with the bevelled edges of their respective legs. The nick at the centre of the instrument will then represent the sought for position of the observer.

**Lesson in manipulation**

In concluding this chapter, the writer hopes he has fully demonstrated the value of "the three-point problem," and the instrument which renders its application so easy in practice. Let the reader not be frightened at the weak points which have been brought under his notice, since a little pains will enable him to steer clear of them, and to utilise to his own benefit an instrument which possesses so much real merit.

**Funk not, but go in and win.**

J. H. Laughton, Mathematical and Naval Instructor at Greenwich, is the distinguished author of an excellent little book on Nautical Surveying, which has been the cherished companion of the writer since first published in 1872. At page 145, when winding up his remarks on the use of the Sextant and Station Pointer, Mr. Laughton puts the thing so clearly and so forcibly that it is impossible not to quote him. He says:—"I have wished, in these last few pages, to show how the position of a ship, when in with the land, may be laid down; how dangers may be avoided; how a course may be steered *without* the compass. In the practice of navigation and pilotage, the attempt to do without the compass would be worse than absurd; it would be blameable in the extreme; but cases may occur, as I have endeavoured to point out, in which the sextant is a safer guide than the compass, or in which it is a most valuable auxiliary to it. To examine into these cases is the Navigator's duty; it is the Surveyor's duty to provide him with the necessary data, accurately laid down."

---

## CHAPTER XI.

### SOUNDING MACHINES AND LOGS.

In days long past, the Ancient Mariner guided his ricketty craft over the ocean principally by "the three L's,"—"Log, Lead, and Lookout." When, later on, the astrolabe and cross-staff were invented, and certain astronomical data became available, another "L" (Latitude) was added to the number. In the present day, when the nautical schoolmaster is abroad, and chronometers almost go begging, this regiment of "L's" is augmented by a fifth and very important comrade, namely, Longitude. Nevertheless, the Veterans still hold their own, and are likely to do so as long as fog and clouds continue to obscure celestial objects from the anxious navigator. The five "L's."

When a ship is stranded through thick weather, the members of the Court of Enquiry very properly lay great stress on the question as to whether proper soundings were taken or not—the omission to do so being considered a grave default. From time immemorial the Lead has been justly looked upon as one of the mainstays of Navigation, and to it, and its companion the Log, will be devoted the present chapter. Legal importance attached to Lead.

Every seaman is familiar with the ordinary "Deep-sea Lead and Line," and although it did very well for our grandsires, who were in no particular hurry, it is obliged in these fast days to make room for a better form of article.

When running up channel before a howling gale of wind, and it became necessary to ask information from the bottom as to the ship's whereabouts, every seaman knows that the operation involved much labour and loss of time, and sometimes considerable peril. The hands had to be called, sail shortened, and the ship rounded to the wind in the face of a dangerous sea. When her way was all but stopped, in obedience to the word "heave," the Difficulty of sounding, old style.

lead was let go from forward, quickly followed by the cry of "watch there, watch," and an experienced man on the weather quarter allowed the line to run through his hands till bottom was obtained. By this time the vessel had drifted to leeward, and according to the quantity of line run out, and the angle it made with the surface when being hauled in, a certain number of fathoms was deducted *by guess* from the gross amount, in order to arrive at an estimation of the true depth of water. After this, the vessel had to be kept away, and sail set, before 'the watch below' could be dismissed. Will any one wonder that masters of ships sounded as seldom as possible? Scarcely!! especially when it is understood that to be of any service the operation must be repeated every few miles. A *single* cast of the lead is *worse* than useless, inasmuch as it may confirm an error in the assumed position of the ship.

**A single cast of no value.**

This necessity for repeated sounding was undoubtedly a hardship, but it can no longer be considered so, as there are now patent machines with which soundings can be taken without stopping the ship or deviating from the course. There are many varieties of these, such as Massey's, Walker's, and others. The one which, in the writer's opinion, immeasurably excels all others, is that invented five or six years ago by Professor Sir William Thomson.

**Sir W. Thomson's Sounding Machine.**

The apparatus, briefly described, consists of a drum, about a foot in diameter and four inches wide, upon which 300 fathoms of steel pianoforte wire are tightly wound. To the wire is attached 9 feet of log-line, and to this is fastened an iron sinker, about twice the length of the ordinary lead, but not so thick. On the log-line, between the wire and the sinker, a small copper tube is securely seized. The lower end of this tube is perforated; the upper end being opened or shut at pleasure by means of a close-fitting cap. When ready for sounding, the copper tube contains a smaller sized glass one. This latter also is open at the bottom end, and hermetically sealed at the other. The interior surface is coated with a chemical preparation of a light salmon colour (chromate of silver). The drum is fitted with a brake cord, which, on a cast being taken, controls its speed, and ultimately arrests it when the lead touches the bottom. A pair of small winch handles wind up the wire again, and the depth is shown by the height of the discoloration on the inside of the glass tube.

**Mode of Action.**

As the lead descends, the water is forced up the tube in obedience to certain well-known laws, discovered quite independently, though about the same time, by Boyle in this country, and Mariotte in

France, and afterwards perfected by Regnault. The chemical action of the salt, where it comes into contact with the salmon colour, turns it to a milky white (chloride of silver). This point of junction of the two colours, when the glass tube is applied to a graduated boxwood scale, tells the depth to which the lead descended. The sinker is "armed" in the usual way. Nothing can be neater than this arrangement. Its advantages are as follows:—

*1st.* Let the speed of the ship be anything up to 16 knots an hour, or even upwards, bottom can be obtained at a depth of 100 fathoms without slowing or deviating from the course. **Advantages of Sir W. Thomson's invention.**

*2nd.* Instead of requiring all hands "to pass the line along," two men and an officer are sufficient to work it under all circumstances.

*3rd.* A cast can be taken in 100 fathoms, and depth correctly ascertained in from 4 to 7 minutes, according to the speed of the ship.

*4th.* This great saving of labour and time admits of soundings being much more frequently taken than formerly, resulting in greater safety to life and property.

*5th.* A regular "*chain*" of soundings, with correct "*time intervals,*" is now not only possible, but easy; and this latter is the *sole* method which can be depended upon to give the place of the ship with any degree of certainty, since a *single* cast is not only useless in the majority of cases, but is apt to prove mischievous in the extreme.

When not wanted, the drum is kept in a tank of lime water, to preserve the wire from rusting. A small pamphlet of directions accompanies the machine; but after seeing it once or twice in operation, the mode of working is so self-evident, as to render the instructions unnecessary. The writer has had it in use for close upon five years, and during that time has had many opportunities of testing it with most convincing results. By its aid he on one occasion, during a thick fog, brought a *new* steamer of 430 feet in length from Belfast to Liverpool, when many of the coasting boats would not venture, and of those that did a large percentage got ashore.*

* Sir W. Thomson has more recently brought out a new form of sounding machine, but the writer does not like it nearly so well as the one described in the text. One of the principal drawbacks to it is that, should the wire break, you are "up a tree," unless there is a second on board, which is scarcely likely, as the apparatus is costly. With the original invention there is sufficient spare gear supplied (inexpensive in its nature) to allow of three or four breakages, which, however, can scarcely all happen in one voyage, except through gross carelessness. It does not appear either that the new form is quite so certain in its action as the other.

Soundings are frequently very unjustly abused, and spoken about as worthless, *from want of knowledge* of how to apply them (in a methodical manner), so as to turn their indications to proper account. It cannot be too forcibly impressed that half a dozen casts taken here and there at random, will seldom fix the ship's position, and indeed under certain circumstances might very seriously mislead. Sir William Thomson, in his "Lecture on Navigation," mentions the *only plan* whereby the lead can be expected to determine the ship's position with any degree of certainty. He says,—

**How to get useful information from the Lead.**

"Take a long slip of card, or of stiff paper, and mark along one edge of it points at successive distances from one another, equal, according to the scale of your chart, to the actual distance estimated as having been run by the ship in the intervals between successive soundings. If the ship has run a straight course, the edge of the card must be straight, but if there has been any change of direction in the course, the card must be cut with a corresponding deviation from the original direction. Beside each of the points thus marked on the edge, write on the card the depth and character of bottom found by the lead. Then place the card on the chart, and slip it about till you find an agreement between the soundings marked on the chart and the series marked on your card."

**Use of Tracing Paper in connection with Soundings.**

The writer has practised this plan for many years, with just a slight difference, to which, on consideration, the reader will probably give the preference.

Instead of cardboard, use *tracing paper*, upon which you have ruled the courses and distances, with corresponding depths.

The advantages consist, for one thing, in the transparency of the tracing paper admitting of the chart soundings being visible in every direction underneath it, which greatly facilitates the task of making the actual soundings "tally" with those on the chart; and again, the ruling in of the courses, &c., on the tracing paper is quicker done, and, in any case, is a more familiar operation to the seaman than the use of the scissors. A meridian line should also be ruled on the tracing paper, so that, when moving the latter about on the chart, it may not get out of "slue."

**Value of Sounding Machine pecuniarily speaking.**

The great superiority of this method, when the navigator has to fall back upon soundings to ascertain his ship's position, cannot be too much dwelt upon. With the machine just described there is no difficulty in putting it in practice. It is true that the first cost of the apparatus is considerable, but with the steamship owner—

perhaps more than most men—"Time is money;" and half a day's "groping" in a large vessel will burn more coal than would pay for it twice over. This is putting all sorts of contingencies due to detention on one side. Every one in the business knows that the loss of a certain tide may entail (directly as well as indirectly) an extra expense of three or four hundred pounds on large steamers running on schedule time. The cost of a sounding machine is very insignificant in comparison with this.

**Principle of other Sounding Machines.**

The other kinds of sounding machines vary in certain minor details, but they nearly all depend upon the principle of the rotating fly. A small cylinder, protected by brass guards, is caused to rotate in its descent through the water by vanes or blades set obliquely to its axis; this communicates motion, by an endless screw or worm, to a train of toothed gearing. On the machine reaching the bottom, an arm falls and locks the rotator, so that it cannot revolve the back way as it is pulled to the surface. An index points to figures on a graduated dial, which indicate the depth of water reached.

**Sounding Machine Index-error.**

These instruments are very good, but they nearly all possess what may be termed an index-error—that is to say, they either show too much or too little. When quite new they are generally correct, but, through wear of the working parts—*or more likely from knocks under the counter in hauling in*—they seldom long remain so. However, their error is easily determined, and an account of it, with date when determined, should be kept in a small pass-book in the box containing the machine.

**To ascertain it in harbour.**

To ascertain the index-error: any time when the vessel is at anchor in tolerably deep water the depth indicated may be compared with the actual depth found by a carefully marked lead-line; should the depth be under 20 fathoms, it is a good plan to take several measurements by the machine *without resetting it*, and divide the last reading by the number of casts; or, what is pretty much the same thing, multiply the actual depth of water by the number of casts, and compare the result with the last reading.

For instance, in 20 fathoms of water, let five casts be taken without resetting the instrument. Now, it is clear that if it indicated truly, the last reading should be 100 fathoms; but supposing it to be 95 fathoms instead, then the index-error is about five per cent., to be added to any soundings which may be taken *until the index-error is again ascertained.*

**To ascertain it at sea.**

A still better plan may be resorted to at sea if any temporary derangement of the engines of a steamer necessitates a short stoppage, or in a calm if a sailing ship.

Set the sounding machine to zero, and attach it to the deep-sea lead and line in the usual way. Make the other end of the line fast to the taffrail, with just enough drift to allow the 100 fathom mark to touch the water when the cast is taken; make the line up into four or five coils of 20 or 25 fathoms each, and let as many men as there are coils hold them over the stern; upon a given signal, let go the lead simultaneously with the first coil, and immediately after, each of the others, taking care to drop them on their flats, proper side up. If the vessel's way is entirely stopped, the machine will of course descend vertically to a depth of 100 fathoms, and should register that water; if not, the difference will be the percentage of error. If there be time, repeat the operation once or twice, and take the mean result as the index-error.

Either before, or immediately after, *test the measurement of your lead-line.*

**Modes of sounding in sailing ships and steamers.**

The foregoing is a correct description of the mode adopted in steamships to sound with these instruments. Should the water be deep, the vessel is slowed down. In sailing ships the machine is usually cast over from forward, and the men with the coils are stationed at intervals along the ship's side in the ordinary way; but they should be instructed *at once* to let go their coils, and not try for bottom, as they would do with the common deep-sea lead. In steamers, the men are stationed across the taffrail, and the coils are dropped over the stern to prevent the bight of the line getting foul of the propeller.

The deep-sea line should be kept on a suitable reel, and protected from wet by a painted canvass cover. When there is no reel, it is handy to coil the line in a small tub, with a hole in the bottom through which to pass the inboard end, so that it may be made fast to a belaying pin, or hitched to a backstay.*

**Deep-sea lead to be always at hand.**

The common deep-sea lead and line ought to be kept on deck ready for use at a minute's notice. Should the vessel at any time appear to be passing through shoal water not marked on the chart, stop her at once, and *arm the lead* before sounding. Do not make certain that you have reached the bottom *unless an unmistakeable specimen of it comes up.*

* Before marking, tow the line astern for some hours with a heavy lead fast to it.

## "VIGIAS."

In the event of falling in with a new danger, such as a rock awash, it is *the imperative duty* of the discoverer to satisfy himself and others on board that it is *really* what they have taken it to be. It should be examined by boat as closely as possible, and soundings taken round it with the hand lead, while the ship, at a safe distance, sounds with the deep-sea lead. If possible to land on it, do so; and chip off a piece of the rock, to make assurance doubly sure.

**Nature of special dangers to be verified.**

In searching for a "vigia," it is difficult to say when its existence is to be considered as disproved. Although experience shows that nine out of ten of the bugbears and blots formerly to be found on Oceanic Charts had been mistakenly placed there from reports of floating whales, wrecks, and patches of vegetable growth taken for discoloured water over a bank, &c.; still the apparently astounding manner in which rocky heads do rise from very deep water, must always make us careful of hastily assuming that no danger exists near a given locality simply because it is known that the depths in the neighbourhood are very great. St. Paul's rocks, near the Equator, may be quoted as a good example of this kind of thing. Were they a few feet *below* water, instead of *above* water, it would be no easy job to find them.

## THE "BLUE PIGEON."

The Hand Lead, or "Blue Pigeon," is *not* by any means as familiar to the seaman as it ought to be. It is a disgrace to the merchant service that so many men calling themselves Able seamen know not how to use it. If officers would but practice their men and boys at this occasionally, instead of putting them to knot rope-yarns for spunyarn, or pass away the watch lazily making sennit, fewer ships would get ashore through unreliable leadsmen. Spunyarn can be purchased at a ship's chandler's, but good leadsmen cannot.

**Hand lead—necessity for practice.**

For use in shallow rivers, such as the Plate, where the vessel is navigated almost entirely by the hand lead, it is convenient to have a small nicely shaped lead, about five pounds in weight, attached to 12 fathoms of cod-line. The line is marked in the usual way, except that at 4 fathoms there is a manilla or coir rope-yarn.

**Shoal-water lead.**

It is unfortunately too common for pilots, when they come aboard off a harbour's mouth, to order the man out of the chains, saying they do not want the lead. The writer never permits this, and squares the matter with the pilot by telling him that he requires the lead hove for his own satisfaction, and to give the man a chance to practise.

Unlit channels—how to navigate.

In navigating an unlit and unmarked channel, where the water shoals pretty gradually on each side, the safest plan is not to attempt to steer a mid-channel course, but to zigzag it, keeping a lead going in both chains. By this plan *you can tell which side you are on*, and how to put the helm to avoid the danger.

Also, when obliged to thread intricate channels between coral reefs, wait, if possible, till the sun is astern or behind you, and direct the course of the ship from the fore-topgallant yard.

## THE COMMON LOG.

Common log not reliable.

Logs, whether patent or common, are entirely unsatisfactory in their indications of speed. The common log does not do so badly up to 10, or perhaps 11 knots, but after that it is not to be depended upon. No two men heaving the log will make the same report, *if* the ship's speed exceeds 12 knots. The short log glass runs 14 seconds, or one second per knot for a ship going 14 knots. Now a second is a very short space of time, and it is not difficult to see that, in consequence, a vessel may very easily be overlogged or underlogged to at least the amount due to this interval. This may be owing solely to the dulness of perception of the man who holds the glass, and does not take into account the possible error of the glass itself, the log-line, the heave of the sea, or the want of skill on the part of the man heaving the log. It is true all these things *may* act in opposite directions, and neutralize each other, and they may *not*.

Again, the common log fails in not affording a *continuous* record of the speed, so that a vessel may go anything during the interval, usually two hours, which elapses between two successive trials. This is not much felt in a steamer, where the rate of speed is not likely to alter greatly in such a short time; or if it does, it can be allowed for. But in a sailing ship it is a serious drawback, and in this respect the patent log has the decided advantage.

## PATENT LOGS.

The patent log—its defects and their causes.

Patent logs depend upon the principle already explained in connection with the sounding machine, but their results, from a variety of causes, are less reliable in affording a correct knowledge of the distance run, than those of the sounding machine in giving the true depth. In the first place, they are more constantly at work, and so wear out sooner; they are liable to be fouled by seaweed, waste, or ropeyarns, &c., thrown overboard from the ship; their indications in a head sea are usually different to those in a following sea, and depend also upon the length of tow-line; they are frequently damaged by blows against the counter in hauling in, and to this they are more often exposed than the patent sounding-machine; lastly, there is no satisfactory way of finding their index-error.

**Off soundings no form of log will indicate current.**

In channel, where there are points of land the distance between which is known, there is usually a tide which renders abortive any attempt to adopt such a mode; and in mid-ocean, there are surface or drift currents depending upon the winds, so that it is next to impossible to arrive at any definite conclusion. In fact, there is no known instrument at the present time which *correctly* gives a vessel's speed *over the bottom* in deep water. Even supposing a patent log to indicate correctly the speed *through the water*, what about current or tide? There is no *deep-sea* log which indicates current; but in shallow rivers like the Plate, what is known as the "Ground log," gives fairly approximate results as to its amount, provided the speed is not too high, and care is exercised in heaving it.

## "GROUND LOG."

**Ground log—its description and use.**

This is simply the common log-line with a hand-lead substituted for the log-ship. When the log is hove, the lead lies on the bottom without dragging, and so gives the speed *over the ground;* and in hauling it in, the *trend* of the line at starting is supposed to shew the *direction* of the current; but this latter is not correct except in a very broad sense indeed, and the writer strongly counsels the navigator not to place the slightest dependence upon it. It is evident that, to get the correct direction of the current, the ship must make a mathematically straight wake during the operation, and her speed must be slow. In a small vessel, with a lumpy sea, the indicated direction would not be worth much, though the speed might be pretty near the mark.

In using the Ground log, some people go to the trouble of fixing a crutch on the taffrail in which to put the line, and underneath it, a painted semicircle of points of the compass, to show the direction; but this, as already stated, is labour entirely thrown away.

## TAFFRAIL LOGS.

Taffrail log.

T. Walker and Son have introduced a patent Taffrail log, which can be consulted and reset as often as necessary, without the trouble incidental to those in which the whole apparatus is towed astern. It has a novel feature of considerable value: by the interval between two consecutive strokes of a small bell, coupled with a short and very simple sum in proportion, the *rate* of speed at any desired moment is found in a few seconds. It is practically free also from the danger of being damaged in the operation of hauling in, as this latter need only be done once at the end of the passage.

In the Taffrail log, the registering portion is secured to the rail, and motion is communicated to it by the rotator through the medium of a long tow-line. There is no doubt this is very convenient, but it appears to the writer that unless great care is exercised in repeatedly oiling it, the works would be liable to heat at a high rate of speed. As the 'harpoon' and other similar logs are towed bodily in the water, and so get plenty of "fisherman's grease," they are not exposed to this danger. As a matter of fact, there are no patent logs yet invented which will stand the wear and tear for any length of time. In slow vessels they will of course last longer than in fast ones. Unless used only on special occasions, such racers as the "Alaska" or "Stirling Castle" very quickly put them out of order.*

From this the reader must not conclude that they are to be abandoned as altogether useless. The writer merely wishes to urge upon the navigator the imprudence of trusting too implicitly to their indications at critical times. Patent logs are more useful in slow steamers than fast ones, and still more useful in sailing ships than steamers. To avoid unnecessary wear and tear, they should only be used when "in with the land." It is found to be a good plan to wrap the line—about a fathom in advance of the log—with sheet lead, to keep the latter from jumping out of the water.

Instance of patent log spoilt by sand ballast.

The writer once knew of a patent log being totally spoilt by sand getting into it. The steamer was bound to an American port in ballast, and, as is usual, got rid of a quantity of it over-

* The writer has lately been using one of Walker's Taffrail logs in a 13-knot steamer with very satisfactory results: for nearly a year the index-error kept between + 2% and 4%, but the log was only towed for 500 miles or so at each end of the passage, and in obedience to a standing order it was oiled every eight-bells by a quarter-master, who made due report of having done so to the officer of the watch.

board during the last two days before arrival. The log was allowed to tow, as no one imagined the sand could reach it, but when it was hauled in at the end of the watch, it was found to be perfectly choked with it; and as the oil-holes, &c., were closed, the puzzle consisted in how the sand reached the interior. The log was duly cleaned, and on the homeward passage tested, but it showed about 30 per cent. too much distance, and was in consequence put away as worthless.

To ensure the best results, a 'harpoon' log should be towed from the outer end of a small spar—a boat's mast, for instance—rigged out on the quarter. This keeps it clear of the dead-water in the ship's wake, and by a simple arrangement of out-haul and in-haul, the log need never strike the ship's side on being taken in for examination.

Before stowing away a patent log for a length of time, it should be immersed for half an hour in a bucket of fresh water, to get rid of the salt, which would otherwise dry and encrust the works, to their manifest detriment.

**Speed calculated by paddle revolutions.**

In certain paddle steamers, probably the best measure of speed is obtained by the revolutions of the wheels. Most of the cross-channel boats depend upon this method of making their runs in thick weather, and the captains of the coast boats of the Pacific Steam Navigation Co. make an invariable practice of tabulating the revolutions between their various ports of call. In vessels such as the Holyhead mail boats, where the passage is short, the vessels of great power, *and their immersion always the same*, the method is susceptible of considerable accuracy. Again, men who are going *constantly* backwards and forwards on a short run, acquire by long experience the knowledge necessary to enable them to make allowance for wind and sea, according as it may be in their favour, or against them. The slip of a screw-propeller is so variable under *apparently* the same circumstances, that in boats so driven the method is of inferior value. Experience shows that the revolutions of a paddle steamer are to be depended upon fully as much as the best patent log yet invented, with the advantage, *that the revolutions do not wear out, and the patent log does.*

## ELECTRICAL LOGS.

Quite recently some experiments have been conducted with an electrical log, which seem to promise well for it. The rotator actuating the electrical portion is placed in a cylinder below the bottom of the vessel, where it has the advantage of working in a body of water of uniform pressure or density, and in this way it is claimed there are none of the inaccuracies of ordinary towing logs, which are affected by so many causes.

The distance run may be shewn by electric agency on one or more dials placed in cabins or chart-room, the stroke of a bell indicating the accomplishment of each tenth of a knot. Though not stated, it is presumed that the arrangement permits of the withdrawal of the instrument in very shallow water, so as to leave no projection below the ship's bottom.

## DEAD RECKONING.

Writing about logs and leads naturally leads to the subject of Dead Reckoning. Sir William Thomson, in his "Lecture on Navigation," has put the matter so clearly and forcibly, that one cannot do better than quote his words. He says,—

Sir W. Thomson's remarks on Dead Reckoning.

"When no landmarks can be seen, and when the water is too deep for soundings, if the sky is cloudy, so that neither sun nor stars can be seen, the navigator, however clear the horizon may be, has no other way of knowing where he is than the dead reckoning, and no other guide for steering than the compass.

"We often hear stories of marvellous exactness with which the dead reckoning has been verified by the result. A man has steamed or sailed across the Atlantic without having got a glimpse of sun or stars the whole way, and has made land within five miles of the place aimed at. This may be done once, and may be done again, but must not be trusted to on any one occasion as probably to be done again this time.

"Undue trust in the dead reckoning has produced more disastrous shipwrecks of seaworthy ships, I believe, than all other causes put together.

"All over the surface of the sea there are currents of unknown strength and direction. Regarding these currents, much most valuable information has been collected by our Board of Trade and Admiralty, and published by the Admiralty in its "Atlas of Wind and Current Charts." These charts show, in scarcely any part of the ocean, less than ten miles of surface current per twenty-four hours, and they show as much as forty or fifty miles in many places. Unless these currents are taken into account, then, the place of a ship, by dead reckoning, may be wrong by from ten to fifty miles per twenty-four hours; and the most accurate information which we yet have regarding them is, at the best, only approximate. There are, in fact, certain currents, of ten miles and upwards per day, due to wind (it may be wind in a distant part of the ocean) which the navigator cannot possibly know at the time he is affected by them.

"I believe it would be unsafe to say that, even if the steerage and the speed through the water were reckoned with absolute accuracy in the "account," the ship's place could in general be reasonably trusted to within fifteen or twenty miles per twenty-four hours of dead reckoning. And, besides, neither the speed through the water, nor the steerage, can be safely reckoned, without allowing a considerable margin for error.

"In the recent court-martial regarding the loss of the Vanguard, the speed of the *Iron Duke* was estimated by one of the witnesses at ten and a half knots, according to his mode of reckoning from revolutions of the screw and the slip of the screw through the water; while other witnesses, for reasons which they stated, estimated it at only 8·2 knots. It was stated in evidence, however, that the only experiments available for estimating the ship's speed in smooth water from the number of revolutions of the screw, had been made before she left Plymouth. If the pressure log, or even the old log-ship and glasses, had been used, there could have been no such great range of doubt. But even with the pressure log (until experimented upon, as it probably will not be except by the Navy, because not needed for thorough practical work except by the Navy) we could scarcely tell with certainty within a quarter of a knot what the actual speed of the ship through the water is at any instant. And, again, the Massey log may be held to have done its work fairly well if it gives the whole distance run by the ship in any interval within five per cent. of the truth.

"Consider further the steerage. In a wooden ship a good ordinary compass, with proper precautions to keep iron from its neighbourhood, may be safely trusted to within a half quarter point; but, reckoning the errors of even very careful steering by compass, we cannot trust to making a course which will be *certainly* within a quarter of a point of that desired. Now you know an error of a quarter of a point in your course would put you wrong by one mile to right or left of your desired course for every twenty miles of distance run. Thus, in the most favourable circumstances, you are liable, through mere error of steerage by compass, to be ten miles out of your course in a run of two hundred.

"In an iron ship, if the compass has been thoroughly well attended to as long as the weather permitted sights of sun or stars, a very careful navigator may be sure of his course by it, within a quarter of a point, when cloudy weather comes on; but by the time he has run three or four hundred miles, he can no longer reckon on the same degree of accuracy in his interpretation of its indications, and may be uncertain as to his course to an extent of half a point or more until he again gets an azimuth of sun or star.

"No doubt an exceedingly skilful navigator may entirely, or almost entirely, overcome this last source of uncertainty when he runs over the same course month after month, and year after year, in the same ship; but it is not overcome by any skill hitherto applied to the compass at sea when a first voyage to a fresh destination, whether in a new ship or in an old one, is attempted.

"All things considered, a thoroughly skilled and careful navigator may reckon that, in the most favourable circumstances, he has a fair chance of being within five miles of his estimated place after a two hundred miles' run on dead reckoning; but with all his skill and with all his care, he may be twenty miles off it; and he will no more think of imperilling his ship and the lives committed to his charge on such an estimate, than a skilled rifle-shot would think of staking a human life on his hitting a bull's-eye at five hundred yards.

"What, then, do practical navigators do in approaching land after a few days' run on dead reckoning? Too many, through bad logic and imperfect scientific intelligence, rather than through conscious negligence, run on, trusting to their dead reckoning. In the course of eight or ten or fifteen years of navigation on this principle, a captain of a mail steamer has made land just at the desired place a dozen times, after runs of strictly dead reckoning of from three or four hours to two or three days. Perhaps of all these times there has only once been a strictly dead reckoning of over thirty hours with satisfactory result. Still, the man remembers a time or two when he has hit the mark marvellously well by absolutely dead reckoning; he actually forgets his own prudence on many of the occasions when he has corrected his dead reckoning by the lead, and imagines that he has been served by the dead reckoning with a degree of accuracy, with which it is impossible, in the nature of things, it can serve any man. Meantime, he has earned the character of being a most skilful navigator, and has been unremitting in every part of his duty, according to the very best of his intelligence and knowledge.

He has, moreover, found favour with his owners, through making excellent passages in all weathers, rough or smooth, bright or cloudy, clear or foggy. At last the fatal time comes, he has trusted to his dead reckoning once too often, he has made a 'centre,' not a 'bull's-eye,' and his ship is on the rocks."

Every seaman of experience will admit the perfect justice of these remarks, even were they not corroborated by the revelations of the wreck register.

**Captain John Miller on Dead Reckoning.**

A very valuable paper on the subject of dead reckoning has been written by the late Captain John Miller, and will be found in the *Mercantile Marine Service Association Reporter*, Vol. III., page 415. It is also given in the May number of the *Nautical Magazine* for 1878. The reader would do well to refer to it.

Do not forget to look to your log-*glass* as well as your log-*line*, especially when nearing land. Test it by the chronometer.

**Permanent deck marks for measuring log and lead lines.**

For convenience of testing the length of the log and lead lines, the required distances should be permanently marked (with copper tacks) on the quarter-deck; 23′ 4″—the length of a knot corresponding to a glass running 14s.—being laid off on the port side, and single fathoms up to five, on the starboard side. It is always best to have the leadlines fitted with *calico* for white marks, *bunting* for red marks, and *serge* for blue marks, because in the dark a man can tell the difference by the feel. Test the measurements of the lines immediately after use, *when they are wet and well stretched.*

The following is from the able pen of Mr. Thomas Gray, to whom sailors of all nations owe a lasting debt for his popular exposition of the Rule of the Road at sea:—

## L. L. L. L.

### THE MARINER'S CREED.

TO BE SAID DAILY, AND ACTED ON ALWAYS.

"I understand L. L. L. L. to be the symbol or sign for four things which I must never neglect; and these things are, Lead, Log, Latitude, and Look-out.

Therefore, I say, use the Lead and the Log; and mind the Latitude and the Look-out.

I believe in the Lead, as it warns me against dangers which the eye cannot see.

I believe in the Log, as it checks my distance run.

I believe in ascertaining the Latitude, as it helps to define my position.

I believe in the Look-out, as it warns me against dangers to be seen.

The lead warns me against dangers invisible, the Log warns me against false distances, the Latitude helps to define my position, and the Look-out warns me against dangers visible.

And I earnestly resolve, and openly declare, that as I hope to sail my ship in safety on the ocean, as I wish to spare the lives of my fellow-creatures at sea, and as I wish to go in safety all my days, so will I steadfastly practise that which I believe.

And I hereby warn seamen, and tell them that if they neglect any one of these four things, either the Lead, the Log, the Latitude, or the Look-out, they or their fellows will some day surely perish."

---

## CHAPTER XII.

### THE MARINE BINOCULAR AND TELESCOPE

These differ, or should do so, from the instruments in use on shore. Such fancy articles as those fitted with revolving eye-pieces, which, according to the particular one employed, constitute them either Marine, Field, or Opera glasses, are quite unsuitable for use on board ship.

**Fancy articles unsuitable.**

Binoculars, when first introduced for sea use, were intended exclusively as *night-glasses*, but from their extreme portability and large field of view, were soon found to be so convenient for general service that, before long, opticians manufactured them of patterns to meet nearly all requirements.

In a work of this practical character, it would be undesirable, even if space permitted, to enter on such complex optical difficulties as 'spherical aberration' or 'confusion,' and 'chromatic dispersion,' but acquaintance with the following simple principles is essential for the wise selection of good and suitable binoculars; and the purchaser, moreover, should fully understand that those adapted for one purpose, are not necessarily so for another.

**Principle of the night glass.**

In all glasses high magnifying power and the acquisition of light are invariably opposed to each other, and it is always necessary that one of these qualities should be more or less subordinated to the other, according to the particular purpose for which the instrument is intended. Consequently, in the Night-glass, where the main desideratum is to collect as much light as possible, to enable that which is looked at to be seen with distinctness, it is evident that we cannot expect much magnifying power.

The amount of light is dependent upon the size and shape of the object lens, and if for the same instrument the magnifying power be increased by a change in the ocular, whilst the object lens remains as before, the light is spread over a larger image, which is necessarily fainter in proportion to its increased size. It is for this reason that the eyes are unduly strained in the endeavour to make out the details of an object as seen through some ill-constructed telescopes of high power and small aperture.

Under such conditions, coloured flags fluttering in the wind are especially difficult to decipher, the colours appearing much less vivid than they should do.

**Object lens—what kind most suitable.**

The object glasses of the binocular should therefore be as large as possible, consistent with a requirement hereinafter to be named; and of short focal length, by which combination you not only gain *good illuminating power*, but also the important advantage of a *wide field of view.*

On a dark night, when sweeping the horizon in quest of ships, land, or buoys, it is obvious that the greater the area embraced, the greater the likelihood of picking up the object sought for.

**How to select binocular for night use.**

From these considerations it will be evident that the proper way to select a binocular for *night* use is, *not* to stand at a shop door in broad daylight, trying how much it *enlarges* some distant clock-face, but to wait until nightfall, and test it by looking up a dark street or passage; and if figures, before only dimly visible to the naked eye, are rendered tolerably clear by the aid of the glasses, you may rest assured you have hit on a suitable instrument.

*The principle aim, therefore, of the night-glasses (as already stated) being to intensify and get as much light and field as possible, you must be prepared to sacrifice magnifying power, which should never exceed four diameters.*

**How to determine magnifying power.**

A simple method of determining this latter quality is to look at any suitable object with one eye unaided, whilst with the other we use one tube of the binocular. The object will then be seen in its natural size, and at the same time as magnified by the instrument. By a little manipulation the two images can be brought side by side, or made to overlap, when it will be easy to see how many times the magnified image is larger than the natural one.

**Width between glasses to correspond with width between eyes.**

Another point essential to be remembered—and this it is which unavoidably limits the size of the object glass—is, *that the centre of curvature of the lenses should be exactly opposite the pupil of each eye; or, in other words, that the distance between the right and left-hand glasses should correspond to the distance between the eyes—centre to centre.* This is capable of easy measurement; so, in choosing your binoculars, those not corresponding to this requirement should be at once rejected, irrespective of other considerations. It is seldom that the distance between the pupils permits of a larger object glass than 2⅜-inches diameter, as it will be apparent to anyone that its measure must be a *little* less than the aforesaid distance, to allow for setting in the frames. Hence a good and well made pair of glasses may suit one man perfectly, and another not at all.

A binocular has been devised, fitted with a hinged joint connecting the twin parts, so that the distance between the barrels can be increased or diminished at pleasure, to suit different eyes, but for several reasons it is not a success. Hinged binoculars.

The best description of binoculars have six lenses in each tube, three being combined to form the object glass, and three to form the eye-piece. In this system some of the lenses are made of crown, and others of flint glass, on account of the unequal *dispersive power* of these two substances. A suitable combination of such lenses gets rid of the fringe of colour which in cheap glasses surrounds the object under inspection like a halo; and the name *achromatic* (derived from the Greek *a*, without; *chroma*, colour) is accordingly given to a telescope or binocular possessing such an arrangement. The medium-priced binoculars have an achromatic object glass of two lenses, and a single eye lens; but in the very common glasses, both the objective and ocular are of the simple form, and the fringe of colour, inseparable from their use, fatigues the sight and impairs the sharp definition of whatever is looked at. Lenses.

Without being in the least colour-blind, it is difficult, when using cheap glasses on a dirty night, to distinguish with certainty the colour of a vessel's lights, especially when the latter happen to be nothing extra in themselves. Under such unpleasant circumstances a white light is apt to have a greenish or reddish tinge, as the case may be; or a green light, as likely as not, is mistaken for a white one. It is important, therefore, to be provided with the best article if you wish to guard against collisions.

The common long-draw binocular is always to be avoided, as with wear the sliding tubes work slack, and the parallelism of their axes being destroyed, the observer "sees double." This remark does not apply to a binocular of superior make now coming much into favour with yachtsmen and tourists. It is to all intents and purposes a small double-barrelled *telescope*, a condition inconsistent with its use as a *night-glass*. For day use, however, these glasses are admirable as a substitute for the telescope, and being easier to hold, recommend themselves greatly Tourists' Binoculars.

to ladies, or to gentlemen who have not got their sea-legs aboard. The high price of the good ones—£10 to £20—restricts their sale, and, after all, they are nothing more than a compromise.

**Eye shields.**

To protect the eyes from a strong cold wind, it is a good plan to have the binoculars furnished with a concave shield of thin brass, made to fit closely to the face, and to ship and unship when required. Any handy engineer on board can do this, and it will be found a great comfort to persons with weak eyes.

Many men, from its greater portability, habitually use the binocular in the day time; but where the distance is great, and the object small, it has to give way to the more powerful telescope.

**Marine Telescope.**

The marine telescope for ordinary use, like the binocular, must not have *too* high a magnifying power, as the greater it is, for the same sized object glass, the fainter the picture, and the narrower the field of view. This latter is a most serious drawback to the telescope for general purposes, as it increases the difficulty (always experienced afloat) of keeping the instrument fixed on the object under scrutiny, the least motion at once putting it out of the field, so that a continuous and steady look is impossible. Can anything be more annoying? Moreover, in misty weather a glass with great magnifying power is unsuitable, as it magnifies the haze as well as the object, and, of course, renders the latter even more indistinct and blurred than before.* Nevertheless, there are times when a powerful glass is suitable.

The writer possesses, and occasionally finds useful, an elegant *compound* telescope (one of Ross's, price £9), which, by means of what is termed a pancratic arrangement, can be made to magnify 30, 40, or 50 times. It has two "draws." For general purposes the one nearest the observer is not pulled out or touched in any way, and the glass then magnifies but 30 times; if, however, an exceedingly bright clear day justifies the use of a higher power, this can be obtained up to 50 by drawing out the small or pancratic tube, which is marked by numbered rings, so as to indicate the precise power employed: the focussing is done with the other tube as before.

**Pancratic eye-piece.**

* Ross, of 112 New Bond Street, London, has acquired a well-deserved reputation as the manufacturer of naval telescopes. He sells a really good glass at £6, having 1¼ times the intensity of those of ordinary construction; but the one sold at £8 is worth the difference of price. Both glasses measure 31 inches when open, and 25 inches when closed, with a power of 20. The £8 glass, however, has an aperture of 2¼ inches—a quarter of an inch more than the other—with the superior advantage of possessing *double* the ordinary intensity, which permits of its use at night or in gloomy weather.

The Calcutta pilots, who have often to look for small channel marks when yet a long way from them, invariably bring on board their own telescopes, and but seldom accept the proffered binocular. It must be remembered, however, that the use of these powerful instruments is, in their case, restricted to clear weather and perfectly smooth water.

**Calcutta Pilots.**

In providing yourself, therefore, with Binocular and Telescope, recollect that each has not only its own important, but its perfectly distinct function. Of all things, beware of "cheap Johns." If you wish for a really good article, you must be prepared to pay a reasonable price for it.*

**Gullability of sailors taken for granted.**

* Some years ago the author's curiosity was excited by the seemingly marvellous statement in the window of a shop, in a certain town, both of which shall be nameless, that a binocular, exhibited for sale, had rendered an "object" visible at the distance of ninety miles. This was attested by a letter to be seen within. On enquiry, the "object" turned out to be none other than the island of Tristan d'Acunha, which, as most southern-going sailors know, is sometimes visible to *the naked eye* at even a greater distance. This reminds one of the anecdote of the Cockney tourist on the summit of Ben Lomond; on remarking to his Scotch guide that they could discern objects at a great distance, the guide replied that if the other would only just wait a couple of hours or so he would be able to see something much further still. Guess the feelings of the tourist when, on enquiring what he would see, he got for answer, "*you'll see the moon.*" Not long since another shop notice caught the author's eye; it was to the effect that the binocular it referred to would enable a person to be recognised at a distance of five miles. Now, when it is known that at that distance a man of average height will only subtend an angle of forty-five seconds (three-quarters of a minute of arc), it will at once be evident that such a statement is ridiculous. On the other hand, *Telescopes* (where large enough) are capable of very much greater feats. For example, Sir Henry Bessemer has in course of construction a reflecting telescope with a speculum of silvered glass 4 feet in diameter. With this instrument placed in his Observatory at Denmark Hill, he expects to be able to read a newspaper posted against the side of the Crystal Palace, 3½ miles away. Lord Rosse's famous telescope has a metal speculum of 4 tons weight and 6 feet in diameter. Its *light gathering* power is consequently enormous, but owing to defects in curvature, its *defining* power is surpassed by smaller but more perfect instruments, such as that belonging to Mr. Ainslie Common, the astronomer of Ealing, which has a silvered glass speculum of 37½ inches in diameter. This last named telescope is thought by some to be the most powerful one in existence.

## CHAPTER XIII.

### SIR WILLIAM THOMSON'S NAVIGATIONAL INSTRUMENTS.

#### 1. NEW FORM OF AZIMUTH AND STEERING COMPASS, WITH ADJUNCTS FOR THE COMPLETE APPLICATION OF THE LATE ASTRONOMER-ROYAL'S PRINCIPLES OF CORRECTION FOR IRON SHIPS.

**First introduction of Compensation.**

Forty odd years ago, Sir George Airy, then Astronomer-Royal, shewed how the errors of the Compass, depending on the influence produced by the iron of the ship, may be perfectly corrected by permanent magnets and soft iron placed in the neighbourhood of the binnacle. Partial applications of his method came immediately into use in merchant steamers; and within the last fifteen years have become universal, not only in the merchant service, but in the navies of England and other countries.

Sir. William Thomson's compasses and binnacles are designed to thoroughly carry out in practical navigation the mathematical theories referred to above; but the general drawback to the complete and accurate realisation of plans for carrying out these principles heretofore, has been the *great size* of the needles in the ordinary compass, which renders one important part of the correction—the correction of the quadrantal error for all latitudes by masses of soft iron placed on the two sides of the binnacles—practically unattainable; and which limits, and sometimes partially vitiates, the other chief part of the correction, or that which is performed by means of magnets placed in the neighbourhood of the compass.

**Compensation taken up by Sir W. Thomson.**

Ten years ago the attention of Sir William Thomson was forced to this subject, through his having been called upon by the Royal Society to write a biographical sketch of the late Mr. Archibald Smith, with an account of his scientific work on the mariner's compass and ship's navigation; and he therefore commenced to make trial compasses with very much smaller needles than any previously in use; but it was only after three years of very varied trials in the laboratory and workshop, and at sea, that he succeeded in producing a mariner's compass with the qualities necessary for thoroughly satisfactory working in all weathers and all seas, and in every class of ships, and yet with small enough needles for the perfect application of the late Astronomer-Royal's method of correction for iron ships.

One result at which Sir William arrived, partly by lengthened trials at sea in his own yacht, and partly by dynamical theory analagous to that of Froude with reference to the rolling of ships, was that steadiness of the compass at sea was to be obtained *not* by heaviness of needles or of compass card, or of added weights, but by longness of vibrational period* of the compass, whatever way the longness may be obtained. Thus if the addition of weight to the compass card improves it in respect to steadiness at sea, it is not because of the additional friction on the bearing point that this improvement is obtained; on the contrary, the dulness of the bearing point, or too much weight upon it, renders the compass less steady at sea, and, at the same time, less decided in shewing changes of the ship's head, than it would be were the point perfectly fine and frictionless, supposing for a moment this to be possible.

**Vibrational period.**

It is by increasing the vibrational period that the addition of weight gives steadiness to the compass; while, on the other hand, the increase of friction on the bearing point is both injurious in respect to steadiness, and detrimental in blunting it or boring into the cap, and so producing sluggishness after a short time of use at sea. If weight were to be added to produce steadiness, the place to add it would be at the very *circumference* of the card.

**Weight of card to be carried at outer edge.**

The conclusion that Sir William Thomson came to was that no weight is in any case to be added, beyond that which is necessary for supporting the card; and that—with small enough needles to admit of the complete application of the late Astronomer-Royal's principles of correction—the length of period required for steadiness at sea is to be obtained, without sacrificing freedom from frictional error, by giving a large diameter to the compass card, and by throwing to its outer edge as nearly as possible the whole mass of rigid material which it must have to support it.

---

* The vibrational period, or the period (as it may be called for brevity) of a compass, is the time it takes to perform a complete vibration, to and fro, when deflected horizontally through any angle not exceeding 30° or 40°, and left to itself to vibrate freely.

Description of card.

In the compass card, of which a representation is here given, these qualities are acquired by supporting its outer edge on a thin rim of aluminium—a strong but exceedingly light metal—and its inner parts on thirty-two silk threads stretched from the rim to a small central boss of aluminium, making thirty-two spokes, as it were, of the wheel. The card itself is of thin strong paper, and all the central parts of it are cut away, leaving only enough to shew conveniently the ordinary points and degree divisions of the compass. The central boss consists of a thin disc of aluminium, with a hole in its centre, which rests on the projecting lip of a small inverted cup made of the same metal, and mounted with a sapphire cap, which, in its turn, rests on a fixed iridium* point, and so sustains the entire card.

* The hardest metal known.

CAP AND BEARING POINT.

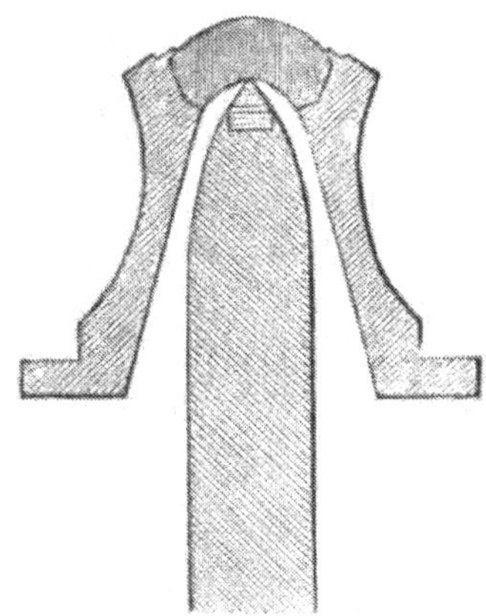

Eight small needles, from 3½ to 2 inches long, made of thin steel wire, and weighing in all 54 grains, are fixed like the steps of a rope ladder on two parallel silk threads, and slung from the aluminium rim by other silk threads rove through eyes in the ends of the outer pair of needles.

The weight of the central boss, aluminium cup, and sapphire cap, amounts in all to about five grains. It need not be more for a 24-inch than for a 10-inch compass.

For the 10-inch compass, the whole weight on the iridium point, including rim, card, silk threads, central boss, and needles, is about 180 grains. The limit to the diameter of the card depends upon the quantity of soft iron that can be introduced, without inconvenience, on the starboard and port sides of the binnacle, to correct the quadrantal error. If, as sometimes may be advisable in the case of a pole or masthead compass, it be decided to leave the quadrantal error uncorrected, the diameter of the compass card may be anything from 12 to 24 inches, according to circumstances. A 24-inch card on this principle will undoubtedly have less frictional error or "sluggishness" for the same degree of steadiness than any smaller size; but a 12-inch card works well even in very unfavourable circumstances, and it will rarely, if ever, be necessary to choose a larger size, unless for convenience of the steersman, to enable him to see the divisions, whether points or degrees.

**Weight of card.**

**Size of card.**

Specimens of 12-inch, 15-inch, and 24-inch Pole compasses have been made. The last mentioned may be looked at with some curiosity as being probably the largest compass in the world, and would require a bowl like a washing tub. It will no doubt be properly condemned as too cumbrous for use at sea, even in the largest ship, but there can be no doubt it would work well in a position in which a smaller compass would be made to oscillate very wildly by the motion of the ship.

**Improved Binnacle top.** The subjoined diagram represents the 10" Standard Compass and upper portion of binnacle. The Azimuth-Mirror is shipped ready for observing, and it will be noticed that a small door in rear of the helmet gives access to it, so that in bad weather an azimuth or bearing can be taken without removing the binnacle-top.

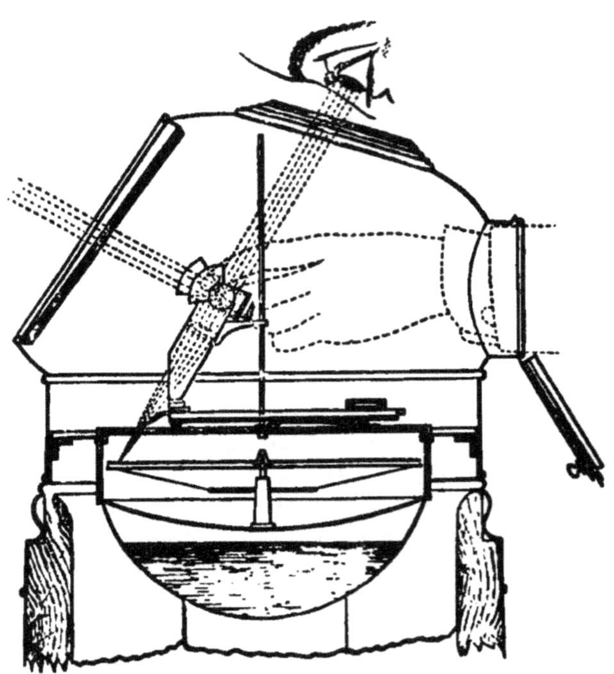

**Steadiness of card.** The "period" of Sir William Thomson's 10-inch compass is in England about 40 seconds, which is more than double the "period" of the A card of the Admiralty Standard Compass, and is considerably longer than that of the ordinary 10-inch compass so much in use in merchant steamers. The new compass ought, therefore, according to theory, to be considerably steadier in a heavy sea than either the Admiralty compass or the *ordinary*

10-inch compass, and actual experience at sea has thoroughly fulfilled this promise. It has also proved very satisfactory in respect to frictional error; so much so that variations of a steamer's course of less than half a degree are shewn instantly and surely, even if the engines be stopped, and the water perfectly smooth.

**Frictional error.**

With the small needles of Sir William's compass, the complete practical application of the late Astronomer-Royal's principles of correction is easy and sure: that is to say, correctors can be applied so that the compass shall be free from Deviation on all points; and these correctors can be easily and surely adjusted at sea as need may arise, so as to remove the smallest discoverable error growing up, whether through change of the ship's own magnetism or of the magnetism induced by the earth according to the geographical position of the ship.

**Quadrantal correctors.**

To correct the quadrantal error, a pair of solid or hollow iron globes are placed on proper supports attached to the binnacle. This mode is preferable to the usual chain boxes, because a continuous globe or spherical shell of iron is more regular in its effect than a heap of chain, and because a considerably less bulk of the continuous iron suffices to correct the same error.

When, in a first adjustment in a new ship, or in a new position of a compass in an old ship, the quadrantal error has been found from observation, by the ordinary practical methods, it is to be corrected by placing a pair of globes in proper positions according to the table on next page.

## TABLE FOR CORRECTION OF QUADRANTAL ERROR.

| Error to be Corrected. | Distances of the Nearest Points of Globes from Centre of Compass. | | | | | | | | | | |
|---|---|---|---|---|---|---|---|---|---|---|---|
| | 10-inch Globes. | 9-inch Globes. | 8½-inch Globes. | 8-inch Globes. | 7½-inch Globes. | 7-inch Globes. | 6½-inch Globes. | 6-inch Globes. | 5½-inch Globes. | 5-inch Globes. | 4½-inch Globes. |
| | Inches. | Inches. | Inches. | Inches. | Inches. | Inches. | Inches. | Inches. | Inches. | Inches. | Inches. |
| 1° | 22·80 | 20·52 | 19·38 | 18·24 | 17·10 | 15·96 | 14·82 | 13·68 | 12·54 | 11·40 | 10·26 |
| 1½ | 19·30 | 17·36 | 16·39 | 15·42 | 14·46 | 13·50 | 12·54 | 11·57 | 10·61 | 9·65 | 8·06 |
| 2 | 17·06 | 15·36 | 14·51 | 13·66 | 12·81 | 11·95 | 11·10 | 10·24 | 9·39 | 8·53 | 7·68 |
| 2½ | 15·48 | 13·94 | 13·16 | 12·39 | 11·61 | 10·84 | 10·07 | 9·29 | 8·52 | 7·74 | 6·97 |
| 3 | 14·28 | 12·84 | 12·13 | 11·42 | 10·70 | 9·99 | 9·28 | 8·57 | 7·85 | 7·14 | 6·42 |
| 3½ | 13·32 | 11·98 | 11·32 | 10·65 | 9·99 | 9·32 | 8·65 | 7·99 | 7·32 | 6·66 | 5·99 |
| 4 | 12·52 | 11·26 | 10·63 | 10·01 | 9·39 | 8·76 | 8·13 | 7·51 | 6·88 | 6·26 | 5·63 |
| 4½ | 11·84 | 10·66 | 10·07 | 9·47 | 8·88 | 8·29 | 7·70 | 7·10 | 6·51 | 5·92 | 5·33 |
| 5 | 11·26 | 10·13 | 9·57 | 9·01 | 8·45 | 7·88 | 7·32 | 6·75 | 6·19 | 5·63 | 5·07 |
| 5½ | 10·76 | 9·67 | 9·13 | 8·59 | 8·06 | 7·52 | 6·99 | 6·45 | 5·91 | 5·38 | 4·84 |
| 6 | 10·40 | 9·27 | 8·75 | 8·24 | 7·72 | 7·21 | 6·70 | 6·18 | 5·66 | 5·14 | 4·58 |
| 6½ | 9·90 | 8·91 | 8·41 | 7·92 | 7·42 | 6·93 | 6·44 | 5·94 | 5·44 | 4·95 | 4·46 |
| 7 | 9·54 | 8·58 | 8·10 | 7·63 | 7·15 | 6·67 | 6·20 | 5·72 | 5·24 | 4·77 | 4·29 |
| 7½ | 9·20 | 8·28 | 7·82 | 7·36 | 6·90 | 6·44 | 5·98 | 5·52 | 5·06 | 4·60 | 4·14 |
| 8 | 8·90 | 8·01 | 7·57 | 7·12 | 6·68 | 6·23 | 5·79 | 5·34 | 4·90 | 4·45 | 4·01 |
| 8½ | 8·62 | 7·76 | 7·33 | 6·90 | 6·47 | 6·04 | 5·60 | 5·17 | 4·74 | 4·31 | 3·88 |
| 9 | 8·36 | 7·53 | 7·11 | 6·69 | 6·27 | 5·86 | 5·44 | 5·02 | 4·60 | 4·18 | 3·76 |
| 9½ | 8·12 | 7·32 | 6·91 | 6·50 | 6·09 | 5·69 | 5·28 | 4·87 | 4·47 | 4·06 | 3·66 |
| 10 | 7·90 | 7·11 | 6·72 | 6·32 | 5·93 | 5·53 | 5·14 | 4·74 | 4·35 | 3·95 | 3·55 |
| 10½ | 7·70 | 6·93 | 6·54 | 6·16 | 5·77 | 5·39 | 5·00 | 4·62 | 4·23 | 3·85 | 3·46 |
| 11 | 7·50 | 6·75 | 6·37 | 6·00 | 5·62 | 5·25 | 4·87 | 4·50 | 4·12 | 3·75 | 3·37 |
| 11½ | 7·32 | 6·58 | 6·22 | 5·85 | 5·49 | 5·12 | 4·76 | 4·39 | 4·02 | 3·66 | 3·29 |
| 12 | 7·14 | 6·43 | 6·07 | 5·71 | 5·36 | 5·00 | 4·64 | 4·29 | 3·93 | 3·57 | 3·22 |

TABLE FOR CORRECTION OF QUADRANTAL ERROR, FROM 12 TO 16 DEGREES.

| Error to be Corrected. | 12-inch Globes. | 11-inch Globes. |
|---|---|---|
| | Inches. | Inches. |
| 12° | 8·61 | 7·89 |
| 12½ | 8·42 | 7·72 |
| 13 | 8·23 | 7·54 |
| 13½ | 8·05 | 7·38 |
| 14 | 7·89 | 7·23 |
| 14½ | 7·73 | 7·09 |
| 15 | 7·58 | 6·95 |
| 15½ | 7·44 | 6·82 |
| 16 | 7·30 | 6·69 |

When the quadrantal error has been thus once accurately corrected, the correction is perfect to whatever part of the world the ship may go, and requires no adjustment at any subsequent time, *except in the case of some alteration in the ship's iron*, or of iron cargo or ballast sufficiently near the compass to introduce a sensible change in the quadrantal error.

The vast simplification of the deviations of the compass effected by a perfect correction of this part of the whole error, has not, until now, been practically appreciated, because, in point of fact, with other compasses this correction has rarely, if ever, been successfully made for all latitudes. The pair of large needles of the compass ordinarily used in merchant ships does not—as has been shewn by Captain Sir Fred. Evans and Mr. Archibald Smith—admit of the correction of the quadrantal error in the usual manner, without the introduction of a still more pernicious error, depending on the nearness of the ends of the needles to the masses of chain, or of soft iron of whatever kind, applied on the two sides of the compass to produce the correction. The Admiralty Standard Compass, with its four needles proportioned and placed according to Archibald Smith's rule, is comparatively free from this fault; so also is the compass described in Chapter II.; but even with them, and still more with the stronger needles of the 12-inch compasses of merchant ships, there is another serious cause of failure, depending on the magnetism induced in the iron correctors by the compass needles, in consequence of which, if the quadrantal error is accurately corrected in one latitude, it will be found over-corrected in high magnetic latitudes, and under-corrected in the neighbourhood of the magnetic equator.

**Difficulty in correcting Quadrantal error.**

Sir William Thomson's compass is specially designed to avoid both these causes of failure in the correction of the quadrantal error; and experiment has conclusively shewn that, with it, the correction by such moderate masses of iron as those indicated in the preceding table, is practically perfect, not only in the place of adjustment, but in all latitudes.

When once the quadrantal error has been accurately corrected, there is no difficulty about the semi-circular deviation, since the binnacle is provided with proper appliances for effecting this part of the adjustment in a speedy and certain manner, and with the minimum of trouble.

**Correcting Magnets.** The objection has often been made to the use of correcting magnets, that their re-adjustment at sea leaves the navigator without the means of judging, when he returns from a foreign voyage, as to how much of the existing error found on re-adjustment depends on changes which have been made in the correcting magnets, and how much on changes of the ship's own magnetism. This objection has been met, in Sir William Thomson's binnacle, by providing that at any moment the correctors can be removed or set to any degree of power to which they may have been set at any time in the course of the voyage, and again re-set to their last position with perfect accuracy.

The appliances for changing the adjustment are under lock and key, so that they can never be altered, except by the captain or some properly authorised officer.

**Graduated scales.** Further to facilitate the use of the correctors, they have scales affixed, which are graduated accurately to correspond to definite variations of the effect which they produce on the compass. Thus as soon as the error has been determined by an azimuth or any other mode, the corrector may at once be shifted to a position certain to compensate it. Of course, whoever is performing the adjustment will satisfy himself of its correctness by a second observation.

The compass-bowl is attached to the suspensory rings by knife-edge gimbals, and, to diminish the shocks incidental to ship-board, the whole affair is slung from an elastic copper grommet. Further, to secure isochronism of the card and bowl, the latter is weighted to the requisite degree by means of castor oil confined in a double bottom. The glass cover is strong, and well secured to the bezel by means of four milled-headed screws; the latter is made to fit air-tight to the bowl, so that dampness cannot get in to cloud the glass; there is consequently never any occasion to meddle with the card. The brass helmet is secured to the binnacle rim without the aid of screws, and can be instantaneously slued to the right or left to get rough eye bearings—a great improvement on the old plan, where the screws were always either mislaid or lost. The binnacle lamps are so placed that the light falls on the *far* side of the card and on the lubber's point, but not *in the eyes of the observer*. In fact, all the details necessary to a satisfactory compass have been carefully considered, and well carried out. **Distinct vision secured**

## 2. THE AZIMUTH-MIRROR.

Some years ago an important objection was raised by Captain Sir Frederick Evans, R.N., against the use of quadrantal correctors in the Navy, that they would prevent the taking of bearings by the prismatic azimuth-ring which forms part of the Admiralty Standard Compass. The azimuth-mirror depicted in the diagram on page 138 was designed to obviate that objection, and happily disposes of many others also. **Its many advantages.**

Its use even for taking bearings of objects on the horizon is not interfered with by the globes constituting the quadrantal correctors, even if their highest points rise as high as five inches above the glass of the compass-bowl.

It is founded on the principle of the camera lucida. The observer, when taking a bearing, turns the instrument round its vertical axis until the mirror and lens are fairly opposite to the object. He then looks through the lens at the degree divisions of the compass-card, and turns the mirror round its horizontal axis till he brings the image of the object to fall on the card. He then reads directly on the card the compass bearing of the object. **Principle upon which it is based.**

Besides fulfilling the purpose for which it was originally designed, to allow bearings to be taken without impediment from the quadrantal correctors, the Azimuth-Mirror has a great advantage in not requiring any adjustment of the instrument such as that by which, in the prismatic azimuth-ring, the hair is brought to exactly cover the object. The focal length of the lens in the Azimuth-Mirror is about 12 per cent. longer than the radius of the circle of the compass-card, and thus, by an elementary optical principle, it follows that two objects a degree asunder on the horizon will, by their images seen in the Azimuth-Mirror, cover a space of 1°·12 of the compass-card seen through the lens. Hence, turning the instrument round its vertical axis through one degree will only alter the apparent bearing of an object on the horizon by 0°·12. Thus it is not necessary to adjust it *exactly* to the direct position for the bearing of any particular object, though as a matter of fact it can be done absolutely without trouble of any kind. If it be designedly put even as much as 9° awry on either side of the direct position, the error on the bearing would hardly amount to a degree.

**Focal Length.** If the instrument were to be used solely for taking bearings of objects on the horizon, the focal length of the lens would be made exactly equal to the radius of the circle of the card, and thus even the small error of 0°·12 in the bearing for each degree of error in the setting would be avoided. But one of the most important uses of the azimuth instrument at sea is to correct the compass by bearings of sun, moon, or stars, at altitudes of from 0° to 50° above the horizon. The actual focal length is accordingly chosen to suit an altitude of about 27°, this being the angle whose natural secant is 1°·12. Thus if two objects, near together, whose altitudes are 27°, or thereabouts, and difference of azimuth is 1°, should be taken simultaneously in the Azimuth-Mirror, their difference of bearings will also be shewn as 1° by the divided circles of the compass card seen through the lens.

**Exact Setting unnecessary.** Hence for taking azimuths of bodies at an altitude of 27°, or thereabouts, no setting of the Azimuth-Mirror by turning round the vertical axis is necessary, except just to bring the object into the field of view, when its bearing will immediately be seen accurately shewn on the edge of the compass-card.

This is a very valuable quality for use in rough weather at sea, or when there are flying clouds which just allow a glimpse of the object to be caught, without allowing time to perform an adjustment, such as that of bringing the thread of the ordinary azimuth ring, or rather, the estimated middle of the space traversed by the thread in the rolling of the ship, to coincide with the object. The same degree of error as on the horizon, but in the opposite direction, is produced by imperfect setting in taking the bearing of an object at an altitude of 38°.

Thus for objects from the horizon up to 38°, the error in the bearing is less than 12 per cent. of the error in the setting. For objects at a higher altitude than 38° the error rapidly increases, but it is always easy, if desired, to set the instrument accurately by turning it so that the red indicator below the lens shall point exactly, or nearly so, to the position on the divided circle of the compass-card occupied by the image of the object; indeed it always suggests itself as the natural thing to do. In no case, however, is it recommended, with this or any other instrument, to take azimuths above 30°.

For taking star bearings the Azimuth-Mirror has the great advantage over the prismatic azimuth-ring, with its then invisible thread, that the image of the object is thrown directly on the illuminated scale of the compass-card. The degree of illumination may be made less or more, according to faintness or brilliance of the object, by holding a binnacle lamp in the hand at a greater or less distance, and letting its light shine only on the portion of the compass-card from which the bearing will be taken. Indeed, with the Azimuth-Mirror, it is almost easier to take the bearing of a planet or moderately bright star by night, than of the sun by day; the star is seen as a fine point on the margin of the card, and it is easy to read off its position instantly by estimation to the tenth of a degree.

**Contrasted with other instruments.**

The most convenient as well as the most accurate method of all, however, is the sun when bright enough and high enough above the horizon to throw a good shadow on the compass-card. For this purpose is the brass shadow-pin which, when required, is inserted in the framework of the instrument in such a position that when the Azimuth-Mirror is properly shipped on the glass of

**Stile or Shadow-Pin.**

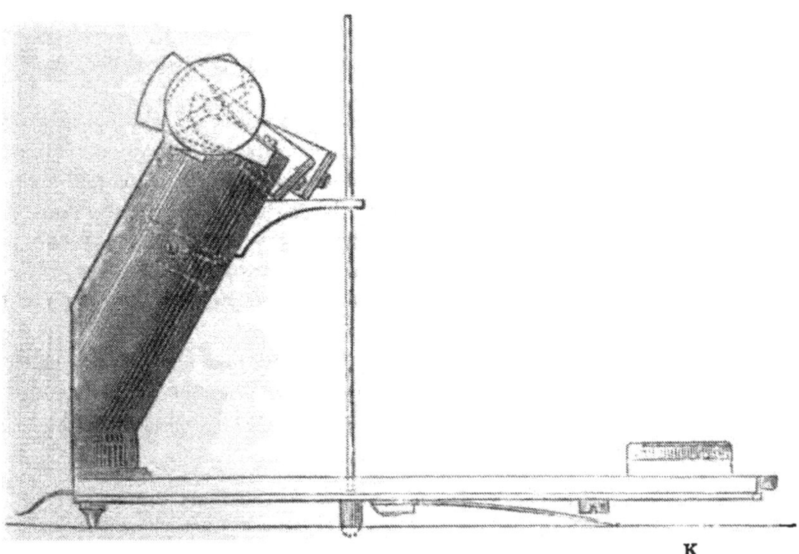

K

the compass-bowl, the pin is perpendicular to the glass, and accurately centred over the bearing point of the card. A small circular level attached to the instrument, shewn on right of diagram, tells at once whether the compass-bowl is out of balance, but in practice this is seldom or never the case. Any way the remedy is simple: a small weight of any kind—say a penny piece—may be moved about on the glass till the bubble of the level remains in the centre of its run, and taken away after the observations are completed.

**How to restore balance.**

Another advantage of the Azimuth-Mirror, particularly important for taking bearings at sea when there is much motion, is that with it, it is not necessary to look through a small aperture in an instrument moving with the compass-bowl, as in the ordinary prismatic arrangement still fitted to the standard compasses of many of the best merchant vessels. In using the Azimuth-Mirror, the eye may be placed at any distance, say from an inch or so to two or three feet from the instrument, according to convenience, and in any position, and may be moved about freely through a considerable range, on either side of the line of direct vision through the lens, without at all disturbing the accuracy of the observation.

**Observer's Freedom of action.**

This last condition is secured by the lens being fixed in such a position that the divided circle of the compass-card is in its principal focus. Thus the virtual image of the divided circle is at an infinite distance, and the images of distant objects seen coincidently with it by reflection in the mirror, show no shifting on it, that is to say, no parallax, when the eye is moved from the central line to either side.

The Azimuth-Mirror is fitted with coloured shades for use when observing the sun; and for bearings of objects on or near the horizon, the mirror can be reversed in a second of time, so as to make the reflected image of the degrees on the card coincide with the object seen by direct vision over the top of the mirror. There are, therefore, two methods of getting the bearings of objects near the horizon, and the observer can please himself as to which he employs.

**Bearings by reversal.**

This little instrument is the quintessence of all that is required to obtain accurate bearings of bodies terrestrial or celestial. When not in actual use it fits into a neat mahogany box.

**3. AN ADJUSTABLE DEFLECTOR, FOR COMPLETELY DETERMINING THE COMPASS ERROR WHEN SIGHTS OF HEAVENLY BODIES, OR COMPASS MARKS ON SHORE, ARE NOT AVAILABLE, AS FOR EXAMPLE IN FOG, OR ON A CLOUDY NIGHT.**

About thirty-five years ago, Sir Edward Sabine gave a method, in which, by aid of deflecting magnets properly placed on projecting arms attached to the prism-circle of the Admiralty standard compass, a partial determination of the error of the compass could be made at any time, whether at sea or in harbour, without the aid of azimuths of heavenly bodies or transit marks on shore. **Origin.**

The adjustable magnetic deflector invented by Sir William Thomson, is designed for carrying out in practice Sabine's method more rapidly and more accurately, and for extending it, by aid of Archibald Smith's theory, to the complete determination of the compass error, with the exception of the constant term "A" of the Admiralty notation, which in almost every practical case is zero, and which in a well made compass, and with a correctly placed lubber line, can only have a sensible value in virtue of some very marked want of symmetry of the iron work in the neighbourhood of the compass. When it exists it can easily be determined once for all, and allowed for as if it were an index-error of the compass card, and it will, therefore, to avoid circumlocution in the statements which follow, be either supposed to be zero, or allowed for as index-error. **Improved instrument.**

The new method of adjustment is founded on the following four principles:— **Principle upon which founded.**

(1.) If the directive force on the compass needles be constant on all courses of the ship, the compass is correct on all courses.

(2.) If the directive force be equal on five different courses it will be equal on all courses.

(3.) Supposing the compass to be so nearly correct, or to have been so far approximately adjusted, that there is not more than eight or ten degrees of error on any course, let the directive forces be measured on two opposite courses. If these forces are equal, the compass is free from semicircular error on the two courses at right angles to those on which the forces were measured; if they are unequal, there is a semicircular error on the courses at right angles to those on which the forces were measured, amounting to the same fraction of the radian that the difference of the measured forces is of their sum.*

* The unit of circular measure is an angle which is subtended at the centre of a circle by an arc equal to the radius of that circle. Such an angle goes by the name of the 'radian,' and is equal to $\frac{180^\circ}{3.1416}$ or 57° 3 nearly

(4.) The difference of the sums of the directive forces on opposite courses in two lines at right angles to one another, divided by the sum of the four forces, is equal to the proportion which the quadrantal error, on the courses 45° from those on which the observations were made, bears to 57°·3.

Its use easily learned.

The deflector may be used either under way or in swinging the ship at buoys. The whole process of correcting the compass by it is performed with the greatest ease and rapidity when under way, with sea room enough to steer steadily on each course for a few minutes, and to turn rapidly from one course to another.

For each operation the ship must be kept on one course for three or four minutes, if under way, by steering by aid of an auxiliary compass, otherwise by hawsers in the usual manner if swinging at buoys, or by means of steam-tugs. A variation of two or three degrees in the course during the operation will not make a third of a degree of error in the result, as regards the final correction of the compass.

The deflector reading is to be taken according to the detailed directions in the printed "Instructions," accompanying the instrument. This reading may be taken direct on the small straight scale in the lower part of the instrument. The divided micrometer circle at the top is scarcely needed, as it is easy to estimate the direct reading on the straight scale to a tenth of a division, which is far more than accurate enough for all practical purposes. This reading with a proper constant added gives, in each case, the number measuring in arbitrary units the magnitude of the direct force on the compass for the particular course of the ship on which the observation is made.

Amount of accuracy attainable.

The adjustment by aid of the deflector is quite as accurate as it can be by aid of compass marks or sights of sun or stars, though on a clear day at any time when the sun's altitude is less than 40°, or on any clear night, the adjuster will of course take advantage of sights of sun or stars, whether he helps himself also with the deflector or not.

The deflector consists of two pairs of small steel bar magnets *bc* attached to brass frames, jointed together and supported on a sole-plate, which is placed on the glass cover of the compass-bowl when the instrument is in use. The two frames carry pivoted screw nuts, with right and left handed screws. A brass shaft *aa* with right and left handed screws cut on its two halves, works in these nuts, so that when it is turned in either direction one of the two pairs of north poles is brought nearer to, or farther from, one of the two pairs of south poles, while the other two pairs of north and south poles are all in the line of the hinged joint between the two frames. This arrangement, which constitutes, as it were, a

**Position of Poles.**

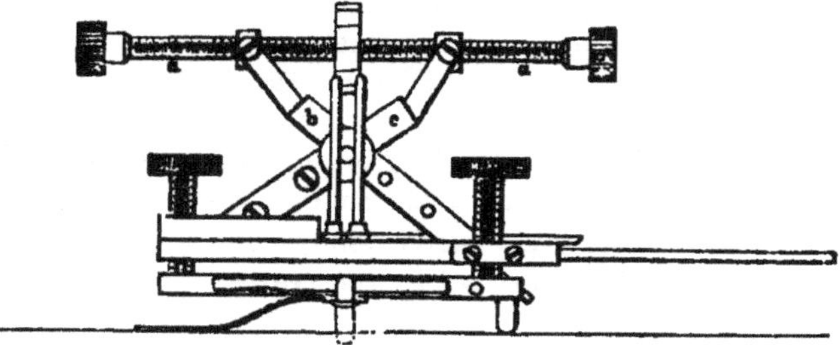


jointed horse-shoe magnet, adjustable to greater or less magnetic moment by increasing or diminishing the distance between its poles through the action of the screw, is so supported on its sole-plate that, when this is properly placed on the glass of the compass-bowl, the effective poles move to and fro horizontally about half an inch above the glass on the two sides of a vertical plane through its centre.

**Sole Plate.**

The sole-plate rests on three feet, one of which, under the centre of gravity of the deflector, rests in the conical hollow in the centre of the glass. It is caused to press with a small part of its whole weight on the other two feet by a brass spring attached to the bottom of the sole-plate, on the other side of the centre from these two feet, and pressing downwards on the glass. This is shewn at bottom and on the left of diagram.

A brass pointer attached to the sole-plate marks the magnetic axis of the deflector. It projects from the centre, on the side of which is the pair of south poles. This is shewn near the bottom and on the right of the diagram. Thus if the deflector be properly placed on the glass of the compass-bowl, with the pointer over the north point of the card, it produces no deflection, but augments the directive force on the needle.

To make an observation, the deflector is turned round in either direction, and the north point of the card is seen to follow the pointer.

**Power, how regulated.**

The power of the deflector is adjusted by the screw, so that when the pointer is over the east or west point of the card, the card rests balanced at some stated degree of deflection, which for the regular observation on board ship is chosen as 85°. A scale, measuring changes of distance, is then read and recorded.

For adjusting a compass by the aid of the deflector, the correcting magnets are so placed that the deflector reading, found in the manner just described, shall be the same for the four cardinal courses; and also for one of the quadrantal courses, if the compass is sufficiently affected by unsymmetrically placed iron to shew any sensible amount of the "E" constituent of quadrantal error.

**Magnetic Scale-value of deflector.**

When the deflector is to be used for determining the ***amount*** of an *uncorrected* error, according to principles (3) and (4) above, the magnetic value of its scale reading must be determined by experiment. This is very easily done on shore, by observations of its deflecting power, when set by its screw to different degrees of its scale.

Under a good teacher, the practical use of this invaluable instrument is soon learnt, and after reasonable practice with it there is no particular difficulty.

### 4. NEW FORM OF MARINE DIPPING NEEDLE, FOR FACILITATING THE CORRECTION OF THE HEELING ERROR.

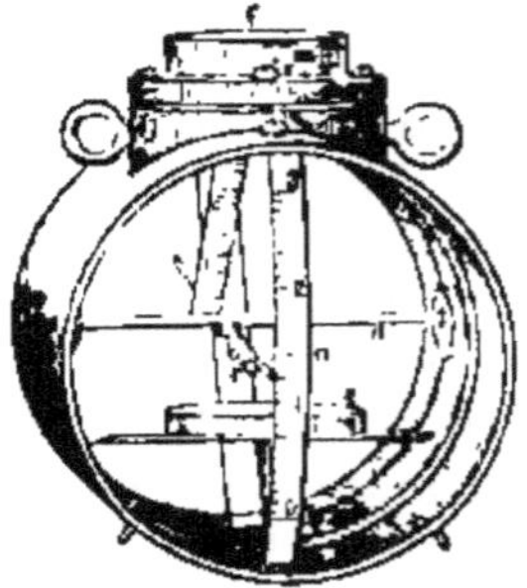

**Vertical Force.**

The marine dipping needle is used for comparing the "vertical force"* on shore with the "vertical force" on board, thereby enabling the vertical magnet in the binnacle to be so adjusted as to correct the heeling error. It consists of a magnetised steel bar *b*,

* "Vertical force" is a short expression for the vertical component of the earth's magnetic force. It is reckoned as positive when the direction of its action upon a red pole is downwards, as in the northern hemisphere; and negative when upwards, as in the southern hemisphere. At the magnetic equator it is zero. The amount of the vertical force at any place is calculated by multiplying the value of the horizontal force, given by the chart of lines of equal horizontal force of the Admiralty Manual, by the tangent of the dip as given by the chart of lines of equal magnetic dip. Thus, for example, the tangent of the dip for the South of England being 2·44, and the horizontal force there being called unity, the vertical force there is 2·44. The tangent of the dip at Aden is ·09, and the horizontal force there is 1·95; hence the vertical force there is ·1755, or about $\frac{1}{14}$ of the vertical force at the South of England.

supported on knife-edges, so as to be capable of turning round a horizontal axis *d*. Before being magnetised, the needle is balanced so as to be truly horizontal when resting on the knife-edges. When magnetised, the north or red end dips, and a paper weight *c* is fitted on the southern half of the needle to restore its balance. This weight can be slid along the needle whenever a change in the "vertical force" renders it necessary. **Marine Dipping-Needle.**

To correct the heeling error on board ship, the instrument is first taken on shore, to a spot free from Local Attraction, and the paper weight adjusted, so that with the bubble of the spirit-level *f* in the centre, the needle is exactly horizontal when resting on the knife-edges. There are marks by which this can be effected.

If the mean directive magnetic force on board were the same as the directive force on shore, the instrument would now be taken on board and placed in the binnacle in such a position that its needle would now occupy the place previously occupied by the needles of the compass card, which latter has to be temporarily removed. It would then be found, probably, that the needle had departed from its horizontal position, and the vertical magnet in the binnacle would have to be moved up or down to restore the level, always bearing in mind to keep the bubble in the centre. But it so happens that the mean force is generally from $\frac{1}{10}$ to $\frac{1}{20}$ less on board than it is on shore, and in order to allow for this, the paper weight must be pushed nearer to the centre of the needle by $\frac{1}{10}$ or $\frac{1}{20}$. This can be done by turning the instrument upside down, so as to make the needle lie along a scale graduated from the centre outwards. This being accomplished, the instrument is taken on board ship, and the compass-bowl having been removed from the binnacle, the instrument is slung by four lanyards, so that its needle shall take up the exact place before occupied by the needles of the compass-card. The vertical magnet is then slid up or down until the needle of the instrument rests truly horizontal when the bubble of the spirit-level is in the centre. **How to use it.**

### 5. NAVIGATIONAL SOUNDING MACHINE.

This important instrument has already been briefly described on pages 114 and 115, but further details will be both useful and interesting.

The sounding machine in question is designed for the purpose of getting soundings from a vessel running at high speed in water of any depth not exceeding 100 fathoms.

**Difficulty in sounding.**

The difficulties to be overcome are twofold; first, to get the lead or sinker to the bottom; and secondly, to get sure evidence as to the depth to which it has gone down. For practical navigation a third difficulty must also be met, and that is, to bring the sinker up again; for although in deep-sea surveys, in water of more than 3000 fathoms depth, it is advisable, even when pianoforte wire is used, to leave the thirty or forty pounds sinker at the bottom, and bring back only the wire with attached instruments—it would never do in practical navigation to throw away a sinker every time a cast is taken; and the loss of a sinker, whether with or without any portion of the line, ought to be a rare occurrence in many casts.

The first and third of these difficulties seemed insuperable, at all events they had not hitherto been overcome with hemp rope for the sounding line, except for very moderate depths, and for speeds much under the full speed of a modern fast steamer.

**Piano forte wire.**

Taking advantage of the great strength, and the small and smooth area for resistance to motion through the water, presented by pianoforte wire, Sir William Thomson has succeeded in overcoming all these difficulties, and with his sounding machine a cast in 100 fathoms can readily be got from a vessel running 15 or 16 knots an hour.

The steel wire weighs nearly 1½ lbs. per 100 fathoms, and bears when fresh, from 230 to 240 lbs. without breaking; its circumference is only ·03 of an inch. By carefully keeping it always, when not absolutely in use, under lime water, in the galvanized iron tank supplied for the purpose, it is preserved quite free from rust, and, barring accidents, will last an indefinite time.

In the most recent pattern, shewn in the diagram on next page, the tank of lime water forms a fixed part of the entire machine, and the drum is so arranged with regard to it, that as soon as the cast is taken the wire can be submerged and kept so till within half a minute of taking the next cast. This is a great improvement. In winding in, one man should guide the wire, to make it lie evenly on the drum, with a piece of canvas wet with lime water. The canvas may be kept in the tank.

**Things requiring attention.**

When taking a cast, not only is the wire *seen* to slacken on the lead touching the bottom, but the *sound* is quite different. When removing the glass gauge-tube from the brass guard-tube, be sure and *keep the open end down;* also in reading off the depth by the box-wood scale, maintain it in this position (vertical, or nearly so) and take the *lowest* part of the red mark for the reading.

| If the Barometer stands at | 29¾″ | add one fathom in | 40. |
|---|---|---|---|
| ” ” ” | 30 | ” ” | 30. |
| ” ” ” | 30½ | ” ” | 20. |
| ” ” ” | 31 | ” ” | 15. |

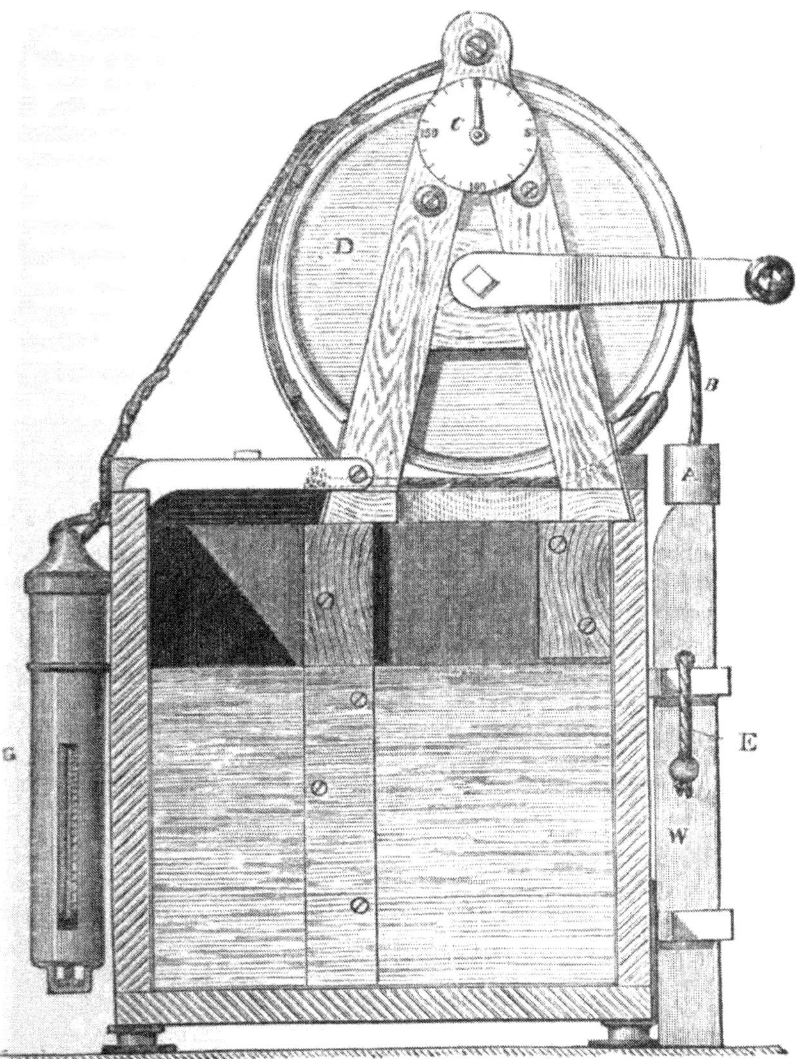


The figure shows the machine with the small weight A resting on the long weight W, and the brake cord B slack, as it is when the wire is being wound in.

To put on the brake:—Lift the long weight W by the hand-rope E, and

Sounding Instructions.

place the small weight A in the recess in the large weight, and then slack the hand-rope again. While a sounding is being taken, the long weight W is held up by the rope E, so as to allow the small weight A to hang freely. As soon as the sinker reaches the bottom, the brake is put on by easing the rope E, and allowing the weight W to be supported, by means of its jaws, on the small weight A. The whole weight of W should not be allowed to come suddenly on A, but it should be eased down gradually. If, when the whole weight of W is resting on A, the wire still continues to run out, the brakesman should press his hand down on the top of W until he stops the wheel. In the figure the new description of sounder is shewn on the left attached to the cod-line, but the writer does not like it nearly so well as the other kind described at foot of page 114.

If the sinker should get jammed in a cleft of rock at the bottom, or against the side of a boulder, the wire will inevitably be lost. Such an accident must obviously be very rare indeed, and any other form of sounding machine is equally liable to the same mishap.

The main care in respect to avoiding breakage of the wire may be stated in three words—*Beware of kinks.*

Precautions.

It should be carefully seen to at all times, when the cod-line* is unbent from the ring, that the ring is securely seized to the hole provided for the purpose in the rim of the drum. If the wire and ring are carelessly allowed to knock about slack on the drum when the drum is being moved to be set up for use, or to be replaced under the lime water, there is a liability to some part of the wire getting a turn which may at the next cast be pulled into a kink, and then, *farewell to the sinker.* All that is wanted in the successful use of this machine is ordinary care and intelligence; lack of these two qualities will occasion the loss of sinkers *and temper.*

* Small line, plaited like signal-halliard stuff, is preferable, as it keeps itself free from turns.

## CHAPTER XIV.

### THE MERCURIAL AND ANEROID BAROMETERS.

As many seamen are but imperfectly acquainted with the fundamental principles of the Mercurial and Aneroid Barometers, a short description will not be out of place.

The word Barometer is compounded of two Greek ones signifying weight and measure, and the instrument is used accordingly to measure the weight of the superincumbent atmosphere. From this knowledge, *coupled with other matters* which will be discussed in the next chapter, conclusions are arrived at with regard to coming changes in the weather. The atmosphere, or invisible air-ocean, extends for many miles above the earth's surface, becoming more and more rarefied in proportion to its height. This latter is variously estimated at from 100 to 200 miles; and beyond this is *luminiferous ether*—an extremely fine imponderable fluid, supposed to pervade all space.

**Barometer—meaning of word.**

**Height of our atmosphere.**

At the level of the sea the pressure of the atmosphere on every square inch of surface is about 15 lbs., or nearly one ton on the square foot, and is exerted equally in *all* directions—*upwards, downwards*, and *sideways*. Without actual proof, it is somewhat difficult to believe this from one's own sensations, but there are a hundred ways of shewing it. The most common method is as follows:—

**Pressure at sea level.**

Let the mouth of an ordinary earthen flower-pot be tightly covered by a piece of bladder, well tied down round the neck. Stand it on the plate of an air-pump, so that the air inside can be exhausted through the hole in the bottom. When this is effected, the weight of the external atmosphere, being no longer counterbalanced by the previous *upward* pressure of the air within the pot, will cause the bladder to stretch and bulge inwards, and finally to burst with a loud report. In a small flower-pot, say of

**Experiment illustrating atmospheric pressure.**

6 inches diameter, if a *complete* vacuum were formed (which, by the way, is impossible), the effect of the downward pressure on

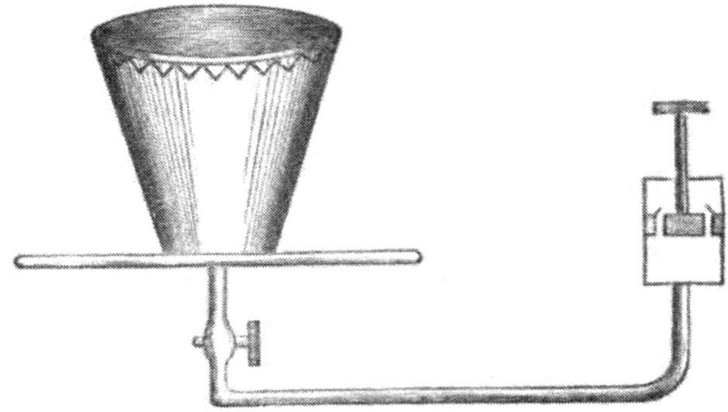

the bladder—supposing it capable of withstanding it—would amount to over 400 pounds.

**Magdeburg Hemispheres.** The same thing may be demonstrated yet more clearly by means of what are known as the Magdeburg Hemispheres. They

are two hollow cups, made to fit on to one another, with an air-tight joint. When pressed together by hand in the ordinary way, they are easily separated, there being, in fact, no appreciable resistance; but if connected with an air-pump, and a vacuum formed within the cups, so that the air is only allowed to exert its force on their *outer* side, it will be found very difficult to pull them asunder, the amount of strain required depending upon the sectional area of the circle: for instance, if the hemispheres should be 14 inches in diameter, they will, after exhaustion, be pressed together with a force of upwards of a ton, and as this is the case *in whatever position they may be held*, it proves that atmospheric pressure is exerted equally in *all* directions.

A familiar and not unpleasant example is afforded by sucking up sherry-cobbler through a straw. By drawing in the breath a vacuum is created in the straw, and the atmosphere pressing upon the liquid in the tumbler, forces it to rush unopposed into the vacant space.

It is supposed that in the vortex of most cyclones the spirally ascending currents cause a partial vacuum, and it has been stated that during the passage of the *calm* centre of a West Indian hurricane, the windows have been forced *outwards* into the street by the greater pressure of the air *within* the houses. **Vortex of cyclones.**

The pressure of the atmosphere having thus been demonstrated, it merely remains to show its particular mode of action on the barometer. This can best be illustrated by the following simple and time-honoured experiment:—

Take a glass tube about 33 inches in length, hermetically sealed at one end. Fill this with pure mercury, and have some more handy in a small vessel, such as a teacup. Press the finger tightly over the open end to act as a stopper, and invert the tube, placing the end covered by the finger in the cup containing the mercury, and when well below the surface, remove the finger. The first assumption would be that *all* the mercury would instantly flow into the cup. Not so, however. The quicksilver will only fall in the tube—leaving a vacant space in the upper **Construction and principle of mercurial barometer.**

end—till the weight of the column is balanced by the atmospheric pressure on the liquid metal *in the cup.* It is evident that there can be no *downward* pressure on the mercury *in the tube*, since the tube is tightly closed at its upper end. The column of mercury remaining within it will be found to be *about* 30 inches in height, and would be equal to the weight of a column of the atmosphere having the same sectional area as the interior of the tube.

**How it weighs the atmosphere.** To put this more plainly—supposing the glass tube to have an internal transverse area of exactly one square inch, and that the height of the column was ascertained to be 30 inches, this would give the contents as 30 cubic inches. Now, one cubic inch of mercury at a temperature of 60° (Fahrenheit) weighs ·491 of a pound, so that the total weight of the mercury in the tube would be equal to 30×·491, or 14·73 pounds, which would *also* be the weight of a column of the atmosphere indefinitely high, having a similar sectional area of one square inch.

Thus we see that the barometer (true to its name) affords a very ready means of determining at any moment the weight or pressure of the atmosphere. This is in fact *all* it is capable of doing when only the reading at one place, as on board ship, can be obtained.

The blank space left at the top of the tube by the descent of the mercury *is the nearest known approach to a perfect vacuum.*

Excepting some small details, it is in this manner mercurial barometers are actually constructed. For example, it is necessary that by means of a lamp the mercury should be boiled in the tube to free it thoroughly from air-bubbles. A suitable cistern is of course substituted for the tea-cup, and a scale of *inches* is affixed, whereby to read off the height of the mercury in the tube above the level of that in the cistern.

**Scale reading—how named.** The reader will therefore understand that the mercury does not rise and fall in the tube merely by its own expansion, or contraction due to temperature, but that it is forced to rise, or suffered to fall, according to the varying pressure of the atmosphere; and that the scale readings represent *inches* and *decimal parts of an inch*, and not *degrees*, as the writer has heard them referred to more than once.

As stated at the commencement of this chapter, the atmospheric pressure or density decreases according as we ascend above the sea-level, which latter is adopted as the datum line for barometrical measurements. It does so in obedience to certain known laws which, it should be said, include considerations of temperature, and not unfrequently we avail ourselves of this knowledge to measure the height of mountains by comparing the readings (taken simultaneously) of two barometers, one at the base or sea-level, and the other at the summit. Roughly, *for small elevations*, a vertical ascent of 900 feet corresponds to a fall of one inch in the height of the barometer. The depth of a mine may of course be measured in the same manner.

**Mountain Heights.**

If water were used in a barometer instead of mercury, the tube would require to be about 36 feet in length. Water, being 13·6 times lighter than quicksilver, would be forced proportionately higher, and when the mercurial column stood at 30 inches, the water column would have a height of 34 feet. It is due to this fact that we are able with a common two-valve suction pump to lift water out of a well from a depth of about 28 or 30 feet.

**Water Barometer.**

The action of a siphon is another instance of atmospheric pressure turned to account in a very ingenious way. The siphon is used to draw off liquids from vessels which it is not convenient or desirable to move, and with care it can be arranged to do this without disturbing sediment at the bottom—sometimes a matter of great importance. A vacuum being first formed in the tube, the liquid enters the immersed leg and fills the place of the exhausted air; and since the pressure on the orifices of the tube is in each case equal to the weight of the atmosphere, *minus the height of the liquid in the respective legs*, it follows that the greater the difference of level between the surface of the liquid to be withdrawn and the orifice of the leg by which it issues, the more rapid will be the flow; and further, that a siphon will cease to act if the height from the surface of the liquid to the bend of the pipe be greater than that of a column of the liquid in use sufficient to counterbalance the atmospheric pressure: consequently, if we were seeking to remove *water* from a vessel by means of a siphon, the difference in height between the bend of the pipe and the surface of the water must be less than 34 feet, and in the case of *mercury* it would require to be under 30 inches.

**How the Siphon acts.**

The following diagram and explanation by J. C. Trautwine, of Philadelphia, ought to make the matter clear.

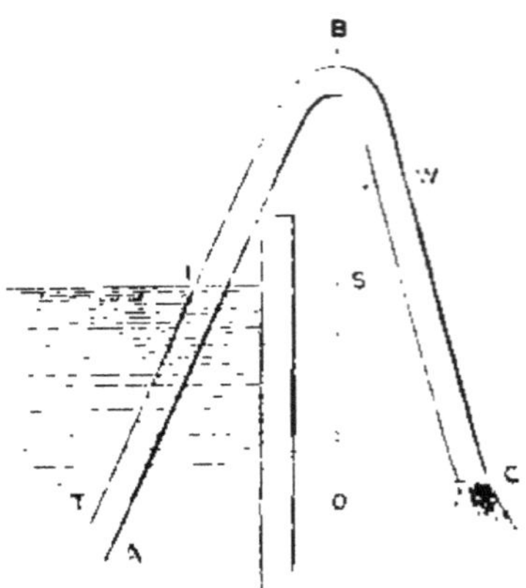


"If one leg *ab* of a bent tube or pipe *abc*, of any diameter, filled with water, and with both its ends stopped, be placed in a reservoir of water, and if the stoppers be then removed, the water in the reservoir will begin to flow out at *c*, and will continue to do so until its level is reduced to *t*, which is the same as that of the *highest* end *c* of the pipe or siphon. The flow will then stop. The parts *ab* and *bc* are called the legs of the siphon, *b* being its highest point; and this is correct so far as relates to it merely as a piece of tube; but considering it purely with regard to its character as a hydraulic machine, the part *ta* below the level of the higher end *c*, may be entirely neglected; for the water in the reservoir will not be drawn down below the level of the higher end, whether that be the inner or the outer one. Therefore, if the discharge end be above the surface of the water in the reservoir, as for instance at W, no flow will take place.

"The vertical height *bo*, from the highest part of the siphon to the lowest level *t*, to which the reservoir is to be drawn down, must not, theoretically, exceed about 33 or 34 feet, or that at which the pressure of the air will sustain a column of water. Practically it must be less, to allow for the friction of the flowing water, and for the air which forces its way in: and still less at places far above sea level, for at such the reduced weight of the atmospheric column will not balance so great a height of water.

"In order readily to understand, or at any time to recall the principle on which the siphon acts, bear in mind that we may theoretically consider the end of the inner leg to be not actually immersed *below* the water surface, but only to be kept precisely *at* it as the surface descends while the water is flowing out; but may regard the vertical distance *bo* as the length of the outer leg; and a varying distance, which at first is *bs*, and finally *bo* (as the surface of the water descends) as the length of the inner leg; and that the flow continues only while *this* outer leg is longer than *this* inner one. The books are wrong which say that the outer leg *bc* *must* be longer than the inner one *ba*, in order that the water may run at all. The principle then is simply this: that both these legs *bc* and *bi* being first filled with water (the part *ia* being considered at first as a portion of the *reservoir*, and not of the siphon), it follows that when the stoppers are removed from the orifices *c* and *a*, the air presses equally against these orifices; but the great vertical head of water *bo* in the outer leg *bc*, presses against the air at *c* with more force than the small head of water *bs* in the inner leg *bi* does against the air at *a* or *i*; consequently the water in *bc* will tend to fall out more rapidly than that in *bi*, and as it commences to fall would produce a vacuum at *b* were it not that the pressure of the air against the other end *a* or *i* forces the water up *ib* to supply the place of that which flows out at *c*. In this manner the flow continues until the surface of the water in the reservoir descends to *t* on the same level as *c*. The pressure of the vertical heads *bo*, *bo*, in the two legs *bc*, *bt*, being then equal, it ceases."

It may be added that, to entirely drain the reservoir, the outer leg would require to be longer than the inner one.

**Water Barometer.** For many reasons a water barometer is unserviceable for scientific purposes, but experiments, attended with a certain amount of success, are being tried with glycerine as a substitute. Mercurial barometers are rapidly going out of fashion for use on board ship, being superseded by the handier *and more sensitive* Aneroid.

**Precautions necessary with mercurial barometer.** It is often difficult to find a suitable spot for the mercurial barometer in the confined cabins of vessels. They are apt to be knocked against and broken. To avoid this, it is not uncommon to see them suspended inside the skylight—the worst possible place. To indicate truly, the sun must not shine on the instrument, nor should it be exposed to currents of air, as is almost certain to happen in such a situation, and in which, moreover, it is not as accessible as it ought to be. Again, should a chance sea break the skylight, the barometer will also come to grief.

Unless the instrument hangs truly vertical, the level of the mercury within the tube will be *too high*. For this reason, therefore, when the ship is rolling, it must on no account be steadied or held in the hand whilst being read off. If anything, such as spiral springs or elastic bands, interfere with its free movement, the readings will be erroneous.

We next come to the Aneroid. This word is derived from three Greek ones, signifying "not of the fluid form," or "without moisture." Where observations are not required for strictly scientific purposes, it is by far the better instrument for use afloat. **Portability.** It is more portable, and occupies much less room; for example, it may be kept in a drawer, on a shelf, or fastened to a panel near one's bed, so as to be visible without effort. As already

Sensitiveness. stated, it is more sensitive than the mercurial barometer, and at all times—more especially in heavy weather—easier to read.

Principle of the Aneroid. In the Aneroid, fluctuations of the atmosphere are measured by its varying pressure on an elastic metallic box, from which almost all the air has been withdrawn, and which is kept from complete collapse by a strong spring. The exterior of this vacuum chamber, as it might be called, is so connected by multiplying levers and springs with the pointer which traverses the face of the instrument, that the slightest increase or diminution of pressure is at once unmistakeably indicated.

From the perfection of make arrived at, and its great portability, the Aneroid is now very commonly used in the determination of mountain heights; also by engineers for contouring, and roughly ascertaining differences of level in a hilly country, when running what are termed "trial lines" as a preliminary to a close survey for a new railway. For these purposes the face of the instrument is graduated on both an inner and outer circle, the one corresponding to inches of mercury, and the other to so many feet of elevation. Taking 30 inches as zero, a reading of 18 inches would correspond to an elevation of somewhere about 14,000 feet. For strictly scientific purposes the Aneroid, as already stated, is inferior to the mercurial barometer.

Occasional comparison with Standard desirable. As the delicate mechanical parts of the Aneroid are liable to suffer from rust, wear and tear, and other causes, it should, as a precaution, be occasionally compared with a standard mercurial barometer.

Mode of adjustment. It is just as well that seamen should know that the Aneroid can at any time be easily adjusted to a higher or lower reading by a deep-set screw at the back. By *carefully* turning this screw to the right or left with a bradawl, the pointer can be moved in the required direction. Before setting a *compensated* Aneroid by a standard mercurial barometer, the reading of the latter should be corrected for temperature by the tables for this purpose.*

Kew Observatory. Parties ordering barometers from opticians may direct them to be forwarded to Kew Observatory, London, for verification. The scale of charges is very moderate.

There is a small pamphlet entitled "The Aneroid Barometer:

---

* Table II., page 152, Adm. Man. Scientific Enquiry. The comparison should be made with the Aneroid in two positions, one in the upright position, or as it would be when suspended; and the other on its flat, as it would be when lying on a table. In nearly every instance there is a difference.

how to buy and how to use it." By a Fellow of the Meteorological Society. It can be procured, post free, for six stamps, from any bookseller, and will be found to contain a full description of this elegant little instrument.

**Descriptive pamphlet on Aneroid.**

---

## CHAPTER XV.

### "WEATHEROLOGY."

Although of late years Meteorology as a science has received much attention, the results, *so far as the navigator is concerned*, are of an almost entirely negative character, and of little *practical* value. To this broad assertion, the wind and current charts, compiled from the logs of vessels supplied with special instruments, are the principal, if not the only exception.

**Difficulty in foretelling weather.**

The highest authorities concur in admitting, that even with the advantage of many combined simultaneous observations at stations some distance apart, such as can be obtained on land by a special and regularly organized service, it is impossible at present to foretell *with certainty*, for even three days in advance, the precise character of the coming weather. Therefore, as might be expected, the results of the storm prophecies telegraphed us from the other side of the Atlantic are far from satisfactory; since, independent of the vaguely wide area embraced, and the impossibility of identifying any particular gale which might be felt off the "British, French, or Norwegian coasts," as the one despatched from American waters, the recorded statistics of the past three years show more failures than successes Nevertheless, one cannot but believe that as time goes on and knowledge increases, our American friends may be enabled with more certainty to forewarn us of the unwelcome visitors they are powerless to restrain.*

**American predictions unreliable.**

* Commencing with the past year (1882) and under the directorship of the Chief Signal Officer of the United States Army, active steps have been taken to secure the co-operation of shipmasters all over the globe in a grand scheme of International Simultaneous Meteorological Observations. The Meteorological Council of London, who have long laboured in this field, are now asking for special observations in the North Atlantic Ocean, to extend over a period of one year. By this it is hoped to connect the weather of the British Isles and the North American Continent with that in the Atlantic in such a manner as will enable a better judgment to be formed of their mutual relationship, and so in time lead to a more reliable system of prediction.

If, then, concerted action avails so little, what chance has an isolated individual, such as the commander of a ship, who has nothing to guide him but his own local observations, of satisfying himself as to the weather he may expect for even a single coming day?

**Barometrical paradoxes.** Where is the sailor who has not been urged to prepare for dirty weather by the warning of an unusually low glass, to find that the disturbance has passed away wide of his position? Let him not, however, regret his trouble, but console himself with the wise "saw" that "it is better to be sure than sorry," and with the knowledge that, though his guide has now deceived him, on the next occasion its monition may be more than justified.

On the other hand, he should bear in mind the fact, that stiff gales sometimes blow with quite a high barometer. This is common enough in the English Channel with the wind at N.E., but it also happens with strong blows from other quarters. For example, though the writer, on the last day of January, 1880, whilst on a passage from Philadelphia to Liverpool, experienced a fresh gale from the *Southward*, with a heavy sea; yet, during the worst of it, the glass never fell below 30"·20, and the sun shone brilliantly, with scarcely a cloud in the heavens. On the previous day, with moderate wind at S.E. by E., it ranged as high as 30"·50.

**Instance of abnormally high pressure** Many people will doubtless remember the anti-cyclone which, in January of 1882, persistently hung over the British Islands for several days, and excited wonder by the high reading of the barometer, which reached 30"·80. The writer was then returning home from the United States, and the following, taken from the log, shews that the region of unusual pressure extended a long way to the westward.

"Noon, Tuesday, January 17th. Lat. 47° 40′ N., and Long. 26° 53′ W. Wind S. ½ W. (true), moderate breeze; light clouds; sun dimly visible at intervals. Barom. 30"·42, Thermom. in open air (shade) 54°.

"Noon, Wednesday, January 18th. Lat. 49° 19′ N., and Long. 19° 52′ W. Wind S. by W. (true), light to moderate breeze. Sun shining brightly. Hazy on horizon. Barom. 30"·70, Thermom. 53°.

"At 9 p.m. Barom. attained its highest reading, viz.:—30"·80.

"Noon, Thursday, January 19th. Lat. 50° 46′ N., and Long. 12° 17′ W. Wind S.E. by S. ½ S (true), light. Sun shewing occasionally through breaks. Horizon very clear and well defined. Barom. 30"·75, Thermom. 47° in open air (shade)."

The point of both examples lies in the *high* glass and *southerly* wind, which latter, in the first one quoted, actually reached the force of a fresh gale.

**Barometric Gradient.**

All this would appear an enigma did we not know, as will presently be explained, that gales depend not so much upon the absolute *height of the glass*, as upon the *difference between two readings* at places some little distance apart.

If, over a given area, the glass be *uniformly high*, or *uniformly low*, there will be but little wind; but when the barometric incline between places of relatively high and low pressure is abrupt, the winds will be violent.

To the sailor, however, who is not behind the scenes, and cannot be in telegraphic communication with other places for comparison of barometers, and has, moreover, his own observations vitiated to a considerable degree by his vessel's onward progress, this knowledge is practically worthless.

What he desires is to be enabled to augur from the study of his own instrument what is likely to take place around him, and, unfortunately, it is but seldom that this is possible to any noteworthy extent.

**Unfailing signs.**

There are, however, certain indications which, when they occur, may be regarded as pretty reliable, and are in consequence worthy of being logged in red ink.

For example, a rising barometer with a southerly wind presages fair weather, whilst a falling barometer with a northerly wind conveys a warning which cannot be disregarded with impunity. To make this applicable to either hemisphere, it would be as well, perhaps, to substitute the words Equatorial for Southerly, and Polar for Northerly.

**Influence of tack on Barometer.**

Another rule of equal importance has reference to the effect of a ship's tack on the barometer. The *cause* will be evident, as explained hereafter; for the present it is sufficient to state the *fact.*

In the Northern hemisphere, with all winds, except when near the equator, the starboard tack takes a ship towards a higher barometer, whilst the port tack takes her towards a lower one. It follows, *that in every case a rising barometer on the port tack is a valuable indication of improving weather, while on the starboard tack, a falling barometer is a great warning.* This order is reversed in the Southern hemisphere.

The cases just quoted, with one or two minor ones which will appear by and by, are the exceptions which prove the rule, that—

opposed though it may seem to older teaching—the barometer, under most circumstances, *when taken singly and unsupported by other indications*, can no longer be regarded as an infallible weather oracle.

**Value of Barometer over-rated as an instrument of *Prediction*.**

Its warnings are uncertain, and, more often than not, its movements are only contemporaneous with the commencement of the disturbance they are supposed to herald, as friction in the tube and inertia must first be overcome before the altered pressure of the air can put the mercury in motion.

Nevertheless there are special instances, and most of us will remember them, when—other indications being wanting—its silent fall has revealed an impending danger. We must therefore by no means cast off our old friend, or too hastily underrate its value.

By English fishermen an echo at sea is considered a sign of coming easterly wind, and it is generally thought that much phosphorescence of the water, or a vivid display of the Aurora, is the prelude to a southerly gale in our own latitudes; whilst lightning in the N.W. never fails, in the North Atlantic, to be followed by a heavy gale from same quarter.

**Barometrical tides.**

In making delicate observations, it should be known by all, that the mercury is subject (quite apart from the weather) to regular daily tidal influences. At between 9 and 10 A.M. and P.M. it is, so to speak, high water. Then commences the ebb, which lasts until between 3 and 4 A.M. and P.M. respectively. The mean range in tropical regions is about the tenth of an inch, but as the latitude increases, the tidal range diminishes, until finally it almost vanishes at the poles.

In our own part of the world this phenomenon is often unnoticed, owing to its lesser degree, and its being frequently masked by accompanying and stronger atmospheric changes. Not so nearer the equator, where the greater tidal range, the more equable character of the weather, and the ordinary barometric fluctuations being both unfrequent and small in amount, render it easily apparent.

The practical lesson to be learned from this noteworthy peculiarity is, that to some extent changes in the barometer are of increased or diminished significance, in accordance as they disagree, or agree, with the regular tidal rise and fall. Thus, if the mercury drop steadily between the hours of 3 and 9, when according to the above law it should be rising, the indication is of more importance than if occurring between 9 and 3, the period of tidal ebb.

So far this singular phenomenon of barometric tides has puzzled physicists, and though many hypotheses have been advanced, none of them seem capable of affording an entirely satisfactory solution.

**Barometer movements in low latitudes.** It must be remembered that though, as before observed, considerable barometric changes are unfrequent near the equator, when they *do* occur they are of proportionately greater significance. In low latitudes, a sudden fall of any magnitude is invariably followed by a hard blow, which, however, is mostly of a transitory character; bearing out the familiar adage, "Long foretold, long last; short notice, soon past."

**Speculations concerning storms.** Now as to Storms themselves. We cannot but feel that to a great extent their origin, nature, shape, and movements, are as yet purely matters of speculation. So much that is contradictory is daily appearing, and such various plausible theories are being propounded, that it is most difficult to arrive at any safe and practical conclusion.

The older writers, such as Capper, Piddington, Thom, Redfield, and Reid, believed in the purely circular character of those terrible convulsions of nature, which, according to location, are variously denominated Hurricanes, Cyclones, or Typhoons; while, on the other hand, the bulk of modern authorities seem in favour of a spirally incurving movement as the probable behaviour of the wind at such times. **Bearing of centre.** In the former case, when facing the wind, the centre of the storm would be at right angles to its direction: in the latter, between about 10 and 11 points from it.

Mr. Meldrum, Director of the Government Observatory at Mauritius, (the very stronghold of tempests), referring to cyclones of the Southern Indian Ocean, is of opinion "that N.E. and Easterly winds often, if not always, blow towards the centre of the storm, and not at right angles to it." **Mauritius Cyclones—anomalous behaviour.** If we assume this to be the case, a vessel in that region having the wind between north and east should make as much easting as possible.

**Jinman's theory.** Captain Jinman, who has apparently devoted much time to this subject, is the author of a small book entitled "Winds and their Courses," in which he seeks to prove that gales blow in arcs of circles intersecting each other at two points, which he names "Confluences."

There would seem to be some truth in his ingenious theory, but it does not appear to have found favour with meteorologists, as one seldom or never hears it quoted by scientific men. Nevertheless the book, from its originality, is worth reading, if only to open up a new train of thought.

Espy considers that, in storms, the wind blows from all quarters alike towards a common centre, and attributes this centripetal motion to the supposed upward rushing of the air in the vortex. It is well known that on the outer verge of cyclones the glass stands abnormally high, shewing great atmospheric pressure, and that its readings are lowest in the focus or vortex, where, accordingly, the pressure is least; thus favouring the "in-blowing" theory, as it seems natural that the outer heavily pressed air should rush into the *comparative* vacuum at the centre. Espy's theory

This very feasible idea is, however, if not entirely demolished, at least very materially weakened by an atmospheric law discovered by Professor Buys Ballot, of Utrecht. It may be thus enunciated.— Buys Ballot's law.

The wind will be nearly at right angles to an imaginary line joining two stations, having respectively a high and a low barometer. In the Northern hemisphere, the low barometer will be on the left, and the high barometer on the right of the wind's course, and the current of air will have enhanced velocity in proportion as the difference of the barometer readings is greater. Thus, if a low glass exists in the north of Scotland, and a high one in the south of England, the wind will certainly be westerly; its strength depending upon the steepness of the barometric gradient connecting the two localities.

This law, even for light winds, is now established beyond all controversy, so far, at least, as moderately high latitudes are concerned, and from it follows, according to Strachan,—

"That in the Northern Temperate Zone the winds will circulate around an area of low atmospherical pressure in the reverse direction to the movement of the hands of a watch, and that the air will flow away from a region of high pressure, and cause an apparent circulation of winds around it in the direction of watch hands." Deduction from Buys Ballot's law

In the Southern hemisphere, of course, this order is reversed. It becomes a question, then, what happens in the neutral vicinity of the equator, where the two hemispheres meet, and the laws pertaining to each would clash, if not gradually modified. In answer to this, Toynbee, in the *Barometer Manual*, says:—

"It seems probable that, with your back to the wind, the lowest pressure faces you. At any rate, most seamen know that in the equatorial doldrums there is a comparatively low barometer, and Toynbee on Equatorial distribution of pressure.

that as they are approached the respective trades d directly from North and South."

It seems now necessary to refer, in passing, to a ph subject of immense importance to the navigator, and w he should be fully conversant.

*Permanent areas of high and low pressure.*

In various parts of the world there are certain *perma* of high and low pressure, which seem to exercise a st influence on the general atmospheric circulation.

The best known of these at present will be found n the accompanying chartlets issued by the Meteorologi and it will be noticed with interest that the directi winds, as shewn by the arrows, conforms to the above la

In addition to the permanent ones, there are certain ot which vary with the season of the year.

The most marked of these extends over Central A appears to cause the N.E. and S.W. monsoons of India.

To return to storms—may it not be, that in the in phenomena known as cyclones, the direction of the wind pounded of the rotatory motion, as indicated by Ballot's the indraught or centripetal theory propounded by Espy a resultant of forces would agree with the spirally incurvin ment already referred to as the probable behaviour of the

**Storm theory of Professor Blasius.**

More recently, Professor Blasius, of Philadelphia, au "Storms: their Nature, Classification, and Laws," has ta entirely new stand-point on this subject. He traces the im origin of gales wholly to conflicting polar and equatoria spheric currents of markedly different temperatures, whose contact he terms "the plane of meeting," as opposed to the sion "barometric gradient," in vogue with other meteorolo

He confines the purely circular or whirling movement wind strictly to the violent local storms known as "Torn and considers, "with regard to meteorological instrument the Thermometer, measuring a primary effect, is, with the meter, at least as important as the Barometer."

**Value of cloud observation.**

Of much more moment than any (and this view seems g ground among our own scientists), he looks upon *cloud obser* as useful in affording information of approaching bad we Upon this point he lays great stress, and supports it with inst in which the notice thus conveyed was 24 hours in advan that given by the Barometer.

The classification of storms, and the cloud formations sup to be typical of each, as given by Blasius, are quoted at le

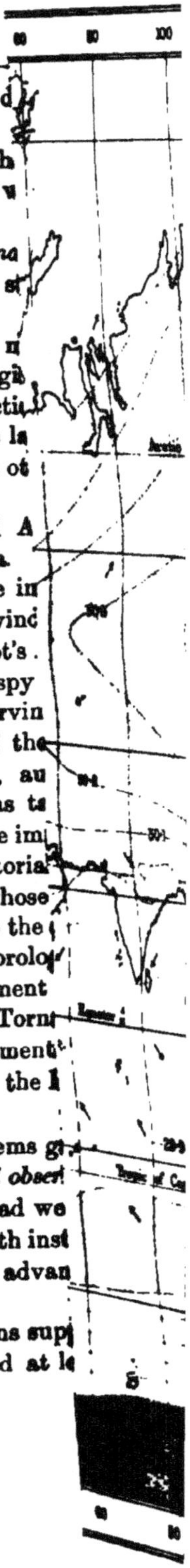

Plate I.

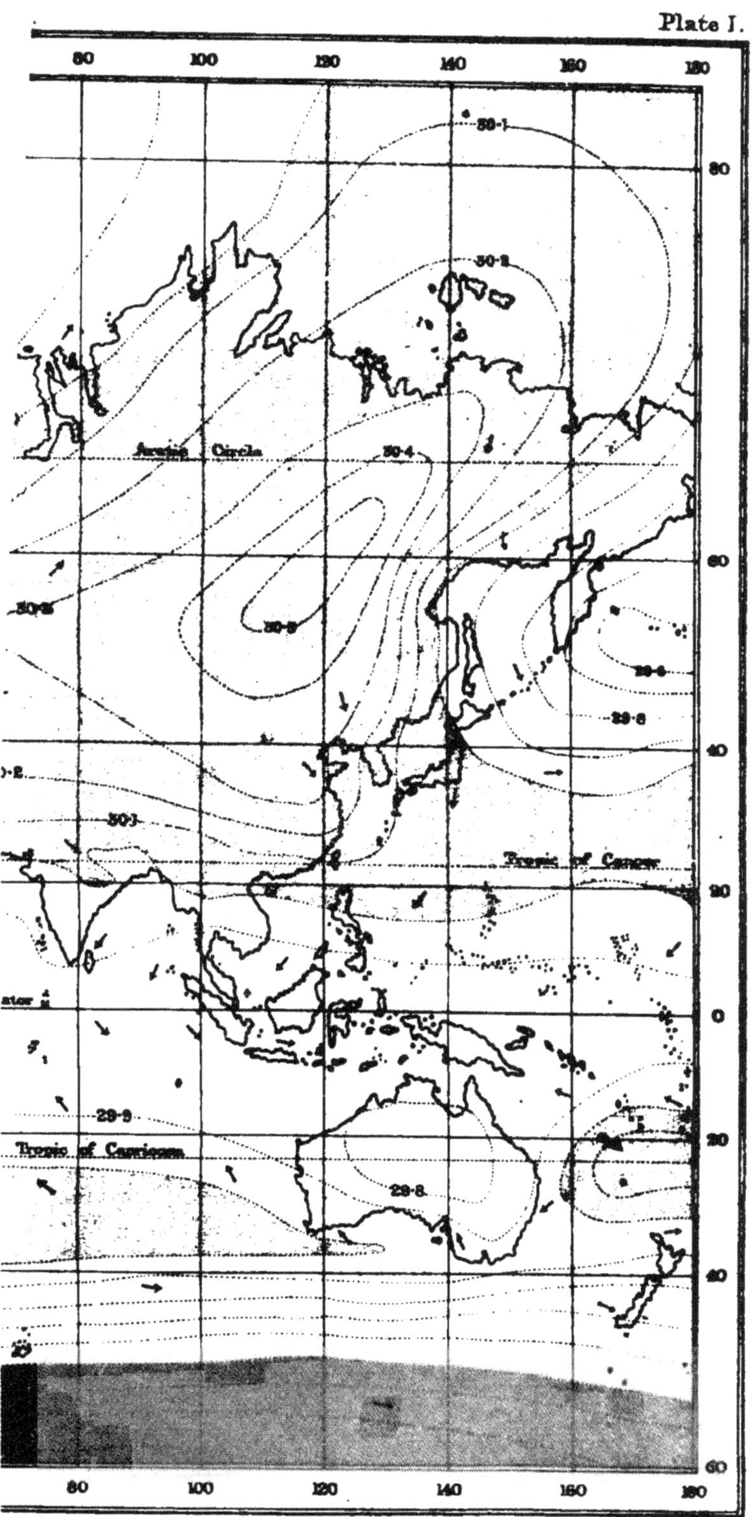


To face Page 170

below. Without pronouncing absolutely at present, either for or against their correctness, the writer considers them well worthy of attention.* He must, however, altogether dissent from this valuation of the Barometer, as compared with the Thermometer and Hygrometer, amounting, as it does, to an almost complete setting aside of the former instrument. By most observers the latter instruments are considered very inferior as weather predicters, owing to the impossibility of obtaining the conditions necessary for accurate observation. In the case of the Barometer, these conditions are either immaterial or easily allowed for.

**Inferiority of Thermometer & Hygrometer as weather predicters.**

Whilst alluding to Nature's own indications of change, it seems an opportune moment to put before the sailor the time-honoured rules of the late Admiral Fitzroy, which, so far as they go, are intrinsically good. They will well repay the trouble of committing them to memory, but it must not be forgotten that many of them have only *local* significance.†

**Admiral Fitzroy's rules.**

---

* "1.—Local or Vertical Storms.
  Stationary. Centripetal. Produced by a tendency of the atmosphere to re-establish in a vertical direction an equilibrium that has been disturbed. *Characteristic cloud*—Cumulus.

2.—Progressive or Lateral Storms.
  Travelling. Produced by a tendency of the atmosphere to re-establish in a lateral direction an equilibrium that has been disturbed. They are of two kinds:—

(*a*)—Equatorial or North-East Storms.
  Winter Storms. Produced by a warm current displacing a cool one, to supply a deficiency towards the poles. Temperature changing from cool to warm. Direction to the north-eastern quadrant. *Characteristic cloud*—Stratus.

(*b*)—Polar or South-East and South-West Storms.
  Summer Storms. Produced by a cool current displacing a warm one, to supply a deficiency towards the equator. Temperature changing from warm to cool. Direction to the southern semicircle. *Characteristic cloud*—Cumulo-Stratus.

3.—Loco-Progressive or Diagonal Storms.
  Travelling locally. Rotatory (tornadoes, hailstorms, sandstorms, waterspouts, &c.) Produced by a tendency of the atmosphere to re-establish the equilibrium of a *polar storm*, which has been disturbed in the plane of meeting by a peculiar configuration of the ground. Direction, the diagonal of the forces of the two opposing currents transversely through the polar storm. *Characteristic cloud*—Conus."

Note.—The word Conus is applied by Professor Blasius to distinguish the tornado cloud, which, from its form (an inverted cone), he thinks makes the appellation a suitable one. The direction by compass applies to the *Northern* hemisphere.

† "Whether clear or cloudy—a rosy sky at sunset presages fine weather: a sickly, greenish hue, wind and rain: tawny or coppery clouds, wind: a dark (or *Indian*) red, rain: a red sky in the morning, bad weather, or much wind (perhaps also rain): a grey sky in the morning, fine weather: a high dawn, wind: a low dawn, fair weather. A 'high dawn' is when the first indications of daylight are seen above a bank of clouds. A 'low dawn' is when the day breaks on or near the horizon, the first streaks of light being very low down.

Among such conflicting opinions regarding storms, sailor is likely to become bewildered. In the writer's the storms themselves are as various in character as th about them. He has seen at times so much in fav

---

"Soft-looking or delicate clouds foretell fine weather, with moder breezes: hard edged oily-looking clouds,—wind. A dark, gloomy blue but a light, bright blue sky indicates fine weather. Generally, the *softe* the less wind (but perhaps more rain) may be expected; and the 'greasy,' rolled, tufted, or ragged,—the stronger the coming wind will pro a bright yellow sky at sunset presages wind: a pale yellow, wet: oran coloured, wind and rain—and thus by the prevalence of red, yellow, gr other tints, the coming weather may be foretold very nearly—indeed, instruments, almost exactly.

"Light, delicate, quiet tints or colours, with soft, indefinite forms o dicate and accompany fine weather: but gaudy or unusual hues, with hard outlined clouds, foretell rain, and probably strong wind.

"Small inky-looking clouds foretell rain:—light scud clouds, driving a masses, show wind and rain; but if alone, may indicate wind only—prop their motion.

"High *upper* clouds crossing the sun, moon, or stars, in a direction dif that of the lower clouds, or the wind then felt below, foretell a chang toward *their* direction. Between the tropics, or in the regions of the Tra there is generally an upper and counter current of air, with very light clo is not an indication of any approaching change. In middle latitudes Currents are not so frequent (*or evident?*) except before a change of weather.

"After fine clear weather, the first signs, in a sky, of a coming change, light streaks, curls, wisps, or mottled patches of white distant cloud, whic and are followed by an overcasting of murky vapour that grows into This appearance, more or less oily, or watery, as wind or rain will prev infallible sign.

"Usually the higher and more distant such clouds seem to be,—the more but general, the coming change of weather will prove.

"Misty clouds forming, or hanging on heights, show wind and rain co they remain, increase or descend. If they rise or disperse, the weather will or become fine.

"When sea birds fly out early, and far to seaward, moderate wind and fair may be expected. When they hang about the land, or over it, sometime inland, strong winds with stormy weather are probable. As, besides bird creatures are affected by the approach of rain or wind, their indications should slighted by an observer who wishes to foresee changes.

"Dew is an indication of coming fine weather. Its formation never *begins* an overcast sky, or when there is much wind.

"Remarkable clearness of atmosphere, especially near the horizon; distant o such as hills, unusually visible, or well defined; or raised (by refraction); and is called 'a good *hearing* day,' may be mentioned among signs of wet, if not w be expected in a short time. Much refraction is a sign of easterly wind.

"More than usual twinkling or apparent size of the stars; indistinctne apparent multiplication of the moon's horns; haloes; 'wind-dogs,'—and the rai are more or less significant of increasing wind, if not approaching rain, with or out wind."

Plate II.

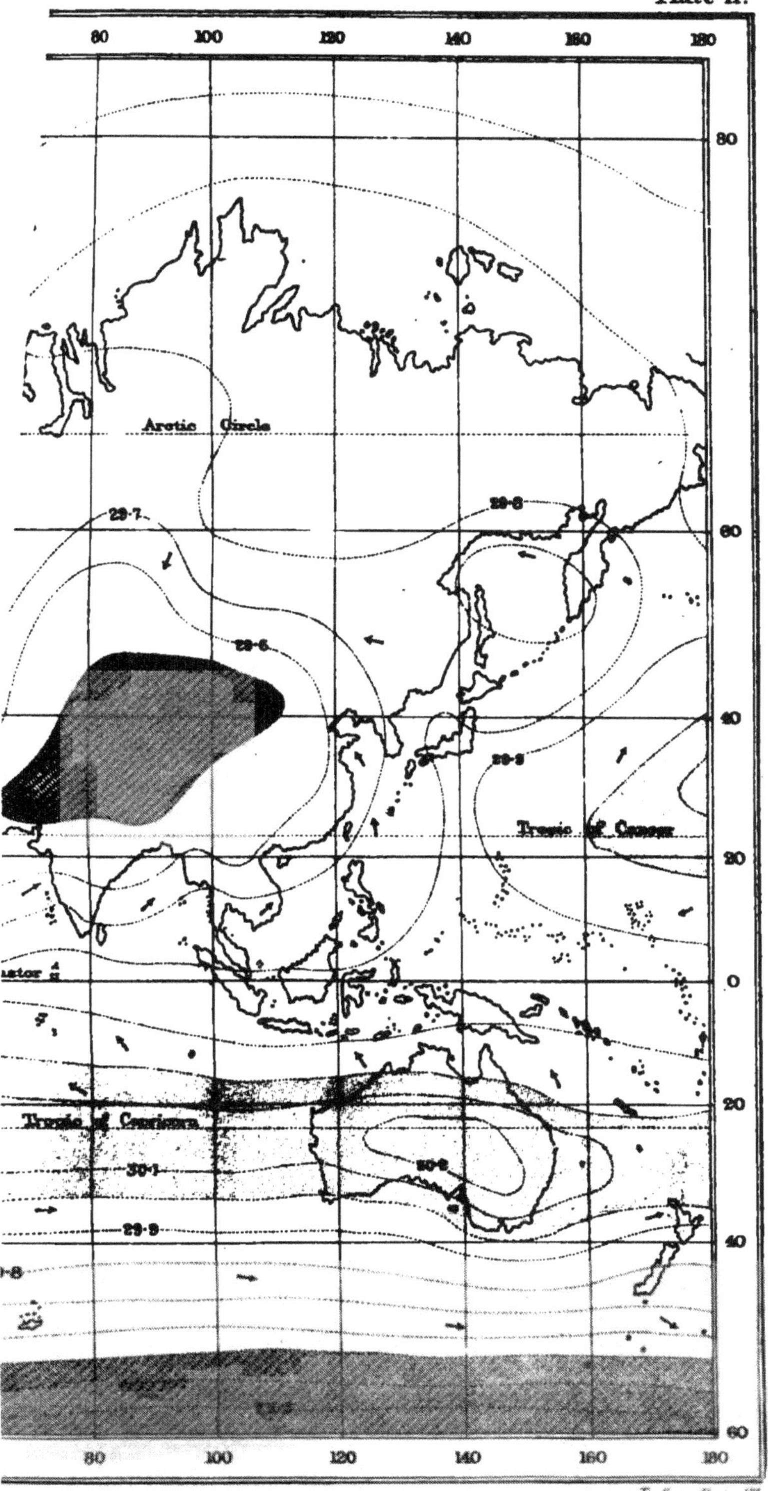


*To face Page 172*

strictly circular theory, that he is led to believe that, in some instances, it may be justifiable. In others, anomalies have presented themselves which, from the impossibility of reconciling them with the law, have rendered it entirely untenable. There remains, also, the general objection to it, *that if one and the same air current were moving in a circle, it would be difficult to explain the rapid thermal changes which certainly take place with the veering of the wind, as the storm passes over us.* If we could only know what was going on in the higher regions of the atmosphere, simultaneously with existing surface conditions, out of apparent chaos might come some sort of order; this however, is a difficulty which seems insuperable.

**Law of Storms a difficult question.**

The writer is disposed to think that each kind of storm is governed by laws only applicable to itself, and it is possible that some of them may be of one type at their commencement, and develop into another before the finish, or even be of a compound character throughout. It is known beyond cavil that land even of moderate height has not only a marked tendency to divert storms from their course, but also to change their very form.

Again, one or more secondary disturbances sometimes hang about on the skirts of the larger ones: these may come into collision, and confusion reign supreme until the one will have merged into the other, the less being absorbed by the greater.

All this would point to great complexity not easily unravelled by the sailor, so completely cut off as he is from all outside help. In the case of actual cyclones, whether they be of a spiral, oval, or strictly circular kind, some of the old rules laid down for the guidance of seamen will, in the absence of better ones, still apply. It is just as well, therefore, to remember them.

**How to manœuvre in Cyclones.**

HEAVE-TO on the starboard tack in the Right-hand semicircle, and port-tack in the Left-hand semicircle, in *both* hemispheres.

CARRY-ON on starboard tack in Northern, and port-tack in Southern hemisphere.

SCUD when on line of progression in either hemisphere; or in Left-hand semicircle in Northern, or Right-hand semicircle in Southern hemisphere.

It will of course be understood that, looking towards the direction in which the body of the storm is moving, the Right and Left-hand semicircles lie respectively on the right and left-hand of the axis line.

In his intercourse with brother seamen, the writer has often heard it contended that the rule saying that if the wind veers to

**Rule to determine semicircle**

the right, the observer is in the Right-hand semicircle, and *vice versâ*, is *not* to be depended on, as in their experience they had sometimes found the very opposite to be the case, which, of course, shook their faith on other points as well. The rule, however, is perfectly sound, *but it is only intended to be used by a vessel that is stationary.*

**Possibility of being misled.**

If the reader will imagine his ship to be *over-running* a *slow moving* circular storm, *which is travelling on the same course as himself*, he cannot fail to see, with the aid of Piddington's Horn Card, or a tracing-paper substitute for it, that when passing through either semicircle, the wind will veer the contrary way to the rule, as it is usually interpreted.

**To ascertain path of storm —heave-to.**

On first falling in with a supposed cyclone, a fair surmise may be made as to the direction in which it is moving, since it is known that these disturbances favour a particular course in each locality, which course is now pretty well mapped out for the various parts of the world; nevertheless, under all circumstances (and bearing in mind the liability to mistake referred to above, and the possibility of unexpected re-curvature), it will be prudent to heave-to until the ship's position with respect to its path is well ascertained. 'In cyclones of both hemispheres, the *west* wind on their equatorial sides is easily dealt with, for they seldom move on a track towards the equator; so the ship may take that route until the barometer rises, and the weather improves.'*

**Distance of centre, impossible to estimate.**

Remember, *whatever may be said to the contrary*, that from the varying area of storms, and the difference of barometric gradients which must therefore exist between their centres and outer edges, *it is quite impossible to estimate the distance of the vortex by the height of the mercury.*

Further, reference to the storm diagrams in the English daily papers will show that the gradients are not uniform on all sides of an area of depression, *and that the latter is not necessarily circular in shape.* In some parts the lines of equal pressure (Isobars) run together much closer than at others, and this is probably the case with tropical cyclones also.

This much, however, is certain—if the barometer rise while the wind diminishes, the meteor is passing away; but if it continue to fall, and the wind and sea to increase, the meteor is approaching, or the depression is deepening and spreading. "He who watches

* TOYNBEE.—*Barometer Manual*, 1871.

his barometer, watches his ship," is therefore more than usually applicable.

Having ascertained, beyond doubt, which semicircle you are in, *wait no longer*, but carry on sail on the starboard tack if in the Northern hemisphere, or port tack if in the Southern hemisphere; and when unable to do so through loss of spars or canvas, heave-to on the starboard tack if in the Right-hand semicircle, or the port tack if in the Left-hand semicircle. By so doing, instead of being continually headed off as the wind veers, you will come up and bow the sea.

**Tack on which ship will bow the sea.**

Again, whilst first hove-to waiting for things to develop themselves, should the barometer fall rapidly, and the indications of an approaching hurricane become stronger, whilst the wind continues to blow steadily, but with increasing violence, *from the same point*, or nearly so, you will know that your vessel is directly in the path of the advancing storm. Then, to escape being involved in the centre and most dangerous part, up helm and scud before the wind, *keeping it, at all hazards, a couple of points or three on the starboard quarter in the Northern hemisphere, or on the port quarter in the Southern hemisphere.*

**Rule for scudding.**

This chapter would manifestly be incomplete without some reference to the Moon as a factor in meteorological matters. It is pretty generally believed by sailors, and farmers, that it exercises some sort of mysterious influence at the Full, Change, and Quarters, and is in fact prime agent in everything that concerns the weather. Patient and laborious research, extending back over half a century, has completely failed to establish such connection. "As an attracting body causing an ærial tide, it has of course an effect, but one utterly insignificant as a mereorological cause."* It is, however, pretty generally admitted that the moon, when near the full, has a tendency to clear the sky of clouds, or, as the sailor phrases it, to "skoff" them up.

**Popular delusion concerning Moon's influence on weather.**

We are all involuntarily much more strongly impressed by the fulfilment than by the failure of our expectations: so it is that the sailor seizes upon an occasional coincidence of this sort, and points triumphantly to it as a proof of the correctness of his theory, whilst he omits to record the many instances in which the weather provokingly failed to behave in the manner he anticipated.

To all but hypercritical folk of the type of Herschel or Arago the evidence that connects the Moon with weather changes is irresistible: old Jobson the carrier finds no difficulty about it at

* Sir John F. W. Herschel, Bart. *Good Words*, 1864.

all, nor do any of his cronies. Their ancient system may be flouted by the learned, but *they* have faith in it, for has it not been handed down from generation to generation? It is quite plain, as the company at "The Jolly Traveller" have remarked over and over again, that when the crescent moon is on her back it is going to be dry, but that when the hollow part is downwards, it will rain. "Plain as turning up this here pot," says old Jobson, who has just finished his pint, and lets the few last drops fall to the ground.

The stars, too, speak with no uncertain voice to this class of weather prophet; if they are clear it is a sign of rain; if they are "misty" it will be wet; if they are clouded the rain is pretty sure to come before long. And curiously enough, down comes the rain, often in less than a week. Who has not met the man with a particular corn which is barometer and thermometer in one, or a faithful knee-joint which has twinges whenever the forces of the air gather themselves for storms?

**Rustic weather prophets.**

Some rustic weather prophets are very amusing: ask one whether it will be a fine day to-morrow, and he will look in his mug, slowly shake his liquor round, take his pipe from his mouth, and say oracularly, "Weather isn't what it used to be." By pressure you get a promise of a fine day, "if the wind don't drop," accompanied by another saving clause that "he don't half like them yaller clouds." He, and two or three other old fellows, who have been shepherds, or have been to sea, bear the burden of the public weather upon their shoulders, for they are consulted by almost everyone they meet as to "what they think of it to-day," and, having reputations to uphold, must be oftentimes much disconcerted by the unstable conduct of the elements. But your weather prophet generally, like the oracle-worker of old, understands the protective possibilities of language, and avails himself of them.

When one considers that the Moon quarters weekly, it would indeed be curious if a change of some kind or another did not occur within a day or so (either way) of that event. And as, in this variable climate, "spells" of weather seldom last more than

**Old style almanacks.**

four or five days, it does not require a very lively imagination to connect them with the constantly recurring phases of the moon. He must therefore be an ill-informed, obstinate, or very credulous fellow who, in the face of the positive dictum of science, continues to pin his faith to the played out fallacies and charlatanism of the old style almanacks.

In reviewing the entire subject, it will be seen that nothing but the hope of better things in the future can save the sailor being disheartened with such little practical result after so many years of investigation. He has, however, always been famed for the faculty (possessed by so few) of doing the best with but indifferent means; and it still remains for him to go to sea almost entirely dependent on his own watchfulness and judgment.

---

## CHAPTER XVI.

### TIDES, CURRENTS, WAVES, AND BREAKERS.

To enter into a disquisition on the complete theory of the tides, would in these pages be both unprofitable and impracticable; for apart from its extent and intricate character, as well as the intimate knowledge required of higher mathematics, "there are perhaps few physical subjects which are still at the present time on the whole more unsatisfactory."*

Tide theory not altogether satisfactory.

Any seaman, therefore, who is desirous of making a *special* study of the tidal theory, must refer to the various works by distinguished men in which this comprehensive subject is treated at great length. These will be found mentioned in the *Admiralty Manual*, in the section devoted to Tides.

The article containing the latest and most complete information is probably that by Sir George Airy (late Astronomer-Royal), in the *Encyclopædia Metropolitana*, and another by Mr. G. H. Darwin, in the *Proceedings of the Royal Society*.

But it is here proposed, after giving a brief sketch of the general laws and features, to draw the seaman's attention to certain points which will have a *practical* interest for him, inasmuch as, upon an understanding of *some* of them at least, the safe navigation of his ship will depend.

To a right appreciation of the subject one must begin at the beginning, and, therefore, a few words about the properties of water, and the nature and origin of waves, are indispensable to lead off with.

There are four descriptions of sea waves, namely, "Wind waves," "Storm waves," "Earthquake waves," and "Tidal waves."

---

* *Admiralty Manual of Scientific Enquiry*, page 79.

**Properties of water.**

Though it has been proved that water is capable of being compressed, it is the case to such a very limited extent, that for our present purpose the property may be disregarded. A forced displacement, therefore, at one point of a liquid surface, is always exactly counterbalanced by a corresponding rise at another. Conversely, a rise at any place can only be effected by a proportionate withdrawal of water elsewhere. This being understood, it is not difficult to see that the first-named kind of wave is produced by a purely *mechanical* action.

**Wind Waves.**

The wind does not blow exactly parallel to the surface, but strikes downward, and causes a depression at the point of impact, which is instantly answered by an equal elevation elsewhere. This elevation or wave—slight at first—must necessarily have the same height *above* the general sea-level or plane of repose that the depression or trough had *below* it.

As the wind increases in strength and duration, these undulations of the water grow larger, and eventually form immense billows, which have been recorded as sixty feet in height from trough to crest.

**Formation of wind waves.**

W. H. White, in his *Manual of Naval Architecture*, says:—"If the wind is at first supposed to act on a smooth sea, and then to continue to blow with steady force and in one direction, it will create waves which finally will attain certain definite dimensions. The phases of change from the smooth sea to the fully formed waves cannot be distinctly traced. It is, however, probable that changes of level, elevations and depressions, resulting from the impact of the wind on the smooth surface of the sea, and the frictional resistance of the wind on the water, are the chief causes of the growth of waves.

"An elevation and its corresponding depression once formed offer direct resistance to the action of the wind, and its unbalanced pressure producing motion in the heaped-up water would ultimately lead to the creation of larger and larger waves. This is probably the chief cause of wave growth, frictional resistance playing a very subordinate part as compared with it. So long as the speed of the wind relatively to that of the wave water is capable of accelerating its motion, so long may we expect the speed of the wave to increase; and with the speed the length, and also the height.

"Finally the waves reach such a speed that the wind force produces no further acceleration, and only just maintains the form unchanged; then we have the fully grown waves. If the wind were now suddenly withdrawn, the waves would gradually decrease in magnitude, and finally die out. This degradation results from the resistance due to the molecular forces in the wave—viscosity of the water, &c.—and when the waves are fully grown, the wind must at every instant balance the molecular forces.

"If the water were a *perfect* fluid (the particles moving freely past one another), and if there were no resistance to motion on the part of the air, the waves once formed would travel onwards without degradation."

**Height of waves depends on "Fetch."**

The height of wind-waves depends on what is called the "Fetch;" that is, the distance from the weather shore or place where their formation commences. According to Mr. Thomas Stevenson (author of *Lighthouse Illumination*), the following formula is nearly correct during heavy gales, when the fetch is not less than about six nautical miles:—height of wave in feet is equal to 1·5 × by the square root of the fetch in nautical miles. As an example, let us suppose that during a violent gale the wave formation commenced at a distance of 625 miles from the observer:—The square root of 625 is 25, which, multiplied by 1·5, gives 37½ feet as the height of the waves at the end of their long journey.

**Occasional groups of large waves during gales.**

Every sailor has noticed the occasional grouping together of three or four huge waves larger than the general run. These are probably caused by the exceptional force of the *squalls* which occur at intervals in nearly every gale of wind. From the inequality in their respective speeds, it follows that any particular set of large waves will not reach the vessel side by side with the wind which produced them. Such a thing would be very unlikely—one might almost say impossible; so that these big fellows, deriving their energy only in part from the blast sweeping over them at any given instant, come rolling along, as often as not, during a lull in the violence of the gale.

**Storm waves.**

"Storm waves" are due to an entirely different source. On the outer or *anticyclone* edge of hurricanes the barometer stands abnormally high, indicative of great atmospheric pressure; whilst at the centre or vortex the mercury falls unusually low; and, accordingly, *there* the pressure is least. Between the centre and outer edge a difference of five inches in the height of the mercury has been recorded; equal to a difference of pressure of 354 pounds on the square foot of surface at these two places. It will readily be seen that the effect of this encircling belt of high pressure, and internal area of low pressure, coupled with the incurving of the wind, is to produce a heaping up of the water under the body of the cyclone, whose highest point is necessarily at the centre, where it is, so to speak, sucked up.

As the hurricane travels bodily onward, this "storm wave"—which, according to the shape of the disturbance, may be likened to an oval dish or a soup plate, bottom up—accompanies it; and has been known more than once to inundate low-lying districts, and cause thousands of human beings to perish at one sweep.

**Earthquake waves, and tidal waves.**

"Earthquake," or "Great Sea Waves," as they are technically styled, differ entirely in their origin from the two preceding. They are frequently spoken of as "*Tidal Waves;*" but as the tides have nothing whatever to do with them, such a designation is obviously wrong.

The term "Great Sea Wave" is used in contradistinction to "Great Earth Wave," which latter is the name given to the disturbance experienced on land.

An earthquake may have its centre of impulse either inland or under the bed of the ocean. In the first case, when the "Great Earth Wave," or superficial undulation, coming from inland, reaches the shores of the sea (unless these be precipitous, with deep water) it may lift the water up, and carry it out on its back, as it were; for the rate of transit of the shock is sometimes so great that the heap of water lifted up has not time to flow away towards the sides.

At Arica, in Peru, and other places, this sudden going out of the sea has made bare the bottom of the bay, and left ships aground which only a few minutes before were riding quietly at anchor in several fathoms of water.

As soon as the shock is over, the body of water thus forced out to sea returns as a huge wave, and, on approaching a sloping shore, rears up like a wall, and breaks with overwhelming force. Sometimes, however, its volume, height, and velocity are so great that it comes ashore *bodily*, and breaks far inland, causing even greater destruction to life and property.

When the seat of disturbance is beneath the ocean, the "Great Sea Wave" rushes in upon the land as before—with this difference, that it is not preceded by the water retiring from the foreshore, as in the first case.

**Curious effect of earthquake waves.**

These submarine shocks are sometimes so severe, that the sensation has been conveyed to those afloat as if the ship were violently bumping over a sunken reef. In one instance which came under the writer's observation, the inkstand on the captain's table of one of the Pacific Company's coast steamers was jerked upwards against the ceiling, where it left an unmistakeable record of the occurrence; and yet this vessel at the time was steaming along in smooth water, many hundreds of fathoms deep. The concussions were so smart that passengers were shaken off their seats, and, of course, thought that the vessel had run ashore. When the non-elastic nature of water is considered, there will be no difficulty in understanding how such an effect could be produced.

**Tidal waves.** Lastly, we come to the purely *vertical* oscillations of water, known as "Tidal Waves."

The distinctive difference between these and "Wind Waves" lies in the fact that the last-mentioned are only *surface* disturbances, which, however violent the gale, reach at no time to a greater depth than 50 fathoms, and are virtually only local and temporary in their action. Whereas "Tide Waves" are the result of an *outside attraction, which continuously affects the whole mass of water on the earth's surface.*

**Tide caused by joint attraction of sun and moon.** The Tides are popularly attributed to the Moon *only*, but in point of fact they are caused by the *joint* attraction of both Sun and Moon; and it is due to this double influence, which sometimes pulls in the same and at other times in a contrary direction, that we have the ever-varying phases in the times and heights of High and Low Water.

The general motion of the Tides consists in an alternate *vertical* Rise and Fall, and *horizontal* Flow and Ebb, occupying an average period of half a Lunar day, or about 12 hours 25 minutes. This vertical movement is transmitted from place to place in the seas, like an ever-recurring series of very long and swift waves.

**Duration of a tide.**

"Tide waves" occur simultaneously at points of the earth's surface diametrically opposite to each other, and are termed Superior or Inferior, according as they are formed on the side next the Moon, or on the one opposite. It will be understood, therefore, that there are *two* tide waves at a fixed distance apart of 180°, measured both in latitude and longitude, and that they are constantly travelling round the earth from East to West.

**Superior and inferior tides.**

Since, as already explained, water may be regarded as practically devoid of elasticity, and cannot be raised at any point without being proportionately lowered at some other, it follows that, midway between each of these waves of High Water, there are depressions of the surface corresponding to what we term Low Water. This is shewn in *Diagrams Nos. 1 and 2*, where, however, for convenience as much as from necessity, the matter of *scale* is entirely disregarded.

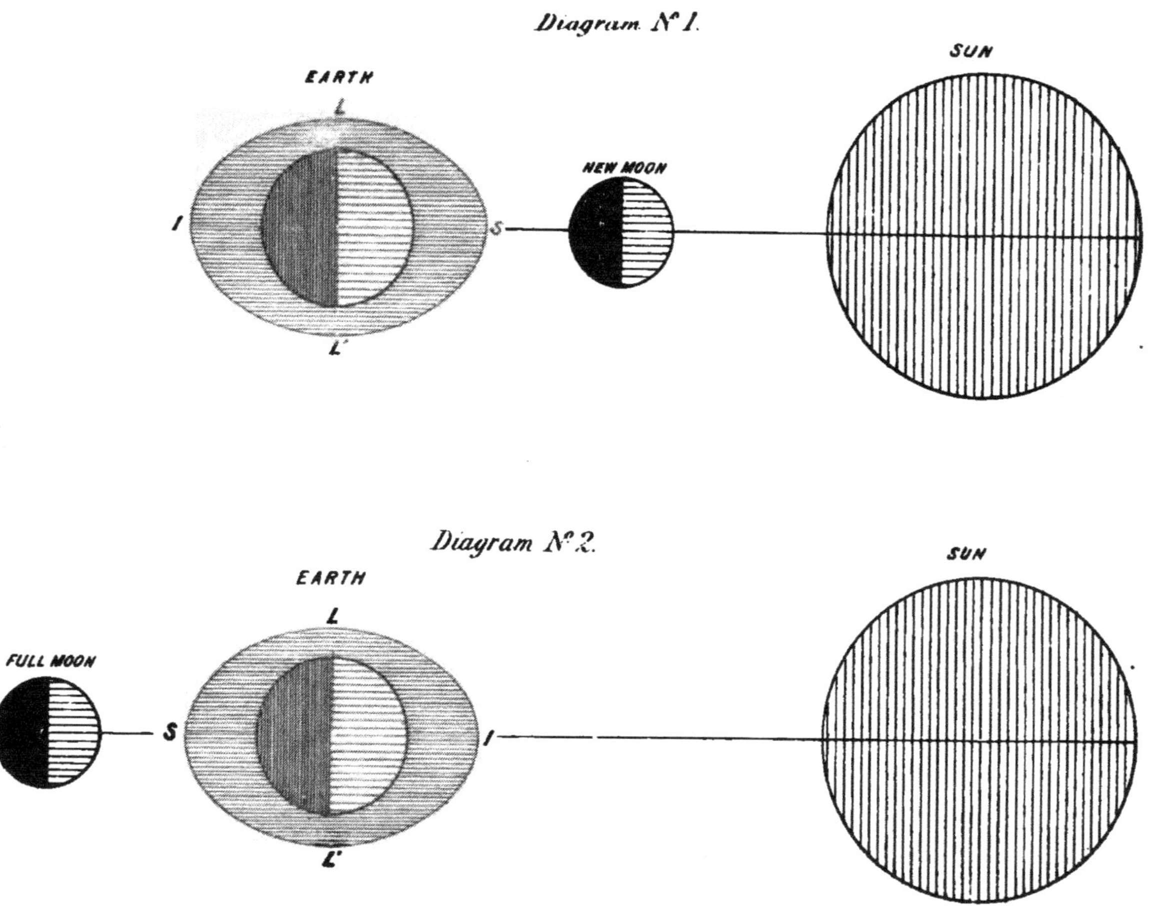


Diagram No. 1.

Diagram No. 2.

To face p.

*S* is the Superior High Water, *I* the Inferior. *L* and *L'* represent Low Water. As may be supposed, the Inferior Tide Wave is a shade smaller than the other.

"Full and change."

At the period of "Change" or New Moon, when it and the Sun are in Conjunction, that is to say, when they are on the same side of the earth, as shewn in *Diagram No.* 1,—and at the period of Full Moon, when they are said to be in Opposition, that is, with the earth between them, as shewn in *Diagram No.* 2,—the greatest tidal effect is produced, as at such times the solar and lunar influences are exerted in the same straight line.* This is the period

* Our satellite, the moon, is a dark globular body, 2,159 miles in diameter, which shines solely by reflected light received from the sun; consequently, at the period termed "new moon," when the sun and moon pass the meridian together at mid-day, the moon is invisible to us, as at such times she occupies a position in the heavens directly between the earth and the sun, and accordingly presents to us her unenlightened face; which is still further hidden by the dazzling brightness of that particular part of the sky (*vide Diagram No.* 1).

But when the moon is at the "full," she passes the meridian at midnight, or 12 hours after the sun, which latter, being then on the opposite side of the earth, illumines the whole of that hemisphere of the moon which is next to us (*vide Diagram No.* 2).

It is obvious that, in the intermediate stages, a greater or less amount of the moon's illumined face must be visible to us.

A day or so after new moon, when its bright portion is crescent-shaped, it is not unusual in clear weather to see the remainder or obscure part also. At such times the brightly illuminated cusps or horns seem to extend *beyond* the darker portion of the disc, and hold it in their grasp. This condition is commonly alluded to as "the old moon with the young in its arms," or "the moon on its back." The phenomenon of the bright part of the moon appearing to encircle the remainder is due to an optical illusion termed "Irradiation," in virtue of which, white objects, or those of a very brilliant colour, when seen on a dark ground, look larger than they really are. The new moon appearing after this fashion, is asserted by some to be the *sure* forerunner of bad weather. A statement so positive in character should have something to support it, but, unfortunately for those who make it, it is not at all justified by the known facts. For example, in many favoured parts of the world, the condition of the atmosphere is mostly *always* propitious to seeing the young moon in the arms of the old; and accordingly, in such localities, it possesses no particular signification. On the other hand, in countries given to a chronic state of mist and haze, the phenomenon, from its rareness, attracts more attention, and indicates an *unusual* clearness in the air, which, according as it is backed up by other signs, may or may not herald the approach of rain or wind. From the roving nature of his calling, the sailor, more than other men, should be on his guard against the *general* application of what are only intended as *local* weather signs. That which denotes one kind of weather in one place may signify something totally different in another; much in the same way that in the northern hemisphere the barometer rises for northerly winds, but falls for the same wind in the southern hemisphere. These remarks apply also to *some* of Admiral Fitzroy's weather signs, given on pages 171 and 172. Now, as the

Spring tides.

of "Springs;" and should it occur when both luminaries happen to be at their nearest approach to the earth, the effect is enhanced, and the term "Extraordinary Springs" is then applied to the tides. In the same manner, the high tides which occur about the latter end of March and September are known as "Equinoctial Springs."

Datum line of soundings on Admiralty Charts.

With the exception of Liverpool, Milford, and Holyhead, and perhaps one or two other ports, the soundings on Admiralty charts and plans are all reduced to *mean low water of Ordinary Springs.*

But when the moon is in quadrature, or 90° distant from the sun—that is to say, when one passes the meridian six hours ahead of the other—their actions neutralize each other to a large extent, by the tendency to produce *four* independent waves: two under the sun, of course on opposite sides of the earth, and two similarly situated under the moon. In this case the action of the sun lowers the waters of the sea at the same point where the moon would raise them, and conversely. Each pulls in a different direction to the other, and thus the tides at such times are less in every way, and get the name of "Neaps."

Neap tides.

It must not be understood, however, that two separate or distinct tide waves are then really traversing the ocean in each hemisphere. Such is not the case. The actual effect is the same as if, after the moon had given a form to the waters, the sun had modified it, both as to size and position; so that the place at which the resultant high water really occurs is at a point intermediate to them both, but nearer to the lunar wave, since it is the greater of the two.

---

moon is only supposed to be rendered visible to us by the light reflected from the side presented to the sun, it may not unreasonably be asked why it is that, as just observed, we sometimes see the obscure as well as the brighter portion. This is easily understood, however, by recollecting that when the moon is one or two days old, the relative positions of the earth, the moon, and the sun, are such as permit the earth to reflect the sunlight back to the moon in sufficient quantity to faintly illumine that hemisphere which is next to ourselves. In fact we give it *Earth-light.*

It is obvious that, to an inhabitant of the moon (if such there could be), our earth must appear as a splendid moon, shining with light borrowed from the sun, and presenting all the moon's own phases as seen from the earth, but possessing more than three times her apparent diameter. We act, therefore, in the same capacity towards the moon that the moon does towards us. It is interesting here to note the opinion of some scientists, that, judging from the moon's physical conditions, life, as we know it, cannot exist there; whilst it is possible, if not probable, that some of the other planets (more especially Mars, which has been termed "the miniature of our earth") may have their inhabitants, though not necessarily b ings of precisely the same order as ourselves.

# Diagram No. 3.

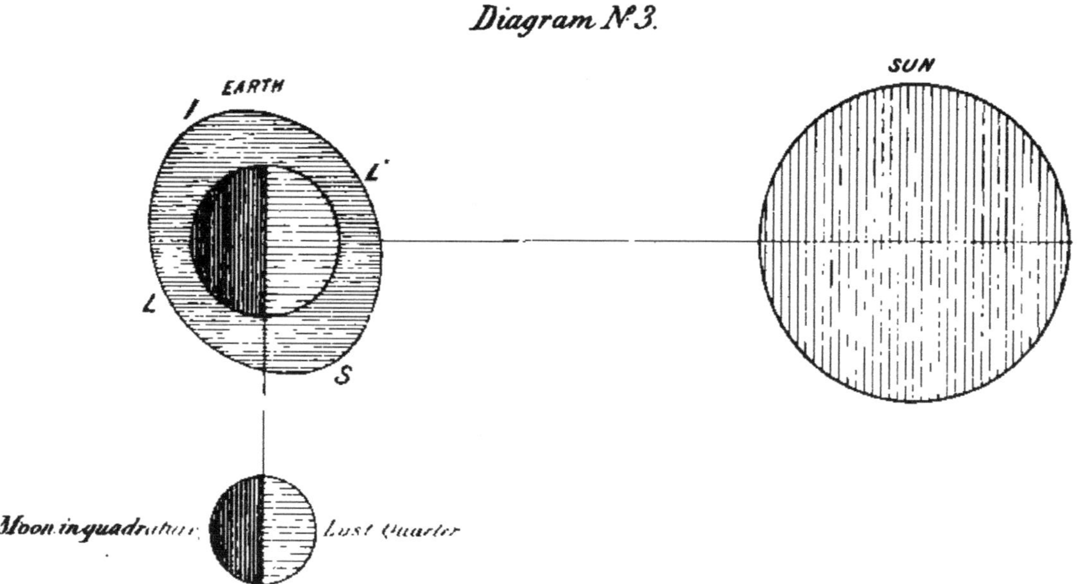


To face Page 1.

Springs are thus *the sum*, and neaps *the difference*, of the co-existing lunar and solar tides.

*Diagram No.* 3 represents neap tides as produced at the last quarter of the moon, and as the effect on the tide at the first quarter is precisely similar, it is not worth while to give the diagram.

The tidal wave is also accelerated or retarded in a way which will now be described. In the 1st and 3rd quarters of the Moon the solar tide is *westward* of the lunar one; and, consequently, the actual High Water (which is the result of the combination of the two waves), will be to the *westward* of the place it would have been at if the Moon had acted alone, and the time of High Water will therefore be hastened. In the 2nd and 4th quarters the general effect of the Sun is, for a similar reason, to produce a retardation in the time of High Water. This effect, brought about by the relative positions of the Sun and Moon, is called the *Priming* and *Lagging* of the tides. It deranges the average retardation, which, from a mean value of 48m., may be augmented to 60m. or be reduced to 36m.

**Priming and lagging.**

A study of the preceding diagrams will shew that the greatest and least water is to be found on a bar at High and Low Water respectively of Spring Tides; whilst at Neaps the tide will neither rise so high nor fall so much. There is therefore more water on a bar at Low Water Neaps than at Low Water Springs. Furthermore, we have the important fact that *at half tide the depth on a bar is always nearly the same, whether it be Springs or Neaps.* Thus at Liverpool, *at the present date*, there are always 24 feet of water on the bar at half-tide, flood or ebb, but of course this depth is subject to alteration by the bar silting up or washing away. Half-tide corresponds to the Mean sea level, which is constant, and should therefore be universally adopted as the standard Plane of reference.

**Half-tide, or mean sea level.**

The following diagram, taken from the Admiralty Tide Tables, is intended to explain the terms Spring Rise, Neap Rise, and Neap Range, as made use of on the Charts and in the Sailing Directions published by the Admiralty:—

**Tidal diagram.**

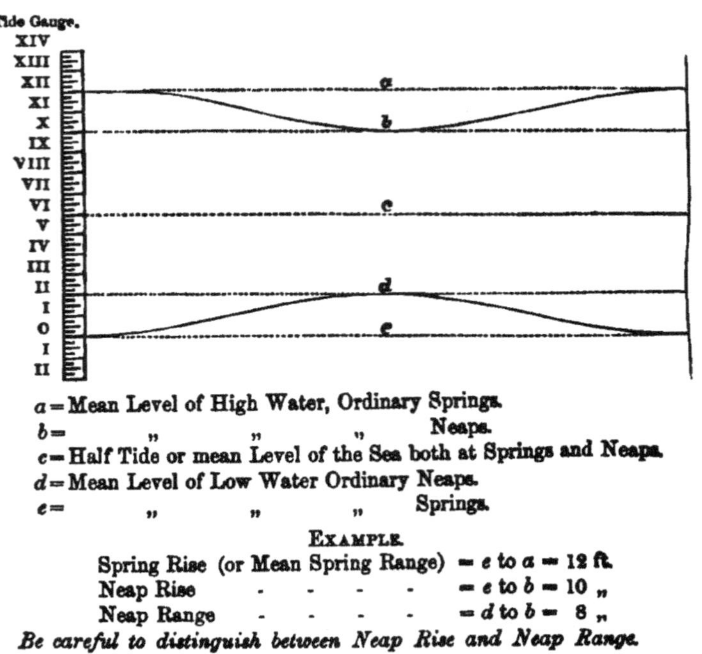


*a* = Mean Level of High Water, Ordinary Springs.
*b* = " " " Neaps.
*c* = Half Tide or mean Level of the Sea both at Springs and Neaps.
*d* = Mean Level of Low Water Ordinary Neaps.
*e* = " " " Springs.

EXAMPLE.

| | | |
|---|---|---|
| Spring Rise (or Mean Spring Range) | = *e* to *a* = | 12 ft. |
| Neap Rise - - - - - | = *e* to *b* = | 10 " |
| Neap Range - - - - - | = *d* to *b* = | 8 " |

*Be careful to distinguish between Neap Rise and Neap Range.*

**Superior and inferior tide waves.**

Now, with reference to a tide wave being formed simultaneously on *both* sides of the earth. In considering this question we will temporarily put the sun on one side, as by so doing matters will be much simplified, without in the least interfering with the general principle.

At first sight it looks strange that the Inferior wave should be produced by the *attraction* of a single body, such as the moon, which of course cannot be on *both* sides of the earth at the same instant of time. Admitting the attractive power of the moon, it is easy to comprehend that the Superior tide may be so formed; but that the other should *also* be the result of a pull in the same direction, is much more difficult to understand, and proves an effectual poser to many who, from want of the key, consider the matter as contrary to common sense. Touching the latter, it must be allowed that common sense is a first rate thing in its way, and happy are those who possess it, but, unfortunately, it is not always equal to unravelling intricate problems, of whatsoever kind. The moon's *attraction* undoubtedly causes *both* tide waves, and, absurd as the idea may appear to many, the fact is capable of sufficiently easy explanation, which we will now attempt.

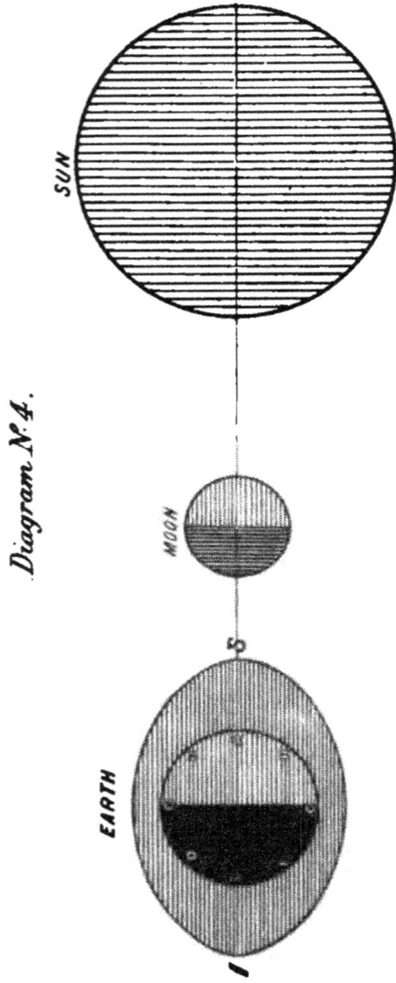


To face Page 87

It is necessary, first of all, to have a clear conception of that species of attraction called Gravitation, which pervades all space—*every particle of matter in this vast universe attracting every other particle.* **Universal attraction or gravitation.**

The laws governing Universal Attraction are well established, and may be thus stated:—

"1. All bodies in nature exert a mutual attraction upon each other, at all distances, in virtue of which they are continually tending towards each other.

"2. For the same distance the attractions between bodies are proportional to their masses.

"3. The masses being equal, the attraction varies with the distance, being inversely proportional to the square of the distances asunder."*

The tides, however, are not due to the simple attraction of the moon upon the waters of the globe, but to the *difference* of its attraction on the near and far sides of the earth. **Explanation of how the tides are formed by attraction.**

Now, the moon attracts the solid earth as well as the waters upon it, and in conformity with law No. 3, she attracts most that which is nearest to her. Therefore, the waters on the side next the moon are most drawn to her, the solid earth in a lesser degree, and the waters on the distant side less still; so that the latter are left behind, as it were, and present the illusory appearance of being *attracted towards I,* which, however, is not the case. See *Diagram No. 4.*

Let the inside letters represent points on the earth's surface, and let us suppose the latter to be uniformly covered with water. Now, the different parts of the earth are at unequal distances from the moon. Hence the attraction which the moon exerts at *a* is greater than that which it exerts at *b* and *h*, and still greater than that which it exerts at *c* and *g*; while the attraction at *e* is least of all.

The attraction of the moon upon the layer of water immediately under it at the point *S* is greater than that which it exerts upon the solid globe; the water will therefore heap itself up over *a*—that is, High Water will take place immediately under the moon. The water which thus collects at *a* is derived from the regions *c* and *g*, where the quantity of water must therefore be diminished—that is, there will be Low Water at *c* and *g*.

* *Ganot's' Popular Natural Philosophy.* A most engaging book, which no officer should be without.

The water at *I* is less attracted than the solid mass of the earth. The latter will therefore recede from the waters at *I*, leaving them behind, so that they will be heaped up also, and produce High Water at the same time as at *S*. The Moon's attraction, as exercised upon our earth, is *differential* in its character, and herein lies the gist of the whole thing.

So much for the Moon; now for the Sun.

**Sun's influence on the tides.**

The sun produces tidal effects similar to those of the moon. He is the centre and controlling force of the system to which we belong; and his attractive power upon the earth, *as a whole*, is vastly greater than that of our comparatively puny satellite; for, though the sun's mean distance from us is nearly 390 times that of the moon, it is more than counterbalanced by his mass, which is 26 million times greater than that of the moon. Nevertheless, the latter's influence upon the tides is nearly 2⅓ times more than the sun.

**Sun's mean distance.**

Here we have another seeming anomaly, but it is explained by the fact that the sun's mean distance is so great (93 millions of miles), that the *inequality* of his attraction on *different* parts of our earth is very small; that is to say, the sun attracts *all* parts of our comparatively small globe in a *nearly* equal ratio, which is not by any means the case with the moon, as the earth's diameter (7,913 miles) bears a considerable proportion to her mean distance from us of 238,830 miles. The moon is only removed from us by a distance equal to 30 of the earth's diameters, whereas it would require nearly 12,000 earths to bridge the space between the sun and ourselves. In other words, the sun's attraction, as applied to our earth, is less *differential* in character than that of the moon.

**Moon's mean distance.**

The term Gravitation is applied more especially to the attraction exerted between the heavenly bodies. The sun being that member of our planetary system which has the largest mass, exerts also the greatest attraction, from which it might seem that the earth and the other planets ought to fall into the sun, by reason of this attraction. This would indeed be the case, if they were *only* acted upon by the force of Gravitation; but owing to their inertia,* the original or primary impulse which they once received constantly tends to carry them away from the sun in a straight line. The *resultant* of this acquired velocity, and of the force of

**Planetary orbits.**

* *Inertia* is a purely negative property of matter. It is that inherent quality of passiveness in bodies which preserves them in a state of perpetual rest when undisturbed, or in perpetual motion unless arrested by some resisting force.

Gravitation, makes the planets describe curves about the sun which are elliptical in shape, and are called their orbits.

**Velocity of tidal wave.**

The moon revolves about the earth once in something under 25 hours, and the earth having a circumference (in round numbers) of 25 thousand miles, the tide wave caused by the joint action of the sun and moon would, if the surface of our globe were uniformly and entirely covered with deep water, have a speed of 1000 miles per hour. As a matter of fact, in mid-ocean, where there are no barriers to its progress, the tide wave is found to travel little short of this rate; but there is a rapid falling off in the speed as well as change in the direction, when the wave is obstructed by land stretching across its natural line of progress, also by the friction of the bottom in shoal water. For example, in the Southern Ocean the hourly rate is nearly 1000 miles; in the middle of the North Atlantic, 700 miles; but in the Irish Channel, between Rathlin and the Isle of Man, the progressive rate of the wave of high water is only 50 miles per hour; and in the southern branch of the same, about half that amount.

Let us remark in passing, that the tides with which our frequenters of the sea shore are acquainted are not the *direct* effect of the moon's attraction. The tides are generated in the Great Southern Ocean, where they are *forced* oscillations, but those that we have in our part of the world are *free* oscillations, started, it is true, by the others, though running up to our latitudes on their own hook, under the action of terrestrial Gravitation. The *direct* tidal effect of the moon in our seas is comparatively small, and is in many places antagonistic to the actual ebb and flow of the waters witnessed by our sea-side visitors.

**Retard or age of the tide.**

Here it is necessary to observe that, owing to fluid-friction, the *inertia* of the water, and other causes, the tide wave is found to lag behind the moon, and on this account the highest tides do not occur when her influence is greatest, but from one to three days after. The tide corresponding to New, or Full moon, can however be detected by its superior height, which accordingly enables us to get at what is termed the *retard* or *age* of the tide. Similarly, High Water at any place is not simultaneous with the moon's passage of the meridian of that place, but occurs an hour or two after.

At this stage of our subject, it is most important to distinguish between the motion of a tidal *wave*, and that of a tidal *current*.

**Difference between tidal wave and tidal current.**

The tide wave is due not nearly so much to the actual horizontal *transfer* of a body of water from one place to another, as to an *elevation* of its surface. Thus the sun and moon do not *draw after them* the mound of water which has been raised by their attraction, but are all the time engaged *in raising the water which is vertically beneath them.* As we have seen, the propagation of this tide *wave* is compatible with immense velocity, whereas the tide *current* rarely exceeds 5 or 6 miles an hour. Were the tide wave one of *translation*, like the tide current, it would carry destruction in its course. The peculiarity of its action may be shewn in this way :—

Let two men stand a few yards apart, each holding the end of a piece of rope stretched loosely between them. Now, if one of the men were to shake the rope smartly in an up and down direction, he would cause undulations or waves in it, which would travel to the other end with great rapidity; nevertheless, from both ends being retained in the hands of the men, the rope, *taken as a whole*, would occupy throughout the same position.

The shaking of a sail, or the fluttering of a flag, serve to illustrate the same effect, therefore we see that it is the *form* alone of the wave which moves, and *not* the water of which it is composed. In other words, the same wave as it advances is not composed of the same water.

**Propagation of light, heat, and sound.**

Light, heat, and sound are transmitted in a similar manner. Let us take the latter by way of further illustration :—

If a long spar be gently tapped at one end, the blow will be readily heard by a person applying his ear to the other end. In this case the sound wave is propagated by the minute but rapid *vibrations* of the atoms of wood composing the spar, but no one for a moment would suppose that the identical *piece* of wood which was struck had travelled to the ear of the listener. Solids, generally, conduct sound much more rapidly than air. Oak, for example, will transmit it with exactly ten times greater velocity. Thus, in the experiment just mentioned, if the spar be struck with sufficient force, the listener will hear two distinct sounds, with an interval between them, depending upon the length of the spar, the first sound transmitted by the wood, and the second transmitted by the air. Iron is a still better conductor.

**Waves of translation.**

Recent investigation, however, goes to prove that every sea wave is *more or less* a wave of translation, setting down each particle of water, or of matter suspended in water, a *little* in advance of where it picked that particle up; but to the ordinary observer this transference of matter is so slight as to be imperceptible. By the seaman, however, it is taken into practical account when he is making allowance for "the heave of the sea."

Shoaling of the water makes a material difference in the character of a wave. Its base is then retarded by the increasing friction of the ascending bottom, and its leading side in consequence becomes steeper and steeper, until at length the crest outstrips the base, and, toppling over, breaks into foaming surf. This may be witnessed any day in the approach of waves to a shelving beach. Where the foreshore happens to slope very gradually, these breakers extend a proportionately long distance seaward; but in such cases the ground friction deprives them of their original height and energy long before reaching the beach.

**Effect on waves of shoaling water.**

**Surf and breakers.**

The name has escaped the writer's memory, but there is a place on the Malabar coast where the water, for miles seaward, shoals so regularly and slowly over muddy bottom, that the force of the heavy seas during the S.W. monsoon is quite spent by the time they get near the land; and it is common for the small craft thereabouts to run in on what is a dead lee shore, and anchor without fear in 4 fathoms.

For conditions of an opposite character take the bar of the Tagus, which shoals *abruptly* from a depth of several hundreds of fathoms existing only a few miles to the westward. During winter gales the deep-water undulations come rolling in upon it in an unreduced form, and break with terrific violence. They have even been known to sweep the decks of large mail steamers that have rashly attempted to enter at such times, though the bar carries not less than 6 fathoms at low water (in the shoalest part). This would give the height of these formidable breakers as upwards of 30 feet, since it is generally accepted that the depth of water where the wave first breaks is equal to the height of its crest above the undisturbed sea level.

**Rule as to height of breakers.**

To give an idea of where broken water will be dashed to in storms, it is related, on good authority, that the fog bell (weighing several cwt.) of the Bishop Rock lighthouse was torn away from its massive fastenings during a severe gale, and the gallery containing the belfry was found thickly strewn with sand, though it had an elevation of 100 feet above high water level.

Engineers have of late years taken advantage of the comparative absence of *horizontal* force in *unbroken* waves, to construct almost perpendicularly the sea faces of such piers or breakwaters as require to be built in exposed positions. Formerly, works of this character had a very long batter or slope, the effect of which—similar to that of a shelving beach—was to cause the waves to curl over and break in a manner which forced out huge blocks of

**Piers and breakwaters—how constructed in present day.**

stone, each very many tons in weight; and this undermining process went on until the solid masonry was completely breached through.

Again, it is not improbable that the reader has seen unbroken waves reflected back from a vertical sea wall; in which case he will have noticed that the reflected outgoing waves pass *through* the incoming ones, and each continues on its course almost as if nothing had happened. The principal visible effect produced by the collision is to momentarily increase the height of the waves at their point of meeting; but after a time the reflected wave is so reduced in speed and size by its repeated encounters with succeeding incoming ones, that it dwindles away, and at last ceases to exist; were they *solid* bodies undergoing translation, the wave with the greater momentum would overcome and carry with it the other one—but, of course, at a reduced speed.

**Properties of unbroken waves.**

To take another example: Every sailor knows that, when hove-to in a gale, his ship, if properly loaded and handled, will ordinarily ride over the monster seas like a duck; and it is clear that such could not be the case if each wave were hurled against the vessel as an independent and separate accumulation of water. But as soon as their free movement is interfered with by friction, no matter how produced, waves have a tendency to "top" and become vicious. For instance, on the edge of the Agulhas Bank, off the pitch of the Cape of Good Hope, it is well known that the seas generated by a W.N.W. gale are often opposed by a strong current setting right in the wind's eye. The result is a hollow, curling sea; and woe betide a deeply laden ship should she meet one of these ugly customers at an awkward moment.* A weather tide in a river is an example of the same thing on a very much smaller scale.

From the foregoing we learn that a wave proper has but a trifling effect in the horizontal transference of floating objects, which do little more than rise and fall on its surface; but the same wave, when transformed into a "breaker" by friction, will carry all before it.

**"Bores."**

The "Bores" peculiar to some rivers are produced in a manner very similar to "breakers." As the Tide wave advances up the river, it is continually checked underneath, not only by the

* Oil slowly dropped into the sea has a *wonderful* effect in preventing it breaking on board. It is common in some parts of England, before beaching a boat, to pull up and down for a few yards, pouring oil on the water, and then row in on the smooth. There have been several interesting articles on this subject in *Chambers's Journal*.

friction of the bottom, but by the resistance of the downward current. These causes operate to dam up the incoming tide, which is nevertheless pushed on by the ever-increasing volume of water behind, until it assumes a steep broken front, and constitutes one continuous breaker, having a long flat back. As the "bore" advances, it is sometimes hemmed in at the sides by a contracting channel, which forces it still more to rise above the ordinary level, since, if the form of the channel cannot accommodate the rush of water in one way, it must in another. In such a case it is not uncommon to see two or three smaller "bores" coming along on the back of the first.

This phenomenon occurs mostly in rivers situated at the head of delta-shaped estuaries, and where these open broadly to the direct course of the Tidal wave, the effect is necessarily more marked.

Chepstow, in the Bristol Channel; Mont St. Michael, in the Gulf of St. Malo; Dungeness Spit, near Cape Virgins; and the Basin of Mines, at the head of the Bay of Fundy,—are all places celebrated for a great Tidal Rise and Fall, which in extreme cases amounts at some of them to 70 feet and upwards.

**Tides in open ocean and inland seas.**

On the other hand, in the open ocean, where the Tide wave is untrammelled, the range is but four feet or so, and in inland seas it is almost insensible. For instance, among the islands of the Pacific Ocean the Rise and Fall varies from 3 to 6 feet, and in the Mediterranean the average Rise and Fall does not exceed 18 inches, though in places—Sphax for example—owing to local causes, the Rise and Fall is fully five feet.

Lakes and inland seas being comparatively small, the attraction of the sun and moon is nearly equal at both extremities, therefore their tides are insignificant. Close investigation backs up the theory that the magnitude of the tidal range depends upon the proportion the size of the lake or sea bears to the diameter of the earth: for instance, the existence of a tide in Lake Michigan has been proved by a series of observations made at Chicago in 1859. The average height of this tide is 1¾ inches; and the average time of H. W. is 30 minutes after the moon's transit. The length of Lake Michigan is 350 miles, or $\frac{1}{23}$ of the earth's diameter; and its tide is about $\frac{1}{23}$ of that which prevails in mid-ocean. Again, the length of the Mediterranean is 2,400 miles, or, roughly, $\frac{1}{3}$ the diameter of the earth, which gives the average height of its tide as $\frac{1}{3}$ what it is in the open sea, and this is confirmed by observation.

**Tide** ***current.***

The Tide Current, then, is caused by Tide waves from the ocean being concentrated and checked by local formation, also by the frictional resistance offered by the bottom and sides of a narrow channel. In passing through contracted spaces, these waves, as already stated, are heaped up and urged on by the continued pressure of the water behind, whose motion is less retarded than that of their own; and thus, in seeking to find its level, an actual current is created.

*Ocean currents.*

The *Tide* Current must not, however, be mixed up with the general *Ocean* Currents, which are progressive movements of the water, due partly to *prevailing winds*, and partly to *differences of temperature and density*, which, by disturbing the equilibrium, cause a constant circulation to be going on in the waters of the globe; and this, be it remembered, takes place in a vertical as well as a horizontal direction.

**Effect on tides of river improvements.**

It is difficult at first to realize that mere friction can play such an important part in connection with tidal currents, but unmistakeable evidence of this is given in a variety of ways. For example, of late years the Tyne has been improved by straightening some of the worst bends, and by dredging its bed. The result is that High Water now occurs at Newcastle some 20 minutes earlier than it did previous to these improvements, though the distance from Tynemouth to Newcastle is but 9 miles or so.

The Tide hour* has been accelerated at Glasgow by similar means, and also at London Bridge, but in a less degree.

**Offing and inshore tides.**

Again, most seamen—especially coasters—are aware that the stream of tide runs longer in the offing than close alongshore. Two causes operate in producing this effect. From the water being deeper in mid-channel, its momentum is proportionately less retarded by bottom friction; whilst the littoral current—affected in a much greater degree by bottom and side friction—has, moreover, to penetrate the bights and follow the bends of the coast. Reference to the accompanying co-tidal map of the British Islands will shew this feature very plainly: it will be noticed more especially in the English Channel, and in the contracted portion of the northern branch of the Irish Channel.†

**Co-tidal map.**

---

* More generally termed "Establishment of the Port."

† Lines connecting all those places which have high water at the same instant of *absolute* time are termed Co-tidal lines. They are useful as marking the progress of the Tide *wave* hour by hour, and are generally drawn for Greenwich Mean Time. They have no reference whatever to Tidal *current*. The map here shewn is taken from a pamphlet by the Rev. Samuel Haughton, M.A. Imray's "*Lights and Tides*" contains an excellent little Chart of the World, shewing the Co-tidal lines between 60°

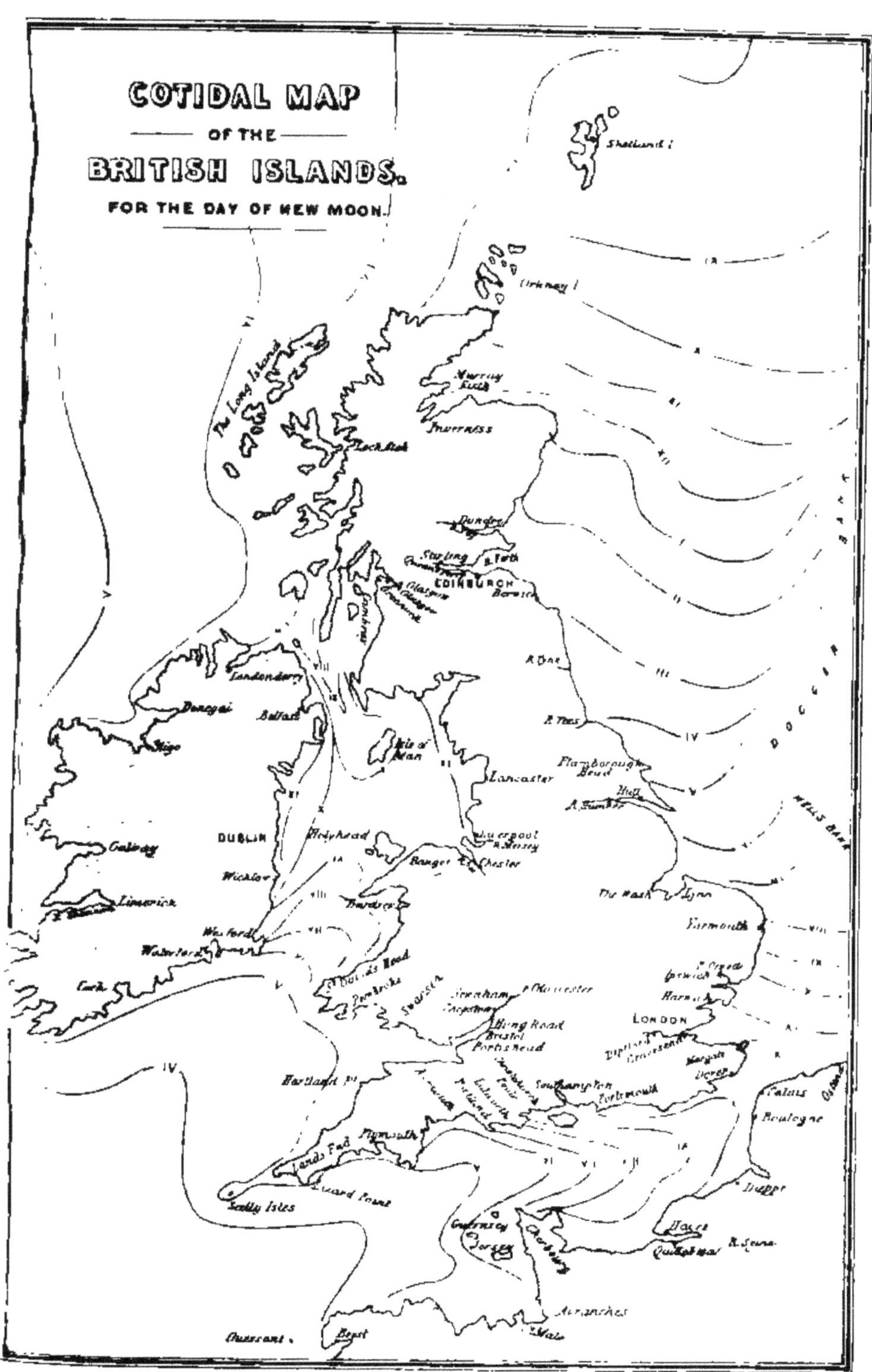
COTIDAL MAP
OF THE
BRITISH ISLANDS.
FOR THE DAY OF NEW MOON.
Shetland I.
Orkney I.
The Long Island
Murray Firth
Inverness
Dundee
Stirling
EDINBURGH
Berwick
Londonderry
Donegal
Belfast
Sligo
Isle of Man
Lancaster
R. Tees
Flamborough Head
Hull
R. Humber
DOGGER BANK
WELLS BANK
Galway
DUBLIN
Holyhead
Bangor
Chester
Wicklow
Limerick
Bardsey
Wexford
Waterford
Cork
St Davids Head
Pembroke
Swansea
Gloucester
Hung Road
Bristol
Portishead
The Wash
Lynn
Yarmouth
Harwich
LONDON
Gravesend
Southampton
Portsmouth
Calais
Boulogne
Hartland Pt
Plymouth
Lands End
Lizard Point
Scilly Isles
Dieppe
Havre
R. Seine
Guernsey
Jersey
Cherbourg
Avranches
Brest
Ouessant

To face Pag.

The Tide current sometimes continues to flow in the offing for three hours after it has turned by the shore, and is then termed "Tide and half tide;" and "Tide and quarter tide" when it only runs for $1\frac{1}{2}$ hours longer. Moreover, the time *at which the stream turns* is often different at different distances from the shore, *but the time of High Water is not necessarily different at these points.* This same peculiarity may be observed in a small way in the Mersey and other rivers, where, though the stream may still be running up in mid-river, it will be at a stand inshore, and the water-level will have fallen several inches at the pier-heads.

**Tide and Half Tide.**

A knowledge of this difference in the turn of the inshore and offshore streams is of great service, more particularly in working to windward, since by keeping close in at the commencement of the tide, and standing out mid-channel towards the last of it, it is possible to carry a favouring tide for nine hours. Indeed, in a smart vessel, *navigated by a man with good local knowledge,* the *flood* may be carried even longer; and in a steamer—from the fact of the turn of the tide in certain cases getting progressively later—the ebb may at times be cheated altogether.

**Carrying the Flood up Channel.**

For example:—Neglecting the odd minutes, it is High Water, Full and Change, at Queenstown at 5 o'clock, and at the Bar Lightship, Liverpool, at 11 o'clock. Now, if on such a day a 17-knot steamer were to leave Queenstown at noon, with the young flood or eastern tide, and round the Tuskar closely, she would carry the tide with her the whole way to the Lightship, a distance of about 226 miles. It should be stated, however, that between Roche's Point and the Coningbeg light-vessel the stream is weak, even at springs. Owing to a peculiarity, which will be alluded to further on, a ship passing through the Straits of Dover, bound to a port on the East Coast, and hitting the tide at the right time, will carry it for nearly twelve hours. The same thing can also happen in the George's Channel.

We now come to another very important phase in the phenomena of tides. It is of the greatest consequence to the navigator that he should not confound the *Rise* and *Fall* of the tide with the *Flow* and *Ebb*.

**Rise and Fall, as distinguished from Flow and Ebb.**

It is too generally supposed that at High Water the flood *current* ceases, and similarly, of course, that at Low Water the ebb

of North and South latitude. The same book has also a variety of other information very useful to the seaman, and is one of those recommended for the Captain's Nautical Library.

*current* ceases; in other words, that the *flood* stream only runs whilst the water is *rising*, and that the *ebb* stream only runs whilst the water is *falling*. Now this is not by any means a necessary consequence; and so far from its being even *generally* the case, such a condition is proved to be extremely rare, and then only to be found in small bays and harbours.

The supposed cessation of the Flood and Ebb streams at High and Low Water respectively, is unfortunately a very prevalent, but at the same time not unnatural, misconception, and has doubtless contributed to many a disaster.

Owing to the momentum of the water, which does not permit of its onward motion ceasing simultaneously with the exciting cause, and owing sometimes to *difference of level*, it is not uncommon to find the Flood run for three hours *after the water has commenced to fall;* and, similarly, the Ebb may continue running out for three hours *after the water has commenced to rise.** Thus, at the actual times of High and Low Water, the Flood and Ebb streams respectively, instead of being "slack," may, on the contrary, be running with their greatest velocity.

**Tides in narrow inlets.** This peculiarity is shewn in a very striking manner at the First Narrows, or eastern entrance to the Straits of Magellan, where it is due almost entirely to excessive difference of water level.

As already stated, in small harbours and bays slack current takes place at the "stand" of the tide at High and Low Water; but where the tide wave enters a narrow inlet, connecting with a great inland basin, the case is different. The basin being nearly tideless, has its surface lying at about the *mean sea level;* therefore, Flood currents can only commence to run in through the Narrows when the surface of the outside water has risen above that of the basin, and the maximum velocity must occur at High Water for the Flood, and at Low Water for the Ebb.

**Tides in Straits of Magellan.** This is precisely what happens in the Straits of Magellan—which, though not an inland sea in the strict sense of the term, nevertheless partakes sufficiently of the characteristics of one. Now, it so happens that, in the gourd-shaped arm of the sea adjoining the contracted cliffy channel forming the water com-

* Most people who have to do with the docking and undocking of vessels will have noticed, by tide-gauges or marks of some sort, how a river rises or "swells" long before the last of the Ebb stream, showing that the Tide *wave* may be going one way, when the *water* itself is actually going another.

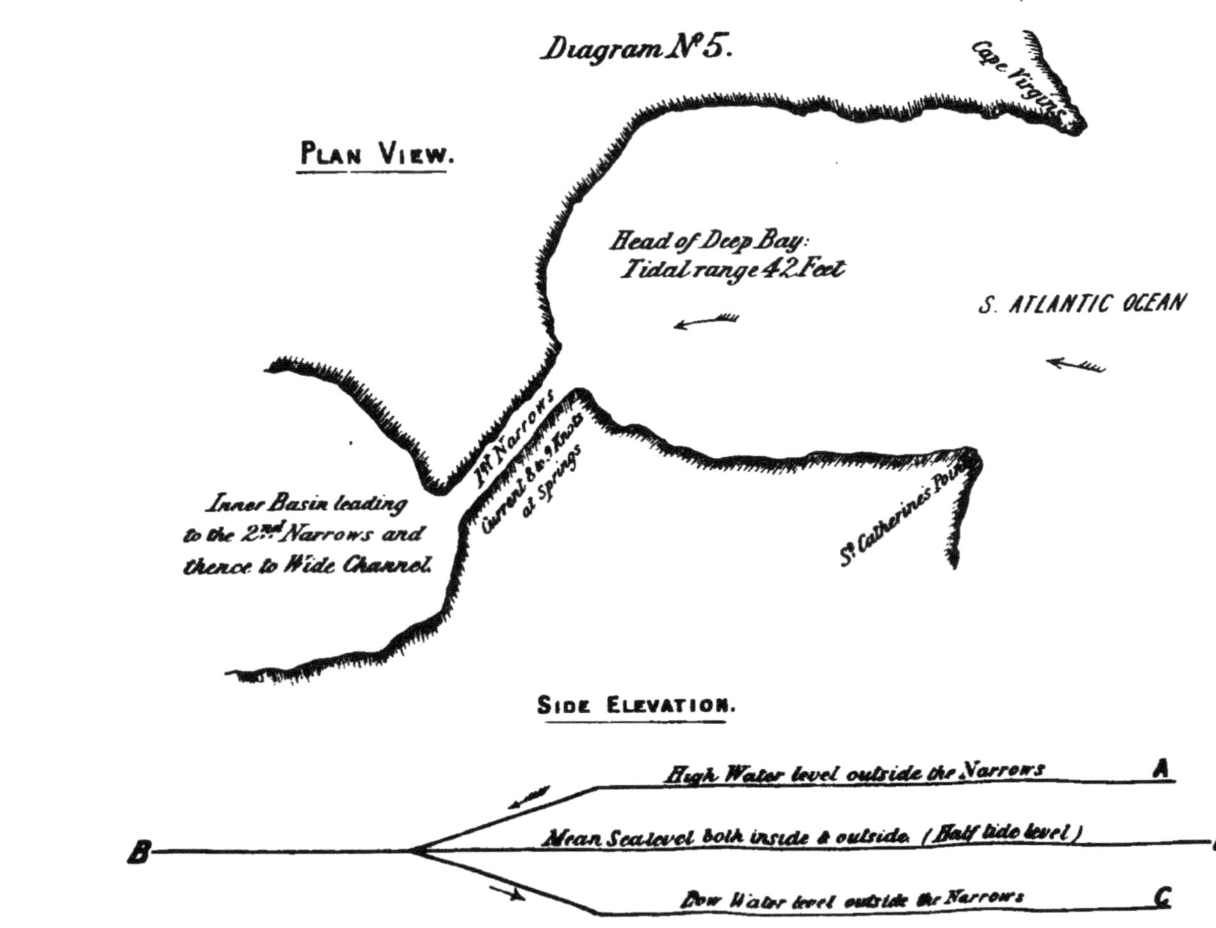
Diagram No. 5.
Plan View.
Cape Virgins
Head of Deep Bay:
Tidal range 42 Feet
S. Atlantic Ocean
1st Narrows
Current 8 to 9 Knots at Springs
St. Catherines Point
Inner Basin leading to the 2nd Narrows and thence to Wide Channel.
Side Elevation.
High Water level outside the Narrows
A
Mean Sealevel both inside & outside. (Half tide level)
B
B
Low Water level outside the Narrows
C

munication between the Straits and the South Atlantic, there is a Rise and Fall of 42 feet. This great tidal range is due to its shape, combined with the fact that it opens invitingly to the direct course of the tide-wave flowing in from the South Eastward. But, in the basin immediately within the Narrows, the range is only 22 feet, and further on it is much less; for, when a large water area has to be filled through a contracted opening, as in the present case, the inner tide suffers a gradual *degradation* as the water composing it spreads itself, and finally becomes nearly insensible; therefore it is that, after passing what is known as the Second Narrows, the Magellan tide virtually becomes spent, and the Rise and Fall insignificant: indeed, the latter would be even less were it not for the numerous water passages communicating with the Pacific Ocean, which act as feeders.

What has been here described as occurring *inside* the Narrows is just the reverse of what takes place *outside* the Narrows. In the latter case the tidal range is continually *augmented* as it proceeds up the estuary, till at or near the head it reaches its maximum.

The annexed diagrams are intended to illustrate the action of the tides at the Eastern entrance to Magellan Straits, and in them we have taken the liberty of supposing the basin on the left to have no Rise or Fall whatever; this is not consistent with the actual fact, but it simplifies the explanation without in any way detracting from the truth of the general principle referred to in the text. The upper diagram does not profess to be anything more than a *very rough* outline of the entrance to Magellan Strait, nor is it even drawn to scale. (See *Diagram No.* 5).

We will begin by supposing it high water outside the Narrows, as represented by the line *A*. The water will then commence to fall; but from its level being 21 feet higher than inside, the flood stream will continue to run in through the Narrows till both basin and estuary have arrived at the same level, which will not happen, however, for 3 hours, by which time it will be half Ebb. The ocean water which has passed through the Narrows cannot, however, do much to swell the inner tide, since its volume is but trifling as compared with the large area over which it has to spread itself. At 3 hours after high water, the surface level being then the same both inside and out, there is a *momentary* stand in the current, which, up till now, has been flowing in; but, as soon as the outside level drops sufficiently to cause an incline in the other direction, the stream will commence to rush *out*, and continue to do so till the common level is again restored, which will not be before half flood. As may well be imagined, the tide in the Narrows seethes like a boiling pot, and makes steady steering an impossibility.

**Popular idea as to Night Tides being higher than Day ones.**

Another popular but erroneous notion is, that the night tides are always higher than the day ones.

Pilots are very prone to this idea, and, without investigation of any kind, it is passed along from father to son as a sort of professional legacy. The *real facts* are as follows :—

In consequence of what is called the Diurnal (or daily) Inequality, it sometimes happens that the night tides are higher than the day tides for weeks together ; but if such be the case at one period of the year, the day tides are higher at another.

Prolonged and properly conducted observations prove conclusively that the height of the tide at a given place is influenced by the *Declination* of the moon ; for as the tide wave ever tries to place its highest point vertically under the body which produces it, when this vertical changes its point of incidence on the surface of our globe, the tide wave must tend to shift with it ; thus, when the moon's declination is 0°, the highest tides should occur along the Equator, and the heights should diminish thence towards the North and South ; but, other things remaining as before, the two consecutive tides at any place should have the same height. (See *Diagram No.* 6).

**Diurnal inequality.**

When the moon has north declination, as shown in the diagram, the highest tides on the side of the earth next the moon will be at places having a corresponding north latitude, as at *A* ; and on the opposite side of the earth from the moon, at those which have an equal south latitude, as at *C*. And of the two consecutive tides at any place, that which occurs when the moon is nearest the zenith should be the greater. Hence when the moon's declination is *North*, the height of the tide at a place in north latitude should be greater when the moon is *above* the horizon, as at *A*, than when she is below it, as at *B*. On the same day, places *South* of the equator have the highest tides when the moon is *below* their horizon, and the least when she is above it. A careful study of the diagram will make this apparent.

In continuation, let us suppose the moon to be "Full," and her declination 28° North. At midnight, therefore, she will be in the *zenith* of a place at *A*, in north latitude, and will produce a *high* night tide. At *D*, situated on exactly the same meridian, but in south latitude, the midnight tide occurring at the same absolute instant of time as the first-named will be a *poor* one, as the *moon's altitude there is low*. On the other side of the globe, the places *B* and *C* have high water at their *noon*, simultaneously with *A* and *D* at their *midnight;* but *C* being in the direct line of the moon's attraction, has much the higher tide of the two.

**Night tides not *always* the highest.**

From these considerations it is obvious that the Inferior or day tide at *C* must be greater than the Superior or night tide at *D*, which completely upsets the idea that "Night tides are *always* the highest."

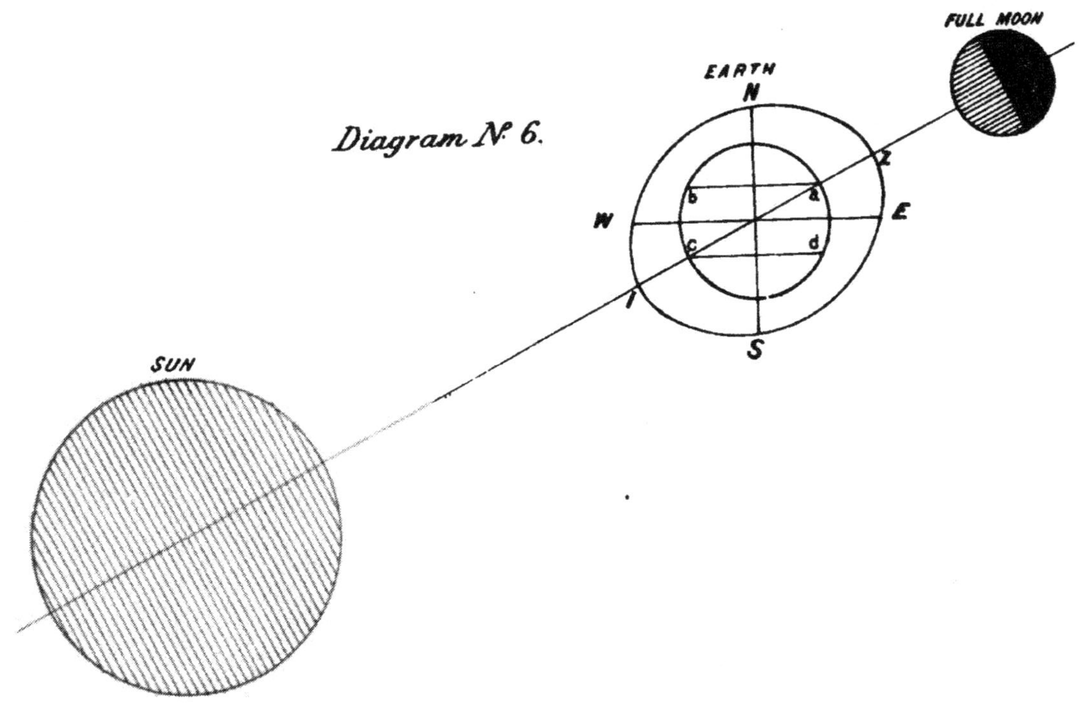


Diagram No. 6.

To face Pag

To go from theory to facts, take for instance what happens at Whampoa docks. In March the day and night tides rise to the same level. From April to October *the day tides are the higher*, and from November to February the lower. At San Francisco, a rock which has three and a half feet water upon it at one Low Water, may be awash at the next succeeding Low Water; but when the moon is on the Equator, the inequality at this port disappears, and the day and night tides become equal.

The Diurnal Inequality varies greatly in amount at different places, but it follows fixed laws at each, and may be predicted. It sometimes becomes so large that for several days there is only one tide in 24 hours: this latter phenomenon is very common on the S.E. coast of China, the coasts of California and Oregon, and in the Gulf of Mexico. On the coasts of Great Britain and Ireland the Diurnal Inequality is small.

**Enumeration of circumstances affecting tides.**

But apart from the irregularities just alluded to, there are other circumstances which also affect the height of the tide, and the times of High and Low Water. These depend upon a variety of things—such as the configuration of the coast, a meeting together of several channels, the direction of the wind, and the height of the barometer. Thus, at Liverpool, a S.W. gale both augments the tide and prolongs it, whilst a blow from the opposite quarter invariably retards and "cuts" it.

A rise or fall of an inch in the barometer is attended with a corresponding fall or rise in the tide, varying from six to sixteen inches, according to situation. At Liverpool it would be equal to twelve inches, which is nearly in the same ratio as the specific gravities of mercury and water.

As these two last influences cannot possibly be predicted in the Almanacs, the tabular times and heights are sometimes considerably in error.

**"Interferences."**

Then, again, there are what are termed "Interferences," whereby two distinct sets of tide waves, in their combination, produce apparent rest. These complications, when they occur, require most careful and lengthened investigation before they can be traced back to their true sources.

**Tidal peculiarity at Southampton.**

At Southampton there is a double High Water, the second occurring within two hours of the first. The fall in the interval does not amount to more than 9 inches, although the Rise and Fall between High and Low Water is 13 feet. The main features of this peculiarity are thus explained:—

The *inshore* eastern or flood stream runs past the Needles into the Solent, and makes High Water at Southampton in the orthodox manner. The tide then falls a little with the last of the stream; but when it turns to the westward inshore, a great body of water, favoured by the shape of the land, unites with the last of the *outside* eastern stream, still flowing round the south-eastern part of the island, and *both* run into the back of the Wight, by way of Spithead. Now, the outlet for it between Hurst Point and the Needles being much smaller than the eastern channel by which it entered, the returning water gets pent up, and, in consequence, there is a general rise in the Solent. At Calshot Castle the tide forks—one branch going out by the Needles, and the other flowing up Southampton Water, which lies open like a trap in the direct course of the main current, and so causes a *second* High Water. This is succeeded by a uniform but rapid fall, lasting about 3½ hours.

To the mariner the knowledge that the High Water at Southampton remains nearly stationary for rather more than two hours, may, in some cases, be important.

**Tidal peculiarity at Havre.**

At Havre, on the north coast of France, though the spring rise is 22 feet, the "stand" at High Water lasts one hour, with a rise and fall of 3 or 4 inches for another hour, and only rises and falls 13 inches for the space of three hours. This long period of nearly slack water is very valuable to the traffic of the port, and permits a larger number of vessels to enter or leave the docks on the same tides than would otherwise be the case.

The tides, then, are not all plain sailing, as might be supposed; and it would be almost impossible for any one man to make himself acquainted with the peculiarities of those on our own coasts alone, unless, indeed, he had no other employment.

**Standard Port of reference for English Channel tides.**

For the direction and rate of the tide in the Channel at any given time or place, the navigator must consult the Admiralty Sailing Directions and Tide Tables. In the latter, the English Channel and North Sea are divided into compartments, in which the Correct Magnetic direction and rate of the tidal streams is given *for every hour of the tide at Dover*. The tables for the Irish Sea are less elaborate, but they contain, nevertheless, much valuable information.

Although in these pages it would be impossible to enter into details, a few words may be said about the general rules which govern the main system of tides round about our shores.

Reference to the Co-tidal Map facing page 194 will shew that the tide wave coming in from the Atlantic splits on the west coast of Ireland. One part, going northward, sweeps round by Inishtrahul and the Giant's Causeway, and enters the George's Channel between Rathlin Island and the Mull of Cantyre; the other part, going to the southward round Cape Clear, enters the same channel between Tuskar and St. David's Head. These streams pursue their respective courses till they meet at the "Head of Tide," which is upon an imaginary line drawn from Dundrum Bay through the Isle of Man, towards Barrow-in-Furness. At the junction of the two tides occurs, as may be expected, the greatest rise and fall, amounting to 15 feet on the Irish side, and double that amount on the English.

**Direction taken by Tidal Wave round Great Britain and Ireland.**

**"Head of Tide" in Irish Channel.**

To the *westward* of the Isle of Man we find an "Interference." The two streams, flowing in exactly contrary directions, here destroy each other, so that no current is at any time perceptible, and the bottom of this region of still water is characterized by a deposit of fine blue mud.

To the *eastward* of the Isle of Man the tidal currents meet at an angle, and flow on together with increased vigour towards Morecambe Bay and Liverpool, making High Water at these places seven hours after its occurrence at their point of separation near the Skelligs.

Offshoots of this same parent tide wave enter the English Channel and German Ocean, the latter coming round "north about." These two tide waves bring High Water to the south and east coasts of England respectively, and also, like those in the Irish Channel, have a place of meeting, or "Head of Tide," which for *them* is found in the Straits of Dover.

**"Head of Tide" in English Channel.**

An investigation of the tidal streams of the Irish Sea, by the late Admiral W. F. Beechey, R.N., brings to light the important fact that, notwithstanding the variety of times of High Water throughout it, *the turn of the stream over all that part which may be called the fair navigable portion of the Channel, is nearly simultaneous.*

The northern and southern streams in both branches of the Channel commence and end *in all the fairway parts* at nearly the same time; and that time corresponds closely with the time of High and Low Water on the shore *at the entrance* of Liverpool and of Morecambe. So that it is necessary only to know the times of High and Low Water at either of these places, to determine the hour when the stream of either tide will commence or terminate in any part of the Channel, *outside the influence of the inshore eddies.* For this purpose the Liverpool Tide Tables may

**Standard Port of reference for Irish Channel tides.**

be used, subtracting 18 minutes from the times there given, in consequence of H.W. at George's Pierhead being that much later than the point which is considered the "Head of Tide."

Now, since it is low water at Queenstown at the same time that it is high water at Liverpool, it follows that, midway between the two there must be a place of comparatively little Rise and Fall; and this in the South channel is found to be on a line joining Courtown and Cardigan Bay, and in the North channel on a line joining Fairhead and the Mull of Cantyre. These are termed the "Nodal points," and here it is that the greatest body of water passes, and the tidal *currents* are strongest.

**"Nodal Points" for Irish Channel tides.**

There are similar effects produced in the English Channel. Careful experiments, systematically carried out by Admiral Beechey and Captain Bullock, R.N., prove that the *channel* streams meeting and separating in Dover Strait, set uniformly in a direction *towards* Dover whilst the water is *rising* at that place, and *away from it* when it is *falling*. To be governed by this law, a vessel must be either in that portion of the channel situated between Beachy Head and a line joining the Start with the Casquets, or between the North Foreland and a line joining the Texel with the Humber.

Off the mouth of the English Channel, *westward* of a line joining Ushant and Scilly, the stream will be found running to the *northward and eastward* while the water is *falling* at Dover, and to the *southward and westward* while it is *rising* at that port.

In the intermediate section included between a line joining Ushant and Scilly, and another joining the Start and the Casquets, there is a *mixed* tide, partaking of the joint directions of the tides east and west of it, which renders a written description impossible; and the Admiralty Tide Tables alone must be consulted for the direction and rate at any particular hour.

**"Nodal Points" for English Channel Tides.**

The nodal points of the two channel streams meeting in Dover Strait are respectively at Swanage and Yarmouth.

One or two other important and interesting features remain to be noticed. The Ebb stream of the Irish and English Channels constitutes the *Flood* of the Bristol Channel; and the Flood of the Irish and English Channels constitutes the *Ebb* of the Bristol Channel: so that, within a line joining Scilly and Tuskar, the tide will be found running eastward towards the Bristol Channel whilst the water is *falling* at Liverpool and Dover, and running out from the Bristol Channel whilst it is *rising* at those places.

**Comparison of English, Irish, and Bristol Channel Tides.**

On its northern side, the Bristol Channel flood sets to the South-eastward, and on its southern side to the North-eastward. It is handy to recollect, also, that when it is High Water at Liverpool and Dover, it is approximately Low Water at Cardiff and Queenstown.

A few pages back it was stated that a vessel navigating the English and Irish Channels might, if she were lucky, carry the tide with her for nearly 12 hours. To show how this could happen, it is necessary to recollect that, at the Head of Tide, the streams meet and separate thus:— **Carrying the Tide for 12 hours.**

*Dover Strait.*

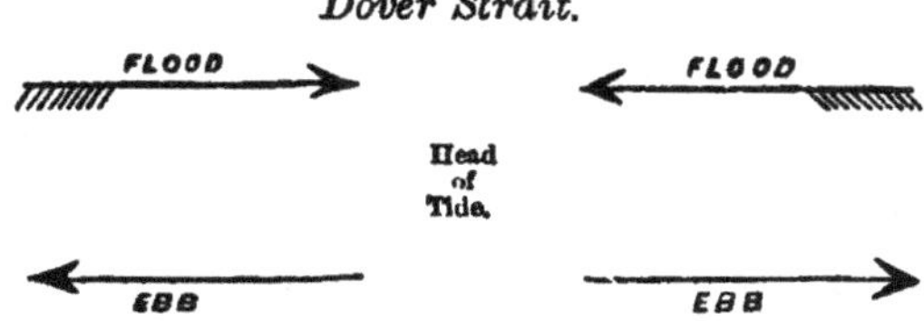


Consequently, if a vessel happens to reach the Head of Tide with the last of the Flood, she will forthwith run into the *opposite* Ebb stream just beginning at that point, and so continue with a favouring tide during the next 6 hours.

Such is a rough outline of the main features of the tides on our coasts; but, for the more detailed information necessary to the safety of a ship working up or down channel in dirty weather, the navigator is referred to the Admiralty publications already alluded to—from which sources the foregoing summary of channel tides has been chiefly compiled.

The Admiralty List* furnishes the Times and Heights of High Water for the morning and afternoon of *every day in the year*, at the 24 principal home ports, including Brest. Also, the depths over the various graving and wet dock sills: these are 223 in number, and comprise 22 ports in the United Kingdom. By aid of a Table of *Tidal Constants*, adapted to certain standard ports of reference, the approximate times and heights of high water *for every day in the year* can readily be found for 231 British, Irish, and European ports, extending as far as Heligoland on the north, and Gibraltar on the south. And, to finish up, the same valuable work gives the time of High Water *at Full and Change*, with the Rise at Springs and Neaps, for no fewer than 3,300 of the principal places on the globe. These last form two distinct **Particulars concerning Admiralty Tide List.**

* Published annually, price 1s. 6d.

tables—one being arranged alphabetically, and the other according to the apparent progress of the Tide Wave.

**Nautical Almanac Tide List.** In the *Nautical Almanac*, also, of each year, the daily *times* of High Water at London Bridge are given, as well as the "Tide Hour," Full, and Change, for 198 harbours and ports in the United Kingdom and adjacent countries.

**"Tide Hour."** The expression "Tide Hour," was first introduced by the late Lieutenant Raper, R.N., and was intended by him to supersede the more obscure phrase, "Establishment of the Port."

The tide-producing influences being the same for each, the time of High Water varies for different ports in the same vicinity, owing to the inertia of the water, and the obstruction it meets with from the configuration of the sea bed, and the narrowness, length, and direction of the channels along which the wave has to travel before reaching the port. It is obviously of great maritime importance to be able to find on any day the time of High Water for the various harbours and ports of the world, and to this end a *standard tide* is fixed upon, indicated by a particular relative position of the moon and sun, from which the time of every succeeding tide may in most cases be deduced. This standard is called the "Establishment of the Port," and is the time of High Water at Full and Change of the moon, *reckoned from Apparent noon;* or, in other words, it is the actual time of High Water after noon of the day upon which the moon, at its upper or lower culmination, passes the meridian at the same time as the sun. It may be roughly determined on the day of Full *or* Change, and is in this case distinguished as the "Vulgar Establishment of the Port."

**Establishment of the Port.**

***Vulgar* Establishment of the Port.**

It is found, however, that in general any particular tide is not due to the moon's transit immediately preceding, but to a transit which has occurred a considerable time before, and which is therefore said to *correspond* to it. This accounts for the highest tides not occurring at time of Full and Change, but from one to three days after. The corrected or "Mean Establishment of the Port" is the interval between the time of the moon's transit and the time of High Water on that particular day which *corresponds* to the day of Full or Change, and may differ considerably from the Vulgar Establishment. The Mean Establishment may be approximately determined by noting each day, for a fortnight, the interval between the moon's transit and succeeding High Water, and taking the mean of them. Those are termed *lunitidal intervals*, and the difference between the greatest and least is

***Correct* Establishment of the Port.**

termed the *semi-mensual*, or *semi-monthly inequality of Times*. This inequality, unfortunately, is not the same for each place; hence the time of High Water at any place cannot always be *accurately* deduced from that at any other place, by merely applying the difference of time between their Establishments.

**Semi-mensual inequality of *Times*.**

In like manner the *semi-mensual inequality of Heights* forbids the height of the tide at any one place being *correctly* inferred from the given height at any other.

**Semi-mensual inequality of *Heights*.**

Owing to this *semi-mensual inequality*, the time of High Water, *as deduced from the Vulgar Establishment*, is open to an error amounting in extreme cases to a couple of hours: it is therefore to be regretted that, from insufficient data, the Admiralty List does not give the Corrected Establishment for *every* port mentioned, nor indeed does it always specify which is which.

This, however, is a defect which, as our tidal knowledge of out-of-the-way places becomes more complete, will be more or less rectified each succeeding year. In the meantime, it may generally be accepted that the Tide Hour of *all* the Home Ports, and that of the *principal* ones abroad, is represented in the list by the Corrected Establishment.

Where the tides are pretty regular, which is mostly, though not always, the case round our own coasts, the table on next page may come in useful when it is required to know the depth of water over a rock, bar, or bank, at some particular hour of the tide.

If the Rise for the day is not exactly known, it may be inferred from the Spring and Neap Rise given on the chart. For instance, if the Mean Spring Rise at Devonport Dockyard is 15½ feet, and the Neap Rise 12 feet, one might fairly assume the Rise midway between Springs and Neaps to be about 13¾ feet.

**How to estimate Tidal Rise for the day.**

From this can be deduced the range for the day as follows:—

| | FT. | IN. | FT. | IN. |
|---|---|---|---|---|
| Mean Spring Range or Rise . . . . . . . . . . | 15 | 6 | | |
| Assumed Rise for the day . . . . . . . . . . . | 13 | 9 | 13 | 9 |
| Difference . . . . . . . . . . . . . . . . | 1 | 9 | 1 | 9 |
| Assumed Rise − Diff. = Mean Range for the day . . . . . . | | | 12 | 0 |

*The following Table shews the approximate height of the tide in feet and decimal parts, for any time before or after High Water, at intervals of twenty minutes:—*

**Table shewing the Depth of Water over the Plane of Reference at any given time of Tide.**

**The range for the day is to be sought for in either side column, and the required quantity will be found on the same horizontal line under the given time from High Water. The table is only suitable to such places as have regular tides.**

| Tidal Range for the day in feet. | TIME OF TIDE BEFORE OR AFTER HIGH WATER. | | | | | | | | | | | | | | | | | | | Tidal Range for the day in feet. |
|---|---|---|---|---|---|---|---|---|---|---|---|---|---|---|---|---|---|---|---|---|
| | 0h. | | | 1h. | | | 2h. | | | 3h. | | | 4h. | | | 5h. | | | 6h. | |
| | m. 0 | m. 20 | m. 40 | m. 0 | m. 20 | m. 40 | m. 0 | m. 20 | m. 40 | m. 0 | m. 20 | m. 40 | m. 0 | m. 20 | m. 40 | m. 0 | m. 20 | m. 40 | m. 0 | |
| 2 | 2.0 | 2.0 | 1.9 | 1.9 | 1.8 | 1.6 | 1.5 | 1.3 | 1.2 | 1.0 | 0.8 | 0.7 | 0.5 | 0.4 | 0.2 | 0.1 | 0.1 | 0.0 | 0 | 2 |
| 4 | 4.0 | 4.0 | 3.9 | 3.7 | 3.5 | 3.3 | 3.0 | 2.7 | 2.3 | 2.0 | 1.7 | 1.3 | 1.0 | 0.7 | 0.5 | 0.3 | 0.1 | 0.0 | 0 | 4 |
| 6 | 6.0 | 6.0 | 5.8 | 5.6 | 5.3 | 4.9 | 4.5 | 4.0 | 3.5 | 3.0 | 2.5 | 2.0 | 1.5 | 1.1 | 0.7 | 0.4 | 0.2 | 0.0 | 0 | 6 |
| 8 | 8.0 | 7.9 | 7.8 | 7.5 | 7.1 | 6.6 | 6.0 | 5.4 | 4.7 | 4.0 | 3.3 | 2.6 | 2.0 | 1.3 | 0.9 | 0.5 | 0.2 | 0.1 | 0 | 8 |
| 10 | 10.0 | 9.9 | 9.7 | 9.3 | 8.9 | 8.2 | 7.5 | 6.7 | 5.9 | 5.0 | 4.1 | 3.3 | 2.5 | 1.8 | 1.1 | 0.7 | 0.3 | 0.1 | 0 | 10 |
| 12 | 12.0 | 11.0 | 11.6 | 11.2 | 10.6 | 9.9 | 9.0 | 8.1 | 7.0 | 6.0 | 5.0 | 3.9 | 3.0 | 2.1 | 1.4 | 0.8 | 0.4 | 0.1 | 0 | 12 |
| 14 | 14.0 | 13.9 | 13.6 | 13.1 | 12.4 | 11.5 | 10.5 | 9.4 | 8.2 | 7.0 | 5.8 | 4.3 | 3.5 | 2.5 | 1.6 | 0.9 | 0.4 | 0.1 | 0 | 14 |
| 16 | 16.0 | 15.9 | 15.5 | 14.9 | 14.1 | 13.1 | 12.0 | 10.7 | 9.4 | 8.0 | 6.6 | 5.6 | 4.0 | 2.9 | 1.9 | 1.1 | 0.5 | 0.1 | 0 | 16 |
| 18 | 18.0 | 17.0 | 17.5 | 16.8 | 15.9 | 14.8 | 13.5 | 12.1 | 10.6 | 9.0 | 7.4 | 5.9 | 4.5 | 3.1 | 2.1 | 1.2 | 0.6 | 0.1 | 0 | 18 |
| 20 | 20.0 | 19.8 | 19.4 | 18.7 | 17.7 | 16.4 | 15.0 | 13.4 | 11.7 | 10.0 | 8.3 | 6.6 | 5.0 | 3.6 | 2.3 | 1.3 | 0.6 | 0.2 | 0 | 20 |
| 22 | 22.0 | 21.8 | 21.3 | 20.5 | 19.4 | 18.1 | 16.5 | 14.8 | 12.9 | 11.0 | 9.1 | 7.2 | 5.5 | 3.9 | 2.6 | 1.5 | 0.7 | 0.2 | 0 | 22 |
| 24 | 24.0 | 23.8 | 23.3 | 22.4 | 21.2 | 19.7 | 18.0 | 16.1 | 14.1 | 12.0 | 9.9 | 7.9 | 6.0 | 4.3 | 2.8 | 1.6 | 0.7 | 0.2 | 0 | 24 |
| 26 | 26.0 | 25.8 | 25.2 | 24.3 | 23.0 | 21.4 | 19.5 | 17.4 | 15.3 | 13.0 | 10.7 | 8.6 | 6.5 | 4.6 | 3.0 | 1.7 | 0.8 | 0.2 | 0 | 26 |
| 28 | 28.0 | 27.8 | 27.2 | 26.1 | 24.7 | 23.0 | 21.0 | 18.8 | 16.4 | 14.0 | 11.6 | 9.2 | 7.0 | 5.0 | 3.3 | 1.9 | 0.8 | 0.2 | 0 | 28 |
| 30 | 30.0 | 29.8 | 29.1 | 28.0 | 26.5 | 24.6 | 22.5 | 20.1 | 17.6 | 15.0 | 12.4 | 9.9 | 7.5 | 5.4 | 3.5 | 2.0 | 0.9 | 0.2 | 0 | 30 |
| 32 | 32.0 | 31.8 | 31.0 | 29.9 | 28.3 | 26.3 | 24.0 | 21.5 | 18.8 | 16.0 | 13.2 | 10.5 | 8.0 | 5.7 | 3.7 | 2.1 | 1.0 | 0.2 | 0 | 32 |
| 34 | 34.0 | 33.7 | 33.0 | 31.7 | 30.0 | 27.9 | 25.5 | 22.8 | 20.0 | 17.0 | 14.0 | 11.2 | 8.5 | 6.1 | 4.0 | 2.3 | 1.0 | 0.3 | 0 | 34 |
| 36 | 36.0 | 35.7 | 34.9 | 33.6 | 31.8 | 29.6 | 27.0 | 24.2 | 21.1 | 18.0 | 14.9 | 11.8 | 9.0 | 6.4 | 4.2 | 2.4 | 1.1 | 0.3 | 0 | 36 |
| 38 | 38.0 | 37.7 | 36.9 | 35.5 | 33.6 | 31.2 | 28.5 | 25.5 | 22.3 | 19.0 | 15.7 | 12.5 | 9.5 | 6.8 | 4.4 | 2.5 | 1.1 | 0.3 | 0 | 38 |
| 40 | 40.0 | 39.7 | 38.8 | 37.3 | 35.3 | 32.9 | 30.0 | 26.8 | 23.5 | 20.0 | 16.5 | 13.2 | 10.0 | 7.1 | 4.7 | 2.7 | 1.2 | 0.3 | 0 | 40 |
| 42 | 42.0 | 41.7 | 40.7 | 39.2 | 37.1 | 34.5 | 31.5 | 28.2 | 24.6 | 21.0 | 17.4 | 13.8 | 10.5 | 7.5 | 4.9 | 2.8 | 1.3 | 0.3 | 0 | 42 |
| 44 | 44.0 | 43.7 | 42.7 | 41.1 | 38.9 | 36.1 | 33.0 | 29.5 | 25.8 | 22.0 | 18.2 | 14.5 | 11.0 | 7.9 | 5.1 | 2.9 | 1.3 | 0.3 | 0 | 44 |
| 46 | 46.0 | 45.7 | 44.6 | 42.9 | 40.6 | 37.8 | 34.5 | 30.9 | 27.0 | 23.0 | 19.0 | 15.1 | 11.5 | 8.2 | 5.4 | 3.1 | 1.4 | 0.3 | 0 | 46 |
| 48 | 48.0 | 47.6 | 45.8 | 44.6 | 42.4 | 39.4 | 36.0 | 32.0 | 28.2 | 24.0 | 19.8 | 15.8 | 12.0 | 8.6 | 5.6 | 3.2 | 1.4 | 0.4 | 0 | 48 |
| 50 | 50.0 | 49.6 | 48.5 | 46.7 | 44.1 | 41.1 | 37.5 | 33.6 | 29.3 | 25.0 | 20.7 | 17.4 | 12.5 | 8.9 | 5.9 | 3.3 | 1.5 | 0.4 | 0 | 50 |

To see how the Table will compare with the one (B) in the Admiralty list, which is specially drawn up for use with the heights given in its own columns, we will create and work out an example or two by both methods.

**Example shewing how to find the Depth of Water over a rock at any given time of Tide.**

The Pollock Rock, in Hamoaze (Plymouth Sound), has 18 feet on it at Mean Low Water Ordinary Springs: What depth will there be over it on the 9th of December, 1881, at 2h. 10m. after High Water in the afternoon?

| | FT. | IN. |
|---|---|---|
| Entering the Table with 12 feet as the assumed Range for the day, and 2h. 10m. after H.W., we find by interpolation . . | 8 | 6½ |
| Depth on the rock at L.W.O.S. . . . . . . . . . . . . . | 18 | 00 |
| Diff. between M.S.R. and Rise for the day . . . . . . . . | 1 | 9 |
| Depth over the rock on December 9th, at 2h. 10m. after H.W. . . | 28 | 3½ |

*According to Admiralty Tables.*

| | FT. | IN. |
|---|---|---|
| Height of Tide above the mean level of L. W. O. S., by the Tables (page 90) December 9th, 1881 - - - - - - - - - - - - - - - - - | 13 | 9 |
| Half Mean Spring Range (given at foot of same column) - - - - - - - | 7 | 9 |
| Height of H. W. above half tide or mean level of the sea, *December 9th* - - - - | 6 | 0 |

| | FT. | IN. |
|---|---|---|
| Half Mean Spring Range - - - - - - - - - - - - - - - - | 7 | 9 |
| By Table (B) 6ft. 0in. and 2h. 10m. give - - - - - - - - - - - - | 2 | 6 |
| Depth on the Rock at L. W. O. S., as per chart - - - - - - - - - - - | 18 | 0 |
| Depth over the Rock on December 9th, at 2h. 10m. after H.W. - - - - - - | 28 | 3 |

In this example the difference is only half an inch, which is not worth talking about. Let us take another, where the datum line for soundings is the low water level of *Equinoctial Springs.*

**Example when the Plane of Reference is below the level of L. W. O. S.**

According to Admiralty Plan No. 2011, the Stag Rock in Holyhead Bay carries 13 feet over it at Low Water. The same plan contains a notice that "the soundings are reduced to an Equinoctial Spring Tide of 20 feet, which is about 2 feet lower than the Ordinary Low Water Springs." What depth will there be over the rock on the 10th December, 1881, at 1h. 40m. before H.W. in the afternoon? The plan gives the *Mean* Spring Rise as 16 feet, and the Neap Rise as 12½ feet; accordingly, the rise in Holyhead Bay on the day in question may be assumed as 14¼ feet above the level of Mean Low Water *Ordinary* Springs. This would give 12¼ feet as the range for the day.

| | FT. | IN. |
|---|---|---|
| Entering the Table with 12¼ feet as the assumed range for the day, and 1h. 40m. before H.W., we find - - - - - - - - - - - - - - - | 10 | 3 |
| Depth over the Rock at L.W., Equinoctial Springs - - - - - - - - - | 13 | 0 |
| *Equinoctial* Springs lower than *Ordinary* Springs - - - - - - - - - | 2 | 0 |
| Diff. between M. S. R. and rise for the day - - - - - - - - - - - | 1 | 9 |
| Depth over the Stag Rock on December 10th, at 1h. 40m. before H.W. - - - - | 27 | 0 |

*According to Admiralty Tables.*

| | FT. | IN. |
|---|---|---|
| Height of H.W. by the Tables (page 95) above the mean level of L.W. Ordinary Springs, December 10th, in the afternoon - - - - - - - - - - | 14 | 3 |
| Half Mean Spring Range - - - - - - - - - - - - - - - - | 8 | 0 |
| Height of H.W. above Half-tide or Mean Sea Level, December 10th - - - - | 6 | 3 |

| | FT. | IN. |
|---|---|---|
| Half Mean Spring Range - - - - - - - - - - - - - - - - | 8 | 0 |
| By Table *(B)*, 6ft. 3in. and 1h. 40m. give - - - - - - - - - - - | 3 | 11 |
| Depth over the rock at L.W. Equinoctial Springs, per chart - - - - - - | 13 | 0 |
| *Equinoctial* Springs lower than *Ordinary* Springs - - - - - - - - | 2 | 0 |
| Depth over the Stag Rock on December 10th, at 1h. 40m. before H W. - - - - | 26 | 11 |

What will be the depth over the Stag Rock at Mean Low Water Ordinary Springs, Mean Low Water Ordinary Neaps, and Low Water of Equinoctial Springs? The plan gives the neap range as 9 feet. Work these out by way of practice, and if you do it correctly the answers will be,—

| | FT. | IN. |
|---|---|---|
| Depth over the Stag Rock at Mean Low Water, Ordinary Neaps | 18 | 6 |
| " " " " " " Springs | 15 | 0 |
| " " " " Equinoctial " | 13 | 0 |

**Tidal Diagram shewing how the Table is constructed.**

The following diagram shews the graphic method by which the preceding Tidal Table is constructed. It is given here in preference to the method by calculation, which last is not nearly so instructive.

To construct the diagram in the first instance. Draw a vertical line as a Tide Gauge to represent the given Rise, say 50 feet.

For the sake of accuracy, choose a fairly large scale for your diagram: $\frac{1}{10}$ of an inch equal to a foot, is a very convenient size. If you should adopt this scale, the vertical line will be exactly 5 inches high, since 5 tens are 50. With an ordinary boxwood or ivory plotting scale, marked decimally, divide the Tide Gauge into feet, working from the bottom upwards. Then from the 25 feet mark as a centre, describe a circle, with a radius of 2½ inches. Divide the right and left hand semicircles, each into 18 equal parts, by stepping round them with a pair of dividers. These 18 parts will represent *hours* and *thirds* of an hour between High and Low water, the duration of a tide being taken in round numbers as 6 hours, which in practice is sufficient. Name them as shewn in the diagram.

Connect similar intervals on each side by parallel horizontal lines: where these lines cut the Tide Gauge will be found the height corresponding to the time of high water. For instance, the line indicating 4h. 20m. before or after high water, cuts the Gauge at 8·9 feet, which accordingly would be the depth above your plane of reference (Mean Low Water Ordinary Springs) at that time of Tide.

This particular circle only shews the tabular values for a Rise of 50 feet. To fill up the remainder of the Table, a circle must be drawn for each Rise given in the side column.

In the diagram here given, the lines outside of the circle—above, below, and to the left—have nothing whatever to do with the construction of the Table. They are merely introduced to assist the Admiralty diagram on page 186 in explaining the

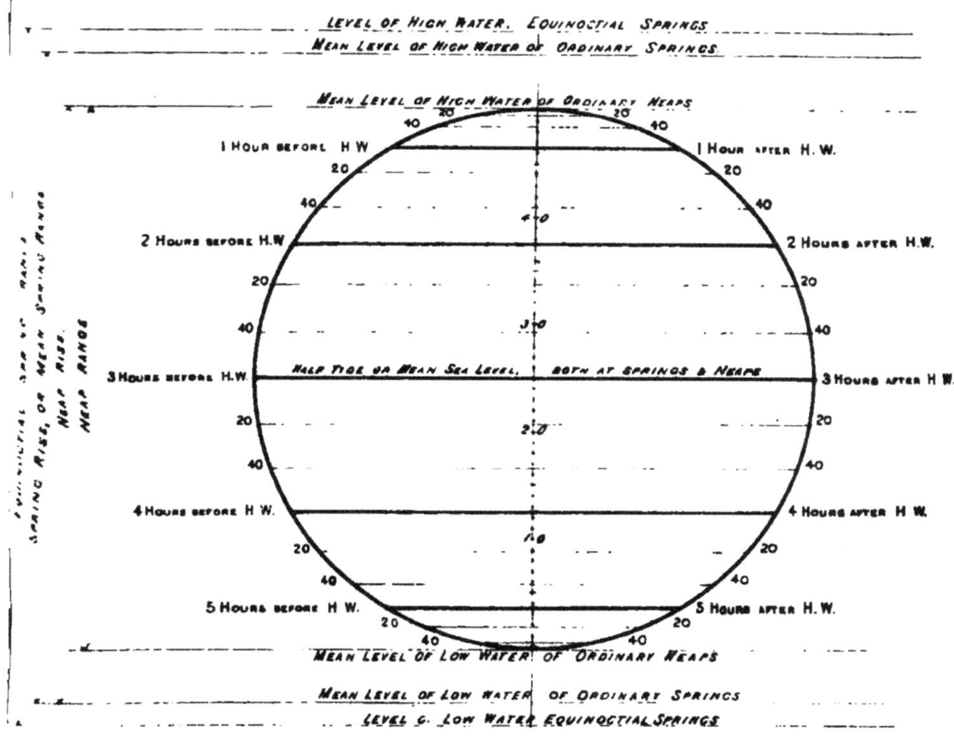


Spring Range 60 Feet. Neap Range 50 Feet. Equinoctial Spring Range 64 Feet.

Scale, ⅛ of an Inch = 1 Foot.

To face Page 208.

meaning of the various terms employed in connection with the Height, and Rise and Fall of the Tide.

**Influence of tides in retarding the rotatory motion of the earth.**

In a foot-note to page 252, some slight reference is made to the frictional effect of the tides in retarding the rotatory motion of the earth. The writer thinks that, by way of a fit conclusion to this chapter, he cannot do better than quote Professor P. G. Tait on this interesting subject.* Speaking of Sir William Thomson's reasoning as to the probable age of the earth, he goes on to say:—

"The second of these arguments of Sir William Thomson depends upon the tidal retardation. In my first lecture I mentioned to you that there was such an effect, and that it had been actually observed by astronomers in a very peculiar way; because, on calculating back from the known present motion of the moon, it was found that there must be some unrecognised peculiarity in that motion which had not been deduced by calculations founded upon gravitation, either as attraction or as disturbance. The moon, in fact, seems to have been moving quicker as time has gone on, since the eclipses of the fifth and eighth centuries before our era. The only way, as Laplace put it, in which it could be accounted for in his time, was by what he called 'secular acceleration of the moon's mean motion.' In other words, the average angular velocity with which the moon moves round the earth appears to have been increasing for the last 2,000 years or more. He shewed that there was a mode of accounting for this by planetary disturbance of the earth's orbit; and, as calculated by him, this explanation seemed to account for exactly the amount of acceleration which was observed in the moon's motion. Using his formulæ, and the numbers calculated from them, and working back to those old days, we find we arrive at almost the circumstances of those eclipses, as described by historians.

"Fortunately, Adams, a few years ago, revised Laplace's investigation, and found that he had neglected a portion of the necessary terms, and that the explanation given by Laplace, when properly corrected, accounted for only one-half of the phenomena observed; so that there still remained one-half of the quantity to be accounted for. This could not be accounted for by the disturbance of other bodies attracting the moon. Why, then, does the moon appear, every revolution, to be moving faster and faster round

---

* See page 170, *et sequitur*, of *Recent Advances in Physical Science*. By P. G. Tait. Macmillan & Co.

the earth? Well, the only way in which we can explain it, after we have made every possible allowance for effects of disturbance by other planets, is simply to enquire—Does our measure of time continue the same?

"We measure the time of the moon's revolution in terms of hours, minutes, and seconds; but these hours, minutes, and seconds are measured for us not by our clocks, as you may at first think. We set our clocks by the earth's rotation, and, therefore, it is in terms of the earth's rotation that we measure the time of the moon's revolution round the earth. So that the moon will appear to be moving quicker round the earth, even supposing her orbit be altogether undisturbed, if the earth itself, which is furnishing the unit of time in which her revolution is to be measured, is rotating slower and slower from age to age.

**Newton's first law of motion.**

"Then comes the question, Is there a cause which tends to slacken the earth's rotation? Newton laid it down, in his first law of motion, that motion unresisted remains uniform for ever; and referred to the earth as a particular instance, where there is nothing in the attraction of the sun or moon, or the disturbance caused by any of the other planets, affecting the rate of its rotation about its axis.

"But it was left to Kant, first of all, to point out, and even to approximate in amount to, a resistance to the earth's rotation, due to the tide-wave; and to shew that the earth—because the tide-wave is lifted up towards the moon, and on the opposite side from the moon—has constantly to rotate inside what is practically a friction-brake. The water is held back by the attraction of the sun and moon, and the earth has to move inside this shell of water. There is, therefore, a source of constant friction, and friction, of course, constantly produces development of heat. The heat must be accounted for by some energy transformed, and what is here transformed is part of the energy of the earth's rotation about its axis. So long as tides go on, there will therefore be constantly a retardation of the rate of the earth's rotation.

"Now, let us see when this relaxation of the earth's rotation would cease. Obviously this would be at the instant when the earth at last ceased to rotate within the tide-wave; in other words, when the tide-wave rotates along with the earth—when it is always full tide at one and the same portion of the earth's surface—the tide-wave being fixed (as it were) upon the earth's surface. But the tide-wave is always, approximately at least, directed towards the moon, so this part of the surface where the tide-wave is fixed for ever must be constantly turned towards the moon. In other words—if there were no sun-producing tides, but the moon only, the final effect of the tides, in stopping or quenching the earth's rotation, would be to bring the earth constantly to turn the same portion of its surface towards the moon, and therefore to rotate about its axis in the same period as that in which the moon revolves about it. This most remarkable ultimate effect we see already produced in the moon,—it is precisely the same thing,—we see the moon turning almost exactly the same portion of its surface to the earth at all times. The little deviation we see occasionally is precisely accounted for by the fact that the moon's orbit is not exactly a circle, and therefore the moon does not move in it with the same rapidity when it is nearest the earth as it does when it is furthest away from the earth. We are thus, as it were, enabled occasionally to see a little round the corner. The moon is now rotating precisely in the way in which the earth will in time rotate, when as much as possible of its energy of rotation is used up in producing heat by tidal friction. And that the moon should already have come into this state so long before the earth has arrived at it, need not surprise us. The moon's seas (when she had them) were of molten lava,—far more viscous than water; and the tide-raising force on her surface depended on the mass of the earth, some *eighty* times greater than that of the moon, which is the main agent in our comparatively puny tides.

**Moon turns but once on its axis whilst making a single revolution round the earth.**

"It being thus established that the rate of rotation of the earth is constantly becoming slower, the question comes: How long ago must it have solidified in order that it might have the particular amount of polar flattening which it shews at present? Suppose, for instance, that it had not consolidated less than a thousand million years ago. Calculation shews us that at that time, on the most moderate computation, it must have been rotating at least twice as fast as it is now rotating. That is to say, the day must have been 12 hours long instead of 24. Now, if that had been the case, and the earth still fluid without, or even pasty, that double rate of rotation would have produced four times as great centrifugal force at the equator as at present, and the flattening of the earth at the poles and the bulging at the equator would both have been much greater than we find them to be.

**Deduction as to age of the earth.**

"We say, then, that because the earth is so little flattened, it must have been rotating at very nearly the same rate as it is now rotating when it became solid. Therefore, as its rate of rotation is undoubtedly becoming slower and slower, it cannot have been many millions of years back when it became solid, else it would have solidified into something very much flatter than we find it. That argument, taken along with the first one, probably reduces the possible period which can be allowed to geologists to something less than ten millions of years."

The foregoing is certainly very wonderful, and philosophers may be correct in their surmises as to the age of the world, but *who* shall say how far distant is the end.

---

## CHAPTER XVII.

### FOG AND FLOATING ICE.

It has been scientifically demonstrated that the air is capable of taking up a certain amount of moisture, and of retaining it suspended in a perfectly invisible gaseous state. As a matter of fact, the ordinary atmospheric air we breathe contains at all times more or less water so suspended. The higher the temperature of the air, the greater its capacity for the retention of water in this invisible form. **Retention of moisture in air.**

Steam, which is nothing more than water at a high temperature, and in a gaseous state, is quite invisible so long as it remains as such; but the moment it comes into contact with anything cold, it gets more or less condensed, and shews itself as a white vapour, to which Dr. Tyndall has given the suggestive name of *water-dust.* **Steam—what it is.**

This fact is strikingly illustrated by a working model of an engine and boiler, both made of glass, in which, although the water is seen to boil, *no steam is visible,* and the engine moves apparently without cause. After passing through various parts, the steam finally enters the condenser, where it is at once chilled and rendered visible by a jet of cold water. **Glass model of engine and boiler.**

When air, whatever may be its temperature, is fully saturated with water, and will hold no more, it is said to be at the "Dew-point." Now, this point being reached, if the temperature be lowered in any way, the moisture loses its aëriform character, and is condensed into white vapour, termed cloud when high in the heavens, and mist or fog when near the earth's surface. **"Dew-point."**

The sea is the great *distillery* or place from which water is drawn up invisibly, in its purest state, into the air; and this is chiefly the case in the seas of the tropics, because there the sun shines with most power all the year round, sending a constant succession of heat-waves to shake the water-particles asunder. It has been found by experiment that, in order to turn 1 lb. of water into vapour, as much heat must be used as is required to melt 5 lbs. of iron; and if one considers for a moment how difficult iron is to melt, and how an iron poker can be kept in the fire and yet remain solid, it helps to realize how much heat the sun must pour down in order to carry off such a continuous supply of vapour as that which afterwards appears to us as rain, cloud, or fog.

This latter result, so very embarrassing at sea, is produced in a variety of ways, and not infrequently—strange though it may appear at first thought—by quite opposite conditions, which, however, it will be seen are obedient to the same law. Thus, when warm air saturated to the "Dew-point" passes over cold water, the temperature of the air is reduced, its moisture is condensed, and fog is the consequence. On the other hand, when a cold wind blows over relatively warm water, the invisible vapour rising from the water is chilled, with precisely the same result. We have a familiar example of this latter mode of fog production each time we take a hot bath, and may notice how, in cold weather, much more vapour *appears* to rise from the water. When a deep ocean current is opposed by a shoal—such, for example, as the Banks of Newfoundland—the cold water from below is driven to the surface; and should it happen to be under the "Dew-point" of the air, fog is the inevitable result.

**Fog—how produced.**

Another cause of fog is the interlacing of currents of greatly varying temperatures, such as are often to be met with in the Gulf Stream. Lastly, it must be borne in mind that a bank of fog may be drifted by the wind to a considerable distance from where it was originated, and encountered by the mariner at a spot where there is little or no difference between the temperatures of the air and surface water; but such fogs rarely last long.

**Drift fog.**

Much has been done by various maritime governments to modify the difficulties which fog presents to navigation. There are others, however, which can only be overcome by great vigilance on the part of the mariner himself. Some fogs—probably when the water is colder than the air—have a tendency to lie in a thin stratum, which extends but 30 or 40 feet above the surface. In such cases it is quite possible to see over it by ascending to the masthead, from which position we may discern land, icebergs, or

**Low lying fog.**

the masts of other vessels, when they are quite concealed to those on deck. Attention should therefore be paid to this point when sailing in fog. On the other hand, there are fogs which do not assume any great density until they have attained several feet of elevation; in which case, of course, it is advisable to get as low down as possible, when objects near the surface, such as rocks and hulls of vessels, may be made out at a distance of half a mile or more.

**Fog-beset coasts—how navigated.** Some coasts are particularly exposed at certain seasons of the year to visitations of fog. This is markedly the case along the coasts of Chili and Peru. But where the water is very deep close up to the shore, and, consequently, the lead next to useless, there are frequently high cliffs, and the coasting captains running between ports only a short distance apart, have no hesitation in cautiously approaching them at very slow speed, knowing that with a good look-out either the roar of the surf, the "booming" of the waves against the cliffs, or the echo of the steam-whistle will be heard in sufficient time to warn of danger. Indeed, sometimes, after groping carefully along, it is only by the cessation of sound shewing a break in the coast-line, that it is known that the vessel has reached the entrance of the port. Of course such things were only done in small paddle boats, by men who, so to speak, knew every foot of the coast, and were well acquainted with the speed of the vessels they commanded.

**Signs indicative of approach to weather shore.** The approach to the eastern coast of Patagonia, which is a weather shore, is frequently notified by the strong smell of the wood and turf fires kindled by the natives. Although in *this* instance the lead *is* a reliable guide, owing to the moderate depth and gradual shoaling of the water, *which also gets smoother under the lee of the land;* in like manner, during a hazy night, the writer on one occasion was apprised of his near approach to an island of the Cape Verde group (Santa Lucia) by the Trade wind coming down to him richly laden with the scent of the orange groves. The setting in or cessation of a ground swell, or a change in the colour of the water, will sometimes notify as to whether the ship is on or off soundings.

All these are indications which the navigator with his senses about him will be fully alive to; while a dull man will let them go by unnoticed, and possibly come to grief in consequence.

**Coasting rule for thick weather.** In the home coasting trade the rule is—"See everything as you pass it;" and this is clearly the right thing to do when the weather is not so thick as to prevent objects being made out in ample time to avoid them, and when the nature of the shore admits of its being made free with, as it is dangerous to *play* with edge-tools. Take care, however, that a *really* good look-out is kept, *and the lead never out of hand*. By obeying this old-fashioned rule, the navigator is able to verify his reckoning from time to time, and get a fresh departure—a matter of no small value where tides run strongly, and it is important to gain a port at a certain time. Should this be neglected in narrow waters, and the fog shut down for a "full due," it is more than probable, in seeking to give danger a wide berth on one side, you will run into it on the other.

When thick fog has lasted some little time in a channel beset with shoals and swift-running tides of great range—such, for example, as the Bristol Channel—the best of navigators is apt to lose the run of his position. In such cases the wisest plan is to *anchor* while there is plenty of water under the vessel's keel. It is sure to clear up before it comes on to blow with any force.

**Advisability of anchoring in fog.**

At any other time of anchoring than Low Water, *do not forget to allow for the fall of the tide*. In the eastern entrance of Magellan Strait, for example, where the rise and fall is 46 feet, and in the Bay of Fundy, where it is yet greater, it would not do to bring up at high water in less than eleven or twelve fathoms.

Southern-going vessels bound down channel, with a fair wind, will gain little or nothing by hugging the shore in thick weather. All *they* require is to shape a *mid-channel* course, keep the lead going, and get out to sea as soon as possible. Again, there is no excuse for a man who gets his ship ashore by running close alongside a nearly straight coast for hundreds of miles without being required to call at any port, and with open water all the time on the other side of him. It is necessary to discriminate in these matters. What is proper and necessary in the one case, may be a foolhardy risk in another.

**High speed in fog unjustifiable.**

A high rate of speed in a fog cannot be justified by any process of reasoning whatsoever. Attempts have often been made to do it; but none of the arguments brought forward will hold water: and he who runs blindly on at such times, especially when near land, and trusting solely to that "stupid old pilot" Dead-Reckoning, is culpable in the highest degree. With proper precautions and slow speed, vessels can be navigated in a fog with a close approximation to absolute safety, so far as the risk of getting on shore is concerned; but there will always be the danger of collision with another vessel, which is even more to be feared.

Within the past few years, many of the more prominent headlands and turning-points have been marked by the establishment of fog signals, such as guns, steam-trumpets, or sirens, and explosive rockets; while less important shoals have been indicated by automatic signal buoys, set in operation by the action of the waves. All these are of the greatest possible service. **Fog signals—various kinds of.**

On one occasion the writer left Liverpool in a dense fog, being guided to the Crosby and Bar lightships by the steam trumpets with which these vessels are fitted. The Skerries were rounded at a distance of three miles in the same manner, the blast of the steam trumpet being audible at double that distance; and when off Holyhead, the reflection of the flash of the fog-gun was distinctly and repeatedly seen in the sky at an elevation of about 30°; this permitted its bearing to be taken, and by listening for the report, and counting by chronometer the number of seconds (twenty) which elapsed, the ship's position was fixed equally as well as cross-bearings could have done it in clear weather. For such observations it is sufficiently correct to allow 5 sec. per mile as the velocity of sound. Of course the lead was kept going unremittingly, and when the depth rendered the hand-lead useless, even more accurate casts were obtained with Sir William Thomson's invaluable sounding-machine.* **Example of fog navigation.**

Allied to fog is the question of danger from ice. It is a popular delusion among passengers on board ship, that by taking the temperature of the water at short intervals, the approach to ice is unfailingly indicated. Unfortunately, such is by no means the fact, and it is time the idea was exploded. More than ordinarily cold water merely shews that the ship is in a part of the ocean where ice may possibly be encountered, and not that it is actually present. **Approach to ice not indicated by water temperature.**

The well-known Labrador Current, for example, is a cold stream flowing from Polar regions, and carrying with it, during spring and summer, enormous quantities of field-ice and bergs, which come down from Davis Strait. It is not the extra-polar ice, however, which causes the cold current, although it is the cold current which brings down the ice; consequently, the experienced navigators of the North Atlantic know full well when the water

---

* From recent investigations it appears that while the mariner may usually expect to hear the sound of the fog-signal normally as to force and place, he should be prepared for occasional aberrations in audition. When approaching a fog-signal from to-windward he should go aloft; and when approaching it from to-leeward the nearer he can get to the surface of the water the sooner he will hear the sound.

temperature falls to the eastward of the Banks, that it is necessary to be on guard against the possibility or probability of meeting ice, according to the time of year.

By kind permission, and on the unexceptional authority of Captains Ballantine, Dutton, and Smith, of the Allan Mail Steamship Line, all men of high standing in the profession, and well acquainted with ice navigation, it is here stated that no appreciable difference in the temperature of the water is caused by the proximity of even the largest icebergs; and when one considers what a poor conductor of heat water is, their statement can be well believed.

**Law of convection.** In conformity with what is known as the law of convection, water will transmit heat readily enough in a *vertical* direction. Thus when the liquid in the bottom of a vessel is warmed by fire, it becomes specifically *lighter*, and accordingly *rises* and makes room for the colder surface water to flow down and fill its place; this cold water gets heated in turn, and so continually ascending and descending *currents* are created, until the temperature of every part alike is raised to the boiling point. **Propagation of heat in a lateral direction.** The propagation of heat in a *lateral* direction does not take place in this manner at all. Heat spreads sideways in water by *conduction* alone, a process which involves no transference of the particles, and is very slow indeed as compared with the other.

For example, the axis of the Gulf Stream in some parts is made up of bands of warm water which alternate with cold ones, but, although running side by side, they do not commingle Further, the separation between the deep blue waters of the Gulf Stream and the cold counter-current which runs down in-shore, is often so well defined, that a ship may be sailing in both at the same moment. From its being so steep-sided, the inner current, at line of meeting with the Gulf Stream, has received the name **"Cold wall."** of "Cold Wall," and has been known to differ 30° in temperature from the one running close alongside it.

On the other hand, if the Arctic Current points to a region where ice may be expected, it by no means follows that it will not be encountered in the Gulf Stream, as bergs have been passed not only *in* the stream, but actually to the southward of it, having been carried there by the *lower* ocean currents. The possibility of this will be recognised when it is stated as a matter of certainty **Icebergs—submersion of** that icebergs are seldom submerged to a less extent than ⅞ of their whole mass, and oftentimes much more. Thus one 15 fathoms high would ordinarily ground in 100 fathoms of water. This measurement is readily derived from the relative specific gravities of fresh and salt water, and the fact that the volume of water is increased 10 per cent. when freezing. With the Barometer at 30 in. and Fahrenheit's Thermometer at 60°, a cubic foot of sea water weighs 64·18 lbs., a cubic foot of fresh water 62·50 lbs., and a cubic foot of ice 58·08 lbs.

Temperature is an important element in this calculation, as it causes the density both of water and ice to vary considerably: thus the *specific gravity* of fresh water is greatest at from 39° to 40° Fahr., and ice reaches its maximum *volume* at 24° Fahr., *below which it contracts.* It is capable of proof that, from this cause, ice at 16° Fahr. *will sink* in water of 50° Fahr.*

The same phenomena take place with other substances; for instance, solid cast-iron will float when put into molten cast-iron at a comparatively low temperature; but if the molten cast-iron is at a white heat, the solid iron will sink.

To revert to the thermometer as a means of detecting the presence of ice by a fall in the water. In a letter to the author Sir William Thomson says:—

"The conducting power of water is so small, that there would be absolutely no cooling effect by conduction to a distance from an iceberg, but there might be a considerable effect by the cold and light fresh water running down from the iceberg, and spreading far and wide over the surface of the sea." **Sir W. Thomson on conducting power of water.**

This seems a reasonable supposition, but it is more than likely that the film of cold fresh water would be broken up by the agitation of the wind and waves, and, in any case, disturbed and turned over by the plough-like action of a vessel's bow going at speed.

Again, it is well known that, about the Banks, the Labrador Current is *sometimes* colder when no ice is to be seen, than it is when the contrary is the case. In winter it even falls to 30° Fahr.† Large icebergs have been actually passed at a distance of

* Sea water differs from fresh water in that it continues to increase in density as the temperature is lowered, till freezing takes place.

† In a letter to the writer on the same subject, Captain H. Toynbee, F.R.A.S., Superintendent of the Meteorological Office, says:—"As to your question whether the thermometer indicates the neighbourhood of icebergs? I fancy it depends upon whether the ship passes through water which has been lately in contact with the iceberg or not. For instance, running before the wind and approaching an iceberg ahead, you might expect the water to get colder as you closed with it, and got into its wake; but I think in other cases it would not be safe to trust to the temperature of

any time on a *clear* night—especially if the moon be up—in obtaining all he may want in the way of reliable sights.*

Youngsters frequently display no little aptitude in becoming acquainted with the stars and planets. This should always be encouraged, and once fairly entered on the subject, they will find the study of the heavens a most absorbing as well as profitable occupation during the long hours of the night watches. A material help to the practical part will be found in the Planisphere published by Mrs. Janet Taylor, which is one of the best of its kind.

**Mrs. Janet Taylor's Planisphere.**

In learning to recognise these bodies, it is just as well to throw on one side as useless—indeed, as misleading—the absurdly grotesque names of the constellations given to them by the ancients. It is much better to engraft them on the memory by aid of the less fanciful figures, such as squares, triangles, &c., which form leading marks to the principal navigational stars, of which there are some fifty-five or sixty.

There is no part of our entire subject which the author is more anxious to press upon the attention of the navigator than this matter of star observation.

No reason exists why every man in command should not be thoroughly proficient at it. It is within the reach of all who choose to try: there are, however, men afloat who *won't* try, and who for downright, double-barrelled, copper-bottomed, bevel-edged bigotry are matchless in all other professions. For such as these this book is not written, as they are hopeless cases, whose pig-headed obstinacy is only equalled by their ignorance. Happily the class will soon become extinct.

It is a true saying that "there is no royal road to learning." Everything requires more or less trouble in its attainment. But for the encouragement of those not yet posted in navigation by the stars, the writer can promise that when once they have taken up the subject with a fixed determination to master it, they will be agreeably astonished at how rapidly the dreaded difficulties will disappear, and their labours be rewarded by the feeling of comfort, and saving of anxiety at critical times, afforded by the certain knowledge of their ship's whereabouts.

**Comfort derived from being familiar with star problems.**

* In connection with this subject, it is interesting to know that, with the aid of a small astronomical telescope, stars *even of the lesser magnitudes* are distinctly visible throughout the entire day; but those in the neighbourhood of the sun can only be discerned by the more powerful instruments of observatories.

This second part of the book is essentially one of figures, and it is desirable at the commencement to dwell upon certain important points in connection with their application.

The writer has frequently seen young officers laboriously working out their sights, schoolroom fashion, to the nearest second, and flattering themselves that because they had done so, the *result* must be equally accurate. This, however praiseworthy in other respects, would ofttimes shew an ignorance of governing principles which it is one of the objects of this book to seek to remove. **Needlessly working to seconds.**

Raper, in the preface to his unsurpassed work on Navigation, says:—

"Very indistinct and erroneous notions prevail among practical persons on the subject of accuracy of computation; and much time is, in consequence, often lost in computing to a degree of precision wholly inconsistent with that of the elements themselves. The mere habit of working invariably to a useless precision, while it can never advance the computer's knowledge of the subject, has the unfavourable tendency of deceiving those who are not aware of the true nature of such questions, into the persuasion that a result is always as correct as the computer chooses to make it; and thus leads them to place the same confidence in all observations, provided only they are *worked* to the same degree of accuracy." **Raper's remarks regarding precision in working.**

This idea is unhappily not confined to the youngsters of the profession: it has taken root in some of the older members as well, and it is therefore incumbent to write strongly against a fallacy which is dangerous in its tendency, and must frequently have contributed to fatal disaster.

In all observations errors must be made: the best instruments have imperfections, and no man, however equable his temperament, can always rely on his making a proper use of his senses.

It has been shewn, in previous pages, that there is often much doubt at sea as to the true place of the visible horizon, so that the altitude is never free from suspicion of inaccuracy. In addition to this, other data, peculiar to the problem, may be more or less unreliable; for example, the latitude is often uncertain to three or four miles. In working out the time at ship, an error to this amount would, under some circumstances, falsify the longitude to a serious degree, whilst, in other cases, a similar error in the same problem would have no appreciable effect. **Uncertainty in much of the data employed in computing.**

Again, we have instrumental defects depending not only upon

errors in workmanship, but upon such as arise from temporary derangement due to a variety of causes.*

It is therefore necessary, not only to exercise judgment as to the degree of close-working any given observation will admit of, and may require, but to endeavour so to select or combine problems and methods, that the errors, of whatever nature they may be, will either neutralize each other in the final result, or so unmistakeably declare themselves as to be capable of easy elimination. The precise way in which this is done will be described under each different observation.

**Working to seconds.**

The sixth chapter of Raper's Introduction, wherein he treats of "limit of error" and "degree of dependence," should be carefully noted in connection with this most important subject.

Whilst the folly of working to seconds in the majority of cases is thus put before the reader, and the striving after an impossible, though pretentious, perfection in so doing, is shewn to be a snare and a delusion, it is by no means to be understood that loose working, or a careless and hasty manner, either of observing or computing, should in any way be practised or tolerated. On the contrary, anything which can *really* increase the accuracy of the observations, or the correctness of the position deduced from them, must be diligently sought for and applied.

It is the possession of the requisite mental activity, or "capacity for taking trouble," and the power of selecting the most advantageous means out of the many at his disposal, which constitute the real test of a man's ability as a navigator, and shew that his knowledge is not superficial, but based on strictly sound principles, which cannot mislead.

As a suitable finish to these remarks, it will probably not come amiss to explain what is meant by Parallax (astronomically considered), and why, in practical Navigation, it is unnecessary to take it into account except in rare instances.

**Moon's Parallax.**

Let us then imagine an inhabitant of the Moon to be regarding our Earth, which, for the time being, we will suppose to be truly circular, and that a tiny speck indicated to him the exact centre of its disc. If now he were to measure with a sextant the angle between this tiny speck and the Earth's limb, or in other words, the Earth's semidiameter, he would obtain a *mean* result of rather

* With regard to these latter, it is the peculiarity of astronomical observations to be the ultimate means of dragging to light all defects of workmanship and adjustment in instruments, which by their minuteness elude every other mode of detection.

less than 1°; or what is the same thing, a base line of 4000 miles would, at the Moon's mean distance from the Earth, subtend an angle of nearly 1°; a simple problem in right-angled trigonometry which any one is equal to.

**Solar Parallax.** Next let us imagine our friend with the sextant to have shifted his observatory to the Sun, and from that far-off luminary to have repeated his measure of the Earth's semidiameter: this time, owing to the greatly increased distance, he would get rather less than 9″ as its mean value, and these two angular quantities would respectively be termed the Moon's and Sun's *Geocentric Horizontal Parallax.*

**Stellar Parallax.** If, proceeding yet further, he winged his way to the *nearest* of the fixed stars—and, travelling as fast as light does, it would take him between three and four years to get there—our celestial traveller, on looking back for this world, which *we* think so immense, would find that it had disappeared by very reason of its insignificance.* But supposing it still discernible, and that it could be watched whilst moving in its orbit round the sun, he would then be able to get the angle subtended by a straight line connecting the centres of the two bodies. This straight line, if measured when the Earth had reached its extreme point of travel either to the right or to the left of the Sun, would give the observer the very respectable base of 93 millions of miles. But notwithstanding the enormous length of such a base, the angle it would subtend at the place of the nearest fixed star would be less than 1″ of arc, and would be spoken of as the Star's *Annual* or *Heliocentric Parallax.*

**Distance of nearest star.** This will convey some faint idea of how far away in space that nearest star must be; expressed in words, it is about twenty billions of miles, whilst

20,000,000,000,000 miles

represents it in figures. In the contemplation of even these numbers the imagination is lost; how then if we seek to gauge the more profound depths of the universe?

The foregoing explains what is meant when allusion is made to the Moon's Parallax, the Sun's Parallax, and Stellar Parallax; but to determine the two latter is no easy job, nevertheless it must be done if we wish to know our distance from these bodies.

**Parallax as affecting navigation.** We will now return to mother Earth, to see in what way Parallax affects Navigation.

* The velocity of light is 187,000 miles per second.

In the theory of Nautical Astronomy—for certain mathematical reasons—all observations of the heavenly bodies are supposed to be made at the centre of our globe, but as this is clearly impracticable (except to gentlemen such as Jules Verne), an allowance has to be made which goes by the general name of *Parallax*. In this connection, therefore, Parallax is the angular difference between the *Apparent* place of a heavenly body as seen by an observer from any station on the Earth's *surface*, and its *True* position as supposed to be seen from the Earth's *centre*.

**Sensible and Rational Horizons.**

With us angular altitudes of the heavenly bodies are of necessity measured from the *Sensible Horizon*, which is a plane passing through the eye of the observer at right angles to a freely suspended plumb-line, whereas they ought to be measured from the *Rational Horizon*, which is parallel to the other, but passes through the Earth's centre.

Now it has been shewn that the distance of the fixed stars is so vast that to them our Sensible and Rational Horizons—though 4000 miles apart—are virtually one and the same thing, so that whether a stellar observation is made at the centre or surface of the Earth matters not; the altitude in either event is exactly the same.

In the case of the Sun it has also been shewn that the *greatest* effect would be less than 9", a quantity so small that in ship work it is not worth notice; and the same may be said of the Planets. But where our next-door-neighbour the Moon is concerned, Parallax is an important element, and cannot be disregarded. Therefore, if altitudes of the Moon could be taken simultaneously from the surface of the Earth and from its centre, they would be found to differ considerably, the altitude observed at the Earth's centre being the *true* one, and the greater of the two. The correction for Parallax, therefore, is always additive.

If the observation were made at the Earth's centre just when the Moon happened to be in the Sensible Horizon of a spectator at the surface, this difference—amounting to nearly 1°—would then be termed the Moon's *Horizontal* Parallax, and would be equivalent to the Earth's semidiameter as measured with his sextant by the "Man in the Moon."

As the altitude of a heavenly body increases, the correction for Parallax decreases, until it absolutely vanishes when the body reaches the zenith.

**Parallax in altitude.**

Except when the body is in the horizon, this correction is spoken of as "Parallax in altitude."

From the foregoing we deduce the practical results that in observations of the stars Parallax is totally insensible, and that in observations of the Sun or Planets it is so small that it may be "left out in the cold" without detriment to Navigation. The Moon, then, is the only body which is seriously affected by it, and as for this and other reasons we decided long ago to send the Moon to Coventry (except when required for Azimuths), Parallax may pack up and go with her.

---

## CHAPTER II.

### LATITUDE BY MERIDIAN ALTITUDE.

The Greenwich Date. In setting about the working of any *astronomical* question in navigation, *the invariable thing to start with is* THE GREENWICH DATE.* All the elements in the *Nautical Almanac* are computed *for noon at the meridian of the Royal Observatory at Greenwich.* Consequently, if an observation be taken *elsewhere*, it becomes necessary to reduce the astronomical data of the calculation to the time at Greenwich corresponding to the instant of observation at the place where it is made.

In the case of the problem under consideration, the only Nautical Almanac element which requires reduction is the sun's declination. This is frequently done by inspection (Table XXI. of *Norie*); but the writer prefers, as the simpler plan of the two, to look at the chronometer as soon as eight bells have been made, and from the Greenwich Mean Time thus found, to correct the declination (taken from page II. for the month) by the hourly difference, in the same way as for an ordinary morning sight.

Easiest mode of correcting Declination.

By this means, as the application of the correction is self-evident, there is less liability to mistake than by the use of the table—markedly so when the sun is very near the equator, and the *correction* for Greenwich time happens to exceed the declination itself.

By reference to the explanation of Table XXI., given in another part of *Norie's Epitome*, a rule will be found to meet this difficulty; but why burthen the memory with *two* rules, when *one* is

---

* For quick reference to the *Nautical Almanac*, it is a good plan, month by month, to cut off half an inch or so of the top right-hand corner, so that the book can at once be opened at pages I. and II. for the current month.

sufficient? The man who can correct his declination for morning or afternoon sights, needs no other method to enable him to correct it for his noon observation; in each case the *object* is the same, and there is no occasion to alter the *process*.

In general, a little mental arithmetic is all-sufficient to calculate this correction, and at the summer and winter solstices, when the change of declination is slow, it can be taken out at sight.

**Mean and Apparent time pages in Nautical Almanac.**

It must be borne in mind that the right-hand page of the *Nautical Almanac* contains the elements for *Mean* time, and that the left-hand page is adapted to *Apparent* time; consequently, whether the reduction in this or any other problem is to be made to Mean or Apparent time, the declination must be taken from the corresponding page.

The column of *Variation in one hour* is only to be found on the left-hand page, and is common to both.

In all the astronomical problems, it will be found handy to work by decimals. Thus, to find the correction for 4 hours and 6 minutes of Greenwich Mean Time, when the variation of declination in one hour is 43″·68, proceed as follows:—

```
Hourly diff.........  43″·7
G.M.T...............× 4·1
                     ------
                      437
                    1748     Correction
                  ---------
               60) 179″·17 ( 2′ 59″·2
                   120
                   ---
                    59
```

In this example, the second decimal figure is dropped as being needlessly exact.

To find the decimal parts of an hour equal to any given number of minutes, divide the latter by 6. Thus 6 minutes equal ·1 of an hour; 30 minutes equal ·5; 45 minutes equal ·75; 3 minutes equal ·05 of an hour, and so on.

**Rough and ready 89° 48′.**

Some men drift into a very common though extremely reprehensible habit of finding the sun's meridian zenith distance by subtracting their noon altitude from the constant 89° 48′; *and this they do under all circumstances*—whether they are standing on the bridge of a high-sided steamer, or the deck nearly awash of a coasting schooner—whether the sun is almost overhead, or only a few degrees above the horizon. Some do it through pure ignorance—others, because never having taken the trouble to investigate the matter, think "it is near enough." But it is *not* near enough; and the man who does such a lazy trick, to save himself at most half-a-dozen figures, is not fit for command.

**Table IX. of Norie.** The proper mode for sea practice, where conciseness is only second to accuracy, is to make use of Table IX. in *Norie's Epitome*, which, however, be it noticed, is calculated for observations of the *lower* limb only.

This tabular correction comprises the joint effect of dip, refraction, parallax, and semi-diameter; but as the latter is a variable quantity, depending upon the earth's distance from the sun,* the correction requires to be itself corrected by another minor one, corresponding to the time of the year which is given at the foot of the table. These corrections are in minutes and tenths of arc; but if it be desired to reduce the tenths to seconds, it is easily done by multiplying them by 6, thus: 7'·3 is equal to 7' 18".

**Correction of meridian altitude.** Therefore, to correct the observed meridian altitude, apply first the sextant index error, if any—which can *always* be done mentally—and to the result add the *corrected correction* from Table IX. This amount subtracted from 90° gives the zenith distance, to which apply the *reduced* declination in the usual way.

As an example of the consequences which might ensue from the use of this slipshod 89° 48', the very possible case will be taken of a vessel bound to Glasgow, entering the North Channel in the month of December. To shew the difference, the latitude will be worked both correctly and loosely.

EXAMPLE.

At noon on Saturday, December 18th, 1880, 0·30 P.M., G.M.T. by chronometer, being in latitude by account 55° 30' North, and longitude by account 7° 40' West, observed the meridian altitude of the sun's lower limb to be 10° 51⅜'. No index error. Height of the eye 32 feet. Weather inclining to be thick with passing drizzles of rain; moderate gale at S.W., freshening gradually.

Rough and ready method supposed to be "near enough."

| | | |
|---|---|---|
| Constant .................... | 89° 48' | |
| Obs. altitude................ | 10 51⅜ | |
| Zen. dist. .................... | 78° 56⅝' | N. |
| Declination ................. | 23 25⅛ | S. |
| Latitude ................. | 55° 31½' | North. |

Short but correct method.

| | | |
|---|---|---|
| Obs. altitude........ | 10° 51⅜' | |
| Corr. Table IX. = 5'·7 } Auxiliary corr. = 0 3 } + | 6 | |
| | 10° 57⅜' | |
| | 90 | |
| Zen. dist. .......... | 79° 2⅝' | N. |
| Declination ........ | 23 25⅛ | S. |
| True latitude .. | 55° 37½' | North |

The difference in the work of the two methods amounts to *five figures*, but

* The earth is nearest to the sun during the northern winter.

the difference in the resulting latitude amounts to *six miles.* This, however, is not all—mark what follows.

About a quarter past ten same morning, when the sun had an altitude of 8°, sights were got for longitude, which were worked up as soon as the necessary latitude had been obtained at noon. Now, at the time the sights were taken, from the sun being so far to the southward, an error of *one* mile in the latitude used for the calculation would produce an error of exactly 4' (minutes)* of longitude—in this case *to the eastward;* and since the error of latitude, as shewn in the preceding example, amounts to six miles, the corresponding error deduced from forenoon sights would be 24' (minutes) of longitude, equal to 13½' (miles) of distance. Consequently, the ship would be 6' miles further north and 13½' miles further east than her captain supposed her to be. Now, assuming the longitude at noon as determined by chronometer to be 7° 25' West, and the latitude 55° 31½' North, according to the "near enough" method, the ship would *apparently* be about 9' miles *north-westward* from Inishtrahull, whereas her *true* position would be in latitude 55° 37½' N., and longitude 7° 1' W., or some 14' miles to the *north-east* of Inishtrahull. Meanwhile the weather rapidly gets thicker, but the captain, feeling satisfied with his observations, and knowing his chronometers cannot be "out" on the short passage from a North American port, runs on with confidence, only to find, in less than three hours, his vessel a total wreck on the rock-bound coast of Islay.† In the Board of Trade enquiry which would be sure to follow, the bewildered captain—if he survived—would probably seek to account for the accident by an unknown error in the compasses, or the influence of a mysterious current. The Court, ignorant of the 89° 48' transaction, would perhaps be equally puzzled to know how the ship got so far out of her course after such an apparently good "Fix" at noon; but in any case it would very properly suspend him for not having verified his position by the lead; and now that Sir William Thomson's invaluable sounding machine enables this to be done without stopping the ship, there is no excuse for the omission. Those who have a blind faith in "sights," without understanding the groundwork of the thing, should take this lesson to heart.

**Declination at noon—*ship time,* must be reduced to corresponding time at Greenwich.**

Doubtless to some the foregoing will appear an exaggerated case, but it is not so. Further, there are men holding Master's certificates who are in the habit of applying the declination (as given in the *Nautical Almanac*) to their noon sight for latitude, without using any correction whatever for the ship's longitude,

* It will be noticed that the word "minutes" is used here instead of "miles." The latter would be decidedly incorrect. *In speaking of Longitude or the divisions of the Sextant,* it is proper to say degrees (°), minutes ('), and seconds ("); strictly speaking, the same thing applies to latitude also, but as a mile of latitude and a nautical mile are practically the same thing all over the world, the looseness of expression is in this last case more pardonable.

† It could be shewn in the same manner, that if the *altitude* were but 1' wrong, and the resulting error in the longitude happened to lie on the same side as the error due to the incorrect latitude, the mistake in the ship's position would be still greater, since 1' of altitude in the case before us is equal to 18ˢ of time, or 4½' of longitude.

or in other words, without reducing it to Greenwich time. They think that the precept, "At apparent noon," heading page I., means that the subjoined declinations, &c., are good for noon *at any place*.

Mere "cramming" to pass examination deprecated.

One would imagine that, with the strict examinations now in force, such misapprehension would be impossible. When we recollect, however, that many worthy young men brought up before the mast, have absolutely no groundwork of education, and pass merely by dint of *hard cramming*, there is no longer occasion to be surprised. Moreover, having obtained their certificates, years may pass before they are called upon to fill a position requiring navigational knowledge; and in the interval they become rusty, and the most of what they have learnt is forgotten.

In the case of finding the latitude just given, it so happened that the declination required no reduction. Let us, then, take an example of a different kind, and work it as recommended for sea practice.

EXAMPLE II.

September 15th, 1880, in longitude by account 74° 30′ West, the meridian altitude of ☉ was 53° 52′, the observer being North of the sun, and the height of his eye 24 feet. Index error — 3′ 24″. When the sun had ceased to rise, the G.M.T. by chronometer was 4h. 54m. 10s. P.M. same date. Required the latitude.

| | |
|---|---|
| Declin. page II. N.A., Sept. 15th | 2° 47′ 3″·5 N. *decreasing*. |
| Reduction for Greenwich date . | − 4 43·7 |
| *Corrected* declination . | 2° 42′ 19″·8 |

| | |
|---|---|
| Observed altitude ☉ | 53° 52′ |
| Index error . . . | − 3½ |
| | 53 48½ |
| Correction table IX. | + 10½ |
| True Altitude . . | 53 59 |
| | 90 |
| Zenith distance . . | 36 1 N. |
| *Corrected* declination | 2 42⅓ N. |
| Latitude | 38° 43⅓′ North. |

Var. in 1 hour 57″·9
G.M.T. . × 4·9
5211
2316
60)283″·71( 4′ 43″·7 correction
240
43

With low altitudes observe sun's upper limb.

When the sun's altitude is low, as in winter, it is advisable to observe the *upper* limb, as being further removed from the influence of the excessive refraction so capricious near the horizon. It is true the after calculation is somewhat lengthened by so doing, and the difference of altitude is not much; still, every little tells, and a trifle in the way of extra labour, when a benefit is to be gained, should not be allowed to weigh for an instant.

In the use of the sextant, the observer should accustom himself from the commencement to the *inverting* telescope. It is rather difficult to manage at first, but practice makes perfect, and its superiority over the direct one is unquestioned. **Inverting telescope.**

At sea, it is a good plan to carry a watch set to *Greenwich Mean Time.* If a common one, it can be regulated every morning when winding the chronometers, but if this be objectionable on the score of the watch's value, it is easy to ascertain its error and make a mental note of it. This watch, then, becomes available for azimuths, ex-meridians, or other work where the exact second is not of consequence, and saves a journey to the chronometer. To have it set to *Apparent Time at Ship* might at first sight be considered preferable, but a moment's reflection will shew that this is continually altering, and in a fast steamer, on east or west courses in high latitudes, does so very rapidly, sometimes as much as 42 minutes in a day, so that the watch would never be correct for an hour on a stretch. Moreover the G.M.T. can with ease be converted into Apparent Time at Ship, Sidereal Time, or any other, just as occasion may require. A strong watch, with water-tight case, which will stand knocking about and yet go sufficiently well for this purpose, can be purchased now-a-days for thirty shillings or two pounds; it should be of the kind known as "key-less," or what the Americans call a "stem-winder." **Hack watch set to Greenw. Mean Time.**

*After* breakfast, all the *clocks* on board should be set to Apparent Time at Ship for *noon* of that day, as determined in advance, by working up the dead reckoning. There is then no fear of missing "sun time," and the plan for many reasons is preferable to the usual one of making eight bells by the sun. **Proper time of regulating clocks on board.**

## LATITUDE BY MERIDIAN ALTITUDE OF A STAR.

*Observations of the stars should be industriously practised.*

The advantage possessed by a man who is well posted in this work, over another who is ignorant of it, cannot be over-estimated. One now and again hears it remarked by old Atlantic navigators, that they have frequently been compelled to make the passage from land to land entirely by dead reckoning, as sights were not to be had. As it is inconceivable that during nine or ten days neither the sun nor stars should ever have been visible, this assertion must surely mean that the sun failed to present itself precisely **Transatlantic passages made solely by dead reckoning!!!!!**

at the orthodox times of 9 A.M. and "high noon;" and when appearing at other hours, could not be utilized for want of a known problem suitable to such irregular visits. Moreover, the stars must have been looked upon only as *theoretical* aids to navigation, being, for *practical* work, quite unreliable. It is hoped a better system of education may serve to dispel such illusions, and that every man in the future will fit himself to take advantage of the heavenly bodies, which are available for his guidance *at all times* when visible.

The problem of finding the latitude by meridian altitude of a star should be more frequently practised, especially when making the land in high latitudes during the winter months. As before stated, morning or evening twilight offers the best horizon for star observation, and reference to Table XLIV. of Norie will give the names of those on the meridian at that time.

**Star observations best during twilight.**

As it may be difficult to bring the star down to the horizon if there is over-much light in the sky, it will be found a capital plan to calculate its meridian altitude beforehand, and having set the sextant to this angle, direct the sight a few minutes before the time of transit to the north or south points of the horizon, as the case may be, and the star's image will be seen either upon or near the horizon. There is then no difficulty in bringing it exactly to the horizon, and keeping it there like the sun, till its greatest altitude is attained, which being read off will give very simply, and with exceedingly few figures, the sought-for latitude.

**How to find the star required.**

The simplicity of this observation is perfectly delightful, *and the star cannot be mistaken*, as no other (except, perhaps, telescopic stars) will have the same meridian altitude at that time. It frequently happens that, by this method, a most perfect observation can be made during twilight, when the unaided eye will entirely fail to pick the same star out in the general brightness of the sky, and it possesses the additional advantage—*that the observer does not even require to be acquainted with the star he is taking.* For this observation, either the inverting or direct telescope may be used; but, as already stated, the first-named is preferable. If, however, the observation be made *after dark*, it will be necessary to employ the *star telescope;* and with regard to this, it may be said that one of inferior quality is worse than none at all.

**Star's previous recognition by eye unnecessary.**

To find the approximate meridian altitude of the star by previous calculation is an easy thing.

**How to *calculate* meridian altitude.**

Work up the latitude by dead reckoning, and by subtracting it from 90° find the co-latitude If the star's declination and the co-latitude be of the same name, add them together; or take their difference if of contrary names. The result is the meridian altitude, to be reckoned from the south point of the horizon when the latitude is north, and the contrary when south. But should the sum exceed 90°, it must be taken from 180°. This last shews that the observer is on the equatorial side of the star, and in that case the altitude must be reckoned from the north in north latitude, and from the south in south latitude.*

EXAMPLE I.

About 8·15 P.M., June 1st, 1881, being in latitude by account 47° 10′ N., wished to observe the star Spica for latitude. On referring to Table XLIV., it is found to pass the meridian on that day about 8·39 P.M. Apparent Time at Ship. Required its approximate altitude at that time, to which to set the sextant. **Example of calculating meridian altitude.**

| | | | | |
|---|---|---|---|---|
| Latitude . . . . | 47° | 10′ | N. | |
| | 90 | | | |
| Co-latitude . . . | 42 | 50 | N. | |
| *'s Declination . . | 10 | 32¾ | S. | See page 345, N. A. |
| Approx. merid. alt. | 32° | 17¼′ | S. | |

EXAMPLE II.

About 4 P.M., July 16th, 1881, being off the Horn, in latitude by account 54° 10′ S., wished to correct the dead reckoning by an observation of the star α Crux, which by Table XLIV. will pass the meridian on that day about 4·35 P.M. Apparent Time at Ship. Required the star's approximate altitude at that time, to which to set the sextant.

| | | | |
|---|---|---|---|
| Latitude . . . . | 54° | 10′ | S. |
| | 90 | | |
| Co-latitude . . . | 35 | 50 | S. |
| *'s Declination . . | 62 | 27 | S. See page 343, N. A. |
| *'s Meridian altitude | 98 | 17 | reckoned from the North. |
| | 180 | | |
| *'s Meridian altitude | 81° | 43′ | reckoned from the South. |

Its declination will always be a guide as to the direction in which to look for a star. According as the former is North or South of the observer's position, so will the latter bear when on **In looking for a star, be guided by its declination.**

* In the N. A. for 1884, the Right Ascensions and Declinations of the stars will be found between pages 319—366.

the meridian. This is so self-evident that there is no occasion to tax the memory by recollecting the rule given further back.

We will now suppose the observation of Spica (Example I.) to have been completed, and that the observed meridian altitude was ascertained to be 32° 22′ S.; eye 30 ft.; no index error. Required the latitude.

| | | |
|---|---|---|
| Observed altitude . . . . . . . . . . | 32° 22′ | S. |
| Correction—Table XV. of *Norie* . . . . – | 6¾ | |
| True altitude . . . . . . . . . . . . | 32 15¼ | |
| | 90 | |
| Merid. zenith distance . . . . . . . . | 57 44¾ | N. |
| ✱'s Declination . . . . . . . . . . . | 10 32¾ | S. |
| True latitude . . . . . . . . . . . . | 47° 12′ | North. |

**Star's declination a fixed quantity.**

This is even shorter and simpler than the latitude by meridian altitude of the sun, *since the star's declination being almost a fixed quantity, requires no correction for Greenwich Mean Time.*

**Correction of altitude.**

Table XV. of *Norie* gives the sum of the corrections for a star in the same manner that Table IX. answers for the sun. It may also be used for correcting the observed altitudes of any of the planets (except the moon), as their semi-diameter and parallax in altitude are not worth consideration; consequently, the operation of finding the latitude by a planet is precisely similar to that by the star Spica, worked out above.

**Planets' declination continually changing.**

The declination of the planets, and their *mean* time of passing the meridian, will be found in the N. A. for 1884, between pages 226—265, under the heading "Mean time." Since the declination of the planets is continually changing, note the time by chronometer when the meridian altitude is observed, and reduce the declination to the Greenwich date by simple proportion. As the "hourly variation" is not given, it will be necessary to take the "variation" for one whole day, and then say—As the change is in 24 hours, so will the change be in the given number of hours.*

EXAMPLE III.

July 3rd, 1881, at 7·39 A.M. *Mean* Time at Ship, in longitude 104° 6′ W., let the observed meridian altitude of the planet Mars (♂) be 22° 50′ N., when a chronometer showed 2h. 35m. 58s.,

* If a rigorously exact reduction be required for any special purpose, "second differences" would have to be employed; see top of page 495 in N. A. for 1884; but for sea use such ultra-refinement is thrown away.

G.M.T., same date. Eye 32 feet; no index error. Required the latitude.

| | | |
|---|---|---|
| Declin. noon July 3rd . . . . | 13° 4′ 3″ N. | Page 245. N. A. |
| Declin. noon July 4th . . . . | 13 18 3 N. | „ „ |
| Change in 24 hours . . . . . | 0 14′ 0″ | |

If the change is 14′ in 24 hours, what will it be in 2·6 hours?

24h. : 2·6h. : : 14′ :

| |
|---|
| 14′ |
| 2·6 |
| 84 |
| 28 |
| 24) 36·4 (1′ 5 |
| 24 |
| 124 |
| 1·0 |

| | |
|---|---|
| Declin. July 3rd. . . . | 13° 4′ 3″ N. |
| Correction for 2·6 hrs. . | + 1 30 |
| Reduced declin. . . . | 13° 5′ 33″ N. |
| Observed merid. alt. . . . | 22° 50′ N. |
| Correction—Table XV. of *Norie* | − 7¾ |
| True alt. . . . . . . | 22 42¼ |
| | 90 |
| Merid. zenith dist. . . . . | 67 17¾ S. |
| Corrected declination . . . | 13 5½ N. |
| Latitude . . . . . . . . | 54° 12¼′ South. |

**Observe stars on both sides of zenith.**

Whenever you can, it is advisable to take stars *both North and South of the observer*, as by so doing all systematic errors, of whatever nature, are eliminated from the *mean* of the results. For example, some men have a *fixed habit* of bringing the object too low—others, not low enough; the astronomical refraction may be greater or less than the amount allowed in the Tables; the instrumental error may be somewhat different to what is supposed; or the horizon may be unduly elevated or depressed, as already explained in a previous chapter.

**Compensation of errors.**

In each and all of these cases the certain cure is to observe stars on both sides of the zenith. If the ultimate effect of these various errors lies on the side of making the altitudes *too great*, the northern star will give the latitude too far north, and the southern star will give it too far south; but the *mean* of the two will be correct, or nearly so.

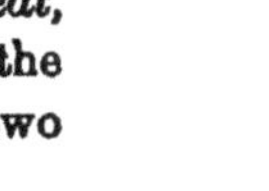

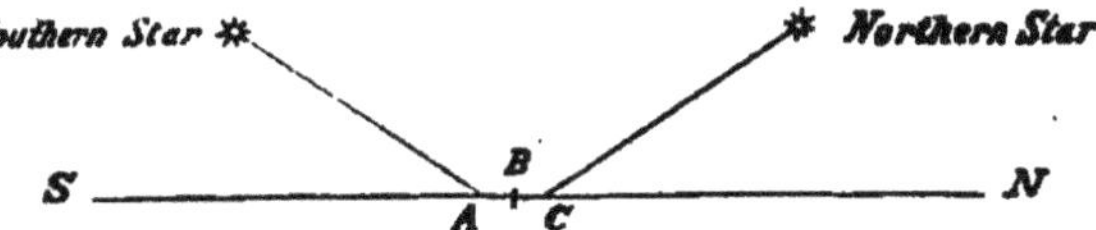


In the diagram, the balance of error in the case of the northern star places the ship at *C*; and as the error is common to both observations if they are taken nearly at the same time, the southern star will place the ship at *A*. In reality she is at *B*, or about midway between the two.

In like manner, if the errors conspire to make the observed altitudes *too small*, the northern star will give the latitude too far south, and the southern star will give it too far north, but the *mean* will be correct as before. The subjoined diagram shews this.

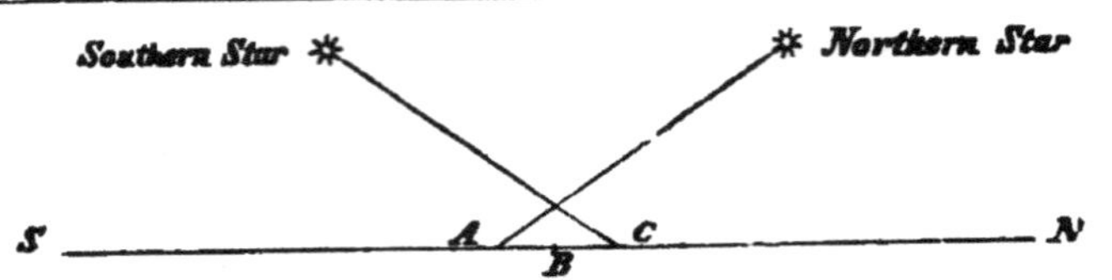


It is well to recollect that the greater the meridian altitude, the greater the correspondence between the latitude of the observer and the declination of the body observed, and *vice versâ*; or, in other words, as we approach an object its altitude increases.

## CHAPTER III.

### LATITUDE BY MERIDIAN ALTITUDE BELOW THE POLE.

We now come to a useful problem, which is very little practised, though it is just as simple, and certainly as short, as any of the preceding.

In high latitudes, certain stars complete their daily revolution round the pole of the heavens without rising or setting, and are consequently termed *Circumpolar stars.* This occurs when their polar distance is less than the latitude of the observer—both being of the same name. These stars having come to the meridian above the pole, which is their highest point, decline towards the westward for six hours, when they gradually curve eastward—still falling, however—till in another six hours their lower culmination is reached, when they are said to be *on the meridian below the pole.*

**Circumpolar stars—their course in the heavens described.**

They then commence to rise, still moving eastward, for another six hours, after which they turn to the westward in their upward course for a further period of six hours, when the circle is completed, and they are again on the meridian *above* the pole. The hours alluded to here are of course *Sidereal* hours, which are nearly ten seconds shorter than mean solar ones.

It will be noticed that during the *lower* half of the star's journey their motion is from *west* to *east.* Attention is particularly called to this, because in observing star azimuths, unless acquainted with it, a beginner is likely to fancy he has made a mistake on discovering that, as his *western* hour angles grow larger after they have exceeded six hours, the star's bearing becomes more *easterly,* which at first sight seems opposed to what

**Azimuths—seeming anomaly when meridian distance is greater than six hours.**

one would expect. The annexed diagram makes the explanation clear.

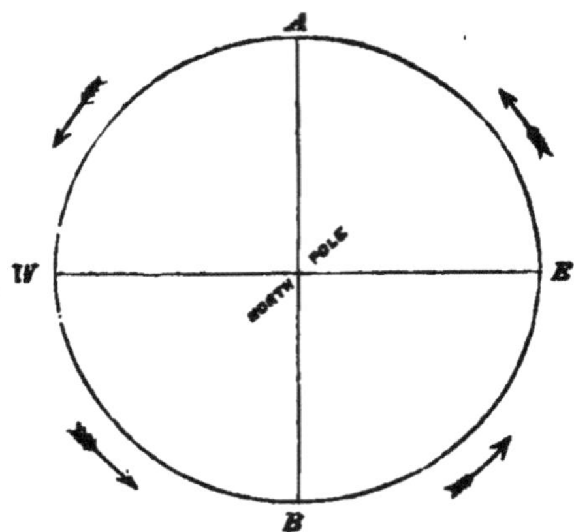


*West* ——————— *Horizon* ——————— *East*

*AWBE* is the diurnal circle of a northern circumpolar star, and the line *AB* represents the meridian of the observer. At *A* the star is at its upper culmination, or, in other words, it is on the meridian *above* the pole, and bears North. During the first six hours, whilst passing from *A* to *W*, it falls towards the *westward;* at *W*, therefore, the hour-angle of the star is 6 hrs. west. During the second six hours, between *W* and *B*, it falls towards the *eastward.* At *B* it is at its lower culmination, or, in other words, it is on the meridian *below* the pole, and again bears North. During the third six hours, between *B* and *E*, it rises towards the *eastward;* at *E* the star's hour-angle may be expressed either as 18 hrs. west or 6 hrs. east of the meridian. And during the last six hours its course is upwards, and towards the *westward*, till, after a lapse of 24 sidereal hours, it again transits at *A*. For southern circumpolar stars the direction of the arrows must be reversed and the letters *E* and *W* change sides.

**Distance of North Star from the Pole.**

If the night be cloudless, it is easy in the northern hemisphere —without reference to the compass—to tell when a star is near the meridian below the pole, by its being vertically under the Pole star, which latter is now scarcely 1½° distant from the pole itself.

In observing the meridian altitude *below* the pole, the sextant readings get *less and less*, until the lowest point is reached, when the star may be said to be "down," in the same sense that at noon we say the sun is "up."

**Rule for finding the Latitude.**

To find the latitude, correct the altitude by Table XV. of Norie. Find the star's polar distance by subtracting the declination from 90°. Add together the polar distance and the true altitude, and the result is the latitude, without further trouble. *It would be a puzzle to find anything more easy.*

EXAMPLE.

Entering Channel after a couple of days of cloudy weather, the sky partially cleared to the northward about 8 o'clock in the evening of November 6th, 1881, when the meridian altitude of star Dubhe *below* the pole was observed to be 21° 58′. Eye, 24 feet. No index error. Required the latitude.

| | | | |
|---|---|---|---|
| Dubhe's declin. Nov. 6th | 62° 23′ N. (page 340, N. A.) | | |
| | 90 | | |
| Dubhe's polar distance | 27 37 N. | *'s observed alt. | 21° 58′ N. |
| „ true altitude | 21 51 N. | Correction (Table XV.) – | 7 |
| Latitude | 49° 28′ North. | *'s true altitude | 21° 51′ |

**How to calculate Meridian Altitude below the Pole.**

To set the sextant for an observation on the meridian below the pole, subtract the star's polar distance from the latitude by dead reckoning, which will give the approximate altitude.

From what has been said, it will be apparent that to find the time of a star's transit below the pole on any particular day, it is only necessary to add 11 hours 58 minutes to the time given in Table XLIV. of Norie. The following is a list of useful circumpolar stars in both hemispheres.

The observer being to the northward of 49° North latitude, the undermentioned are available:—

**List of useful Circumpolar Stars in Northern Hemisphere.**

| | | | | H. | M. |
|---|---|---|---|---|---|
| Dubhe, or α Ursæ Majoris . | Magnitude | 2.—Right | Ascen. | 10 | 56 |
| γ Ursæ Majoris . . . . | „ | 2.3 | „ | 11 | 47 |
| Benetnasch, or η Ursæ Majoris . | „ | 2. | „ | 13 | 43 |
| Rastaban, or γ Draconis . . | „ | 2.3 | „ | 17 | 54 |
| α Cepheus, or Alderaimin . . | „ | 3.2 | „ | 21 | 16 |

North of 51° North latitude, the following may be added to the list:—

| | | | | H. | M. |
|---|---|---|---|---|---|
| Capella, or α Aurigæ . . . | Magnitude | 1.—Right | Ascen. | 5 | 8 |
| α Cygnus, or Deneb . . . | „ | 2.1 | „ | 20 | 38 |

In high Southern latitudes, observations below the pole are of greater utility than with us in the more favoured hemisphere, where the Pole star is on duty all through the night. It is a pity the Southern celestial pole is not furnished with a similar sentinel. However, it has half-a-dozen stars of great brilliancy, which, though not quite so ready to hand, go far to make up the deficiency.

**List of useful circumpolar stars in Southern hemisphere.**

| | | | | | H. | M. | | |
|---|---|---|---|---|---|---|---|---|
| Achernar . | Mag. | 1 | —Right | Ascen. | 1 | 3: | Available to the Southward of | 42° S. |
| Canopus . | „ | 1 | „ | „ | 6 | 21 | „ | 47½° S. |
| α Crucis . | „ | 1 | „ | „ | 12 | 20 | „ | 38° S. |
| β Centauri . | „ | 1 | „ | „ | 13 | 55 | „ | 40½° S. |
| α Centauri . | „ | 1 | „ | „ | 14 | 32 | „ | 40° S. |
| α Pavonis . | „ | 2 | „ | „ | 20 | 16 | „ | 42° S. |

## CHAPTER IV.

### LATITUDE BY THE NORTH STAR (POLARIS).

The student of the heavens should make himself practically acquainted with the constellations of the Great and Little Bear as starting points in search of the rest. The first-named is very conspicuous; and the figure formed by the seven principal stars is variously termed—the Plough, the Skillet, the Cleaver, the Dipper, the Waggon, and Charles's Wain.

**The "Great Bear" or "Plough."**

With the exception of the Pole Star, those in the Little Bear are much less bright, and at times somewhat difficult to make out. The star at the extremity of the tail of the Great Bear (or handle of the Plough) is named BENETNASCH, and the corresponding one in the Little Bear is POLARIS, or the "North star," formerly called RUCCABAH, before it was entitled to its present designation. The two stars at the leading end of the Plough are called the "POINTERS," because a line through them, if produced, will pass close to the North star—which, by the way, is the best means of finding it. Of these two, the one nearer the North star is known as DUBHE. Both *Benetnasch* and *Dubhe* are in the Nautical Almanac Catalogue.

**The "Little Bear."**

**The "Pointers."**

The North star (Polaris) is particularly accommodating in affording seamen a ready means of determining the latitude at any hour of the night. This invaluable guide is now a degree and a third ($1\frac{1}{3}°$) distant from the Pole of the heavens; and as the diameter of its diurnal circle ($2\frac{2}{3}°$) is small in consequence, the star's apparent revolution round the Pole is very slow, being only about a minute of arc (1′) in three minutes of time. This enables observations for latitude to be made regardless of whether it is on or off the meridian, as an error in the time used in the computation—unless very considerable—has but little effect on the result.

**The North star—particularly useful for finding the latitude.**

Did the North star but occupy the exact position of the Pole, it would be a fixed point, and its altitude, when corrected for instrumental error, dip, and refraction, would give the latitude of the observer without any calculation whatever. To make this fully understood, the writer takes the liberty of quoting from W. H. Rosser's book—*The Stars: How to Know Them, and How to Use Them.**

**Elevation of the Pole equal to Latitude of place.**

"The *elevated* Pole is that Pole which is above the horizon; and the *Elevation* of the Pole is the *Altitude* of the Pole above the true Horizon, and is equal to the Latitude of the place. This may be shewn as follows:—

"An observer under the Pole (in Lat. 90°) has the Pole and Zenith in one—therefore, 90° above the Horizon; in which case, also, the Horizon coincides with the Equinoctial or Equator. By as many degrees as the observer goes from the Pole towards the Equator, by so many degrees does his Horizon go below the Equator on one side, and approach the Pole on the other side; therefore, the Pole approaches the Horizon by the same number of degrees as the Zenith approaches the Equator—*i.e.*, the *elevation* of the Pole above the Horizon is equal to the *distance* of the Zenith from the Equinoctial, which is equivalent to the *distance of the observer from the Equator*; or, in other words, to the latitude of the place."

Again, it may be put this way:—In the diagram Z represents the zenith, N the nadir, PP the poles, EQ the equator, HH the horizon.

Then ZE is the arc of the meridian intercepted between the Zenith of the place and the Equator, and is therefore equal to the Latitude, also PH is the altitude of the Pole.

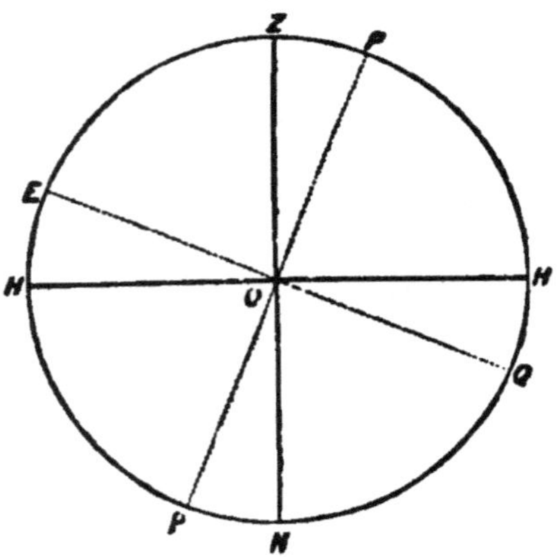


* London: James Imray and Son.

Now PE is equal to 90°, and ZH is equal to 90°; therefore, PE is equal to ZH. Take away the common part ZP. Then ZE is equal to PH, or, the latitude is equal to the altitude of the Pole.

The foregoing explanations are probably as simple as they can well be made; nevertheless, to understand them requires concentration of thought. Therefore, when they are being studied, one must not be dreaming about something else, or the result will be unprofitable.

**Vega the future Pole star.**

At present the Pole is approaching the North star, and in a century and a quarter will have reached within half a degree of it, when it will commence to recede, and gradually come nearer to the bright star Vega, which, in about 12,000 years—owing to what is known as the *Precession of the Equinoxes*—will then become the Pole star.

**How to find the North Pole of the heavens.**

The imaginary point representing the Pole of the heavens may be found by drawing a line from $\epsilon$ Ursæ Majoris (the first star in the tail) to within a degree and a third of the North star. These two stars are consequently on diametrically opposite sides of the Pole. When $\epsilon$ Ursæ Majoris is six hours from the meridian, the North star will be so also, and its altitude in that position will be nearly the same as the elevation of the Pole. It will be known when this is the case by a line through $\epsilon$ Ursæ Majoris and Polaris being parallel with the horizon. The eye can guess this pretty accurately. At the same time, a line from $\beta$ in the Little Bear, drawn midway between $\epsilon$ and $\zeta$, will also be horizontal, and, of course, parallel with the other.

**How to know when Pole star has same elevation as the Pole.**

An altitude at such times, simply corrected by Table XV. of *Norie*, will give a rough shot at the Latitude. This is mentioned, not to advocate such a slap-dash mode of finding it, but to exhibit the principle.

As a matter of fact—for an *accurate* determination—the Pole star is then in its worst possible position, as at such times its vertical motion is most rapid, and an error in the time produces its greatest effect, namely 1′ of latitude for every three minutes of error in the time. On the other hand, when the Pole star is near the meridian either above or below the pole, its motion in altitude is least, and an error in the time is of little or no consequence. Reference to Table XVII. of *Norie* will shew that for half an hour on either side of the meridian the altitude will barely change 1′, so that the observer has ample time to get a good sight without being embarrassed by the rising or falling of the star. This, then, is the best time for observing.

**Best time for observing Pole star.**

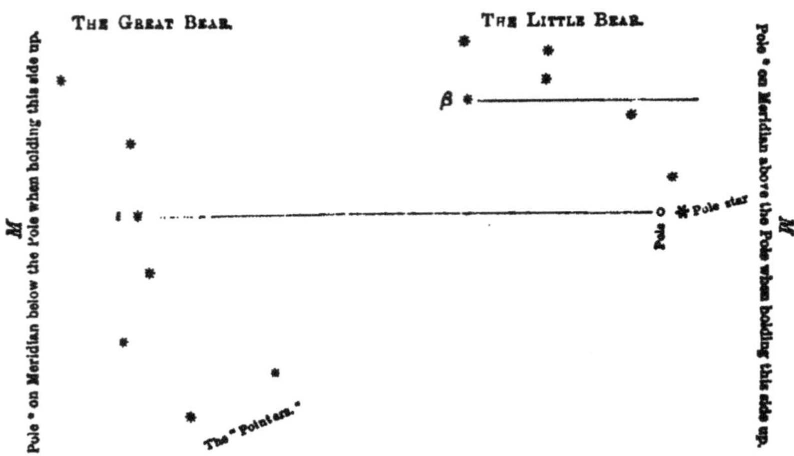


**How to know best time for observing.** The time of transit may be found by consulting Table XLIV. of *Norie*, or by the appearance of the Great and Little Bear. When ε Ursæ Majoris (sometimes called *Alioth*) is vertically above or below Polaris, or when a line from β traced midway between ε and ζ of the Little Bear is "up and down," the North star will be on or near the meridian. The diagram will exhibit this state of affairs by slueing it a quarter of the way round, so that one of the sides marked *M* shall face the reader. γ and β in the Little Bear are sometimes called "the Guards."

**Latitude by Pole star—two methods.** There are two ways of working out the latitude by Polaris; one is known as the *Nautical Almanac*, and the other as the *Epitome*, method. The former is the more exact, and as the difference in the length of the calculation is so trifling as not to be worth speaking about, the preference is given to it, especially since it possesses the decided advantage of familiarizing the navigator with Sidereal Time in the precise form employed in certain of the stellar problems herein treated of. *Therefore, mark well how it is arrived at.* It is a matter of importance, in the first place, to select a good form of working, *and then to stick to it.* This has been made a leading feature in "Wrinkles."

EXAMPLE.

At about 8·10 P.M., May 19th, 1880, when in Latitude and Longitude by account 41° 47′ N. and 55° 45′ W., observed the altitude of star Polaris to be 40° 36¾′, when a chronometer which was 3m. 56s. slow of G.M.T. shewed 11h. 41m. 31s. P.M. same date. Eye 32 feet. Index error + 45″.

| | H. | M. | S. | |
|---|---|---|---|---|
| | 11 | 41 | 31 | Time by chronometer. |
| + | | 3 | 56 | Error of chronometer. |
| | 11 | 45 | 27 | G.M.T. |
| − | 3 | 43 | 00 | Longitude in time W. |
| | 8 | 2 | 27 | Mean time at ship. |
| + | 3 | 50 | 8 | Sid. time at Greenwich mean noon. |
| + | | 1 | 56 | Acceleration for 11h. 45m. 27s. |
| | 11 | 54 | 31 | Sidereal time of observation at ship, or, in other words, the Right Ascension of the Meridian of observer. |

| | | ° | ′ |
|---|---|---|---|
| Observed alt. of Polaris .. .. | | 40 | 36¾ |
| Index error .. .. .. .. | + | | ¾ |
| | | 40 | 37½ |
| Correction, Table XV. of *Noris* .. | − | | 6½ |
| True altitude .. .. .. .. | | 40 | 31 |
| Constant correction .. .. .. | − | | 1 |
| Reduced altitude .. .. .. | | 40 | 30 |
| 1st corr. Table I. N.A., page 483 .. | + | 1 | 15¼ |
| 2nd corr. Table II. N.A., page 484 | | 0 | 00 |
| 3rd corr. Table III. N.A., page 484 | + | | 1 |
| Latitude | | 41° | 46¼′N. |

Nautical Almanac method.

This looks formidable on account of the explanatory writing at the sides, which is inserted as a guide to the learner; but in actual practice most of this is omitted, and the figures themselves are not many.

In the N.A. method (*vide* above example) there is a *constant* correction of 1′ subtractive; and as the question has often been asked *why* the true altitude should *always be diminished* by this amount without any apparent reason, the explanation is now given:—In the construction of Table II. the Polar Distance and Right Ascension of the North Star are assumed to be invariable throughout the year, but this is not the case, as may be seen by turning back to the Table on page 311 of the *N.A.* for 1884.

Table III., which is an auxiliary to Table II., depends on the *difference* between the *true* and *assumed* values of the P.D. and R.A., and contains the necessary correction, *increased by* 1′ for the sake of rendering the quantities *always* additive; and as it would not do to allow this convenient unit to remain to vitiate the result, it is quietly got rid of near the beginning of the problem.

## CHAPTER V.

### LATITUDE BY EX-MERIDIAN ALTITUDE OF THE SUN.

**Towson's Ex-meridian method the best.**

Of the various methods for computing the reduction to the meridian, Towson's—which is independent of the latitude by account—is undoubtedly the easiest, as well as the most accurate for sea practice. His tables, however, only extend to 23° 20' of declination, so that if stars be observed whose declination exceeds this quantity, it is advisable to have recourse to the method given on page 211 of *Norie's Epitome* (20th edition).

**Towson's tables, limited to 23½° of declination.**

**Norie's method comes to the rescue.**

When the sky is cloudy, the sun or other celestial body, though it may happen to be obscured so that the *meridian* altitude is unattainable, nevertheless frequently appears for short intervals both before and after its meridian passage. If not observed at these times, the Latitude may be lost for the day; and as the finding of the Longitude is generally dependent upon a correct knowledge of the Latitude, the morning sights will have been taken to little purpose.

**Advantages of Ex-meridians.**

In addition to the extreme simplicity of the Ex-meridian problem, it has this to recommend it,—that neither is the patience taxed, the eye fatigued, nor the instrument unnecessarily exposed by the usual weary waiting for the Meridian altitude, as *one* observation within the prescribed limits suffices for the correct determination of the Latitude, if the Apparent Time at Ship be known with tolerable accuracy. Were it not, indeed, that the wide application of this most useful problem is somewhat restricted, it would deserve to rank *before* that of the Meridian altitude, which latter—since the introduction of an easy solution of the Ex-meridian problem—is certainly no longer of the same importance.

**Application limited in low latitudes.**

If the value of the problem under consideration be somewhat lessened owing to its unsuitability in low latitudes, it must not be forgotten that in such regions there is generally but little difficulty in getting the sun exactly at noon, so that the inapplicability of the method at such times is not much felt.

The rule regulating the limits within which Ex-meridians may be taken is easily remembered, namely—*The hour angle of the sun, or time from noon, should not exceed the number of degrees in the sun's* MERIDIAN *zenith distance.* Therefore, if the sun's *meridian* altitude be about 80°, the time from noon of an Ex-meridian observation should be less than ten minutes. In Towson's method, the Tables admit of a 20 minute hour angle with an altitude of 74°, beyond which it is not prudent to go, as the results would be doubtful. **Rule regulating Hour Angle.**

The correctness of the Latitude deduced from the method of reduction to the meridian, depends upon the accuracy with which the Apparent Time at Ship is known, *and the higher the altitude the greater is the precision required in the time.* If sights have been taken *at a suitable hour* in the morning (see chapter on Longitude by Chronometer), there should be no hitch on this account. But admitting the Apparent Time to be in error somewhat, there is still a way of circumventing the difficulty. *Get a P.M. Ex-meridian as well as an A.M. one, and endeavour that both shall have about the same altitude.* The *mean* of the two resulting latitudes—*after each has been reduced to noon*—will be within a fraction of the truth. In a note Towson says:— **Dodge when Hour Angle is faulty.**

"If equal altitudes be taken before and after the meridian passage, half the elapsed time may be employed as the hour angle for determining the reduction. Or, when the altitudes before and after noon differ by only a few minutes,* the mean of the two may be reduced by employing half the elapsed time as the hour angle for reducing the mean altitude." **Towson's dodge.**

In these rules no allowance is made for observer's change of position; and though they may be sufficiently accurate in a slow moving vessel when the hour angle is small, or where the course is nearly East or West, it would scarcely do in a fast steamer, steering North or South with a large hour angle. So if these rules should at any time be employed, care must be taken to see that the circumstances are not objectionable. **Results affected by ship's change of position.**

There is yet another dodge, when the time is uncertain, by which it may be approximately corrected. If two *equally good* Ex-meridian altitudes, with an interval between them of say ten

* Minutes of arc (′) are of course meant.

minutes, be taken on the same side of noon; and the second latitude, on being worked back to the place of the first by allowing the correction due to the course and distance in the interval, does not agree with it, the Time is probably in error; in which case the *mean* latitude is *not* to be taken as the true latitude, *from the fact that an error in the time affects least the observation nearest the meridian;* which latter is accordingly to be preferred. It will be easy then to find *by trial* the hour angle which will make the first result agree with the last; and thus the Apparent Time may be *approximately* corrected.

**Mode of approximately correcting Hour Angle.**

It is unnecessary in these pages to give the rules for working "Ex-merids."* as the two recommended will be found respectively in Towson's pamphlet and *Norie's Epitome.* The Apparent Time at Ship is deduced from the chronometer time in the manner already explained in the chapter about "Azimuths."

The student will do well to take his books and pencil, and follow out the work in the subjoined example, which is solved by each of the two methods above referred to. By so doing, certain "important simplicities" will in each case be forced upon his attention.

EXAMPLE.

November 18th, 1881, about seven bells in the forenoon, in Latitude by account 51° N., and Longitude 11° 30′ W., the observed altitude of the sun's lower limb was 19° 20½′ S., when a chronometer which was 4m. slow of G.M.T. shewed 0h. 2m. 30s. P.M. same date. Eye 24 feet. Required the latitude at instant of observation, *and also at noon;* the ship making S. 14° W. (true), 14 knots per hour.

### "EX-MERID." (TOWSON'S METHOD.)

| | H. M. S. |
|---|---|
| Time by chronometer .. .. | 0 2 30 |
| Chronometer slow .. .. .. | + 4 00 |
| Greenwich Mean Time .. .. | 0 6 30 |
| Equation of Time .. .. .. | + 14 36 |
| Greenwich Apparent Time .. .. | 0 21 6 |
| Longitude in Time W. .. .. | − 46 0 |
| Apparent Time at Ship .. .. | 11 35 6 |
| | 12 |
| Sun's hour angle .. .. | 0h. 24m. 54s. |

| | |
|---|---|
| Sun's observed altitude .. .. | 19° 20½′ S. |
| Correction, Table IX. (Norie) .. | + 8½ |
| Augm., Table II.—Index 61 .. | + 6½ |
| Augmented true alt. .. .. | 19 35½ |
| | 90 |
| | 70 24½ N. |
| Augmented declin. .. .. | 19 27 S. |
| Lat. *at time of observation* .. | 50 57½ N. |
| Correction for run till noon .. | − 5½ S. |
| Latitude *at noon* .. .. .. | 50° 52′ North. |

| | |
|---|---|
| Sun's declin., corrected for G.M.T. .. .. | 19° 20′ 43″ S. |
| Augmentation, Table I. Index 61.. .. .. | + 6 22 |
| Augmented declination .. .. .. | 19° 27′ 5″ S. |

* Commonly so called for shortness.

**Relative length of Towson's and Norie's methods.**

The observation on last page is given below, worked according to *Norie's Epitome,* and since the finding of the hour angle and the correcting of the sun's declination is the same in each case, they are both left out to avoid unnecessary repetition. This, however, must not be allowed to mislead in estimating the relative length of the two methods. Towson's is much the shorter and easier; nevertheless, if compelled to fall back upon Norie's method for stars whose declinations exceed 23½°, the navigator will find no trouble whatever in mastering it.

### "EX-MERID." (NORIE'S METHOD.)

| | | | | | |
|---|---|---|---|---|---|
| Sun's hour angle, 0h 24m. 54s. .. | | .. .. .. .. .. | | Log. rising Table XXIX. | 2·77051 |
| Latitude by account 51° N... | | .. .. .. .. .. | | ,, cosine .. .. | 9·79887 |
| Sun's corr. declin., 19° 20¾' S. | | .. .. .. .. .. | | ,, cosine .. .. | 9·97476 |
| | | Natural number .. .. | 350·1* | Log... | 2·54414 |
| Sun's true altitude .. | 19° 29¼' .. | Natural sine .. .. | 333601 | | |
| Merid. zen. distance .. | 70° 18' N. | Natural cosine .. .. | 337102 | | |
| ☉'s corr. declin. .. | 19 20¾ S. | | | | |
| Latitude .. .. .. | 50° 57½' N. *at time of observation.* | | | | |
| Correction for run .. – | 5¾ S. | | | | |
| Latitude .. .. .. | 50° 51¾' N. *at noon.* | | | | |

**Ex-meridian gives latitude at time of observation.**

It is *very* important to understand that the above meridian zenith distance, 70° 18', was the sun's actual meridian zenith distance *at the place where the altitude was taken;* and the resulting latitude, 50° 57½' N., *was the latitude of the ship at the time of the observation* (*not* at noon). *Therefore, always bear in mind that the Latitude found by an Ex-meridian altitude is the Latitude of the ship at the instant of observation, and if afterwards you should require to know what it is at noon, you must correct it by the difference of latitude (out of the traverse tables) due to the course and distance which the ship has made in the interval.*

**Common misconception.**

Ignorance of this has been a fruitful source of error with *many* seamen of the writer's acquaintance, who, until it was fully explained to them, were inclined to dispute the truth of the above statements. It is easy to see that, in a case similar to the imaginary one pictured on pages 230—231, if the latitude were found by an "Ex-merid.," instead of the meridian altitude, *and if the reduction to noon were not made,* a like catastrophe might well ensue.

* Attention is called to the footnote in Norie's later editions, which says,—"This 'natural number' had better *always be taken out to one place of decimals* (as shewn in the example), as then the nat. sine of the true altitude can be taken to *six figures.* If *no decimal* figure be taken, the nat. sine must only be taken to the *first five figures.*" The writer considers it quite unnecessary to work to six figures, so the decimal had better always be omitted, and the nat. sine of the true altitude only taken out to *five* figures.

## CHAPTER VI.

### TIME.

Before going any deeper into the various star problems which are considered of practical value, it is as well that the reader should be thoroughly at home in the subject of *Time*—especially *Sidereal Time*. The word *Sidereal* means—of or belonging to the stars, and is derived from the Latin *Sidus*, a star.

**Sidereal day.** A *Sidereal day* is the period in which the earth performs one complete revolution round its axis, and, setting fractions on one side, is equal to 23h. 56m. 4s. of *mean time*, as measured by our clocks or watches; so that the common expression, that the world revolves once in twenty-four hours, is incorrect, unless *Sidereal* hours are either specified or understood.*

A *Sidereal day* is shorter than a *mean Solar day* by 3m. 56s.; consequently, the stars come to the meridian of any place nearly four minutes of clock time *earlier* on each succeeding day. Their

**Daily revolution of stars perfectly regular.** revolution in the heavens† may be taken as perfectly regular, since our distance from the stars is so inconceivably great, that the earth's annual motion in space is quite imperceptible when compared with it.‡ With the sun it is otherwise. Owing to the

* The interval occupied by the earth in performing one revolution round its axis is taken as the *standard* for the measurement of time. The velocity of rotation is considered never to vary in the slightest degree; but Sir William Thomson (Professor of Natural Science at the University, Glasgow), supposes, from certain mathematical investigations made by him, that this may not be altogether true. These investigations lead him to believe in the possibility of the earth's motion being infinitesimally retarded by the tidal wave, which, moving in the opposite direction, acts upon it after the manner of a friction brake. From the impossibility at present of constructing clocks to go with sufficient regularity, there is no direct way of testing this idea.

† In the language of nautical astronomy, the earth (for sake of convenience) is considered as standing still, and the heavens to be moving round it.

‡ See page 225.

non-coincidence of the Equator with the Ecliptic, and the unequal motion of the sun in the latter,* due to the eccentricity of the earth's orbit, the solar days are of varying length. The period between two successive transits of the sun is known as an *Apparent Solar Day;* but, from its irregularity, it would be impossible to get clocks which would conform with it, so as always to point to 12 when the sun was on the meridian. **Solar days vary in length.**

To get over this and other difficulties, astronomers conceived the idea of creating an *imaginary sun*—which, like the stars, would be uniform in its motion. The interval between two successive transits of this imaginary sun is termed a *Mean Solar Day, and is equal to the mean or average of all the Apparent Solar Days in a year.* It is this to which our clocks and chronometers are adjusted, as well for navigational as the every-day purposes of life; but, in observatories, it is also customary to have an additional clock regulated to *Sidereal Time,* on account of its greater convenience in connection with certain of the astronomical observations. The dial of this clock is numbered up to 24 hours, so that the short hand makes but one round of the circle in the day.† **Imaginary or Mean Sun.** **Sidereal clock face—how marked.**

The difference between the place of the real and imaginary sun is familiarly known to sailors as the *Equation of Time.* Sometimes the imaginary sun is ahead of the real one, and sometimes it is astern of it, according to the period of the year. The fact as to which of the two is leading decides the application of the equation of time, as set forth in the precept at the head of its column in the *Nautical Almanac.* **Equation of Time.**

A sun-dial shews *Apparent* time, and consequently its indications will only agree with *Mean* or clock time when the real and imaginary suns happen to coincide, or pass the meridian at the same instant. This actually occurs four times in a twelvemonth, namely, about April 14th, June 13th, August 31st, and December 23rd. Accordingly, on these days—at a particular moment—the Equation of Time is *nil.* **Apparent Time, and difference between Sun-dial and Clock Time.**

The foregoing explanations ought to make clear the meaning of the terms *Apparent Solar day* (apparent time), *Mean Solar day* (mean time), and *Sidereal day* (sidereal time). Until the

* See footnote on page 230.

† In parenthesis, let it be here remarked, that chronometers for use on ship-board should have their faces figured in a similar manner. Were it so, it would save many mistakes.

reader feels that he perfectly comprehends them he had better not attempt to go further.

**Mean Time.** *Mean time* begins (that is, a mean solar clock points to 0h. 0m. 0s.) at *mean noon;* or what is the same thing—at the instant of the passage of the *imaginary* sun across the meridian.

**Sidereal Time.** *Sidereal time* begins (that is, a sidereal clock points to 0h. 0m. 0s.) when the first point of *Aries* is on the meridian, and is counted straight through 24 hours till the same point returns again. The hour angle or meridian distance of this point is accordingly *Sidereal time.*

**First point of Aries.** It is now necessary to know what is meant by the first poiut of *Aries.* It is that point in the heavens which the sun's centre occupies at the *Vernal equinox* when its declination changes from South to North; or, as sailors say, when the sun *crosses the Line* bound North.

This point, like the mean sun, is purely an imaginary one, as nothing exists to mark its place, nor would it be any particular advantage were it otherwise; moreover, the point itself is liable to a certain slow movement westward,—so slow, however, as not to affect perceptibly the interval of any two of its successive returns to the meridian, although in a year the amount of retrogression (50″), as it is called, is quite appreciable.

**Equivalents of Right Ascension and Declination.** It is from this point as zero that the *Right Ascensions* of all celestial bodies are measured. The *Right Ascension and declination of a point in the heavens corresponds to the Longitude and Latitude of a station on the earth.*

**Definition of Right Ascension.** *Right Ascension,* which we come across so frequently in Nautical Astronomy, may be defined as an arc of the equator included between the first point of *Aries* and the celestial meridian of the body it refers to, and is reckoned on the *celestial* equator exactly as the *Longitude* of places on the earth is reckoned on *our* equator; with this distinction, however, that *Right Ascension is reckoned continuously through* 24 *hours from west to east,* or in the opposite direction to the apparent diurnal motion of the heavenly bodies, —whereas *Longitude* is counted as east *or* west of Greenwich, or any other arbitrary meridian, such as Paris, or Cadiz, according to caprice. Moreover, as the stars do not preserve that constant position with respect to the meridian which they do with respect to the equator, there cannot be that correspondence between *Right Ascension* and *Longitude* which *does* exist between *Declination* and *Latitude.*

This being understood, we next come to the term *Hour angle,* or

*Meridian distance* as it is sometimes called. It may be defined as the angle at the Pole, included between the meridian of the observer and the celestial meridian of the body referred to. Like the *Right Ascension*, the *Hour angle* is measured on the *celestial* equator in the same way that *Longitude* is measured on the *terrestrial* equator.* **Definition of Hour Angle.**

In turning these definitions over in the mind, one must try not to get "mixed," as will, however, very likely be the case with those whose attention has only been seriously called to them now for the first time. Do not be disheartened and tempted to skip, but try back, and each fresh reading will give more insight, until the whole is as plain as *A B C.* Often it is a good plan to sleep on a matter difficult to understand, and attack it again in the morning when the brain is vigorous. **"Time"—a difficult study.**

*Time* is an essential element in navigation, and, entering as it does into all of the astronomical problems, is as necessary to be understood as the points of the compass. Unfortunately there is no "royal road" to these more abstruse questions—nothing for it but to hammer away at them with all possible concentration of thought till the victory is gained.

If the reader has got a clear conception of the foregoing, he will scarcely require to be told that the *Hour angle* of the first point of *Aries* is equal to the *Right Ascension of the Meridian* of an observer, which again is precisely the same thing as *Sidereal Time.* From this it follows that *difference* of *Right Ascension* may with perfect propriety be considered *as a portion of Sidereal time, or as Longitude.* **Equality in differences of Longitude and Right Ascension.**

Thus, if a certain star were on the meridian of any place—say New York—at the same instant that another star was on the meridian of Greenwich, the *difference* of the *Right Ascensions* of these two stars would be equal to the Longitude of New York.

By turning to page II. for the month in the *Nautical Almanac*, it will be found that the last or right-hand column is headed "SIDEREAL TIME." In the words of the explanation given on page 495 of the N. A. for 1884, this "SIDEREAL TIME" "is the angular distance† of the first point of *Aries*, or the true vernal equinox from the meridian‡ at the instant of Mean noon. It is, therefore, the Right Ascension of the Mean sun, or the time shewn by a sidereal clock at Greenwich, when the mean time clock indicates 0h. 0m. 0s." In proof of this it will be noticed on the

* It must not be forgotten that longitude is reckoned in *time* as well as in *arc*.

† Reckoned in *time*, not in *arc*. ‡ At Greenwich.

same page that the *Equation of Time* is equal to the difference between the *Apparent Right Ascension* of the sun at Mean noon, and the *Sidereal time* at Mean noon.

By the foregoing, it ought to be again made evident that *Sidereal Time* and *Right Ascension of the meridian* are one and the same thing. Now, since the measure of *Sidereal time* is identical with the measure of Longitude, if by any means we can know the *Sidereal time at Greenwich* corresponding to the *Sidereal time at Ship*, we have at once the Longitude of the ship as measured from Greenwich.

**Similarity of Sidereal and Mean Time intervals.**

In the thoughtful mind the question may be raised as to whether Longitude, when measured by an interval of *Sidereal* time, is the same as when measured (numerically speaking) by a similar interval of *Mean* time, seeing that sidereal and mean time have different absolute values. Raper, in a foot-note,* disposes of this question thus:—

"The diff. long. is found as well by means of the motion of a star as of the sun; that is, by means of a clock or chronometer regulated to Sidereal time, as well as by one regulated to Mean time. For although the absolute interval of time employed by a star in moving from one meridian to the other, is less than that employed by the sun, yet it is divided into the same number of hours, minutes, and seconds, but which are of smaller magnitude, and thus the difference of time results, in numbers, the same."

In finding the longitude at sea, the *Sidereal Time at Ship* is obtained by calculation from observations of the stars themselves, but the *Sidereal Time at Greenwich*, with which to compare it, is dependent upon the accuracy of the chronometers employed in the operation, and is found as follows. To the chronometer time of observation apply its error, which, of course, gives Greenwich Mean Time. To this add the Sidereal time for the *preceding* Mean noon, taken from the last column on page II. of the month.

**How to change Clock Time into Star Time.**

It now becomes necessary to change the given Greenwich Mean Time into sidereal measure by *adding* to it the *acceleration* taken from a table of time equivalents to be found on page 480 of the N.A. for 1884. This table is also given in *Norie's Epitome*, where it is numbered XXXVIII., and is used for converting intervals of mean solar time into equivalent intervals of sidereal time. In actual practice the hundredths would be rejected.

* Page 157, thirteenth edition.

EXAMPLE.

Required the Sidereal Time *at Greenwich* on March 28th, 1881, when a chronometer which was 5m. 42s. fast of G.M.T. shewed 9h. 15m. 18s. same date:— **Example of Sidereal Time at Greenwich.**

| | H. | M. | S. |
|---|---|---|---|
| Time by chronometer | 9 | 15 | 18·00 |
| Chronom. fast of G.M.T. – | | 5 | 42·00 |
| Greenwich Mean Time | 9 | 9 | 36·00 |
| Sidereal time at *preceding* mean noon, viz., March 28th. | 0 | 24 | 9·57 |
| By Table, the acceleration for 9h. of Green. Mean Time is + | | 1 | 28·71 |
| " " 9m. " " + | | 0 | 1·48 |
| " " 36s. " " + | | 0 | 0·10 |
| Required Sidereal Time at Greenwich | 9 | 35 | 15·86 |

9h. 35m. 15·86s. is accordingly the *Sidereal Time at Greenwich* at the instant of 9h. 9m. 36s. Mean Time at that place, and is equal to the *Right Ascension of the meridian* of an observer at Greenwich; or, in other words—at that moment, and at that place—the *Hour angle* of the first point of *Aries* is 9h. 35m. 15·86s. West.

The approximate *Sidereal Time at Ship* may, in a somewhat similar manner, be determined from the chronometer time and the longitude by account.

EXAMPLE.

Required the Sidereal Time *at Ship* on November 18th, 1881, when a chronometer, which was 2m. 42s. slow of G.M.T., shewed 11h. 54m. 33s. same date. Longitude by account, 60° 15′ W. **Example of Sidereal Time at ship.**

| | H. | M. | S. |
|---|---|---|---|
| Time by chronometer | 11 | 54 | 33·00 |
| Chronom. slow of G.M.T. + | | 2 | 42·00 |
| Greenwich Mean Time | 11 | 57 | 15·00 |
| Longitude of ship in time | 4 | 1 | 00·00 |
| Mean Time at ship | 7 | 56 | 15·00 |
| Sidereal Time at *preceding* mean noon, viz., Nov. 18th | 15 | 50 | 39·98 |
| By Table, the acceleration for 11h. of Green. Mean Time is. + | | 1 | 48·42 |
| " " 57m. " " + | | 0 | 9·36 |
| " " 15s. " " + | | 0 | 0·04 |
| The required Sidereal Time at Ship, *or* Right Ascension of the Meridian | 23 | 48 | 52·80 |

This last is what is required in the problem, "Latitude by an Ex-meridian Altitude of a star." Then, to ascertain from it the star's

**How to find and name Star's Hour Angle.**

hour angle, you have merely to take the difference between the *Right Ascension of the meridian*, as above, and the *Right Ascension of the star*, as given in the *Nautical Almanac*.

In working "Ex-merids.," it is not always necessary to know whether the hour angle is East or West; but, should it be required, the following rule is not difficult to remember. In all cases, if the *Right Ascension of the meridian* exceed 24h., subtract that amount from it; then, if it be greater than the Right Ascension of the star, the hour angle is west. When the contrary is the case, it is east. Should the hour angle thus found exceed 12h., subtract it from 24h., and reverse its name.

**Check to avoid mistakes.**

To prevent any gross mistakes creeping into this work, it is easy to check the result by Norie's Table XLIV. Thus: take the difference between the Apparent Time at Ship (roughly found by clock) and the stated time of star's meridian passage, as given in the table, which will be sufficiently near the true hour angle to enable any *great* blunder in the regular work to be detected.

**Gain or loss of a day in circumnavigating the Globe.**

In connection with *Time*, there is one point which deserves more than a passing notice. It is the picking up or dropping of a day, according as the globe is circumnavigated east or west about.

One who is not familiar with the subject finds it difficult to realize that at the same moment there should be a difference of time at various parts of the earth's surface—nor is this really the case so far as *absolute* time is concerned. The *present moment* here in England is equally the *present moment* in Sydney, Australia, although the clock there marks some ten hours later than it does with us. This is accounted for by the fact that the sun, which is the divider of day and night, and all over the world the recognized marker of Time, crosses the meridian of Sydney some ten hours before it reaches ours.

**Sun the domestic timekeeper of the world.**

In the daily course of the sun, his advent at each meridian on the earth's surface marks the hour of noon for all places on that meridian. It is thus the sailor, more especially, reckons his time. No matter what seas he may be navigating, he considers it noon the moment the sun is "up," or on his meridian. Now, if his course lies from east to west, or if he and the sun are moving in the same direction, clearly at the instant the sun arrives at his meridian, and he strikes 8 bells, it must be past noon at the places he left yesterday, and is not yet noon at the place he hopes to reach by to-morrow.

**Explanation of how time is gained or lost in navigation.**

On the other hand, if he is sailing eastward, he is moving in an opposite direction to the sun—which, therefore, instead of overtaking him, as it did when he was bound towards the west, now advances to meet him, and consequently, before it has reached the spot where he took his mid-day observation of yesterday, it will be past noon with him to-day, and getting on towards one bell. In plain language, as he goes eastward he shortens his day, and as he goes westward he lengthens it, in exact proportion to the difference of longitude made good—the constant rate in all latitudes being 1 hour for every 15° of his advance.

Let then the navigator—having started presumably from Greenwich in an easterly direction—arrive at the meridian of 180° at 1 o'clock on the morning of Tuesday the 16th (ship time); it will then be only 1 o'clock at Greenwich in the afternoon of Monday the 15th, as by meeting the sun he has got ahead of the folks at home, and anticipated their time by 12 hours. It will be midnight with him when it is only mid-day with them. If he continues on in the same direction, and completes the other half of the voyage without altering his date, he will have gained another 12 hours on arrival at Greenwich, *no matter how long he may be in getting there,* and would probably imagine the day of his return to be, say Friday noon, when in reality it was only Thursday noon.

**What to do on arriving at the meridian of 180°.**

To avoid this, on passing the meridian of 180° E., he should have reckoned Monday the 15th *twice over,* which would have brought things straight at the finish. On the contrary, when reaching 180° in a westerly direction, the navigator would be exactly 12 hours *behind* Greenwich, so that if it were then 1 o'clock on Tuesday morning the 16th by *his* reckoning, it would be 1 o'clock in the afternoon of the same day at Greenwich. If he pursued his voyage westward without making the requisite alteration in his calendar, he would arrive at Greenwich, say at noon on Friday, and be surprised to learn that with the inhabitants it was noon of Saturday. To avoid this, he should have skipped a day when at 180° W. He should have called the day Wednesday, and have overlooked Tuesday altogether.

**Pay attention to Greenwich date *shewn by chronometer.***

The great point for the practical navigator to attend to is *to hold on to his Greenwich date by chronometer,* otherwise he may make the not uncommon blunder of taking out the *Nautical Almanac* elements for the wrong day, and so get adrift as to his true position.

**Chronometer face—how it should be marked.**

Here the marking of the chronometer face from 1 up to 24 hours would be of great service. As the dial is figured at present, there are no means of distinguishing the XII. noon from XII. midnight; whereas, if marked as suggested, 24 hours would always refer to noon, and 12 hours to midnight.

If, however, a man, when winding his chronometer, were to take the trouble from the very beginning of the voyage, to enter every day, on a slip of paper kept in the case, the hour A.M. or P.M., day of the week, and day of the month—*Greenwich time*—of his doing so, he could not possibly get astray. When, by-and-by, he found his own or ship date differing from that of Greenwich, he would merely have to adopt the latter, whatever it might be. Thus, having passed the meridian of 180° E., on going to wind his chronometer at 8 o'clock on Tuesday morning the 16th, he would find by his slip that at Greenwich it was 8 o'clock on Monday evening the 15th, and would accordingly instruct his chief officer to consider the day as Monday over again, and so enter it in his log.

**How to avoid confusion.**

Going east or west round the world, there will be no *real* gain or loss of a day. Otherwise a man, by continually sailing round east about, might be considered—from the frequent repetition of a day which it entailed—to have lived longer than another who had stopped at home. In the case of the traveller, he only *appears* to gain a day, as each one of those he has lived whilst on his journey has been shorter by a certain number of minutes—which has arisen from the difference of longitude traversed between two consecutive arrivals of the sun on his meridian; whilst the day of the man who remained behind has always contained the complete 24 hours.

**No *absolute* gain or loss of time in circumnavigating the world.**

Again, if two men, *A* and *B*, started at the same instant on a journey round the world, the first going east and the other west, and neither made any alteration in their dates from time of setting out till their return together on the same day, this is what would happen: *A* would believe he had arrived, say on Sunday, and *B* would persist in considering it as Friday. There would be a difference of two whole days in their reckoning; but no one would seriously entertain the idea that on this account *A* had lived 48 hours longer than *B*. The actual day of the week would, of course, be Saturday, and the *actual* time occupied by each on the journey would be precisely the same.

**Curious illustration of difference of date caused by circumnavigating in opposite directions.**

The reader will understand from this that *Time* may be *relative* as well as *absolute*.

To shew this yet more clearly, let us take a very exaggerated case. Supposing it were possible for a pedestrian to walk round either pole of the earth, say at a fixed distance from it of 10 miles, the circumference of the circle which he would describe would be 60 miles, and at the rate of 2½ miles per hour he would accomplish the entire circuit in one day. If, then, he started at noon, Apparent Time at place, and walked always in a westerly direction, preserving the above steady rate, he would keep pace exactly with the sun, and have it bearing either north or south, as the case might be, apparently stationary on his meridian as long as he chose to keep up his walk. His *local time* would *never* alter. If he started, say at noon on Sunday, so long as he continued to walk, *local time* would cease to progress, and it would remain noon on Sunday; but *absolute time* would go on as usual, as his weary feet and the watch in his pocket would plainly tell him.

**Distinction between *relative* and *absolute* time explained.**

The following problem is so instructive in first principles that, although it scarcely belongs to the subject, and is not rigorously correct, it would be a pity to omit it.

**Curious but instructive problem.**

The question is—In what way could a navigator who has no knowledge of his position, and has lost all record of time, ascertain not only his correct latitude and longitude, but recover the day and date? It is presumed that he is provided with the usual nautical instruments and books.

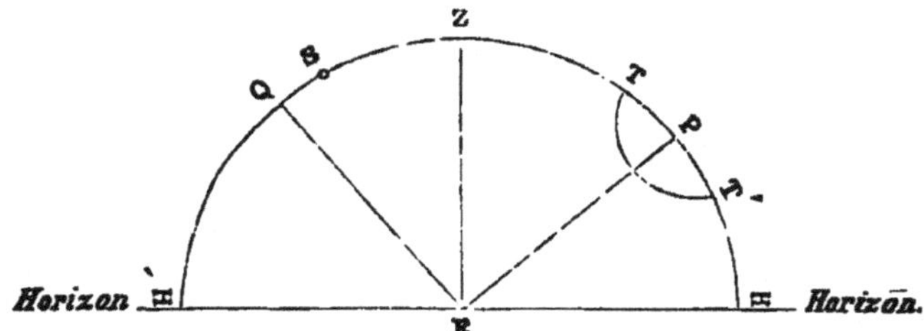


Let the above figure be a projection of the sphere on the plane of the meridian. *P* is the elevated pole; *Z*, the zenith, *EQ*, the equator; and *TT'*, any circumpolar star.

To solve the question, let the navigator observe the altitude of any circumpolar star at both its upper and lower culminations, as at *T* and *T'*; the half sum of these altitudes will give him the altitude of the pole, which is equal to the latitude of the place of observation—that is, it will give him the arc *QZ*. Then let the ship be hove-to, so as to keep on the same parallel of latitude until noon of next day. At noon, observe the meridian altitude of the sun; thus, the arc *SH'* becomes known, *S* being the position of the sun when on the meridian. Subtract *SH'* from *ZH'*, and we have the arc *SZ*.

*QS* is the declination of the sun. Now we know *QZ* and *SZ*; hence we have $QZ - SZ = QS$, or we thus ascertain the declination at noon of the sun. This quantity is tabulated in the *Nautical Almanac* every noon; it is a constantly varying quantity—hence there can be only *one* noon to which the known declination corresponds; so by hunting this up in the *Nautical Almanac*, the day, month, and year are at once determined.

A second method of determining the date is to measure the distance between the sun and moon with a sextant (Lunar observation), or the distance between the moon and one of the principal stars. These distances are tabulated in the *Nautical Almanac*. They differ from day to day, and the difference between any two days is sufficient to fix the date. The "Lunar" would give the longitude from Greenwich. The intelligent reader will not need to be told that there are insuperable difficulties to the carrying out of the foregoing in actual practice.*

**Days of the week distinguished by symbols.**

To wind up the chapter on *Time*, it is well to know that with us the days of the week are named after the deities in the Scandinavian mythology; but in astronomy they are represented by symbols having reference to the sun and certain of the planets.

☉ Sunday (the Sun).

| | |
|---|---|
| ☾ Monday (the Moon). | ♃ Thursday (Jupiter). |
| ♂ Tuesday (Mars). | ♀ Friday (Venus). |
| ☿ Wednesday (Mercury). | ♄ Saturday (Saturn). |

Sometimes, when jammed for room, it is convenient to use these symbols, and they are soon learned.

**Difference in duration of Northern and Southern Summer.**

It may also be interesting to know that in the northern and southern hemispheres the duration of summer is not the same. The northern summer is the longer of the two, since the sun is on our side of the equator for 186½ days, and to the southward of it for the remaining 178¾ days.

In this chapter there has been no little repetition and much harping upon the same thing; but the writer will not regret the loss of space or literary effect, if thereby he has succeeded in making this (generally speaking) hazy subject of *Time* any clearer to the understanding of seamen.

---

* Captain S. P. H. Atkinson has cleverly pointed out that, as the observer could not tell whether the sun was moving North or South, it would be necessary to wait and take *two* meridian altitudes to determine which side of the solstice he was on. Also, that as the observer's longitude is unknown, and as the elements in the N.A. are computed for noon *Greenwich Date*, and not for noon *at Ship*, our Nautical Rip Van Winkle would still be in a mental fog as to the exact date. To overcome this, Captain Atkinson proposes that the Lunar should be taken near the time of getting the meridian altitude, and the interval measured by watch, and allowed for in comparing with the N.A.

This, *coupled with* the meridian altitude, would fix the Greenwich Date, and the Lunar would give the G.M.T. as closely as the moon's Sem. and Hor. Parall. taken out for the approximate G.M.T. (determined by roughly corrected App. Dist.) would allow.

The Lunar then worked afresh with the elements corrected by the last found G.M.T. would give a still better determination.

## CHAPTER VII.

### LATITUDE BY EX-MERIDIAN ALTITUDE OF A STAR.

**Similarity between "Ex-merid." of Sun and Stars.**

With the exception of finding the hour angle (meridian distance) *this work is exactly the same as that for the sun.* The stars, however, have manifold advantages, inasmuch as, among other things, it is generally possible to choose those which will give the best results, whereas with the sun we have to take it as we find it.

As shewn in the previous chapter, much depends in this problem on a correct knowledge of the *Time* employed in the calculation, consequently *it is important to choose such stars as will be least affected by any error in this element.*

From the slowness of their motion in altitude, it follows that the stars near either pole are the best adapted for this observation. Always give the preference, therefore, to such as have large declinations, of which the following is a list, in the order of their Right Ascensions; but the examples given further on will shew that it is by no means necessary to confine one's self to these alone.

**Suitable stars—limit of visibility in opposite hemispheres.**

| | Declin. | visible to | | Declin. | visible to |
|---|---|---|---|---|---|
| Achernar | Declin. 58° S. | visible to 22° N. | α Perseus | Declin. 49° N. | visible to 31° S. |
| Canopus | ,, 53 S. | ,, 27 N. | Capella | ,, 46 N. | ,, 34 S. |
| ι Argo Navis | ,, 59 S. | ,, 21 N. | Dubhe | ,, 62 N. | ,, 18 S. |
| α Crux | ,, 62 S. | ,, 18 N. | γ Ursæ Majoris | ,, 54 N. | ,, 26 S. |
| β Centaur | ,, 60 S. | ,, 20 N. | Benetnasch | ,, 50 N. | ,, 30 S. |
| α Centaur | ,, 60 S. | ,, 20 N. | β Ursæ Minoris | ,, 75 N. | ,, 5 S. |
| α Triangula Australis | ,, 69 S. | ,, 11 N. | Rastaban | ,, 51 N. | ,, 29 S. |
| α Pavo | ,, 57 S. | ,, 23 N. | Vega | ,, 39 N. | , 41 S. |
| α Grux | ,, 48 S. | ,, 32 N. | Deneb | ,, 45 N. | ,, 35 S. |

The above latitudes of visibility are in each case calculated for a meridian altitude of 10°, but in clear weather, and under ordinary conditions of temperature and atmospheric pressure, these limits may be exceeded, as it is possible to see stars at much lower altitudes—sometimes, indeed, on rising or setting, when they are not unfrequently mistaken for a steamer's mast-head light. Owing, however, to the uncertainty of refraction near the horizon, it is not usually prudent to observe bodies having a less altitude than 7° or 8°. When compelled to do so, however, it is advisable to note the barometer and thermometer, also the sea temperature, and if the conditions are abnormal, correct the mean refraction by the Auxiliary Table III.* of Norie. In such cases, endeavour to get an observation on the opposite side of the zenith as well, which will enable you, as already explained, to detect any unusual refraction.

**Precautions with low altitudes.**

**Increased opportunities of observation at favourable times.**

Another point wherein the *ex*-meridian altitude has a pull over the altitude *on* the meridian, is, that during twilight (the best time for observing) it may so happen that there is no star then culminating; whereas it would be hard lines indeed if one or two could not be found, the smallness of whose hour angle east or west permitted the use of this method. The reader cannot fail to see that, by it, the opportunities of getting the latitude are materially increased.

Again, to watch for the transit of a star on a dark night requires no little patience, and it has a decidedly fatiguing effect on the eye. This is avoided by the ex-meridian, where one good sight—without the bother of waiting, on a possibly wet deck—is all that is required. Nor does the sextant in this latter case suffer by unnecessary exposure to the damp night air, which, by clouding the glasses, requires a frequent application of the chamois leather; and this, in its turn—unless carefully done—is apt to put the instrument out of adjustment.

**Ex-Meridians of stars better than the observation on the Meridian.**

All things considered, Ex-meridians are preferable to the Meridian altitude. Compared with the gain, the extra work is trifling.

About 3 A.M. on Sunday, June 6th, 1880, the following "Ex-merids." for latitude were taken on board the s.s. "*British Crown.*" Eye 22 feet; no index error; chronom. slow of G.M.T. 3m. 57s.: barometer, 30″·52; air temperature, 58° Fahrenheit.

| Chronometer. h. | m. | s. | | | | ° | ′ | |
|---|---|---|---|---|---|---|---|---|
| 16 | 34 | 12 | June 5th, observed alt. | | ✱ Altair, | 50 | 17 | S. |
| 16 | 43 | 13 | „ | „ | ✱ Polaris, | 48 | 33¾ | N. |
| 16 | 53 | 00 | „ | „ | ✱ Altair, | 49 | 38¾ | S. |

At noon, June 6th, the same chronometer shewed 1h. 20m. 00s. (25h. 20m. reckoning from previous day), and the ship's position was 48° 44′ N., and 20° 53′ W. Between 3 A.M. and noon, the ship made N. 70° E. (true), 12·2 knots per hour; therefore, at the time the chronometer shewed 16h. 43m. 13s., we have for the position by account—Latitude 48° 8′ N., and Longitude 23° 22′ W.

Example of "Ex-merid." by Towson's method.

### EXAMPLE I. *(Towson's Method.)*

| | H. M. S. |
|---|---|
| Time by chronometer .. .. .. | 16 34 12 |
| Chronom. slow.. .. .. .. .. + | 3 57 |
| G M.T... .. .. .. .. .. .. | 16 38 09 |
| Longitude in time .. .. .. .. | 1 33 40 |
| Mean time at ship .. .. .. .. | 15 04 29 |
| Sidereal time at *preceding* G.M. noon. .. .. .. .. | 4 57 09 |
| Acceleration for 16h. 38m. 09s. .. + | 2 44 |
| Right Ascension of the meridian. | 20 04 22 |
| Right Ascension of * Altair .. | 19 44 59 |
| | M. S. |
| *'s hour angle. .. .. .. .. .. | 19 23W. |

| | ° ′ |
|---|---|
| *'s observed alt. .. .. .. .. .. | 50 17 S. |
| Correction—Table XV. of *Norie*. − | 5½ |
| *' true altitude. .. .. .. .. .. | 50 11½ |
| Augm. Table II., Index 46.. ..+ | 14¾ |
| Augmented altitude .. .. .. | 50 26¼ S. |
| | 90 |
| | 39 33¾ N. |
| *'s Augmented declin... .. .. | 8 35 N. |
| Latitude .. .. .. . .. .. | 48° 08¾′N. |

| | ° ′ ″ |
|---|---|
| Altair's declin., page 358, N.A. .. .. .. .. .. | 8 33 12 N. |
| Augm. Table I. of *Towson*, Index 46 .. .. .. ..+ | 1 48 |
| Augmented declination .. .. .. .. .. .. .. | 8° 35′ 00″N. |

Example of "Ex-merid." by Norie's method.

### EXAMPLE II.

| | H. M. S. |
|---|---|
| Time by chronometer .. .. .. | 16 53 00 |
| Chronometer slow .. .. .. ..+ | 3 57 |
| G.M.T. .. .. .. .. .. .. | 16 56 57 |
| Longitude in time .. .. .. .. | 1 33 16 |
| Mean time at ship .. .. .. .. | 15 23 41 |
| Sidereal time at *preceding* G.M. noon. .. .. .. .. .. | 4 57 09 |
| Acceleration for 16h. 57m. .. ..+ | 2 47 |
| Right Ascension of the meridian. | 20 23 27 |
| Right Ascension of * Altair .. | 19 44 59 |
| *'s hour angle .. .. .. .. .. | 38 28W. |

| | ° ′ |
|---|---|
| *'s observed altitude .. .. .. | 49 38¾ S. |
| Correction—Table XV. of *Norie* − | 5½ |
| *'s true alt. .. .. .. .. .. | 49° 33¼′S. |

NOTE.—As this observation lies beyond the scope of *Towson's* Tables, recourse is had to *Norie's* method. The difference in length will be apparent.

| | M. S. | | | |
|---|---|---|---|---|
| Time from meridian .. .. | 38 28 W. | .. .. .. .. .. .. | Log rising .. | 8·14779 |
| | ° ′ | | | |
| Latitude by account .. .. | 48 9 N. | .. .. .. .. .. .. | Cosine .. .. | 9·82425 |
| *'s declination. .. .. .. | 8 33½ N. | .. .. .. .. .. .. | Cosine .. .. | 9·99514 |
| | ° ′ | | Natural Number .. .. .. | 927 = 2·96718 |
| *'s true altitude .. .. .. | 49 33¼ S. | .. | Natural sine .. .. .. | 76106* |
| Merid. zen. distance .. .. | 39 37 N. | .. | Natural cosine .. .. .. | ..77033 |
| *'s declination .. .. .. | 8 33½ N. | | | |
| Latitude .. .. .. .. .. | 48° 10½′ N. | | | |

Reduction of several obs. to one time for sake of comparison.

The latitude as found by the Pole star was 48° 10′ N., and by allowing for the ship's run in the interval between sights, the first

* Do not take this out to more than *five* places of figures.

"Ex-merid.," reduced to time of observation of Pole star, gives the latitude at that moment as 48° 9½′ N., and the second "Ex-merid.," reduced in like manner, gives it as 48° 9½′ N. also.

The following "Ex-merids." were taken on board the s.s. "*British Crown*" about 8·40 P.M. on the evening of June 6th, 1880. The position by dead reckoning at 9h. 51m. 12s. by chronometer (which shewed 1h. 20m. at preceding noon) being, latitude 49° 21′ N., and longitude 18° 18′ W. Eye 22 feet for all but the North star, which was observed from the bridge, where the eye was 32 feet. Ship supposed to be making N. 70° E. (true), 12·7 knots per hour since noon. Chron., 3m. 57s. slow of G.M.T. No index error. Barom., 30″·32. Therm., 57° Fahr. To economize space, only the first and last sights are shewn worked out, but the reader can work the others by way of practice, if so inclined.

| Chronom. H. M. S. | | | | | Answers. |
|---|---|---|---|---|---|
| 9 42 3 | obs. alt. | * Arcturus . | 59° 41′ S. | For sake of comparison the answers are reduced to time of observation of Polaris, namely 9h. 51m. 12s by chronometer. | Lat. 49° 24′ N. |
| 9 51 12 | " | * Polaris . . | 48 10¾ N. | | " 49 23¾ " |
| 9 53 49 | " | * Arcturus . | 60 7¾ S. | | " 49 24¾ " |
| 9 57 14 | " | * Spica . . | 29 44½ S. | | " 49 24½ " |
| 10 5 2 | " | * Spica . . | 29 29¾ S. | | " 49 25 " |

### EXAMPLE III.

| | H. M. S. |
|---|---|
| Time by chronometer. . . . . . . . | 9 42 3 |
| Chronometer slow . . . . . . . . . | + 3 57 |
| G.M.T. . . . . . . . . . . . . . | 9 46 00 |
| Longitude in time . . . . . . . . . | 1 13 24 |
| Mean time at ship . . . . . . . . . | 8 32 36 |
| Sidereal time at *preceding* G.M. noon . | 5 1 6 |
| Acceleration for 9h. 46m. . . . . . . | + 1 36 |
| Right Ascension of the meridian . . . | 13 35 18 |
| Right Ascension of * Arcturus . . . | 14 10 14 |
| *'s hour angle . . . . . . . | 34m. 56s. E. |

| | |
|---|---|
| Observed altitude * Arcturus . . | 59° 41′ S. |
| Correction, Table XV. of *Norie*. . | − 5 |
| *'s true altitude . . . . . . . . | 59° 36′ S. |

*Note.*—As this observation exceeds the limits of Towson's Tables, recourse is had to Norie's method.

| | | | | |
|---|---|---|---|---|
| Time from meridian, 34m. 56s. E. . . . . . . . . . | | | Rising | 3·06428 |
| Latitude by account, 49° 20′ N. . . . . . . . . . | | | Cosine | 9·81402 |
| *'s declination, 19° 48½′ N. . . . . . . . . . | | | Cosine | 9·97352 |
| | | Natural number, 711 | = | 2·85182 |
| *'s true altitude . . | 59° 36′ . . . . . . . . | Natural sine . 86251* | | |
| Merid. zen. distance . | 29 35 N. . . . . . . . . | Natural cosine . 86962 | | |
| *'s declination . . | 19 48½ N. | | | |
| Latitude . . . . . | 49° 23½′ N., at instant of observation. | | | |

* Do not take this log. out to more than *five* places of figures.

Example IV. (Towson's Method).

| | H. M. S. |
|---|---|
| Time by chronometer . . . . . . . | 10 5 2 |
| Chronometer slow . . . . . . . . | + 3 57 |
| G.M.T. . . . . . . . . . . . . . | 10 8 59 |
| Longitude in time . . . . . . . . | 1 13 2 |
| Mean time at ship . . . . . . . . | 8 55 57 |
| Sidereal time at *preceding* G.M. noon. | 5 1 6 |
| Acceleration for 10h 9m. . . . . . . | + 1 40 |
| Right Ascension of the meridian . . | 13 58 43 |
| Right Ascension of * Spica . . . . | 13 18 55 |
| *'s hour angle . . . . . . . . . | 39m. 48s. W. |

| | |
|---|---|
| * Spica's observed altitude . . . | 29° 29¾′ S. |
| Correction, Table XV. of *Norie* . | − 6½ |
| *'s true altitude . . . . . . . | 29 23¼ S. |
| Augm. Table II.—Index 102 . . | + 28¾ |
| Augmented altitude . . . . . | 29 52½ |
| | 90 |
| | 60 7½ N. |
| *'s augmented declination . . . | 10 41⅞ S. |
| Latitude at time of observation . | 49° 26′ N. |

| | |
|---|---|
| * Spica's declination, page 345, N.A. . . . . . . | 10° 32′ 24″ S. |
| Augmentation, Table I.—Index 102 . . . . . . | + 9 26 |
| *'s augmented declination . . . . | 10° 41′ 50″ S. |

It will be noticed that Towson's solution is independent of the latitude by dead reckoning, which is entirely excluded from the calculation. On this account, combined with the brevity and accuracy of the method, give it the preference whenever it is possible to do so. It may here be mentioned that the arrangement for making the correction from Table I. *always additive*, is effected on a somewhat similar principle to the one already described in connexion with the *Nautical Almanac* method of latitude by the Pole star, and is made purely for convenience. **Towson's method independent of the latitude.**

In example III. the number of minutes in the hour angle exceeds the number of degrees in the meridian zenith distance—which, in a star like Arcturus, having small declination, is an unfavourable condition; nevertheless, the observation is worked out to shew that, if carefully made, and the time used be reliable, the result will still be good. **Unfavourable condition.**

The foregoing examples are *bona fide*, having been actually taken on board the "*British Crown*" on a North Atlantic passage. They were selected at hap-hazard from among a large number of others equally good, and prove very conclusively the splendid results which may be obtained by the use of the ex-meridian problem.

When the time is in error, the reductions on one side of the meridian will be too great, and on the other too small; if, therefore, two stars on opposite sides of the meridian—having nearly equal hour angles—be observed within a few minutes of each other, the mean of the two results (each being first reduced to the same instant of time) will be free from any error due to this cause. Or, what amounts to the same thing, it may be possible to get the *same* star at nearly equal distances on *both* sides of the meridian, but in this last case the ship should be stationary, or nearly so, or allowance made for change of position (see page 303).

**"Ex-merid." table, by A. C. Johnson, R.N.**

Mr. A. C. Johnson, R.N., of H.M.S. "*Britannia*," has brought out a capital little ex-meridian table,* which is extremely convenient when the observer keeps well within the limits assigned to this problem. It occupies but one small page, and, with the rule for using it, can easily be pasted on the fly-leaf of the *Epitome*. Of course, in a table of such modest proportions, *very* great accuracy must not be looked for; but it is sufficiently exact for the ordinary purposes of navigation when in open water, and requires even less time to get out the result than Towson's method.

**"Ex-merids." of planets.**

Ex-meridians of the planets Venus, Mars, Jupiter, and Saturn, are worked in a similar manner to the fixed stars. As, however, their Right Ascensions and Declinations are constantly varying (the Latin word *Planeta* means a *wandering star*), it is necessary to correct them for the Greenwich Date.† They will be found in the *Nautical Almanac* for 1884, between pages 226 and 265. In other respects the problem is precisely the same, even to the correction of the observed altitude,‡ so that an example is unnecessary.

**"Ex-merids." *below* the Pole.**

So far, ex-meridians *above* the Pole have only been treated of; but as occasion may offer to observe them *below* the Pole, and the results derived from this problem being just as correct as any other, it is proper to give a few examples. Unfortunately, in this case, Towson's tables are disqualified for use in the ordinary navigable waters of the globe. To be of service, the observer would require to be on the polar side of 70° of latitude; therefore Norie's method, slightly altered, must be used instead.

On board the S.S. "*British Crown*," about 11 P.M. on Saturday, June 19th, 1880, the clouds were seen to break low down on the northern horizon, and disclose a bright star shining in the midst of a small clear space. To the eye there was nothing by which this solitary star could be recognized. A bearing of it by standard compass, when corrected for variation and deviation, gave its *true* azimuth as N. 2° W., making it evident that the star—whichever it might be—was approaching its lower culmination.

* Table II., page 21, in his very excellent pamphlet "*On finding the Latitude and Longitude in cloudy weather, and at other times.*" Published in London by J. D. Potter, 31, Poultry.

† "The GREENWICH DATE is the time at Greenwich corresponding to any given time elsewhere." See Raper, para. 481, page 157, ninth edition.

‡ Parallax may be disregarded. In the case of Jupiter and Saturn it is an utterly insignificant quantity; and in that of Venus, seldom exceeds 15". Since it is, in all cases, the estimated *centre* of the radiant point which will be brought down to the horizon, semi-diameter may also be disregarded.

Reference to Table XLIV. of Norie shewed that Capella had passed the meridian *above* the Pole at 11h. 9m. in the forenoon, and would consequently pass the meridian *below* the Pole at 11h. 7m. on that very night. This, therefore, must be the star which, out of the many in the heavens, happened to be the only one visible. On computing Capella's meridian altitude,* its close agreement with that observed made the identity of the star no longer a matter of conjecture. It was accordingly decided to secure sights, to be worked up *as ex-meridians below the Pole,* and also, if possible, to get its *Lower meridian altitude.*

**How to compute meridian altitude *below* the Pole.**

As a check on Capella—the altitude being so very small—it was important to get a star to the southward, and on referring again, with this in view, to the same Table in Norie, it was discovered that the star Ras Alhague (*a* Ohpiuchi) would pass the meridian to the southward at 11·34 P.M. But as the sky was completely clouded over, with the exception of the aforesaid small break to the northward, and as, moreover, the writer was unacquainted with this particular star, it was not likely the wish would be gratified; *nevertheless the meridian altitude of Ras Alhague was computed, in readiness to place upon the sextant in the event of the clouds breaking up.* This actually occurred shortly after, and through a rift in the clouds the needful sight of the coveted star was obtained.

**How to be ready for flying shots.**

Had the approximate altitude not been calculated beforehand, and the sextant set to it, the observation would certainly have been lost; as the star, with three or four others, only remained visible for half a minute or so, and could not, even if recognized, have been brought down to the horizon with exactness in so short a time.

The following are the observations as actually taken, but want of space does not permit of them all being worked out:—

| | Chronometer. H. | M. | S. | | | ° | ′ | |
|---|---|---|---|---|---|---|---|---|
| (*a*) | 12 | 33 | 32 | observed alt. | ✱ Capella | 5 | 32¼ | N. |
| (*b*) | 12 | 43 | 45 | ” | ” | 5 | 27½ | ” |
| (*c*) | 12 | 50 | 24 | ” | ” | 5 | 25¼ | ” |
| (*d*) | 12 | 53 | 00 | ” | ” | 5 | 25½ | ” |
| (*e*) | 12 | 57 | 9 | ” | ” | 5 | 25¾ | ” |
| (*f*) | 13 | 10 | 1 | ” | ” | 5 | 28 | ” |
| (*g*) | 13 | 20 | 48 | ” | ” | 5 | 34¾ | ” |
| (*h*) | 13 | 26 | 19 | ” | ✱ α Ophiuchi | 53 | 22¼ | S. |

Eye 30 feet. Index error + 45″. Chronometer slow of G.M.T. 4m. 00s.

Barometer, 29″·40. Air, 56°. Water, 57°. Position by account at 12h. 53m. 00s. by chronometer: Latitude, 49° 15′ N.; Longitude, 25° 53′ W. Ship making S. 70° W. (true) 11·2 knots per hour.

For sake of comparison, the various latitudes in the answers are all reduced, for the run of the ship, to 12h. 53m. by chronometer, at which time Capella was *on the meridian below the Pole.*

* Rule for computing the approximate meridian altitude *below* the Pole:—From the latitude by account subtract the star's polar distance. Simple enough! Isn't it?

## Example I. (*a*).

| | H. M. S. |
|---|---|
| Time by chronometer - - - - - - | 12 33 32 |
| Chronometer slow - - - - - - - | + 4 00 |
| G.M.T. - - - - - - - - - - - - | 12 37 32 |
| Longitude in time - - - - - - - | 1 43 00 |
| Mean time at ship - - - - - - - | 10 54 32 |
| Sidereal time at *preceding* G.M. noon - - - - - - - - - - - - | 5 52 21 |
| Acceleration for 12h. 37m. 32s. - - - | + 2 5 |
| Right Ascension of the meridian - | 16 48 58 |
| Right Ascension of * Capella - - | 5 7 51 |
| Capella west of the meridian, *above* the pole - - - - - - - - - - | 11 41 07 |
| | 12 |
| Capella's hour angle west of the meridian, *below* the pole - - - | M. S. 18 53 |

| | |
|---|---|
| Observed alt. of * Capella - - - - | 5° 32½' N. |
| Index error - - - - - - - - - - - | + ½ |
| | 5 33 |
| Correction—Table XV. of *Norie* - - | — 14¾ |
| *'s true altitude - - - - - - - - | 5° 18¼' N. |
| *'s declination, page 328, N.A. - | 45° 52½' |
| | 90 |
| *'s Polar distance - - - - - - - | 44° 07½' |

| | | |
|---|---|---|
| Time from the meridian below the pole, 18m. 53s. - - - - - - - | Rising | - 2·53073 |
| Latitude by account, 49° 13½' N. - - - - - - - - - - - - - - | Cosine | - 9·81501 |
| *'s declination, 45° 52½' N. - - - - - - - - - - - - - - - - | Cosine | - 9·84275 |
| | Natural number - - | 154* = 2·18849 |
| *'s true altitude, 5° 18¼' - - - - - - - - - - | Natural sine - - - | - 09244 |
| Lower meridian zenith distance - 84° 47' - - - | Natural cosine - - | - 09090 |

| | |
|---|---|
| Lower meridian zenith distance | 84° 47' |
| | 90 |
| True lower meridian altitude - - | 5 13 |
| *'s Polar distance - - - - - - - | 44 7½ |
| Latitude - - - - - - - - - - | 49 20½ N. |
| Reduction for ship's run - - - - | — 1¼ |
| Latitude - - - - - - - - - | 49° 19¼' N. at 12h. 58m. by chronometer. |

## Example II. (*b*).

| | H. M. S. |
|---|---|
| Time by chronometer - - - - - - | 12 43 45 |
| Chronometer slow - - - - - - - | + 4 00 |
| G.M.T. - - - - - - - - - - - - | 12 47 45 |
| Longitude in time - - - - - - - - | 1 43 11 |
| Mean time at ship - - - - - - - - | 11 04 34 |
| Sidereal time at *preceding* G.M. noon | 5 52 21 |
| Acceleration - - - - - - - - - | + 2 6 |
| Right Ascension of the meridian - | 16 59 1 |
| Right Ascension of * Capella - - - | 5 07 51 |
| Hour angle west of meridian, *above* the pole - - - - - - - - - - | 11 51 10 |
| | 12 |
| Hour angle west of meridian, *below* the pole - - - - - - - - - - | M. S. 8 50 |

| | |
|---|---|
| * Capella's observed altitude - - | 5° 27½' N. |
| Index error - - - - - - - - - | + ½ |
| | 5 28 |
| Correction, Table XV. of *Norie* - | — 14¾ |
| * Capella's true altitude - - - - | 5° 13¼' N. |

* In ex-meridians *below* the Pole, the natural number must be *subtracted* from the natural *sine* of the true altitude.

| | | | | |
|---|---|---|---|---|
| Time from the meridian, 8m. 50s. W. - - - - - - - - - - - - - | | | Rising | - 1·87080 |
| Latitude by account, 49° 13½′ N. - - - - - - - - - - - - - - | | | Cosine | - 9·81501 |
| *'s declination, 45° 52½′ N. - - - - - - - - - - - - - - - | | | Cosine | - 9·84275 |
| | | | Natural number - - 84 = | 1·52856 |
| *'s true altitude - - - - | 5° 13½′ N. | - - - - - | Natural sine - - - | ·09100 |
| Meridian zenith distance - | 84 48 | - - - - - | Natural cosine - - | ·09066 |
| | 90 | | | |
| True meridian altitude - | 5 12 N. | | | |
| *'s polar distance - - - | 44 7½ N. | | | |
| Latitude - - - - - - - | 49 19½ N. at time of sight. | | | |
| Correction for ship's run - | — ½ | | | |
| Latitude - - - - - - - | 49° 19′ N. at 12h. 53m. by chronometer. | | | |

EXAMPLE III. (*d*).

In strictness, this example, not being an ex-meridian, belongs to a previous chapter, but it is introduced so that the resulting latitude may be compared with that given by the other sights.

| | ° ′ |
|---|---|
| Observed alt. of * Capella on the merid. *below* the pole | 5 25¼ N |
| Index error- - - - - - - - - - - - - - - - - - | + ¾ |
| | 5 26 |
| Correction, Table XV. of *Norie* - - - - - - - - - - | − 14¾ |
| * Capella's true meridian altitude - - - - - - - - | 5 11¼ N. |
| * Capella's polar distunce - - - - - - - - - - - | 44 07½ N. |
| Latitude - - - - - - - - - - - - - - - - | 49° 18¾′ N. at 12h. 53m. |

EXAMPLE IV. (*g*).

| | H. M. S. |
|---|---|
| Time by chronometer - - - - - | 13 20 48 |
| Chronometer slow - - - - - - - | + 4 00 |
| G.M.T. - - - - - - - - - - - - | 13 24 48 |
| Longitude in time - - - - - - - | 1 43 57 |
| Mean time at ship - - - - - - - | 11 40 51 |
| Sidereal time at *preceding* G.M. noon | 5 52 21 |
| Acceleration - - - - - - - - - | + 2 13 |
| Right Ascension of the meridian - | 17 35 25 |
| Right Ascension of * Capella - - | 5 7 51 |
| Hour angle *west* of meridian, *above* the pole - - - - - - - - - - - | 12 27 34 |
| | 12 |
| | M. S. |
| Hour angle *east* of meridian, *below* the pole - - - - - - - - - - - | 27 34 |

| | |
|---|---|
| * Capella's observed altitude - - | 5° 34¾′ N. |
| Index error - - - - - - - - - - - | + ¾ |
| | 5 35½ |
| Correction, Table XV. of *Norie* - - | — 14¾ |
| *'s true altitude - - - - - - - - | 5 20¾ N. |

NOTE.—Attention is called to the change in name of the hour angle. As the *westerly* hour angle *above* the pole is greater than 12 hours, the excess is of necessity equal to the hour angle *east* below the pole. Refer to diagram on page 240.

| | | | | |
|---|---|---|---|---|
| Time from the meridian, 27m. 34s. E. - - - - - - - - - - - - | | | Rising - - | 2·85884 |
| Latitude by account, 49° 13½ N. - - - - - - - - - - - - | | | Cosine - - | 9·81501 |
| * Capella's declination, 45° 52½′ N. - - - - - - - - - - - | | | Cosine - - | 9·84275 |
| | | | Natural number - - 329 = | 2·51660 |
| * Capella's true altitude - - - - | 5° 20¾′ | - | Natural sine - - - | ·09317 |
| Lower meridian zenith distance - | 84 50½ | - | Natural cosine - - | ·08988 |
| | 90 | | | |
| True lower meridian altitude - - | 5 9½ N. | | | |
| * Capella's Polar distance - - - | 44 7½ N. | | | |
| Latitude - - - - - - - - - - - | 49 17 N. at time of sight. | | | |
| Correction for ship's run - - - - | + 1¾ | | | |
| Latitude - - - - - - - - - - - | 49 18¾ N. at 12h. 53m. by chronometer. | | | |

### EXAMPLE V. (*h*), Towson's Method.

* Ras Alhague *above* the pole to the southward. Taken as a check on Capella.

| | H. M. S. |
|---|---|
| Time by chronometer | 13 26 19 |
| Chronometer slow | + 4 00 |
| G.M.T. | 13 30 19 |
| Longitude in time | 1 44 6 |
| Mean time at ship | 11 46 13 |
| Sidereal time at *preceding* G.M. noon | 5 52 21 |
| Acceleration for 13h. 30m. 19s. | + 2 13 |
| Right Ascension of the meridian | 17 40 47 |
| Right Ascension of * Ras Alhague | 17 29 25 |
| Hour angle of Ras Alhague (α Ophiuchi) | 11m 22s. W. |

| | ° ′ |
|---|---|
| Obs. alt. of * Ras Alhague | 53 22¾ S. |
| Index error | + ½ |
| | 53 23¼ |
| Correction—Table XV. of *Norie* | — 6 |
| | 53 17¼ |
| Augm. Table II., Index 15 | + 5½ |
| Augmented alt. | 53 22¾ |
| | 90 |
| | 36 37¼ N. |
| Augmented declination | 12 39¾ N. |
| Latitude at time of sight | 49 17 N. |
| Correction for run | + 2 |
| Latitude at 12h. 53m. | 49° 19′ N. |

| | ° ′ ″ |
|---|---|
| Declination of * Ras Alhague | 12 38 53 N. page 354, N.A. |
| Augm. Table I., Index 15 | + 53 |
| Augmented declination | 12° 39′ 46″ N. |

About 9·15 P.M., Monday, June 21st, 1880, being in latitude by acc. 45° 20′ N., and longitude 37° 57′ W., from the bridge of the s.s. *British Crown*, Capella and the North Star were observed for latitude. On referring to Norie's Table XLIV., the former was found to be west of the meridian below the Pole, and the North Star east of it. Eye 32 feet. Index error, + 30″. Chronometer slow of Greenwich mean time, 4m. 00s. Barometer, 29″·98. Air, 56°. Water, 59°.

Chronometer 11h. 38m. 34s., observed alt. * Capella - - - 4° 51½′ N.
" 11h. 41m. 20s., " " North Star - - 44° 13½′ N.

### EXAMPLE VI.

| | H M S. |
|---|---|
| Time by chronometer | 11 38 34 |
| Chronometer slow | + 4 00 |
| G.M.T. | 11 42 34 |
| Longitude in time | 2 31 48 |
| Mean time at ship | 9 10 46 |
| Sidereal time at *preceding* G.M. noon | 6 00 14 |
| Acceleration for 11h. 43m. | + 1 56 |
| Right Ascension of the meridian | 15 12 56 |
| Right Ascension of * Capella | 5 7 51 |
| *'s hour angle west of meridian, *above* the pole | 10 5 5 |
| | 12 |
| *'s hour angle west of meridian, *below* the pole | 1 54 55 |

| | ° ′ |
|---|---|
| Observed alt. * Capella | 4 51½ N. |
| Index error | + ½ |
| | 4 52 |
| Dip | — 5½ |
| | 4 46½ |
| Refraction | — 10½ |
| *'s true altitude | 4° 36½′ N. |

| | | | | |
|---|---|---|---|---|
| Time from meridian, 1h. 54m. 55s. W. | | Rising | | 4·09025 |
| Latitude by account, 45° 20′ N. | | Cosine | | 9·84694 |
| * Capella's declination, 45° 52½′ N | | Cosine | | 9 84275 |
| | ° ′ | Natural number | 6025 = | 3 77994 |
| *'s true altitude | 4 36½ | Natural sine | 08027 | |
| Lower meridian zenith distance | 88 51 N. | Natural cosine | 02003 | |
| | 90 | | | |
| True lower meridian altitude | 1 9 N. | | | |
| *'s polar distance | 44 7½ N. | | | |
| Latitude | 45° 16½′ N. | | | |

EXAMPLE VII. (Pole Star *N. A.* Method).

| | H. M. S. |
|---|---|
| Time by chronometer | 11 41 20 |
| Chronometer slow | + 4 00 |
| G.M.T. | 11 45 20 |
| Longitude in time | 2 31 48 |
| Mean time at ship | 9 13 32 |
| Sidereal time at *preceding* G.M. noon | 6 00 14 |
| Acceleration for 11h. 45m | + 1 56 |
| Right Ascension of the meridian | 15 15 42 |

| | ° ′ |
|---|---|
| Observed alt. Pole star | 44 13½ |
| Index error | + ½ |
| | 44 14 |
| Correction—Table XV. of *Noris* | — 6½ |
| | 44 07½ |
| Constant | — 1 |
| Reduced altitude | 44 6½ |
| First correction | +1 9½ |
| Second correction | + 0½ |
| Third correction | + 0½ |
| Latitude | 45° 17′ N. |

The very close agreement of all these results might lead those not well posted in star work to suspect that they had been "cooked." Such, however, is not the case. Wherever the name of the ship is given, the observations are those which were actually taken, *and have not been altered in any way whatsoever*. In many instances (of which this is one) the stars were observed and calculated in the presence of the officers of the vessel, who can answer for the perfect honesty of the work. This is mentioned to dispel any doubts as to what stars are really capable of. The *beginner* can scarcely hope for such a nice accordance of results, but a moderate amount of perseverance will prove the truth of the adage—"Practice makes perfect."

In Example VI. Capella has been treated as an ex-meridian for latitude, but from its very large hour angle (1h. 54m. 55s.) putting it beyond the prescribed limits, it must be regarded as an extreme case, and is expressly chosen on that account to assist in illustrating what will presently be said about the North star. An error of 15′ in the *latitude* by account used with Capella will not appreciably affect the result, but an error of 15′ in the *longitude* (equal to 1 minute in the Time) would put the answer wrong some three miles, shewing the impropriety of placing dependence on ill-conditioned observations. If Capella's declination were but

**Why stars near the Poles should be chosen for "Ex-merids."**

larger (say 70° instead of only 46°) a similar error in the time would not affect the result nearly so much, proving that greater liberties in this respect can be taken with the stars near the Poles, such for example as Dubhe, and the brilliant one in the foot of the Southern Cross.

To these, therefore, the rule for the sun, that the number of *minutes* in the hour angle should not exceed the number of *degrees* in the meridian zenith distance, does *not* apply.

The most notable instance of this is to be found in the North star, which is so close to the Pole that (as previously stated) an error in the time of half an hour, when near its upper or lower meridian passage, will fail to produce an error of even one mile in the answer.

**Pole Star problem merely an "Ex-merid." *in disguise.***

It has probably never occurred to the nautical reader, when figuring out the "Latitude by Pole star," that to all intents and purposes he is working an ex-meridian. Such, however, is really the case, though ninety-nine out of every hundred are deluded into believing it to be a *special* problem, peculiar to this star alone.

The plain fact is, that the North star's extreme slowness of motion, due to its small diurnal circle, permits of a handy table being calculated to do away with the tedium of the longer process.* A somewhat similar table might, indeed, be computed for

---

* To shew that the familiar North star problem is nothing more than an ex-meridian *in disguise*, Example VII. is here given over again, worked out similarly to Capella.

| | H. M. S. |
|---|---|
| Right Ascension of meridian, as before | 15 15 42 |
| Right Ascension of Pole star, N.A., page 314 | 1 14 43 |
| Hour angle west of meridian *above* the pole | 14 00 59 |
| | 12 |
| Hour angle east of meridian *below* the pole | 2 00 59 |

| | |
|---|---|
| Declination of Pole star | 88° 40′ N. |
| | 90 |
| ✱'s polar distance | 1° 20′ N. |

| | | |
|---|---|---|
| Time from the meridian, 2h. 00m. 59s. E. | Rising | 4·13394 |
| Latitude by account, 45° 20′ N. | Cosine | 9·84694 |
| Declination of Pole star, 88° 40′ N. | Cosine | 8·36678 |
| | Natural number 222 = | 2·34766 |

| | | |
|---|---|---|
| True altitude of Pole star | 44° 7½′ N. | Natural sine 69628 |
| Lower meridian zenith distance | 46 3 | Natural cosine 69406 |
| | 90 | |
| Lower meridian altitude | 43 57 N. | |
| ✱'s polar distance | 1 20 N. | |
| Latitude | 45° 17′ N. The same as before. | |

The writer is not aware of ex-meridians *below the Pole* having been treated of in any other work on navigation. It is hoped their practical utility has been fully demonstrated.

any other circumpolar star, but in no sense would it pay to do so. If the reader be curious to know how this table is formed, he will find a very easily understood account of it in the explanation to Norie's Table XVII. **Construction of table for use with Pole star.**

The two books of Towson—his *Ex-meridian Tables,* and *Practical Information on the Deviation of the Compass,* &c.—should, for convenience, be put together in one strong binding; and the reader is recommended to adopt this plan with regard to them. **Bind Towson's books together for convenience.**

To finish with this problem—Do not forget that the latitude found by an ex-meridian (whether above or below the Pole) is that of the ship *at the moment of observation,* and if required for any other time, must be reduced to it, according to the course and distance made in the interval. BEAR THIS IN MIND.

---

## CHAPTER VIII.

### LONGITUDE BY CHRONOMETER.

If, in the determination of *latitude*, *Time* be an element of *importance*, it becomes an absolute *necessity* where *longitude* is concerned—this latter being invariably found afloat by a comparison of the time at ship with the time at some other place which may happen to be chosen as a starting point from which to measure.

**First meridian—the Royal Observatory at Greenwich.** With us this starting point is the meridian of the transit instrument at the Royal Observatory of Greenwich; and it is probable that, by international consent, this will in future be considered the *First Meridian* for the entire globe, and foreign charts graduated accordingly.

**Longitude—how defined and measured** The *longitude* of a place, therefore, by our reckoning, may be defined as *an arc of the equator*, included between the meridian of Greenwich and the meridian of the particular spot referred to; and is measured either in *space* (° ′ ″), or in *time* (hrs. m. s.). Or, since the meridians all run together to a point at the poles, the longitude of any place on the earth's surface may also be defined as the *angle at the Pole*, included between the meridian of the place and some assumed *First Meridian*, such as Greenwich.

Owing to this *convergence* of the meridians just alluded to, a

**Value in different latitudes.** degree of longitude has different absolute values, according to the latitude in which it is measured. Thus, a degree of longitude on the equator is equal to 60 nautical or geographical miles. In the latitude of Christiania, in Norway (60° N.), it is equal to 30 miles; in 83° 20½′ N.—the highest latitude attained by Captain Markham in the recent Arctic Expedition under Captain Sir George Nares—a degree of longitude is only 7 miles; and at the North Pole itself, in latitude 90°, longitude has no existence whatever, and the sun always bears true south during the six months of the year that it is visible.

When referring, therefore, to a measure of longitude, it is improper to use the word *miles.* The symbols °′″ should be spoken of as degrees, *minutes*, and seconds.

As the sun, which is the great timekeeper for the world, returns every 24 hours, or thereabouts, to the same meridian, after describing a complete circle, or 360°,—it follows, by simple division, that *one hour of time* is equal to 15° (degrees) of longitude; *one minute of time* is equal to 15′ (minutes) of longitude; and *one second of time* is equal to 15″ (seconds) of longitude.

**Longitude in time, how converted into arc.**

As mentioned in a previous chapter, there are several astronomical modes of taking account of time, but that which regulates the business of life is naturally reckoned by the sun, which divides the 24 hours into alternate periods of day and night—light and darkness. It is mid-day, or noon, at a place when the sun is on its *upper* meridian, and midnight when on its *lower* meridian, at which latter time it has accomplished half (180°) its journey round the earth. Owing to the earth revolving left-handed on its axis, the sun passes the meridian of places to the eastward before it comes to us, so the time at such places must necessarily be in advance of ours; consequently, a citizen of New York, in 74° west longitude, may (about 7 in the morning of *his* time) receive a cablegram from a friend in London telling him of his marriage, which had taken place that same forenoon at 11 o'clock, and of his intention to embark for a honeymoon tour in America. In this case electricity, in conveying the news, had outstripped the sun in the race across the Atlantic—in fact, had beaten him by several hours—since the New Yorker at 7 in the morning (perhaps while still in bed) had intelligence of what had *already* occurred in London at 11 A.M. of the same day.

**News by electricity—difference between absolute and relative time.**

According as to whether his own time is ahead of Greenwich or behind it, the navigator is enabled to decide whether he is in east or west longitude; and one is saved the trouble of even *thinking* over this question by the well-known rhyme—

**Rule for naming longitude east or west.**

"Longitude west, Greenwich time best.
Longitude east, Greenwich time least."

As an astronomical question, the determination of longitude resolves itself into the determination of the difference of time *reckoned at the two meridians at the same* ABSOLUTE *instant.* For seamen, the only *really* practical methods of effecting this are—

first by the chronometer, and secondly by Lunars. These last, however, are rapidly dying out, and are mostly looked upon now as "fancy navigation." Excellent chronometers can be purchased brand new for £25 to £30; when second-hand, and equally good, for much less; in fact, they are becoming a drug in the market. The better class of vessels seldom carry fewer than three.

**Money value of chronometers.**

Till Harrison's invention of the first useful artificial marine chronometer was given to the world in 1765, through the well-judged beneficence of the British Government, the only chronometer generally available for finding longitude at sea was that great natural chronometer presented by the moon in her orbital motion round the earth.

Imagine a line joining the centres of inertia of the earth and moon to be, as it were, the hand of a great clock, revolving round the common centre of inertia of the two bodies, and shewing time on the background of stars for a dial.

**"Lunar Theory."**

If the centres of inertia of the moon and earth moved uniformly in circles round the common centre of inertia of the two, the moon, as seen from the earth, would travel through equal angles of a great circle among the stars in equal times; and thus our great lunar astronomical clock would be a perfectly uniform timekeeper.

This supposition is only a rough approximation to the truth; and the moon is, in fact, a very irregular chronometer.

But thanks to the mathematicians, who from the time of Newton have given to what is called the "Lunar Theory" in Physical Astronomy the perfection which it now possesses, we can tell, for years in advance, where the moon will be relatively to the stars, at any moment of Greenwich Time, more accurately than it can be observed at sea, and almost as accurately as it can be observed in a fixed observatory on shore. Hence the error of the clock is known more exactly than we can read its indications at sea, and the accuracy with which we can find the Greenwich Time by it is practically limited by the accuracy with which we can observe the moon's place relatively to sun, planet, or star. This, unhappily, is very rough in comparison with what is wanted for navigation.

**Moon's motion in her orbit.**

The moon performs her orbital revolution in 27·321 days, and, therefore, moves at an average rate of 0°·55 per hour, or ·55 of a minute of angle per minute of time. Hence to get the Greenwich Time correctly to one minute of time, or longitude within 15′, it is necessary to observe the moon's position accurately to half a minute of angle. This can be done, but it is about the most that can be done in the way of accuracy at sea.

It is done, of course, by measuring, with the sextant, the angular distance of the moon from a star, as nearly as may be, in the great circle of the moon's orbital motion. Thus supposing the ship to be navigating in tropical seas, where a minute of longitude is equal to a mile of distance, a careful navigator, with a good sextant, whose errors he has carefully determined, can, by one observation of the lunar distance, find the ship's place within 30 miles of east and west distance. If he has extraordinary skill, and has bestowed extraordinary care on the determination of the errors of his instrument, he may, by repeated observations, attain an accuracy equivalent to the determination of a single lunar distance within a quarter of a minute of angle, and so may find the ship's place within 7 miles of east and west distance; but, *practically*, we cannot expect that a ship's place will be found within less than 20 miles, by the method of lunars, in tropical seas, or within 10 miles in latitude 60°; and to be able to do even so much as this is an accomplishment which not even a good modern navigator, now that the habit of taking lunars is so much lost by the use of chronometers, can be expected to possess.

**Amount of dependence.**

To be able, therefore, to place any reliance on Lunars, requires a really first-class observer, and constant practice, and even then the results are at best but approximate, "inasmuch as the errors of observation are multiplied in their effects on the resulting longitude by a factor whose mean value is about 30; consequently an error of only 10″ in a Lunar Distance (and we presume that under the most favourable circumstances we have no right to expect less—and in most cases it would probably be very much more) becomes 300″ or 5′ in the resulting longitude deduced from it, and this, be it observed, is independent of an additional error of from 6′ to 8′ due to a small uncertainty still existing in the place of the moon as given in the Tables."*

**Lunars almost obsolete.**

Raper also says,—"Great practice is necessary for measuring the distance successfully; and the application of so many small corrections as are necessary where accuracy is required is, even with extraordinary care and some skill, scarcely compatible with extreme precision."

Also in a footnote on page 333 of his 13th ed. we find the

* See Admiral Sir Chas. Shadwell "*On the Management of Chronometers.*"

following:—"The Rev. G. Fisher, in the appendix to Captain Parry's second voyage, states that the mean of 2500 Lunars observed in December differed 14′ from the mean of 2500 observed in March following; and that the mean of the observations made in the same summer differed 10′ from these last, or 24′ from the first." Captain King, in his survey of Australia, notices a discrepancy of a similar kind to the amount of 12′ at the Golbourn Islands.

**Lunar discrepancies.**

Sir W. Thomson, who is considered one of the most profound mathematicians of our time, referring to this question in his "Lecture on Navigation," says,—"I shall say nothing of Lunars at present, except that they are but seldom used in modern navigation, as their object is to determine Greenwich Time, and this object, except in rare instances, is now-a-days more correctly attained by the use of chronometers than it can be by the astronomical method."

**Cheap Sextants of no use for Lunars.**

In the class of vessels most likely to need Lunars (namely, those small craft which, for sake of economy, carry but one chronometer), it is not likely that an expensive Sextant or Quintant will be found; and if by chance it were, it is questionable whether the requisite expertness in observing and calculating would accompany it.

In the ordinary cheap sextants the divisions of the arc are unreliable—sometimes to the extent of 2′—which puts them entirely out of the question for Lunars. In poor instruments, also, the cutting of the vernier and arc at any given angle will often not coincide exactly, and judgment may assign the wrong reading.

Once upon a time, Lunars used to be the crucial test of a good navigator, but that was in the "good old days" when ships were made snug for the night, and the East India "Tea-waggons" took a couple of years to make the round voyage.

The writer of these pages, during a long experience at sea in all manner of vessels, from a collier to a first-class Royal Mail steamer, has not fallen in with a dozen men who had themselves taken Lunars or had even seen others do so. Whether Lunars are worth cultivating or not may, in the minds of some people, still be open to question, but certain it is they have fallen into disuse, and, without in the least being endued with the mantle of prophecy, the writer ventures to say they will never be resurrectionised, for the best of all reasons—they are no longer required.

Nor is there the same necessity for them as of yore. Steam is superseding sail, and voyages generally are shorter than formerly. Now-a-days, also, as the longitude of most places on the globe has been correctly determined, there are infinitely greater opportunities for rating chronometers.

Thanks to the persevering research of Mr. Hartnup, the able astronomer at Bidston, who has experimented for this purpose with over 3000 chronometers, the fluctuations of rate due to temperature are fully understood, and rendered capable of easy application. It may, therefore, be confidently stated that there is now no reason why (on board steamers, at least) the correct Greenwich Time should not always be known within eight or ten seconds *at the very outside.*

**Correct Greenwich time now easily obtained.**

*On shore*, differences of longitude can be determined with marvellous accuracy by means of the electric telegraph, used in connection with the Transit instrument, Astronomical clock, and Electro-chronograph. This last-mentioned instrument may be regarded as an appendage of the clock, and is a contrivance for visibly recording on a sheet of paper each successive beat of the clock. This is very simply and readily accomplished by electricity. The instant of the occurrence of any celestial phenomenon is *also* registered on the same slip, in such a manner, that it can be referred to the preceding clock-beat with great precision. In fact, the interval between two successive beats of the clock can be *easily* divided by scale, so as to admit of the time of the occurrence being read off to the one-hundredth part of a second. The Chronograph, therefore, by subdividing minute portions of time, performs a similar office for the clock that the Vernier does for the Sextant.

**Differences of longitude, how determined *on shore.***

**Instruments used.**

In ascertaining differences of longitude, the usual method now employed is to note the time occupied by a certain star in passing from the one meridian to the other. Roughly stated, the mode of carrying out this operation in practice is as follows:—At *each* station there is a properly adjusted Transit instrument, also a Chronograph, and at *one* of the stations an Astronomical clock, the *rate* of which has been carefully ascertained. Further, it is necessary that the stations should be placed in direct telegraphic communication with each other.

**Actual mode of operation.**

When the star agreed upon enters the field of the transit instrument at the eastern station, the assistant to the observer sets the Chronograph in motion, and, by a preconcerted signal, notice is given to the observer at the western station to do the same. The clock, then, by suitable electric connections, records its beats on *both* Chronographs simultaneously, and the instant of the star's transit is *also* recorded at the proper time, by the observer touching a small spring known as a "signal key." This constitutes the first half of the business. When the star, in due course, arrives at the meridian of the western station, the foregoing signals are there repeated in a precisely similar manner, which completes the operation.

The Chronographic Registers are then consulted, and the interval measured by the clock (*after being corrected for its rate*) is, of course, the difference of longitude between the two stations. The foregoing is but one of several telegraphic methods for determining differences of longitude on shore.

**Differences of longitude, how determined *at sea*.**

*At sea* there is no means of exactly noting the transit of a heavenly body, so local time on shipboard is always found from an *altitude* of some celestial object, observed with the Sextant, and measured from the Sea horizon. The computation of the hour angle or meridian distance is then made, and the resulting local or ship time is compared directly with the Greenwich Time given by the chronometer at the instant of the observation. Next to the meridian altitude, this problem is about the most familiar to the navigator, and yet experience proves that it is but very imperfectly understood by the majority. *It is quite commonly supposed that the error in the longitude is strictly proportional to the error in the altitude*:—thus, if on a hazy day, the observation is in doubt some 3′ or 4′, it is innocently considered that this also is the limit of error of the longitude. Not so, however, as will presently be shewn; the error in the longitude may *easily* be treble the error in the altitude. (See Table II., page 291).

**No direct ratio between errors of observation and errors in the result.**

**Proper time to take sights for longitude.**

*For sights to give the longitude correctly, they must be taken at the right time*:—that is, when an error either in the latitude of the observer, or in the altitude observed, will produce the least effect on the hour angle. To fulfil this condition, *the body must be observed when it is on the Prime Vertical*. These two last appear big-sounding words, and some people allow themselves to be unnecessarily scared by them, although they are capable of very simple explanation.

**Prime Vertical.**

A celestial body is said to be *on the Prime Vertical* when it bears true east or west; so that it is merely a term used in opposition or contradistinction to the well known expression "*on the Meridian*," which latter refers to an object having a true north or south bearing. *The Prime Vertical, therefore, is at right angles to the Meridian*. To get the *latitude*, seamen are very familiar with *the*

"*Meridian altitude*," and for finding the *longitude*, they should be on equally good terms (to coin an expression) with the *Prime Vertical altitude.*

When a celestial object is observed "*on the meridian*," the latitude is found without the *time* being known with greater accuracy than is necessary to correct the declination for the Greenwich date. In the same manner, when an object is observed "*on the Prime Vertical*," the longitude can be found without the necessity of the *latitude* being accurately known—indeed, sometimes an error of 30′ or 40′ will not perceptibly affect the result. To carry out the comparison:—when an "ex-meridian" for *latitude* is observed, a knowledge of the correct *time* is necessary; and the *further* the object is *from the Meridian*, the more important such knowledge becomes. Similarly, when, to determine the *longitude*, an object is observed which is "*Ex-Prime Vertical*," it is essential to a correct result that the *latitude* should be accurately known; and the *further* the object is *from the Prime Vertical*, the more important such knowledge becomes.

**Latitude of but little importance when observation is made on the Prime Vertical.**

Time sights should be taken, therefore, when the body observed bears true east or west, or as near thereto as possible. According to the latitude and declination, this occurs at various hours in the day, and it sometimes happens in the tropics that the most accurate results are to be got from sights taken *within half an hour of noon.* At such times, also, the horizon is free from that fierce glare which so often dazzles the eye, and renders the horizon indistinct when the altitude is low. This latter important advantage is also gained with stars observed during twilight, when the horizon as a rule is strongly marked.

**Good sights for longitude can *at times* be had within 10 or 20 minutes noon.**

When the observer is on the equator, the Prime Vertical becomes identical with the Celestial Equator. In this case, if the declination be 0°, the sun will rise exactly at east, and *continue* on that bearing till the instant of noon, when it will be directly overhead or in the zenith, and have no compass bearing whatever, and its altitude (90°) may be observed *from any point of the horizon.* Immediately that it has passed the meridian, it will bear west, and *continue* to do so till it sets at six o'clock.

When, as just mentioned, the latitude and declination both happen to be 0°—which, by-the-bye, will seldom happen to any one individual—there is little or no calculation required to find the hour angle or meridian distance. (Don't forget that these two mean the same thing.)—Take a sight at *any* altitude; correct it, as usual, by Table IX. of Norie · find the zenith distance by subtracting it from 90°; turn this zenith distance into time, and you have at once the hour angle; or the Apparent Time at Ship, if the object be the sun, and the time be afternoon. Of course in the forenoon you will subtract the hour angle from 12 hrs. or 24 hrs. to get A.T.S., according to the way you wish to apply it.

**Parallels of latitude.**

*Parallels of latitude* encircle the globe in an east and west direction, and to determine which of the parallels we are situated upon, we select celestial objects at right angles to this direction, or as nearly north and south as we can get them.

**Meridians.**

*Meridians* pass from pole to pole in a north and south direction; and, following out the above argument, to determine which of the meridians we are situated upon, we select celestial objects at right angles to their direction, or as nearly east and west as possible. A special reason will be given for this in the next chapter; meanwhile, the reader will kindly accept the statement as reliable.

It is *very* important that attention should be paid to this point in observing for time, as neglect of it may entail serious disaster.

**Table shewing by inspection the Hour Angle and Alt. of a body when on the Prime Vertical.**

In the majority of epitomes *there is a table which shews the hour angle of a celestial object when it is on the Prime Vertical,* and daily reference should be made to it, so as to get sights at the most favourable moment. In *Norie's Navigation*, the table is numbered XLV.,* and in the one following will be found the true *altitude* of the body when it is on the Prime Vertical, so that either may be used at pleasure. Of course if the time at ship be not known within a handful of minutes, it will be preferable to use the *altitude.* The sextant can be set to it, *after correcting it backwards, by subtracting the quantity in Table IX.*, and all possibility of mistake thus avoided.

The nearer the bearing is to east or west the better, but in practice it may be a little on either side of it without signifying greatly; and, indeed, clouds and other causes will often interfere to prevent the sight being taken *exactly* at the instant of passing the Prime Vertical. Sailors think nothing of waiting for the *Meridian* altitude to get the latitude: Why not wait for the *Prime Vertical* altitude to get the longitude? The one thing is as reasonable as the other.

The reader is strongly counselled to look over the explanation to the tables above specified: it is given on page xxxii. of Norie.

Another mode of ascertaining the time that a celestial object will bear east or west, is by reference to Burdwood's or Davis's

* Table XXIX. of Raper.

Azimuth Tables, where, by opening at the latitude of the observer (*same* name as declination), and running down the proper column, the required *hour angle* will be found in the *right-hand* margin, opposite the bearing of 90°. As these tables do not extend beyond 23° of declination, they can only be used with a body whose declination does not exceed that amount. In Norie, the limit for declination is 50°, and for latitude 70°.

**P. V. observations only possible when Lat. and Declin. have same name.**

A celestial object *can* only bear true east or west when its declination is of the *same* name as the latitude, *and less in amount.* When the declination is of the same name, but *greater* than the latitude, the object will not pass the Prime Vertical, *but its nearest approach thereto* will be when its diurnal circle coincides with an azimuth circle. This will be rendered clearer by supposing a case, and referring it to Burdwood or Davis.

**Lat. and Declin. having *contrary* names—best time to observe.**

For example:—In latitude 10° N., the sun's declination being 23° N., when will it be at its nearest approach to the Prime Vertical, and what will be its bearing in the forenoon at that moment? Open Davis at page 81, and it will be found that, with the data given, the sun will rise bearing N. 66° 37′ E.; its bearing will gradually get *more easterly* till 7·36 A.M., when it will be N. 69° 11′ E., and at its nearest approach to the east and west points; after which it will become *more northerly,* till it arrives on the meridian at noon. In this case, therefore, half-past seven in the morning, or half-past four in the afternoon, will be the best time to take sights for longitude; for though the sun will not be on the Prime Vertical, and therefore not in the most favourable position for giving the time, it is the best that can be got under the circumstances. With the conditions just cited, an error of 1′ *in the latitude* will only cause an error in the hour angle of a second and a half; and an error of 1′ *in the altitude* will only cause an error of rather more than four seconds and a quarter.

As before stated, when the object is *exactly* on the Prime Vertical, an error in the latitude of even 30′ or 40′ will not appreciably affect the result. This knowledge is of incalculable value, as it shews the navigator how the longitude may be obtained when the latitude by account is possibly very much in error. The correct time, thus acquired, may be afterwards used to get the latitude by an "Ex-meridian," when the conditions of the "Ex-meridian" might unavoidably be such, that without the *correct* time the result deduced might be considerably astray.

When the latitude and declination are of *contrary* names, the object *cannot* bear east or west, but will be nearest to these points at rising and setting—consequently, in such a case, the least unfavourable time for observing will be when the object is near the horizon, but not at a less altitude than 5° or 6°, unless, from the state of the atmosphere, and the relative temperatures of the air and sea, one is led to believe that there is not an unusual amount of refraction.

**How to detect excessive refraction.**

This can in general be guessed pretty nearly, by noticing the shape of the sun at rising or setting. If it appears flattened, or it its limbs spread out on touching the horizon, or cling to it on leaving, you may be sure there is excessive refraction. On the other hand, if the sun retains its circular shape, and the contact of the limbs is well defined, there is but little refraction. In this latter case, however, it may be *less* than the tabular value, which of course would introduce an error on the *other* side; so that, as a rule, even though the mean refraction be corrected for the height of the barometer and thermometer, observations very near the horizon should be avoided. The careful reader will see from the foregoing, *that the determination of the longitude by the sun in high latitudes during the winter, must be very unsatisfactory.*

**During winter, sun unsuitable for determination of longitude.**

If a low altitude be used, it is open to errors of refraction; but in winter one seldom gets the chance of *any* altitude till the sun has strength to break through the clouds, at which time its bearing is so far from the Prime Vertical, that any error either in the altitude or latitude will produce a very large one in the longitude. On this account, for four or five months in the year, navigation in our own latitudes is a much less ticklish affair when the stars are brought into action. In most cases they can be selected on, or nearly on, the Prime Vertical during twilight, and will then give a *very* reliable longitude. It has already been demonstrated that there is no difficulty in getting a good latitude by Meridian or Ex-meridian altitudes of these friendly guides.

**Stars suitable at all seasons.**

Even supposing that inexpertness in taking stars may cause some error at first, the chances are that it will be less (if the objects selected be well-conditioned) than the inherent error arising from an ill-conditioned observation of the sun, which is concealed, and beyond the observer's control.

Table I., (pages 288, 289), inserted by the generous permission of its author,* gives the error of longitude due to an error of 1′ in the *Latitude*, for every second degree of bearing from 10° up to 90.° This is a most valuable table, shewing at a glance what to

* Mr. A. C. Johnson, R.N.

expect from an incorrect latitude. The writer, following up Mr. Johnson's idea, has had Table II, (pages 290, 291) computed for him by one of his officers, Mr. George C. Burton, which, in a similar manner to Table I, gives the approximate error in the longitude due to an error of 1′ in the *Altitude*. Of course an error in the Polar distance (the third element in the problem for finding the time) should never occur, and, accordingly, is not taken into consideration.*

**Tables shewing errors in result due to errors of latitude and altitude.**

To avoid confusing Table I. with Table II., the latter is printed in red ink.

Reference to the top right hand corner shews that in high latitudes, when the bearing is only 15° or 20° from the meridian, the error in the longitude may be very large—conceive, then, the difficulties of Polar navigation. Even in the very ordinary case given on page 231, where the morning sights were taken at 10·15 o'clock, when the sun had a bearing of S. 23½° E., an error in the *Altitude* of only 2′ (nothing very uncommon with a poor horizon or a poor sextant) would put the longitude out 9′. Should this by chance conspire with the error caused by working with the wrong *Latitude*, the total error in the longitude of the ship, *from both causes acting in concert*, would in this particular instance amount to 33′. This will explain some of the bad land-falls made in winter, which at the time were wrongly imputed to the chronometer, or perhaps to an extraordinary "set."

**Explanation of bad land-falls.**

The quantities in these two tables, it will be seen, depend upon the latitude of the observer and the bearing of the object. The latter is easily arrived at by the Azimuth Tables, or, if great accuracy be a matter of no moment, by a compass bearing corrected for Variation and Deviation. To change the tabular values into seconds of time, multiply by 4.

In working out sights at sea, it is perfect folly to work to seconds of arc; the nearest quarter of a minute (15″) is quite close enough, and in this Raper helps materially by his Table 68, *where the log. sines, &c., are given for every half minute* (30″) *of arc.* Raper deserves the thanks of seamen for many things, and this is not one of the least of them.

**Folly of working to seconds of arc.**

Nor is it necessary to take out the logarithms to more than five figures, any greater exactness being incompatible with the com-

* In this Edition, Table II. is quite accurate, having been kindly overhauled by Capt. S. P. H. Atkinson, who lent a hand with one or two other things which have also been improved upon.

## TABLE I.

*Showing the error in the Longitude produced by an error of 1′ in the Latitude.*

| Bearing. | LATITUDE. | | | | | | | | | | | | | | |
|---|---|---|---|---|---|---|---|---|---|---|---|---|---|---|---|
| | 0° | 4° | 8° | 10° | 12° | 14° | 16° | 18° | 20° | 22° | 24° | 26° | 28° | 30° | 32° |
| 10° | 5·67′ | 5·70′ | 5·73′ | 5·76′ | 5·79′ | 5·85′ | 5·91′ | 5·97′ | 6·03′ | 6·12′ | 6·21′ | 6·30′ | 6·42′ | 6·55′ | 6·69′ |
| 12 | 4·71 | 4·72 | 4·75 | 4·78 | 4·81 | 4·85 | 4·89 | 4·95 | 5·01 | 5·08 | 5·16 | 5·28 | 5·34 | 5·43 | 5·55 |
| 14 | 4·01 | 4·02 | 4·04 | 4·06 | 4·09 | 4·12 | 4·16 | 4·20 | 4·26 | 4·32 | 4·38 | 4·46 | 4·54 | 4·63 | 4·73 |
| 16 | 3·49 | 3·50 | 3·52 | 3·54 | 3·56 | 3·59 | 3·62 | 3·66 | 3·70 | 3·76 | 3·82 | 3·88 | 3·94 | 4·02 | 4·11 |
| 18 | 3·08 | 3·09 | 3·11 | 3·13 | 3·15 | 3·18 | 3·20 | 3·24 | 3·28 | 3·32 | 3·37 | 3·43 | 3·49 | 3·55 | 3·63 |
| 20 | 2·75 | 2·76 | 2·78 | 2·79 | 2·81 | 2·83 | 2·86 | 2·89 | 2·92 | 2·96 | 3·01 | 3·06 | 3·12 | 3·17 | 3·24 |
| 22 | 2·47 | 2·47 | 2·48 | 2·50 | 2·52 | 2·54 | 2·57 | 2·60 | 2·63 | 2·66 | 2·70 | 2·75 | 2·80 | 2·86 | 2·92 |
| 24 | 2·25 | 2·26 | 2·27 | 2·28 | 2·30 | 2·32 | 2·34 | 2·37 | 2·39 | 2·43 | 2·46 | 2·50 | 2·55 | 2·59 | 2·65 |
| 26 | 2·05 | 2·05 | 2·07 | 2·08 | 2·10 | 2·11 | 2·13 | 2·15 | 2·18 | 2·21 | 2·24 | 2·28 | 2·32 | 2·37 | 2·42 |
| 28 | 1·88 | 1·88 | 1·90 | 1·91 | 1·92 | 1·94 | 1·96 | 1·98 | 2·00 | 2·03 | 2·06 | 2·09 | 2·13 | 2·17 | 2·22 |
| 30 | 1·73 | 1·73 | 1·75 | 1·76 | 1·77 | 1·78 | 1·80 | 1·82 | 1·84 | 1·87 | 1·89 | 1·92 | 1·96 | 2·00 | 2·04 |
| 32 | 1·60 | 1·60 | 1·62 | 1·63 | 1·64 | 1·65 | 1·66 | 1·68 | 1·70 | 1·73 | 1·75 | 1·78 | 1·81 | 1·85 | 1·89 |
| 34 | 1·48 | 1·48 | 1·49 | 1·50 | 1·51 | 1·53 | 1·54 | 1·56 | 1·57 | 1·60 | 1·62 | 1·65 | 1·68 | 1·71 | 1·75 |
| 36 | 1·38 | 1·38 | 1·39 | 1·40 | 1·41 | 1·42 | 1·44 | 1·45 | 1·47 | 1·49 | 1·51 | 1·53 | 1·55 | 1·59 | 1·62 |
| 38 | 1·28 | 1·28 | 1·28 | 1·29 | 1·30 | 1·31 | 1·32 | 1·34 | 1·35 | 1·37 | 1·39 | 1·41 | 1·44 | 1·48 | 1·51 |
| 40 | 1·19 | 1·19 | 1·20 | 1·21 | 1·22 | 1·23 | 1·24 | 1·25 | 1·27 | 1·28 | 1·30 | 1·32 | 1·35 | 1·38 | 1·41 |
| 42 | 1·11 | 1·11 | 1·12 | 1·13 | 1·14 | 1·14 | 1·15 | 1·17 | 1·18 | 1·20 | 1·22 | 1·24 | 1·26 | 1·28 | 1·31 |
| 44 | 1·04 | 1·04 | 1·04 | 1·05 | 1·06 | 1·07 | 1·08 | 1·09 | 1·10 | 1·12 | 1·13 | 1·15 | 1·17 | 1·20 | 1·22 |
| 46 | 0·97 | 0·97 | 0·98 | 0·98 | 0·99 | 1·00 | 1·01 | 1·02 | 1·03 | 1·04 | 1·06 | 1·07 | 1·09 | 1·11 | 1·14 |
| 48 | 0·90 | 0·90 | 0·91 | 0·91 | 0·92 | 0·93 | 0·94 | 0·95 | 0·96 | 0·97 | 0·99 | 1·00 | 1·02 | 1·04 | 1·06 |
| 50 | 0·84 | 0·84 | 0·85 | 0·85 | 0·86 | 0·87 | 0·87 | 0·88 | 0·89 | 0·91 | 0·92 | 0·93 | 0·95 | 0·97 | 0·99 |
| 52 | 0·78 | 0·78 | 0·79 | 0·79 | 0·80 | 0·80 | 0·81 | 0·82 | 0·83 | 0·84 | 0·85 | 0·87 | 0·88 | 0·90 | 0·92 |
| 54 | 0·73 | 0·73 | 0·73 | 0·74 | 0·74 | 0·75 | 0·75 | 0·76 | 0·77 | 0·78 | 0·79 | 0·81 | 0·82 | 0·84 | 0·86 |
| 56 | 0·67 | 0·67 | 0·68 | 0·68 | 0·69 | 0·69 | 0·70 | 0·71 | 0·71 | 0·72 | 0·73 | 0·75 | 0·77 | 0·78 | 0·79 |
| 58 | 0·63 | 0·63 | 0·63 | 0·63 | 0·64 | 0·64 | 0·65 | 0·66 | 0·66 | 0·67 | 0·68 | 0·69 | 0·71 | 0·72 | 0·74 |
| 60 | 0·58 | 0·58 | 0·59 | 0·59 | 0·59 | 0·60 | 0·60 | 0·61 | 0·62 | 0·62 | 0·63 | 0·65 | 0·66 | 0·67 | 0·68 |
| 62 | 0·53 | 0·53 | 0·54 | 0·54 | 0·54 | 0·55 | 0·55 | 0·56 | 0·56 | 0·57 | 0·58 | 0·59 | 0·60 | 0·61 | 0·63 |
| 64 | 0·49 | 0·49 | 0·50 | 0·50 | 0·50 | 0·51 | 0·51 | 0·52 | 0·52 | 0·53 | 0·54 | 0·55 | 0·56 | 0·56 | 0·57 |
| 66 | 0·45 | 0·45 | 0·45 | 0·45 | 0·46 | 0·46 | 0·46 | 0·47 | 0·47 | 0·48 | 0·49 | 0·50 | 0·50 | 0·51 | 0·52 |
| 68 | 0·40 | 0·40 | 0·40 | 0·41 | 0·41 | 0·41 | 0·42 | 0·42 | 0·43 | 0·43 | 0·44 | 0·45 | 0·45 | 0·47 | 0·47 |
| 70 | 0·36 | 0·36 | 0·36 | 0·37 | 0·37 | 0·37 | 0·37 | 0·38 | 0·38 | 0·39 | 0·39 | 0·40 | 0·41 | 0·42 | 0·43 |
| 72 | 0·33 | 0·33 | 0·33 | 0·33 | 0·34 | 0·34 | 0·34 | 0·34 | 0·35 | 0·35 | 0·36 | 0·36 | 0·37 | 0·37 | 0·38 |
| 74 | 0·29 | 0·29 | 0·29 | 0·29 | 0·30 | 0·30 | 0·30 | 0·31 | 0·31 | 0·31 | 0·32 | 0·32 | 0·33 | 0·33 | 0·34 |
| 76 | 0·25 | 0·25 | 0·25 | 0·25 | 0·25 | 0·26 | 0·27 | 0·27 | 0·27 | 0·27 | 0·27 | 0·28 | 0·28 | 0·29 | 0·29 |
| 78 | 0·21 | 0·21 | 0·21 | 0·21 | 0·21 | 0·22 | 0·22 | 0·22 | 0·22 | 0·23 | 0·23 | 0·23 | 0·23 | 0·24 | 0·25 |
| 80 | 0·18 | 0·18 | 0·18 | 0·18 | 0·18 | 0·18 | 0·18 | 0·18 | 0·19 | 0·19 | 0·19 | 0·20 | 0·20 | 0·20 | 0·21 |
| 82 | 0·14 | 0·14 | 0·14 | 0·14 | 0·14 | 0·14 | 0·14 | 0·15 | 0·15 | 0·15 | 0·15 | 0·15 | 0·15 | 0·16 | 0·17 |
| 84 | 0·10 | 0·10 | 0·10 | 0·10 | 0·10 | 0·10 | 0·11 | 0·11 | 0·11 | 0·11 | 0·11 | 0·11 | 0·11 | 0·12 | 0·12 |
| 86 | 0·07 | 0·07 | 0·07 | 0·07 | 0·07 | 0·07 | 0·07 | 0·07 | 0·07 | 0·08 | 0·08 | 0·08 | 0·08 | 0·08 | 0·08 |
| 88 | 0·03 | 0·03 | 0·03 | 0·04 | 0·04 | 0·04 | 0·04 | 0·04 | 0·04 | 0·04 | 0·04 | 0·04 | 0·04 | 0·04 | 0·04 |
| 89 | 0·01 | 0·01 | 0·01 | 0·02 | 0·02 | 0·02 | 0·02 | 0·02 | 0·02 | 0·02 | 0·02 | 0·02 | 0·02 | 0·02 | 0·02 |
| 90 | 0·00 | 0·00 | 0·00 | 0·00 | 0·00 | 0·00 | 0·00 | 0·00 | 0·00 | 0·00 | 0·00 | 0·00 | 0·00 | 0·00 | 0·00 |

## TABLE I.

***Showing the error in the Longitude produced by an error of 1′ in the Latitude.***

| Bearing. | LATITUDE. | | | | | | | | | | | | | |
|---|---|---|---|---|---|---|---|---|---|---|---|---|---|---|
| | 34° | 36° | 38° | 40° | 42° | 44° | 46° | 48° | 50° | 52° | 54° | 56° | 58° | 60° |
| 10° | 6′·84 | 7′·01 | 7′·20 | 7′·40 | 7′·63 | 7′·88 | 8′·16 | 8′·48 | 8′·82 | 9′·21 | 9′·65 | 10′·14 | 10′·70 | 11′·33 |
| 12 | 5·67 | 5·81 | 5·97 | 6·14 | 6·33 | 6·54 | 6·77 | 7·03 | 7·32 | 7·64 | 8·00 | 8·41 | 8·88 | 9·41 |
| 14 | 4·84 | 4·95 | 5·09 | 5·23 | 5·40 | 5·58 | 5 77 | 5·99 | 6·24 | 6·51 | 6·82 | 7·17 | 7·57 | 8·02 |
| 16 | 4·21 | 4·31 | 4·43 | 4·55 | 4·69 | 4·85 | 5·02 | 5·21 | 5·42 | 5·66 | 5·93 | 6·24 | 6·58 | 6·97 |
| 18 | 3·71 | 3·80 | 3·90 | 4·02 | 4·14 | 4·28 | 4·43 | 4·60 | 4·79 | 5·00 | 5·24 | 5·50 | 5·81 | 6·15 |
| 20 | 3·31 | 3·39 | 3·49 | 3·59 | 3·70 | 3.82 | 3·95 | 4·11 | 4·27 | 4·46 | 4·67 | 4·91 | 5·19 | 5·49 |
| 22 | 2·98 | 3·06 | 3·14 | 3·23 | 3·33 | 3·44 | 3·56 | 3·70 | 3·85 | 4·02 | 4·21 | 4·43 | 4·67 | 4·95 |
| 24 | 2·71 | 2·77 | 2·85 | 2·93 | 3·02 | 3·12 | 3·23 | 3·36 | 3·49 | 3·65 | 3·82 | 4·02 | 4·24 | 4·49 |
| 26 | 2·47 | 2·53 | 2·60 | 2·68 | 2·76 | 2 85 | 2·95 | 3·06 | 3·19 | 3·33 | 3·49 | 3·66 | 3·87 | 4·10 |
| 28 | 2·27 | 2·32 | 2·39 | 2·45 | 2·53 | 2·61 | 2·71 | 2·81 | 2·92 | 3·05 | 3·20 | 3·36 | 3·55 | 3·76 |
| 30 | 2·09 | 2·14 | 2·20 | 2·26 | 2·33 | 2·41 | 2·49 | 2·60 | 2·69 | 2·81 | 2·95 | 3·10 | 3·27 | 3·46 |
| 32 | 1·93 | 1·98 | 2·03 | 2·09 | 2·15 | 2·22 | 2·30 | 2·39 | 2·49 | 2·60 | 2 72 | 2·86 | 3·02 | 3·20 |
| 34 | 1·79 | 1·83 | 1·88 | 1·93 | 1·99 | 2·06 | 2·13 | 2·22 | 2·31 | 2·41 | 2·52 | 2·65 | 2·80 | 2·96 |
| 36 | 1·66 | 1·70 | 1·74 | 1·80 | 1·85 | 1·91 | 1·98 | 2·06 | 2·14 | 2·24 | 2·34 | 2·46 | 2·60 | 2·75 |
| 38 | 1·54 | 1·58 | 1·62 | 1·67 | 1·72 | 1 78 | 1·84 | 1·91 | 1·99 | 2·08 | 2·18 | 2·29 | 2·41 | 2·56 |
| 40 | 1·44 | 1·47 | 1·51 | 1·55 | 1·60 | 1·66 | 1·72 | 1·78 | 1·85 | 1·94 | 2·03 | 2·13 | 2·25 | 2·38 |
| 42 | 1·34 | 1·37 | 1·41 | 1·45 | 1·49 | 1·54 | 1·60 | 1·66 | 1·73 | 1·80 | 1·89 | 1·99 | 2·09 | 2·22 |
| 44 | 1·25 | 1·28 | 1·31 | 1·35 | 1·39 | 1·44 | 1·49 | 1·55 | 1·61 | 1·68 | 1·76 | 1·85 | 1·95 | 2·07 |
| 46 | 1·16 | 1·19 | 1·23 | 1·26 | 1·30 | 1·34 | 1·39 | 1.44 | 1·50 | 1·56 | 1 64 | 1·73 | 1·82 | 1·93 |
| 48 | 1·09 | 1·11 | 1 14 | 1·17 | 1 21 | 1·25 | 1·30 | 1·35 | 1·40 | 1·46 | 1·53 | 1·61 | 1·70 | 1·80 |
| 50 | 1·01 | 1·04 | 1 06 | 1·09 | 1·13 | 1·16 | 1·21 | 1 25 | 1·31 | 1·36 | 1·43 | 1·50 | 1·58 | 1·68 |
| 52 | 0·94 | 0·96 | 0 99 | 1·01 | 1·05 | 1·09 | 1·12 | 1·17 | 1·22 | 1·27 | 1·33 | 1·40 | 1·47 | 1·56 |
| 54 | 0·88 | 0·90 | 0·92 | 0·95 | 0 98 | 1 01 | 1·04 | 1·09 | 1·13 | 1 18 | 1·23 | 1·30 | 1·37 | 1·45 |
| 56 | 0·81 | 0·83 | 0 85 | 0·88 | 0 91 | 0·94 | 0 97 | 1·01 | 1·05 | 1·10 | 1·15 | 1 21 | 1·27 | 1·35 |
| 58 | 0·75 | 0 77 | 0·79 | 0·81 | 0·84 | 0·87 | 0·90 | 0·93 | 0·97 | 1 01 | 1·06 | 1·12 | 1·18 | 1·25 |
| 60 | 0·70 | 0 71 | 0·73 | 0·75 | 0·78 | 0·80 | 0·83 | 0·86 | 0·90 | 0·94 | 0·98 | 1·03 | 1·09 | 1 15 |
| 62 | 0·64 | 0·66 | 0·67 | 0·69 | 0·72 | 0·74 | 0·76 | 0·79 | 0 83 | 0 86 | 0·90 | 0·95 | 1 00 | 1·06 |
| 64 | 0·59 | 0·60 | 0·62 | 0·64 | 0 66 | 0·68 | 0·70 | 0·73 | 0·76 | 0·79 | 0·83 | 0·87 | 0 92 | 0·97 |
| 66 | 0·54 | 0·55 | 0·56 | 0·58 | 0·60 | 0·62 | 0·64 | 0·66 | 0·69 | 0·72 | 0·76 | 0·79 | 0·84 | 0·89 |
| 68 | 0·49 | 0·50 | 0·51 | 0·53 | 0·54 | 0·56 | 0·58 | 0·60 | 0·63 | 0 65 | 0·69 | 0·72 | 0·76 | 0·81 |
| 70 | 0·44 | 0·45 | 0·46 | 0·47 | 0·49 | 0·51 | 0·52 | 0·54 | 0·57 | 0·59 | 0·62 | 0·65 | 0·68 | 0·73 |
| 72 | 0·39 | 0·40 | 0·41 | 0·42 | 0·44 | 0·45 | 0 47 | 0·49 | 0·51 | 0·53 | 0·55 | 0·58 | 0·61 | 0 65 |
| 74 | 0 34 | 0·36 | 0·36 | 0 37 | 0·38 | 0·40 | 0·41 | 0·43 | 0·44 | 0·46 | 0·49 | 0·52 | 0·54 | 0·57 |
| 76 | 0·30 | 0·31 | 0·31 | 1·32 | 0·33 | 0·34 | 0·36 | 0·37 | 0·39 | 0·40 | 0·42 | 0·45 | 0·47 | 0.50 |
| 78 | 0·25 | 0·26 | 0·27 | 0·28 | 0·29 | 0·29 | 0.30 | 0·32 | 0·33 | 0·34 | 0.36 | 0·38 | 0·40 | 0·42 |
| 80 | 0·21 | 0·22 | 0·22 | 0·23 | 0.24 | 0·24 | 0·25 | 0·26 | 0·27 | 0·29 | 0·30 | 0·31 | 0·33 | 0·35 |
| 82 | 0·17 | 0·17 | 0·18 | 0·18 | 0·19 | 0 19 | 0·20 | 0·21 | 0·22 | 0·23 | 0·24 | 0·25 | 0·26 | 0·28 |
| 84 | 0·13 | 0·13 | 0·13 | 0·14 | 0·14 | 0·14 | 0 15 | 0·16 | 0·16 | 0·17 | 0·18 | 0·19 | 0·20 | 0·21 |
| 86 | 0·08 | 0·08 | 0·09 | 0·09 | 0·09 | 0·10 | 0·10 | 0·10 | 0·11 | 0·11 | 0·12 | 0 12 | 0·13 | 0·14 |
| 88 | 0·04 | 0·04 | 0·04 | 0 04 | 0·05 | 0·05 | 0·05 | 0·05 | 0·05 | 0·06 | 0·06 | 0 06 | 0·07 | 0 07 |
| 89 | 0·02 | 0·02 | 0·02 | 0·02 | 0 02 | 0·02 | 0·02 | 0·03 | 0·03 | 0·03 | 0·03 | 0·04 | 0·05 | 0 05 |
| 90 | 0·00 | 0·00 | 0·00 | 0·00 | 0 00 | 0·00 | 0·00 | 0·00 | 0·00 | 0·00 | 0 00 | 0·00 | 0·00 | 0·00 |

## TABLE II.

*Showing the error in the Longitude produced by an error of 1′ in the Altitude.*

| True Azimuth | Latitude 4° | 8° | 10° | 12° | 14° | 16° | 18° | 20° | 22° | 24° | 26° | 28° | 30° | 32° | 34° | 36° | 38° | 40° | 42° |
|---|---|---|---|---|---|---|---|---|---|---|---|---|---|---|---|---|---|---|---|
| 10° | 5·77 | 5·82 | 5·85 | [illegible] | [illegible] | [illegible] | [illegible] | 6·13 | 6·21 | 6·30 | [illegible] | 6·52 | [illegible] | 6·70 | [illegible] | [illegible] | 7·31 | 7·52 | [illegible] |
| 12 | [illegible] | [illegible] | [illegible] | [illegible] | [illegible] | [illegible] | [illegible] | 5·12 | [illegible] | 5·27 | 5·35 | [illegible] | [illegible] | [illegible] | [illegible] | [illegible] | [illegible] | [illegible] | [illegible] |
| 14 | [illegible] | [illegible] | [illegible] | 4·23 | [illegible] | [illegible] | 4·35 | [illegible] | [illegible] | 4·53 | [illegible] | [illegible] | [illegible] | [illegible] | [illegible] | [illegible] | [illegible] | [illegible] | [illegible] |
| 16 | [illegible] | [illegible] | 3·68 | 3·71 | 3·74 | 3·77 | [illegible] | 3·86 | 3·91 | [illegible] | [illegible] | 4·11 | [illegible] | [illegible] | [illegible] | [illegible] | [illegible] | [illegible] | [illegible] |
| 18 | [illegible] | 3·27 | [illegible] | 3·31 | [illegible] | 3·37 | [illegible] | [illegible] | [illegible] | [illegible] | [illegible] | [illegible] | [illegible] | [illegible] | [illegible] | [illegible] | [illegible] | [illegible] | [illegible] |
| 20 | 2·93 | [illegible] | [illegible] | [illegible] | 3·01 | 3·04 | 3·07 | 3·11 | 3·15 | 3·20 | 3·25 | 3·31 | [illegible] | [illegible] | [illegible] | [illegible] | [illegible] | [illegible] | [illegible] |
| 22 | 2·68 | 2·70 | 2·71 | 2·73 | 2·75 | [illegible] | 2·81 | [illegible] | [illegible] | 2·92 | 2·97 | 3·03 | [illegible] | [illegible] | [illegible] | [illegible] | [illegible] | [illegible] | [illegible] |
| 24 | 2·47 | 2·48 | [illegible] | 2·52 | 2·54 | [illegible] | [illegible] | 2·62 | [illegible] | [illegible] | 2·71 | [illegible] | [illegible] | [illegible] | [illegible] | [illegible] | [illegible] | [illegible] | [illegible] |
| 26 | [illegible] | [illegible] | 2·31 | 2·33 | 2·35 | 2·37 | [illegible] | 2·43 | [illegible] | [illegible] | [illegible] | [illegible] | [illegible] | [illegible] | [illegible] | [illegible] | [illegible] | [illegible] | [illegible] |
| 28 | 2·14 | 2·15 | 2·16 | 2·18 | 2·20 | 2·22 | [illegible] | [illegible] | [illegible] | [illegible] | [illegible] | [illegible] | [illegible] | [illegible] | [illegible] | [illegible] | [illegible] | [illegible] | [illegible] |
| 30 | [illegible] | [illegible] | [illegible] | [illegible] | [illegible] | [illegible] | [illegible] | [illegible] | [illegible] | [illegible] | [illegible] | [illegible] | [illegible] | [illegible] | [illegible] | [illegible] | [illegible] | [illegible] | [illegible] |
| 32 | [illegible] | [illegible] | [illegible] | 1·93 | [illegible] | [illegible] | [illegible] | 2·01 | [illegible] | 2·07 | 2·10 | [illegible] | [illegible] | 2·23 | [illegible] | [illegible] | [illegible] | [illegible] | [illegible] |
| 34 | [illegible] | [illegible] | [illegible] | [illegible] | [illegible] | [illegible] | [illegible] | [illegible] | [illegible] | [illegible] | [illegible] | [illegible] | [illegible] | 2·11 | [illegible] | [illegible] | [illegible] | [illegible] | [illegible] |
| 36 | 1·71 | 1·72 | [illegible] | [illegible] | [illegible] | 1·77 | [illegible] | 1·81 | [illegible] | [illegible] | [illegible] | [illegible] | [illegible] | [illegible] | [illegible] | [illegible] | [illegible] | [illegible] | [illegible] |
| 38 | 1·63 | [illegible] | [illegible] | [illegible] | 1·67 | [illegible] | 1·71 | 1·73 | 1·75 | [illegible] | [illegible] | [illegible] | [illegible] | [illegible] | [illegible] | [illegible] | [illegible] | 2·12 | [illegible] |
| 40 | [illegible] | 1·57 | [illegible] | [illegible] | [illegible] | 1·62 | [illegible] | [illegible] | [illegible] | [illegible] | [illegible] | [illegible] | [illegible] | [illegible] | [illegible] | [illegible] | [illegible] | [illegible] | [illegible] |
| 42 | [illegible] | [illegible] | [illegible] | [illegible] | [illegible] | [illegible] | [illegible] | [illegible] | [illegible] | [illegible] | [illegible] | [illegible] | [illegible] | [illegible] | [illegible] | [illegible] | [illegible] | [illegible] | [illegible] |
| 44 | [illegible] | [illegible] | [illegible] | 1·47 | [illegible] | [illegible] | 1·51 | 1·53 | [illegible] | [illegible] | [illegible] | [illegible] | [illegible] | [illegible] | [illegible] | [illegible] | [illegible] | [illegible] | [illegible] |
| 46 | [illegible] | [illegible] | [illegible] | [illegible] | 1·43 | [illegible] | [illegible] | [illegible] | [illegible] | [illegible] | [illegible] | [illegible] | [illegible] | [illegible] | [illegible] | [illegible] | [illegible] | [illegible] | [illegible] |
| 48 | [illegible] | [illegible] | [illegible] | [illegible] | [illegible] | [illegible] | [illegible] | [illegible] | [illegible] | [illegible] | [illegible] | [illegible] | [illegible] | [illegible] | [illegible] | [illegible] | [illegible] | [illegible] | [illegible] |
| 50 | 1·31 | 1·32 | [illegible] | [illegible] | 1·35 | [illegible] | 1·37 | [illegible] | [illegible] | [illegible] | [illegible] | [illegible] | [illegible] | [illegible] | [illegible] | [illegible] | [illegible] | [illegible] | [illegible] |
| 52 | 1·27 | [illegible] | [illegible] | [illegible] | 1·31 | [illegible] | [illegible] | [illegible] | [illegible] | [illegible] | [illegible] | [illegible] | [illegible] | [illegible] | [illegible] | [illegible] | [illegible] | [illegible] | [illegible] |
| 54 | 1·24 | 1·25 | [illegible] | [illegible] | [illegible] | [illegible] | [illegible] | [illegible] | [illegible] | [illegible] | [illegible] | [illegible] | [illegible] | [illegible] | [illegible] | [illegible] | [illegible] | [illegible] | [illegible] |
| 56 | 1·21 | 1·22 | [illegible] | 1·23 | [illegible] | [illegible] | [illegible] | [illegible] | [illegible] | [illegible] | [illegible] | [illegible] | [illegible] | 1·42 | [illegible] | [illegible] | [illegible] | [illegible] | [illegible] |
| 58 | [illegible] | [illegible] | [illegible] | 1·21 | 1·22 | 1·23 | [illegible] | 1·25 | [illegible] | [illegible] | [illegible] | [illegible] | [illegible] | [illegible] | [illegible] | [illegible] | [illegible] | [illegible] | [illegible] |
| 60 | 1·16 | 1·17 | [illegible] | [illegible] | [illegible] | [illegible] | [illegible] | [illegible] | [illegible] | [illegible] | [illegible] | [illegible] | [illegible] | [illegible] | [illegible] | [illegible] | [illegible] | [illegible] | [illegible] |
| 62 | [illegible] | 1·14 | [illegible] | [illegible] | 1·17 | [illegible] | [illegible] | [illegible] | [illegible] | [illegible] | [illegible] | [illegible] | 1·31 | [illegible] | [illegible] | [illegible] | [illegible] | [illegible] | [illegible] |
| 64 | 1·12 | 1·12 | [illegible] | [illegible] | [illegible] | [illegible] | [illegible] | [illegible] | [illegible] | 1·22 | [illegible] | [illegible] | [illegible] | [illegible] | [illegible] | [illegible] | [illegible] | [illegible] | [illegible] |
| 66 | [illegible] | 1·11 | 1·11 | 1·12 | [illegible] | [illegible] | [illegible] | [illegible] | [illegible] | [illegible] | [illegible] | [illegible] | [illegible] | [illegible] | [illegible] | [illegible] | [illegible] | [illegible] | [illegible] |
| 68 | [illegible] | [illegible] | [illegible] | [illegible] | [illegible] | [illegible] | [illegible] | [illegible] | [illegible] | [illegible] | [illegible] | [illegible] | [illegible] | [illegible] | [illegible] | [illegible] | [illegible] | [illegible] | [illegible] |
| 70 | [illegible] | [illegible] | [illegible] | [illegible] | [illegible] | [illegible] | [illegible] | [illegible] | [illegible] | [illegible] | [illegible] | [illegible] | [illegible] | [illegible] | [illegible] | [illegible] | [illegible] | [illegible] | [illegible] |
| 72 | [illegible] | [illegible] | [illegible] | [illegible] | [illegible] | [illegible] | [illegible] | [illegible] | [illegible] | [illegible] | [illegible] | [illegible] | [illegible] | [illegible] | [illegible] | [illegible] | [illegible] | [illegible] | [illegible] |
| 74 | [illegible] | [illegible] | [illegible] | [illegible] | [illegible] | [illegible] | [illegible] | [illegible] | [illegible] | [illegible] | [illegible] | [illegible] | [illegible] | [illegible] | [illegible] | [illegible] | [illegible] | [illegible] | [illegible] |
| 76 | [illegible] | [illegible] | [illegible] | [illegible] | [illegible] | [illegible] | [illegible] | [illegible] | [illegible] | [illegible] | [illegible] | [illegible] | [illegible] | [illegible] | [illegible] | [illegible] | [illegible] | [illegible] | [illegible] |
| 78 | [illegible] | [illegible] | [illegible] | [illegible] | [illegible] | [illegible] | [illegible] | [illegible] | [illegible] | 1·12 | [illegible] | [illegible] | [illegible] | [illegible] | [illegible] | [illegible] | [illegible] | [illegible] | [illegible] |
| 80 | [illegible] | [illegible] | [illegible] | [illegible] | [illegible] | [illegible] | [illegible] | [illegible] | [illegible] | [illegible] | [illegible] | [illegible] | [illegible] | [illegible] | [illegible] | [illegible] | [illegible] | [illegible] | [illegible] |
| 82 | [illegible] | [illegible] | [illegible] | [illegible] | [illegible] | [illegible] | [illegible] | [illegible] | [illegible] | [illegible] | [illegible] | [illegible] | [illegible] | [illegible] | [illegible] | [illegible] | [illegible] | [illegible] | [illegible] |
| 84 | [illegible] | [illegible] | [illegible] | [illegible] | [illegible] | [illegible] | [illegible] | [illegible] | [illegible] | [illegible] | [illegible] | [illegible] | [illegible] | [illegible] | [illegible] | [illegible] | [illegible] | [illegible] | [illegible] |
| 86 | [illegible] | [illegible] | [illegible] | [illegible] | [illegible] | [illegible] | [illegible] | [illegible] | [illegible] | [illegible] | [illegible] | [illegible] | [illegible] | [illegible] | [illegible] | [illegible] | [illegible] | [illegible] | [illegible] |
| 88 | [illegible] | [illegible] | [illegible] | [illegible] | [illegible] | [illegible] | [illegible] | [illegible] | [illegible] | [illegible] | [illegible] | [illegible] | [illegible] | [illegible] | [illegible] | [illegible] | [illegible] | [illegible] | [illegible] |
| 89 | [illegible] | [illegible] | [illegible] | [illegible] | [illegible] | [illegible] | [illegible] | [illegible] | [illegible] | [illegible] | [illegible] | [illegible] | [illegible] | [illegible] | [illegible] | [illegible] | [illegible] | [illegible] | [illegible] |
| 90 | [illegible] | 1·01 | 1·01 | 1·02 | [illegible] | [illegible] | [illegible] | [illegible] | [illegible] | [illegible] | [illegible] | [illegible] | 1·15 | [illegible] | [illegible] | [illegible] | [illegible] | [illegible] | [illegible] |

# TABLE II.

*Showing the error in the Longitude produced by an error of 1′ in the Altitude.*

| True Bearing. | LATITUDE. 44° | 46° | 48° | 50° | 52° | 54° | 56° | 58° | 60° | 62° | 64° | 66° | 68° | 70° | 72° | 74° | 76° | 78° | 80° |
|---|---|---|---|---|---|---|---|---|---|---|---|---|---|---|---|---|---|---|---|
| 10° | 8′01 | 8′29 | 8′61 | 8′96 | 9′35 | 9′80 | 10′30 | 10′87 | 11′52 | 12′27 | 13′14 | 14′16 | 15′37 | 16′84 | 18′64 | 20′89 | 23′80 | 27′70 | 33′16 |
| 12 | 6·69 | 6·92 | 7·19 | 7·48 | 7·81 | 8·18 | 8·60 | 9·08 | 9·62 | 10·24 | 10·97 | 11·83 | 12·84 | 14·06 | 15·56 | 17·45 | 19·88 | 23·13 | 27·70 |
| 14 | 5·75 | 5·95 | 6·18 | 6·43 | 6·71 | 7·03 | 7·39 | 7·80 | 8·27 | 8·81 | 9·43 | 10·16 | 11·05 | 12·09 | 13·38 | 15·00 | 17·09 | 19·88 | 23·80 |
| 16 | 5·04 | 5·22 | 5·42 | 5·64 | 5·89 | 6·17 | 6·49 | 6·85 | 7·26 | 7·73 | 8·28 | 8·92 | 9·69 | 10·61 | 11·74 | 13·16 | 15·00 | 17·45 | 20·89 |
| 18 | 4·50 | 4·66 | 4·84 | 5·03 | 5·26 | 5·51 | 5·79 | 6·11 | 6·47 | 6·89 | 7·38 | 7·96 | 8·64 | 9·46 | 10·47 | 11·74 | 13·38 | 15·56 | 18·64 |
| 20 | 4·06 | 4·21 | 4·37 | 4·55 | 4·75 | 4·97 | 5·23 | 5·52 | 5·85 | 6·23 | 6·67 | 7·19 | 7·81 | 8·55 | 9·46 | 10·61 | 12·09 | 14·06 | 16·84 |
| 22 | 3·71 | 3·84 | 3·98 | 4·15 | 4·33 | 4·54 | 4·78 | 5·04 | 5·34 | 5·68 | 6·10 | 6·57 | 7·12 | 7·80 | 8·63 | 9·70 | 11·03 | 12·85 | 15·37 |
| 24 | 3·42 | 3·54 | 3·67 | 3·83 | 4·00 | 4·18 | 4·40 | 4·64 | 4·92 | 5·24 | 5·62 | 6·05 | 6·57 | 7·20 | 7·97 | 8·93 | 10·17 | 11·85 | 14·15 |
| 26 | 3·17 | 3·29 | 3·41 | 3·55 | 3·70 | 3·88 | 4·08 | 4·30 | 4·56 | 4·86 | 5·20 | 5·61 | 6·09 | 6·67 | 7·38 | 8·27 | 9·43 | 10·95 | 13·15 |
| 28 | 2·96 | 3·07 | 3·19 | 3·32 | 3·46 | 3·62 | 3·81 | 4·02 | 4·26 | 4·54 | 4·86 | 5·23 | 5·67 | 6·23 | 6·90 | 7·73 | 8·80 | 10·25 | 12·25 |
| 30 | 2·78 | 2·88 | 2·99 | 3·11 | 3·25 | 3·41 | 3·58 | 3·78 | 4·00 | 4·26 | 4·56 | 4·92 | 5·33 | 5·85 | 6·47 | 7·27 | 8·27 | 9·60 | 11·50 |
| 32 | 2·62 | 2·72 | 2·82 | 2·94 | 3·06 | 3·21 | 3·37 | 3·56 | 3·77 | 4·01 | 4·31 | 4·64 | 5·04 | 5·52 | 6·09 | 6·86 | 7·79 | 9·09 | 10·87 |
| 34 | 2·49 | 2·57 | 2·67 | 2·78 | 2·90 | 3·04 | 3·20 | 3·38 | 3·58 | 3·82 | 4·08 | 4·40 | 4·77 | 5·23 | 5·79 | 6·49 | 7·39 | 8·59 | 10·26 |
| 36 | 2·37 | 2·45 | 2·54 | 2·65 | 2·77 | 2·90 | 3·04 | 3·20 | 3·40 | 3·63 | 3·88 | 4·18 | 4·54 | 4·97 | 5·51 | 6·17 | 7·04 | 8·21 | 9·81 |
| 38 | 2·26 | 2·34 | 2·43 | 2·53 | 2·64 | 2·76 | 2·91 | 3·07 | 3·25 | 3·46 | 3·71 | 3·99 | 4·34 | 4·75 | 5·25 | 5·88 | 6·71 | 7·82 | 9·37 |
| 40 | 2·16 | 2·24 | 2·33 | 2·42 | 2·53 | 2·65 | 2·78 | 2·93 | 3·11 | 3·31 | 3·55 | 3·82 | 4·15 | 4·55 | 5·03 | 5·64 | 6·43 | 7·48 | 8·96 |
| 42 | 2·08 | 2·15 | 2·23 | 2·32 | 2·43 | 2·54 | 2·67 | 2·82 | 2·99 | 3·18 | 3·41 | 3·68 | 3·95 | 4·35 | 4·85 | 5·41 | 6·17 | 7·17 | 8·63 |
| 44 | 2·00 | 2·07 | 2·15 | 2·24 | 2·34 | 2·45 | 2·58 | 2·72 | 2·88 | 3·06 | 3·28 | 3·55 | 3·85 | 4·20 | 4·67 | 5·23 | 5·95 | 6·93 | 8·30 |
| 46 | 1·93 | 2·00 | 2·08 | 2·16 | 2·26 | 2·37 | 2·49 | 2·62 | 2·78 | 2·96 | 3·18 | 3·43 | 3·71 | 4·07 | 4·50 | 5·04 | 5·75 | 6·70 | 8·00 |
| 48 | 1·87 | 1·94 | 2·01 | 2·09 | 2·18 | 2·29 | 2·41 | 2·54 | 2·69 | 2·87 | 3·07 | 3·31 | 3·59 | 3·94 | 4·35 | 4·89 | 5·58 | 6·48 | 7·77 |
| 50 | 1·82 | 1·88 | 1·95 | 2·03 | 2·12 | 2·22 | 2·33 | 2·46 | 2·61 | 2·78 | 2·98 | 3·21 | 3·49 | 3·82 | 4·22 | 4·73 | 5·37 | 6·27 | 7·53 |
| 52 | 1·77 | 1·83 | 1·90 | 1·98 | 2·06 | 2·16 | 2·27 | 2·39 | 2·54 | 2·71 | 2·90 | 3·12 | 3·39 | 3·71 | 4·10 | 4·60 | 5·25 | 6·10 | 7·30 |
| 54 | 1·72 | 1·78 | 1·85 | 1·92 | 2·01 | 2·10 | 2·21 | 2·33 | 2·47 | 2·63 | 2·82 | 3·04 | 3·30 | 3·61 | 3·99 | 4·49 | 5·12 | 5·93 | 7·13 |
| 56 | 1·68 | 1·74 | 1·80 | 1·88 | 1·96 | 2·05 | 2·16 | 2·28 | 2·41 | 2·57 | 2·75 | 2·97 | 3·22 | 3·52 | 3·89 | 4·37 | 4·97 | 5·77 | 6·93 |
| 58 | 1·64 | 1·70 | 1·76 | 1·83 | 1·91 | 2·00 | 2·11 | 2·23 | 2·36 | 2·51 | 2·69 | 2·90 | 3·15 | 3·45 | 3·84 | 4·28 | 4·86 | 5·66 | 6·70 |
| 60 | 1·61 | 1·67 | 1·73 | 1·80 | 1·88 | 1·97 | 2·07 | 2·19 | 2·32 | 2·47 | 2·64 | 2·85 | 3·10 | 3·40 | 3·76 | 4·20 | 4·77 | 5·57 | 6·66 |
| 62 | 1·57 | 1·63 | 1·69 | 1·76 | 1·84 | 1·93 | 2·03 | 2·14 | 2·26 | 2·41 | 2·58 | 2·78 | 3·02 | 3·31 | 3·67 | 4·11 | 4·67 | 5·46 | 6·51 |
| 64 | 1·55 | 1·60 | 1·66 | 1·73 | 1·81 | 1·89 | 1·99 | 2·10 | 2·22 | 2·37 | 2·54 | 2·74 | 2·97 | 3·25 | 3·61 | 4·04 | 4·61 | 5·36 | 6·41 |
| 66 | 1·52 | 1·57 | 1·63 | 1·70 | 1·78 | 1·86 | 1·96 | 2·07 | 2·19 | 2·33 | 2·50 | 2·69 | 2·92 | 3·20 | 3·54 | 3·97 | 4·51 | 5·27 | 6·31 |
| 68 | 1·50 | 1·55 | 1·61 | 1·68 | 1·75 | 1·83 | 1·93 | 2·04 | 2·16 | 2·30 | 2·46 | 2·65 | 2·88 | 3·16 | 3·50 | 3·93 | 4·46 | 5·20 | 6·20 |
| 70 | 1·48 | 1·53 | 1·59 | 1·66 | 1·73 | 1·81 | 1·90 | 2·01 | 2·13 | 2·27 | 2·43 | 2·62 | 2·84 | 3·11 | 3·45 | 3·86 | 4·41 | 5·11 | 6·12 |
| 72 | 1·46 | 1·51 | 1·57 | 1·64 | 1·71 | 1·79 | 1·88 | 1·98 | 2·10 | 2·24 | 2·40 | 2·59 | 2·81 | 3·07 | 3·40 | 3·81 | 4·35 | 5·05 | 6·06 |
| 74 | 1·45 | 1·50 | 1·56 | 1·62 | 1·69 | 1·77 | 1·86 | 1·96 | 2·08 | 2·22 | 2·37 | 2·56 | 2·78 | 3·03 | 3·37 | 3·77 | 4·30 | 5·00 | 6·00 |
| 76 | 1·43 | 1·48 | 1·54 | 1·60 | 1·67 | 1·75 | 1·84 | 1·94 | 2·06 | 2·20 | 2·35 | 2·54 | 2·75 | 3·01 | 3·34 | 3·74 | 4·25 | 4·95 | 5·91 |
| 78 | 1·42 | 1·47 | 1·53 | 1·59 | 1·66 | 1·74 | 1·83 | 1·93 | 2·04 | 2·18 | 2·33 | 2·51 | 2·73 | 2·99 | 3·31 | 3·71 | 4·21 | 4·91 | [illegible] |
| 80 | 1·41 | 1·46 | 1·52 | 1·58 | 1·65 | 1·73 | 1·82 | 1·92 | 2·03 | 2·16 | 2·32 | 2·50 | 2·71 | 2·97 | 3·28 | 3·68 | 4·18 | 4·88 | 5·85 |
| 82 | 1·40 | 1·45 | 1·51 | 1·57 | 1·64 | 1·72 | 1·81 | 1·91 | 2·02 | 2·15 | 2·30 | 2·48 | 2·70 | 2·95 | 3·27 | 3·67 | 4·17 | 4·85 | 5·81 |
| 84 | 1·40 | 1·45 | 1·50 | 1·56 | 1·63 | 1·71 | 1·80 | 1·90 | 2·01 | 2·14 | 2·29 | 2·47 | 2·68 | 2·94 | 3·25 | 3·65 | 4·16 | 4·83 | 5·79 |
| 86 | 1·39 | 1·44 | 1·50 | 1·56 | 1·63 | 1·71 | 1·79 | 1·89 | 2·00 | 2·14 | 2·29 | 2·46 | 2·67 | 2·93 | 3·24 | 3·64 | 4·14 | 4·81 | 5·77 |
| 88 | 1·39 | 1·44 | 1·50 | 1·56 | 1·63 | 1·70 | 1·79 | 1·89 | 2·00 | 2·13 | 2·28 | 2·46 | 2·67 | 2·93 | 3·24 | 3·64 | 4·14 | 4·80 | 5·76 |
| 89 | 1·39 | 1·44 | 1·49 | 1·55 | 1·62 | 1·72 | 1·79 | 1·89 | 2·00 | 2·13 | 2·28 | 2·46 | 2·67 | 2·92 | 3·23 | 3·63 | 4·13 | 4·80 | 5·76 |
| 90 | 1·39 | 1·44 | 1·49 | 1·55 | 1·62 | 1·72 | 1·79 | 1·89 | 2·00 | 2·13 | 2·28 | 2·46 | 2·67 | 2·92 | 3·23 | 3·63 | 4·13 | 4·80 | 5·76 |

paratively rude nature of the observation, and in consequence thrown away.

**Equation of Time—*when* to apply it.**

Usually, the Equation of Time is applied to the Apparent Time at Ship to reduce it to Mean Time, but you can steal a little march by applying it to the Greenwich Mean Time *at the commencement* of the work. There is then so much less to do when the calculation is completed at noon. When applied to Greenwich Mean Time in this manner, the equation must be added or subtracted as directed on page II. of the N.A.

About as good a way as any for finding the time at ship is Method I. of Norie, which will accordingly be here used in the examples.

**Delusive "short methods."**

It is necessary to beware of those so called "short methods" which appear from time to time. They generally only *look* short, because good care is taken to apply the various corrections *beforehand*, and the unsuspecting reader is deceived by this device. It is seldom, however, that there is a *real* difference of half-a-dozen figures, and the mathematical correctness of the problem is sometimes more than doubtful.

**Martelli's short method.**

As a case in point we will take the small but expensive pamphlet by Mr. Martelli, which contains rules and tables for finding the longitude by chronometer.

When his so-called "short method" is properly overhauled and compared with Norie's Method I., we get the following startling result:—Martelli, 56 figures and 5 logarithms, against Norie's 59 figures and 5 logarithms, required to produce the same result. So that by the first method we have the enormous (!!!) gain of *three figures*. Furthermore, Mr. Martelli's pamphlet contains several glaring errors which make one rather dubious about the general correctness of the tables, although (for all the writer knows to the contrary) the mathematical principle of his method may be correct enough.

Another pamphlet came out some years ago wherein it was stated that chronometers were quite unnecessary to find the longitude at sea, and that it could be done equally well by the method set forth in the pamphlet. But, some way or other, its author has not as yet succeeded in converting the public to his views, and the chronometer trade is more brisk than ever.

To illustrate what has been said relative to the great advantage of taking observations on the Prime Vertical, when desirous of finding the longitude, a few examples will now be given.

EXAMPLE. ⊙ bearing N. 89° 53′ W. (true).

On board the s.s. "*British Crown*," about 4 P.M. June 25th, 1880, a chronometer (which was 4m. 00s. slow of G.M.T.) shewed 7h. 43m. 57s. same date, when the alt. of the ⊙̲ was 37° 49¾′. Eye 32 feet. No index error. Lat. 40° 00′ N., and Long. 57° 12′ W., both by dead reckoning. Required the longitude. **Example shewing advantage of observations on Prime Vertical.**

| | H. M. S. |
|---|---|
| Time by chronometer | 7 43 57 |
| Slow | + 4 00 |
| G.M.T. | 7 47 57 |
| Equation of Time | − 2 30 |
| Greenwich Apparent Time | 7 45 27 |

⊙̲ 37° 49¾′
+ 9 Table IX.
⊙ 37° 58¾′

0·52s. hourly diff.
7·8 G.M.T.
416
364
+ 4·056
2 25·760
Corrected Equation of Time - 2m. 29·82s.

4·6″ hourly difference of declination
7·8 G.M.T.
368
322
− 35·88
23° 23′ 14·40″ declin. at G.M. noon.
23° 22′ 39″ corrected declin.
90

| | | | |
|---|---|---|---|
| Polar distance | 66° 37¼′ | Cosecant | 0·03720 |
| Latitude | 40 00 | Secant | 0·11575 |
| Altitude | 37 58¾ | Cosine | 9·48292 |
| | 144 36 | Sine | 9·75114 |
| ½ sum | 72 18 | | 9·38701 = 3h. 56m. 42s. Apparent Time at Ship. |
| Remainder | 34 19¼ | | 7 45 27 " " Greenwich. |

Longitude in time - 3h. 48m. 45s. = 57° 11¼′ W.

Same sight worked with latitude 39° 20′ N., or 40′ in error.

| | | |
|---|---|---|
| P.D. | 66° 37¼′ | 0·03720 |
| Lat. | 39 20 | 0·11156 |
| Alt. | 37 58¾ | 9·49076 |
| | | 9·74742 |
| | 143 56 | 9·38694 = 3h. 56m. 41s. App. Time at Ship. |
| ½ Sum. | 71 58 | 7 45 27 " " Greenwich. |
| Rem. | 33 59¼ | 3 48 46 = 57° 11½′ West. |

In this case, with the sun on the Prime Vertical, an error in the latitude of 40′ caused an error in the longitude of only 0¼′.

Venus and Jupiter are often on or near the meridian, when sights of the sun are taken in the morning or afternoon; and, therefore, the latitude found by them serves to work the sights, *and is free from the errors of the run.* This is so manifest an advantage, that the N.A. should occasionally be consulted, to see if either of these planets are available. Their Right Ascensions **Venus or Jupiter for latitude, simultaneous with sun for longitude.**

should differ from that of the sun by *at least* two hours, otherwise they will be rendered invisible, by being in the very bright part of the sky surrounding the latter.

**Mode of observing planets in daylight.**

The proper plan is to set the sextant to the *computed* meridian altitude. Use either the direct or inverting telescope (whichever you are most accustomed to), but the last, as it has more power, is to be preferred. *Screw it close down to the plane of the instrument*, and having directed the sight to the north or south point of the horizon, the planet ought to be seen *in the silvered part of the glass.* Of course that part of the sky must be *entirely* free from even the most filmy clouds, and unless the sextant glasses are perfectly clean, and the silvering of the mirrors in good order, there is little use in attempting this observation.

About 1·45 P.M. June 15th, 1882, on board the s.s. "British Prince," homeward bound from Philadelphia, in Latitude 48° 33½′ N., and Longitude 24° 30′ W., both by account; Barom. 30″·22; Therm. in the shade on deck 63°; wind S.S.W., light breeze, with smooth water, fine clear weather. Having found by reference to the N.A. (page 237) that Venus (♀) would pass the meridian at 2·7 P.M., decided to observe it, and accordingly set the sextant to the computed altitude 64° 38′ (see rule, page 234).

On looking for the planet near the appointed time, it was seen beautifully distinct a little below the horizon, and no difficulty was experienced in getting the exact meridian altitude, notwithstanding that the midsummer sun was shining *brilliantly* in a cloudless sky, and the fact that there were but two hours difference of Right Ascension between him and Venus.

| | H. M. |
|---|---|
| Mean Time at ship June 15th | 2 7 |
| Longitude in Time .. .. .. | 1 38 |
| Mean Time at Greenwich .. | 3 45 |
| | ° ′ ″ |
| Declin. of Venus June 15th | 23 8 39 N. |
| " " June 16th | 22 56 55 N. |
| Variation in 24 hours .. .. | 11′ 44″ |
| | 60 |
| | 704″ |
| G.M.T. .. .. .. .. × | 3·75 |
| | 3520 |
| | 4928 |
| | 2112 |
| | 24)2640″·00(110″=1′ 50″ |
| | 24 |
| | 24 |
| | 24 |

| | ° ′ ″ |
|---|---|
| Declin. of Venus June 15th .. | 23 8 39 N. |
| Decrease in 3hrs. 45m. .. .. − | 1 50 |
| Declin. corrected for G.M.T. | 23° 6′ 49″ N. |
| | ° ′ |
| Obs. alt. of Venus .. .. .. | 64 38¾ |
| Corr. Table XV. of Norie .. − | 5 |
| True alt. .. .. .. .. .. | 64 33¾ |
| | 90 |
| Merid. zen. dist. .. .. .. | 25 26¼ N. |
| Corrected declin. .. .. .. | 23 6¾ N. |
| Latitude .. .. .. .. .. | 48° 33′ N. |

Now, the apparent diameter of Venus on this occasion was only

12″, and when the reader is informed that at inferior conjunction it amounts to as much as 67″, it will be seen that in the absence of clouds there should be usually no difficulty about picking it out even in strong sunlight.

**Phases of Venus.**

Here, however, it is necessary to put in a word or two. Venus is an inferior planet, that is to say, its orbit lies between the earth and the sun; it therefore exhibits well marked phases resembling those of our moon, and the best time for an observation such as described above, is when the planet is about five weeks from inferior conjunction, or its nearest approach to the earth. Its apparent diameter is then about 40″, and the breadth of the illuminated part nearly 10″, so that rather less than ¼ of the entire disc is illuminated; but this small portion transmits more light at such times than do phases of greater extent, because the latter correspond to greater distances of the planet from the earth.

Year by year in the N.A. the date is given when Venus attains its greatest brilliancy; thus, on page 461 of the N.A. for 1884, under the heading of PHENOMENA, this is shewn to occur on August 17th.

To find the *latitude*, it has been said that slow-moving stars near the Poles are best; but to find the *longitude*, select bodies on the Prime Vertical, as their motion in altitude is then the greatest. It does not signify whether their declination be large or small, since *for any given latitude* the motion in altitude on the Prime Vertical is the same, no matter what the declination.

**Observations for longitude best near the Equator.**

Again, "Since the change of altitude of any celestial body is greatest at the Equator, and nothing at the Pole, the time deduced by means of altitudes is more correctly determined in low than in high latitudes."*

In the two following examples of stars taken *near* the Prime Vertical, the formal rule for working them is left out, as the method (with one or two easily noticed exceptions) is so similar to that by the sun. In star observations, the longitude is the difference between the Sidereal Time at Ship, and the Sidereal Time at Greenwich.

Ere this the reader must be pretty familiar with the conversion of Mean Time and Sidereal Time, and should experience no difficulty in mastering what follows. To avoid perplexing him by anything strikingly different to what is contained in the examples

* Raper.

of stars already given, the Epitome method, wherein the sun's Right Ascension is used with the Equation of Time, is not introduced. This adherence to one rule when practicable, is in accordance with the recommendation at foot of page 228.

**Examples of stars on the Prime Vertical.**

On board the s.s. "*British Crown,*" about 8·30 P.M. June 22nd, 1880, the following observations were made to determine ship's position.

| | H. M. S. | | | | | | |
|---|---|---|---|---|---|---|---|
| Chron. | 11 16 50 | obs. alt. | ✱ Altair | 14° 43½′ | bearing S. 88° E. true. | Eye 32 feet. | |
| ,, | 11 24 21 | ,, ,, | ✱ Polaris | 42 15 | ,, N. 1 E. | ,, | ,, ,, |
| ,, | 11 30 49 | ,, ,, | ✱ Regulus | 22 18½ | ,, S. 86¼ W. | ,, | ,, ,, |

Position by account, Lat. 43° 20′ N. Longitude 43° 24′ W. No index error. Chron. slow of G.M.T. 4m. 00s. Ship making S. 58° W. (true) 11 knots. Polaris, when worked out, gives the latitude as 43° 23¾′ N.

### EXAMPLE I. ✱ ALTAIR.

| | H. M. S. |
|---|---|
| Time by chronometer .. .. | 11 16 50 |
| Slow .. .. .. .. .. | + 4 00 |
| G.M.T. .. .. .. .. .. | 11 20 50 |
| Sidereal time at G.M. noon .. | 6 4 11 |
| Acceleration for 11h. 21m. .. .. | + 1 52 |
| | H. M. S. |
| Sidereal time at Greenwich .. .. | 17 26 53 |

| | ° ′ |
|---|---|
| ✱'s observed altitude .. .. .. | 14 43½ |
| Table XV. of *Norie* .. .. .. | − 8¼ |
| ✱'s true altitude.. .. .. .. | 14 35¼ |

| | ° ′ | | |
|---|---|---|---|
| | 90 | | |
| ✱'s Declination .. .. | 8 33¼ N. | | |
| ✱'s Polar distance .. .. | 81 26¾ | ....Cosecant .. .. | 0·00486 |
| Ship's latitude .. .. | 43 24½ | ....Secant .. .. | 0·13878 |
| ✱'s altitude .. .. .. | 14 35¼ | Cosine .. .. | 9·53982 |
| | | Sine .. .. | 9·91407 |
| | 139 26¼ | | |
| | | | 9·59753 |
| Half sum.. .. .. .. | 69 43¼ | | |
| Remainder .. .. .. | 55 08 | | |

| | H. M. S. | |
|---|---|---|
| ✱'s Hour angle .. .. .. | 5 11 54 | E., = true azimuth S. 83° E., by Burdwood. |
| ✱'s Right Ascension .. .. | 19 44 59 | page 358, N.A. |
| Sidereal Time at Ship .. .. | 14 33 05 | |
| Sidereal Time at Greenwich .. | 17 26 53 | |
| | H. M. S | |
| Longitude in time .. .. | 2 53 48 | = 43° 27 W. |

### SAME SIGHT WORKED WITH LATITUDE 40′ IN ERROR.

| ° ′ | |
|---|---|
| 81 26¾ | 0·00486 |
| 44 04½ | 0·14362 |
| 14 35¼ | 9·53292 |
| | 9·91582 |
| 140 6½ | |
| | 9·59722 |
| 70 3½ | |
| 55 28 | H M. S. |
| | 5 11 46 E. |

Here, notwithstanding that Altair is 2° from the Prime Vertical, the large error of 40′ in the latitude only produces a difference of 8s. in the hour angle, or 2′ in the longitude. It will be noticed that the main feature wherein this example differs from the sun is, that the *Sidereal Time at Greenwich* is compared with *the Sidereal Time at Ship*. The Declination and Right Ascension are taken out direct from the N.A. *without the necessity for the smallest correction*—another advantage over the sun. When the hour angle is east, *subtract* it from the ✱'s Right Ascension, which will give the Right Ascension of the Meridian, or, in other words, the Sidereal Time at Ship.

**Declinations of stars require no correction for G.M.T.**

EXAMPLE II.— ✱ Regulus.

| | H. M. S. |
|---|---|
| Time by chronometer.. .. .. | 11 30 49 |
| Slow .. .. .. | + 4 00 |
| G.M.T. .. .. | 11 34 49 |
| Sidereal time at G.M. noon .. .. | 6 4 11 |
| Acceleration for 11h. 35m. .. .. | + 1 54 |
| Sidereal Time at Greenwich .. | 17 40 54 |

| | ° ′ |
|---|---|
| ✱'s obs. alt. .. .. .. .. | 22 18¼ |
| Table XV. of Norie .. .. .. | − 7½ |
| ✱'s true alt. .. .. .. .. | 22° 10¾′ |

| | ° ′ | | |
|---|---|---|---|
| | 90 | | |
| ✱'s Declination .. .. .. | 12 33 N. | | |
| ✱'s Polar distance .. .. | 77 27 | .... Cosecant .. .. .. | 0·01050 |
| Ship's latitude .. .. | 43 23½ | .... Secant .. .. .. | 0·13863 |
| ✱'s altitude .. .. .. | 22 10¾ | Cosine .. .. .. | 9·50129 |
| | 143 01 | Sine .. .. .. .. | 9·87994 |
| | | | 9·53036 |
| Half sum .. .. .. | 71 30½ | | |
| Remainder .. .. .. | 49 19¾ | | |

| | H. M. S. | |
|---|---|---|
| ✱'s Hour angle .. .. | 4 44 56 W. | = true azimuth, S. 86½° W., by Burdwood. |
| ✱'s Right Ascension .. | 10 2 1 | Page 338, *N.A.* |
| Sidereal Time at ship .. | 14 46 57 | |
| Sidereal Time at Greenwich | 17 40 54 | |
| Longitude in time .. .. | 2 53 57 | = 43° 29¼′ W. |
| Correction for run between sights | | − 3 |
| Longitude corresponding to that by Altair | | 43° 26¼′ W. |

SAME SIGHT WORKED WITH LATITUDE 40′ IN ERROR.

| ° ′ | |
|---|---|
| 77 27 | 0·01050 |
| 44 3½ | 0·14346 |
| 22 10¾ | 9·49366 |
| | 9·88210 |
| 143 41 | |
| | 9·52972 |
| 71 50½ | |
| 49 39¾ | H. M. S. |
| | 4 44 41 W. |

The hour angle being west, is *added* to the ✱'s Right Ascension to procure the Sidereal Time at Ship.

Regulus being further from the Prime Vertical than Altair, the error in the hour angle is of course greater. Still it is not large, amounting only to 15s., or $3\frac{3}{4}'$ of longitude for an error of 40′ in the latitude.

The difference in the longitude of the ship as given by Altair and Regulus (the one east and the other west of the meridian) is only $0\frac{3}{4}'$, proving the practicability of getting first-class results from star observations when made at the right time and in the proper manner.

**Advice to novices at star work.**

ADVICE TO BEGINNERS.—Do not despair because your first efforts are unattended with particularly good results. PERSEVERE. "Rome was not built in a day." Practice in *fine* weather, so as to gain confidence, and feel perfectly at home with the work in case of requiring its aid in *bad* weather, or on an emergency. If you do this, you will soon get out of conceit with the sun.

**Johnson's method of correcting sights for an error in the latitude worked with.**

Morning sights, as a rule, are only partially calculated pending the determination at noon of the true latitude, which of course is referred back to the time of observation by the course and distance made in the interval; but Mr. A. C. JOHNSON, in his valuable pamphlet already alluded to, shews how the sights can *at once* be worked out in full with the latitude *by account*, and *afterwards* corrected by Table I. for any error in the latitude worked with. The plan is so simple and convenient that an example is given.

About 9·45 A.M. on board the s.s. "*British Crown*," July 7th, 1880, took following observation for longitude. Eye 28 feet. Chronometer slow of G.M.T., 4m. 3s. Position by account—latitude 39° $51\frac{1}{4}'$ N., and longitude 53° 1′ W. Ship making east (true) 12 knots.

| | H. M. S. |
|---|---|
| Chronometer time .. .. | 1 18 37 |
| Slow .. .. | + 4 3 |
| | 1 22 40 |
| Corrected Equation of Time .. | − 4 42 |
| Greenwich Apparent Time .. | 1 17 58 |

| | |
|---|---|
| Observed altitude .. ☉ | 56° $44\frac{1}{2}'$ |
| | + 10 |
| ☉ | 56° $54\frac{1}{2}'$ |

| | ° ′ | | |
|---|---|---|---|
| | 90 | | |
| Corrected declination .. | 22 $31\frac{3}{4}$ | | |
| P. D. .. .. | 67 $28\frac{1}{4}$ | Cosecant .. .. | 0·03447 |
| Latitude by account .. .. | 39 $51\frac{1}{4}$ | Secant .. .. .. | 0·11482 |
| Altitude .. .. | 56 $54\frac{1}{2}$ | Cosine .. .. .. | 9·13722 |
| | | Sine .. .. .. | 9·62932 |
| | 164 14 | | |
| | | | 8·91583 |
| Half sum .. .. | 82 7 | | |
| Remainder .. | 25 $12\frac{1}{2}$ | | |

| | H. M. S. | |
|---|---|---|
| ☉'s Hour angle .. .. | 2 13 26 | = true azimuth S. 68° E. nearly, by Burdwood. |
| Apparent Time at Ship .. | 9 46 34 | |
| Apparent Time at Greenwich | 13 17 58 | |
| Longitude in time .. .. | 3 31 24 | = 52° 51′ W. at sights. |
| | | — 34½ for run till noon. |
| Longitude by sight .. .. | | 52° 16½′ W. brought up till noon. |
| Latitude by account .. | | 39° 51¼′ N. brought up till noon. |

At noon the *true* latitude was found to be 39° 41′ N., or 10¼′ S. of that by account. By Table I., the error of longitude due to an error of 1′ in the latitude is 0′·52, which, multiplied by 10′·2, gives 5¼′, to be applied as a correction to the above longitude. We have, therefore, for the true position at noon, latitude 39° 41′ N., and longitude 52° 21¾′ W.

**Johnson's rule for applying the correction.**

Johnson gives a very ingenious, and at the same time simple, method of determining whether the correction is to be added or subtracted.* The plan adopted by the writer, being based upon a graphic representation of the problem, is more instructive, and on that account to be preferred. Here it is. Imagine a line through the ship's position on the chart, drawn at right angles to the bearing of the sun, thus:—

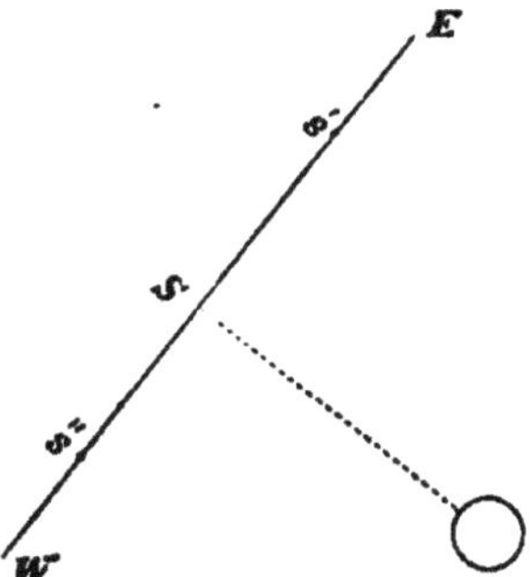


**Method used by writer for same purpose.**

For the reasons *why* the ship may be conceived to be on a line at right angles to the sun's bearing, see next chapter, where the subject is fully explained.

To make the case as plain as possible, let the sun be supposed to bear S.E. Then the line will run N.E. and S.W., as above. Let the point S. in the diagram represent the position of the ship as determined by sights worked with the latitude by account. If this turn out to be wrong, and the true latitude be further north, say at s′, the diagram shews, when this latitude is pricked off on the line, that the true longitude is more to the eastward. If, however, the true latitude be south of the latitude by account,

* See page 324.

say at s″, then the longitude is thrown to the westward. This can easily be done mentally. The plan holds good for a bearing in any quadrant of the compass.

Let us suppose another case, where the celestial object bears N.E. Then the imaginary line would run N.W. and S.E., thus :—

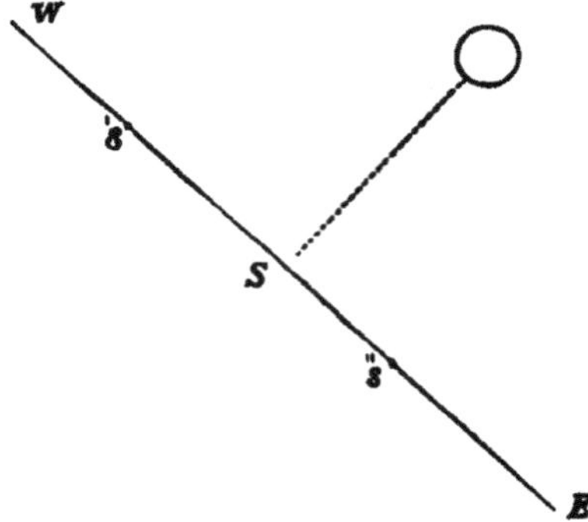


In this case, if the actual latitude be south of the one worked with, as at s″, the longitude will be thrown to the eastward, but if north, it will be thrown to the westward; just the reverse of the preceding example. The reader can test for himself the effect in the other two quadrants.

We will now imagine the sun to bear east, and see what effect is produced on the longitude by an error in the latitude.

Diagram shewing advantage of observations on the Prime Vertical.

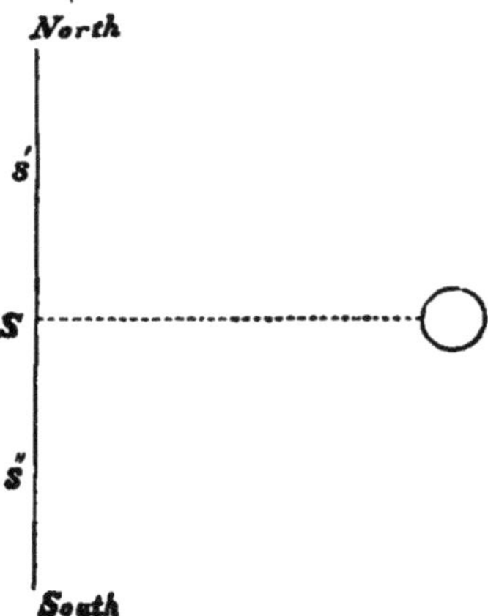


Evidently there is no effect at all, as in this case the imaginary line runs north and south. *Hence the advantage of taking sights for longitude when the celestial object is on the Prime Vertical, as a considerable error in the latitude has no effect on the result.* There is, however, a limit to this use of an indiscriminate latitude, which will be fully explained in the next chapter. In the meantime, one more illustration.

Let the sun be supposed to bear S. by E. What effect will then be produced on the longitude by an error in the latitude?

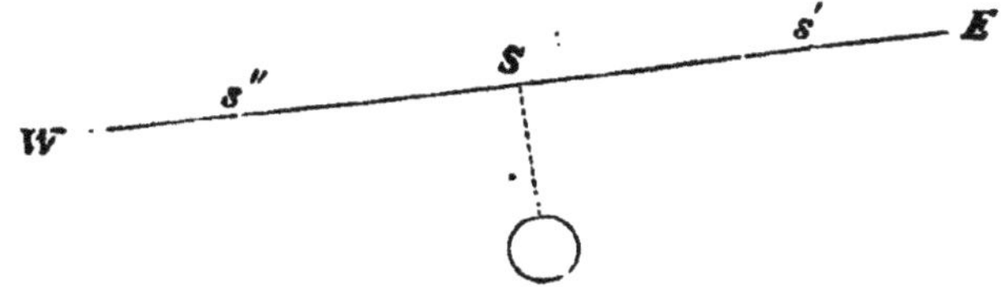


Diagram shewing disadvantage of observs. for time near the meridian.

It will now be evident that a small error in the latitude will produce a very large one in the longitude; *shewing the impropriety of taking sights for Time when the bearing of the object is near the North or South points.*

When applying the correction to the longitude by the mental process, it is always well to imagine the sun or star to have a four-point bearing, such as S.W., N.W., N.E., or S.E., although the *actual* bearing may be quite near to one of the cardinal points. This exaggeration of the case puts more forcibly to the mind the direction in which the correction is to be applied; but until thoroughly proficient, it is certainly advisable to draw the lines roughly on a slip of paper. A little practice, however, will soon do away with the necessity for even this.

Proper way of looking at a chart.

It may here be remarked, in parenthesis, that when looking at a chart, for any purpose whatsoever, it should be laid on the table with the north side from you. The mind thus acquires a fixed habit of considering the positions of places with regard to their true bearings from each other. Some men, on the contrary, if sailing south for example, turn the chart with the north side to them, so as more readily (?) to lay off bearings, &c. But this twisting and turning of the chart according to the course steered is not to be recommended, and conveys an unstable idea of geographical position.

### SHORT EQUAL ALTITUDES.

Equal altitudes at sea.

There is one other mode of finding the longitude by chronometer, which, from its extreme simplicity and the few figures required, is very alluring. Unfortunately for everyone, it is restricted in its application, and the results cannot be depended upon as more than roughly approximate. The method referred to is that of Equal Altitudes taken a few minutes before and after noon.

If the course in the interval be east or west, or the vessel be stationary, and the altitude not under 75°, the longitude will probably be somewhere near the truth, so that sailing ships lying becalmed near the line may find it convenient; but if the course be towards the north or south, and the vessel's speed at all considerable, there will be a large error due to the observer's change of latitude unless it is allowed for: this, however, is easily done as follows:—

Ascertain by the Traverse Tables the difference of latitude which will be made good between sights, and add this to, or subtract it from, the observed forenoon altitude, according as to whether the ship has sailed towards or from the sun in the interval. Set the sextant to this corrected altitude, and, when the sun falls to it, note the chronometer time.

Should the celestial object be the sun, an altitude sufficiently great cannot be obtained in high latitudes, and in low ones there are generally better modes available. If the quantities in Table II., (pages 290, 291), be multiplied by 4, so as to convert them into seconds of time, it will be seen that, even in moderately high latitudes, the change of altitude near noon is very slow. Inversely, an error of even 1′ in the altitude means a large error in the time or longitude. For these and other reasons the method of "Equal altitudes at sea" is not to be recommended. It may, however, be given a place among those auxiliary problems which science places as a reserve, but which should only be resorted to when, without them, the battle would be hopelessly lost.

### Rule.

Rule for Equal Altitudes at sea.

From 10 to 15 minutes before noon, observe the sun's altitude, and note the time by chronometer. When the sun has fallen to the same altitude P.M., corrected as above for difference of latitude made good in the interval, again note the time by same chronometer; the mean or half sum of these times, when corrected for the chronometer error, will be the Mean Time at Greenwich corresponding to Apparent Noon at Ship. Reduce the Greenwich *Mean* Time to Greenwich *Apparent* Time, by adding or subtracting the Equation, according to the precept at head of page II. of the *Nautical Almanac.* If the longitude be west, the Greenwich Apparent Time turned into arc will be the longitude; but if it be east, subtract the G.A.T. from 12 hours, and *then* turn it into arc.

### Example I.

Ship stationary, or steering either East or West (true).

August 3rd, 1881. Observed altitude, ⊙ 80° in West Longitude.

| | | H. | M. | S. | |
|---|---|---|---|---|---|
| Time by chronometer .. .. .. | | 8 | 2 | 10 | at A.M. altitude. |
| Time by chronometer .. .. .. | | 3 | 14 | 20 | at P.M. altitude. |
| | | 6 | 16 | 30 | |
| Middle time .. .. .. .. .. | | 3 | 8 | 15 | |
| Chronom. slow of G.M.T. .. .. .. | + | | 4 | 17 | |
| Greenwich Mean Time .. .. .. | | 3 | 12 | 32 | |
| Corrected Equation of Time .. .. | − | | 5 | 55 | Page II., N.A. |
| | | H. | M. | S. | |
| Longitude in time .. .. .. .. | | 3 | 6 | 37 | = 46° 39½′ W. at Noon. |

### Example II.

Where ship has changed her Latitude between sights.

August 3rd, 1881.—In east longitude, and about latitude 4° 10′ N., the eye being elevated 22 feet, the altitude of ⊙ was observed to be 76° 00′ (rising), when a chronometer which was 10m. 20s. fast of G.M.T. shewed 8h. 30m. 42s. A.M. at Greenwich same date. After a lapse of half an hour, during which time the ship had made good N. 33° E. (true) 6 knots, the sun was observed to be approaching the same altitude. After taking out the difference of latitude (5′) due to this course and distance, the Sextant was set to 76° 5′, and when the ⊙ had dropped to this altitude the same chronometer shewed 9h. 1m. 18s. Required the latitude and longitude at noon.

Note:—As the ship had been sailing *towards* the sun in the interval between sights, the difference of latitude made good had to be *added* to the first or forenoon altitude.

| | | H. | M. | S. | |
|---|---|---|---|---|---|
| Time by chronometer at A.M. observation .. | | 8 | 30 | 42 | .. .. ⊙ 76° 0′ |
| Time by chronometer at P.M. " .. | | 9 | 01 | 18 | .. .. ⊙ 76° 5′ |
| | | 17 | 32 | 00 | |
| Middle time by chronometer .. .. .. .. | | 8 | 46 | 00 | |
| Chronometer fast of G.M.T. .. .. .. .. | − | | 10 | 20 | |
| Greenwich Mean Time .. .. .. .. .. | | 8 | 35 | 40 | |
| Corrected Equation of Time .. .. .. .. | − | | 5 | 56 | Page II., N.A. |
| Greenwich Apparent Time .. .. .. .. | | 8 | 29 | 44 | |
| Apparent Time at Ship = noon, or .. .. | | 12 | 00 | 00 | Corresponding to middle time by chronometer. |
| | | H. | M. | S. | |
| Longitude in time .. .. .. .. .. .. .. | | 3 | 30 | 16 | = 52° 34′ East at Noon. |
| Latitude at noon = 4° 12½′ North. | | | | | |

*Do not abuse this method by using it at improper times, and be sure that both observations are made with eye at same height above the sea-level.*

In sight-taking, should an assistant not be available to note the chronometer time, the observer himself can very well manage with the aid of a 28s. log-glass. Turn the glass when the altitude is taken, walk to the chronometer and note the time when the sand has run out: from this subtract the running time of the glass to get the correct instant of observation. *Test the glass.*

## CHAPTER IX.

### "SUMNER LINES."

This and the following chapter are probably the most important in the book, as explaining and illustrating the geometrical process —underlying the calculation by logarithms which is performed every day by the practical navigator, but the meaning of which he has very often no conception of whatever. He only knows that by certain arithmetical formulæ (learnt off like a parrot) certain results are produced, but *how*, is a mystery. Let us open the pages of this sealed book, by which the navigator may learn to reason for himself, instead of trusting entirely to rules which, when forgotten, leave him adrift on his beam ends.

**The *principle* of a problem being understood, one is not dependent on memory for the rules.**

In the present chapter it is proposed to shew *to what extent* a single altitude of a heavenly body (say the sun) will reveal the whereabouts of a ship, *the latitude being completely unknown*, and how, when combined with certain *non*-astronomical data, it may be made to give her actual position.

It is of course assumed that the correct Greenwich Time is obtainable by means of chronometers.

We have already seen that a single altitude *on the Meridian* will give the *Latitude* with but trifling calculation; and that a single altitude *on the Prime Vertical* will give the *Longitude*, even though the latitude be but imperfectly known. It remains to shew more particularly *why* this is so, and also, *by using the latitude by dead reckoning*, what information is to be derived from a celestial body which occupies neither the one nor the other of these important positions.

By way of the simplest illustration, imagine an ordinary flag-staff in a park, and let its base—from the ground to the height of the eye—be painted a different colour from the rest. Let our

**Illustration of "Circle of Equal Altitude."**

experimentalist lay off, in any direction from it, a distance of say 100 yards, and having marked the spot by a stake, measure with the sextant the angular altitude of the flagstaff from its truck to the paint-stroke.

Suppose this to be 25°. Now let him go to any number of positions round about the flagstaff, approaching or receding from it, until in every case the same angle (25°) is obtained. At each such spot plant a stake. Connect these various points by some "small-stuff" and if they are sufficiently close together, a circle will be formed, every part of which will be exactly the same distance from the flagstaff in its centre. It is evident that an observer getting an angle of 25° must be *somewhere* on this circle, which accordingly may be termed "*a circle of equal altitude;*" since, if the angle be *greater*, he will be *within* it, and *nearer* to the flagstaff; whilst if the angle be *less*, he will be *outside* of it, and *further* from the flagstaff.

Now, conceive a number of such circles to be described at various distances from the flagstaff. If furnished with a set of tables giving the distance of each from the flagstaff, and its corresponding angle, the observer, on measuring such an angle at any point, will only know that he is *somewhere* on a circle, at a definite distance from the flagstaff. Thus, if the angle obtained were 8° 50′, reference to the tables would merely tell him that he was on a circle every point of which was 300 yards distant from the flagstaff; but if this latter and the circles were enclosed by a very high wall, which shut out from view all external objects, he could not possibly tell his position on that circle with regard to those external objects. He might just as likely be at the point marked *C* in the diagram as at *A* or *B*. If he wished to go to any particular place in the park outside the wall—say to the house at *D*, or to the fish-pond at *E*—he would not know in which direction to shape his course, or by which door to go out.

**Circle of Position illustrated.**

Let it be supposed, however, that the surface of the ground round about the flagstaff varies very much in character—that in one direction it consists of clay, in another of shells, in another of sand, and so on; and that, in addition to his set of tables, the observer is provided with a plan of the park, shewing the flagstaff and this peculiarity of the ground in its vicinity. So aided, he would at once be able to tell by the *angle* which of the circles he belonged to, and by the *nature of the ground* under his feet what particular part of it he was on, and, consequently, his position relative to the invisible objects outside the wall.

DIAGRAM ILLUSTRATING "CIRCLES OF EQUAL ALTITUDE."

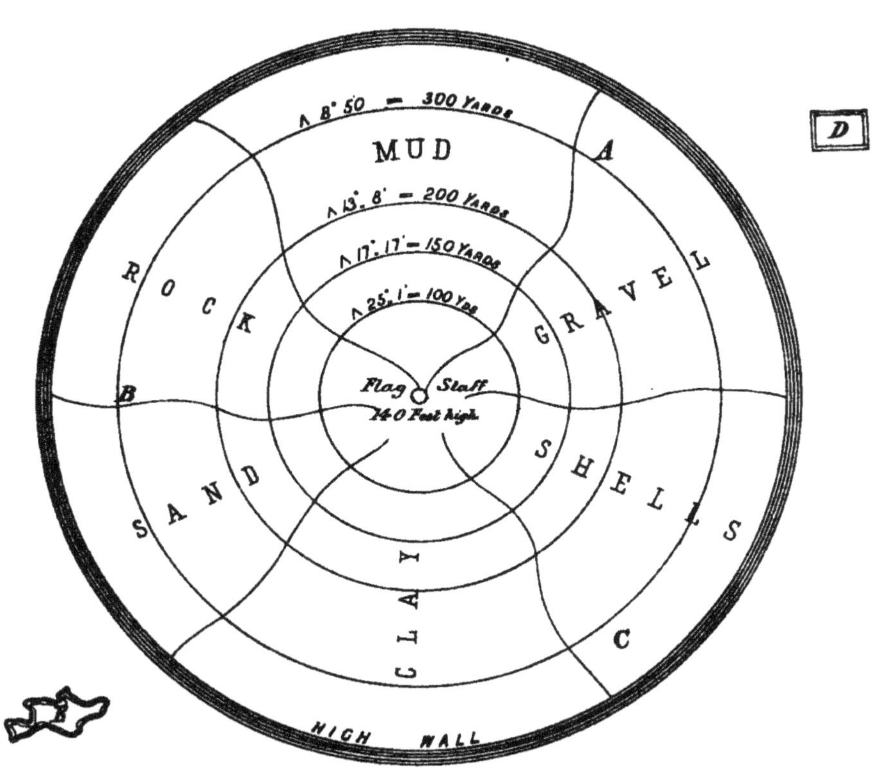

Now this is pretty much what can be done on board ship by substituting the Sun for the truck of the flagstaff, the Horizon for the paint-stroke, the *Epitome* and *Nautical Almanac* for the tables, a Chart for the plan of the park, and Soundings for the surface peculiarities of the ground.

Next come the various astronomical facts for which the foregoing simile is intended to pave the way.

**Circle of Illumination.** At any given instant of time the sun is vertically above—or, as it is termed, *in the zenith* of—some point on the earth's surface, and its rays directly illumine that half of the globe nearest to it, the other half being in darkness, more or less complete, according to circumstances. To avoid complications, imagine for the time being the earth to be arrested in its motion, so that the sun remains steady over one particular spot. At this spot an observer with a sextant would find the true altitude of the sun's centre to be 90°, and being therefore exactly overhead, upright objects would throw no shadow. On the other hand, if the observer were situated on any part of the Great Circle* separating the dark from the enlightened half of the globe, the sun would be on his horizon, and its altitude would be 0°. These represent the two *extreme* cases. We have more especially to deal with the first and intermediate ones.

If the Latitude and Longitude of the sun were known,† the Latitude and Longitude of the spot over which it was vertical would also be known, and *vice versâ*. Now, with the *Nautical Almanac* it is very easy to find the sun's position in the heavens at any given moment, and if it were possible to drop a plumb-line from it to the earth's surface, the latitude and longitude of the point of contact would correspond with that of the sun.

**Circle of Equal Altitude.** If, however, an observer were so situated that, instead of getting 90° as the sun's true altitude, he found it to be only 89°, his position would then be uncertain, since he would only be *somewhere* on the circumference of a "small circle," the centre of which would be the spot where the sun was vertical at the instant of observation. *The radius of this circle would be equal to the sun's zenith*

* This is sometimes called "The Circle of Illumination."

† These terms, as here applied, are not used in their *celestial* sense, since the *longitude* of a celestial object is measured *on the Ecliptic* from the first point of Aries, and the *latitude* is measured *from the Ecliptic* towards its poles. These terms being utterly at variance with their *terrestrial* signification, where *latitude* is measured *on a meridian* and *longitude on the Equator*, are apt to cause much confusion, and should be abolished by common consent.

*distance*, which, in the case just cited, is 1°. As the observer shifts his position away from the sun, its distance from his zenith will of course become greater, and his "Circle of equal altitude" proportionately larger, thus rendering his whereabouts more and more uncertain.

It will be seen, therefore, that, so far, the observer can only be sure of his precise position when the sun happens to be exactly in his zenith; at other times it is indefinite, and becomes more so the greater his distance from the sun. From a consideration of the foregoing, "a Circle of equal altitude" may also be designated "a Circle of position."

**How to find position of Sun at any given instant.**

To find the place on the chart over which the sun is vertical at a given Greenwich time, is very easy, *when you know how.* Since the earth revolves steadily on its axis, any place whose latitude happens to be the same as the declination of the sun at the instant of its meridian passage, must of necessity have the sun vertical at noon; and as Greenwich Apparent Time is equal to the sun's hour angle—or, in other words, to its meridian distance from Greenwich—the required longitude is found by simply turning the Greenwich Apparent Time into arc by Table XIX. of *Norie.*

Briefly, therefore, the sun's declination (corrected for the given Greenwich time) is equal to the latitude of the place; and the Greenwich Apparent Time is equal to the longitude in time, which is always to be reckoned towards the west, since the sun moves in that direction.

To project this on the chart is easy enough *in theory*, but not so easy *in practice.* Suppose "a Circle of position" is required to be drawn with the following data:—

**March 7th, 1880, at 1h. 11m. 3·8s., G.M.T., an observer, who was in complete ignorance of his position, found the sun's true altitude to be 50°. To what extent would this enlighten him?**

| | H. | M. | S. |
|---|---|---|---|
| Greenwich Mean Time | 1 | 11 | 3·8 |
| Corrected Equation of Time .. .. | — | 11 | 3·8 |
| Greenwich Apparent Time .. .. | 1 | 00 | 00·0 = Long. 15° W |

| | ° | ′ | ″ | |
|---|---|---|---|---|
| ☉'s Declination at apparent noon | 5 | 00 | 18 | S. |
| Correction for 1h., G.A.T. .. | – | | 58 | |
| ☉'s Corrected declination .. | 4 | 59 | 20 | S. |

Prick off a point in 4° 59¼′ South and 15° West (see *Chartlet No.* 1). Here the sun will be vertical at the Greenwich time specified. Subtract the observed true altitude (50°) from 90°, which will give 40° for the distance of the sun from the zenith of the observer. Take this amount in the dividers, and, with the

CHARTLET No. 1

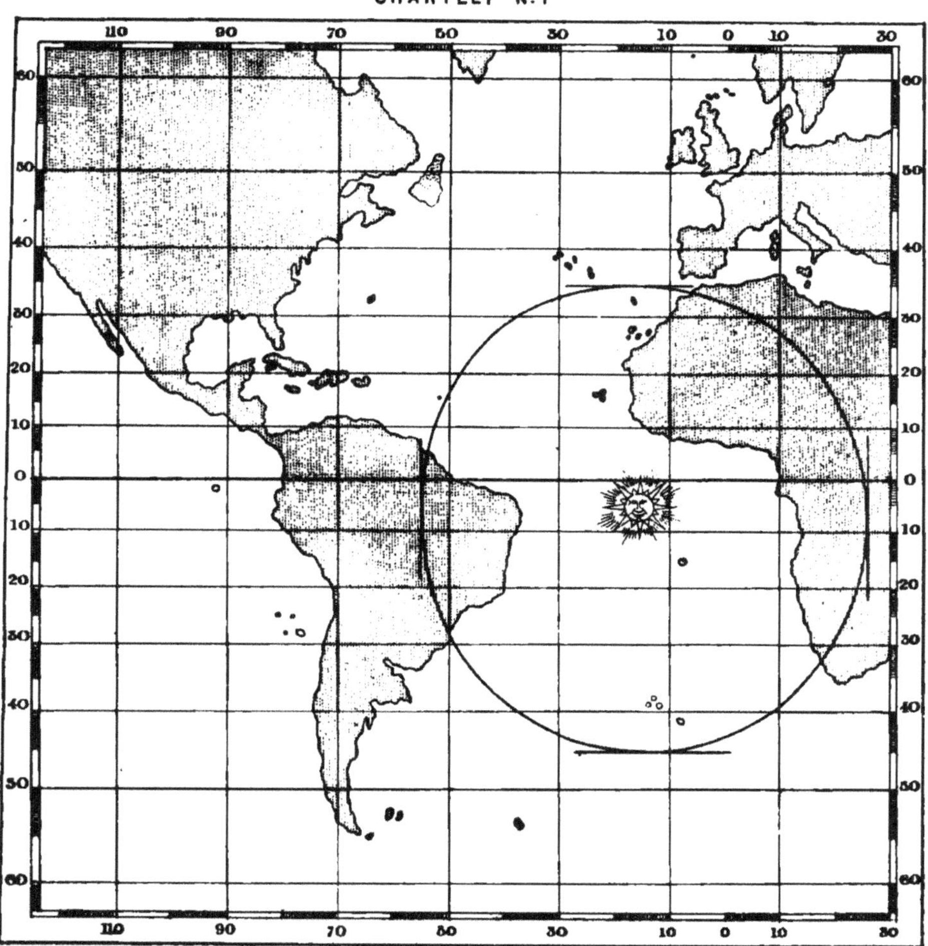


To face Page 308.

above position as a centre, describe a circle. There will now be no difficulty in understanding that for *all* ships on this circle—no matter what part of it—the sun would have an altitude of 50°. Each master would know that he was *somewhere* on this particular circle—neither inside nor outside it, but *on* it. Excepting the certainty that his ship was not on the *land* portion of it, this, however, is all he would know, unless aided in some way yet to be described; and reference to the chartlet will shew that the circle covers a goodly portion of the globe, leaving him plenty of room to guess.

**What a circle of Equal Altitude teaches.**

Place him, however, in the ordinary circumstances of the navigator, and give him his latitude by account. Then, by laying this off on the circle, he would get an *approximate* position; but such knowledge is not always sufficient where the navigation is intricate; nevertheless, poor as it is, *it may sometimes be used to great advantage*, as will be shewn further on.

**Position on Circle determined by Sounding.**

The individual in the park determined his whereabouts on the circle by the character of the ground, and, similarly, it is often possible for the navigator to fix the ship's position on it *by the depth of water and character of the bottom*. Bear this in mind, as it is important.

**On Chart, Circles of Position appear as irregular ovals.**

Passing by other methods for the present, the reader's attention is invited to sundry striking points developed by the subject. On scrutinizing *Chartlets Nos.* 1 *and* 2 more closely, it will be seen that the so-called "Circles of position" are not fairly entitled to the name—that, in fact, they are *irregular ovals*, and not true circles.

It will be remembered that it is stated in the chapter on Charts, that Mercator's projection gives a distorted representation of the earth's surface, and here we have another proof of it. Owing to the degrees of latitude being extravagantly drawn out as the Poles are approached, a true circle, when shewn correctly on a Mercator's chart, is made to assume a somewhat elliptical form, having its longer axis in a north and south direction. This feature makes the drawing of the circle in actual practice a matter of some difficulty. The usual way of arriving at it, is to calculate a number of longitudes from one sight, retaining in each case the same Polar distance and Altitude, but changing the Latitudes by suitable quantities, say 5° where the scale of the chart is small. As a check against using an *impossible* latitude in the computation, it is as well to know that in the chronometer problem, the sum of the Polar distance, Latitude, and Altitude cannot exceed 180°.

**How to draw Circle on Chart.**

Should the addition shew an excess, it proves that the computer made choice of too high a latitude, and he must reduce it accordingly.

*When the sum is exactly equal to* 180°, *it shews the polar limit of the latitude, as the body in such a case is on the meridian.* When a sufficient number of points have been thus determined, they can be pricked off on the chart, and connected by a free curve drawn with a pliable ruler, which will give the figure with tolerable exactness, and when so drawn, it may be termed "a Curve of position," or "Curve of equal altitude." This, however, would be endless work, and totally unsuited to the wants of the sailor. Happily it is not required.

**Curve of Equal Altitude.**

When the sun passes nearly overhead, the Circle of position is small, and as the observer approaches the sun it becomes yet smaller; until finally, when he has it in its zenith, it vanishes in a point, and this point, as already stated, represents his position on the globe. Conversely, as the observer recedes from the sun, the circle becomes larger, and this brings us to a feature of the very highest importance.

*Chartlet No.* 2 shews that *when the circle is large*, small portions of it (say an arc of 30′ or 40′) *may be treated as a straight line* without deviating much from the truth; and the larger the circle the nearer any part of its circumference approaches to this condition. This will be apparent by contrasting *Chartlets Nos.* 1 *and* 2, which have straight lines drawn on four of their sides. We see that in *Chartlet No.* 2, where the circle is large, the straight line touching it coincides for a much greater distance with the circumference, and this would be even more marked if the circle in *No.* 1 were say half the size. It is very necessary to retain a good mental grip of this point, as it plays an important part hereafter.

**Unnecessary in practice to draw complete circle.**

Now, in actual practice, the navigator always knows his latitude within half a degree or so, and it is therefore quite unnecessary to draw the *complete* circle on the chart. He only requires to draw that portion of it which is included between a position say 30′ North, and another 30′ South of his latitude by D.R., and as explained above (*when the circle is large*), this included arc may safely be considered as a straight line.* To this end he merely works his chronometer sight twice over; the first time with a latitude 30′ in excess, and the second time with a latitude 30′ in

* The straight line is spoken of mathematically as a *tangent or chord to the curve.*

## CHARTLET No. 2.

Sunday, March 7th, 1880, at 5h. 11m. 1·2s. mean time at Greenwich, an observer in the Northern hemisphere found the sun's true altitude to be 33° 17′ 45″.

| | H. | M. | S. | |
|---|---|---|---|---|
| Greenwich Mean Time . . | 5 | 11 | 1·2 | |
| Corrected Equation of Time . | − | 11 | 1·2 | |
| Greenwich App. Time . . . | 5 | 0 | 0·0 | =Longitude 75° W. |

| | ° | ′ | ″ |
|---|---|---|---|
| ☉'s Declin. at Greenw. App. noon . | 5 | 00 | 18 S. |
| Correction for 5 hours Greenw. App. Time | − | 4 | 52 |
| ☉'s corrected Declin. . . | 4 | 55 | 26 S. |

Therefore at the time specified the sun was vertical to a spot in Lat. 4° 55′ 26″ S., and Long. 75° W.

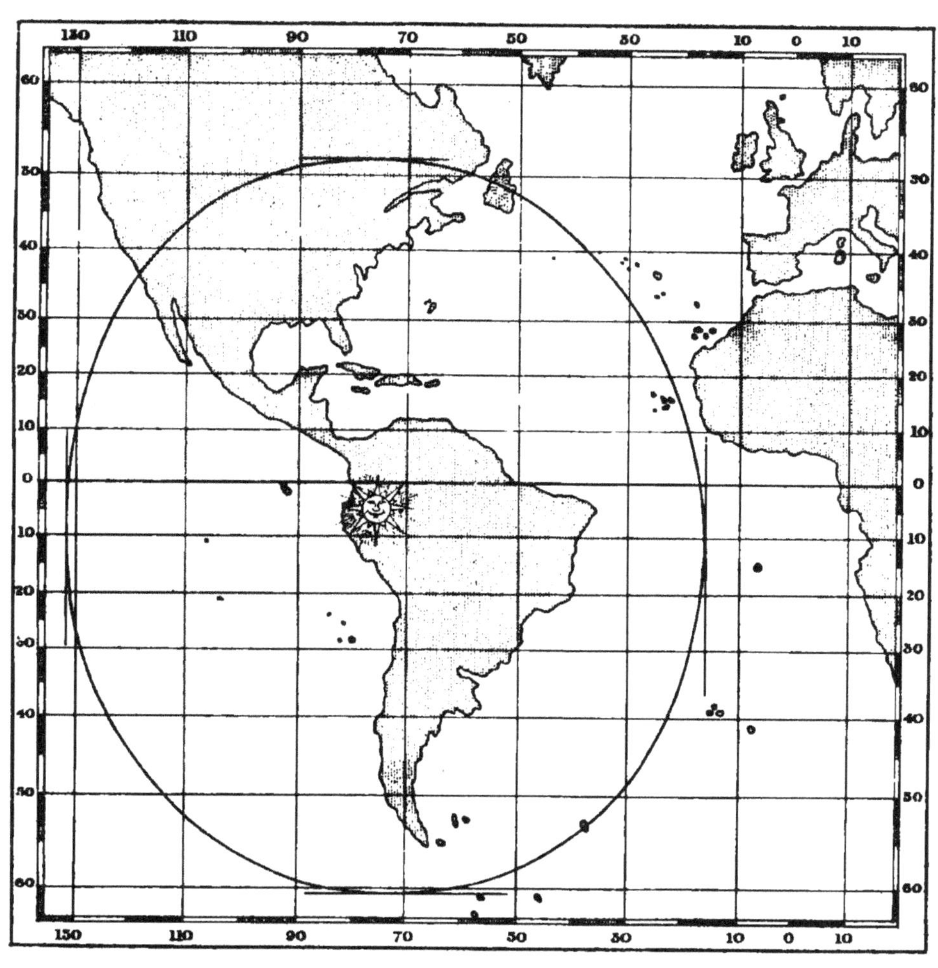

defect of his position by account. The two resulting longitudes, with the latitude proper to each, he then pricks off on the chart, and connects them by a straight line, which is really an arc of the Circle of equal altitude. Unless the error of the latitude is greater than that assumed, the ship *must* be somewhere on this "Line of position,"* which, for convenience, will henceforth in these pages be termed a "Sumner line," after the American seaman who first brought this useful problem prominently to the notice of the profession. **Sumner Lines.**

Having got so far in the knowledge of his position, if some kind friend were but able to communicate the *actual* latitude, it would be easy to prick it off on the "Sumner line," and the ship's place would at once be accurately established.

This matter of the "Sumner line" leads to another point of immense value. If we take any portion of the circumference of the circle, and consider it as a straight line (Sumner line), a noteworthy fact stands revealed—the importance of which it is almost impossible to overrate—namely, *that the bearing of the sun is invariably at right angles to this line.* Conversely, a "Sumner line" lies at right angles to the bearing of the sun, so that if either be known the other can be found. **Direction of Sumner Line always lies at right angles to bearing of Sun.**

Among other things, this explains why noon is the best time to obtain the latitude. For example, when the sun is on the Meridian it bears either north or south, and if the "Circle of position" be then drawn, that portion of the circumference at right angles to these bearings (when treated as a straight line) will run east and west, or, in other words, will constitute *a parallel of latitude*, upon which the observer must be situated (*vide* Chartlets). Again, when the sun is on the Prime Vertical, it bears either east or west, and is, accordingly, in the best position for determining the longitude, since an observer at such times will be on the "Sumner line" running due north and south, and, therefore, independent of his *exact* latitude. This is also shewn on the Chartlets. **What Sumner Lines teach.**

There is, however, a very wide difference in these two cases, which it may be as well to refer to. If the sun left a mark on the earth's surface as it moved over it from east to west, the latitude of this mark would everywhere be the same,† and would

* As before stated, the Greenwich Time is supposed to be accurately known, otherwise the line will be moved bodily to the *eastward* or *westward*, in proportion to the amount and direction of the error, 4s. being equal to 1' of longitude. The latitude, however, is not in any way affected by an error in the Greenwich Time.

† This is a broad statement, as no account is taken of the constant change in the declination.

be equal to the declination, and therefore, if the observer but knew his distance north or south of this line, he would know his latitude also. That is easily understood.

Now, as the meridian altitude subtracted from 90° gives the distance from the sun, and, consequently, from the mark, the rest is the simplest kind of arithmetic.

**How latitude is arrived at.**

For example, let the sun's declination at noon be 20° S., and the observer's zenith 40° to the *southward* of the sun, then his latitude will be 20° S. *plus* 40° S., equal to 60° S. Or, suppose the observer's zenith to be 40° *north* of the sun; then, as the sun is 20° *south* of the Equator, and the observer is 40° to the *north* of the sun, he must be 20° *north* of the Equator, which is his latitude.

Now, to ascertain the longitude, we might calculate in the same way if we only had a second sun moving round us from north to south, but we have not, and so the matter needs to be treated in some other form.

**How longitude is arrived at.**

The latitude, as already seen, may be obtained by *direct* instrumental measurement, being nothing more than the sun's angular distance *from the observer's parallel*, plus or minus the sun's distance from the Equator. This is done every day at noon, and the operation is to a large extent independent of a knowledge of the longitude. In ascertaining the latter, the distance of the sun is taken *from the observer's Meridian*; but excepting in the one particular case, when the observer is on the Equator, and the declination is 0°, this is not susceptible of *direct* measurement. In this special case, the sun describes a "Great Circle" round the world, rising due east, and setting due west.* At such times the *Meridian Distance* is obtained *directly*, by merely subtracting the true altitude from 90°, and turning the remainder into time, which of course is the Hour Angle. At all other times the Meridian Distance is obtained by computing the spherical triangle, of which the arguments are the Polar Distance, Latitude, and Altitude, constituting the after-breakfast problem so familiar to all "South Spainers."

**Sumner Line shews bearing of land.**

But we must get back to the "Sumner line," as it possesses yet another property of very considerable convenience to the navigator. If the line on the chart be extended till it meets a point of land, *it shews the bearing* of that land, and although the exact distance will not be known, we have only to sail on this line till

* *Vide* foot-note, page 311.

the place is arrived at. On this account the "Sumner line" is frequently termed a "Line of bearing."*

When entering the English Channel in winter, this knowledge may be of great service. The course of homeward-bounders is generally a north-easterly one, so that the south-easterly bearing of the sun in the forenoon is well adapted to give such a direction to the line as will cause it to strike some part of the coast.

**How to make Sumner Line pass through any given point.**

When the "Sumner line" happens to pass rather wide of a place which would make a suitable landfall, the difficulty can be circumvented by ruling through the desired point a second line parallel to the first, and so shaping the course as to get on to this new line as quickly as possible. Just as though in a strange town you were directed to a shop some distance ahead on the opposite side of the street, your first move would naturally be to cross over, and then resume your walk in the same direction, knowing that you are bound to come to it in time, and only require a good look-out till you do so.

**Best way of laying down Sumner Line.**

Instead of laying down a "Sumner line" by working a sight with *two* assumed latitudes, and pricking them off with their respective longitudes, *half* of the labour may be saved by recollecting *that the "Sumner line" runs at right angles to the sun's true bearing*, therefore, if the sun's bearing be known, it is easy to lay down the "Sumner line." To do this, work the sight *once only*, using the latitude by account, and mark the resulting position on the chart. Open the "Red Book,"† and find the sun's true bearing, employing for this purpose the hour angle just found, and the same latitude and declination. Rule a line through the chart position at right angles to the sun's true azimuth, and you have the "Sumner line" as before.

Here a word of caution is necessary. When the sun's altitude is high, the circle is small; and if even a trifling portion of the circumference be then taken, it will be found considerably curved, and the azimuth of the sun as measured from the two extremes of the arc will appreciably differ; so that the "line of bearing" is not altogether so reliable as it would be if the altitude were low, and the circle proportionately large. However, as this problem is more likely to be used in winter than summer, such a case will scarcely arise in practice. Nevertheless, it is well to bear it in mind.

* Seamen of the old school (when chronometers were more scarce than now) are familiar with the plan commonly adopted long before Sumner's time, of running down their easting or westing on the parallel of the port bound to. This was nothing more than sailing on a 12 o'clock "Sumner line."

† *Burdwood's* or *Davis's Azimuth Tables.*

The practicability having already been pointed out, of fixing a ship's position on the "Sumner line" by a cast of the lead, it remains to shew another mode of doing so by the bearing of a distant object.

**How to fix position on Sumner Line by bearing of distant land.**

It is essential in this case that the sun should be either pretty much in the same or contrary direction to the object of which the bearing is taken. Should the sun bear either exactly over it or in the contrary direction, the "cut" will be a right-angled one; and in proportion to the difference of the bearing of the sun and object, so will the angle of intersection of the two lines be more or less favourable. If, for example, the sun bears two points to the right or left of the object, the "cut" will have an angle of six points, which is very good, but the nearer it is to eight points the better. If the object be a long way off—say 40 to 50 miles—it is necessary to take the bearing with great care. A method of doing this with the utmost accuracy will be given further on. An error of 1° at 50 miles would throw out the ship's position nearly one mile. As the sun's position can be laid down on the chart at any time, this method may be regarded as a mode of fixing the ship's position by cross bearings; a short object being used for one bearing, and the sun for the other.

**Dangerous places safely navigated by Sumner Lines.**

An example will now be given, accompanied by a chartlet, to demonstrate the many great advantages of the "Sumner line" in cases of critical navigation. *It will vrove the practicability of sailing in absolute safety, and without losing distance, round dangerous shoals, when neither the latitude nor longitude of the ship are more than approximately known.*

The observations here detailed were actually made by the author when commanding the Pacific Co.'s steamship *Galicia*, but the date has been altered to suit the Nautical Almanac for the present year.

On the morning of October 24th, 1881, the steamship *Galicia*, being bound to Monte Video, was steering N. 29° E. (true), 12 knots per hour, the intention being to pass outside the French, Astrolabe, and English banks.

At 7h. 8m. A.M. App. Time at Ship, a cast of the lead was taken in 15 fathoms, sandy bottom, and the following observation was made to get a "Sumner line," by which to keep clear of the shoals.

| | H. | M. | S. | | |
|---|---|---|---|---|---|
| G.M.T. | 10 | 34 | 23·6 | A.M. same date. | -☉- True Alt 20° 40′ |
| Corr. Equa. | + | 15 | 44·2 | | |
| G.A.T. . . . | 10 | 50 | 7·8 | | |

CHARTLET No 4.

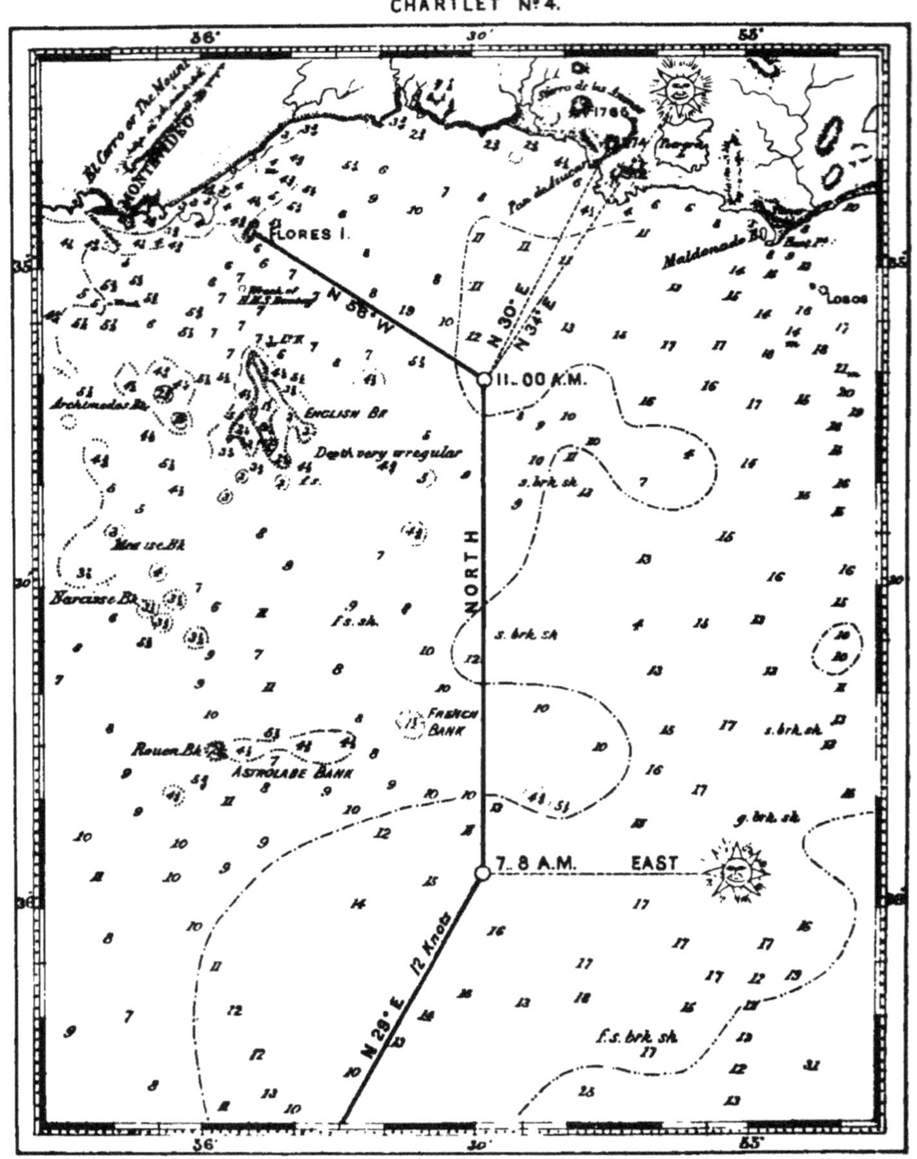

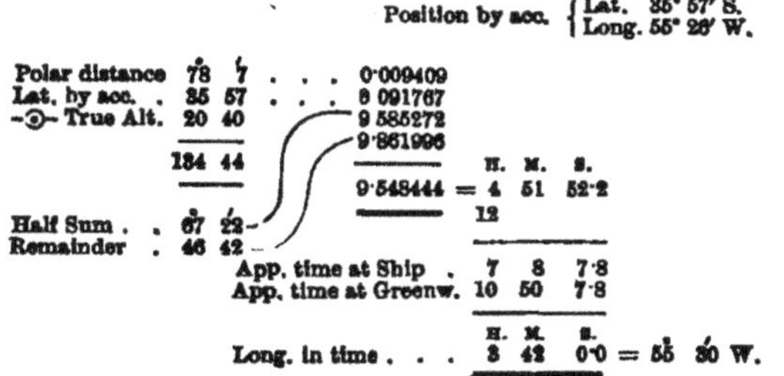

Position by acc. { Lat. 35° 57′ S. / Long. 55° 26′ W.

```
Polar distance   78°  7′ . . . 0·009409
Lat. by acc.  .  35  57  . . . 8 091767
-☉- True Alt.    20  40        9 585272
                 ------        9·861996
                 134  44       --------     H.  M.  S.
                 ------        9·548444  =  4   51  52·2
Half Sum .  .    67° 22′       --------     12
Remainder   .    46  42                    -----------
          App. time at Ship   .             7    8   7·8
          App. time at Greenw.             10   50   7·8
                                           -----------
                                            H.  M.  S.
          Long. in time . . .               3   42  0·0 = 55° 30′ W.
```

Accordingly, Latitude 35° 57′ S., and Longitude 55° 30′ W., were pricked off on the chart. Next Burdwood was opened at page 65, and under declination 12°, and opposite 7h. 8m. A.T.S., the sun's true bearing was found to be 90°, or East. Therefore, a North and South "Sumner line" was ruled through the ship's position.

Now, in accordance with what has already been stated, the ship must be *somewhere* on this line; and as it trended due North and South, owing to the *sun being on the Prime Vertical*, the exact *longitude* was a matter of certainty, and the soundings seemed to indicate that the latitude by D.R. was pretty correct. Looking at the line on the chart, it is evident, let the latitude be what it may, that if the ship was steered upon it, she would go clear of danger. This was done, and the ship's course then became North (true). *As a precaution the lead was kept going, to guard against a westerly set of the tide or current.*

About 10 A.M. high land was sighted a little on the starboard bow, and at 11 A.M. the Pan de Azucar (a mountain 1374 feet high) was recognized, bearing N. 30° E. (true). Its vertical sextant angle—*measured on and off*—was 0° 26′ 45″, eye 28 feet. Immediately an observation was made to get a second "Sumner line," as the sun was favourably situated for crossing it with the bearing of the mountain. A cast was also taken in 11½ fathoms, mud.

```
               H.  M.  S.
G.M.T.         2   26  16·6 P.M. same date.        -☉- True Alt. 63° 6′
Corr. Equa.  + 15  45  3
              -----------
G.A.T. . .     2   42  1·9
              ===========
                                  Position by acc. { Lat.  35° 10′ S.
                                                   { Long. 55° 30′ W.

Polar distance   78°  3′ . . . 0·009515
Lat. by acc.  .  35  10  . . . 0 087523
-☉- True Alt.    63   6        8 507014
                 ------        9·626895
                 176  19       --------     H.  M.  S.
                 ------        8 230947  =  0   59  58·1
Half Sum .  .    88°  9½′      --------     12
Remainder   .    25   3½                   -----------
          App. time at Ship   .            11   00   1·9
          App. time at Greenw.             14   42   1·9
                                           -----------
                                            H.  M.  S.
          Long. in time . . .               3   42  0·0 = 55° 30′ W.
```

This position was duly pricked off, and as Burdwood does not give the azimuth when the altitude exceeds 60°, recourse was had to Towson's handy tables,* page 72, where, by a very few figures, the sun's true bearing was determined to be N. 34° E. A "Sumner line" at right angles to this (N. 56° W. true) being ruled through the chart position, was found to lead in safety round the north-eastern edge of the English Bank, and strike the island of Flores. This course was steered with every confidence, and in three-quarters of an hour the lighthouse was made dead ahead. When the "Sumner line" was cut by laying off on the chart the bearing of the "Pan de Azucar," it gave a position agreeing exactly with the one by D.R., and further corroboration was found in the soundings, which tallied to a nicety. The distance of the mountain was calculated from the observed vertical angle, and found to be 24½ miles. The measurement on the chart proved to be the same.†

**Distance of land by Vertical Angle of same.**

Here we have as good an example as could well be selected, of the immense value of the "Sumner line" when making the land, or dodging round shoals. It is necessary to observe that the chronometers had been rated a few days before at Sandy Point, in the Straits of Magellan, so that the longitude of the "Sumner line" could be depended upon as correct, otherwise it would have been imprudent to skirt the banks so closely. In laying off "Sumner lines" on the chart, the navigator is strongly recommended to use Field's Parallel Ruler, which will be found very handy for this and similar purposes.

**Field's Parallel Ruler.**

By way of practice, the reader can work out the following observations, which were made going up the Irish Channel:—

Tuesday, June 8th, 1880, at 3h. 4m. P.M., the s.s. *British Crown* passed one mile S.E. of Tuskar lighthouse, and shaped a course up the George's Channel N. 31½° E., the speed over the bottom varying from 9 knots per hour against the ebb, to 14½ knots with the flood.

**Instructive examples for Student.**

In every case the correct Greenwich Mean Time is referred to. The courses and bearings are by Sir William Thomson's standard compass *reduced* to true. Eye 24 feet. No index error. The exact position of the ship was ascertained from time to time by bearings of the land, and horizontal angles laid down with the Station Pointer. In two instances *vertical* sextant angles of Croghan

* "Practical Information on the Deviation of the Compass, for the use of Masters and Mates of Iron Ships." By J. T. Towson.

† The writer has brought out a small book (pocket size), entitled "The Danger Angle and Off-shore Distance Tables," whereby a ship's distance from the coast may be taken out by simple inspection. It can be procured from the publishers of this work, and other nautical booksellers. (Price 4s. 6d.)

Hill—*measured on and off the arc*—were taken as a check, and coincided beautifully with the other determinations. The observations were made by the writer singlehanded, and the chronometer times taken by an officer. Had there been an assistant to permit of the observations being made simultaneously, of course it would have been easier, but the close agreement of the results shews what can be done by trying. The chart used was Admiralty Sheet No. 1825 B. The reader is recommended, before going into the calulations, to lay off the ship's position corresponding to the various times of observation. This is easily done by starting at one mile S.E. of Tuskar, and ruling a light pencil line with Field's Parallel Ruler in the direction of N. 31½° E. true. Upon this lay off the ship's position at 5h. 28m. 16s.—5h. 45m. 00s.—6h. 10m. 19s.—6h. 37m. 00s.—7h. 51m. 53s. and 8h. 15m. 8s. When working out the Sumner lines, use a latitude expressly in error some 10′, so that the perfection of the method may be fully demonstrated.

4h. 4m. 00s. P.M. Lucifer Shoals lightvessel abeam, distant about 4¾ miles.

5h. 28m. 16s. ☉ 25° 57′. Slieve Boy N. 75¼° W. Position by bearings, &c., 52° 33′ 7″ N., and 5° 50′ 00″ W. Position by "Sumner line" crossed with bearings of Slieve Boy 52° 33′ 00″ N., and 5° 49′ 37″ W.

5h. 33m. 40s. ☉ 25° 7¾′. Croghan Hill N. 54° W. ∧ 0° 43′ 50″ = 23′ distant against 22¾′ by bearings, &c., which latter gave position 52° 34′ 8″ N. and 5° 49′ 10″ W. Position by "Sumner line" crossed with bearing of Croghan Hill 52° 34′ 5″ N. and 5° 49′ 45″ W.

5h. 45m. 00s. South Arklow lightvessel bore N. 43¼° W., distant nearly 8′.

6h. 10m. 19s. ☉ 19° 36′. Croghan Hill N. 72¾° W. ∧ 0° 42′ 10″ = 23½′, distant, agreeing exactly with following position by bearings, &c., 52° 40′ 50″ N. and 5° 42′ 30″ W. By "Sumner line" crossed with bearing of Croghan Hill 52° 40′ 55″ N. and 5° 43′ 00″ W.

6h. 23m. 54s. ☉ 17° 34½′. Croghan Hill N. 79½° W. Observed horizontal angles as follows:—Mt. Leinster 18° 45′ Croghan Hill 45° 34′ Great Sugar Loaf. Which gave position 52° 43′ 20″ N. and 5° 40′ 00″ W., against 52° 43′ 12″ N. and 5° 38′ 30″ W., by "Sumner line" cut by Croghan Hill.

6h. 37m. 00s. Wicklow Head lighthouse bore N. 48¼° W.

7h. 51m. 53s. ☉ 5° 30′. Summit of Bardsey Island, in the *opposite* direction to the sun, bore S. 54¼° E., distant about 27½ miles. The sextant angle between Croghan Hill and the sun's nearest limb was 53° 57′. Position 53° 1′ 50″ N. and 5° 23′ 00″ W., against 53° 2′ 5″ N. and 5° 23′ 40″ W., by "Sumner line" cut by Bardsey. In this case the bearing of Croghan Hill was found by first getting out the sun's azimuth from the "Red book," and then applying to it the horizontal angle measured between it and Croghan Hill. The method of doing this will be given in another chapter.

8h. 15m. 8s. The final position of the ship was 53° 6′ 40″ N. and 5° 18′ 50″ W. The horizontal angle between the Great Sugar Loaf and the sun's nearest limb was 30° 45′, the sun having an altitude of *about* 2° 45′. At the same time, nearly, the horizontal angle between Holyhead Mountain and the summit of Bardsey was 74° 40′.

## CHAPTER X.

### "DOUBLE ALTITUDES."

**Pre-eminence given to Double Altitudes.**

That very distinguished authority, Sir W. Thomson, in alluding to Sumner's method of "Double Altitudes," is credited with having said in the course of a lecture at Glasgow, "that it would be the greatest blessing to navigators, both young and old, if every other method of ordinary navigation could be swept away." When one considers that the "Double Altitude" problem—not Ivory's, or Riddle's, or the method by natural sines, but the "Double Altitude" problem as *now* practised—gives the Latitude, Longitude, and Azimuth, *all at one working*, the learned Professor's remark seems more than justified.

The chief virtue of this powerful problem consists in utilizing observations taken at any hour of the day, so that one is rendered gloriously independent of the 9 o'clock sight, and the time-honoured Meridian Altitude. Of all others, therefore, this is the problem to which the navigator should devote his most serious attention.

In the last chapter it is shewn how a single altitude of the sun gives a "Circle or Curve of position," upon some part of which the observer must be. If, then, after an interval, during which the sun has travelled sufficiently to the westward, *another* altitude be taken, a second "Circle of position" will be obtained, upon some part of which the observer must likewise be. Now, since he is *somewhere* on *both* of the circles, he must of necessity be at their point of intersection, which is the only place that can satisfy the twofold condition. It is true that the circles intersect each other at *two* points, but these are *generally* wide apart—perhaps in opposite hemispheres—and surely the observer knows his whereabouts within a handful of degrees. It will be evident, therefore,

CHARTLET Nº 3.

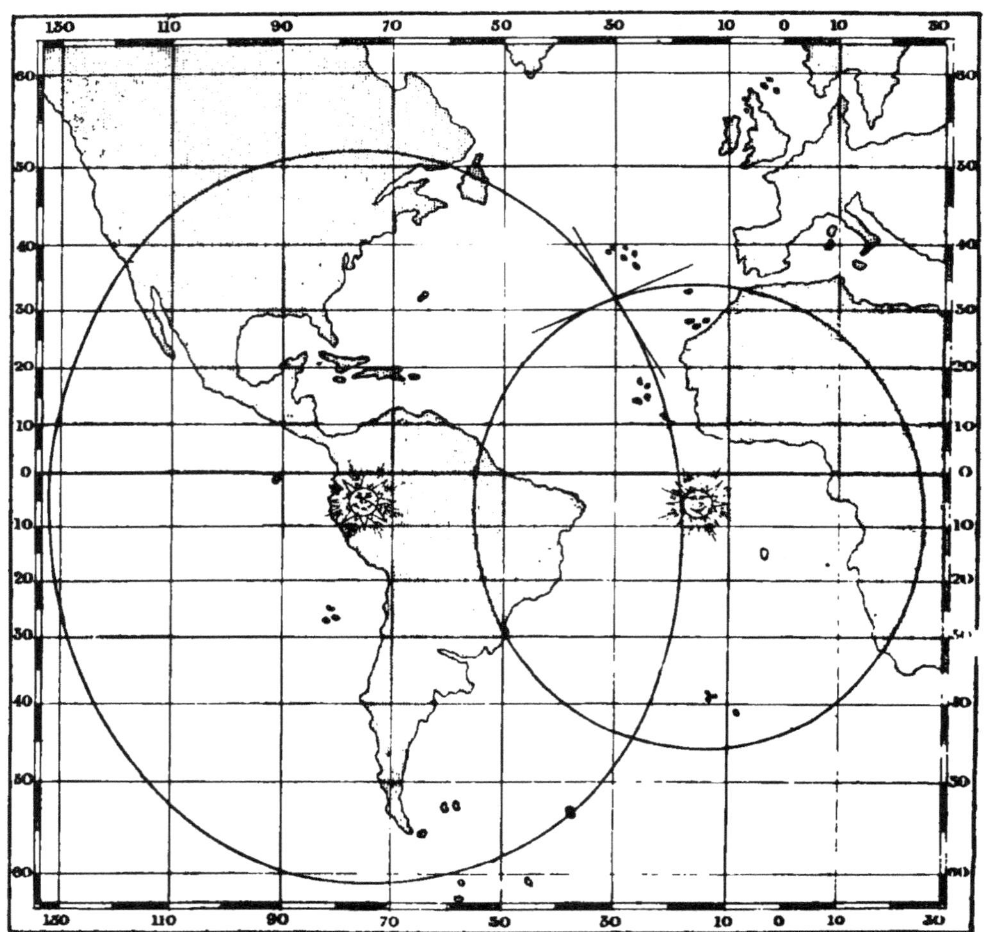


To face Page

that the "Double Altitude"* problem is nothing more than the operation detailed in the last chapter, repeated after a suitable interval. *Chartlet No.* 3 illustrates this. The circles in it are those which have already been separately given. They are now combined, to exemplify the method, and the data belonging to each presented to the reader in a complete form.

MARCH 7TH, 1880.

**Example of Double Altitude.**

About 11 A.M. Apparent Time at Ship, an observer *in the Northern hemisphere* found the sun's true altitude to be 50°, when a chronometer shewed 1h. 11m. 3·8s. of G.M.T.

After an interval of four hours, the same observer, at 5h. 11m. 1·2s. of G.M.T., found the sun's true altitude to be 33° 17′ 45″. Required his Latitude and Longitude; also the sun's true azimuth at each observation.

Reference to the chartlet will shew that the circles intersect in Latitude 32° 23′ N., and Longitude 30° W. The sun's azimuth at the first observation was S. 23¾° E. and S. 57½° W. at the last one. The "Sumner lines" are at right angles to these bearings, and of course cut each other at the same point that the circles do. Considering them as "*Lines of bearing*," if the ship were sailed on the first "Sumner line," she would fetch Vigo in one direction, or the West India Islands in the other. If she were sailed on the second "Sumner line," she would fetch either Sierra Leone or Baffin's Bay.

**"Astronomical cross bearings."**

This method may be considered as a means of determining the ship's place *by astronomical cross-bearings;* the first bearing of the sun being taken when convenient, and its position at that moment laid down on the chart; and the second, or *cross-bearing*, after an interval sufficient to allow the requisite change in the sun's position. In the example before us, the bearings cross at an angle of 81½°, which, being nearly a right angle, gives a very favourable "cut."

**How to manage when ship shifts position between observations.**

In practice, the ship is very seldom stationary between the observations, and if it be required (as is customary) to know her position at the *last* one, the first circle must be moved *bodily* to the same distance and in the same direction as the ship has sailed in the interval. When dealing with the "Sumner lines," the same rule of course holds good: the first one must be trans-

* Raper finds fault with this term, and suggests "Combined Altitudes," but its meaning is so thoroughly established among the seafaring community, that any attempt to change it would be questionable wisdom.

ferred *parallel with itself*, according to the course and distance made good between sights. *Then* its point of intersection with the second "Sumner line" will be the ship's place as required.

In sea-going practice, to find the latitude and longitude by this method, take two altitudes of the sun, with such an interval between them as will give a difference of bearing of *at least* three points, but the nearer to eight points the better—same rule in fact as in taking cross-bearings of the land, where the place of the ship is most distinctly marked when the pencil lines have a good square crossing. Work the altitudes separately, using the Latitude by account and Polar distance proper to each, and find the respective azimuths by the "Red book." Through each resulting position on the chart, rule a "Sumner line," differing 90° in direction from the sun's true bearing. Take *any* point in the 1st line, and from it draw a 3rd, to represent the ship's run between the observations. Through the end of this 3rd line draw a 4th, parallel to the 1st, and the point at which it cuts the 2nd Sumner line is the place of the ship.

**Double Altitudes.**

To prevent confusion, it is better not to draw the 2nd "Sumner line" till the 1st one has been projected for the run of the ship: there need then be but one point of intersection, as in the figure. It might serve to make this transference of the 1st "Sumner line" better understood, if we were to imagine it something the ship could carry with her, and drop *at the correct angle*, at the

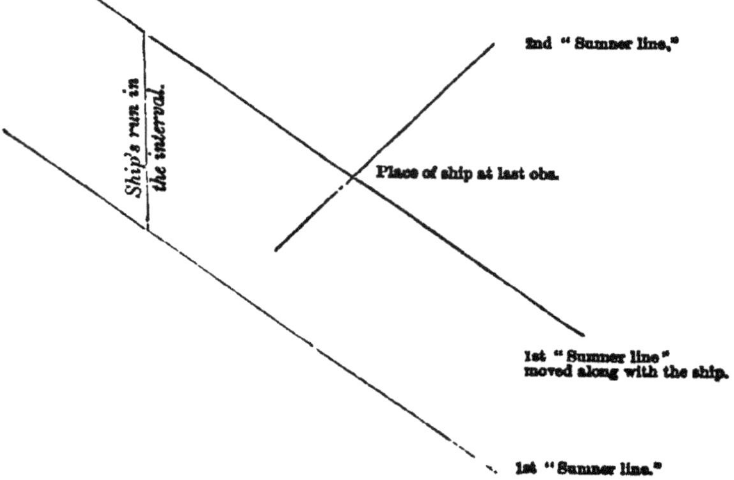

instant of making the observation which was to cross it with the 2nd "Sumner line."

Now, it is not always convenient to draw "Sumner lines" on a chart. Moreover, to define the "cut" clearly and accurately, it is necessary to use a well-sharpened pencil, to have a chart on a fairly large scale, and that the difference in the sun's bearing be not less than three points,—the two latter of which conditions are unfortunately not always obtainable. Again, if "Double altitudes" be practised daily—as most assuredly they ought to be—constantly plotting the "Sumner lines" would soon disfigure the chart. It may be graphic, but it is also clumsy.

**Calculation better than "plotting."**

**Calculation by Sumner's own method too tedious.**

To avoid all this, and ensure the greatest accuracy the method is capable of, it is advisable to do the whole thing *by calculation from first to last.* But the "Double altitude" problem, when worked out in full, *according to Sumner*, is a formidable affair, and the rules at the finish are so complicated as to scare most ordinary seafaring men.

The easier method recently introduced by Mr. A. C. Johnson, M.A., Naval Instructor on board Her Majesty's training ship "Britannia," is therefore a most welcome improvement.* It is short, easily understood, and accurate, and there is little in the whole calculation with which the navigator is not already familiar. Let us now contrast the two methods, and the reader can judge for himself which gives most value for an equal number of figures. The example, of which the figures are here given, is the one already presented graphically to the reader in chartlets 1, 2, and 3.

**Johnson's Double Altitude Problem the best.**

* "*On finding the Latitude and Longitude in Cloudy Weather.*" London: J. D. Potter, 31, Poultry.

## SUMNER'S STYLE OF CALCULATING A "DOUBLE ALTITUDE."—(ROSSER'S ARRANGEMENT).

Assumed Latitude, 32° 15′ N.

| | H. | M. | S. | |
|---|---|---|---|---|
| Greenwich Mean Time . . . . | 1 | 11 | 3·8 | -☉- True Alt. 50° 00′. |
| Corrected Equation of Time . . | — | 11 | 3·8 | |
| 1st Greenwich App. Time . . . | 1 | 0 | 0·0 | |

| | H. | M. | S. | |
|---|---|---|---|---|
| Greenwich Mean Time . . . . | 5 | 11 | 1·2 | -☉- True Alt. 33° 17¾′. |
| Corrected Equation of Time . . | — | 11 | 1·2 | |
| 2nd Greenwich App. Time . . . | 5 | 0 | 0·0 | |

| (a) | | (b) | | (c) | | (d) | |
|---|---|---|---|---|---|---|---|
| 94° 59¼′ | 0·00165 | 94° 55¼′ | 0·00161 | 94° 59¼′ | 0·00165 | 94° 55¼′ | 0·00161 |
| 32 00 | 0·071 8 | 32 00 | 0·07158 | 32 40 | 0·07478 | 32 40 | 0·07478 |
| 50 00 | 8·42032 | 33 17¾ | 9·23481 | 50 00 | 8·31189 | 33 17¾ | 9·22005 |
| | 9·79407 | | 9·86283 | | 9·79723 | | 9·86519 |
| 176 59¼ | | 160 13 | | 177 39¼ | | 160 53 | |
| | 8·28762 | | 9·17083 | | 8·18555 | | 9·16163 |
| 88° 29½′ | | 80° 6½′ | | 88° 49½′ | | 80° 26½′ | |
| 38 29½ | | 46 49 | | 38 49½ | | 47 09 | |

| | H. | M. | S. | | H. | M. | S. | | H. | M. | S. | | H. | M. | S. |
|---|---|---|---|---|---|---|---|---|---|---|---|---|---|---|---|
| Hour ∠ . . | 1 | 4 | 2 | | | | | Hour ∠ . . | 0 | 56 | 54 | | | | |
| A T S. . . | 10 | 55 | 58 | . . . . . . . | 3 | 1 | 8 | . . . . . . . | 11 | 3 | 6 | . . . . . . . | 2 | 59 | 7 |
| A.T.G. . . | 13 | 00 | 00 | . . . . . . . | 5 | 0 | 0 | . . . . . . . | 13 | 0 | 0 | . . . . . . . | 5 | 00 | 0 |
| Long. in Time | 2 | 4 | 2= | | 1 | 58 | 52= | | 1 | 56 | 54= | | 2 | 00 | 53= |
| Long. (a). . | 31° 00¼′ W. | | | Long. (b) . . | 29° 43′ W. | | | Long (c) . . | 29° 13½′ W. | | | Long. (d) . . | 30° 13¼′ W. | | |

With Latitude 32° N. (D. 40′).

| | | |
|---|---|---|
| 1st observation—Longitude (a) | 31° 00¼′ | W. |
| 2nd observation—Longitude (b) | 29 43 | W. |
| Diff (A) . . . . . | 1 17¼ | E. |
| (B) . . . . . | 0 59¾ | W. |
| As (A + B) . . . | 2 17 | . . . . Prop. Log.—(ar. com.) 9·8822 |
| is to (A) . . . | 1 17¼ | . . . . . . . . . . Prop. Log. 3660 |
| so is (D) . . . | 0 40 | . . . . . . . . . . Prop. Log. 6532 |
| Correction . . . | +0 22½ | N. . . . . . . . . . Prop. Log. ·9014 |
| Lesser Latitude . . . . . . | 32 00 | N. |
| True Latitude . . . . . . . | 32° 22½′ | N. |

With Latitude 32° 40′ N.

| | | |
|---|---|---|
| Longitude (c) . . | 29° 13½′ | W. |
| Longitude (d) . . | 30 13¼ | W. |
| (B) . . | 0° 59¾′ | W. |

| | | | |
|---|---|---|---|
| Longitude (a) . . | 31° 00¼′ | W. | |
| Longitude (c) . . | 29 13½ | W. | |
| (C) . | 1° 47′ | W. | |
| | | | 9·8822 |
| | | | 3660 |
| (C) 1° 47′ Prop. Log. . | | | 2259 |
| Correction . . . | —1° 0¼′ | E. | ·4741 |
| Longitude (a) . . | 31 0¼ | W. | |
| True Longitude . . | 30° 00′ | W. | |

Note.—When the ship has changed her position between the observations, there is even more work, and also an additional rule to remember.

## SAME "DOUBLE ALTITUDE" CALCULATED BY A. C. JOHNSON'S METHOD.

### Assumed Latitude, 32° 15′ N.

| | H. | M. | S. | |
|---|---|---|---|---|
| Greenwich Mean Time . . . | 1 | 11 | 8·8 | -⊙- True Altitude 50° 00′ |
| Corrected Equation of Time . | — | 11 | 8·8 | |
| 1st Greenwich App. Time . . | 1 | 0 | 0·0 | |

| ° ′ | |
|---|---|
| 94 59½ | 0·00165 |
| 32 15 | 0·07277 |
| 50 00 | 8·38276 |
| | 9·79526 |
| 177 14½ | 8·25244 |
| 88° 37′ | |
| 38 37 | |

| | H. | M. | S. | |
|---|---|---|---|---|
| Hour ∠ . . . | 1 | 1 | 29 | = S. 24° E. ex "Red Book," page 28. |
| A.T.S. . . | 10 | 58 | 31 | |
| A.T.G. . . | 13 | 00 | 00 | |
| Long. in Time | 2 | 1 | 29 | = |

1st Longitude 30° 22¼′ W.
2nd Longitude 29 53¾ W.

8·4) 28·5 (8′·4 Correction for Lat.
272
———
130
136

| | ° | ′ | |
|---|---|---|---|
| Assumed Latitude . . | 32 | 15 | N. |
| Correction . . . . . | + | 8¼ | |
| True Latitude . . . | 32° | 23¼′ | North. |
| 1st Longitude . . . . | 30 | 22¼ | W. |
| Correction . . . . . . | − | 22¼ | |
| True Longitude . . . | 30° | 00′ | West. |

| | H. | M. | S. | |
|---|---|---|---|---|
| Greenwich Mean Time . . . | 5 | 11 | 1·2 | -⊙- True Altitude 33° 17¾′ |
| Corrected Equation of Time . | — | 11 | 1·2 | |
| 2nd Greenwich App. Time . . | 5 | 0 | 0·0 | |

| ° ′ | |
|---|---|
| 94 55¼ | 0·00161 |
| 32 15 | 0·07277 |
| 33 17¾ | 9·22952 |
| | 9·86369 |
| 160 28¼ | 9·16759 |
| 80° 14′ | |
| 46 56¼ | |

| | H. | M. | S. | |
|---|---|---|---|---|
| A.T.S. or Hour ∠ . | 3 | 0 | 25 | = S. 57¼° W. ex "Red Book," page 28. |
| A.T.G. . . . . | 5 | 0 | 00 | |
| Long. in Time. . . | 1 | 59 | 35 | = |

| | ° | ′ | |
|---|---|---|---|
| 2nd Longitude . . . | 29 | 53¾ | W. |
| Correction . . . . | + | 6¼ | |
| True Longitude . . | 30° | 00′ | West. |

Table I., page 288.

⊙ Bearing S. 24° E. — 2′·65 × 8′·4 = 22¼′ correction for 1st Long.
⊙ Bearing S. 57¼ W. — 0′·75 × 8′·4 = 6¼′ " 2nd "

Sum 3·40

NOTE.—Here we have about 280 figures, including the suns azimuths, against about 530 by Sumner's Method; or nearly double the number without the azimuths.

### THE FOLLOWING IS THE RULE FOR THIS METHOD.*

**Johnson's Rules.**

I. Let two chronometer observations be taken at an interval of about an hour and a half, or two hours, if possible,† and let the first be worked out with the lat., D.R. at the time of observation.

II. Let the lat., D.R., and longitude thus obtained, be corrected for the run of the ship in the interval between the observations, and let the second observation be worked with this corrected latitude. Name these longitudes (1) and (2), and take their difference.

III. The bearing of the sun at each observation is to be taken from an Azimuth Table. In every case they are to be considered as less than 90°; so that when the Tabular bearings exceed 90°, we must subtract them from 180°, and reckon them from the opposite point of the compass; thus N. $122\frac{1}{2}$° W. would be S. $57\frac{1}{2}$° W., and so on.

IV. Enter Table I. (pages 288, 289,) with the latitude and bearings, and take from it two numbers (*a*) and (*b*), of which take the difference or sum, according as the bearings are in the same or different quarters of the compass. The difference between the longitudes (1) and (2), divided by this difference or sum, gives the correction for the second latitude; and (*a*) and (*b*), multiplied by this correction for latitude, gives the corrections for the two longitudes.

V. *To apply the corrections for the longitude.*

When the observations are in the *same* quarter of the compass, allow the corrections *both* to the East, or *both* to the West,

When the observations are in different quarters of the compass, correct the Easterly longitude towards the West, and the Westerly longitude towards the East,

in such a manner as to make the two longitudes *agree*. If they do not agree, they shew that the corrections have been wrongly applied; and herein, as Mr. Johnson says, we have a valuable safeguard against error, peculiar to this method only.

VI. *To apply the correction for the latitude.*

Under the sun's bearing at the time of observation write the *opposite* bearing, and suppose the letters to be connected diagonally; then that connected with the name of the correction for longitude will be the name of the correction for the latitude. Thus, if the

* Inserted with Mr. Johnson's permission.

† Provided that the sun's bearing has changed not less than a point and a half, or two points.

correction for the longitude were $6\frac{1}{4}'$ W., and the sun's bearing S. $57\frac{1}{2}°$ W.,

We should write down S. W.

and under it N. E.

Then, as the letter which stands diagonally opposite to W. (the name of the correction for the longitude) is N., the correction for the latitude has to be allowed towards the North: and so on in other cases.

A consideration of the direction in which the "Sumner lines" trend, will give the reason for Rule VI. The reader can also refer back to those in *Chartlet No.* 3, and to the explanation on page 299, *et sequitur*.

An example from actual observation on board ship is given on the following page, to shew the complete working of the method advocated.

**Similarity of principle between Rosser's and Johnson's methods.**

This of Johnson's may be regarded as a convenient adaptation of Rosser's method of "Double Altitudes by Logarithmic Tabular Differences." The two are virtually the same in principle; and although Rosser's is *very* first-rate, Johnson's has undoubtedly cut it out. The greater brevity of the latter, its freedom from even *the suspicion* of algebra—a regular bugbear to some men—and fewer rules to remember, are all good points to score. The writer used Rosser's method almost daily for a number of years, but has abandoned it in favour of Johnson's.

**Preference given to Johnson.**

Sir W. Thomson, much impressed with the value of Sumner's method in his own nautical experience, which is not inconsiderable, has gone to the trouble and expense of publishing a set of tables to facilitate the working, but they do not seem to find general favour, and Johnson's method—taken all round—is hard to beat.

In actual practice, the first half of the "Double Altitude" observation is worked out as soon as possible; and it is well to take the 2nd altitude about an hour or so after the first, in case a more desirable one should not be obtained later on. It can be kept as a "stand by," and need not be worked out if a better turn up.

**Winter better than Summer for Double Altitudes.**

As the sun's bearing changes more rapidly in high latitudes than in low—in winter than in summer—the interval between the observations may at such times be correspondingly smaller. This fits in admirably with the sailor's requirements, as it is just in winter he happens most to need the aid of this problem. The

On board the (s.s.) "*British Crown*," at 8·38 A.M. and 10·38 A.M. on January 17th, 1880, the following observations were made to find the latitude and longitude by Johnson's "Double Altitude" method. Course and distance in the interval, S. 74° W. (true), 25½ miles, =7′ diff. of lat. and 32¼′ diff. of long.

Pos. by Acc. { Lat. 40° 23½′ N. / Long. 69° 41′ W. } at 1st. obs.

| | H. | M. | S. | | | | |
|---|---|---|---|---|---|---|---|
| Chronometer | 1 | 25 | 22 | | ☉ . . . | 13° | 2¼′ |
| Slow of G.M.T. | + | 4 | 23 | | Eye 24 feet | + | 7¾ |
| G.M.T. | 1 | 29 | 45 | | -☉- | 13° | 10′ |
| Corrected Equa. of Time | — | 10 | 16 | | | | |
| | 1 | 19 | 29 G.A.T. | | | | |

| | | | |
|---|---|---|---|
| 110° | 47¾′ | . . . | 0·02925 |
| 40 | 23¼ | . . . | 0·11822 |
| 13 | 10 | | 9·13401 |
| | | | 9·97018 |
| 164 | 21 | | 9·25166 |
| 82 | 10½ | | |
| 69 | 00½ | | |

| | H. | M. | S. | |
|---|---|---|---|---|
| Hour ∠ | 3 | 19 | 57 | = S. 47½° E. |
| A.T.S. | 8 | 40 | 06 | |
| A.T.G. | 13 | 19 | 29 | |
| Long. in Time | 4 | 39 | 26 | = |
| Long. at 1st obs. | 69° | 51¼′ | W. | |
| Run | + | 32¼ | W. | |
| Long. (1) | 70 | 23½ | W. | |
| Correction | — | 6¼ | E. | |
| True Longitude | 70° | 17¼′ | West at time of 2nd obs. | |

Sun's Bearing S. E.
The Contrary N. W.
Therefore apply the correction for the latitude to the North.

Table L, page 269.

☉ Bearing S. 47½° E. — 1′·22 × 5′·14 = 6¼′ corr. for Long. (1).
☉ Bearing S. 21½° E. — 3′·36 × 5′·14 = 17¼′ „ (2).
Diff. 2′·14

| | H. | M. | S. | | | | |
|---|---|---|---|---|---|---|---|
| Chronometer | 3 | 25 | 17 | | ☉ . . . | 25° | 49′ |
| Slow of G.M.T. | + | 4 | 23 | | Eye 24 feet | + | 9¼ |
| G.M.T. | 3 | 29 | 40 | | -☉- | 25° | 58¼′ |
| Corrected Equa. of Time | — | 10 | 17·5 | | | | |
| | 3 | 19 | 22·5 G.A.T. | | | | |

| | | |
|---|---|---|
| 110° | 46¾′ | 0·02920 |
| 40 | 16¼ | 0·11747 |
| 25 | 58¼ | 8·41550 |
| | | 9·94806 |
| 177 | 01¼ | 8·51023 |
| 88 | 30½ | |
| 62 | 32 | |

| Long. (2) | 70° | 34½′ | W. |
|---|---|---|---|
| Correction | — | 17¼ | E. |
| True Long. | 70° | 17¼′ | West. |

At second observation.

| | H. | M. | S. | |
|---|---|---|---|---|
| Hour ∠ | 1 | 22 | 56 | = S. 21½° E. |
| A.T.S. | 10 | 37 | 04 | |
| A.T.G. | 15 | 19 | 22·5 | |
| Long. in Time | 4 | 42 | 18·5 | = |
| Long. (2) | 70° | 34½′ | W. | |
| Long. (1) | 70 | 23½ | W. | |

2·14)11·00(5·14′ Correction for Lat.
10·70
300
214
860
856

| Latitude by Acc. | 40° | 16¼′ | N. |
|---|---|---|---|
| Correction | + | 5¼ | |
| True Latitude | 40° | 21½′ | North at time of second observation. |

NOTE.—The accuracy of this position was fully confirmed at noon.

writer has frequently worked out "Double altitudes" by this method with only three-quarters of an hour interval, for want of a longer, and found them to come out with wonderful accuracy. The difference in bearing in such cases would be less than a point, and if the "Sumner lines" were drawn on the chart, they would be found *to run together*, and their intersection would be very ill defined indeed. Therefore it is that in many instances calculation is preferable to laying down the lines, &c., on the chart, which latter operation is technically styled "plotting" the work.

**Double Altitudes applicable to all Heavenly Bodies.**

What has been stated in this and the previous chapter, with regard to "Circles of Equal Altitude," "Sumner lines," and "Double altitudes" generally, is equally applicable to Sun, Moon, Planet, or fixed Star—the principle is the same; but as there can be no possible reason on a clear night to *wait* for a "Double altitude" of a star, when the Heavens are full of objects in the most suitable positions for simultaneous *Astronomical Cross-bearings*, it is proposed to devote the next chapter to the method of finding the latitude and longitude by *simultaneous* altitudes of two or more fixed stars.

**Simultaneous Altitudes of Stars.**

If the reader be desirous of going very thoroughly into the fundamental principles of "Double altitudes," let him read an excellent article on the subject in the first three numbers of the *Nautical Magazine* for 1880. The problem is there handled in a masterly style, and in language suitable to the indifferent mathematical training of the merchant seaman.

# CHAPTER XI.

## SIMULTANEOUS ALTITUDES.

**How to ascertain position of Star at any given instant.**

The problem of the "Circle of Equal Altitude" may be extended to any celestial body. The pole of the circle will always be the place whose longitude is the Greenwich hour angle of the object (reckoned westward), and whose latitude is the same as the declination of the object.

The Greenwich hour angle of a star is as easily obtained as that of the sun; since, if there is extra work in one part, it is made up for by the fact that we take out at sight the Declination and Right Ascension without having to make any corrections. Thus:—

Over what places on the earth's surface were the stars Sirius and Benetnasch vertical at 7h. 27m. 46s. G.M.T., on February 21st, 1880?

| | * Sirius. | | * Benetnasch. | |
|---|---|---|---|---|
| | H. M. S. | | | |
| Greenwich mean time | 7 27 46 | | | |
| Sidereal time at G.M. noon | 22 8 10·9 | | | |
| Acceleration for G.M.T. | + 1 13·5 | | H. M. S. | |
| Sidereal time at Greenwich | 29 32 10·4 | | 29 32 10·4 | |
| *'s Right Ascension | 6 39 53·7 | | 13 42 51·2 | |
| Longitude in time | 22 52 16·7 | W. | 15 49 19·2 | W. |
| | 24 | | 24 | |
| Longitude in time | 1 7 43·3 | E. | 8 10 40·8 | E. |
| Longitude | 16° 55′ 50″ | East | 122° 40′ 12″ | East. |
| *'s Declination | 16 33 20 | South | 49 54 18 | North. |

Having thus found the centres of the circles, their size at any given moment will depend entirely upon the altitudes obtained at the place of the observer. In the case before us—to which this is the introduction—the circles are very large, as the observed altitudes happen to be both small.

The true altitude of Sirius is 15° 56½′, and that of Benetnasch 16° 24½′; and the circles intersect in Latitude 51° 1′ N., and Longitude 17° 43′ W. The "Sumner lines" cut at a good angle —121°; and, as usual, each lies at right angles to the bearing of the star to which it pertains.

Attention is here directed to the fact that in that geographical position, when the altitude of Sirius was 15° 56½′ the corresponding altitude of Benetnasch could only be 16° 24½′—*neither more nor less.* This amounts to saying that if, at a specified time, the altitude of any visible star be given to a computer whose own position is known, he can calculate what the altitude of any other visible star would be at the same instant and at the same place; or, in other words, the two sets of data are interchangeable. Again: take notice of the difference in the longitude of the centres or poles of the two circles. It amounts to 105° 44′ 22″ in arc, or 7h. 2m. 57·5s. in time, which is exactly equal to the difference of the Right Ascensions of the stars. A second reading of the chapter on "Time" will brighten up the memory as to how this can be.

Having endeavoured briefly to explain some of the groundwork of the problem, we will now get on to the more practical part.

**Advantages of simultaneous Star Altitudes**

Unlike "Double altitudes" of the sun, in which the observer has to air his patience waiting till the difference of bearing is such as will give a sufficiently good "cut," *Astronomical Cross-bearings* (as the writer chooses to call them) can be obtained from *simultaneous* observations of the stars or planets without any interval whatever. This method possesses several striking advantages.

I. Stars may always be selected in such positions as will give the very best results, while the sun, on the contrary, is restricted in its application, the conditions not generally being matters of choice. Hence this method may be practised with equal success in all latitudes, and with high as well as low altitudes, although the latter are preferable, for reasons with which the reader is no doubt by this time familiar.

II. Since there is no interval between the observations, the method is free from possible errors in the ship's run, which errors, even when comparatively small, may seriously affect the result.

III. Several pairs of stars may be taken at the same time—one as a check upon the other.

IV. One observation of either sun or star gives a "Line of bearing," which, valuable as it may be—so far as it goes—does not give a complete result. But it will be rare indeed that there will be any occasion to plot a "Line of bearing" by a single star; since, if one is visible, there are generally others also, some of which can be taken simultaneously, and so make it possible to define the ship's position exactly.

With the stars also, calculation throughout is preferable to the chart, though in their case there is not altogether the same need for it as with the sun; since, if the stars be well chosen—and there is no reason why they should not be—the "Sumner lines" will not be open to the objection of making a bad "cut." However, this may be considered a matter of taste; but, for those who prefer calculation, Johnson's method is again available.

A few examples of the working will now be given. Instead of computing an imaginary series of observations, these are selected at random from among a number of others, taken on the same evening. The results in every case agreed within a 1′ or so. Were it not that the writer *knows* the great accuracy attainable with stars, and how superior they are to the sun, he would scarcely take up time and space to advocate their adoption.

It is necessary to notice two points of importance about the work of the ✱ Benetnasch.

(1.) As its declination exceeds 23°, the azimuth cannot be taken out by inspection from the "Red Book." This will sometimes occur in practice, but the difficulty, as already explained on page 93, may be got over by the use of Towson's Table VII. When, however, the star employed is not one of those in the table, its bearing must be worked out in the old-fashioned way, by the Alt-azimuth problem (*vide* Norie, page 228, *et seq.*) The calculation is in all respects the same as the one employed for the sun. *Norie* only gives examples of the latter, but, as there is no difference, the omission does not signify.

**Star Azimuths.**

(2.) Benetnasch being a circumpolar ✱ does not set to an observer North of 40°, and, consequently, it may have any hour angle up to 12 hours east or west of the meridian.

In the preceding example, its hour angle or meridian distance is 9h. 23m. 38s., which is not contained in Table XXXI. of Norie. It will be found, however, in Table 69 of *Raper's Epitome*, which extends up to 12 hours. Should the navigator not possess the latter epitome, he need not consider the battle lost, as there is an easy dodge by which the desired end may be attained.

At 6h. 11m. on Saturday evening, February 21st, 1880, the following simultaneous observations of Sirius and Benetnasch were made on the bridge of the (s.s.) "*British Crown.*" Eye 30 feet. No index error. Cold fresh breeze at N.W.; moderately rough sea; clear, with passing clouds and light showers. Ship making S. 79° W. (true), 11 knots.

Position by D.R. { Latitude 51° 00¾′ N. / Longitude 17° 42′ W.

```
                                H. M. S.
Time by chronometer . . . .    7 23 25 . . . Observed altitude * Sirius . 16° 5′ E. . . . . . . . Observed altitude * Benetnasch . . . 16° 33′ E.
Chronometer slow  . . . . .  + 4 21          Table XV. of Norie . . . . . — 8½             Correction . . . . . . . . . . . . . — 8¼

G.M.T. . . . . . . . . . .     7 27 46       *'s true altitude . . . . . 15 56½            *'s true altitude . . . . . . . . . . 16 24¾
Sidereal time at G.M.N. . .   22 03 10·9
Acceleration for 7h. 28m. .  + 1 13·5

Sidereal time at Greenwich .  29 32 10·4

*'s Declination . .  16° 33½′ S.                                   *'s Declination . . . .  49° 54¼′
                     90                                                                     90

Polar distance . . .  106 33½   0·01839                            Polar distance . . . .   40  5¾    0·19107
Assumed latitude . .   51 10¾   0·20273                            Assumed latitude . . .   51 10¾    0·20273
*'s true Altitude  .   15 56½   8·74226                            *'s true Altitude  . .   16 24¾   9·77091
                                9·97539                                                              9·78374
                      173 40                                                               107 40¼
                                8·93877                                                              9·94845
Half sum . . . .      86 50                                                                 53 50⅛
Remainder . . . .     70 53½                                                                37 25⅜
```

| Bearing of * S. E. |
|---|
| The contrary N. W. |
| Therefore, apply the correction for latitude to the South. |

| Bearing of * N. E. |
|---|
| The contrary S. W. |
| Therefore, apply the correction for latitude to the South. |

```
                                   H. M. S.                                                       H. M. S.
Hour ∠ . . . . . . . . . .        2 17  7·1 E.=S. 34° E. ex Red Book.     Hour ∠ . . . . . . . .  9 23 33·0 E.=N. 25° E. ex Towson.
*'s Right Ascension . . . .       6 39 53·7                               *'s Right Ascension . . 13 42 51·2

Sidereal Time at Ship . . . .     4 22 46·6                               Sidereal time at ship . . .  4 19 18·2
Sidereal Time at Greenwich        5 32 10·4                               Sidereal time at Greenwich .  5 32 10·4

Longitude in time . . . . .       1  9 23·8 =                             Longitude in time . . . .  1 12 57·2 =

Longitude . . . . . . . .        17° 21′ W. by Sirius.                    Longitude . . . . . . . . 18° 14¼′ W. by Benetnasch.
Correction . . . . . . . .      + 21¾ W.                                                            17 21  W.
                                                                                             5·75) 53·2′ (9·26′ correction for latitude.
True longitude . . . . .         17 42¾ West.                                                      51·75
                                                                                                     1500
                                                                                                     1150
                                                                                                      350
```

TABLE L, page 289.

```
Bearing of Sirius . .     S. 34° E. — 2·35 × 9′·26 = 21¾′ Correction for Long.
Bearing of Benetnasch    N. 25° E. — 3·40 × 9′·26 = 31½′ Correction for Long.

Sum, being in different quarters . 5·75
```

```
Assumed latitude .  51° 10¾′ N.          Longitude by Benetnasch . 18° 14¼′ W.
Correction . . . .  — 9¾                 Correction . . . . . . .  — 31½  E.

True latitude . . . 51  1  North.        True longitude . . . . .  17 42¾ West.
```

**How to find Hour Angle when the regular Table is not available.**

Take out the log. sine of *half* the log. of the hour angle; *double* it and turn it into *time*, and you have what you want. The log. of the hour angle is 19·94845; halve it = 9·974225; the log. sine of this is 70° 27′ 17″, which, doubled, is 140° 54′ 34″ = 9h. 23m. 38s.

**How to select Stars for Simultaneous Altitudes.**

To select fitting stars for *Simultaneous Altitudes* is a simple matter. Choose any star or planet whose bearing from the meridian exceeds 10° or 12°. Face it squarely, and, extending the right or left arm upwards from the side, notice if it points to any other known star of the first, second, or third magnitude. Such a star will bear at right angles to the first one, and be in the best possible position for pairing with it. If you fail to find a star or planet so situated, take the next best you can get, but endeavour to avoid the difference in the bearings being *less* than 60°, or *more* than 120°.

In working *Simultaneous Altitudes* by Johnson's method, it is by no means essential that they should be taken exactly at the same instant. The idea that two observers were required for this problem has often proved a bar sinister to its use. This we must remove forthwith, and shew that, by having all preparations made beforehand, one sextant is quite equal to the occasion.

Place an officer at the chronometer, and take the sights yourself from behind the shelter of the bridge-cloth—*in clear weather, the higher the better.* Let a quartermaster attend with a bull's-eye or binnacle lamp by which to read off, and in this manner the two stars can easily be taken by an expert observer in from one to two minutes of each other, which is close enough together if the sights are good.

The two following examples, taken in this fashion, may be worked for practice. To convince yourself of the value of the method, work with a latitude purposely 10′ or 20′ in error—say 51° 10½ N., as in the preceding example:—

**Examples for Practice.**

FEBRUARY 21ST, 1880, OBSERVED AS FOLLOWS.

| | H. M. S. | | ° ′ | |
|---|---|---|---|---|
| Time by chron. | 7 25 5 | ✱ α Cygni (Deneb) | 20 34¼ W. | To be worked as a pair. |
| „ „ | 7 27 7 | ✱ Dubhe | 40 34 E. | |
| „ „ | 7 34 28 | ✱ Alpheratz | 35 37¼ W. | To be worked as a pair. |
| „ „ | 7 36 10 | ✱ Dubhe | 41 25 E. | |

All conditions the same as in the worked example.

These observations are *bona fide*, and although they come out well together, the evening was not by any means a favourable one; and the writer might easily have selected stars out of his work books agreeing closer, but these are preferred as a *fair average sample.*

As a specimen of *accurate* observation, take the following, made on the present voyage. About 7h. 22m. P.M., August 1st, 1880, the stars Altair (E.), and Arcturus (W.), gave *precisely* the same longitude; the third—Benetnasch (W.), differing only 1′. The Pole ✱ was observed for latitude, and differed only *half a mile* from Antares to the Southward, the latter being worked as an Ex-meridian, with an hour angle of 11m. 9s.

The observations were taken and calculated in the presence of the Chief Officer and Surgeon, and afterwards examined by them, so that "cooking" was impossible. They are not mentioned here **"Cooking."** in self-glorification, but merely to shew what can be done with the stars, and what extremely satisfactory results are to be obtained, when one understands and has practice at the work.

Of course simultaneous altitudes of two Planets, or of a star and a Planet, can be worked out in a precisely similar manner. An example of a star and a Planet coupled together is given over the leaf.

At 5h. 56m. on Monday evening, February 27th, 1882, the following nearly simultaneous observations of Procyon (E.) and planet Saturn (W.) were made on the bridge of the (s.s.) "*British King.*" Eye 30 feet. No index error. Moderate breeze at S.W.; smooth sea; fine and clear. Ship making N. 76° E. (true), 12½ knots per hour.

Position by D.R. { Latitude 40° 10¾′ N. / Longitude 55° 41′ W.

**Procyon**

| | H. M. S. |
|---|---|
| Time by Chronometer | 10 9 38 |
| Chronometer fast | − 10 53 |
| G.M.T. | 9 58 45 |
| Sidereal Time at G.M.N. | 22 28 52 |
| Acceleration for 10 hours | + 1 39 |
| Sidereal Time at Greenwich | 8 29 16 |

| | ° ′ |
|---|---|
| Observed Alt. ✱ Procyon | 39 11 |
| Table XV. of Norie | − 6¾ |
| ✱'s true altitude | 39 4¼ |

✱'s Declination . . 5° 21¼′ N.
90

| | ° ′ | |
|---|---|---|
| Polar Distance | 84 28¾ | 0·00201 |
| Latitude by D.R. | 40 10¾ | 0·11688 |
| ✱'s true altitude | 39 4¼ | 9·15069 |
| | | 9·83209 |
| | 163 44 | 9·10167 |
| Half Sum | 81 52 | |
| Remainder | 42 47¾ | |

Bearing of Procyon S. E.
The contrary N. W.
Therefore, apply the correction for latitude to the North.

| | H. M. S. |
|---|---|
| Procyon's Hour Angle | 2 46 35 = S. 58¼° E., *ex* Red Book. |
| " Right Ascension | 7 33 10 |
| Sidereal Time at Ship | 4 46 35 |
| Sidereal Time at Greenwich | 8 29 16 |
| Longitude in Time | 3 42 41 = 55° 40¼′ W. |
| Correction | − 3 applied to the East. |
| True Longitude | 55° 37¼′ W. |

**Saturn**

| | H. M. S. |
|---|---|
| Time by Chronometer | 10 10 36 |
| Chronometer fast | − 10 53 |
| G.M.T. | 9 59 43 |
| Sidereal Time at G.M.N. | 22 28 52 |
| Acceleration for 10 hours | + 1 39 |
| Sidereal time at Greenwich | 8 30 14 |

| | ° ′ |
|---|---|
| Observed alt. ✱ Saturn | 47 59 |
| Table XV. of Norie | − 6¾ |
| ✱'s true altitude | 47 52¼ |

✱'s Declination . . . 12° 4′ N.
90

| | ° ′ | |
|---|---|---|
| Polar distance | 77 56 | 0·00970 |
| Latitude by D.R. | 40 10¾ | 0·11688 |
| ✱'s true altitude | 47 52¼ | 9·08615 |
| | | 9·75985 |
| | 165 59½ | 8·97258 |
| Half Sum | 82 59¾ | |
| Remainder | 35 7 | |

Bearing of Saturn S. W.
The contrary N. E.
Therefore, apply the correction for latitude to the North.

| | H. M. S. |
|---|---|
| Saturn's Hour Angle | 2 22 44 = S. 58¼° W., *ex* Red Book. |
| " Right Ascension | 2 25 13 |
| Sidereal Time at Ship | 4 47 57 |
| Sidereal Time at Greenwich | 8 30 14 |
| Longitude in time | 3 42 17 = 55° 34¼′ W. by Saturn. |
| | 55° 40¼′ W. by Procyon. |

1·6) 6·0 (3′·75 corr. for latitude.
48
120
112
80
80

| | ° ′ |
|---|---|
| Latitude worked with | 40 10¾ N. |
| Correction | + 3¾ |
| True Latitude | 40 14½ N. |
| Longitude by Saturn | 55 34¼ W. |
| Correction | + 3 applied to the W. |
| True Longitude | 55° 37¼′ W. |

TABLE I., page 289.

Bearing of Procyon . . S. 58¼° E. = 0′·8 × 3′·75 = 3′ correction for longitude.
Bearing of Saturn . . S. 58¼° W. = 0′·8 × 3′·75 = 3′ correction for longitude.

Sum 1′·6 being in different quarters.

At 10h. 5m. 13s. by the same chronometer, the observed altitude of the North ✱ was 41° 9½′; and at 10h. 15m. 13s. the observed altitude of the ✱ Rigel to the southward was 41° 21½′, all conditions same as above. When reduced to time corresponding to that of Procyon and Saturn, the North ✱ gives the latitude 40° 15′ N., and Rigel worked as an ex-merid., with an hour angle of 16m. 27s., gives the latitude as 40° 15¼′ N. By a pure coincidence, Saturn happened to have precisely the same bearing West that Procyon had East. The error in the longitude, due to an error in the latitude worked with, was therefore the same for each of them.

## CHAPTER XII.

### COMPASS ADJUSTMENT.

An exhaustive enquiry into this most important subject must involve a whole book on it alone, whilst in these pages we can but afford it a chapter. For more complete information, the student cannot do better than read up the books in the *Nautical Library* marked by an asterisk, taking them in the order there numbered 4, 5, and 6. Even here, however, before treating of the *practical* part of the work, it is *absolutely necessary* to explain some of the principal features of the *theory*, since it is certain that any one who attempts Compass Adjustment by mere "rule of thumb," without clearly comprehending the laws upon which it is based, can never hope to perform it satisfactorily.

**The Earth a Magnet.**

The Earth itself is a huge magnet, whose magnetic poles (two in number) are entirely distinct from its poles of rotation. That in the northern hemisphere is situated to the N.N.W. of Hudson Bay, in British North America, and has been actually reached by man; whilst the other lies to the South of Tasmania, but, owing to impenetrable barriers of ice, has not quite been reached, but so nearly that its position was without difficulty ascertained by calculation.

**Position of Magnetic Poles.**

Unlike the *Geographical Poles*, which are represented by a mere point, the *Magnetic Poles* include a considerable area of the earth's surface, amounting perhaps to 50 square miles.

**Magnetic Polarity distinguished by colour.**

"As the magnetism of the north end of a needle is of the opposite kind to that of the north pole of the earth, physicists are not agreed as to which should be called *north* magnetism; and it has therefore been found convenient to distinguish them by colour, calling the first red, the second blue. The distinction may be easily remembered, by supposing the needle coloured, and from R occurring in noRth and in Red; U in soUth and in blUe."*

At the north magnetic pole, the red or north end, and at the south magnetic pole, the blue or south end, of a freely-suspended needle, points vertically downwards; or in other words, at both these places the "dip" is 90°.

**First law in Magnetism.**

Here may be stated the first general law in magnetism—namely, that *opposite* poles *attract*, and *similar* poles *repel* each other. From which it follows, that if we decide to colour red that end of the needle which points to the north, the magnetism of that part of the earth must be considered as blue.

*Variation of the compass* is the angle, measured at the place of the observer, between the earth's nearest true and magnetic poles. If he be so placed in either hemisphere that the true and magnetic poles of that region are in transit, there will be no Variation. On the other hand, were an observer situated directly *between* them, he would have 180°, or the greatest possible amount of Variation. And here a curious anomaly presents itself. Starting from the *north magnetic pole*, one would have to steer due *south by compass* to reach the *true or geographical north pole*, since the needle points not to the *true*, but to the magnetic pole.

**Variation of the Compass.**

A compass needle, perfectly free from the effects of iron or other magnetic substance, in obedience to the earth's influence, will rest in the plane of the magnetic meridian; or, in other words, its red end will point towards the north magnetic pole. The angular amount it is pulled to the right or left of this direction by the ship's iron is termed the "Error" or "Deviation of the Compass." The first is the better word of the two.† It is also defined as the angle between the north and south line of the card and the *Correct Magnetic* north and south line. It is to be regretted, however, that some writers—*combining Variation with Deviation*—have defined "Error" (or "Total error") as the angle between the north and south line of the compass and the astronomical or *true* north and south line; for "this definition conveys an altogether wrong idea of what the compass *ought* to do, and is not in any respect convenient."‡ *Deviation and Variation* arise from entirely different causes, and should never be mixed up with each other in this manner. It is possible, by compensation, to

**Deviation of the Compass.**

---

* Captain Sir F. J. Evans, R.N., K.C.B., F.R.S.

† Throughout these pages, both words are used indifferently to express the same thing.

‡ Sir W. Thomson.

free the compass from the one, and not from the other. The Deviation or Error is said to be easterly when the north point of the card is pulled to the right or east of north *Correct Magnetic*, and westerly when it is pulled to the left or west of north Correct Magnetic. The confusion which sometimes arises as to the effect of Deviation on the ship's course may be got over by standing in imagination at the centre of the compass, and conceiving the ship to be sailing thence along any desired point to the margin of the card. Now, since easterly Deviation pulls the card to the right, *and the ship follows the card*, it is clear that she also is thrown to the right, and *vice versâ*. "Local Attraction" is the term used to express the disturbance of the compass by magnetic influence existing *outside* of the ship, such as may be found in docks and other confined water spaces.

**Effect of Deviation on ship's course.**

**Local Attraction.**

At the earth's magnetic poles all compass action ceases; since there a freely-suspended needle, pointing straight up and down, *has no horizontal force to give it direction*—hence the very apparent sluggishness of the compass in high latitudes, and its *complete uselessness* in the neighbourhood of the magnetic poles. Indeed, were it not for the conical shape of the pivot and cap which compels the card of a mariner's compass to assume a horizontal position, it would tip over end as the magnetic poles were approached.

**Compass useless near Magnetic Pole**

Now, if the earth has *Magnetic Poles*, it has also a *Magnetic Equator*. This magnetic equator is a sinuous curve encircling the earth, and crossing the geographical equator in two places nearly diametrically opposite to each other, something after the fashion of the Ecliptic. One crossing is on the eastern side of the Atlantic, about the meridian of Greenwich, and the other is in the Pacific, about the longitude of 168° W. Its greatest divergence from the true equator is in Brazil, in latitude 16° S., and longitude 45° W.; is next greatest in the Arabian Sea, at a point in latitude 11° N., somewhere between Socotra and the Laccadives.

**Magnetic Equator.**

At all places on the magnetic equator a freely-suspended needle takes a true horizontal position; or, in other words, the dip is 0°. One might imagine that here would be found the strongest lines of horizontal or directive force; but most careful observations prove that such is not the case—in fact, that of the two, they rather evince a preference for the geographical equator.

**Action of freely suspended needle on Magnetic Equator.**

To recapitulate:—If a freely-suspended needle be taken to the *north* magnetic pole, its *red* end will point vertically downwards. As the needle is carried south, it will *gradually* approach a horizontal position, which will be exactly attained on the magnetic equator. Proceeding still south, its *blue* end will next begin to dip, and at the *south* magnetic pole will point vertically downwards. These facts have direct reference to the magnetic change which goes on in the iron of a ship, as she alters her *magnetic* latitude in the course of a voyage.

**Difference between hard steel and soft iron.**

The next most important point to be remembered is the difference between a magnet made of *hard steel* and one made of *soft iron*. That of hard steel will not reverse its poles, no matter at what part of the earth or in what position it may be held. Its magnetic *character* is absolutely permanent, and will so remain even though its red end be directed towards the south, and its blue end towards the north. Hard steel displays no particular haste to receive magnetism, but, once acquired, it does not like to part with it. In this respect it resembles self-taught people; their knowledge—often hard bought—is deeply rooted, and abides with them. Not so, however, with soft iron, which possesses no independent magnetism of its own. In *its* case the magnetism is of a purely transient kind, ceasing with the removal of the producing cause, and being just as easily and quickly reproduced with reversed poles in the same bar.

**Experiments with kitchen poker and boat's compass.**

The experiment may be easily tried with an ordinary kitchen poker and a boat's compass. But, first, it will be necessary to explain that a bar of *soft iron*, if held in the earth's "Line of force," will *instantly* become magnetic, though it may not have been so before. Now, what *is* the earth's "Line of force?" It is the position which a *freely-suspended* needle—when undisturbed by iron—would take up if left entirely to itself. In the first place, it would point towards the magnetic pole; and, in the second place, one end would incline downwards at an angle below the horizon corresponding to the "dip" at the place. The "dip" at Liverpool is now about 69½°. When, accordingly, the poker is held in this direction, it *at once* becomes magnetic by induction—its *lower* end or point acquiring *red* magnetism in our hemisphere, and its *upper* end or handle acquiring *blue* magnetism. This may readily be tested by placing the compass near it. If held a few inches from the lower or red end, the *south* point of the needle will be attracted by the poker; while, if held near the upper or blue end, the *north* point of the needle will be attracted. This invisible force, exerted by the poker, is termed "*induced magnetism*," or "*magnetism of position*," and only remains so long as the poker is held in that particular manner. To destroy it, it

**"Line of Force."**

**"Dip."**

**Induced Magnetism.**

is merely necessary to hold the poker in an east and west direction, or at right angles to the "Line of force," when it will no longer appreciably affect the compass.

This shews that soft iron has no *fixed* polarity. Percussion exercises a marked influence on both the inducing and dispelling of this kind of magnetism. If, therefore, the poker be hit a few taps with a hammer whilst held in the "Line of force," its magnetic power will be intensified; and, again, when the position is altered so as to dissipate the force, it will be found that the tapping hastens that process also.

**Percussion—its effect.**

Let the poker be once more held in the "Line of force"—but this time with the point up and handle down—it will again become magnetic; *but the blue and red magnetism will be found to have changed ends.* The red will have shifted its quarters to the handle, because it is now the lower end, and the blue to the point, because it is now the upper end. Just like water and oil behave in a bottle: the oil will unfailingly be found at the top, no matter which way the bottle may be held.

The facility with which soft iron acquires or parts with magnetism may be shewn in another way. Take the kitchen poker, in imagination, to the north magnetic pole, and hold it vertically, point down. The lower end, as before, will acquire "red," and the upper end "blue" magnetism. *Holding it still in the same way,* transport it to the magnetic equator; it will there be entirely free from magnetism of any description. *Still holding it in the same manner,* transfer it to the south magnetic pole; it will once more be magnetic, *but,* the lower end will now have "*blue,*" and the upper end or handle, "*red*" magnetism. The rapidity of the change will correspond to the time occupied on the journey.

**Change produced in soft iron by geographical change of place.**

As before stated, *this will not happen with a magnet of hard steel,* whose poles remain unchanged in character, no matter what way it is held, or in what hemisphere it may be placed. Keep this in mind, as it bears directly upon the behaviour of the iron in a ship.

Thus, in north (magnetic) latitude the upper end of all vertical soft iron, such as funnel, masts, stanchions, davits, rudder, sternpost, &c., has *blue* magnetism, and *attracts* the north end of the compass needle. While as the ship sails south, such iron becomes gradually weaker in its effect, and on the magnetic equator—being then at right angles to the "Line of force"—produces none whatever. On the other hand, in south (magnetic) latitude the upper end of this same vertical iron acquires *red* magnetism, *and repels*

**Effect of vertical iron.**

*the end of the needle it had previously attracted*, doing so with continually augmented force as high latitudes are gained.

**Action of vertical iron not dependent on direction of ship's head.**

Further, be it remembered that in any given locality the magnetic intensity of a vertical bar of soft iron, such as the rudder post, remains undiminished *no matter what may be the direction of the ship's head;* but its *disturbing* effect on the compass depends upon its position relative to the needle, being greatest when at right angles to the direction of the needle's length, and ceasing when in a line with it (*see Diagrams Nos.* 1 *and* 2). We have now done with *vertical* iron for the present.

**Behaviour of horizontal iron.**

A *horizontal* bar of soft iron at the magnetic pole has no magnetism whatever, since there it is at right angles to the "Line of force." It is, in fact, in the same harmless condition that the vertical bar found itself on the magnetic equator. When taken, however, into low latitudes, it gradually becomes magnetic *if kept pointing towards the magnetic pole*, and has its greatest power in the vicinity of the equator. The *red* magnetism will always be found in the end which points to the north, *no matter which*, turn it about as you may.

As the south magnetic pole is approached, a horizontal bar of soft iron loses force, and at the point of 90° dip, has again ceased to be magnetic. In brief; vertical iron is most magnetic at the poles, and horizontal iron, held in the direction of the meridian, is most magnetic on the equator.

**Action of horizontal iron dependent upon the angle it makes with the magnetic meridian.**

Another very marked distinction between vertical and horizontal iron must here be noted. The magnetic intensity of the latter depends not only upon its proximity to the equator, *but on the angle it makes with the magnetic meridian.* Thus, when held in a north and south direction (Correct Magnetic) it is at its best; on being turned in azimuth it loses power, and when held exactly east and west (C.M.) has none at all. Therefore, unlike vertical iron, horizontal iron on board ship has a varying action upon the compass, *depending on the direction of the ship's head as well as the position of its poles relative to the compass needle.*

**Horizontal iron produces same deviation in all latitudes.**

This is an important distinction; but there is yet another. Horizontal iron produces the same deviation in *all* latitudes; for though its power varies with that of the earth, the ratio between the two is constant; and since the first is the *disturbing* force of the needle, and the other the *directing* force, it follows that the deviation arising from the induced magnetism of horizontal iron is the same at any part of the globe.

A magnet possesses the peculiar power of producing magnetism

*Diagram No. 1.*

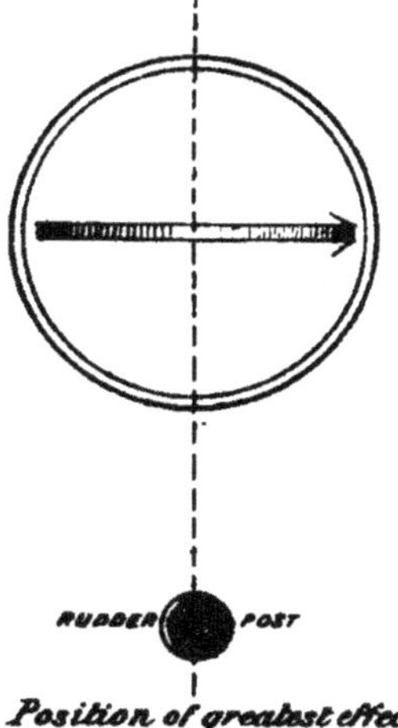


*Position of greatest effect*

*Diagram No. 2*

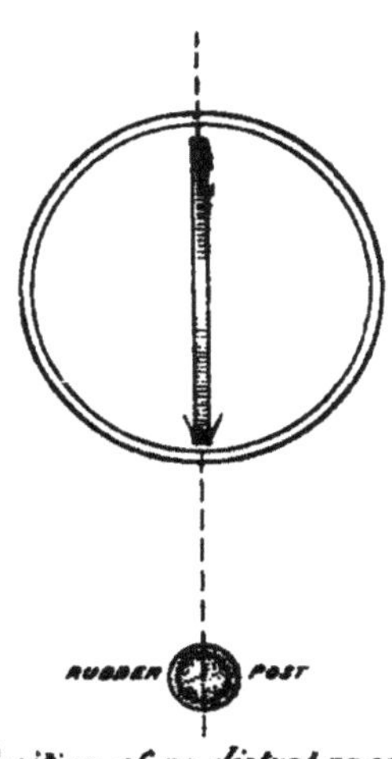


*Position of no disturbance*

To face Page 340

in a bar of iron or steel without loss to itself, and so is capable of propagating its own species to any extent. Therefore, when trying experiments with a slice, crowbar, or kitchen poker, it must not be placed *too* close to the compass needle, as the latter, if strong, will of itself induce magnetism in the poker when, from the position in which it may be held at the time, none would otherwise exist. Thus, if a common spike nail be held near one pole of a powerful magnet, the latter will first *induce* magnetism in the nail of a *contrary name to itself*, and then the law which says that *opposite poles attract each other* will come into operation, and the nail in obedience will fly to the magnet.

**By one magnet an indefinite number can be made.**

In the process of making a permanent magnet, which is variously done by "touching" a bar of glass-hard steel with the natural lodestone, with another magnet, or by electricity, the one under treatment should be surcharged with the magnetic fluid. It never, however, retains all its original strength; but, after a while, settles down into a certain definite state known as "the saturation point," which, if the steel be of the proper temper, it will maintain for years without appreciable loss, and accordingly gets named a *permanent magnet.*

**"Saturation Point."**

**Permanent Magnet.**

Whatever the process of magnetisation may be, it produces two opposite and *equal* forces in the ends of the steel bar, from which it follows that there will be a neutral point about the centre of the bar totally devoid of magnetism of any kind. It is well to know this; since, if it be compulsory to put a compass near vertical iron, it may be possible to raise or lower it to the level of the neutral point, and so render the iron incapable of mischief, so long at least as the ship is upright.*

**Neutral point.**

---

* Magnetism has recently been used for a very curious purpose, as the following account taken from *Chambers's Journal* for Nov., 1880, will shew :—"It is well known that in working iron, such as welding two pieces together, and even in its manufacture, hollow places or flaws occur, with merely an outside skin over the defective parts, which any test but a destructive one would fail to discover. * * * To test the homogeneity of the metal, Captain Saxby takes a bar of iron and places it on the equatorial line"—(that is to say, in an east and west direction.—*Author.*) "He next passes a compass with a very sensitive needle along in front of the bar—the needle, of course, pointing at a right angle to it. If the bar is perfectly solid through its whole length the needle will remain steady. If, however, there should be a flaw or hollow place in the bar, the needle will be deflected as it passes from the solid to the hollow place, *backwards* towards the solid iron ; passing on over the hollow place, the needle will come within the range of the solid iron at the other end of the flaw, and will again be deflected *forward.* If the bar be cut through anywhere between these two points of deflection, a flaw will invariably be found. Many thousands of pieces of iron—some prepared for the purpose of testing this method of trial, others in the ordinary course

An iron ship may be correctly looked upon as in itself a large permanent magnet. She became so in the process of construction; for, although the materials of which she is built are not such as by themselves retain magnetism permanently, it is found that, when united in the form of a ship, and subjected to percussion by rivetting, &c., they acquire this property in a greater or less degree.

**Sub-permanent Magnetism.**

After launching and reversal of the ship's head as it was on the building slip, the magnetism undergoes very rapid diminution; but in no case does it depart *entirely*, and that which is left when the saturation point is reached is accordingly styled *Sub-permanent.* So far there is a great correspondence between the ship, taken as a whole, and the steel magnet.

It is evident that the position of the poles of the ship's Sub-permanent magnetism must depend—first, upon the direction of her head when building; and, secondly, upon the "dip" at the part of the world in which she was built. If, for example, a ship were built at the North Magnetic Pole—direction of her head in this case immaterial—her magnetic constitution would be shewn by diagram *No.* 3.

**Direction of ship's Sub-permanent Magnetic Poles.**

If built on the Magnetic Equator (head North), *Diagram No.* 4 would represent the state of affairs.

*Diagram No.* 5 represents a ship built at the South Magnetic Pole, and in this case also the direction of her head would not signify: and *Diagram No.* 6 shews one built at Liverpool—head South.

Endless diagrams might be drawn to shew the effect of the combination of geographical position, with the direction of the ship's head at time of building, on her Sub-permanent magnetic character, but the foregoing are sufficient to illustrate what is meant; and the reader, having mastered the principle, can draw for himself any special case he may desire.

We have now shewn that the compasses of a ship are acted upon, first, by her *general* magnetic character, which, so to speak, was

---

of business—have been operated upon with the same unvarying result. Captain Saxby has called to his assistance Nature, who never makes mistakes in her operations."

Note:—The writer of this article has made a mistake in giving Mr. Saxby the title of Captain. He was Principal Instructor of Naval Engineers in Her Majesty's Steam Reserve, and at no time belonged to the Executive branch of the service. By way of light and pleasant reading, sailors would do well to take the journal just quoted. It contains also the latest scientific "tips" on all subjects.

*Diagram Nº 3.*

SIDE ELEVATION

DECK PLAN

*Diagram Nº 4.*

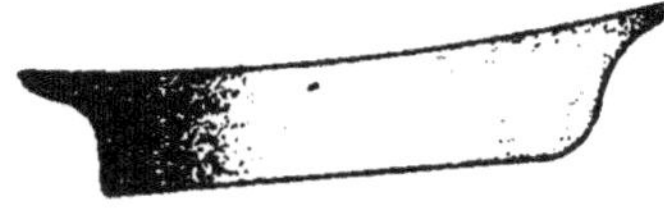

SIDE ELEVATION

DECK PLAN

*Diagram Nº 5.*

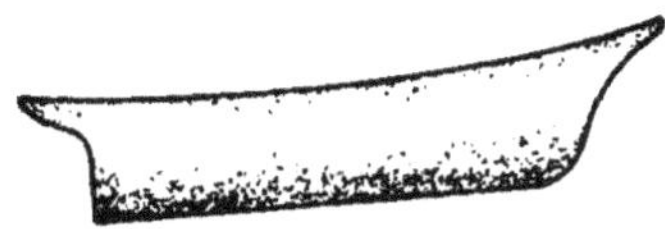

SIDE ELEVATION

DECK PLAN

*Diagram Nº 6.*

SIDE ELEVATION

DECK PLAN

born with her, and secondly, by the *induced* magnetism of individual masses of vertical and horizontal iron.

**Stability of Sub-permanent Magnetism.**

The general magnetism, after a time, becomes stable in amount, irrespective of geographical position, and the colour of its poles is not subject to change; the *induced* magnetism never becomes so, and the colour of its poles depends, in the case of vertical iron, upon the magnetic latitude the ship may be in at the moment; and in the case of horizontal iron, upon the direction of the ship's head.

**Varying effect of Sub-permanent Magnetism.**

Although the Sub-permanent portion of the ship's magnetism remains constant in all latitudes, its *effect* upon the needle is very different. Near the equator, the horizontal or *directive* force of the needle is at its best, and, accordingly, it is then most fit to resist the disturbing pull of the fixed portion of the ship's magnetism just referred to. But, as we know, the needle *loses* its directive force as polar regions are approached, and, consequently, at such times comes more and more under the domination of the ever vigorous Sub-permanent magnetism. It is consequently necessary to compensate these various effects *by means suitable to each.*

**Duty of Steel Magnets.**

The *Permanent* portion of the ship's magnetism, which causes *Semicircular or Polar deviation,* is compensated by *steel magnets,* whose magnetism is likewise permanent; and that part due to induction in *vertical* iron, which goes and comes with change of latitude, and likewise causes Semicircular deviation, is compensated by *vertical* bars of ordinary wrought-iron, which similarly become magnetic by terrestrial induction, and are influenced in a corresponding degree by such changes of latitude as both may be exposed to.

**Duty of vertical wrought-iron bars.**

**Quadrantal deviation.**

Another part of the ship's magnetism, namely, that arising from the induction of *horizontal* iron, produces *Quadrantal* deviation—which, as before stated, is the same for all latitudes, and is compensated by *horizontal* cylinders of soft iron. These are usually cast.

The correct principle, therefore, to go upon in adjusting compasses appears to be that "Like cures like," when applied on the opposite side to the disturbing influence.

The many diverse causes shewn to operate on the compass at one and the same time, combine in producing a certain sum total of effect, but as these forces do not always act in harmony either as regards direction or amount, it is clear that their joint effect cannot be compensated by any single magnet whose power is the same at all times and in all places. Here the knowledge of the

Necessity for magnetic analysis.

*skilled* compass adjuster comes in, as by certain mathematical rules, by no means difficult of attainment, he is able to *analyse* the magnetic character of the ship, apportion to *each kind* of deviation its *proper value*, and apply the *right kind* of remedy.

Tracing semicircular deviation to its true cause.

To distinguish Quadrantal from Semicircular deviation is quite easy, but to separate that part of Semicircular deviation caused by *vertical iron*, from that part which is produced by the ship's *Sub-permanent magnetism*, is a more difficult task by far; yet, in vessels continually changing their magnetic latitude, this is of the highest importance.

To adjust a compass, it is necessary to put the ship's head on two adjacent cardinal points, such as North and East; also on any one of the four principal inter-cardinal points, such as N.E.

Ship's head North or South—cause of Deviation.

The Deviation (semicircular) existing when the ship's head is either North or South, is caused by the attraction of the port or starboard side of the ship, according as the attracting pole of her magnetism lies to one side or the other, and is compensated by steel magnets placed athwartships. The compass being placed in the midship fore-and-aft line of the vessel, and the iron on each side of it being *in general* equally and symmetrically distributed, there is no occasion to compensate the induced magnetism of vertical iron, as that on the port side counteracts that on the starboard side.

In a ship built either due North or South, the poles of her Sub-permanent magnetism would exist in the bow and stern, rendering thwartship magnets unnecessary, as there would be no deviation on either of these two points; that is, supposing the iron on each side of the compass to be the same in amount and position.* The only effect would be to *increase* the directive force of the needle when the ship's head was on the *opposite* point to that on which she had been built, and to *diminish* it when on the *same* point.

Ship's head East or West—cause of Deviation.

When the ship's head is either due East or West, the Deviation (semicircular) is caused by the attraction of the bow or stern of the vessel, according as the attracting pole of her Sub-permanent magnetism lies forward or aft, *and according to whether the greatest effect of vertical iron is found before or abaft the compass.* The compensation in this case is effected *partly* by *steel* magnets placed fore and aft, *and partly by a vertical pillar of wrought-iron.*

* When, on the other hand, a compass is flanked by a donkey boiler, or the iron pedestal of an engine-room telegraph on the bridge, compensation on the North and South points would be necessary.

Diagram No. 7

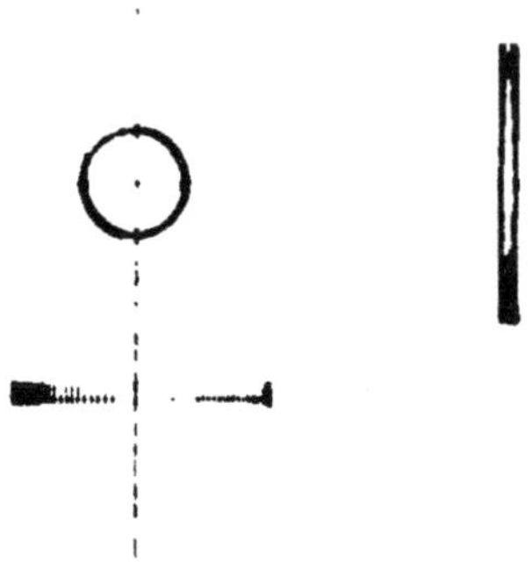

Diagram No. 8

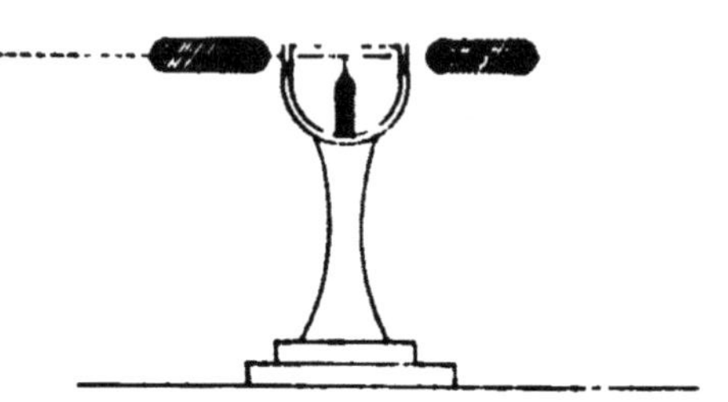

To face Page

In a ship built either due East or West, the poles of her *Sub-permanent* magnetism would lie to starboard and port, *rendering fore and aft steel magnets unnecessary*, as there would be no Deviation *from this cause* with the ship's head on either of these points, and the rule as to the directive force of the needle would be the same as before.

**Knowledge conveyed by being acquainted with direction of Ship's head on building sling.**

It is seldom or never that a ship is built with her head *exactly* on one of the cardinal points, so that both fore-and-aft and athwartship magnets are almost invariably required; and when the compass is so placed as to be free from the effects of vertical iron (which, now-a-days, is seldom the case), it is possible, by comparing the natural deviation on the north and south points with that on the east and west, to determine pretty accurately the direction of the ship's head at time of building; *or, knowing this latter and the natural deviation on north and south, it is possible to determine how much of the deviation on east and west is due to sub-permanent magnetism, and how much to the induced magnetism of vertical iron. This knowledge is very important.**

**Quadrantal Correctors.**

When the ship's head is either N.E., S.E., S.W., or N.W., the remaining deviation (quadrantal) is got rid of by cylinders, or, better still, by hollow globes of cast iron, placed on each side of the compass bowl. The athwartship and fore-and-aft magnets are usually, but not necessarily, placed on the deck *below* the compass. Sometimes it is more convenient to place them on the deck *above*, or on a bulkhead, or inside the binnacle itself. In reality, it matters not whether they are placed above or below the compass, so long as the middle of the magnet's length is in the vertical plane, passing fore-and-aft or athwartships—as the case may be—through the centre of the compass card. (*See Diagram No.* 7.)

**How to place magnets.**

On no account are *steel* magnets to be applied *end on* to the compass, neither should they be placed vertically, excepting the one used for correcting the heeling error. Therefore, athwartship magnets must be placed either before or abaft the compass, and fore-and-aft ones to starboard or port.

**Size of magnets and distance from card.**

It is preferable to use large magnets at a considerable distance, than small ones close to. The rule is, that the magnet should not

* Rule: Enter the traverse tables, with the correct magnetic direction of the ship's head at time of building, as a course. In the departure column look for the number corresponding to the deviation on north or south, and against it in the latitude column will be found the value of the sub-permanent magnetism on east or west, which, subtracted algebraically from the quantity actually observed on one or other of these points, will leave the amount due to vertical iron.

be nearer to the centre of the card than twice its own length; thus, a 30″ magnet should not be within 5 feet. But some are so weak that at this distance their effect would be next to nothing. Well-made magnets of equal size will sustain each other's weight.

**How to place Quadrantal Correctors.**

The cast-iron cylinders or globes—on suitable brackets—are placed on each side of the bowl, *so that their centres may be as nearly as possible on the same level as the compass needles,* and that a horizontal thwartship line through the centre of the card may pass through their centres also. *(See Diagram No. 8.)*

**How to place vertical iron pillar.**

The wrought iron vertical pillar is generally from 3 to 4½ inches in diameter, and of such a length that, when secured in its place, the *upper* end may be about 2 inches or so *above* the level of the card. It is more usually placed on the *fore side* of the compass, and exactly in a direct fore-and-aft line with the centre of the card; but cases may arise where the balance of effect of the ship's vertical iron lies *itself* on the fore side of the compass, in which case the compensating pillar might have to be placed on the *after* side. The rule is simply this—that the pillar must be placed so that the pole on a level with the compass card may be of such a name as will counteract the pull of the ship's vertical iron; and to accomplish this, the pillar may be placed in various positions, being sometimes on the same and sometimes on the opposite side to the force it is intended to compensate. Occasionally it will be found necessary to bolt it to the deck overhead (as in a wheelhouse), so that its *lower* end may hang a couple of inches *below* the level of the card. A good example of this kind of adjustment is shewn facing page 354.

In the Admiralty method of adjusting the sub-permanent magnetism, only *one* magnet is used. This is placed horizontally with the middle of its length exactly under the centre of the card, at such a distance from it, and at such an angle with the fore-and-aft line of the ship as will produce the desired effect. The explanation of its action is simple:—it is merely the *resultant* of the forces which affect the needle when two magnets—one athwartships and the other fore-and-aft—are employed.

This is a very elegant method, but somewhat more difficult than the ordinary one in vogue on board merchant vessels. For details see *Bedford's Sailors' Pocket-book*, p. 45, 3rd Ed.

**Preparations previous to adjusting.**

When intending to adjust, choose a fine day with smooth water, provide a number of steel magnets of various sizes,* and mark

* Magnets for use on board ship are usually soldered in watertight cases of copper, to protect them from rusting.

their centres. Hold them one by one near a compass, and a couple of inches or so of that end which attracts the north end of the needle, paint blue, and the other end, red.

It will also help matters to tint red the northern semicircle of each compass card, and its southern half blue. This can be done with the ordinary coloured pencil. It will do no harm to allow it to remain so always, and, indeed, compass cards might with advantage be coloured this way by the makers in the first instance.

**Draw chalk lines on deck.** Plumb under the centre of the compass, draw on the deck two chalk lines, one fore-and-aft, and the other athwartships, as represented in *Diagram No.* 7. In the case of a wheelhouse compass, do the same *on the underside of the deck overhead.* We will suppose the vessel to be at sea, and that it is intended to use the bearing of the sun.* Work up the position from last observations, and set your hack watch to *Apparent Time at Ship,* as explained in the chapter on the Pelorus. **Set watch to A.T.S.** Take out of the "Red book" the sun's *true* bearing for every four minutes of the time during which you will be occupied adjusting, and convert it into the *Correct Magnetic* bearing by applying the Variation at place, taken from the *Variation chart,* and duly corrected for annual change, which latter in some parts of the globe is too large to be neglected. Write down neatly, in a small pass book, these Correct Magnetic bearings and corresponding times. **Make list of sun's correct magnetic bearing.**

To find the Correct Magnetic bearing from the true, you must apply westerly Variation to the right, and easterly to the left. Thus, if the *true* bearing be East, and the Variation two points westerly, the *Correct Magnetic* bearing will be E.S.E.

**Lubber lines of compasses truly fore-and-aft.** If a steamer—take in all sail, *trim her perfectly upright* by filling the boats with water or otherwise, slow the engines so as not to waste coal, provide copper tacks and a hammer, *and see that the lubber-lines of the compasses to be adjusted are truly fore-and-aft.* Place the Pelorus in one of its stands—near to the man at the wheel, if possible—and appoint an officer who has some "Nous," and is thoroughly familiar with the instrument, to put the ship's head as required, whilst attending yourself to the compasses. Begin with the Standard, being the most important, and leave the Steering compass to the last; although there is no reason why its deviation on the various points, as the ship goes round, should

* The writer, many years ago, using *the moon* for this purpose, adjusted a new steamer at night in the Sunderland Dock.

**How to use Pelorus.** not be noted by another officer. All being ready, let the lubber's point of the Pelorus be secured at North, and the sight vanes clamped to the sun's Correct Magnetic bearing, then starboard or port the helm until the sun's reflected image is seen in the speculum or mirror fairly bisected by the thread of the vane.

The vessel's head will now be North *Corr. Mag.*,—that is to say, in the direction of the north magnetic pole, as would be indicated by a well-made compass in a wooden ship without a particle of iron on board, either in her construction, equipment, or cargo. If, now, the compasses were correct, they would agree with the Pelorus in shewing the ship's head to be North; if, however, influenced by the iron of the ship, they fail to do so, the amount each differs from it will be the *Deviation* due to that particular compass *on that particular course.*

**To adjust on North.** Accordingly, if the north or red end of the compass-card be attracted—say three points to starboard—the ship's head will appear N.W. by N. by compass; or in other words, the deviation will be three points easterly (+). To counteract this blue *attracting* force of the Sub-permanent magnetism on the starboard side, place athwartship on the deck—either before or abaft, above or below the compass, as most convenient—a steel magnet, *with its red end to starboard,* and, consequently, *its blue end to port of the compass.* The red end of the magnet will of course repel the red end of the needle *from* the starboard side, and be aided in doing so by the equally strong attractive force *to* port of the blue end of the magnet.

To avoid setting up a swinging motion, let the magnet at first be placed a considerable distance from the compass—say four or five feet—and put its centre mark exactly on the fore-and-aft chalk line. Then move it gradually closer, until the ship's head is North by the card.

The pull of the starboard side will now have been neutralized by the combined action of the poles of the magnet, which may be lightly tacked down in its place. This is shewn in *Diagram No.* 9. Adjust each of the other compasses in a similar manner, placing the red or *repelling* end of the correcting magnet to starboard or port, according as the north end of the compass-needle is *attracted* to starboard or port by the ship. If one magnet be insufficient to correct the Deviation, apply another—putting it, if possible, on the opposite side of the compass to the first; or, if the first be on the deck *under* the compass, the second may, if desired, be tacked to the deck *above* it. *But in every case similar colours must*

Diagram No 9.

SHIP'S HEAD NORTH, COR: MAG:

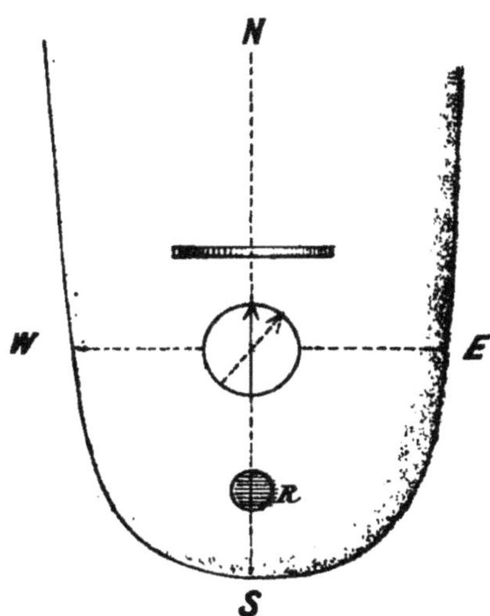


To face Page 348

*Diagram № 10.*

SHIP'S HEAD EAST. COR: MAG:

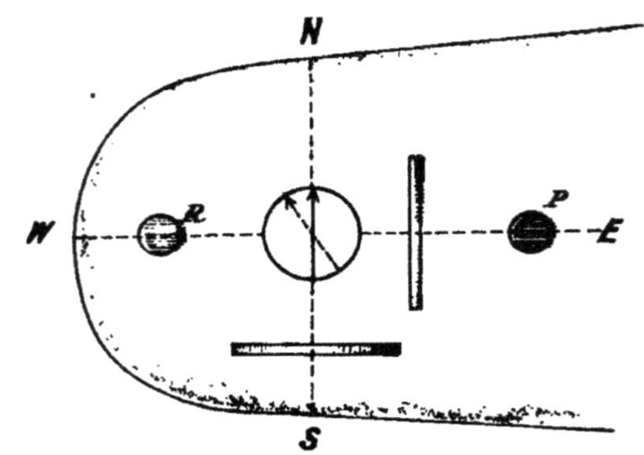


To face Page 349

*point in the same direction, or they would neutralize each other.* All this time the officer at the Pelorus—duly provided with watch and pass-book—is altering the setting of the sight vanes for every half degree of alteration in the sun's bearing, and is conning the ship *with small helm*, so as to keep her steady on the North point (C.M.), signalling by whistle whenever she is exactly so.

Having taken a second look at each of the compasses, and made any little alteration which may be required, screw the lubber line of the Pelorus to East; and, keeping the vanes set to the sun's C.M. bearing, bring the ship's head round with port helm until the sun's image is once more seen in the speculum, and *steady her* carefully on this fresh course. The various compasses, if correct on this point, ought *also* to show the ship's head as East. Should they fail to do so, the difference is the Deviation, which must be corrected *partly* by fore-and-aft magnets of steel, and *partly* by the upright iron pillar. **To adjust on East.**

The means taken to determine *how much* is to be corrected by one, and how much by the other, will be shewn further on; in the meantime, imagine half the deviation to be corrected by the pillar, and half by the steel magnet. If, now, with the ship's head at East (C.M.), the needle be drawn two points towards the stern,* the ship's head by compass will be E.S.E. To counteract this, place a steel magnet fore-and-aft ways, either to starboard or port of the compass, with its red end *also* towards the stern, and centre mark on the thwartship chalk line. Move it slowly towards the compass till half of the westerly Deviation is corrected. The ship's head will now be E. by S. by compass. Next place the upright pillar *forward* of the binnacle at such a distance as will cause the ship's head to appear due East, when it may be securely bolted down to the deck. It is preferable, however, that the lower end of the pillar should be let down some distance *through* the deck, and rest either on the one below, or on some firm support provided for the purpose. The object is not only to intensify its power, but to keep the *lower* pole of the pillar from being so near as to counteract the opposite effect of the *upper* one. The compass at this stage is shewn in *Diagram No.* 10. *R* stands for the rudder post, which in this case is the active vertical iron, and *P* for the pillar which is intended to counteract it.

* When speaking of the needle being attracted or repelled, its *north* end is always meant, unless otherwise specified.

The *Semicircular* deviation of all the compasses is now corrected. We have still, however, to deal with the *Quadrantal.*

**To adjust on N.E.**

Put the ship's head *by Pelorus* on any one of the four principal inter-cardinal points—say N.E. correct magnetic. In 99 ships out of 100 the compasses will exhibit *Easterly* Deviation on this point, amounting to as much sometimes as 10° or 12°. Should this be the case, a cast-iron cylinder or globe must be placed on each side of the compass-bowl, and moved nearer to or further from it, till the ship's head points correctly to N.E. *by compass* also.

This adjustment, once properly made, does not require touching ever after, unless, indeed, the ship were to load a cargo of iron, or some alteration made in the iron-work near the compass.

**Rule as to placing Quadrantal Correctors.**

The ends of the correctors must not, however, be nearer to the centre of the card than 1¼ times the length of the longest needle. They effect their purpose by becoming magnetic by terrestrial induction. For example, with ship's head N.E., their *port* ends exhibit *red* magnetism, and in this position compensate *easterly* Deviation; but on turning the ship round to N.W., their *starboard* ends acquire red magnetism, and in this fresh position compensate *westerly* Deviation. Chain boxes, though in very common use for this purpose, are not to be recommended. The best corrector of Quadrantal Deviation is a couple of hollow cast-iron globes or shells, the introduction of which, like many other things sailors have to be thankful for, is due to Professor Sir W. Thomson.

**Magnetic effect of hollow iron.**

Here may be mentioned incidentally a curious and often-times important fact with respect to all hollow iron bodies, whether globular or square, such as water-tanks, &c.—namely, that as soon as the thickness of the sides has reached to $\frac{1}{10}$ of the thickness or diameter of the whole body, the magnetic effect is the same as if the body were a solid piece of iron.

The compass is now shewn fully adjusted in *Diagram No.* 11.

**Semicircular and Quadrantal Deviation, why thus named.**

*Semicircular* Deviation is so termed because it has the *contrary name* and maximum value in *opposite semicircles*—thus, if it is easterly on North, it will be westerly on South. On the other hand, *Quadrantal* Deviation is so termed because it is greatest on the four inter-cardinal points. It has the *same name* in *opposite quadrants*, and the *contrary name* in *adjacent* ones:—thus, if it is easterly on N.E., it will be easterly on S.W. also, but westerly on S.E. and N.W. So you see the two kinds of Deviation are vastly different.

Steel *fore-and-aft* magnets produce their greatest effect on East

Diagram Nº II.

SHIP'S HEAD N.E. COR MAG:

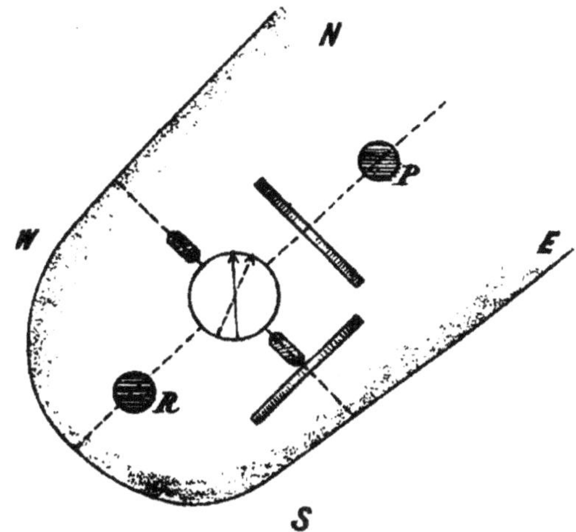


To face Page 350

and West, diminishing to nothing on North and South, when they become parallel to the compass needle. A vertical iron pillar placed on the centre line before or abaft the compass acts in the same way. Steel *thwartship* magnets produce their greatest effect on North and South, diminishing to nothing on East and West, when they become parallel to the compass needle.

**Variable effect on compass needle of compensating Magnets.**

Quadrantal correctors produce their greatest effect on N.E., S.E., S.W., and N.W., tapering off to nothing at North and South, East and West. When the ship's head is on North or South (C.M.), the poles of cast-iron cylinders, being at right angles to the "line of force," are powerless to affect the compass; and when the ship's head is on East or West (C.M.), though the cylinders are then magnetic, they cannot affect the compass, as their poles are parallel to the needle. In the case of cast-iron globes, their magnetic poles are parallel to the needle on all four of the last-named points, but the effect is the same as with the cylinders.

**Variable effect of Quadrantal Correctors.**

Any one following out this system of compensating magnets, with their ever varying effects, cannot but be struck with the beauty of the arrangement which permits of so many discordant elements being made obedient to natural laws.

When the process described above is accurately carried out, and the compasses well made and properly situated, they will be *nearly* correct on *every* point. Nevertheless, it is prudent to steam the ship completely round, steadying her on every fourth point by Pelorus, to determine remaining errors.

Then, should any compass be found to have considerable deviation—say 4° or 5°—on the *opposite* points to those on which it has been adjusted, *halve the error between the two.* If, for example, you find a compass correct on North, but 4° out on South, move the thwartship magnet so as to reduce the error on South to 2°, which will, of course, cause 2° of error on the North point also. When necessary, do the same on the West and S.W. points likewise. After which, swing ship for a table of remaining deviations on every *second* point. When this inequality occurs, it shews that the ship's iron is not symmetrically distributed round about the compass in question.

**Final corrections.**

Having finished up, resume Course, nail the magnets down for good, and cover them at your leisure with neat cases of hardwood.

If the operator knows what he is about, adjusting in this manner should not occupy more than from two to three hours, and is worth a hundred swingings in a close dock, where there is probably any amount of *Local Attraction* by cranes, bridges, roof

**Sea Adjustment preferable to Dock Adjustment.**

girders of sheds, water pipes, &c., not to speak of other iron vessels round about.

**Caution as to Steam Tenders and Tug-boats.**

Few people are alive to the fact that in high latitudes even a *wooden* tugboat may be a source of trouble to the compass, if, when fast alongside, the upper end of the funnel, as will probably be the case, is about the level of the bridge or Standard compasses, and not many feet from them. An instance of this occurred not a month since in Queenstown harbour, when the Standard compass of this ship was affected to the extent of 3° by the funnels of the passenger tender. Thus an apparently trivial cause might lead to serious results, and shews the necessity for being *continually* on the alert.

It is now necessary to go back a little, and explain the manner of getting at the *correct* amount of Deviation to be compensated by the vertical pillar of soft iron. When the ship's head is either East or West, any deviation then existing arises partly from Sub-permanent magnetism resident in the bow and stern (which must be compensated by a permanent steel magnet), and partly from the induced magnetism of vertical iron predominating more at one end of the ship than the other. This latter must be compensated by a like cause applied in the opposite direction. Thus, if vertical iron situated *abaft* the compass pulls the needle towards it, another piece of vertical iron can be put *forward* of the compass to pull it back again; or it may even be placed *abaft* the compass, on the same side as the disturbing force, if the deck fittings will permit of its *repelling* pole being placed on a level with the card.

**How to know the amount of Deviation to be corrected by vertical pillar.**

It has been shewn that on the Magnetic Equator vertical iron ceases to be magnetic, and is consequently powerless to affect the compass. *If, then, the Deviation be ascertained on the cardinal points when the ship is on the Magnetic Equator, it is certain that it cannot be due to vertical iron.* It must be owing either to *Sub-permanent* magnetism, or to *Retentive* magnetism, to be explained hereafter. For the present let us assume that it is Sub-permanent only, and correct it by a steel magnet; which being done, let the vessel proceed to high latitudes, and let the Deviation be again determined. Then, that arising from Sub-permanent magnetism having already been cured on the equator, and being, moreover, *when compensated*, not sensibly affected by change of geographical position, we know that whatever now exists is principally due to vertical iron, and should therefore be corrected by a vertical iron pillar, applied as already explained.

In practice, the experiment on the equator is only tried on the East and West points, as vertical iron, from its symmetrical arrangement in the ship, seldom disturbs the compass on the north and south points.

**Effect of ship built head North.** Again, supposing a vessel to have been built with her head due North: this will have constituted her a Sub-permanent magnet, whose axis lies exactly fore-and-aft, the bow being the red, and the stern the blue pole. When such a ship is placed head East, the red bow repels the needle, causing westerly Deviation; and unless she proceeds to the Magnetic Equator, there is no way of telling how much of it arises from the cause just mentioned, and how much from the induced magnetism of vertical iron.*

**Effect of ship built head East.** On the other hand, suppose the ship's head to have been due East when building, then the entire port side would be Sub-permanently red, and the starboard side blue. Now, what Deviation would this cause when the ship's head was East or West at any after time? None whatever! Since the poles of the ship's Sub-permanent magnetism and the needle itself would lie in the same straight line, *the only effect would be to diminish or increase the directive force of the needle.* Nevertheless, on trial, there is found to be large Deviation on these points. If so, it must be due to masses of vertical iron situated either before or abaft the compass, according to the direction of the pull, and is capable of easy cure by one or more upright pillars applied in the proper manner.

**Diminished directive force—sluggish Compasses.** There is another point in connection with the *diminished* directive force of the needle which should not be overlooked; namely, that when the ship is steering in the same direction as that in which she was built, the compass, *when uncompensated,* will be both sluggish and fickle. Therefore, every master of an iron ship should endeavour to learn in what direction his ship was built, and, when sailing on that course, be more than ever on his guard against the seemingly mysterious pranks of his compass.

**Example of difficult Compass Adjustment.** The forward wheelhouse compass of the s.s. "————" commanded by the writer, from its extremely bad situation, affords a good example of difficult compass correction. Previous to adjustment, this compass—although an excellent 12″ liquid one, by Cairns of Liverpool—had enormous natural deviations. *Diagrams* 12 *and* 13, drawn to a scale of 0″·3 to the foot, shew the steps taken to correct it.

---

* This is the extreme case (never likely to occur), which is put to give more point to what follows. Ordinarily, the rule given in the footnote on page 345 would be used.

**Iron mainmast a magnet.**

From the very close proximity of the mainmast, which acted as a powerful magnet, it was evident from the outset that strong measures would have to be taken with this compass. Experiment shewed that, at the level of the card, which was below the "neutral point" of the mainmast, the latter had north or red polarity, and exerted a strong repellant action on the needle.

In due course the ship was swung, and her *natural deviations* carefully ascertained all round. Having been built with head N. 68° E. (C.M.), the deviation on north should have been twice and a half as much as that on east, *were the compass undisturbed by vertical iron.** Knowing what it actually was on both these points, it became a comparatively easy matter to roughly separate the Inductive from the Sub-permanent. Accordingly, two round bars of wrought-iron, each 4″ in diameter, were used to counteract the mainmast. The after one—48″ in length—was let down through the top of the wheelhouse, and the other—42″ in length—was bolted to the deck just abaft the mast.

**Separating Inductive and Sub-permanent magnetism.**

It will be noticed, on looking at *Diagram No.* 13, which represents the ship's head in an easterly direction, that the north end of the needle was forcibly *repelled* by the mast. Now the *upper end* of the vertical pillar between the compass and the mast strove to *pull* it back again, and in this it was aided by the *lower end* of the pillar abaft the steam-steering wheel, which repelled or pushed it back in the same direction. The distance of these pillars from the compass was so arranged, that when in position, they about compensated the deviation due to the inductive magnetism of vertical iron; the remaining deviation on the east and west points was corrected by two 16″ steel magnets, tacked on fore-and-aft ways to the *under side* of the deck *above* the compass. The deviation on the north and south was compensated by one 30″ thwartship magnet tacked on to the outside of the forward bulkhead; and the *Quadrantal* deviation (10°) by two cast-iron cylinders with globular ends, something like the old-fashioned clock weights, each being 12″ long by 3¼″ in diameter.

**Heeling error.**

This formidable array of magnets reduced the huge errors of the compass within more manageable bounds, but afterwards, when at sea and the ship listed over, the heeling error was excessive, and had to be compensated in the usual way, by a *vertical steel magnet,* placed exactly under the centre of the card when the vessel was upright. Two iron ventilators marked V were also

* *Vide* Traverse Tables.

*Diagram №12.* **SIDE ELEVATION.**

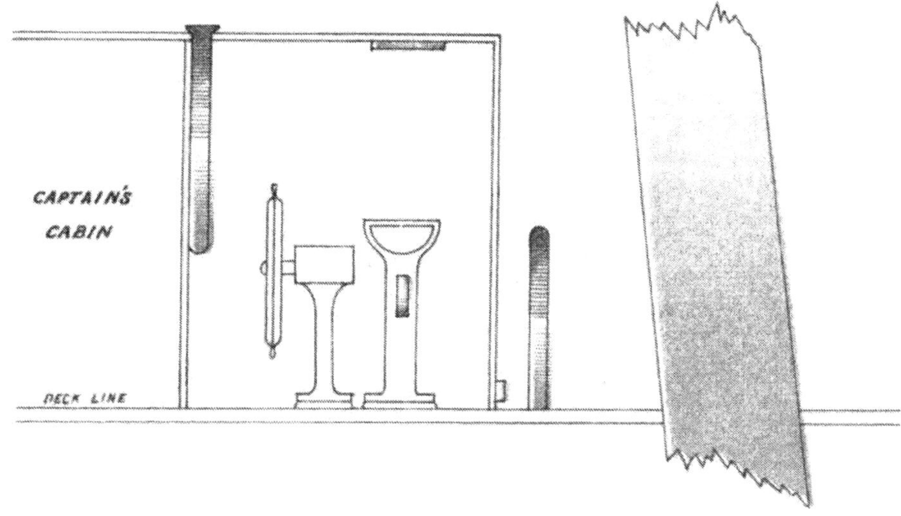


*Diagram №13.* **GROUND PLAN.**

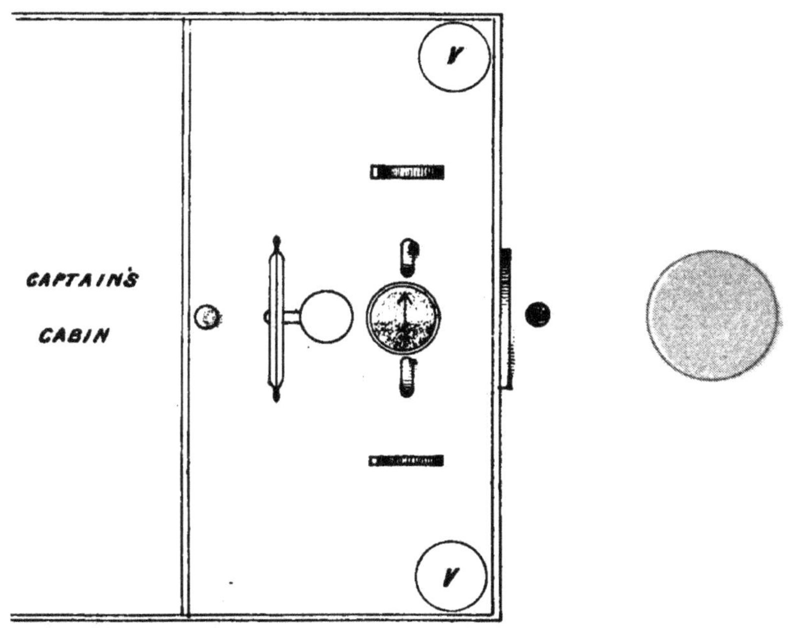


To face Page 354

removed. Nevertheless, this compass was extremely wild and fickle during the first and second voyages, and although it afterwards behaved somewhat better when the ship's magnetism had settled down, it could not be said to give very satisfactory results at any time. Of course the builders should never have placed the wheelhouse in such a ridiculously unsuitable place; but being there, and no way of improving matters short of putting in a wooden mainmast, it was necessary that the Captain should know how to make the best of a bad job.

The reader will perceive, from the very unusual character of the conditions named, that in the case just quoted, the amount of deviation to be compensated by the wrought-iron pillars could only be approximately inferred; and it is probable that, if ever this ship gets down to the Magnetic Equator, some little alteration of these arrangements will be found advisable.

**Retentive magnetism.**

To avoid confusion of ideas, it has been considered wise to leave for separate consideration that part of the ship's magnetism which is known by the term "Retentive." It plays, however, a very important part in the deviation of compasses, and will be found to modify to some extent what has been said in the previous pages.

It has been stated that when the kitchen poker is held in the "Line of force," it *instantly* becomes magnetic; or more correctly, that the latent or dormant magnetism within it has undergone excitation when held in that particular manner. This statement is correct so far as it goes, but it is necessary to supplement it by saying, that the longer the poker is so held, the more magnetic it becomes—up to a certain point. Again, when the poker is held at right angles to the "Line of force," it loses its magnetism; but if it has previously stood *for a long time* in the "Line of force," it will not lose it instantaneously, but will require a longer or shorter period to get rid of the magnetic charge, according to its intensity, and the quality of the iron in which it was excited—soft iron parting with it more readily, and *vice versâ*.

Now this is just what happens when a ship's head has been in one direction for a long time. She becomes temporarily magnetised by the earth's inductive force, and this action is intensified by the sea striking her; and also, in the case of a steamer, by the tremor imparted to the hull by the engines. The poles of the magnetism are of course parallel to the Magnetic Meridian. Thus, if the ship sailed due south for a week or so, her stern would acquire red and her bow blue magnetism—the new charge being superimposed on what may be called the ship's *natural* magnetism, and, to a certain extent, masking it.

**Duration of Retentive magnetism.**

"Retentive" magnetism remains for a considerable time after the cause is removed—frequently for days—unless the direction of the ship's head be exactly reversed, when it goes more quickly, giving way to the opposing influence of the magnetism proper to the new direction of the ship's head.

This is a *most important phase* in the magnetic character of a ship, and any one who chooses to investigate it will see, *that for this reason alone* an Adjuster's *Deviation Table* is comparatively worthless. Thus, if a ship had been laying up in a dock—say head south for several months, or even weeks—and was then most carefully adjusted, and replaced in her original berth to load for sea, but with her head in the reversed direction, it would be found before sailing that her compasses had comparatively large deviations, though when the adjuster left the vessel a fortnight previously they were practically free from error. Every one entrusted with the navigation of an iron ship should keep this fact continually before him. The immediate effect of *Retentive magnetism* upon the compass of a ship at sea is to cause her, on a change of course, *to deviate invariably in the direction of the last one.* If a vessel has been steering—let us say South—for some time, and is then hauled-up West, it will be found that the deviation previously existing on that point will be increased if it has been westerly, and diminished if easterly—*the change frequently amounting to a point and upwards;* so that, unless allowed for, she will infallibly be thrown to the southward of her intended course. Even in shaping a fresh course, differing only a couple of points from the last one, this propensity of the compass must be taken into account according to circumstances, as it varies much in different ships, and in different compasses on board the same ship.

**Retentive magnetism—effect when course is changed.**

**Tendency towards last course.**

**Effect of Retentive magnetism entering New York Bay or the Delaware.**

As an illustration, we will take the case of the lines of steamers running constantly between Liverpool and New York or Philadelphia. On the outward passage these vessels have their heads in a westerly direction for upwards of a week, and consequently the poles of their *Retentive magnetism* lie to starboard and port—the red pole on the starboard, and blue pole on the port side. The tendency on subsequent northerly courses will be to throw the ship to the westward. Thus, entering New York Bay by the south channel, the Swash Range Lights come in one bearing N. 40° W. (C.M.); but if, when in one, the vessel be steered directly for them, the direction of her head *by compass* will probably be about N. 33° W., or even more to the northward. The same effect will be still better shewn when hauled up for Fort Hamilton. The course, keeping the Range Lights in one astern, is N. 13¼° E. (C.M.), but the chances are in favour of the vessel having to steer about N. 23° E. *by compass*, or, at all events, considerably to the eastward of the proper course.

The same thing occurs in the Delaware. From Cape Henlopen to the Brandywine Lighthouse, the course—keeping the ranges in one astern—is N. 2¾° W. (C.M.): it is quite common, however, to steer about N. 12° E. by compass.*

**Effect of Retentive magnetism in Irish Channel.**

On the homeward passage, these steamers, having had their heads to the eastward for a week, get magnetised in the opposite direction. It is the *port* side which now has *red* magnetism; and, in consequence, when hauled up at Tuskar for the Skerries or South Stack, instead of steering N. 58° E. (C.M.), they have generally to shape a *compass course* many degrees to the northward.

**How to eliminate Retentive magnetism.**

As the effects due to crossing the Atlantic are about equal, going and coming, it is not a difficult matter to adjust the compasses with accuracy for the ship's Sub-permanent magnetism on the North and South points. If, for example, outward bound, with head North by compass in the Delaware, the deviation is found to be 8° *westerly;* and homeward bound, with head North outside Queenstown, it is found to be 20° *easterly*—the amount of *Sub-permanent* magnetic attraction to be compensated by the thwartship magnets is 6° easterly. Accordingly, at one or other of these places the magnets should be moved to shew 14° of deviation—westerly in the Delaware, easterly at Queenstown; *and this amount would then be solely the effect of Retentive magnetism*, which would quickly disappear if the circumstances producing it were reversed.

It is evident that were it due to *Sub-permanent magnetism*, it could not, on the same point, be easterly at one time, and westerly at another. But, in making these observations and corrections, *do not forget that the ship must be perfectly upright, or the results will be vitiated.* From half-passage over either way, it will be easy to adjust on the East and West points, as by

* In Trans-Atlantic Steamers it is a good plan to have one of the deck compasses adjusted for the American port frequented, and another for the English port. The writer keeps his Bridge compass adjusted for the Delaware inward-bound, and the Standard or Navigating compass for the Irish Channel, outward-bound.

that time the Retentive magnetism due to steering towards the North or South will have disappeared.

No possible amount of care or scientific knowledge in an adjuster can provide against *Retentive Magnetism*. There is, however, one dodge by which its effects can, in some minor degree, be modified. In those regular liners always sailing on the route just specified, it will probably be found useful to *over*-compensate *the Quadrantal deviation*. The correctors diminish westerly deviation in the N.W. quadrant, and easterly deviation in the N.E. quadrant; therefore, by *over*-compensation, the effect of the Retentive magnetism would be partially neutralized in one semicircle of the compass at both ends of the voyage; and so long as the course lay within that semicircle, there would be undoubted advantage. On the other hand, those liners who run principally in a North and South direction, and have occasion to make abrupt changes of course near the end of the passage, should have their Quadrantal deviation *under*-compensated, or, if small, neglected altogether.

**Over compensation of Quadrantal Deviation.**

These last are not so fortunately situated as the first named, since the application of correctors for Quadrantal deviation has not only the effect of increasing the directive force of the needle, but lessens very considerably the error due to heeling.* Each one, therefore, must judge for himself how far these suggestions are suitable to his own particular route and ship. Pole compasses, *when well placed*, are comparatively exempt from the effects of Retentive magnetism, and Masthead compasses are almost entirely so.

Now this matter of *Retentive magnetism* has a very important bearing upon compass adjustment. It is evident that if its effects get mixed up with the ship's *permanent* or *congenital* magnetism, the adjuster will be compensating something which would ultimately have disappeared of itself, or perhaps have taken an opposite name. This is another reason why a *Deviation Table* cannot be trusted, and by imparting undue confidence, is more likely to lead into trouble than to keep one out of it. It shews also that, before the Captain of a ship undertakes to meddle with his compasses, he should be tolerably certain that they are free from this fleeting but troublesome error, or else know by experience how much to allow for it.

If, soon after launching and masting, a ship be experimentally swung for compass errors, and then be completed for sea with her

* The Quadrantal deviation in all these cases is supposed to be of the kind due to the coefficient + D; that is, easterly in the N.E. and S.W. quadrants, and the contrary in the other two.

head in the opposite direction to that which it had whilst on the building slip, it will be found on next swinging her that a wide discordance will exist between the first and last Deviation Tables. Now, as already stated on page 342, an iron ship becomes a magnet during the process of construction, but only a portion of the magnetism thus acquired is fixed or *Permanent*, the remainder is *Retentive;* and to get rid of this surplus charge before the compasses are adjusted for sea, it is highly expedient that an iron vessel should have the direction of her head reversed as soon as possible after she leaves the stocks, *and kept so* till she is taken away to be adjusted. This unfortunately is too often neglected, as builders generally are averse to the trouble, or it may not always suit their convenience in other respects. But, seeing its great importance, owners ought to make reversal obligatory by inserting a clause to that effect in their specification, for instance, that the vessel should have the building direction of her head reversed for at least ten days previous to adjustment. When reversal is neglected, the adjustment made just before going to sea is only so much time and money scattered to the winds, not to speak of the positive danger likely to accrue from the omission if the vessel should have a beating wind and thick weather when going down channel.

**First Adjustment of new vessels.**

The writer has a lively remembrance of a case in point. Not a hundred years ago it was his fortune to command a fine new steamer, which the builders, in spite of all entreaty, refused to reverse after launching. When the day for it came, the adjustments were carefully made by himself and a professional of considerable reputation. The vessel then started on a trial trip which lasted some 36 hours. During the greater portion of this time, however, the writer was kept briskly on the move, shifting magnets and readjusting according as the vessel parted with her *retentive* magnetism. No doubt the builder, in his happy ignorance, thought the extra fuss was all a "fad" of the Captain's. Luckily, throughout the trip, the weather was beautifully clear and the sea like a mirror, but had it been thick and stormy, that builder might have left the ship in a sadder, if not a wiser, mood.

The Latin proverb, when paraphrased, tells us that experience teaches even *wise* men.

**Facilities for adjustment of Eastern going steamers.**

The numerous lines of steamers running to Eastern ports through the Suez Canal have a splendid opportunity for adjusting their compasses in the most perfect manner. In the first place, between Aden and Ceylon—a distance of over 2000 miles—

*they are steaming nearly due east on the magnetic equator,* during which time, of course, vertical iron has no effect whatever on the compass. Therefore, when about half passage over, let the ship's *Sub-permanent magnetism* be carefully compensated with fore-and-aft magnets of steel on East (C.M.)

As, however, the deviation existing on the east course may be due partly to the ship's *natural* magnetism, and partly—though in a less degree—to the *Retentive* magnetism picked up coming down the Canal, Gulf of Suez, and Red Sea, it will be proper, at the same place, on the return passage, to ascertain the deviation on the West point. Should there be any, it ought to be reduced one-half, by shifting one of the fore-and-aft magnets in the required direction, and when the ship gets up by Beachy Head or Dover, *again* determine the deviation on the East point.

**How to arrive at amount of deviation due to vertical iron.**

It may now be pretty large, *and if not mixed up with Retentive magnetism, will be due wholly and solely to the influence of vertical iron. Now* is the time to place the upright iron pillar, and let it be at such a distance as will compensate all the deviation on East, unless there is reason to believe that some of it arises from that troublesome *Retentive* magnetism, in which case allow, say, a couple of degrees to remain. It is not, however, likely that there will be much "Retentive" left by the time Beachy Head is reached; but if the weather is fine, you can make tolerably sure by yawing the vessel right off to *South* for 20 minutes or half-an-hour—going slow—and then putting her on East (C.M.) to be adjusted.

Should the iron pillar be made to bolt to the deck on which the binnacle rests, it will be merely necessary to move it nearer to or further from the compass, till the ship's head points to East (C.M.) by compass as well as by Pelorus. But if, as recommended, the pillar has been made to let down through the deck, you must ascertain *beforehand* the effect, at various distances, produced by it on this particular compass, *taking care that the experiment is made in the same magnetic latitude as that in which it is intended to ship the pillars.*

**Experiment with iron pillar.**

When the writer was in the S.S. "*City of Mecca,*" this plan was adopted with complete success. The deviation on East was ascertained off Dover, and noted. On arrival in London, a round wrought-iron pillar, 5 feet long and 4¼ inches in diameter, was procured, and its inductive power tested as follows. The compass (12-inch card, 4 needles) was taken on shore in the S.W. India Dock, and placed on some cotton bales, at such a height that the pillar stood a couple of inches above the level of the needles. As soon as the card had ceased vibrating, a piece of marline was stretched across the centre of the compass in an east and west direction, *and made fast.* The iron pillar, *which had purposely been left standing on end for some hours,* was next, with the assistance of an impromptu plumb-line, placed *vertically* under the marline, in which position it was of course at right angles to the direction of the needles, and consequently exerting its greatest influence. Having measured the distance of the pillar from the compass—centre to centre—and noted the effect produced, it was advanced—*still under the marline*—a little nearer, the measurement repeated, the effect again noted, and so on.

**Magnetic effect of iron pillar.**

The following shews the results, and may be useful to others under similar circumstances, but only as a rough guide, since different qualities of iron, and a different construction of compass, may increase or diminish the values here given.

| Distance. ft. | in. | Effect. ° |
|---|---|---|
| 7 | 6 | None. |
| 6 | 7½ | 1½ |
| 4 | 7¾ | 3 |
| 3 | 6⅛ | 6¼ |
| 2 | 9⅓ | 11¼ |
| 1 | 11¼ | 25 |

Having by this method determined the distance at which the pillar would compensate the amount of deviation ascertained off Dover, a hole was bored in the deck at the same distance from the compass, and the pillar let down until its upper end stood about two inches above the level of the card, and the heel rested on a strong wooden cleat or bracket, screwed to a bulkhead below. The partners were then wedged up with soft wood, and a duck coat put on over all, and painted, to preserve the pillar from rust.

This compass was sworn by ever after, so perfect was its behaviour.

**Adjusting on North and South in Suez Canal.**

To adjust compasses on the North and South points, there is a capital place for these eastern-going ships in the Suez Canal. Just after leaving Port Said, there is one unbroken "straight" of 26 miles, the Correct Magnetic course down which is S. 4° W. the whole way; and as the speed in the Canal rarely exceeds 7 knots, there will be 3½ hours available for adjusting. It is true the vessel's head cannot be put *exactly* on South (C.M.); but if the thwartship magnets are placed to make the compass show S. 4° W.

when the vessel is pointing straight down the Canal, this will be found quite near enough.

The next matter is how to get rid of the *Retentive* magnetism acquired whilst steaming on Easterly courses in the Mediterranean, which will naturally produce its greatest temporary effect now that the vessel's head is South, or at right angles to its former direction.

**Port Said.**

It is usual to coal at Port Said; or if a steamer arrives late in the afternoon, it is seldom that she can proceed before the next morning. If, during this unavoidable detention, the pilot can be prevailed upon to put the vessel into the Ismail Basin, she will there head to the N.W.; or in the opposite direction, to the courses steered down from Malta; and will be almost sure to have lost all her *Retentive* magnetism before the following morning.

Even should it be found impossible to get the ship's head in this direction, the ordinary berth for waiting steamers runs about S.W., or some 10 points from her last course, which will go a long way to remove the unwelcome visitor. If in any doubt, however, the compasses can again be tried on South, when emerging from the Canal into Suez Bay, by which time they will certainly be free from the effects of the "Retentive" acquired on Easterly courses.*

**Compensation of Quadrantal Deviation not affected by Retentive Magnetism.**

The compass has now been corrected on the cardinal points, but there is yet the *Quadrantal deviation* to deal with. Fortunately, *in this case* the presence of any amount of *Retentive magnetism* does not signify in the slightest degree. At any convenient time or place, steam the ship right round the circle, steadying her sufficiently long on N.E., S.E., S.W., and N.W., *by compass*, to get the deviation on these points with accuracy. Mark easterly deviation by the plus (+) sign, and westerly by the minus (−) sign, and then proceed as follows:—*Reverse* the sign of the deviation observed on S.E. and N.W., then add together those which have the same sign; take the difference between the two dissimilar quantities thus found, and prefix the sign of the greater. Divide this difference by 4, *retaining its sign*, and the result will be the *Quadrantal deviation*, which, in its natural state, without correctors, will nearly always be + in name; and as it is due to horizontal

---

* In the so-called *steel* ships now coming into fashion, the writer finds, as might be expected, that their magnetism is of a more fixed character as compared with iron ones. The Deviations of the compasses in steel vessels are therefore somewhat more constant, which in itself is a great advantage, since in general it is not so much the *amount* of Deviation that is complained of in compensated compasses, as its perplexing variability.

iron, will retain the same value in any latitude, unless, indeed, the construction of the vessel be materially altered, or large quantities of iron be shipped as cargo. The following example is taken from the Record of the "*British Crown's*" compasses.

BELFAST LOUGH. Monday, 6/10/79.

**How to ascertain amount of Quadrantal Deviation.**

The natural deviation on N.E. was − 6°, on S.E. − 62°, on S.W. + 32°, and on N.W. + 48°.

| | | |
|---|---|---|
| N.E. − 6° | S.E. + 62° sign reversed. | + 94° |
| N.W. − 48 sign reversed. | S.W. + 32 | − 54 |
| − 54° | + 94° | 4) + 40 |
| | | + 10° = Quadrantal deviation |

To compensate it; if the sign is + as in the example, put the ship's head the same number of degrees *to the left* of N.E. as the value of the Quadrantal deviation; and, keeping her exactly in this direction by the aid of some other compass, place the correctors, and move them closer to, until her head is N.E. by the compass under treatment. Ships are so seldom found having Quadrantal deviation with a − sign, that it is unnecessary to enter upon its compensation.

**Quadrantal more embarrassing than Semicircular Deviation.**

Although the Quadrantal error is rarely large in amount, like the Semicircular, it is for many reasons very important that it should be corrected. Not the least is the fact, that for the same amount of maximum error, the Quadrantal changes *twice* as rapidly as does the Semicircular error; and, therefore, a Quadrantal error of 10° is much more embarrassing than a Semicircular error of the same amount. The true significance of this will be seen when it is explained that a Quadrantal error of 10° implies a rapid change in the deviation of the compass, amounting to as much as half a point, with so small a change as a point and a half in the ship's course from one side to the other of any of the four cardinal courses. *Imagine the difficulty of trying to steer by such a compass!*

**Heeling error.**

This concludes the adjustment of a ship *on even beam*, in which only the pull of the *horizontal* portion of the ship's magnetism has duly been considered. Some iron vessels, however, have excessively large deviations, due to magnetic force *below* the compass, since the poles of the ship's magnetism can only lie in the *horizontal* plane in such ships as have been built on or near the magnetic equator. *Vide* page 342. This heeling error has been known to amount to as much as 2° for every 1° of heel. It is greatest when the ship's head is on the North or South points, and becomes reduced to a very small quantity on East or West. Thus a ship changing her heel from 10° port to 10° starboard, may change her deviation as much as 40°, which no one will deny is a very serious matter.*

**Compensation by "Dipping needle."** It is seldom or never possible to list a ship in dock to ascertain her peculiarity in this respect, as doing so costs too much time and money in these days of rapid movements and economy; but it may be approximately arrived at in another and much easier way. Get an optician *of repute* to make you a delicately poised "Dipping needle," mounted on a suitable stand, carrying a couple of spirit levels, and protected with a glass cover. Let the needle-point traverse a vertical scale of degrees, and be fitted with a small sliding balance weight, so that whatever part of the world you may be in, by moving the weight you can set the needle to zero of the scale, when the spirit levels indicate that the instrument is perfectly horizontal.† Now, to test the vertical force of the ship on any compass, take your "Dipping needle" on shore, *in a spot free from Local Attraction*, and adjust it to zero: then, returning on board, remove the compass, and put the "Dipping needle" in its place, bedding it up with wood or otherwise until it is perfectly levelled, and occupies *exactly* the same position and direction the compass needles did. Then, if it be found deflected from zero, it shews the existence of vertical magnetic force *below* the compass, commensurate with the amount of such deflection. This can be compensated by inserting a vertical steel magnet in a suitable receptacle, directly underneath the very centre of the instrument; which magnet is to be slid up or down till the point of the "Dipping needle" again rests at 0°, when it is to be secured in place, and the compass returned. Generally it is the red pole of the magnet which requires to be uppermost, but this is very easily seen on trial.

This is a very important adjustment in all ships, but more especially in those whose cargo is largely composed of iron; and as it is certain that such vessels cannot be heeled every voyage, owing to the unceasing hurry-scurry in mercantile affairs, such a simple and inexpensive mode of effecting it should not be neglected. Unfortunately, this adjustment, as at present effected, only holds good for the Magnetic Latitude in which it is made.

---

* See *Appendix*.

† Sir W. Thomson has patented a very neat arrangement for determining the vertical force below the compass. See Chapter XIII., Part I.

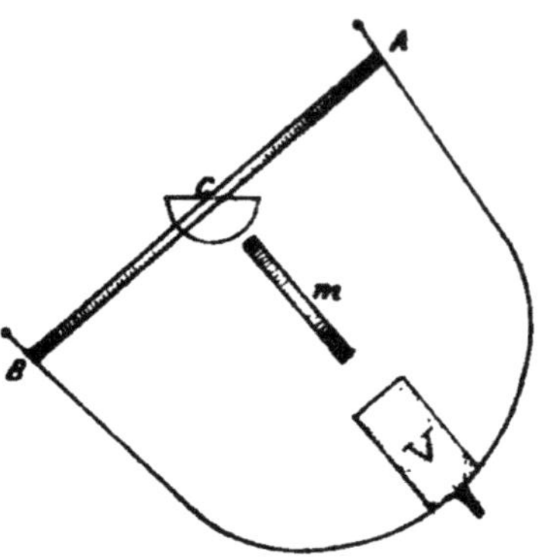


Diagram No. 14

SHIP'S HEAD NORTH C.M.

B
C
A
m
V

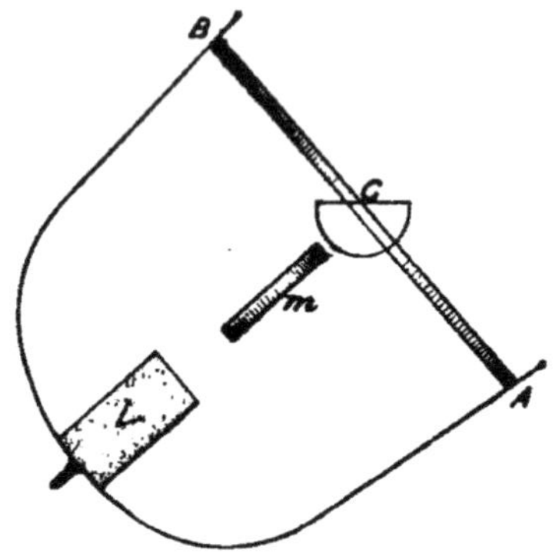


To face Page [illegible]

The vertical force below the compass is compounded of Induced as well as Sub-permanent magnetism; and we have shewn that these require different treatment, inasmuch as the *transient* induced magnetism of soft iron cannot be satisfactorily compensated by *permanent* steel magnets. Moreover, iron which was horizontal with the ship upright, partakes also of the nature of vertical iron when she heels over, which at once introduces a fresh disturbing element. This adjustment, therefore, can only be considered reliable in such *foreign-going* vessels as the Atlantic liners before alluded to—which, in the run from the United Kingdom to New York, are all the time *practically* in the same Magnetic Latitude, the difference not amounting to 3°.

**Adjustment of heeling error only good in magnetic latitude in which it was made.**

To see what a great advantage a vessel has whose heeling error is compensated over another where it is not so, just suppose them to be on northerly or southerly courses in a rough beam sea. In the one case, each time the ship rolls, the vertical magnetic force below the compass will come out now on one side, and now on another, causing the card to be alternately pulled to starboard and port at every roll; and should this pull happen to coincide with the period of vibration due to the motion of the ship, *the swing of the card will be so great as to render it perfectly useless.* In such cases, a man ignorant of the science of compass adjustment will be almost certain to attribute the excessive swing to some inherent fault of the compass, and inwardly curse the maker. On the other hand, the properly compensated compass will remain comparatively steady under all circumstances, and any little swing will be due to purely mechanical causes. In the latter case, the swing may be lessened by affixing deep wings of talc to the under side of the card, on its outer edge. These will help to steady it, by their resistance to the air.

**Advantages of heeling error compensation.**

In diagram No. 14, facing this page, let *V* in each of the figures represent the vertical component of the ship's magnetism, and its effect on the compass-needle, when the vessel rolls, will be easily understood. *B* represents the deck beams, *C* the compass, and *M* the compensating magnet.

It has already been shewn how necessary it is that the ship's magnetism, causing the deviation on East and West, should be resolved into its constituent parts, and each compensated by the means suitable to it; but to impress it more vividly on the mind, just consider what happens when this has been neglected.

Take the case of a southern-going vessel, having—say 5 points natural deviation on East, 3 of which are due to vertical iron.

**Result of improper compensation.**

The adjuster having no time given him to sift the matter, compensates all 5 points, in happy-go-lucky fashion, by means of *permanent steel magnets*, and so the compass is rendered correct *for the time being*. But as the vessel goes south, the vertical iron loses its power over the compass, and on the Magnetic Equator exerts none whatever; the steel magnet, on the contrary, is as strong as before, and having now all its own way—(Happy Magnet!!)—causes an error of three points. By the time the vessel has got off Cape Horn, vertical iron has *again* become strongly magnetic, *but now with reversed poles, so that it pulls in the same direction as the steel magnet, and both acting together*, cause 6 *points of deviation*. Not only is this large error a trouble in itself, *but the directive force of the needle is so reduced* as to make the compass sluggish, and almost worthless to steer by.

Many uninformed men in this fix take up the magnets altogether, which certainly may mend matters, but won't cure them. They even eye the magnets themselves as something dangerous, actually throw them overboard, are rather proud of the exploit, and boast of having done so to their nautical chums.

**How to keep spare magnets.**

If ignorant of the principles of compass adjustment, the more rational plan would be to tie the magnets together in pairs of equal size—the red end of one touching the blue end of the other—and consign them to the forepeak, or the carpenter's storeroom. When so fastened together, they retain their magnetic force unimpaired, while they effectually neutralize each other's action, and so cannot play tricks with a compass *or chronometer*, should they *accidentally* be placed near them. In this way they will be ready for use when next required, and the expense of buying others will be saved.

**Advisability of determining natural Deviations before adjusting.**

Before adjusting a new vessel, it is advisable to swing her on the eight principal points *by each compass*, and ascertain the Co-efficients,* which, when recorded, are afterwards useful in connection with the magnetic history of the ship; but with three or four compasses the process is a tedious one, occupying at least a whole day, irrespective of the time required at the finish for putting down the magnets; and it is only in rare cases, such as yachts, or men-of-war, where time is of less importance, that this would be practicable. *When the natural errors are not too large*, time may be saved and several swingings avoided, by the use of Napier's diagram, but extreme cases, which often occur in practice, cannot be treated this way.

* Towson, page 23.

Enough has been said to convince anyone that *reliable* compass adjustment is beset with difficulties, and cannot be lightly undertaken. What dependence, then, can be placed on the hurried performance which is daily witnessed in some of our largest ports, when a lot of magnets are slapped down as the vessel leaves the dock gates, and a Deviation Card handed to the Captain worth little more than the paper it is written on? This, however, is seldom or never the Adjuster's fault, but is the result of a vicious system against which conscientious men dare not shew fight, since less scrupulous competitors are ever ready to step in and adjust (?) in half the time, if necessary, and for half the money. Strange to say, any one with sufficient money or credit to rent a shop can style himself a Compass Adjuster, as no Government test "exam." is required; so, for legal purposes, Tom, Dick, or Harry suit equally well.

**Comparative uselessness of Deviation Cards.**

In the course of a voyage, many opportunities present themselves for adjusting or forming a Deviation Table, and such chances should be carefully sought for and utilized. The man responsible for the navigation of an iron vessel cannot be too zealous in this respect.

**Ports on Magnetic Equator.**

The ports of Callao, Bahia, Calabar, Aden, Madras, Colombo, and many others, are practically on the magnetic equator, and ships lie at anchor in them for weeks, during which their captains might perfect the Sub-permanent and Quadrantal portion of the adjustment; and be prepared to complete it, as already explained, on return to high latitudes.

This being satisfactorily accomplished, and the adjustment being in all respects carried out in conformity with the foregoing rules, it is strongly recommended not to fiddle-faddle afterwards with the magnets, in, what would only be, vain attempts to correct the subsequent comparatively small errors *sure to arise* from time to time. Unless the vessel be new, or has had alterations made affecting the compass, these errors will be due entirely to Retentive Magnetism, over which, from their "come-and-go" character, it is impossible to exercise any permanent control.

To keep a compass exactly correct at all times and places, the magnets would have to be everlastingly shifted about, than which —it is almost needless to say—nothing could be more injudicious.

The proper way to circumvent the difficulty is to keep a Compass Record in some such form as that given on page 379. This particular one is kept in stock by the publishers of "Wrinkles."

When the writer was in the service of the P. S. N. Co., and had to touch regularly at a couple or three dozen ports on the round trip, it was his practice to avail himself of the natural marks for swinging ship to be found in many of the harbours. For example, when at anchor in a port like Rio de Janeiro, it is easy to ascertain the correct magnetic bearing of a distant object, such as a mountain peak, well-defined hill top, or small island, by taking its *true* bearing off the harbour plan with a Field's Parallel Ruler, and applying to it the *corrected* variation. The difference between this and the compass bearing, as the ship swings round to wind or tide, is, of course, the Deviation for the particular point on which the ship's head may be at time of observation. This method is independent of the sun, which will not always show itself when wanted, and in the tropics may have too high an altitude to be serviceable; with the additional advantage that, *as the bearing of the object is constant, no calculation is necessary.*

**Adjusting by bearing of distant object.**

In Rio, the steamers of the P.S.N. Company invariably anchored off the small island of Mocangué, which was their coaling station. From this position, the conspicuous peak of Tijuca (3,316 feet high) bore S. 66° W. correct magnetic, distant 9¼ miles, and was therefore fairly adapted for this purpose. A remarkable peak in the Organ Mountains, from its greater distance, was a better object, and could be used indifferently with Tijuca, when one or other happened to be shut out by the masts or funnel. This last peak was not laid down on the harbour plan; but its bearing was ascertained in the simplest manner by *merely taking the horizontal sextant angle between it and Tijuca.**

**Adjusting marks in Rio de Janeiro.**

At this anchorage a couple of excellent *transit* marks are also available for compass work. On the eastern side of the harbour are two forts, viz., Gravata and Santa Cruz. Their western faces are in one on the bearing of due South C.M.; and *in the same line*, and close to the anchorage, is a low-lying rock off the S.W. corner of Mocangué.

The lighthouse on Raza Island, in transit with this rock, bears S. 6½° W., C.M. As the ship swings to wind and tide, one or other of these two transit marks is pretty sure to be "on;" but in any case a good eye can always estimate the difference when they happen to be a little open of each other. Whether in transit or not, be sure and observe the bearing of the *back* object.

**Always observe transit bearing of *back* object.**

* On these occasions, should the angle exceed the limits of your sextant, it can be measured at twice by using some intermediate object lying in the same horizontal plane.

Should the navigator, however, not be provided with a large scale plan of the harbour, or the sun not be visible, the *mean* of two bearings on East and West *by compass* will give the *corr. mag.* bearing of the distant object. The old advice on this subject was to observe the compass bearing on *every* point as the ship swung round, dividing by 32 to get the required C.M. bearing; but Towson* has shewn conclusively that the first method is more correct, as well as more convenient. Thus, if with head west by compass, the observed bearing is S. 81° W., and with head east it is N. 63° W., we have

**How to obtain the *Corr. Mag.* bearing of an object from its *compass* bearing.**

N. 63° W.
N. 99° W.
2) 162°
Corr. mag. bearing of . . . N. 81° W. . . distant object.

Should the sun be visible, there is a very correct mode of finding the required bearing, which can be put into practice whenever there is a true sea horizon. *In a confined harbour this may be obtained from a boat alongside, if the shore line is not nearer than 1½ miles.*

**How to obtain Astronomical *true* bearing of distant object.**

Measure with the sextant the oblique angular distance between the sun's nearer limb and the object selected, *taking a point at the water-line* (imaginary or otherwise) *vertically under the latter.* At the same instant let another observer take the sun's altitude in the usual way, and note the time. Then, neglecting minor corrections, proceed as follows:—Find the sun's true altitude by Table IX. of Norie. Add 16′ to the observed angular distance, to reduce it to the sun's centre. Next, from the log. Cosine of the distance subtract the log. Cosine of the altitude, and the result will be the log. Cosine of the *horizontal angle* between the sun's centre and the object. Thus:—

EXAMPLE I.

| | ° ′ | | |
|---|---|---|---|
| Corrected angular distance . | 76 40 | . Cosine . | 9·3629 |
| ☉'s true altitude . . . . | 28 10 | . Cosine . | 9·9453 |
| Horizontal angle between ☉ and object. } = | 74 50 | . Cosine . | 9·4176 |

* Page 124. 2nd Ed.

EXAMPLE II.

| | ° ′ | | | |
|---|---|---|---|---|
| Corrected angular distance . | 98 20 | . | Cosine . | 9·1612 |
| ⊙'s true altitude . . . . | 30 10 | . | Cosine . | 9·9368 |
| | 80 21 | . | Cosine . | 9·2244 |
| | 180 | | | |
| Horizontal angle = . . . | 99° 39′ between ⊙ and object. | | | |

In the last example the angular distance exceeds 90°, and it is therefore necessary to take the *supplement* of what would otherwise have been the required horizontal angle. The sun's true bearing, at the time the observations were made, having been found, either by the "*Red Book*" or the old alt-azimuth problem, apply to it the horizontal angle just obtained, and you get the *true* bearing of the object. To this apply the *corrected* variation at place, and you have the desired *corr. mag.* bearing with even more than the necessary precision. *The three log. cosines make this problem easy to remember.* To ensure an accurate result, the angular distance must be *at least* double the sun's altitude.

**Arica—facilities for Compass Adjustment.** Captains of vessels plying regularly to certain ports might keep a memorandum of the C.M. bearings of distant peaks, &c., as seen from the anchorage they frequent. Thus at Arica, in Peru, there are several capital marks, as under:—

| | | |
|---|---|---|
| Morro de Sama.............. | N. 59¼° W.C.M. | (distant 41 miles). |
| Notch Peak .................. | N. 13¼° W. | " |
| Left Peak ..................... | N. 20¼° E. | " |
| Right Peak .................. | N. 23½° E. | " |
| Sajama ........................ | N. 53¾° E. | " |
| Centre of Table Mount ... | N. 80¼° E. | " |

These bearings—which, from there being no appreciable annual change in the variation at this part of the coast, will hold good for an indefinite time—were determined at anchor, with the new mole S.E. ½ E. (C.M.), 3½ cables distant; but from the great distance of these mountains, the ship might shift her position very considerably without affecting the bearings. Taking the Morro de Sama—one of the nearest—a vessel would have to shift her berth ¾ of a mile *at right angles to its line of direction* before causing an alteration in the bearing of even 1°. Therefore, to adjust compasses, a vessel might steam slowly round the Bay. Here the Pelorus, or Sir W. Thomson's Azimuth Mirror, would come in tip-top.

**Plymouth—special buoys provided for swinging ship**

At Plymouth, the Admiralty have a couple of mooring buoys just inside the breakwater, which are specially provided to swing men-of-war. From the eastern one, Sheepstor—a hill eleven miles inland—bears N. 45° E. (C.M.), and from the western one N. 47° E. (C.M.) As a general rule, when at single anchor in a tideway, the distance of a selected object should not be less than 10 miles; but if the vessel is taut moored, and the observing compass be well forward, five miles will suffice.

**Observations unreliable when ship swings rapidly.**

When swinging pretty fast, with wind and tide in the same direction, the observations will not be nearly so reliable, owing to friction causing a heavy card to drag with the ship, in opposition to the directive force of the needle. A light card, like Sir W. Thomson's, has a great advantage in this respect, as friction on the bearing point is reduced to a minimum. To counteract the dragging tendency, keep quietly moving the compass in the gimbals as the ship goes round.

**River Mersey, Vauxhall Chimney.**

In the Mersey, ships may determine their deviations by the bearing of Vauxhall chimney, in transit with any one of a system of figures painted in large characters on the dock walls and sheds. These figures give the C.M. bearing of the chimney, reckoning from north towards south by the east. Thus 110° would be read as N. 110° E., or S. 70° E.

Similar facilities are also given at Kronstadt. Capt. J. Belavenetz, of the Russian Imperial Navy, has made the following arrangement in the commercial port of Kronstadt to enable mariners to determine the deviations of their compasses, as resulting from the effects of the iron of the ship, or the cargo on board, whilst lying at anchor in the great roadstead of that port: viz.—

The true bearings of the foundry chimney from various parts of the western wall of the commercial port of Kronstadt are indicated by a series of marks, ranging between the bearings of N. 89° E. and S. 79° E., painted on the western face of the wall.

The degrees are marked in figures legible from the roadstead of Kronstadt, the even figures being on a black ground, and the odd figures on a red ground, in the following order, indicating as here stated, under each figure,—

| 9 | 80 | 1 | 2 | 3 | 4 | 5 | 6 | 7 |
|---|---|---|---|---|---|---|---|---|
| S.79°E. | S.80°E. | S.81°E. | S.82°E. | S.83°E. | S.84°E. | S.85°E. | S.86°E. | S.87°E. |

| 8 | 9 | 90 | 9 |
|---|---|---|---|
| S.88°E. | S.89°E. | East. | N.89°E. |

There is quite a similar arrangement at Cherbourg, and to

facilitate adjusting there are eight warping buoys in a circle with one in the centre.

**Deviation of wooden vessels marked on Compass Card.**

In the absence of cargoes containing iron, *wooden* vessels going short voyages have their deviation nearly constant, in which case it is not a bad plan to write it neatly on each point of the compass card for ready reference. Do not, however, *when correcting a bearing,* commit the blunder *of taking the deviation from the bearing point.* It must, of course, be taken from the one which corresponds to the direction of the *ship's head* at time of observation. *This mistake has frequently been made.*

Leaving Liverpool in winter, it often happens on the approach of a southerly gale that the atmosphere is more than ordinarily clear, although the sky may be quite overcast. At these periods it is possible to see almost fabulous distances; and in the absence of the sun—a rare visitor in winter—transit bearings of lighthouses, mountains, and other shore marks can be used to give the deviation with all needful accuracy. *Then comes one of the advantages of having large scale Admiralty Coast Sheets, from which to get the true bearings.*

**Transit bearings of shore marks.**

For example, almost immediately after passing the Crosby Light-vessel, the Hoylake lights come in range bearing S. 28¾° W. corr. mag. (1884), and about 7 miles after passing the North-West lightship, Great Orme Head lighthouse (readily distinguished with the binocular) will be seen in one with the conspicuous peak of Penmaen Mawr. Six miles further on, the latter comes in transit with a lofty mountain named Carnedd Llewelyn. But Carnedd Llewelyn, from this point of view, is not readily picked out by a stranger. Again, the bearing of the Skerries and South Stack lights, when in one, happens by good fortune to coincide with the fairway course down the Irish Channel, passing within nice range of Bardsey and the Smalls; so that, if when in transit they are brought either right ahead or astern—the latter is preferable—these lights will prove additionally an invaluable guide. Of course, by taking their transit bearing in passing, the deviation will be found for any point on which the ship's head may happen to be at the moment.

**How to name the Deviation.**

In *naming* deviation ascertained in this manner, recollect that if the *shore bearing* is to the right of the *compass bearing,* the deviation is easterly, and *vice versa.*

Now, in regard to transit bearings, there is a point to be noted. The further off the back object is so much the better, for then the bearing is "tender," and the exact moment of transit is easily noted. On the other hand, when the objects lie tolerably close together, and the observer some little distance from them, it is difficult to discover when they are actually in one, and an error of 2° or 3° in consequence is quite possible.

Furthermore, when observing, be sure to take the compass bearing of the *back object*, which shifts but slowly, and note the reading at the instant the other object is seen to transit. The more rapid change in the bearing of the *near object*, renders it difficult to follow and get correctly at the proper moment. Sometimes, when *one* of the objects is indistinct, an assistant with a binocular to tell you when the objects are exactly "on" is a great help.

There are literally thousands of suitable marks all round our coasts; and a few are now given, which will be found convenient, especially by vessels navigating the George's, Bristol, or English Channels. Those marked thus * are only available in fine clear weather.

**List of useful transit marks.**

| Marks | Bearing | |
|---|---|---|
| Turret on pier and New Brighton church spire (River Mersey) | S. 88¾° W. | – |
| Rock lighthouse and New Brighton church spire | S. 35¼ W. | – |
| Great Orme Head lighthouse and Penmaen Mawr | S. 51¼ W. | – |
| *Penmaen Mawr and Carnedd Llewelyn | S. 28¾ W. | – |
| *Penmaen Mawr and Y Foel Fras | S. 23 W. | – |
| Tower on Puffin Island and Penmaen Mawr | S. 15¾ E. | + |
| *Moelfra Island and Snowdon | S. 4 W. | – |
| *Beacon on Dulas Rocks and Snowdon | S. 2¾ W. | – |
| *Point Lynas lighthouse and Snowdon | S. 1¼ W. | – |
| Point Lynas lighthouse and Penmaen Mawr | S. 31½ E. | + |
| *Middle Mouse and Snowdon | S. 9¼ E. | + |
| Middle Mouse and Point Lynas lighthouse | S. 57½ E. | + |
| Beacon on West Mouse and Coal Rock shore marks—three in one | S. 39¼ W. | – |
| *Beacon on West Mouse and Snowdon | S. 18½ E. | + |
| *Mount Pengarn and Snowdon | S. 20 E. | + |
| Skerries and South Stack lighthouses | S. 46½ W. | – |
| Skerries lighthouse and Pen Gybi (Holyhead Mountain) | S. 41½ W. | – |
| *Skerries lighthouse and Snowdon | S. 21 E. | + |
| Skerries lighthouse and Mount Pengarn | S. 30¼ E. | + |
| *Holyhead Breakwater lighthouse and Snowdon | S. 30 E. | + |
| *Pen Gybi (Holyhead Mountain) and Snowdon | S. 34½ E. | + |
| *South Stack lighthouse and Snowdon | S. 36¼ E. | + |
| *Pen Gybi (Holyhead Mountain) and Carnedd Llewelyn | S. 48½ E. | + |
| *South Stack lighthouse and Carnedd Llewelyn | S. 50 E. | + |
| Left xme of North Stack touching Breakwater lighthouse | S. 80¾ E. | + |
| *Mynydd Mawr and Snowdon | S. 68 E. | + |
| *Wicklow Head lighthouse and Lugnaquilla Mountain | N. 68¼ W. | + |
| *Wicklow Head lighthouse and Thonagee | N. 48 W. | + |
| *Wicklow Head lighthouse and Great Sugar Loaf | N. 5 W. | + |
| Wicklow Head Lighthouse and Little Sugar Loaf | N. 2¼ E. | – |

| | | |
|---|---|---|
| *Slieve Boy and Mount Leinster | N. 80¼ W. | + |
| *Arklow Rock and Crogan Hill | N. 55 W. | + |
| *Tara Hill and Crogan Hill | N. 12¼ W. | + |
| Tuskar lighthouse, Greenore windmill, and Forth Mountain | N. 41 W. | + |
| *Coningmore Rock and Slieve Coiltia | N. 15¼ W. | + |
| *Hook lighthouse (Waterford) and Tory Hill | N. 6¼ W. | + |
| *Tory Hill, seen between Brownstown Head towers | N. 18¾ E. | − |
| *Metal-man tower (Great Newton Head) and Tory Hill | N. 29¼ E. | − |
| *Minehead lighthouse and Knockmealdown Mountain | N. 18¼ W. | + |
| *Capel Island tower and Knockmealdown Mountain | N. 15¾ E. | − |
| *Ballycotton lighthouse and Knockmealdown Mountain | N. 28¼ E. | − |
| Right face of Dognose (Queenstown) and Roche Pt. lighthouse | S. 7½ W. | − |
| Left xmes of Weaver Point (known by its signal station) and Cork Head | S. 40 W. | − |
| Reanie's Head and Little Sovereign | S. 83¼ W. | − |
| Reanie's Head and Big Sovereign | S. 82 W. | − |
| Fastnet lighthouse and Mizen Peak | N. 36 W. | + |
| *Fastnet lighthouse and Hungry Hill | N. 2¼ E. | − |
| Man-of-War Sound white beacon, and Leamcon Tower | N. 23 E. | − |
| Fastnet lighthouse, and Leamcon tower open left of white beacon | N. 23¼ E. | − |
| *Left xme of Sheep Head and Hungry Hill | N. 39¼ E. | − |
| Calf Rock lighthouse and summit of Skariff Island | N. 21¾ E. | − |
| The Cow and summit of Skariff Island | N. 28¾ E. | − |
| The Bull and summit of Skariff Island | N. 35¾ E. | − |
| North Bishop Rock and Ramsay Hill | S. 10 E. | + |
| North Bishop Rock and Llaeithty Peak | S. 70¼ E. | + |
| Carreg Rhoson and Llaeithty Peak | S. 89¾ E. | + |
| Right xme of St. David's Head and Ramsay Hill | S. 48¾ W. | − |
| South Bishop lighthouse and Ramsay Hill | S. 80¾ E. | + |
| South Bishop lighthouse and Llaeithty Peak | N. 78¼ E. | − |
| South Bishop lighthouse and left xme of St. David's Head | N. 72¼ E. | − |
| South Bishop lighthouse and North Bishop Rock | N. 39¼ E. | − |
| Smalls lighthouse and Grassholme Island (highest part) | S. 73 E. | + |
| Smalls and S. Bishop lighthouses and xme of St. David's Head | N. 72¼ E. | − |
| Grassholme Island and S. Bishop lighthouse | N. 40¾ E. | − |
| South-West xmes of Skokham Island and St. Ann's Head | S. 58¼ E. | + |
| Great Castle Head range lights (Milford Haven) | N. 61¼ E. | − |
| St. Ann's Head range lights | N. 22¾ W. | + |
| Wolf and Longships lighthouses | N. 38¼ E. | − |
| Lizard lights | S. 81 E. | + |
| Killiganoon House and Penarrow Point (Falmouth) | N. 0¼ W. | + |
| Eddystone lighthouse, and chapel crowning Rame Head | N. 31¼ E. | − |
| " " and Picklecombe Fort | N. 40¼ E. | − |
| " " and Rifle Butt on Staddon Heights | N. 49¼ E. | − |
| South Foreland lights | N. 83¼ W. | + |
| Ushant lights, in one | S. 88 E. | + |
| Les Pierres Noires, and Pte. St. Mathieu | S. 81¼ E. | + |
| Ar Men Rk., and Tevennec (The Saints lights.) | S. 80 E. | + |
| Ar Men Rk., and Pte. du Raz (The Saints lights.) | S. 67 E. | + |
| Ar Men Rk., and Isle de Sein (The Saints lights.) | S. 65¾ E. | + |
| Isle de Sein, and Tevennec (The Saints lights.) | N. 76 E. | − |

**These bearings are all *correct magnetic*, and adapted to the year 1834. To adapt them to subsequent years, those in the N.E. and S.W. quadrants must be diminished,**

and those in the N.W. and S.E. quadrants increased, at the rate of 8′ per annum, or a degree in seven years. To facilitate the application of this correction, the proper sign has been placed after each bearing.

It may happen, however, when sailing along shore, that a distant conspicuous object presents itself which is laid down on the chart, but has nothing suitable to transit with it, in which case the Station Pointer comes in *very* handy. Select, in accordance with the rules laid down in the chapter on this instrument, three known and well-defined objects, and at the same instant that the ship's place is fixed by the horizontal sextant angles between them, let a third observer take the compass-bearing of the distant object, which may or may not be one of those already in use. Then lay off the ship's place on the chart with the Station Pointer, and, using Field's Parallel Ruler or the horn protractor, find therefrom the *true* bearing of the distant object. To this apply, as usual, the Variation at place *reduced for annual change,* which will give its *correct magnetic* bearing, in readiness to be compared with the observed *compass* bearing.

**Adjustment by bearing of one distant object.**

If the object chosen is a very distant one—say Snowdon in Wales, Sca Fell in Cumberland, Snae Fell in the Isle of Man, or Slieve Donard in the Co. Down (all visible from the Irish Channel) —a steamer may be slowed down, and steamed half round, so as to get the Deviation on every second point in that semicircle of the compass she would be most likely to use during the next few days. The half hour thus spent will not only conduce to the ship's safety generally, but may, if thick weather comes on, save many a half hour's groping about.

For new vessels requiring their compasses adjusted, or ships lying wind-bound in Belfast Lough, the following transit bearings observed by the writer, will be found of service. The *true* bearings, in most instances, were determined by Theodolite and sun, and converted into *corr. mag.* bearings for the year 1884, by applying the variation taken from the Admiralty Magnetic Chart of the World. The marks here given are very conspicuous, but to pick them out a stranger would in most cases require the assistance of some one locally acquainted.

Holywood Hill House, in one with

| | ° | |
|---|---|---|
| Power's House on Kinnegar and Bellevue, the three houses in one | S. 41¼ E. | + |
| Holywood Bank Pile Lighthouse | S. 85¼ E. | + |
| Holywood Episcopal Church Spire | S. 2¾ W. | – |
| Tudor Hall (centre) | S. 15¼ W. | – |

**Correct Magnetic Transit Bearings in Belfast Lough.**

GRAY'S HOUSE (HAZELBANK), in one with

| | ° |
|---|---|
| Glengormley Mill Chimney | N. 62 W. + |
| Carnmoney Summit (Δ) | N. 31½ W. + |

NOTE.—Glengormley chimney stands conspicuously in the saddle midway between Cavehill and Carnmoney summit. Hazelbank may easily be recognised by a walled-in garden close to shore, on west side of lawn. When house and chimney transit, the shore-road entrance is also about in the same line.

HOLYWOOD BANK PILE LIGHTHOUSE, in one with

| | ° |
|---|---|
| Strandtown Episcopal Church Tower | S. 25¾ W. – |
| Garmoyle Pile Lighthouse | S. 28 W. – |
| Albert Clock Tower (Belfast) | S. 56½ W. – |

MOSLEY MILL CHIMNEY, in one with

| | ° |
|---|---|
| Monkstown Mill Chimney | N. 44½ W. + |

NOTE.—Mosley chimney stands in centre of factory buildings; whilst Monkstown chimney (the nearer of the two in question) stands among trees, no building being visible about its base. A small red-brick house (supposed to be Jordanstown Railway Station) lies on the observer's side of the chimneys, and transits with them.

GREY POINT (xme), in one with

| | ° |
|---|---|
| Copeland Lighthouse | S. 76 E. + |
| Glenghana House | S. 61½ E. + |
| Mrs. Connor's Turret (flag-pole) | S. 55½ E. + |
| Foster Connor's House (Seacourt) | S. 51½ E. + |
| Tower of Carnalea House | S. 32¾ E. + |
| Mount Divis | S. 90 W. – |
| McArt's Fort (Cavehill) | N. 82½ W. + |

CARRICKFERGUS CASTLE, in one with

| | ° |
|---|---|
| Carnbilly Summit (Δ) | N. 30½ W. + |
| Carrick Church Spire | N. 16 W. + |
| Burleigh Hill House | N. 6½ W. + |

HELEN'S TOWER,* in one with

| | ° |
|---|---|
| Craigdarrah House | S. 18½ E. + |
| Clandeboye Coast Guard Station | S. 14½ E. + |
| Rockfield Cottage | S. 11½ E. + |
| Cramsie's Villa (turret) | S. 10 E. + |
| Clandeboye Railway Station (turret) | S. 9½ E. + |

* Helen's Tower—crowning a hill in the background—about 2½ miles S.W. of Bangor, is quite unmistakable, as is also Scrabo Monument, which lies about an equal distance further off, in the same direction.

| | | |
|---|---|---|
| **Pattison's House** | S. 7½ E. | + |
| **Centre of Helen's Bay Quarry** | S. 1¾ E. | + |
| **Crawfordsburn House** | S. 0¼ W. | – |
| **McNeill's Square Villa** | S. 11¾ W. | – |
| **Carnalea House (tower)** | S. 15 W. | – |
| **Ruin in Smelt Mill Bay** | S. 25 W. | – |
| **Foster Connor's House (Seacourt)** | S. 31¼ W. | – |
| **Cochrane's House** | S. 32 W. | – |
| **Cochrane's New Villas** | S. 33 W. | – |
| **Bangor Church Spire** | S. 41½ W. | – |
| **Presbyterian Church Steeple** | S. 43¾ W. | – |
| **Bangor Castle (turret)** | S. 46 W. | – |
| **Mrs. Connor's Turret (flag-pole)** | S. 46¼ W. | – |
| **Ulster Royal Yacht Club House** | S. 46¾ W. | – |
| **Stewart's House** | S. 48¼ W. | – |
| **Islet Hill Farm House** | S. 57½ W. | – |
| **Ballyholme Windmill** | S. 59½ W. | – |
| **Groomsport Presbyterian Church** | S. 62¼ W. | – |
| **Groomsport Irish Church** | S. 64 W. | – |
| **Maxwell's House, Groomsport** | S. 65½ W. | – |
| **Orlock Point Coast Guard Station** | S. 73¼ W. | – |
| **Copeland Lighthouse** | S. 75¾ W. | – |
| **Donaghadee Church** | N. 80 W. | + |
| **Killeghy Spire** | N. 64 W. | + |
| **Mill Isle Windmill** | N. 57¾ W. | + |
| **Carrowdore Church** | N. 44½ W. | + |

SCRABO MONUMENT, in one with

| | ° | |
|---|---|---|
| **Carnalea House (tower)** | S. 27¼ W. | – |
| **Cochrane's House** | S. 35¼ W. | – |
| **Helen's Tower** | S. 38 W. | – |
| **Bangor Church Spire** | S. 39 W. | – |
| **Ballyholme Windmill** | S. 49½ W. | – |
| **Islet Hill Farmhouse** | S. 49¾ W. | – |
| **Groomsport Irish Church** | S. 54 W. | – |
| **Copeland Lighthouse** | S. 66 W. | – |
| **Donaghadee Lighthouse** | S. 80¾ W. | – |
| **Killeghy Spire** | S. 86 W. | – |
| **Mill Isle Windmill** | N. 85 W. | + |
| **Carrowdore Church** | N. 69½ W. | + |

BALLYHOLME WINDMILL, in one with

| | ° | |
|---|---|---|
| **Foster Connor's House (Seacourt)** | S. 53½ E. | + |
| **Mrs. Connor's Turret (flag-pole)** | S. 37 E. | + |
| **Ulster Royal Yacht Club House (flag-pole)** | S. 29¾ E. | + |
| **Stewart's House** | S. 24½ E. | + |
| **Ladies' Bathing Hut** | S. 16½ E. | + |
| **Groomsport Presbyterian Church** | S. 69¼ W. | – |
| **Groomsport Irish Church** | S. 74½ W. | – |
| **Maxwell's House (Groomsport)** | S. 77½ W. | – |
| **Copeland Lighthouse** | S. 86 W. | – |

Presbyterian Church Steeple,* in one with

| | ° | |
|---|---|---|
| Cochrane's House ........................................ | S. 37⅛ E. | + |
| Foster Connor's House (Seacourt).......................... | S. 25 E. | + |
| Copeland Lighthouse ...................................... | S. 89¼ W. | − |

Bangor Church Spire, in one with

| | ° | |
|---|---|---|
| Ruin in Smelt Mill Bay ................................... | S. 21⅛ E. | + |
| Cochrane's House.......................................... | S. 1¾ E. | + |
| Foster Connor's House (Seacourt) ......................... | S. 2½ W. | − |
| Sea View House (Ritchie's) ............................... | S. 8¼ W. | − |
| Presbyterian Church Steeple .............................. | S. 58 W. | − |
| Ulster Royal Yacht Club Flag-pole ........................ | S. 58¼ W. | − |
| Stewart's House .......................................... | S. 63 W. | − |
| Ballyholme Windmill ...................................... | N. 86¼ W. | + |

**Note.—The variation in Belfast Lough in 1884 is estimated at 22°, and decreases about 1° in seven years.**

**Compasses unaccountably "jumping" a point or two.**

One sometimes hears wonderful stories of compasses suddenly "jumping a point or two," without actual alteration of the ship's head, and this is attributed to all sorts of fantastic causes, such as shallow water, attraction of the land, and so on. Some even go so far as to say that in the Red Sea, the sun beating fiercely on one side of the vessel in the morning, and on the other in the afternoon, will cause a change in the Deviation of several degrees. Very careful experiments made in that locality by the writer, have satisfied him on the impossibility of this latter supposition; and consequently, if the A.M. and P.M. azimuths disagree, or whenever these perplexing alterations take place, they will doubtless be due to some cause within the ship herself—such as *change of heel*, errors of centring, bent shadow-pins, loose iron placed in the 'tween decks or anywhere near the compass, boats' davits turned in that had previously been swung out, or some other simple but overlooked cause.

**Supposed causes.**

**Probable causes.**

**Wheelhouse Lockers.**

It is quite common in wheelhouses to find lockers close on each side of the compass, which are nominally for flags only, but in reality soon become a stowhole for quartermaster's gear. Have them taken down as quickly as possible.

**Deviation Cards unreliable.**

Because *Deviation Cards* are condemned in these pages, it is not to be understood that a properly kept *Compass Record* is worthless: on the contrary, the commander of every iron vessel should keep a daily account of the behaviour of his compasses.

* At present there are but two churches with spires in Bangor, and the Presbyterian one is the nearer of the two.

*Register of Deviations and Daily Comparison of Compasses on board the Steamship "British Crown," from Liverpool to Philadelphia.*

| Voyage No. 9. Date. 1880. | | Ship's Position | | Variation by Chart (corrected to date). | Ship's Head Corr. Mag. | Ship's Head by | | | Heel. | Deviations of | | | Body Observed | Remarks. |
|---|---|---|---|---|---|---|---|---|---|---|---|---|---|---|
| | | Lat. | Long. | | | Standard Compass. | Bridge Compass. | After Compass. | | Standard Comp's. | Bridge Compass. | After Compass. | | |
| ♄ September | 4 | 41¼° | 49¾° | −25° | N.71¼°W. | N.70°W. | N.72° W. | N.70° W. | 5° S. | −1¼° | +0¾° | −1¼° | ✱ Jupiter. ✱ Saturn. | Most excellent obs. and compars. |
| ☉ " | 5 | 41¼ | 54½ | −22⅓ | N.69 W. | N.70W. | N.72 W. | N.69 W. | 7 S. | +1 | +3 | None. | ⊙ | Good obs. & compars. |
| ☾ " | 6 | 41 | 58 | −21 | N.72¼W. | N.74W. | N.75½W. | N.72 W. | None. | +1¾ | +3¼ | −0¼ | ⊙ | Excellent " |
| ♂ " | 7 | 41 | 64 | −16 | N.74¼W. | N.76W. | N.76 W. | N.72½W. | 1 S. | +1¾ | +1¾ | −1¾ | ✱ Capella ✱ Arcturus | " " |

Note.—This form is just ⅗ the original size.
The entries under Ship's Head Corr. Mag. should always be made in red ink.

In regular Lines it will be found that the compasses of vessels that have already made several voyages on the one route, under similar circumstances will shew time after time pretty nearly the same deviations in the same localities. This, however, should not lead to neglect in observing azimuths, as nothing but constant watchfulness can ensure safety.

**Useful form of Compass Record.**

A form of Compass Record is here inserted, which those who try it will be sure to like. One need only run the eye down the deviation columns to see at a glance the action of each compass during any given period. Some men, on the contrary, set *deviation* altogether on one side, and to correct their courses take the difference between the *true* and *compass* bearing. This

**"Total Error."**

"Total error," as it is called, they also enter in their compass book, which is both meaningless and inconvenient. For "Total error" being compounded of *Variation* and deviation, must necessarily be a *constantly changing quantity;* and, therefore, a record of it is of no value until it has undergone a troublesome sifting process, which would better have been done in the first instance.

**Modes of finding Deviation from an Azimuth.**

There are two modes of determining the Deviation from an azimuth. One is used by Towson in his examples, but the writer much prefers the other, as tending to practise the navigator in the every-day application of Variation and Deviation to the true courses he may wish to steer.

| 1st Mode. | | 2nd Mode. | |
|---|---|---|---|
| ☉'s true bearing | S. 57° W. | ☉'s true bearing | S. 57° W. |
| ☉'s compass bearing | S. 84 W. | Variation per chart | 22 Wly. |
| Correction, or total error | 27 Wly. | ☉'s *correct magnetic* bearing | S. 79 W. |
| Variation per chart | 22 Wly. | ☉'s *compass* bearing | S. 84 W. |
| Deviation | 5° Wly. | Deviation | 5° Wly. |

The number of figures is the same in each case, but in the first mode an unnecessarily new process is originated; whereas in the mode advocated, the navigator is familiar with the term "Correct Magnetic," with the rule for naming the Deviation according as the *compass bearing* is to the right or left of the *correct magnetic bearing*, and has not to tax his memory with any fresh formula, this being very similar to the way he would set about turning a *true* course into one by *compass*. Thus:—

| | |
|---|---|
| True course - - - - - - | S. 57° W. |
| Variation per chart - - - - | 22 Westerly. |
| Correct magnetic course - - - | S. 79 W. |
| Deviation - - - - - - | 5 Westerly. |
| Compass course to steer - - - | S. 84° W. |

In the Compass Record suggested, after the date, &c., the comparisons are first jotted down; next the ship's head corr. mag. is entered in *red ink* by way of distinction, this important direction being got by applying the ascertained Deviation to the compass by which it was ascertained—generally the Standard. The Deviations of the remaining compasses are arrived at by simply taking the difference between the ship's head C.M. and the ship's head as shewn by each compass. The left-hand pages are left blank for remarks, &c. **Explanation of Compass Record.**

In the *Proceedings of the Royal Geographical Society* (No. III., Vol. XXII.) will be found a very interesting and instructive paper on the Earth's Magnetism, by Captain Sir F. J. Evans, R.N., K.C.B., Hydrographer to the Admiralty.* It embodies all that is known up to the present time, and is well worth perusal. **Valuable Paper on the Earth's Magnetism.**

Captain W. Barrett's very ingenious diagram will also be found useful to the student in compass adjustment, as giving a strikingly graphic representation of the terms into which the Deviation of the compass in iron ships may be separated. **Barrett's Deviation Diagram.**

There have been many discussions from time to time as to the propriety of adjusting compasses by magnets, some men contending that the better plan was to leave the compass to follow its own bent, and to navigate by the aid of a Table, giving the *natural* deviations: but iron is now so largely and *recklessly* used in deck fittings, &c., that compass errors have assumed a magnitude quite unknown when iron vessels first came into vogue. Formerly, also, more care was exercised in the selection of suitable positions for the compass, and the theory of adjustment was not so well understood. Thus it is that adjustment now cannot be dispensed with, or the majority of compasses would be quite unmanageable. Scarcely any one, now-a-days, will be found so ignorant as to advocate non-adjustment.

Sir George Airy, late Astronomer-Royal, thus sums up the advantages in favour of compass adjustment:— **Advantages of Compass Adjustment—Sir Geo. Airy.**

* Procurable from Dorrell & Son, 15, Charing Cross, London. Price One Shilling.

| "NON-CORRECTED COMPASSES. *Using a Table of Errors.* | "CORRECTED COMPASSES. *The Binnacle being adjustable.* |
|---|---|
| (1.) The directive power on the compass is extremely different on different courses. | (1.) The directive power on the needle is sensibly constant. |
| (2.) The principal part of the tabulated errors arises from sub-permanent magnetism, whose effects in producing Deviation vary greatly in different parts of the earth. | (2.) The magnets which perfectly correct the sub-permanent magnetism in one place, will also perfectly correct it in another. |
| (3.) It is therefore absolutely necessary, from time to time, to make a new table of errors, by observations in numerous positions (not fewer than eight) of the ship's head. | (3.) Only when there is suspicion of change in the ship's magnetism are new observations necessary, and then two are sufficient. |
| (4.) In difficult navigation, as in the channels of the Thames or the Mersey, especially with frequent tacks, the use of a Table of Errors would be attended with great danger." | (4.) In any hydrographical difficulty, the corrected compass is right on all tacks, and its use is perfectly simple." |

No. 2 of the above applies equally to the Deviation arising from the inductive magnetism of vertical iron.

## CHAPTER XIII.

### TO FIND THE ERROR AND RATE OF A CHRONOMETER.

Hitherto the recommendation has been to effect this by "Equal Altitudes" of the sun, A.M. and P.M., taken with the Artificial Horizon. This method, however, though short and simple, so far as the figures go, is open to many objections. The operation cannot be completed at one time, since several hours must elapse before the second half of the observations can be made. During this tedious interval, the conditions which existed in the morning may be considerably changed. For example, the refraction may have increased or diminished, owing to a shift of wind or fall of rain; the observer's "Personal Equation," as it is termed, may have varied; and the divisions of the sextant may have altered, through the effect of heat or cold in expanding or contracting the metal. **Equal Altitudes not recommended**

Raper says—"The method, even under the most favourable circumstances, can rarely be considered as affording extreme precision;" and all the things just mentioned tend to vitiate the accuracy of the result in a greater or less degree. Furthermore, the setting in of cloudy weather may cause the morning's work to be so much labour thrown away, by rendering impossible the corresponding P.M. altitudes; and, in any case, there is the inconvenience (sometimes very great) of a double journey to and fro the ship, and a repetition of chronometer comparing. It is true the A.M. sights could be used as "Absolutes," but every one accustomed to this sort of work knows the suspicion which attaches to observations taken only on one side of the meridian. **Disadvantages enumerated.**

The term "Personal Equation," though very familiar to astronomers, may be new to many sailors, so it is as well to explain it. **Personal Equation.**

It has been found that most men have a fixed habit of "making contact" either too soon or too late, depending for amount upon their peculiar nervous organization and bodily state at the time, whether of rest or fatigue, sickness or health. It is even found that an easy or constrained position of the individual at the moment of observation may exercise considerable effect on the result. Thus the excitable man, fearing to miss the event, is apt to forestall it; while the man of phlegmatic disposition is more likely to be too late. The human eye, in its measurement of distance, varies in different people. One man may consider the sun's limb to be just touching the horizon, whilst another, using the same sextant, will consider it a trifle above it; and a third be impressed with the idea that the sun is too low, and that both the others are wrong. No doubt, to this, as much as to instrumental errors, is to be attributed the difference among officers in the common operation of taking the sun at noon.

These may seem insignificant trifles to some, but the process of chronometer rating is itself a delicate one; and it must be remembered that, in the necessary splitting of seconds, we are dealing with quantities susceptible of the most minute influences.

The principle of finding the error of a Time-keeper by "Equal Altitudes" is, that the earth revolving at a uniform rate, equal altitudes of a fixed body on either side of the meridian will be found at equal intervals from the time of transit of that body over the meridian, and that, therefore, the mean of the times of such equal altitudes will give the time at transit, which for the sun is noon.

**How to eliminate Errors of Observation.**

The better mode—taken all round—is to observe stars east and west of the meridian, within a few minutes of each other—by which *all* systematic errors, whether atmospheric, instrumental, or personal, are practically neutralized in the *mean* result. Moreover, with "Equal Altitudes," it unavoidably happens, when the latitude and declination are of contrary names, that the sun being badly situated, from the slowness of its motion in altitude, cannot be expected to give good results. Now this need never be the case with the stars; a couple on or near the Prime Vertical, east and west, can always be found at some hour of the night, let the latitude be what it may. When selecting stars, choose those that have about the same altitude, and will therefore be equally affected by refraction. To avoid error due to a want of parallelism in the surfaces of the glass roof of the Artificial Horizon, reverse it for opposite stars, *so that the same side may, in*

**Reversal of Artificial Horizon.**

*every case, be next to you.** If the regular mercurial horizon is not to be had, an extempore one can easily be rigged up with a soup plate, and some oil or treacle. On a *calm* evening this makes an A1 substitute.

**Professor Knorre's method of observing Stars.**

In the observation of the altitude of a star with the Artificial Horizon, it is always troublesome to bring down the image of the star reflected from the sextant mirrors to the image reflected from the mercurial horizon, or *vice versâ;* and sometimes, when two bright stars stand near each other, there is danger of employing the reflected image of one of them for that of the other. A very simple method of avoiding this danger, and of facilitating the observation, has been suggested by Professor Knorre, of Russia.

"It can be proved geometrically, that whenever the direct and reflected images of any star are made to coincide in the field of view of the sextant, the index glass will be inclined at a constant angle to the horizon. (This angle is equal to the inclination of the sight-line of the telescope to the horizon glass.) If, therefore, we attach a small spirit level to the index arm, so as to make with the index glass an angle equal to this constant angle, the bubble of this level will play, whenever the two images of the same star are in coincidence, in the middle of the field of view.

"With a sextant thus furnished, we begin by directing the sight-line towards the image in the mercury; we next move the index until the bubble plays, taking care not to lose the image in the mercury. The reflected image from the sextant mirrors will then be found in the field, or will be brought there by a slight vibratory motion of the instrument about the sight-line.

"A sextant is easily fitted up on this principle, the level being made out of a small glass tube of little more than one inch in length. In sextants of the usual construction, the reading lens is attached to a stem that turns round a short pillar fixed at right angles to the index arm; in these cases, the level may be attached to the same pillar, rotating stiffly round it to admit of preparatory adjustment, and then fixed once for all in its proper position."†

**Chronometer rating in Suez Canal.**

When made fast for the night in the Suez Canal—now the great highway to the East—the writer has found it very convenient to ascertain the errors of his chronometers by the method above

* In taking "absolutes" or independent observations of the sun (not Equal Altitudes), the roof must be reversed when half way through the desired number.

† *Hints to Travellers; by a Committee of Council of the Royal Geographical Society.* London: Edward Stanford, 15, Charing Cross, S.W. Price 2/6.

advocated. The Admiralty plan gives the exact latitude and longitude of each end of the canal, from which, with a little care and neat-handedness, the geographical position of any other point may be determined. But for the convenience of those who may distrust their own measurements, a few positions are subjoined, from which others can more readily be fixed.

| | Latitude. ° ′ ″ | Longitude. ° ′ ″ |
|---|---|---|
| Port Said high lighthouse . . . . . . . | 31 15 45 N. . | 32 18 45 E. |
| The 25′ post at Kantara siding . . . . . | 30 50 45 N. . | 32 18 45 E. |
| Palace at Ismaïlia . . . . . . . . . | 30 35 30 N. . | 32 16 45 E. |
| The 52′ post at northern entrance to Great Bitter Lake . . . . . . . . . . | 30 25 45 N. . | 32 21 00 E. |
| The 74′ post near Chalouf . . . . . . . | 30 8 15 N. . | 32 34 24 E. |
| South Pier Head of Port Ibraham. . . . | 29 56 3 N. . | 32 33 12 E. |

**Principle of getting the correct G.M.T. by observation on shore.**

The correct latitude and longitude of a place being known, the principle of determining Greenwich Mean Time, whereby to ascertain the error of a chronometer, may be explained in a few words. Every navigator is aware that his daily sights give him the *Apparent Time at Ship*, and that by applying the Equation of Time he gets *Mean Time at Ship.* Of course the same thing applies to the determination of *Mean Time on Shore.* Now, if he knows (from the chart or otherwise) the exact longitude of the spot where he took his sights, and turns it into time, he has merely to add or subtract it (according as it is west or east) to or from this *Mean Time at Place*, to obtain at once the correct *Mean Time at Greenwich.* This, compared with the corresponding time by chronometer, gives its error, fast or slow, as the case may be.

**"Original Error," and "Accumulated Rate."**

Here it is necessary to be clear on one point. When this comparison is made of the Chronometer time with the Greenwich time, it is to be distinctly understood that the "*Original error*" and "*Accumulated rate*" are to be entirely disregarded, and not allowed to enter into this part of the calculation. The actual difference then existing between the Chronometer and Greenwich times is to be taken as a *new* original error—entirely independent of the first one, which is no longer to be employed. This is particularly dwelt upon, from the fact that many men compare the *corrected* Chronometer time with the Greenwich Mean Time, and in after work apply *both* errors, and even carry on the old rate, when they have all the materials for getting a new and more correct one.

**Rating Chronometers by sights at Sea.**

Sometimes, also, the error of the longitude by chronometer is found by the ordinary sights taken off an island or headland passed in the course of the voyage; and this error—say 12′—is improperly applied as a constant correction to all longitudes subsequently determined, instead of working out the error in *time* of the chronometer, and so arriving at the *sea rate* for future use.

With reference to this custom of taking sights at sea when the ship's position is fixed by cross-bearings of well-known land, it is certainly very useful as a rough check *if the vessel has been away from port for a considerable time:* for example, it might be done with advantage by a homeward East Indiaman when passing Cape Agulhas, or by an outward-bounder when passing St. Paul's rocks, near the equator.*

But if the chronometers have been *recently* rated on shore, the errors inseparable from such observations at sea would probably exceed the errors in the rate given by the maker. Thus many smart vessels pass Madeira when only a week out, and this might be considered a good opportunity for testing the chronometer rates; but though sights so taken might be useful in detecting gross errors, if such were suspected, *they could not be relied upon* under ordinary circumstances to give the time with the needful precision for *rating* purposes. More useful results might indeed be obtained if the vessel were becalmed, so as to combine P.M. with A.M. observations; or in the event of her passing in the afternoon a second point of land equally well determined with the first. In either case the mean of the two sets would perhaps give a fair approximation to the truth.

**Interval necessary for Rating.**

To find, on shore, the *rate* of a chronometer, its error on Mean Time must be known on two days, separated by an interval of not less than six, or more than ten days. Then the difference between the two errors, divided by the number of days in the interval, will give its daily rate for the time being. Where the interval is a long one, say a month or six weeks, during which the temperature has varied considerably, the *mean* daily rate is that which will be obtained, and may differ considerably from the performance of the chronometer at time of last observation. This goes to prove the necessity of adopting *Temperature rates*, as recommended by Mr. Hartnup.

To watch the performance of a chronometer on shore, it is not by any means necessary for the observer to know his longitude,

* Both these are very accurately determined positions:—

| | | |
|---|---|---|
| St. Paul's Rocks.......... | Lat. 0° 55′ 30″ N..... | Long. 29° 23′ 00″ W. |
| Cape Agulhas Lighthouse.. | Lat. 34° 49′ 46″ S..... | Long. 20° 0′ 36″ E. |

as the error of the chronometer on *Local* Mean Time is all that is wanted. It may be done also by simply noting the time of the successive disappearances of any star (not a *planet*) behind a smoothly-planed straight-edged board, nailed in a truly vertical position against some firm support. The observer's eye must be always at the same point, such as a small hole in a tin plate, also nailed to an immovable support, at a distance of say 30 or 40 feet from the board, and to the north or south of it, according to the particular star selected.

**Rating by Transit of Star.**

This is a very excellent practical method, and one capable of much precision. To carry it out, proceed as follows:—On any given evening, note the time by chronometer of the star's disappearance, which—from a star being a mere luminous point, without sensible diameter—is so sudden as to be at first quite startling; and after an interval, say of six days, do the same again. On account of a Sidereal day being shorter than a Mean Solar day, the star will disappear sooner each evening by 3m. 55·9s.; therefore multiply this quantity by the number of days between the observations, and subtract the result from the time shewn by chronometer at first observation.

If the chronometer is keeping exactly Mean Time, the first and second times will now agree; if they do not, the difference is the loss or gain of the chronometer. If the second time is greater than the first, it is evident the chronometer is gaining, and the difference divided by the number of days gives its daily rate.

EXAMPLE.

**Example of Rating by Star Transit.**

At Philadelphia, on October 16th, 1880, the star Fomalhaut was observed to disappear at 14h. 2m. 18·5s. by chronometer.

On Oct. 22nd the disappearance was timed at 13h. 38m. 34·0s. Required the daily rate of chronometer.

| | | H. M. S. | | M. S. |
|---|---|---|---|---|
| Oct. 16. | Star disappeared at - | 14 2 18·5 | | 3 55·9 |
| | | − 23 35·4 | | × 6 |
| | | 13 38 43·1 | | 23 35·4 |
| Oct. 22. | Star disappeared at - | 13 38 34·1 | | |
| | Loss in 6 days - - | 6) 9·0 ( | 1·5s. daily rate losing. | |
| | | 6 | | |
| | | 30 | | |
| | | 30 | | |

We will now give an example of finding the *Error* of a chronometer on Greenwich Mean Time by observations of stars east and west, taken with an Artificial Horizon on shore. The observations are *bonâ fide*, and selected at random from among quite a large number, taken on the same occasion. They were expressly made to determine the meridian distance between Valparaiso and Tongoy, the latter being a port of which the author was then engaged in making a trigonometrical survey.*

**To find the Error of a Chronometer by Stars East and West.**

Sunday, August 15th, 1875.—The following sights were taken at Valparaiso, in front of the Port Captain's office, in latitude 33° 2′ 8″ S., and longitude 4h. 46m. 32·1s. W.; Fort San Antonio being taken at 71° 38′ 00″ west of Greenwich. Index error + 1′ 30″. Chronometer, from previous observations at Arica, assumed to be 51·6s. slow of Greenwich Mean Time.

⁎ Spica, bearing about N. 88° W. true.

| | H. | M. | S. |
|---|---|---|---|
| Time by chronometer - - - - | 13 | 3 | 32·0 |
| Assumed error - - - - - - - | | + | 51·6 |
| G.M.T., August 15th - - - - - | 13 | 4 | 23·6 |

| | ° | ′ | ″ |
|---|---|---|---|
| Observed angle ⁎ Spica - - - - | 46 | 51 | 10 |
| Index error - - - - - - - - - - | + | 1 | 30 |
| | 2 ) 46 | 52 | 40 |
| ⁎'s apparent altitude - - - - - | 23 | 26 | 20 |
| Refraction (Table XVIII. of *Norie*) | — | 2 | 10 |
| ⁎'s true altitude - - - - - - - - | 23 | 24 | 10 |

| | ° | ′ | ″ | | |
|---|---|---|---|---|---|
| | 90 | | | | |
| ⁎'s Declination | 10 | 30 | 41 S. | | |
| Polar distance - | 79 | 29 | 19 | Cosecant | 0·007350 |
| Latitude - - - | 33 | 2 | 8 | Secant - | 0·076584 |
| Altitude - - - | 23 | 24 | 10 | | |
| | 135 | 55 | 37 | | |
| Half sum - - | 67 | 57 | 49 | Cosine - | 9·574257 |
| Remainder - - | 44 | 33 | 39 | Sine - - | 9·846130 |
| | | | | | 9·504321 |

| | H. | M. | S. |
|---|---|---|---|
| Sidereal time at G.M. noon, Aug. 15th - - - - - - - - - | 9 | 33 | 56·83 |
| Acceleration for 13h. - - - - - - | + | 2 | 8·13 |
| ,, ,, 4m. - - - - - - - | + | | ·66 |
| ,, ,, 24s. - - - - - - - | + | | ·06 |
| Right Ascension of mean ☉ - - | 9 | 36 | 5·68 |

| | H. | M. | S. | |
|---|---|---|---|---|
| 9·504321 = Star's hour ∠ - - - | 4 | 35 | 18·00 | W. |
| ⁎'s Right Ascension | 13 | 18 | 37·61 | |
| Right Ascension of the meridian - - | 17 | 53 | 55·61 | or Sidereal time |
| Right Ascension of the mean ☉ - - - | 9 | 36 | 5·68 | at place. |
| Mean time at place - - - - - - - | 8 | 17 | 49·93 | P.M. |
| Longitude of observation spot - - - | 4 | 46 | 32·10 | W. |
| Mean time at Greenwich - - - - - | 13 | 4 | 22·03 | |
| Time by chronometer - - - - | 13 | 3 | 32·00 | |
| | | | S. | |
| Chronometer slow of G.M. time - - | | | 50·03 | |

For an explanation of the term Right Ascension of the Mean ☉ refer back to page 255.

Fomalhaut, the other star of the pair, is worked out on the next page in a manner exactly similar to the foregoing: its hour angle, however, being East, has to be *subtracted* instead of added.

* The plan of Tongoy, with others from the same source, has since been published by the Hydrographic Office of the Admiralty.

✱ Fomalhaut, bearing about S. 72° E. true.

| | H. M. S. |
|---|---|
| Time by chronometer | 13 20 00·0 |
| Assumed error | + 51·6 |
| G.M.T., August 15th | 13 20 51·6 |

| | ° ′ ″ |
|---|---|
| Observed angle ✱ Fomalhaut | 62 53 20 |
| Index error | + 1 30 |
| | 2 ) 62 54 50 |
| ✱'s apparent altitude | 31 27 25 |
| Refraction (Table XVIII. of *Norie*) | — 1 32 |
| ✱'s true altitude | 31 25 53 |

| | ° ′ ″ | | |
|---|---|---|---|
| | 90 | | |
| ✱'s Declination | 30 16 46 S. | | |
| Polar distance | 59 43 14 | Cosecant | 0·063699 |
| Latitude | 33 2 8 | Secant | 0·076584 |
| Altitude | 31 25 53 | | |
| | 124 11 15 | | |
| Half sum | 62 5 37 | Cosine | 9·670272 |
| Remainder | 30 39 44 | Sine | 9·707550 |
| | | | 9·518105 = ✱'s hour ∠ |

| | H. M. S. |
|---|---|
| Sidereal time at G.M. noon, Aug. 15th | 9 33 56·83 |
| Acceleration for 13h. | + 2 8·13 |
| " " 20m. | + 3·23 |
| " " 52s. | + 14 |
| Right Ascension of mean ☉ | 9 36 8·33 |

| | H. M. S. | |
|---|---|---|
| ✱'s hour ∠ | 4 40 20 60 | E. |
| ✱'s Right Ascension | 22 50 48·00 | |
| Right Ascension of the meridian | 18 10 27·60 | or Sidereal time at place. |
| Right Ascension of the mean ☉ | 9 36 8·33 | |
| Mean time at place | 8 34 19 12 | P.M. |
| Longitude of observation spot | 4 46 32·10 | W. |
| Mean time at Greenwich | 13 20 51·22 | |
| Time by chronometer | 13 20 00·00 | |
| | S. | |
| Chronometer slow of G.M. time | 51·22 | |

Both stars—Spica especially—were favourably situated in azimuth, and their very close agreement (the difference amounting only to 1·19s.) proves conclusively that not only were the altitudes and times accurately observed, but that all the conditions must have been normal.

The mean of the two results gives 50·62s. as the error of the chronometer on August 15th.

At Arica, on August 7th, the same chronometer was 46·40s. slow of G.M.T., shewing that in the interval of 8 days it had lost 4·22s., equal to a daily rate of 0·53s.

It will be noticed that in comparing the Chronometer time of observation with the Greenwich Mean Time of observation, the *original error* 51·6s. was not taken into account. At the commencement of the calculation, however, it was used to get the *Greenwich date* as closely as possible, whereby to reduce correctly any of the data requiring it, such as the Sidereal Time at Greenwich mean noon, &c.

It is evident that if the chronometer error were neglected, when at all large, many of the elements used in the calculation would be inaccurate. This is less the case, however, with the stars (which may be regarded as fixed) than it would be with the sun or planets. In the case of the moon, which alters its Declination and Right Ascension very rapidly, the error would be excessive. For this and other reasons the moon is never used in this connection.

In the Suez Canal, under certain conditions, sights may very well be taken on board ship, and when this can be done it is of course much more convenient and pleasant than squatting down on a sandhill. Acting on the suggestion of Captain Lee of the Transport "Capella," the writer tried this several times during the war in Egypt, and got results in every way satisfactory.*

As a stand for the Artificial Horizon, a small table was placed close over on the starboard side of the saloon deck, and the observer was comfortably seated in a chair with a Quarter Master standing by with a bull's eye lamp, kept dark till required for reading off. The 2nd officer sat *behind* the observer (back to back), with the chronometer and lamp facing him on a third chair. In this way three sets (of three in a set) were taken of the Eastern star, and after shifting the gear over to the port side, a similar number were taken of the western star.

To make this plan possible, it is necessary to wait till all hands have turned in, as the most cautious footfall on deck is at once revealed by the star's image dancing in the quicksilver: even the donkey engine for feeding the boilers must be stopped for the time-being. If there is any wind, the Artificial Horizon and observer may be sheltered by a weather-cloth, rigged up for the purpose; and, with the awning overhead, you are as comfortable as in a regular observatory—*always barring the Musquitoes.*

About 11 o'clock P.M. Wednesday, September 20th, 1882, the following sights were taken on board Her Majesty's Transport *British Prince*, then moored for the night to the west bank of the Suez Canal, midway between mile posts 36·6 and 36·7. This position when laid off on the Admiralty plan gave the latitude 30° 39′ 30″ N., and the longitude 32° 20′ 00″ E. Index error − 40″. Chronometer, from previous observations taken on the mole at Alexandria, assumed to be 2m. 14s. slow of G.M.T.

* Mr. H. S. Blackburne, of the P. & O. steamer "*Carthage*," mentions, in his "A and B Tables for Correcting the Longitude," having repeatedly tried this plan with complete success.

### ✱ Saturn, bearing N. 87¼° E. true.

| | H. M. S. |
|---|---|
| Time by chronometer | 9 10 14·5 |
| Assumed error | + 2 14·0 |
| G.M.T., September 20th | 9 12 28·5 |

| | ° ′ ″ |
|---|---|
| Observed angle ✱ Saturn | 61 2 30 |
| Index Error | − 40 |
| | 2)61 1 50 |
| Saturn's apparent altitude | 30 30 55 |
| Refraction (Table XVIII. of *Norie*) | − 1 37 |
| Saturn's true altitude | 30 29 18 |

| | ° ′ ″ | | |
|---|---|---|---|
| Polar distance | 73 00 20 | Cosecant | 0·019391 |
| Latitude | 30 39 30 | Secant | 0·065339 |
| Altitude | 30 29 18 | | |
| | 134 9 8 | | |
| Half sum | 67 4 34 | Cosine | 9·590516 |
| Remainder | 36 35 16 | Sine | 9·775285 |
| | | | 9·450581 |

| | H. M. S. |
|---|---|
| Sidereal Time at G.M. noon, September 20th | 11 57 5·86 |
| Acceleration for 9h. 12m. 29s. | + 1 30·76 |
| Right ascension of mean ☉ | 11 58 36·62 |

| | H. M. S. |
|---|---|
| 9·450581 = Saturn's hour angle | 4 16 42·8 E. |
| Saturn's reduced Right Ascension | 3 37 7·8 |
| Right Ascension of the meridian | 23 20 25·0 |
| Right Ascension of the mean ☉ | 11 58 36·6 |
| Mean Time at ship | 11 21 48·4 P.M. |
| Longitude of ship in time | 2 9 20·0 E. |
| Mean Time at Greenwich | 9 12 28·4 |
| Time shewn by chronometer | 9 10 14·5 |
| | M. S. |
| By ✱ Saturn, chronometer slow of G.M.T. | 2 13·9 |

So much for the eastern star, now we will see what the western one says.

### ✱ Altair, bearing S. 81° W. true.

| | H. M. S. |
|---|---|
| Time by chronometer | 9 29 57·8 |
| Assumed error | + 2 14·0 |
| G.M.T., Sept. 20th | 9 32 11·8 |

| | ° ′ ″ |
|---|---|
| Observed angle ✱ Altair | 62 20 00 |
| Index error | − 40 |
| | 2)62 19 20 |
| Altair's apparent altitude | 31 9 40 |
| Refraction (Table XVIII. of *Norie*) | − 1 34 |
| Altair's true altitude | 31 8 6 |

| | ° ′ ″ | | |
|---|---|---|---|
| Polar distance | 81 26 9 | Cosecant | 0·004870 |
| Latitude | 30 39 30 | Secant | 0·065339 |
| Altitude | 31 8 6 | | |
| | 143 13 45 | | |
| Half sum | 71 36 53 | Cosine | 9·498869 |
| Remainder | 40 28 47 | Sine | 9·812364 |
| | | | 9·381492 |

| | H. M. S. |
|---|---|
| Sidereal Time at G.M. noon, September 20th | 11 57 5·86 |
| Acceleration for 9h. 32m. 12s. | + 1 33·97 |
| Right Ascension of mean ☉ | 11 58 39·83 |

| | H. M. S. |
|---|---|
| 9·381492 = Altair's hour angle | 3 55 3·0 W. |
| Altair's R.A. | 19 45 5·0 |
| Right Ascension of the meridian | 23 40 8·0 |
| Right Ascension of the mean ☉ | 11 58 39·8 |
| Mean Time at ship | 11 41 28·2 P.M. |
| Longitude of ship in time | 2 9 20·0 E. |
| Mean Time at Greenwich | 9 32 8·2 |
| Time shewn by chronometer | 9 29 57·8 |
| | M. S. |
| By ✱ Altair, chronometer slow of G.M.T. | 2 10·4 |

The mean of the two results gives 2m. 12·2s. as the error of the chronometer on September 20th. Seven days afterwards, when at Malta, the Greenwich Mean Time, carried on from these observations, was found to differ only a second and a half from the Time Ball.

Where delicate observations are required, the planets Jupiter and Venus are out of the running, from the fact that they are so very much bigger and brighter than the mere speck which a star presents; the latter, therefore, is to be preferred, but in this, as in many other matters, external circumstances control our wishes, and it is often a case of do-with-what-you-can-get without being too fastidious: or in other words, be thankful for the bread even if it is not buttered. On this account it is deemed advisable to give an example shewing the working of a planet, which it will be noticed is precisely the same as the working of a fixed star, if we except the necessity for reducing the Declination and Right Ascension to the Greenwich Mean Time of Observation. In the case of Saturn the reduction is very small.

**A number of observations should be worked out separately.**

When several altitudes of each star have been taken, which is the proper thing to do, they should be worked out *separately*, and not in groups, or sets, of three or five. By so doing, palpable mistakes in reading off the sextant, or taking the time, &c., declare themselves at the finish, and the particular observations which contain them, if incapable of adjustment, can be rejected *in toto*. It is true this very materially increases the labour of calculation, but the man who strives to be accurate will not grudge it. Having thrown out the bad ones, the mean results of the remainder will then be reliable.

**Time Signals.**

Since the recent telegraphic determination of the longitude of the principal places on the globe, Time signals have been established at a great number of ports for the benefit of shipping. Annexed will be found a complete list. When the signal is made by gun fire, the time of the *flash* must be noted; but if from any cause this cannot be seen, it will be necessary to fall back upon the *report*. In which case, allow for the velocity of sound in air at the rate of 1,093 feet per second, when the thermometer registers 32° Fahr. As the temperature increases, the velocity increases at the rate of 1·11 of a foot for each degree, decreasing in the same proportion for temperatures lower than 32°. Thus at 55° Fahr. we have the velocity = 1,118 feet per second, and at 80° Fahr. it is 1,146 feet per second. Taking into account so many facilities, the error in the Greenwich Mean Time of any sailing ship should

**Flash and Report of Time-Gun.**

**Velocity of Sound in Air.**

never exceed 20s., and in steamers should certainly not amount to half this quantity.

Time signal arrangements vary much at different places, as may be seen by reference to the Table, and it is of importance that those desirous of profiting by them should make themselves fully acquainted, by enquiry from the proper authorities, with the exact nature of the local regulations concerning them. At many ports, the error (if any) in making the signal is published in the next day's papers; here, for example, is a specimen cut out of the New York "World."

WESTERN UNION TIME-BALL.

NEW YORK, February 22.—The time-ball on the Broadway tower of the Western Union Telegraph Company's building, which is dropped at New York noon (12h. 0m. 0s.) by the standard time of the United States Naval Observatory at Washington, was dropped to-day exactly at noon.

New York, east of Washington, 0h 12m. 10·47s.
New York, west of Greenwich, 4h. 56m. 1·65s.

The Harbour Master's office is generally the best place to institute enquiry.

## TIME SIGNALS.

| Place. | Signal. | Position of Signal. Latitude. | Longitude. | Local Mean Time of Signal. | Greenwich Mean Time of Signal. | Remarks. |
|---|---|---|---|---|---|---|
| | | | | H. M. S. | H. M. S. | |
| Greenwich .......... | Ball | Royal Observatory | | 1 00 00·0 P.M. | 1 00 00·0 P.M. | |
| Hull .............. | .. | .. | .. | 10 00 00·0 A.M. | 10 00 00·0 A.M. | |
| Deal ............... | Ball | Royal Naval Yard | | 1 00 00·0 P.M. | 1 00 00·0 P.M. | |
| Dover ............. | Gun | Fort on Heights | | Noon. | Noon. | |
| Portsmouth ........ | Ball | Royal Dockyard | | 1 00 00·0 P.M. | 1 00 00·0 P.M. | |
| Cardiff............. | Ball | .. | .. | 10 00 00·0 A.M. | 10 00 00·0 A.M. | |
| Plymouth .......... | Cone | Mount Wise, Devonport | | 1 00 00·0 P.M. | 1 00 00·0 P.M. | Repeated five minutes later. |
| " .......... | " | " | " | 1 5 00·0 P.M. | 1 5 00·0 P.M. | |
| West Hartlepool .... | Gun | .. | .. | 1 00 00·0 P.M. | 1 00 00·0 P.M. | |
| Birkenhead ........ | Gun | Morpeth Dock, Pier Head | | 1 00 00·0 P.M. | 1 00 00·0 P.M. | |
| Swansea ........... | Gun | .. | .. | 1 00 00·0 P.M. | 1 00 00·0 P.M. | |
| North Shields ...... | Gun | .. | .. | 1 00 00·0 P.M. | 1 00 00·0 P.M. | |
| Sunderland ........ | Ball | .. | .. | 1 00 00·0 P.M. | 1 00 00·0 P.M. | Private enterprise. |
| Edinburgh .......... | Gun | Edinburgh Castle | | 1 00 00·0 P.M. | 1 00 00·0 P.M. | |
| Dundee ........... | Gun | .. | .. | 1 00 00·0 P.M. | 1 00 00·0 P.M. | |
| Glasgow ........... | Gun | .. | .. | 1 00 00·0 P.M. | 1 00 00·0 P.M. | |
| Dublin.............. | Ball | .. | .. | 0 34 38 P.M. | 1 00 00·0 P.M. | |
| Cork .............. | Gun | .. | .. | 0 34 38 P.M. | 1 00 00·0 P.M. | |
| Queenstown ........ | Gun | .. | .. | 0 34 38 P.M. | 1 00 00·0 P.M. | |
| Toulon.............. | Ball | Observatory in N.W. part of town | | 11 00 00·0 A.M. | 10 36 18·6 A.M. | Repeated two minutes later. |

## TIME SIGNALS—*continued.*

| Place. | Signal. | Position of Signal. Latitude. | Position of Signal. Longitude. | Local Mean Time of Signal. | Greenwich Mean Time of Signal. | Remarks. |
|---|---|---|---|---|---|---|
| | | | | H. M. S. | H. M. S. | |
| Toulon | Ball | Observatory in N.W. part of town | | 11 2 00·0 A.M. | 10 38 18·6 A.M. | |
| Brest | Flag | Nautical School Observatory | | Mean noon. | 0 17 58·4 P.M. | |
| Cherbourg | Disc | Marine Observatory | | 11 44 6·5 A.M. | 11 50 89·0 A.M. | Disc falls at Paris mean noon. |
| L'Orient | Ball | Harbour Tower | | Mean noon. | 0 13 25·1 P.M. | |
| Fouras, R. Charente Basque Roads | Ball | Pier of Fouras, North Harbour | | 11 58 27·0 A.M. | 0 2 50·4 P.M. | Repeated at 0 0 27·0 P.M. =0 4 50·4 G.M.T. |
| Rochefort | Ball | St. Louis Tower | | 11 59 00·0 A.M. | 0 2 50·4 P.M. | Repeated at 0 1 0·0 P.M. =0 4 50·4 G.M.T. |
| Wilhelmshaven | Ball | East Tower of Observatory | | Mean noon. | 11 27 24·8 A.M. | |
| Bremerhaven | Ball | 53° 33′ 00″ N. | 8° 34′ 7″ E. | Mean noon. | 11 25 43·5 A.M. | Repeated. |
| ,, | ,, | ,, | ,, | 0 34 16·5 P.M. | Mean noon. | |
| Cuxhaven | Ball | 53° 52′ 00″ N. | 8° 42′ 30″ E. | Mean noon. | 11 25 10·0 A.M. | Repeated. |
| ,, | Ball | ,, | ,, | 0 34 50·0 P.M. | Mean noon. | |
| Hamburgh | Ball | 53° 32′ 30″ N. | 9° 58′ 57″ E. | 0 39 53·7 P.M. | Mean noon. | |
| Hellevoetsluis | Discs | 51° 49′ 19″ N. | 4° 7′ 40″·5 E. | Mean noon. | 11 43 29·2 A.M. | |
| Nieu Diep | Discs | 52° 57′ 50″ N. | 4° 46′ 36″ E. | Mean noon. | 11 40 58 6 A.M. | |
| Swinemunde | Ball | 53° 54′ 37″ N. | 14° 16′ 4″ E. | Mean noon. | 11 2 55·7 A.M. | Repeated. |
| ,, | ,, | ,, | ,, | 0 57 4·3 P.M. | Mean noon. | |
| Kiel | Ball | 54° 20′ 30″ N. | 10° 8′ 52″ E. | Mean noon. | 11 19 24·5 A.M. | |
| Newfahrwassen | Ball | 54° 24′ 24″ N. | 18° 39′ 48″ E. | Mean noon. | 10 45 20·8 A.M. | |

# TIME SIGNALS—*continued.*

| Place. | Signal. | Position of Signal. | | Local Mean Time of Signal. | Greenwich Mean Time of Signal. | Remarks. |
|---|---|---|---|---|---|---|
| | | Latitude. | Longitude. | H. M. S. | H. M. S. | |
| Flushing, Walcheren Island ............ | Discs | 51° 26′ 33″ N. | 3° 35′ 48″ E. | Mean noon. | 11 45 36·8 A.M. | |
| Rotterdam ........ | Discs | 51° 54′ 30″·2 N. | 4° 28′ 50″·5 E. | Mean noon. | 11 42 4·6 A.M. | On Tower of Yacht Club Buildings. |
| St. Petersburgh .... | Gun | 59° 56′ 30″ N. | 30° 18′ 20″ E. | Mean noon. | 9 58 41 4 A.M. | |
| Nicolaev .......... | Ball | At the Observatory | | Mean noon. | 9 52 4·9 A.M. | |
| Kronstadt .......... | Ball | 59° 59′ 24″ N. | 29° 45′ 54″ E. | Mean noon. | 10 00 56·7 A.M. | |
| Trondhjem.......... | Drum | Staff on roof of Observatory | | Mean noon. | 11 18 11·3 A.M. | |
| Bergen ............ | Ball | N.E. corner of Observatory | | Mean noon. | 11 38 45·0 A.M. | Saturdays only. |
| Christiania ........ | Ball | On roof of Observatory | | Mean noon. | 11 17 6·3 A.M. | Wednesday and Saturday. |
| Stockholm .......... | Ball | 59° 19′ 10″ N. | 18° 4′ 42″ E. | 1 12 18·8 P.M. | Mean noon. | |
| Gothenburg ........ | Ball | School of Navigation | | 0 47 52·0 P.M. | Mean noon. | |
| Copenhagen ........ | Ball | 55° 40′ 42″ N. | 12° 34′ 48″ E. | 1 00 00·0 P.M. | 0 9 40·8 P.M. | |
| Elsinore ............ | Ball | Entrance to Harbour | | 0 50 29·6 P.M. | Mean noon. | |
| Lisbon .............. | Ball | Marine Observatory | | 1 00 00·0 P.M. | 1 36 33·6 P.M. | |
| Cadiz .............. | Ball | 36° 27′ 40″ N. | 6° 12′ 24″ W. | 1 00 00·0 P.M. | 1 24 49·6 P.M. | |
| Gibraltar .......... | Ball | Signal Tower on Summit of Rock | | 9 38 34·2 A.M. | 10 00 00·0 A.M. | Dropped automatically by current direct from Greenwich. |
| Genoa .............. | Gun | Fort Castellacio | | Mean noon. | 11 24 18·6 A.M. | |
| Pola ................ | Ball and Gun | S.W. Bastion of the Harbour Castle | | Mean noon. | 11 4 36·5 A.M. | |
| Fiume .............. | Gun and Ball | Staff at end of Mole | | Mean noon. | 11 2 13·1 A.M. | |

## TIME SIGNALS—*continued.*

| Place. | Signal. | Position of Signal. | | Local Mean Time of Signal. | Greenwich Mean Time of Signal. | Remarks. |
|---|---|---|---|---|---|---|
| | | Latitude. | Longitude. | | | |
| | | | | H. M. S. | H. M. S. | |
| Trieste ............ | Ball and Gun | N.W. side of Lighthouse | | Mean noon | 11 4 58·2 A.M. | |
| Malta .............. | Ball | Port Captain's Office | | Mean noon. | 11 1 55·0 A.M. | |
| Alexandria ........ | Ball | .. | .. | Enquire. | Enquire. | |
| New York .......... | Ball | Western Union Telegraph Office, 195, Broadway | | Mean noon. | 4 56 1·7 P.M. | Error (if any stated daily in *New York Herald.* |
| " ............ | " | Equitable Life Assurance Co. | | Exactly at every hour of G.M.T. throughout the day. | | |
| Philadelphia ...... | Ball | Union Telegraph Office, Walnut Street | | Enquire. | Enquire. | |
| Boston ............ | Ball | Equitable Life Assurance Co. | | Mean noon | 4 44 15·5 P.M. | By signal from Harward College Observatory. |
| Washington ........ | Ball | Naval Observatory | | Mean noon | 5 18 12·1 P.M. | |
| St. John's, Newfoundland .. | Gun | Near Block House on Signal Hill | | Mean noon | 3 30 43·0 P.M. | |
| St. John, New Brunswick .. | Ball | New Custom House | | 1 00 00·0 P.M. | 5 24 15·0 P.M. | |
| Quebec ............ | Ball | At the Citadel | | 1 00 00 0 P.M. | 5 44 50·3 P.M. | Ball dropped by electricity from the Observatory |
| Montreal .......... | Ball | Harbour Commissioners' Building | | Mean noon | 4 54 13·0 P.M. | Ball dropped by electricity from the Observatory |
| Paramaribo ........ | Disc | 5° 49′ 30″ N. | 55° 9′ 54″ W. | Mean noon | 3 40 39·7 P.M. | Main yard-arm of Guard Ship. |
| Bermuda .......... | Ball | Ireland Island. Flagstaff on Western Jetty | | Mean noon | 4 19 26·2 P.M. | Saturdays only. |
| St. Anne, Curacoa . | Red flag | 12° 6′ 45″ N. | 68° 56′ 44″ W. | Mean noon | 4 35 46·9 P.M. | |
| Demerara .......... | Ball | Flagstaff near General Post Office | | Mean noon | 3 52 46·0 P.M. | Wednesday and Saturday. |
| St. Paul de Loando . | .. | .. | .. | 1 00 00·0 P.M. | Enquire. | |
| Cape Coast Castle .. | Ball | 5° 5′ 25″ S. | 1° 12′ 05″ 0 W. | Enquire. | Enquire. | |

## TIME SIGNALS—*continued.*

| Place. | Signal. | Position of Signal. | | Local Mean Time of Signal. | Greenwich Mean Time of Signal. | REMARKS. |
|---|---|---|---|---|---|---|
| | | Latitude. | Longitude. | | | |
| | | | | H. M. S. | H. M. S. | |
| Ascension .......... | Ball | Flagstaff at Master's Cottage, Southward of Hayes Hill | | 0 2 18·0 P.M. | 1 00 00·0 P.M. | |
| St. Helena.......... | Ball | James Town Valley | | Mean noon. | 0 22 50·0 P.M. | Also at flagstaff on Ladder Hill. |
| " .......... | " | Ladder Hill | | 0 37 10·0 P.M. | 1 00 00·0 P.M. | |
| Rio de Janeiro...... | Ball | Imperial Observatory 22° 54′ 24″ S. | 43° 10′ 21″ W. | Mean noon | 2 52 41·4 P.M. | |
| Cape Town* ........ | Gun | On Imhoff Battery | | 1 00 00·0 P.M. | 11 46 5·3 A.M. | |
| " .......... | Gun | Entrance of Alfred Dock | | Mean noon | 10 46 5·3 A.M. | See footnote |
| Simon's Bay ........ | Disc | 34° 11′ 30″ S. | 18° 25′ 45″·0 E. | 0 59 48·3 P.M. | 11 46 5·3 A.M. | The Disc falls at 1 o'clock, *Cape Observatory time* |
| Algoa Bay .......... | Disc | Lighthouse, Port Elizabeth | | 1 28 34·6 P.M. Lady Donkin's Monument. | 11 46 5 3 A.M. | The Disc falls at 1 o'clock, *Cape Observatory time* |
| Port Alfred ........ | Ball | .. | .. | 1 33 41·9 P.M. | 11 46 5·3 A.M. | Do. Do. |
| East London........ | Ball | .. | .. | Enquire. | Enquire. | |
| Durban, Natal ...... | Ball | .. | .. | Enquire. | Enquire. | |
| Port Louis, Mauritius ........ | Ball | Signal Mountain | | 1 00 00·0 P.M. | 9 9 46·0 A.M. | Monday, Wednesday, and Friday only. |
| Melbourne .......... | Ball | Gellibrand Point, Williamstown | | 1 00 00·0 P.M. | 3 20 5·2 A.M. | |
| " .......... | Ball | Telegraph Office, Geelong | | 1 00 00·0 P.M. | 3 20 5·2 A.M. | |
| " .......... | Flag | At Signal Station, Queenscliff | | 1 00 00·0 P.M. | 3 20 5·2 A.M. | |
| Adelaide .......... | Ball | At the Semaphore | | 1 00 00·0 P.M. | 3 45 30·0 A.M. | |

* True Local Time is also shewn by a clock at dock entrance. It is controlled from the Observatory by electricity, and is consequently extremely useful for getting G.M.T. and for rating chronometers. The first stroke of the bell in the clock tower may be relied on as a true signal of Local Mean Time. The Royal Observatory is 1h. 13m. 54·74s. East of Greenwich.

## TIME SIGNALS—*continued.*

| Place. | Signal. | Position of Signal. | | Local Mean Time of Signal. | Greenwich Mean Time of Signal. | Remarks. |
|---|---|---|---|---|---|---|
| | | Latitude. | Longitude. | | | |
| | | | | H. M. S. | H. M. S. | |
| Sydney, N.S.W. .... | Ball | 33° 51′ 54″ S. | 151° 12′ 42″ E. | 1 00 00·0 P.M. | 2 55 9·2 A.M. | |
| Auckland ......... | .. | .. | .. | 1 00 00·0 P.M. | Enquire. | |
| Hobart Town, Tasmania ........ | Ball | 42° 53′ 32″ S. | 147° 21′ 13″ E. | 1 00 00·0 P.M. | 3 10 35 A.M. | Also Gun. |
| Newcastle, N.S.W... | Ball | 32° 55′ 50″ S. | 151° 48′ 21″ E. | 1 00 00 0 P.M. Sydney M. time | 2 55 9·2 A.M. | |
| Lyttelton, N.Z. .... | Ball | Tower on the Heights | | 1 00 00·0 P.M. | 1 30 00 A.M. | |
| Wellington, N.Z..... | Ball | 41° 17′ 15″ S. | 174° 47′ 45″ E. | Mean noon. | 0 30 00 A.M. | |
| Port Nicholson, N.Z. | .. | .. | .. | Mean noon. | Enquire. | |
| Bombay ........... | Ball | 18° 54′ 45″ N. | 72° 49′ 35″ E. | 1 00 00·0 P.M. | 8 8 44·3 A.M. | |
| Colombo........... | Ball | Flagstaff adjoining Master Attendant's Office | | 1 00 00·0 P.M. | 7 40 34·6 A.M. | |
| Madras ........... | Semaphore | Marine Office Flagstaff | | 8 00 00·0 A.M. | 2 30 0·7 A.M. | Repeated six hours later. |
| " ........... | " | " | " | 2 00 00·0 P.M. | 8 30 0·7 A.M. | |
| Calcutta ........... | Ball | Tower in Fort William. | | 1 00 00·0 P.M. | 7 6 41·3 A.M. | |
| Batavia ........... | Disc | 6° 7′ 37″ S. | 106° 48′ 25″·5 E. | Mean noon. | 4 52 46 3 A.M. | |
| " ........... | " | " | " | 1 7 13·7 P.M. | 6 00 00·0 A.M. | |
| Fourth Point, Sunda Strait .......... | Discs | 6° 4′ 17″·3 S. | 105° 52′ 48″ E. | Mean noon. | 4 56 28·3 A.M. | Or at any time by Signal. |
| Surabaya, River Kali-mas.......... | Discs | 7° 12′ 10″ S. | 112° 42′ 58″ E. | Mean noon. | 4 29 4·1 A.M. | Near New Landing Pier. |
| Shanghai .......... | Gun | Senior Naval Officer's Ship. | | Mean noon. | Enquire. | |
| Hong Kong ........ | Ball | 22° 16′ 40″ N. | 114° 10′ 00″ E. | 1 00 00·0 P.M. | 5 22 20 0 A.M. | H.M.S. "Victor Emanuel." |

## CHAPTER XIV.

### SHAPING THE COURSE.

At first sight this seems a simple enough affair; and yet there are often, if not always, many matters of moment which require due deliberation before the actual Course to be steered can be given to the helmsman.

Until within a recent period, the Course was set to the nearest quarter point; and with short junks of vessels—which, especially when running, yawed a handful of points either way—this was near enough, perhaps; but the old "three-handled serving mallet" is fast disappearing. The high-pressure navigation of to-day demands much greater precision; and, in large steamers at all events, the Course is now rarely given otherwise than in *degrees*. Indeed, some of the new pattern compass-cards are so graduated as to leave it no longer optional.

**Course now set in Degrees instead of Quarter Points.**

To the man unaccustomed to it, this steering to degrees seems rather absurd, as he is almost certain to regard it as a vain striving after the impossible. But when he discovers that, day after day, the long and finely-modelled vessels of present build actually *make* the desired Course, his unbelief gives place to astonishment, and he is fain to admit that the world progresses.

To conduct a vessel from one place to another, when out of sight of land, involves a knowledge of the TRUE COURSE, the CORRECT MAGNETIC COURSE, and the COMPASS COURSE.

**The True Course.**

The TRUE COURSE is the angle made with the meridian by a straight line on the chart, drawn to connect the ship's position with the place bound to. This angle is readily ascertained, after the manner already described, by means of the Protractor, Field's Parallel Ruler, or the common ebony one (the latter being used in conjunction with the *true* compass diagram on the chart); also by calculation.

**The Correct Magnetic Course.**

The CORRECT MAGNETIC COURSE is derived from the True Course by applying to it the Variation at place of ship, which may be obtained with accuracy from the *Magnetic Chart of the World.* Easterly variation is applied to the left, and westerly variation to the right of the true course. Thus, if the TRUE COURSE is North, and the variation is 20° Easterly, the CORRECT MAGNETIC COURSE would be N. 20° W.

**The Compass Course.**

THE COMPASS COURSE, or course to steer, is found by applying the Deviation to the CORRECT MAGNETIC COURSE—Easterly to left, and Westerly to the right, *just as you would with Variation.* Consequently, when these two elements in the Course are of the *same* name, they are to be applied in the *same* direction, and *vice versâ.*

***Plus* and *minus* signs used to express the *name* of Variation or Deviation.**

It is usual to speak of Easterly Variation and Deviation as *plus* (+), and of Westerly Variation and Deviation as *minus* (−). Thus, if the CORRECT MAGNETIC COURSE is N. 20° W., and the Deviation is − 20°, the COMPASS COURSE would be North.

This manner of distinguishing the name of the Variation and Deviation by the *plus* and *minus* signs, though purely arbitrary, is convenient when one has become accustomed to it. Thus, in the example just given, we have North for the TRUE COURSE, with + 20° of Variation, and − 20° of Deviation: since, as Algebraists are aware, these two quantities neutralize each other, being equal in amount, but of opposite names, it is evident that the COMPASS COURSE must be North, or the same as the TRUE COURSE.

As a further illustration, let the TRUE COURSE be N. 40° E., the Variation − 38°, and the Deviation + 18°. Then, taking their difference (being of contrary names), we have − 20° as the remainder; or, in other words, the *correction* is 20° Wly., which makes the COMPASS COURSE N. 60° E.

| | | | |
|---|---|---|---|
| Variation . . . . . . . | − | 38° | Being of contrary names, |
| Deviation . . . . . . . | + | 18° | take their difference. |
| *Correction* . . . . . . . | − | 20° | Apply to the right, being Westerly. |
| TRUE COURSE . . . . | N. | 40° E. | |
| COMPASS COURSE . . . | N. | 60° E. | |

The tyro must guard against the mistake of using the prefixes *plus* and *minus* in their arithmetical sense, since in the process just described, a *minus* correction, though subtractive in the S.E. and N.W. quadrants, is additive in the N.E. and S.W. quadrants.*

To give a case where the Variation and Deviation have the same sign, and consequently act in unison, let the TRUE COURSE be S. 75° W., the Variation + 24°, and the Deviation + 16°; the *Correction* would be + 40°, making the COMPASS COURSE S. 35° W.

| | | |
|---|---|---|
| Variation . . . . . . . | + 24° | Being of same name add |
| Deviation . . . . . . . | + 16° | them together. |
| *Correction* . . . . . . . | + 40° | Apply to the left, being Easterly. |
| TRUE COURSE . . . . | S. 75° W. | |
| COMPASS COURSE . . . | S. 35° W. | |

In all iron vessels, and indeed in most wooden ones (since the compasses, even of the latter, are seldom altogether free from the influence of iron), the above "rendering down" of the TRUE COURSE into the COMPASS COURSE is absolutely necessary.

**Magnetic Chart of the World.** The navigating outfit of a foreign-going vessel is incomplete without a Magnetic Chart of the World. The Admiralty publish one, giving single degree curves of equal Variation,† and many, if not all, of their Ocean Charts give the curves for every fifth degree. On the first-named, which is now issued for the year 1880, there is a chartlet shewing the *annual change* in the Variation. A knowledge of this change is important, as in many parts of the world it is very rapid, and after a few years the correction becomes quite a consideration. **Annual change in the Variation.** Thus, on the North Coast of Ireland the Variation is decreasing at the rate of about 1° in seven years, which soon mounts up; and in the English Channel the rate is about 1° in eight years. In some localities the Variation is nearly stationary, and in others it is increasing.

Pilots are not always acquainted with this peculiarity of terrestrial magnetism, and, in consequence, many of the old ones give Courses which may have been the correct thing when they were apprentices, but are so no longer. **Liability to change of Corr. Mag. bearings.** For example, quite recently a very experienced Channel pilot gave the *correct magnetic* bearing of the South Foreland lights when in one as W. by N., though in reality it is now little better than W. ½ N.; and on being told so,

* The reader will remember that when the daily rate or the accumulated error of a chronometer is marked with the prefix +, it means that the one is gaining, and that the other is fast, and *not* as an indication that they are quantities to be *added*.

† These are termed "Isogonic Curves."

said he was certain he was right, as he recollected hearing it thus given *since he was a boy, and he was not aware that the light-houses had ever been moved from their original places.*

Where there is a wide expanse of shoal water, and only a narrow channel, half a point in thick weather or at night may just make all the difference between danger and safety. In a run of ten miles it would throw the ship *one mile* out of her proper course.

**Tables of Channel Courses.**

Certain cheap and useful almanacs, much in favour with coasters, contain tables of Channel Courses; but it is evident, from what has just been stated, that in a comparatively short time these tables must need revision. A man *with* a chart does not require such dry nursing, and a ship navigated *without* one is not safe.

There are parts of the world, also, where a trifling change in the ship's position means a comparatively large change in the amount of Variation. These localities are easily recognized on the Magnetic Chart by the crowding together of the Variation curves; and when the ship's track happens to lie *across* these curves, it is necessary to be more than usually careful with the compass courses.

Between Nantucket and Cape Race, for example, a fast steamer will increase the Variation as much as 10° in a single day's run; and a want of due appreciation of this fact, through not having a Variation Chart, has probably been *one* of the causes which have led to so many cases of stranding in this neighbourhood.

**Periodical change of course to allow for geographical change of Variation.**

When shaping a course in such a locality, it is advisable to measure off on the Magnetic Chart the probable run during the ensuing 24 hours, and so ascertain the change which will take place in the amount of the Variation in that time; then alter course every "eight bells" to the required extent. Supposing the change of Variation in a day's run to be 6°, it would be properly met by altering the course 1° every four hours. This is a long way better than employing the *mean* value of the Variation at both ends of the run, and steering *one course throughout.*

It is evident that if this last mentioned and more common plan should be pursued, the vessel's track will be actually a curve instead of a straight line; and if the course should happen to be a "fine" one, set to pass within a few miles of an outlying shoal, this loose manner of doing it might lead to disaster *in those cases where the convex or outer side of the curve chanced to lie on the same side as the danger.*

Sometimes, when steering on a Great Circle track, the Variation accidentally alters in the same proportion as the TRUE COURSE, so that there is no necessity for changing the COMPASS COURSE as long as this condition prevails.

**Retentive Magnetism the possible cause of Wreck.**

The reader now comes to a point demanding special attention. At first it may be a little difficult to understand, but its importance will not allow it to be overlooked. It has reference to this periodical changing of the Course in accordance with the increase or decrease of Variation as the vessel progresses, and the bothering effect of Retentive Magnetism. Many iron steamers bound to New York have got ashore at various times on the "Georges" and Sable Island, when those in command thought they were well to the Southward. An unusual set of current generally gets the blame in these cases; the writer hopes to make it clear, however, that current was not *necessarily* the cause of the stranding, though it may sometimes have contributed to it. A number of petty things, when acting in the same direction, will produce a large effect; therefore it is necessary to notice those which, taken by themselves, would be seemingly trivial.

By consulting the Magnetic Chart, it will be seen that the amount of variation on the coasts of New England and Nova Scotia changes very rapidly in a short distance. Now a careful navigator would undoubtedly allow for this by steering a more southerly compass course as the *Westerly Variation decreased;* but he might lose sight of the fact that this change of course—small as it might be—would probably cause almost a proportionate *increase* in the *Easterly Deviation* of his compasses, and thus counteract the effect he desired to produce.*

It has been shewn in a previous chapter that compasses, when under the influence of *Retentive Magnetism,* always hang back in the direction of the last course. Now, in vessels crossing the Atlantic, this effect is very marked when, near the end of the passage, they come to be put upon Northerly or Southerly courses; and badly placed compasses, which may be nearly correct, say on West, speedily acquire a large + error as the course is changed towards the South, and a − one as it is changed towards the North, on points where previously no error existed.† This error

* Consult Towson, page 15, on this point.

† Iron is now so much used for deck fittings of all kinds, that it is often extremely difficult to hit upon even a fairly good place for the compasses. A subject of such *vital importance,* however, should have the best attention of both owners and builders

may grow with such rapidity at every change in the course as very nearly to equal the amount of that change, and thereby frustrate its intention.

"Critical Points."

The neutral line which separates the + and – Deviations consequent on Retentive magnetism, may be termed the "Critical point;" and, for Trans-Atlantic steamers, it is about East going one way, and West when going the other.

Near the termination of the Eastern passage the retentive magnetism causes a *minus* error on Southerly courses, and a *plus* one on Northerly courses. Reverse this for a west-bound ship.

After a straight run of several days, it is not uncommon, when the compass is badly placed, to find the Deviation increase fully half a degree for every degree of alteration in the compass course. For example, on W. by S. ½ S. (by compass) let the Deviation be half a point easterly; but if the course be altered to W.S.W. (by compass), the Deviation will probably increase to three-quarters of a point.

Difficulty of steering by a badly placed Compass.

In the first case, the *actual* direction of the ship's head (correct magnetic) would be W. by S.; and in the second case it would be only W. by S. ¼ S. (correct magnetic), or a *quarter* of a point more to the southward, though *by compass* apparently *half* a point to the southward of the original course. This is one of the great evils of a badly placed compass; and if, in addition to this drawback, the adjustment be of an indifferent character, the evil will be augmented; and when, to the direct effect of the Retentive magnetism just mentioned, is added the swing of the card produced by the incessant and perhaps violent motion of the ship—*which, in its turn, allows the magnetic disturbing force to act upon the needle at angles which are constantly varying*—to make a good course is clearly a hopeless matter. Under such circumstances the unfortunate Quartermasters too often get roundly rated for careless steering, when the truth is, the best of helmsmen would be puzzled to keep the ship's head straight on *any* course for even two minutes at a time.

It follows that the navigator, when hauling to the Southward in the locality named, should bear in mind this tendency of the ship to hang to the Westward, and make ample allowance for it, according to existing circumstances. If sun, moon, or stars be

*when the vessel is being designed.* No matter how skilful the Adjuster, or how well made the compass, the latter cannot act satisfactorily, if recklessly placed in the vicinity of large bodies of iron. (See chapter on *Compasses*.)

visible, azimuths will speedily tell him the true state of the case; but if these are not available, *there is nothing like the Deep-Sea Lead*, which, on the Eastern coasts of the United States, may be depended upon as a reliable guide to avoid danger.

**Great Circle Sailing.**

We now come to Great Circle Sailing. Most people sturdily refuse to admit that a curve joining any two places constitutes a shorter distance between them than a straight line would; and in this they are perfectly correct. A straight line *is* the shortest distance between any two points; and it is because the opposite idea is conveyed—unintentionally, of course—by an imperfect or badly put explanation of Great Circle Sailing, that there are still sailors who refuse to believe in it; or if otherwise, it is solely because they have a vague idea that the distance is lessened on account of the degrees of longitude being shorter in high latitudes, forgetting that to arrive at these short degrees of longitude, *additional* degrees of latitude would have to be sailed over. As a matter of fact, the short degrees of longitude have nothing to do with it. When the Great Circle track is laid down on a Mercator's Chart, and compared with a straight line* ruled between the same points, it certainly does seem odd to be told that the curved track is the shorter of the two, and that to sail on the straight line (as laid down on the chart) would be to go over unnecessary ground.

The key to the puzzle lies in the fact already stated, that a chart on Mercator's projection gives a distorted representation of the earth's surface; and its construction is such, that the shortest distance between any two points on the globe is represented, *not by a straight line*, but by a certain *curved* line termed a Great Circle, which, if carried round the world, would divide it into two equal portions, and whose plane would in every case pass through its centre. The only exceptions to this rule are those where the straight line on the chart happens to coincide with the equator, or with a meridian, since both these are Great Circles in themselves. It follows, with these exceptions, that a straight line between any two places on a Mercator's Chart is always a round-about route, being more so in polar regions than in equatorial ones.

**Meridians & the Equator, the only straight lines on Mercator's Chart which represent Great Circles.**

This is easily put to a direct and simple test by means of a good terrestrial globe, say two feet in diameter, and a general chart of the North Atlantic on Mercator's projection. Let it be required to find the shortest possible distance between the lighthouse on

* This straight line is known as a Rhumb line, or Loxodromic Curve.

the island of Inishtrahul, off the north coast of Ireland, and that on Belle Isle, at the entrance to the straits of the same name.

**How to determine a Great Circle on the globe.**

On the globe, at each of the places mentioned, drive in a common brass pin, and stretch a piece of fine silk thread tightly from one to the other.* Every one will admit readily enough that this thread marks the shortest possible road between the two places; there can be no doubt of that. This, then, is the required Great Circle track, and if carried right round the globe, would be found to divide it exactly in half. SMALL CIRCLES, on the other hand, divide the earth into two *unequal* portions, and in consequence, their planes cannot pass through its centre. Now examine the angle the thread makes with the various meridians it crosses, and in each case the angle will be seen to be different, *shewing that on a Great Circle the* TRUE COURSE *is continually altering.*

**To prove that the arc of a Great Circle is the shortest distance between two places.**

Next measure with care the exact latitude in which the thread cuts each of the meridians on the globe, and prick off on the chart the several positions thus ascertained. Connect them in a free-hand by pencil lines, and it will be seen that the nearest distance between Inishtrahul and Belle Isle is represented *on the chart* by a curve, differing very widely from the straight line drawn between the two places on the same chart. Next, by way of proof, try what *the straight line on the chart* looks like *when transferred to the globe:* so just reverse the last process, and prick off *on the globe* the latitude of the straight line where it cuts the meridians *on the chart.* Drive in a pin at each such point; and from one to the other, and on their southern or convex side, stretch a second piece of thread, and it will be seen with half an eye that *the straight line on the chart* is actually a round-about one when laid down on the globe. This will be made still more apparent by removing the intermediate row of pins last inserted, when the second thread will become quite slack, which could not be the case if it had been the measure of the shortest distance between the places.†

A ship navigated on the straight-line course of the chart, never has her head in the exact direction of the port bound to

* What do carpenters when they wish to mark a perfectly straight line between two points?

† For the purpose of actual demonstration on the globe, the distance in this example is rather small. The principle would be better shewn by a similar comparison of the Mercator and Great Circle tracks between Cape Horn and the Cape of Good Hope, or from the latter place to Hobart Town, Tasmania.

*until it is in sight.* On the other hand, a vessel's head, when following the Great Circle track, is *all the time* pointed exactly towards the port bound to. If it were only possible at starting to *see* her destination from the masthead, and the ship was steered unswervingly for it, she would, in such a case, be sailing on the Great Circle between the two places; and it would be found by a series of azimuths, taken as the voyage progressed, that the TRUE COURSE—or, in other words, that the angle her track made with the meridian—was continually changing, though the *absolute* direction of the ship's head did not vary a single degree from first to last. But if the vessel were navigated on the Mercator's course, it would be seen that, at starting, her head pointed considerably towards the equatorial side of the port bound to, and only turned gradually towards it as the voyage progressed. Azimuths taken from time to time would shew no change in the TRUE COURSE.

**True Course on a Great Circle is constantly changing.**

**True Course on a Mercator's track is the same throughout.**

This will, perhaps, be better understood from a consideration of the fact that the Mercator's track cuts all the meridians *at the same angle;* and since *on the globe* these meridians are *not* parallel to each other, it follows that, to enable this condition to be fulfilled by the ship, she must pursue a circuitous route. The saving in distance is not always the only advantage gained by Great Circle sailing. It often happens, in a sailing ship especially, that a foul wind, *according to the Rhumb or straight line course,* is actually a fair one. Raper says:—

"Indeed it is only on laying down the Great Circle, which alone shews the *real* direction of the port, that it can be decided whether the wind is foul or not for a distant port."

**Windward Great Circle Sailing.**

Take, for instance, the case of a vessel bound from Quebec to Greenock or Liverpool. The true course and distance *by chart* from Belle Isle lighthouse to Inishtrahul lighthouse is N. 83° E., 1,722 miles; but the distance on the Great Circle is 1,690 miles, or 32 less; whilst the course at starting is N. 63½° E., or 19½° more to the northward. Now, if a sailing-ship, on clearing the Strait, has the wind at E. ½ N., it would at first seem immaterial, on looking at Mercator's chart, which tack she was put upon; but if placed on the starboard tack, she would lie up within 3½ points of the *true* direction of her port; whilst, if placed on the other tack, instead of approaching her port, *she would be actually going away from it.*

The following is a still better example of the advantage gained by Great Circle sailing. It is taken, by permission, from a first-class *practical* Epitome of Navigation, written by Captain William C. Bergen, of Sunderland:—

"Given the ship, off Flinders Island, Bass Strait, in lat. 40° 0′ S., long. 148° 30′ E., bound to Callao, in lat. 12° 4′ S., long. 77° 14′ W. It is required to compare the Great Circle and Mercator's tracks.

**Example from Bergen's Epitome.**

To compare the Courses.

The Mercator course is E. by N. ¼ N., and the first Great Circle course is S.E. ½ E.; the difference, therefore, is 4¾ points. Suppose the wind to come from E. by N. ¼ N., that is, right ahead by the Mercator track. To a person ignorant of Great Circle sailing, it would appear a matter of indifference, so far as the wind was concerned, on which tack the vessel were put. Suppose one vessel to be put on the starboard tack, and that she could make a course good six points from the wind. Then her course made good would be N. ¾ E., which differs from the Great Circle course 10¾ points, and the vessel would lose 50 miles in the first 100 sailed.

Suppose another vessel to be put upon the port tack. Then her course made good would be S.E. ¾ S., that is, within 1¼ points of the first Great Circle course, and she would gain 97 miles in the first 100 sailed.

The two ships sail each 100 miles, and one is 50 miles further from her port than when she started; the other is 97 miles nearer than when she started; thus, in this case, making a difference of 147 miles in less than one day's sail in favour of Great Circle sailing.

Again, suppose the wind to come strong, say half a gale, from the N. ¾ E. Then the vessel on the Mercator track would lie her course, but she would be close-hauled, and it would be necessary to reduce sail in order to ease the vessel, so that she would be forging ahead at the rate of from 1 to 3 miles an hour, and at the same time making from 2 to 4 points leeway; but the vessel on the Great Circle track would have the wind on the quarter, she would carry double-reefed topsails, mainsail, and jib, and would be going at the rate of from 6 to 8 miles an hour.

Again, suppose the wind to increase to a heavy gale from the North, and cause a high sea. Then the ship may run South until the fury of the gale is spent, and she will at the same time gain 63 miles in the first 100 sailed."

* * * * * * * * * * *

To compare the Distances.

The distance by the Mercator track is 7321 miles, and that by Great Circle is 6772 miles, which therefore is shorter than the Mercator by 549 miles, and it therefore should be adopted, if polar regions, land, shoals, winds, and currents will allow."

**Certain occasional advantages of Great Circle Sailing.**

When these two tracks are at their greatest point of separation, they are about 1500 miles apart, and it will be readily understood that this may mean a very different state of things in regard to winds, weather, and currents. This is strikingly exemplified in the example just given, in which everything is in favour of the Great Circle track.

It is also shewn on the route between Liverpool and Philadelphia. To follow the Great Circle track on this voyage, the vessel must leave by the northern branch of the Irish Channel, which, being shorter than the other, is of course much sooner cleared. The time occupied from land to land by a fast steamship is less than five days, a circumstance in itself very reassuring to passengers, who, when they see Cape Race, consider the dangers of the voyage as practically at an end. The weather is undoubtedly less stormy, though perhaps a trifle colder than that experienced in the trend of the Gulf Stream. Should any rotatory gales be crossing the Atlantic, the chances are greater for the ship being on their easterly wind side. Fewer vessels are met with, and consequently less risk of collision: and lastly, the adverse current of the Gulf Stream is completely dodged by getting inshore of it at Cape Race, from which point, down inside Sable Island, to the Delaware, there is nearly always a favouring current, and much less sea in the North-West gales. Unfortunately this route, from the liability to encounter fog and ice at other seasons, is only safe during the late autmmn and winter months.

There are many modes of *calculating* the data for Great Circle tracks, but all are tedious, more or less; and it is very desirable that there should be some graphic method of doing this, so as to enable the navigator to see at a glance whether it is practicable or not, also what winds and currents he may expect by following it. This desideratum has been well supplied by Captain W. C. Bergen, already referred to, who has recently published a very admirable series of Great Circle track charts. These are so constructed, that a *straight line* drawn on them between any two places, represents the required Great Circle track.

**Bergen's Great Circle Charts.**

Once satisfied, by reference to these useful charts, of the advisability of the route thereon indicated, the track should be transferred for greater convenience to a Mercator's chart of larger scale: this is usually done by measuring the latitude of the straight line where it is intersected by the various meridians, and pricking off on the working sheet the points thus ascertained. When the meridians are only drawn at every 10th degree of longitude, this is scarcely sufficient for accuracy; in which case the latitude and longitude of the line, at as many intermediate points as may be deemed necessary, should be determined and transferred in the same manner. By connecting these points in pencil, the Great Circle track, as shewn on a Mercator's chart, is at once obtained, and that, too, by a very simple operation, which need not occupy more than a few minutes, and is familiar to every one. A protractor of novel construction is supplied with each chart, for laying off the course at any part of the route; and the instructions for its use are very plain, so that the navigator can please himself as to how he does it.

The principle upon which Captain Bergen has constructed his charts has been fully endorsed by the late Astronomer-Royal, and other eminent mathematicians. For laying down Great Circle tracks, it may be said with confidence that there is nothing half so handy as these charts, and their very low price places them within reach of all.

**Track on Polar side of Great Circle.**

Another important point in connection with this subject here presents itself. It must not be overlooked that, as the Great Circle track is the shortest possible, there must be another *on its polar side* equal in length to the Mercator's track; so that, if from any cause it should be deemed expedient to adopt this last route, or if forced on to it by head winds or obstructions, it is consoling to know that, though to the eye it is *apparently* a terrible round, such is not *really* the case, or, at all events, that it is not more so than the Mercator course.

One lesson to be derived from the foregoing is, that when in doubt for the moment as to the tack to go upon with a head wind, no very great harm can be done by putting the vessel on the one which lies *on the polar side of the Mercator course.*

The principle of Great Circle sailing may be made yet plainer by a consideration of the following case. Suppose three very lofty mountains—each 100 miles apart from the other—to be situated in some high latitude, such as Scotland, or Tierra del Fuego; and that an observer on the most *eastern* summit found that all three peaks lay *precisely* in the same straight line; and that the *true bearing* of that line, *as measured from his own meridian*, by careful theodolite observations of the heavenly bodies, was *exactly* West (90°). If this same observer next ascended the most *Western* peak, he would of course find, on looking back, that the three mountains were still in line as before; *but* on taking their *true bearing* from this new position, he would now discover that instead of its being due East—the exact reverse of what he obtained at the first station—it would be about E. 2½° N.* The explanation is, that each bearing was measured from

**Why the initial courses of a G. C. track are dissimilar.**

* Quite a feat has lately been performed in California by the United States Coast Survey. With the aid of an instrument known as the Heliograph, which reflects the

a different meridian; and as these meridians on the globe do not run parallel to each other, like they are *made* to do in the construction of a Mercator's chart, it follows that the true bearings could not possibly be the reverse of each other, as one unlearned in such matters would imagine they ought to be. This accounts for the courses at each end of a long Great Circle track being so very different to each other.

In the comparatively short one between Belle Isle and Inishtrahul, the true course at starting from Belle Isle is N. 63½° E.; but the true initial course from Inishtrahul is N. 77° W. On the other hand, the construction of Mercator's chart is such that the true course between any two places is the same as starting as at the finish, or at any intermediate point. In the case just mentioned, it is N. 83° E. in the one direction, and S. 83° W. in the other.

To revert to the three mountains: If the observer were a surveyor, and it was his duty to lay their positions down on a Mercator's chart, he would first ascertain very accurately the latitude and longitude of each, and then prick off these positions on the chart.

**Mercator's Chart does not shew Objects in their true relative positions.**

One not acquainted with chart construction would suppose that, if in nature the mountain peaks existed all in the same straight line, they would do so also on the chart; but it would not be so. If correctly laid down according to their ascertained latitudes and longitudes, they would form a curve, the centre one lying considerably on the polar side of a straight line joining the other two.

This again goes to prove that the Mercator's chart depicts falsely the geographical features of the earth, but here disparagement ends, for of all the known projections it is the one best suited to the *general* requirements of the navigator.

By Bergen's charts, COMPOSITE Great Circle sailing is rendered quite simple; they have, moreover, the advantage of shewing at once whether the preference should be given to it or to the strict Great Circle. A pamphlet containing a full explanation of the different applications of Great Circle sailing accompanies each chart. But all this is somewhat of a digression, and we must return to the subject which has given a title to this chapter.

---

sun's rays in the required direction, the reciprocal true bearings of Mount Helena and Mount Shasta were easily obtained, though the observers were 192 miles apart. This is the longest connection of the kind yet made.

To allow for a known current or tide when shaping a course, is only an application of the "Composition of Forces." In the parallelogram *RGSC*, the direction *SR*, in which the ship is steered, gives one component; the direction of the current *SC* is another; and the course made good *SG* is the resultant.

Let *P*, the port, bear N. 35° E. from *S.*, the ship, whose rate of sailing is 8 knots per hour: let the arrow represent the *direction* of a 3-knot current setting S. 77° E. From *S* lay off on the arrow the hourly drift *SC*, taking the measurement from any convenient scale, say half an inch to the mile. Using the same scale, take in the dividers the vessel's hourly speed; and placing one foot at *C*, the other will fall upon the line *SP* at the point *G*. Draw the dotted line *GC*, and rule *SR* parallel to it: also dot *RG* parallel to *SC*. The Parallelogram is now complete, and its opposite sides are equal to each other.

**Current Sailing.**

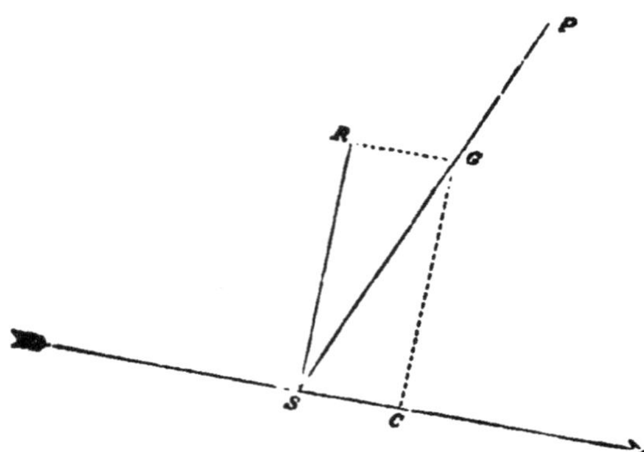


By steering in the direction *SR* = N. 14° E., the vessel will make good her intended course *SP*, and keep the port all the time on the same line of bearing. So long as the angle *GSC* is *less* than the angle *GCS*, the current is favouring the vessel—in the present case to the extent of half an knot an hour. The figure need not necessarily be drawn on the *face* of the chart; the *back*, or any spare piece of paper, will do equally well; and the scale may be anything that is desired. Should the chart scale be employed, it will generally be necessary to multiply the vessel's speed and the drift of the current by some convenient factor—say 5—so as to get a good working size for drawing the figure. If 5 be used, the side *CG* will equal 40 of the chart scale, and the side *SC* will equal 15 of the chart scale. A protractor, or Field's parallel ruler, can be used for laying off the angles.

From a consideration of the diagram it will be readily seen that a fast vessel in channel, when running between any two points, is not so much influenced by tide as a slow one.

**Leeway, and heave of the Sea.**

In making up the reckoning, leeway and heave of the sea must be allowed for *according to judgment*, as it varies in different vessels according to their build; and in the same vessel according to her draft and trim for the time being. It depends also upon the amount of wind and sea, and the sail carried, so that no fixed rule for estimating it can be laid down. The leeway table one usually sees in books on Navigation is therefore but of little value.

There is, however, a somewhat important matter to be considered in connection with leeway. Suppose a vessel, on a wind heading N.W. by N., under short canvas, and looking up within 3 points of her port, which accordingly bears north; but, owing to its blowing hard, she is making 2½ points leeway. Clearly this vessel is only *making good* a N.W. by W. ½ W. course, which is 5½ points from the direction of her port. Let her speed under these conditions be, say 4 knots per hour. Now if the yards be checked in a point or so, and the vessel be kept off N.W. by W., she will slip away much faster through the water, and probably will make not more than half a point leeway. This keeps the course *made good* exactly the same as before, with the advantage of increased speed. Therefore, if you can possibly avoid it, do not allow your vessel to sag to leeward by jamming her up in the wind. KEEP YOUR WAKE RIGHT ASTERN, unless it be found from the bearing of the port that the course *made good* is actually taking the vessel away from it, in which case it is obvious that the less the speed the better.

**Expediency of keeping a Steamer away in strong Head Wind.**

In steamers it is often a matter for consideration whether, by keeping away in a head wind, and setting fore-and-aft canvas, the increased speed will compensate for the extra distance sailed over. It may be accepted as a fact, that by keeping away in full-powered steamships, there is no advantage gained under *ordinary* conditions of wind and sea. Generally, now-a-days, the sails of large steamers are so disproportionate to the size of hull, that their *propelling* effect is but trifling, though their *steadying* effect may be considerable.

When blowing a gale, however, with a heavy head sea smothering everything fore and aft, it is probably advantageous to ease a fast steamer by keeping off sufficiently to get the fore-and-afters to stand with the booms nearly amidships. By this means she would take the sea more kindly, and the canvas would keep her side down, but she would probably lose in the matter of nearing her port. On the other hand, in an under-powered boat of small or moderate size, it would undoubtedly be a gain to assist her with canvas. Against a strong wind and head sea such vessels will do absolutely next to nothing. In addition to want of power, their propellers are too near the broken surface water; and being short vessels, they "race" heavily in a head sea, which necessitates shutting off steam just at the time it is most required.

In the long deep draught vessels of the trans-Atlantic lines, pitching is reduced to a minimum, and the screw, from being well immersed, has a good grip of the water, and is better able to stand up to its work. When a steamer is thus kept away under sail, and a port is not far distant, a point will be reached when, to avoid losing ground, it will be necessary to haul up and steer directly for it. The seafaring community are indebted to Captain W. B. Duncan, of the Marine School, South Shields, for the investigation of the rule for what he proposes to call "Triangular Sailing." By permission it is here inserted nearly verbatim from *Bergen's Epitome*.

**Triangular Sailing.**

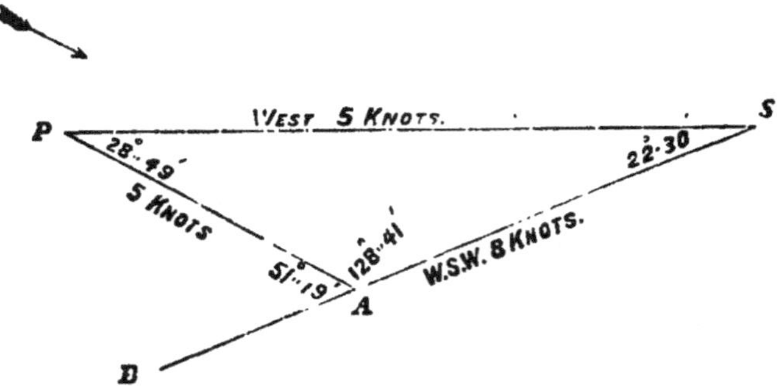


In the above figure, let $S$ be the ship's place, $P$ her port; let the arrow denote the direction of the wind, $PSA$ the angle that the ship must be kept away in order that the sails may pull; $A$ the place where the ship must be hauled up direct to her port; $AP$ its bearings at that time; and let the rate of speed in the direction $SP$, $SA$, and $AP$, be respectively 5, 8, and 5 knots an hour; then we have the following

### Rule.

Put the rates of sailing in the form of a vulgar fraction, of which the numerator is the lesser rate, and the denominator the greater rate;* reduce this fraction to a decimal, find the angle of which this decimal is the natural cosine. It will be the anglo *PAB* between the ship's track, *SAB* when she is kept away, and the bearing of the port *AP* at the time she ought to be hauled up for it.

Taking the preceding rates, we have by the rule $\frac{5}{8}$ = ·625000, which is the natural cosine of 51° 19′, that is, 4½ points roughly. Let the ship be on the starboard tack, and her course *SAB* when kept away W.S.W.; then N.W. × W. ½ W. is 4½ points from W.S.W., and is therefore the bearing of the port when the ship is hauled up for it.

### To find the point *A* on the Chart.

Through *S*, the ship's place, draw *SAB*, to represent the course W.S.W.; and through *P*, the port, draw *PA*, the bearing N.W. × W. ½ W. The points where these two lines intersect will determine *A*. The distances *SA* and *AP* can then be measured, and the time of going these distances compared with the time of going the distance *SP*.

### By Calculation.

Referring to the figure: In the triangle *APS*, let *SP* = 100 miles; then, by Trigonometry,

$$SA : SP :: \text{sine } P : \text{sine } A.$$
$$AP : SP :: \text{sine } S : \text{sine } A.$$

Let the angle $S = 2$ points; then the angle $A = PAS = 180° - PAB = 180° - 51° \, 19' = 128° \, 41'$.

And the angle $P = 180° - (A + S) = 180° - (128° \, 41' + 22° \, 30') = 28° \, 49'$. Hence we have as follows:—

| To find *SA*. | | | | To find *AP*. | | |
|---|---|---|---|---|---|---|
| Angle *P* 28° 49′ | Sine | 9·683055 | Add | Angle *S*. 22° 30′ | Sine | 9·582840 |
| Angle *PAB* 51° 19′ | Cosec. | 0·107565 | | Angle *PAB* 51° 19′ | Cosec. | 0·107565 |
| *SP* 100′ | Log. | 2·000000 | | *SP* 100′ | Log. | 2·000000 |
| *SA* 61′·75 | Log. | 1·790620 | | *AP* 49′·02 | Log. | 1·690405 |

* "A *Fraction* is a quantity which represents a part or parts of an integer or whole. A *Vulgar* (that is, a common) fraction, in its simplest form, is expressed by means of two numbers placed one over the other, with a line between them. The lower of these is called the *Denominator*, and shews into how many of equal parts the whole is divided; the upper is called the *Numerator*, and shews how many of those parts are taken to form the fraction. Thus, ¾ denotes that the whole is divided into four equal parts, and that three of them are taken to form the fraction."—Colenso.

2 D

To find the Time saved.

| | MILES. | | KNOTS | | HOURS. |
|---|---|---|---|---|---|
| *SA* | 61·75 | ÷ | 8 | = | 7·72 |
| *AP* | 49·02 | ÷ | 5 | = | 9·80 |
| | | | | | 17·52 |
| *SP* | 100 | ÷ | 5 | = | 20·00 |

Time saved = 2·48 that is, nearly 12½ per cent.

**Notes.—(1) If a change of wind occur, the chances that it will be in favour of the vessel are as 16 to 3. (2) If the wind be blowing so hard that a small-powered vessel cannot steam against it, tack her when the port is right abeam.**

## CHAPTER XV.

### THE DANGER ANGLE, AND CORRECT DETERMINATION OF DISTANCE FROM LAND.

As laid down in a previous chapter, every captain and officer on board ship should keep a note of the height of the eye above the load-line corresponding to the bridge, upper, and main decks. If this be known for any given draft, it is, of course, easily ascertained for any other. Such information is useful, not only for the correct application of the "Dip" in every-day sight taking, but it is of importance in arriving at the approximate distance from a beacon light when it first pops into view above the horizon in clear weather.* It also affords a ready means of estimating by eye alone the distance of an object, by referring its water-line to the sea horizon.

**Acquaintance with height of the eye useful in estimating Distance.**

The distance of the visible horizon depends mainly upon two things, namely, the curvature of the earth's surface, which is constant, and the height of the observer's eye, which, of course, varies with circumstances; and this distance happens to correspond *approximately* to the square root of the height of the eye, "an accidental relation"—as Raper puts it—"easy to remember." Thus, if the height of the eye be 25 feet, the distance of the visible sea horizon will be *about* 5 nautical miles: if the height of the eye be 36 feet, the distance will be about 6 miles, and so on.

**Distance of the visible Horizon.**

To get a more exact result, multiply the square root of the height in feet by 1·06.

---

* By Beacon light is meant any one of the various coast lights exhibited for purposes of navigation.

The general tendency, however, of terrestrial refraction is to throw up the horizon, and slightly increase the distances thus obtained.

If an observer, whose eye is elevated say 16 feet above the sea level, is passing a small island, rock, ship, or other object, whose *water-line* appears one unbroken continuation of the sea horizon, he knows that his distance from it is rather more than four miles. If the water-line of the object appears *nearer* to him than the horizon, he knows that the distance must be *less* than four miles: and if the water-line is invisible, and consequently *beyond* the horizon, he knows it must be *greater* than four miles. Indeed, by ascending or descending till the water-line of the object comes on a new horizon, corresponding to the altered level, it is possible to make a very fair shot at the actual distance.

**Distance from Beacon Light.**

Similarly, in clear weather, when a beacon light first shows itself above the horizon, the approximate distance from it may be found as follows:—take the square root of the elevation of the observer's eye, and the square root of the elevation of the light, both in feet. Add them together, and you have the distance required. Let the eye, for example, be 16, and the light 169 feet above the sea level. The square of 16 is 4, which, added to 13, the square root of 169, gives 17 nautical miles as the approximate distance of the light when first sighted.* *(Do not forget to note the time, and the greater the speed of your ship the more necessary is this caution).*

The following table, in which refraction is taken into account, gives a still closer approximation.

---

* What is here stated refers only to such lights (1st and 2nd order) as have sufficient power to be seen at distances corresponding to their elevation. It is necessary to discriminate between the *Luminous* range and the *Geographical* range; the one depends upon the power of the light, and the other upon its elevation. For example, the light on San Lorenzo Island, Callao, has the absurd elevation of 980 feet, which should give it a range of 41 miles, but it is such a poor affair (1880) that 10 or 12 miles is about its outside limit of visibility. On account of greater liability to obscuration by fog or mist hanging over hill-tops, 200 feet should be the maximum elevation for beacon lights, but peculiarities of position sometimes *force* engineers to place them higher.

## TABLE OF DISTANCES, BY ALAN STEVENSON.

*Table of Distances at which objects can be seen at sea, according to their respective elevations, and the elevation of the eye of the observer.*

| Heights in feet. | Distances in geographical or nautical miles. | Heights in feet. | Distances in geographical or nautical miles. | Heights in feet. | Distances in geographical or nautical miles. |
|---|---|---|---|---|---|
| 5 | 2·565 | 70 | 9·598 | 250 | 18·14 |
| 10 | 3·628 | 75 | 9·935 | 300 | 19·87 |
| 15 | 4·443 | 80 | 10·26 | 350 | 21·46 |
| 20 | 5·130 | 85 | 10·57 | 400 | 22·94 |
| 25 | 5·736 | 90 | 10·88 | 450 | 24·33 |
| 30 | 6·283 | 95 | 11·18 | 500 | 25·65 |
| 35 | 6·787 | 100 | 11·47 | 550 | 26·90 |
| 40 | 7·255 | 110 | 12·03 | 600 | 28·10 |
| 45 | 7·696 | 120 | 12·56 | 650 | 29·25 |
| 50 | 8·112 | 130 | 13·08 | 700 | 30·28 |
| 55 | 8·509 | 140 | 13·57 | 800 | 32·45 |
| 60 | 8·886 | 150 | 14·22 | 900 | 34·54 |
| 65 | 9·249 | 200 | 16·22 | 1,000 | 36·28 |

EXAMPLE: A tower, 200 feet high, will be visible to an observer whose eye is elevated 15 feet above the water, 21 nautical miles; thus, from the table:

| | | | | |
|---|---|---|---|---|
| 15 feet elevation, | distance visible | | 4·44 | nautical miles. |
| 200 | " | " | 16·22 | " |
| | | | 20·66 | " |

To check Light ranges by this table is always advisable, as it not unfrequently happens that books and charts give this item very incorrectly; and in any case it is manifest, from what has been said, that the range must depend upon the varying height of the observer's eye—whether he be on the lofty bridge of a large steamer, or on the main deck of a small vessel.

**Elevation of Beacon lights calculated from High Water level.**

In the Admiralty Light List of the British Isles, the range is calculated for a height of eye of 15 feet, the elevation of the lights themselves being in all cases taken as *above high water*. To remember this last point is of importance where the rise and fall of tide is considerable—as, for example, in the Bristol Channel, the Bay of Fundy, or the Gulf of St. Malo. With a tidal range of 30 feet, there would be a difference of six miles in the visibility of a light, according as it happened to be high or low water at the time of observation. Low water gives the greatest range of visibility.

The range of the Cies Island light, on the coast of Spain, is given at 20 miles, but the writer has often seen it at 33 miles.

**Necessity for checking Light Ranges by the Distance Table.**

Reference to the table will shew that the latter is the distance at which, if it is a 1st order light, it ought to be visible to an observer elevated 25 feet, since its own height above the sea level is 604 feet. Now, there is a vast difference between 20 and 33 miles, and in many cases a departure, based upon such incorrect data, would lead to grief.

After all, even when every care has been taken, this mode of getting at the distance of lights by their presumed range is but guess-work. A great deal depends upon the clearness of the atmosphere, and more still upon the vagaries of refraction. For this latter it is impossible to make a correct allowance, and its effect is sometimes very startling.

**Visibility of Lights unduly increased by Abnormal refraction.**

At the commencement of the year 1881, the writer, then in command of the (s.s.) "*British Queen*" on her first voyage, was astonished, when making the American coast, to see—a full hour and a quarter before the proper time—a light, which, from its characteristics, could be no other than Cape May, unless, indeed, some alteration had been made of which he was not aware. As the vessel's position had been determined with great accuracy only a couple of hours previously, both by stellar observations and soundings, the unexpected appearance of this light was, for the moment, quite puzzling. When in doubt, the trump card to play in a case of this kind *is to stop*, which was done forthwith, and a careful bearing of the light taken by standard compass, the Deviation on the course then steered being well known from previous observations. Whilst busy getting a cast of the lead, the officer of the watch reported the sudden appearance of a fixed light on the starboard beam. Both lights shone with brilliancy. To get the correct bearing of this new light the horizontal angle between it and the first one was measured by sextant.

**One bearing and a horizontal angle give a better "fix" than Cross Bearings.**

*This mode of doing it was rendered all the more necessary as the vessel's head had fallen off in the meanwhile to a point of the compass upon which the deviation was only imperfectly known.*

The ship's place was first laid off by the course and distance made since the "fix" by stars, and the soundings on the chart were found to tally exactly with the cast just taken.

To make assurance doubly sure, the North ⋆ was next observed for latitude, which also agreed. There could, therefore, be but little doubt as to the vessel's true position. Assuming the lights to be those of Absecom and Cape May, their bearings, which crossed at a good angle (69°), were then laid down, and intersected most exactly at the position assigned to the ship, which of course was conclusive; so the engines were started ahead, and the course was resumed. From this point to Cape May the distance was 35 miles, and to Absecom 29 miles.

The first-named light is 152 feet above the sea level, and should not have been seen further than 21 miles; whilst Absecom is 167 feet, and should not have been seen further than 22 miles. In fifteen minutes, however, owing to some atmospheric change, the lights gradually lost brilliancy, and at last vanished altogether; and it was not until the vessel was some miles inside the *ordinary* range of Cape May light that it reappeared, although we were steadily approaching it all the time. In due course the Five-fathom Bank lightship was sighted and passed, and the position of our own vessel at time of stopping fully confirmed. The river was full of ice at the time, and this may have had something to do with it.

Some years previous to this occurrence, the writer saw the flash light on Sankaty Head at a distance of 38 miles, or 17 miles outside its usual range. In both these cases abnormal refraction had temporarily lifted the lights above the horizon, and made them visible at a point where, under ordinary conditions, such a thing would have been impossible. The reverse of this phenomenon occasionally happens.

This goes to shew that extraordinary departures from the general rule will sometimes occur, and points out the necessity for extreme caution; also the value of an *independent* check in cases where any error might lead into danger. There is no other profession whose members are obliged to be so constantly on the alert against accident brought about by freaks of nature, rendering unreliable the very materials they have to work with.

**On first seeing a light, to know distance ship will pass from it.**

If a vessel be provided with a good Azimuth Compass, the horizontal angle between the ship's course and a beacon light on its first appearance, can be used to determine the approximate distance at which the latter will be passed when abeam, provided always the same course be steered *and made good*. Having ascertained by the range tables the distance of the light, open the traverse tables at the given angle, and, with this distance in its column, take out the corresponding amount in the departure column, which will be the passing distance required.

Suppose a vessel to be steering North by compass, and on the first appearance of a beacon light its bearing is taken as N. 16° E., and its range calculated at 20 miles. Open the Traverse Tables at 16° and in the departure column will be found 5½ miles, opposite 20 in the distance column. But the navigator should not rest content with such an assurance, since tide or current, leeway or bad steering, might altogether falsify it.

**Sir William Thomson's Azimuth Mirror.**

For an observation of the kind here referred to, Sir William Thomson's Standard Compass is invaluable, as it is provided with what is in all respects a most perfect little instrument for taking *accurate* bearings by night or day. Friend's Pelorus is also good, and has the advantage of being portable, so that if the object of which the bearing is sought should be concealed in one position, the Pelorus can readily be moved to another. It has already been said that there should be a proper stand for the Pelorus on *each* side of the bridge. To use it for this purpose, clamp the lubber line to the course steered, and at the instant that an assistant intimates that the vessel is exactly on her course, take your bearing by Pelorus.

As the light is approached, a more accurate method of getting its distance when abeam becomes available.

**Distance by Four-point bearing.**

It is known as "Distance by Four-point Bearing." This method recommends itself to favour from its extreme simplicity and comparative accuracy. It is as follows:—When the light or other fixed object bears by compass four points (45°) from the course, note the exact time by watch or clock, and again do so when it bears on the beam, or 90° from the course. The distance run by the ship in the interval is the distance of the object when abeam.

For example, let a ship be steering North by compass, at a speed of 14 knots per hour. At 9·00 A.M. a lighthouse is observed to bear N.E., and at 9·30 it bears East. In the interval of half-an-hour, the ship ran 7 miles, which, accordingly, is her distance off the lighthouse when abeam

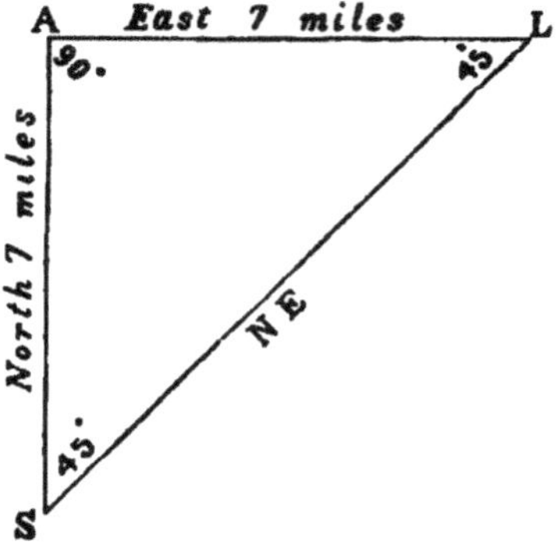

*S* is the position of the ship at 9 o'clock, when *L* bore N.E., or 4 points on the bow.

*A* is the position of the ship at 9·30, when *L* bore due East, or on the beam.

The line *SA* is the run in the interval, = 7 miles, and represents latitude. The line *AL* is the distance of the lighthouse when abeam, = 7 miles, and represents departure.

To prove this, open the Traverse Tables at the angle 45°, and the latitude and departure will be found equal to each other.

Should it be required to know the ship's distance from the lighthouse at the time of its bearing 4 points *abaft* the beam, recourse must be had to the Traverse Tables; and in the *distance* column, under the angle of 45° will be found the required information.

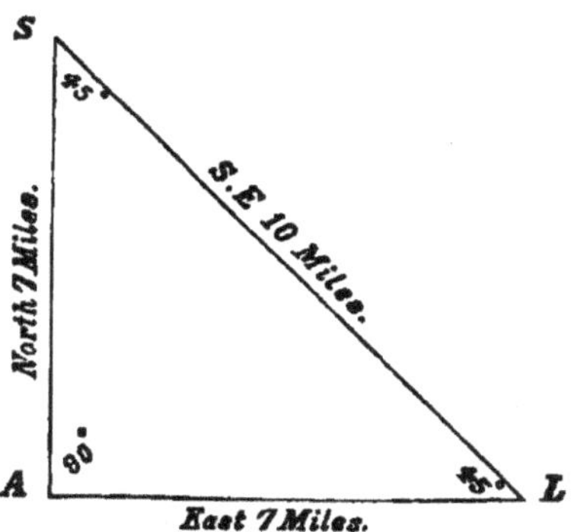


Thus, the ship having sailed on for another half-hour, = 7 miles, at which time *L* bore S.E., or 4 points *abaft* the beam, her distance from it would be 10 miles, and would serve as a departure.

This 4-point method of ascertaining distance is most convenient in practice, as the very trifling calculation required can be performed mentally without leaving the deck, and needs no reference to the chart. It is manifest, however, that it cannot be considered *rigorously* exact, since either the speed or the course (upon both of which it depends) may have been influenced by tide or current. Still the method is a good one, *and the practice of it on all occasions should be a standing rule.* Indeed, it often happens—at night especially—that no other method is available which does not depend upon the same principle.

It often happens, also, that a light or other fixed object is not visible till nearly abeam. In such cases the 4-point method is

**When light is only seen when nearly abeam.**

not available, but the approximate distance of the object can be found as follows:—

Note the time carefully when it bears exactly $1\frac{1}{4}$ points (14°) before the beam, and again when it has the same bearing abaft the beam. *Twice* the distance run in the interval is very nearly the distance of the object when it bore exactly on the beam.

EXAMPLE.

At 9 o'clock a light bore 14° before the beam; at 9·15 it was abeam, and at 9·30 it bore 14° abaft the beam. Ship steaming 12 knots per hour against a 2-knot tide or current. Required the approximate distance from the light at 9·15 when it was abeam.

*Answer.*—10 miles, which is *double* the distance the ship made *over the ground* in the interval between first and last bearing.

---

**"Rake of the eye."**

Pilots, in the absence of definite leading marks, are in the habit of judging their position by what they term "the rake of the eye"—a loose plan, which, to say the least of it, is unsatisfactory, since no three individuals on board ship will agree in their *estimate* of distance or of height, and, at times, appearances deceive even the most experienced; so that, under certain conditions of coasting, *exact* methods become a necessity. Fortunately there are such methods; and the opportunity for employing them is both greater and less troublesome than is generally supposed. Comparatively few men are aware what a powerful ally they possess in the Sextant for the determination of distance, and to enable them to fix a ship's position with all needful precision when in sight of land. Judgment may be at fault—for man is not infallible; but angular measurements are reliable matters of fact.

**"Fix" by *vertical* angle and Compass bearing.**

In the chapter on the Station Pointer, it was shewn how two simultaneous horizontal angles, subtended by three well defined objects, gave an exact "fix;" also, how an angle between two objects in transit and a third, was equally good, if not better. In these cases the angles measured are *horizontal* ones; but it is now proposed to shew that *vertical* angles, combined with a compass bearing or not, as the case may be, will fulfil the same purpose, and sometimes be available when the others are not.

On the Admiralty charts, the heights of all beacon lights are given, as well as those of most of the islets, rocks, hills, cliffs, and mountains along a line of coast. Each of these, then, are available as bases in a right-angled triangle, by which to determine their distance; but when the vertical angle is small, *and the dis-*

*tance considerable*, the angle must be measured with all possible accuracy. To do so, the sextant telescope should be employed, and the angle observed both "on and off" the arc. The mean of the two readings will then be free from index error. But if the object be near,—say a lighthouse on the edge of a cliff, about a mile or so away,—it will be sufficient to measure its altitude in the usual manner, and apply the index error previously determined.

**Arc of excess.**

The divisions of the limb of every sextant are continued for a few degrees to the right of zero, and this is known as the "Arc of excess." For example, suppose it were required to measure the vertical angle between the summit of a *distant* mountain and the sea horizon underneath it. This is a case in which, unless the ship were steering directly towards or from the mountain, the angle would alter very slowly, and is one where the "on and off" reading should be employed. By moving the index bar of the sextant *forward* from zero, the reflected image of the *summit* would be brought *down* to the actual horizon, as seen directly through the horizon glass, and the reading would be made in the ordinary way. Starting again from zero, and moving the index *backwards*, the reflected image of the *horizon* will be brought *up* to the actual summit of the mountain, as seen by direct vision through the horizon glass.

**"On and off" measurement.**

To get the value of the angle in this last case, both the limb and the vernier must be read *from left to right*. Suppose the sextant limb to be divided to 10′, the 10′ of the vernier would have to be considered 0′ or zero, the 9′ taken as 1′, the 8′ as 2′, the 7′ as 3′, and so on. A little practice will soon overcome any difficulty which may at first be experienced in doing this. To utilise quickly the vertical angle, and to render the method complete, a set of tables is necessary, so that the required distance may be taken out by inspection.

**Becher's Masthead Angles.**

There is a handy little book by Captain A. B. Becher, R.N., (published by Potter, the Poultry, London), in which the angles are calculated for heights from 30 to 280 feet, and distances varying from a cable's length to four miles. The small compass of this book, however, only fits it for use where the object of which the angle is measured lies at a less distance than the visible horizon. The author's intention was that it should be employed more particularly in experimental squadrons, for finding the distance of one ship from another by her masthead angle.

To give a wider scope to this vertical method, the writer has

**Lecky's Off-shore Distance Tables.**

published an extended set of somewhat similar Distance Tables, in which angles are given for heights from 50 to 18,000 feet, and distances from a tenth of a mile up to 100 miles. Part I. of the Tables is intended to be used with objects not exceeding 1,000 feet in height, which lie *on* or *within* the radius of the observer's horizon; and Part II., where curvature has to be taken into consideration, is for more elevated objects lying *beyond* the observer's horizon.*

By these Tables (Part I.) the distance from an object can be taken out absolutely *at sight*, without the necessity for any figuring whatsoever. It may now and again happen, however, that the height of the object exceeds 1000 feet, the limit of Part I., in which case use the following rule.

*Multiply the height in feet by ·565 and divide by the number of minutes in the angle between the summit and the water-line: the quotient will be the distance in nautical miles and decimals of a mile.*

Thus, in passing Ailsa Craig (Firth of Clyde) it subtended an angle of 1° 57′ when abeam, the observer being elevated 26 feet. The given height of the Craig is 1097 feet, but for sake of round numbers call it 1100 feet. Required the distance to a point vertically under the summit.

```
                        1100 feet.
                         ·565 constant factor.
                        ─────
                         5500
                        6600
                       5500
                      ──────────
Sextant angle 117′ ) 621·500 ( 5·312 m distance.
                       585
                      ─────
                        365
                        351
                       ─────
                        140
                        117
                        ────
                         230
                         234
                        ────
```

This method requires pencil and paper, and involves delay; whilst, therefore, it is not so handy as the Tables, it serves well

* The Danger Angle, and Off-shore Distance Tables. Price 4s. 6d. Philip, Son and Nephew.

on a pinch, and is perfectly accurate. It is restricted to objects *on* or *within* the observer's horizon.

In July, 1882, Commodore J. G. Walker, Chief of Bureau of Navigation, United States Navy, courteously sent the author a "Diagram for finding Distances and Heights." On comparing the results obtained by this ingenious contrivance with those taken out of Part II. of the Tables, they proved in every case identical. This correspondence between calculation and construction served of course as a voucher for the accuracy of each. The diagram, however, is not so handy for reference as the Distance Tables—especially on deck, where its size (24" × 19") would render it liable to be taken charge of by every puff of wind, as well as injured by rain or spray. The diagram also lacks the advantages to be derived from Part I. of the Distance Tables. The inventor is H. Von Bayer, C.E., and the price one dollar.

**Vertical Danger Angle.**

To shew the practical utility of this vertical angle method, let us suppose that the navigator, for some important reason, such as meeting a crowd of vessels, is forced to round more closely than he otherwise would, the Skerries lighthouse on the coast of Anglesea. He knows, however, that at 3 cables from it there is the hidden African rock, which he had better pass at least two cables outside of to ensure safety; this makes in all 5 cables from the lighthouse. His chart gives the height *of the light* as 117 feet above the level of high water. Opening the Distance Tables, therefore, at 120 feet (since it is scarcely likely to be high water at that precise moment) he finds opposite 5 cables the angle 2° 17′ 26″. This when corrected for index error, is placed upon the sextant, and so long as the angle subtended between *the centre of the lantern* and the water-line beneath it does not exceed this amount, he knows he is at, or outside the prescribed distance.

**Points of measurement.**

Attention is here called to the fact that the angle is measured *not* to the cowl or top of the lighthouse, but to *the centre of the glass lantern*, or, in other words, to a point representing the height of the focal plane of the light above the level of the sea. If it be desired to measure from the extreme top of the lighthouse to its water-line, the following is the approximate number of feet to be added to the given height of the light:—

| | | |
|---|---|---|
| 1st Ord. light, from centre of the light to the vane is *about* | 15 feet. |
| 2nd " - - - - " - " | 11 |
| 3rd , - - - - " - " | 10 |
| 4th " - - - - " - " | 8 |
| 5th " - - - - - " | 7 |
| 6th " - - - - , - " | 6 |

**Precautions to be observed in measuring Vertical Angles.** In connection with this matter of taking vertical angles, one point deserves notice. When the object is near, the observer should get as low down as possible, to lessen the error which would arise from his eye not being on the level of the water-line, to which the angle is measured.

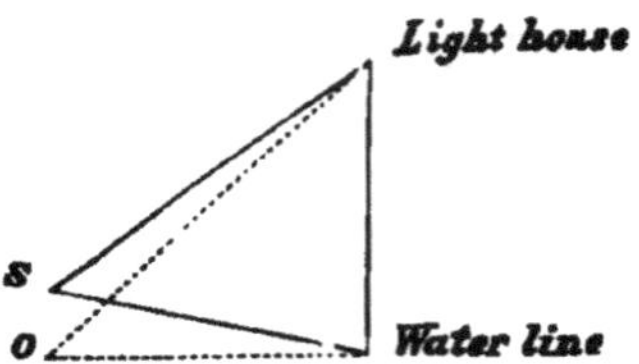


*S* represents the angle as measured from the bridge, and *O* what it would be if measured from the sea level. Except, however, in exaggerated cases, the difference is not large; and as the angle at *S* is greater than the angle at *O*, the error lies on the safe side, if the injunction to descend is disregarded, so long as there exists no danger *outside* of the ship.

This second case is one to be guarded against, as the error involved is considerable. It represents a ship passing a lighthouse, standing on a hill, say some two miles inland; whilst in the foreground, at *W*, is a low rocky point. The angle *S*, subtended by *L* and *W*, is clearly too great; it ought to be measured between *L* and *V*; but as this is impossible from there being no way of ascertaining the whereabouts of the imaginary point *V*, the difficulty is practically got over by descending to as near the point *O* as you can get.

On the other hand, when measuring the vertical angle of objects *beyond the horizon*, it is desirable that the observer should be as high as he can conveniently get. The words water-line and horizon must not be understood to mean the same thing. The horizon is the natural boundary line where the sea and heavens apparently meet each other, and its distance—a direct consequence of the earth's curvature—depends upon the elevation of the observer. The distance of an object's water-line, on the contrary, has nothing to do with the elevation of the observer. Attention to these and other delicate points constitutes the *expert* navigator.

**Distinction between *Water line* and *Horizon*.**

When a distant mountain peak is visible above the sea horizon, a ship's position may be fixed, with a near approach to accuracy, by measuring its "on and off" altitude, and laying off on the observed line of bearing the corresponding distance taken out from the tables by inspection. Or the Compass may be dispensed with altogether if the Astronomical bearing be found by a second observer in the manner indicated on page 369.

**"Fix" by two vertical angles without bearing.**

Should *two* summits be observed simultaneously, or nearly so, which are separated by a considerable horizontal angle—the nearer to 90° the better—the ship's place will be found by simply sweeping the distance from each with the dividers. It is true the circles will intersect at *two* points, but the eye alone, or a rough bearing, will easily determine which is the ship's position.

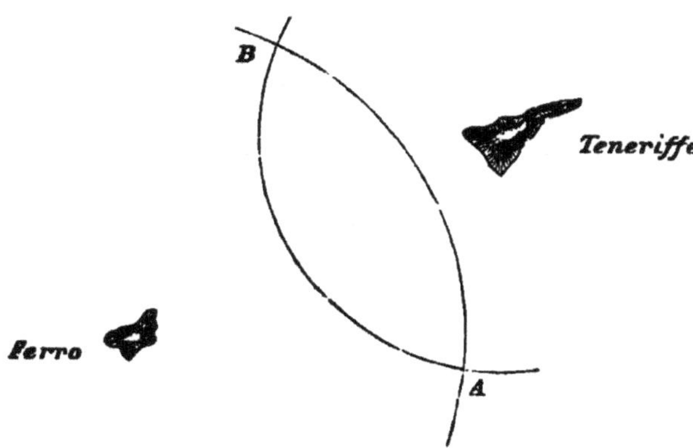


Let the diagram be supposed to represent any two neighbouring islands—say Ferro and Teneriffe, both of which are lofty—and let the arcs of circles represent their respective distances from the ship. Then the latter must either be at $A$ or at $B$; and it is almost needless to say there can be no difficulty in deciding which. In all these cases where vertical angles are measured, the greater the height of the object, and less acute the observed angle, the more reliable will be the result.

When well out in the offing, known mountain peaks are frequently visible, and form salient features, when the coast-line—indistinct through distance or haze—offers no points by which to get a "fix." This is very much the case on the coasts of Chili and Peru. Moreover, should a vessel be standing in from seaward to make her port, what a source of satisfaction it is to be able to define her *precise* position, and shape a correct course for it before the coast-line is even visible, and this with scarcely any trouble.

**The Danger Angle.**

The Sextant has a vast superiority over the Compass in a number of cases. This is particularly well shewn in the problem known as the "Danger Angle," where the compass is scarcely of any service whatever. It is no disparagement, however, to the compass to say that it cannot do *everything*, or that there are other instruments which, in particular cases, should supersede it.

**Vertical Danger Angle.**

The "Danger Angle" may be measured either vertically or horizontally, according to the features of the coast. Let us take a vertical one first—of which a good example has already been given in the case of the Skerries Lighthouse and African Rock. It was there shewn that so long as the angle did not exceed 2° 17′ 26″, the vessel would pass two cables' lengths outside the danger. Similarly with the South Rock off Tuskar. This can be rounded in safety if the angle between the water-line and the top of the lighthouse is not allowed to exceed 1°; but in such a situation, where the tide runs strongly, the angle would require to be narrowly watched; and, unless pressed in by having to port for another vessel at the critical moment, there is no object in making such very close shaves with plenty of sea room on one side—although at the same time, be it said, ordinary skill and care should obviate the necessity for throwing distance away as if it cost nothing. Moreover, there are thousands and thousands of spots where dangerous shoals *have* to be threaded without the aid of a pilot, and then this sort of knowledge is worth a Jew's eye.

The peculiar and very convenient property of the circle, namely, the equality of angles in the same segment, permits of the second or horizontal application of the "Danger angle."

**Horizontal Danger Angle.**

In the diagram the line *ABCDEFG* represents the course of a ship as she rounds a promontory, off which lie several dangerous rocky shoals. Having decided to give the reefs a berth of half a mile or so, a circle is drawn passing that distance outside of them, and through the church and windmill on the cliff. Then measure with a protractor the angle at *D*, subtended by the aforesaid church and windmill, which of course, in an accurate survey, will be laid down in their proper places on the chart. The angle in the present instance is 25°, and will be found the same for *all*

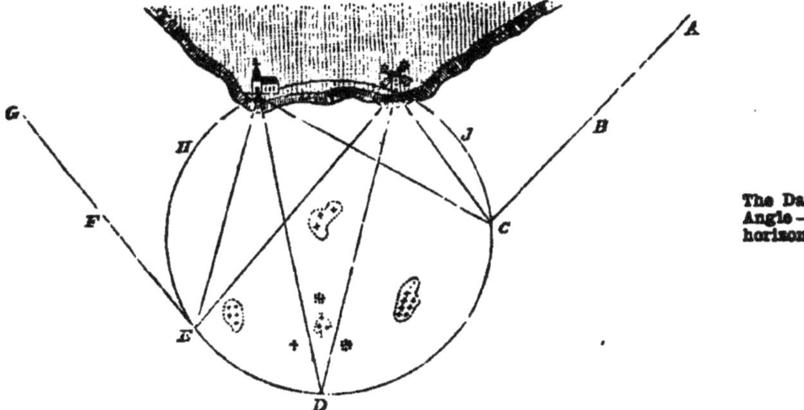


**The Danger Angle—horizontal.**

parts of the circumference of the circle seaward of the two marks, no matter whether measured at *J, C, D, E,* or *H*. Therefore, so long as the angle is *less* than 25°, the vessel must be outside of the circle, and *in safety;* but if the angle be *greater* than 25°, she is evidently *inside* the circle, and *in danger*.

As depicted above, the vessel is standing alongshore on the line *ABC*, but as she approaches the pitch of the cape her commander, who is on the alert with his sextant, gets the "Danger angle" at the point *C*. Thus warned of his being too close in, he at once starboards and hauls off, steering so as to avoid increasing or unnecessarily diminishing the angle until the point *E* is gained, when the course *EFG*, along the coast, causes the angle rapidly to decrease, and tells the danger is passed.

It is manifest that compass cross-bearings here would be of no use, since the cut made by a difference in the bearings of only 2¼ points is too acute to be in the least reliable.

Supposing the height to be known of the cliff or of the church, a second observer could independently verify the distance by the *vertical* "Danger angle," so that not only could the navigation be conducted with the utmost safety, but without losing ground.*

* As a rule it is safer to navigate in the vicinity of doubtful ground during roughish weather than during fine, since sunken rocks, carrying only three or four fathoms over

This horizontal method may be employed in a great variety of ways, and has the special advantage that the man in charge of the navigation, after having once drawn his circle and measured the danger angle, has no need to leave the deck and attempt hurriedly to lay off unsatisfactory bearings on a chart. He has a hard and fast angle, and so long as he does not *increase* it, he knows without any other guide that his ship is safe. For those running steadily in certain trades, it is advisable to have the "Danger angles" tabulated for the various parts of their route requiring them. Less would then be heard of losses through "errors in judgment."

**Abrolhos reefs.** For example: off the coast of Brazil, the Abrolhos* lighthouse stands on one of a small group of islets out of sight of land, which islets are surrounded by sunken coral reefs extending seaward several miles. This group of islets is circular in shape; and so long as they subtend a horizontal angle not greater than 7° 20′, it is impossible to touch the reefs on the eastern side.

Liverpool navigators, running in the North Atlantic steam trade, are all familiar with an awkwardly situated danger on the **Pollock Rock.** south coast of Ireland known as the Pollock Rock. The Admiralty surveyors found on it not less than 4½ fathoms, but the local fishermen say that it has a spot with only 3 fathoms. Every one experienced in such work knows how extremely difficult it is to find the shoalest points of a reef, principally on account of the lead slipping off when the rocks are cone-shaped, and as this ridge is some 400 feet in extent, it is quite likely the fishermen may be right.

Lying, as it does, slap in the eastern fairway to and from Queenstown, it is a regular *Bête noire*, and from the absence of good clearing marks, in hazy weather or at night, requires a wide berth.

Here the "Danger angle" comes in as a perfect God-send. So long as the horizontal angle between the fog-trumpet on Poor

---

them, will not break in smooth water, but will unmistakeably do so when there is any sea.

Note.—*Have an intelligent quick-eyed officer at the masthead under such circumstances.*

In Magellan Straits and other parts of the world sunken dangers are buoyed, so to speak, by "Kelp," and this is almost an unfailing guide during daylight; but it should be known that where the currents are strong, "Kelp" is often run under. "Live Kelp"—which is the term given to the weed when rooted to the rock—is easily distinguished from loose or "dead Kelp:" the one is oily looking, combed out and streaky; the other drifts about in tangled masses.

* Abrolhos is compounded of two Portuguese words, signifying "Open your eyes."

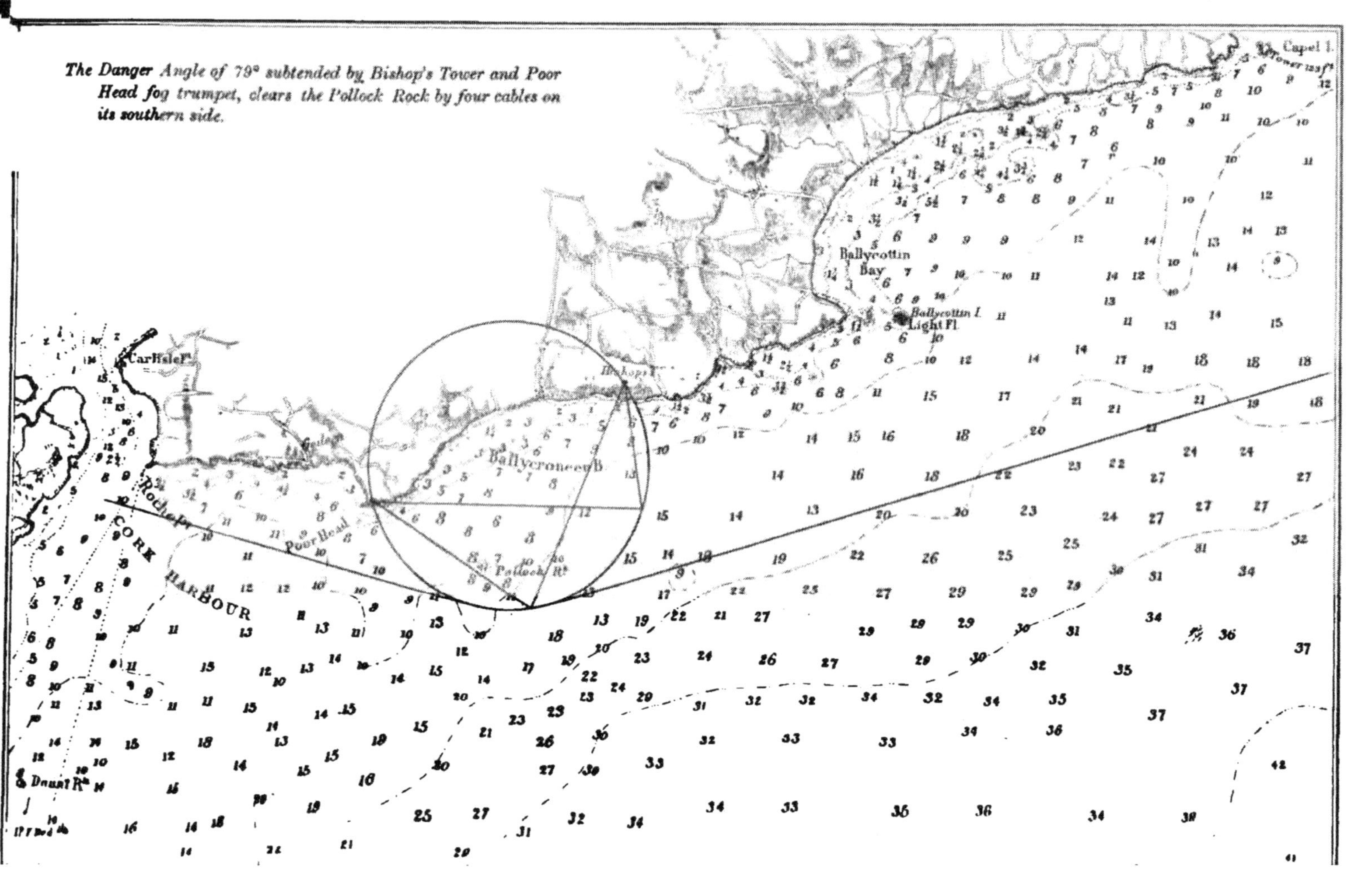


*The Danger Angle of 79° subtended by Bishop's Tower and Poor Head fog trumpet, clears the Pollock Rock by four cables on its southern side.*

Head and Bishop's Tower, some 3½ miles to the eastward, does not *exceed* 79°, you will—when at nearest approach—pass four cables outside the rock. To strike it the angle would require to be about 93°.

The fog-signal station on Poor Head, with its white boundary wall, is unmistakeable, and the trumpet is quite conspicuous at the western end of the enclosure. Bishop's Tower is situated on high ground midway between Poor Head and Ballycottin lighthouse. With the binocular it is easily got hold of, and once recognised and impressed on the memory there is no after trouble in doing so.

**Horizontal Danger Angle.**

To ascertain the "danger angle" for any place possessing suitable marks is a simple matter:—choose two conspicuous objects which are laid down on the chart, and if possible let them lie about an equal distance on each side of the danger. Put a pencil dot on the chart at the distance you wish to pass from the danger, and then draw a circle through the two selected objects and the pencil dot. The centre of the circle may be found by trial or as described in foot-note.* Next connect the pencil dot

* To find the "Danger angle" (horizontal), it is necessary to know that a circle can be drawn to pass through any three given points, no matter how situated, provided they do not lie in the same straight line. In the subjoined figures, a circle, whose centre is at *C*, is drawn through the given points *ABD*. The centre is found by the intersection of the dotted lines *FC* and *GC*. *Vide* Chapter X., on *Station Pointer.*

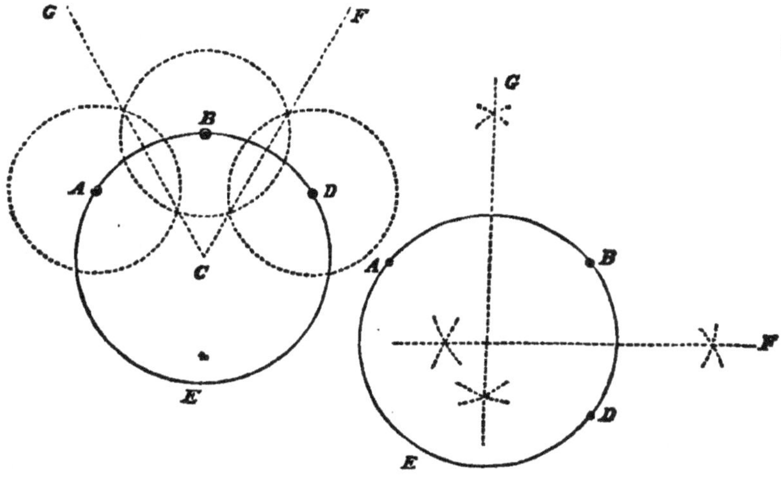


For a solution of this and other equally interesting Problems in Practical Geometry, see *Norie*, pages 19 to 25; also *Raper*.

with each of the marks by a fine straight line, and, with a protractor of any kind, measure the contained angle. This angle, as already stated, will be found to be the same at *any* point in the circumference of the circle.

Of course if it were desired to pass *inside* the Pollock Rock, another circle could be drawn to suit the new condition. In this case, to give the rock a berth of 4 cables on the inshore side, the "Danger angle" must not be *less* than 117°—an inconveniently large angle to measure with the sextant, but it might be possible to select more suitable objects. When taking the inside passage *beware of the "Hawk" and other sunken rocks off Poor Head.*

**Pearl Rock.** Entering or leaving Gibraltar Bay on the west side, the Pearl Rock (on which H.M's.S. *Agincourt* was nearly lost) has to be guarded against. The horizontal "danger angle" to pass 2½ cables (or a quarter of a mile) outside it, is 74°. This angle is to be measured between two very conspicuous square towers, the one situated on a hill overlooking the lighthouse on Carnero Point, and the other on the hill above Frayle Point.

Whether measured at the points in the diagram marked *A, B, C, D,* or any other part of the circle *seaward* of the towers, the angle is still 74°.

**Entering River Tagus by Danger Angle.** Again, in going into the port of Lisbon after dark, before the present range lights were established, the only guides to avoid the North and South Cachopos were the Compass bearings of San Julian and Bugio lights; but it often happened in winter that there was a heavy run on the bar, which sent the compass-cards spinning, and so rendered them utterly useless at the time of all others when most wanted; besides, in any case it would have been impossible to leave the bridge to lay off bearings at such a critical time.

The writer, however, has entered with comparative ease on very stormy nights, when no pilot could be had, by steering so as to maintain the "Danger angle" of 71° between Guia and San Julian lights, until those of Bugio and San Julian subtended nearly the same angle (68°), when the worst was passed, and it merely remained to con the vessel by eye midchannel between the two last-mentioned lights.

If, by bad steering or otherwise, the "Danger angle" between the first pair of lights was allowed to be greater or less than 71° at the moment the "Danger angle" came on between San Julian and Bugio, it shewed the vessel was not in mid-channel. In the event of the angle being greater than 71°, she was on the North

PEARL ROCK "DANGER ANGLE." (74°).

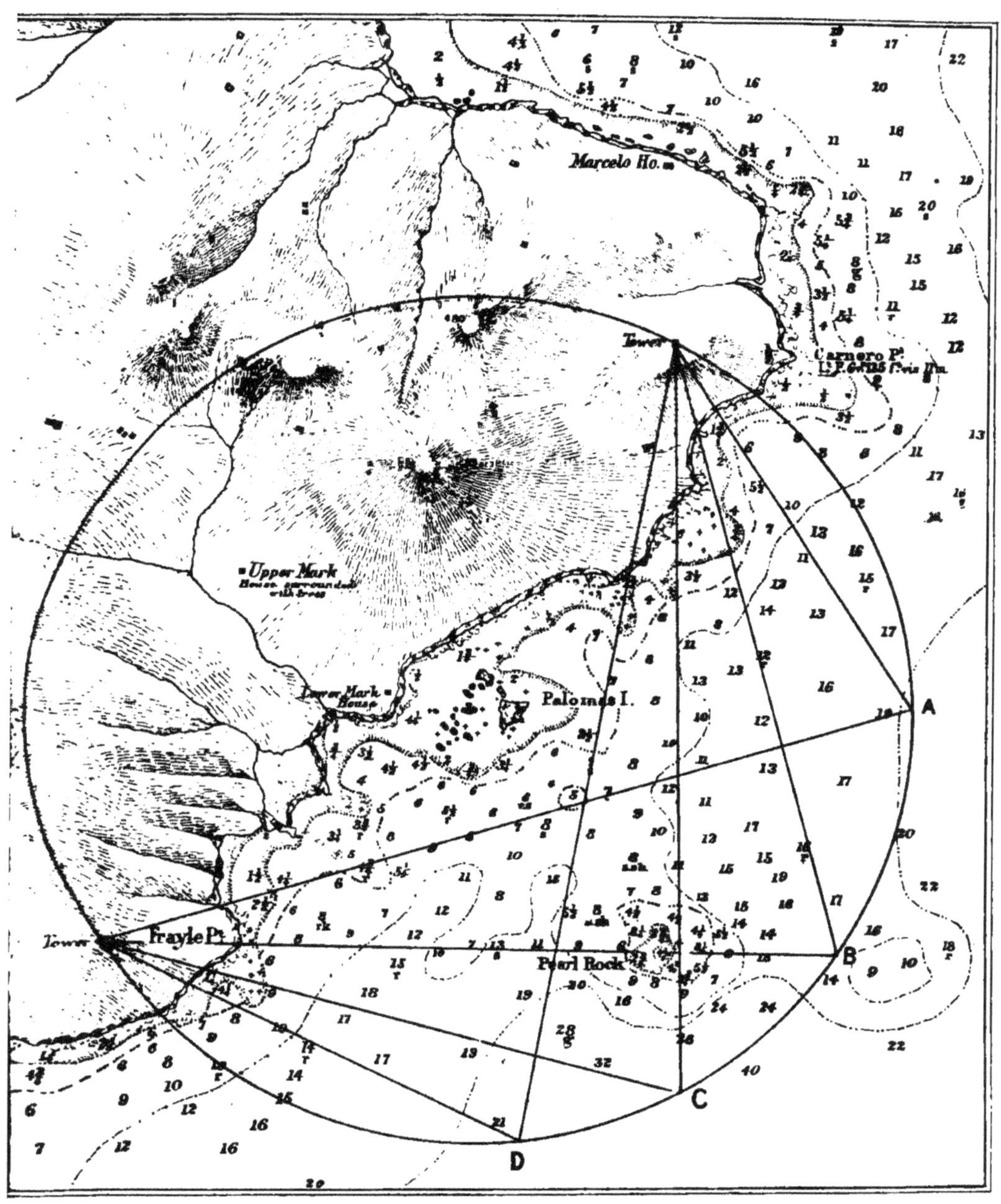


To face Page 436

side of the fairway; and if less, it placed her on the South side. So long, however, as the "Danger angle" between Guia and San Julian did not exceed 90°, or be under 55°, there was no cause for alarm.

By way of practice, these "Danger angles" might be laid off on Admiralty Plan No. 89, which gives the entrance of the River Tagus.

**Sextant versus Compass.**

It would hardly be wise, however, to make one's *first* experiment with the "Danger angle" under critical conditions such as those just described, nor would it be fair play to the method. Better, by far, to practice where no risk is incurred, until a perfect mastery of the principles gives confidence in their power. The foregoing examples afford conclusive proof that the Sextant is often of greater use in pilot waters than the Compass—not that the latter, after centuries of good service, is to be despised and forsaken; that time has not yet come. Each of the two instruments is good in its place; and it is the object of these pages to point out more particularly those cases where, with advantage, one may be employed in preference to the other.

**Best way to take *accurate* Cross-bearings.**

To conclude this subject, it should always be borne in mind that, in taking cross-bearings, the better plan is to observe but *one* compass bearing—whichever is most conveniently situated for the purpose—and then, with the sextant, take the horizontal angle between the two selected objects. The second bearing is, of course, got by applying the sextant angle to the right or left of the first one, as the case may require.

Get into a habit, and make your officers do the same, of noting and marking down *there and then* the exact time of all such observations.

EXAMPLE.—Being off Holyhead, observed the Skerries lighthouse to bear S. 84° E. by compass at 10·7 A.M. by watch, the sextant angle between it and the South Stack lighthouse being 80° at the same moment. The latter, therefore, bore S. 4° E. by same compass; and the cut being nearly a right angle, gives a good "fix."

## CHAPTER XVI.

### THE COMPOSITION AND RESOLUTION OF FORCES AND MOTIONS.

**Knowledge of this subject very important to seamen.** A full understanding of the Composition and Resolution of Forces and Motions is of so much importance to the sailor, from the infinite number and diversity of their application to *every* branch of his business, that it is hoped the introduction of a chapter savouring at first sight more of mechanics than navigation, will not be considered out of place. Indeed, there are few problems in physical science with which the principles herein to be explained are not intimately blended. Their relation to navigation, generally, is close; but it is seen more particularly, perhaps, in *Current Sailing*, and also when it becomes necessary to trace the total effect on the compasses of an iron ship to its various causes.

**Motion and Force.** *Motion* is the direct outcome of *force*, and the composition and resolution of *motions* are in all respects analagous to those of *forces*. It is therefore quite admissible, and will be convenient here, to deal with them as synonymous or convertible terms.

**A Single Force, how represented on paper.** A single force may be represented on paper by an arrow-headed straight line; the commencement of the line indicating the *Point of application* of the force—the direction of the line, the *Direction* of the force—and the length of the line, the *Magnitude* or *Intensity* of the force, according to the scale made use of.

The smallest number of *inclined* forces which can balance each other is three. To do so, these three forces must act through one point, and in one plane. Their relation to each other depends on

**Parallelogram of Forces and Velocities.** the following principle in mechanics, known as the *Parallelogram of Forces*, or, where motion is alluded to, as the *Parallelogram of Velocities.* The law is thus expressed. If two forces be represented in magnitude and direction by the adjacent sides of a parallelogram, an *equivalent* force will be represented in magnitude and direction by its diagonal. The two side forces are termed the *Components;* and the diagonal, the *Resultant* or product of their joint effect; whilst the junction of all three is called the *Point of application.*

A Parallelogram may be defined as any four-sided straight-lined figure, of which the opposite sides are parallel, and the diagonally opposite angles are equal to each other; its Diagonal, as the straight line joining two of its opposite angles. Thus a Square is a Parallelogram, and the subjoined Rhomboid is another. There are yet two, namely, the Rectangle and Rhombus.

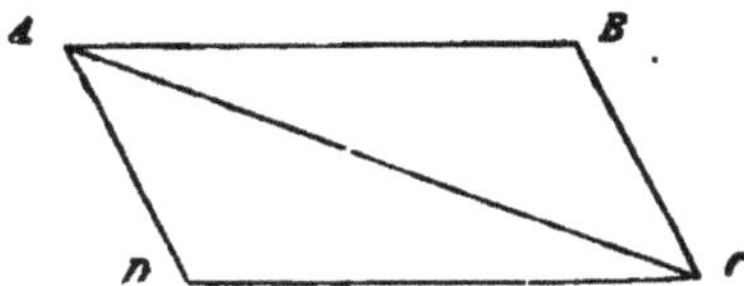

Thus the side $AB$ is parallel to the side $DC$; and $AD$ is parallel to $BC$. The angle $A$ is equal to the angle $C$; and $B$ is equal to $D$; whilst $AC$ is the diagonal. If $AB$ and $AD$ be taken as two forces, $A$ will be their *Point of application.*

**Given one angle in a parallelogram to find the other three.**

In any parallelogram the four angles amount to four right angles, or 360°; and from the fact above stated, that any two diagonally opposite angles are equal to each other, if *one* angle be given, *the other three* can readily be found. Thus if the angle $D$ be 116°, the angle $B$ will be 116° also. These two added together, and subtracted from 360°, leave 128° as the sum of $A$ and $C$; and as these are also equal to each other, their values must be respectively half of 128°, or 64°.

The following is an example of the *Composition of Motions,* which should be familiar to every seaman.

**Example of Composition of Motions.**

In the subjoined figure let $DC$ represent the course and hourly speed of a steamer; say due East, 14 knots: and let $AD$ represent the true direction of the wind, and its hourly velocity, say N.E. by N., 10 knots.

If the atmosphere were calm, the wind caused on board the vessel by her onward progress would appear to come from right ahead at a rate exactly equal to her speed: therefore the line $CD$ may be taken to represent a wind blowing in the direction of the arrow with a velocity of 14 knots per hour. Then $AD$ and $CD$ are the two components of the resultant $BD$, which latter shews the *apparent* direction and velocity of the wind as felt by an observer on the deck of the vessel, viz.; E.N.E. nly., 21¼ knots per hour: this result being due to the *combined* directions and velocities of the true wind and that produced by the motion of the steamer.

*Scale ⅛-inch to the mile.*

Parallelogram of Velocities.

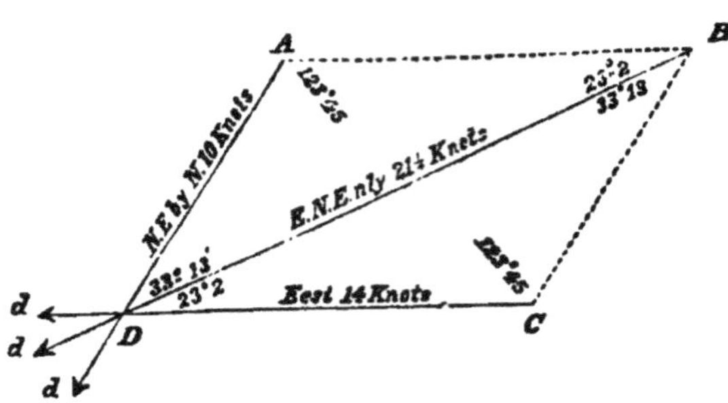


As is here shewn, this problem is very easily solved by construction, but when great accuracy is required, it can also be calculated as follows. Consider the parallelogram as two triangles, then we have,—

*To find the angles* DBC *and* BDC.

Side $AD$ = 10 — As the sum of $AD$ and $CD$ = 24 . . . . . . 1·380211
Side $CD$ = 14 — is to their difference = 4 . . . . . . 0·602060
Sum . . 24 — So is tang. of half the sum of angles $DBC$ and $BDC$ } 28° 7½′ . . . . 9·727957
Difference 4

10·330017
1·380211

| | 180° | | To tang. of half their difference | 5° 5½′ = 8·949806 |
|---|---|---|---|---|
| Angle $C$ . . . | 123 | 45 | | 28 7½ |
| Sum of Angles $DBC$ & $BDC$ | 56 | 15 | Sum gives greater angle $DBC$ | 33 13 |
| | | | Difference gives less angle $BDC$ | 23° 2′ |
| Half sum . . . | 28° | 7½′ | | |

*To find the resultant* BD.

| | |
|---|---|
| As sine of the angle $BDC$ = 23° 2′ . . . . . . . . . . . . . | 9·592473 |
| is to the side $BC$ = 10 knots . . . . . . . . . . . . . | 1·000000 |
| So is sine of the angle $C$ = 123° 45′ . . . . . . . . . . . . | 9·219846 |
| To the side $BD$ = 21·25 knots . . . . . . . . . . . . . | = 1·327373 |

Knowing how to compound two forces acting at a point, it is possible to compound or determine the resultant of any number.

**Resolution of Forces.**

The *Resolution of Forces* is the converse of the foregoing example. To resolve or decompose a given force or velocity $d'$, whose direction and magnitude is *BD*, into two forces or velocities acting in any direction that may be chosen, as $Ad''$ and *Cd*, we have only to draw parallels through *D*, which determine the lines *AD*, *CD*, representing the magnitude of the forces required. It is evident that there are an infinite number of pairs of forces into which *BD* might be resolved. It is usual, however, to resolve a force into forces that are at right angles to each other.

**Important illustration shewing how strains can be calculated.**

Subjoined is one more example of the practical value of understanding the *Parallelogram of Forces*.

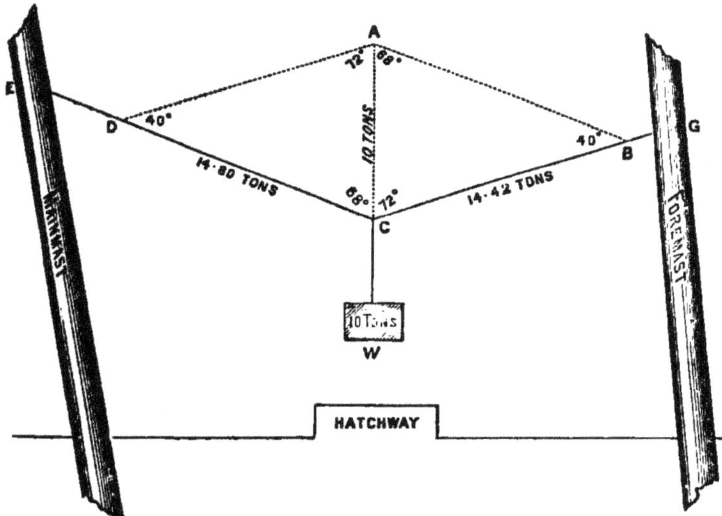


In the diagram, *W* is a weight of ten tons which is suspended without motion from a span between two masts. Let the angle $DCB = 140°$, and the angle $ACB = 72°$, then the angle $ACD$ will $= 68°$.* Draw *AC* to represent 10 tons on any convenient

* The Euclid scholar will have no difficulty in seeing how the values of the remaining angles are arrived at, but for the information of such as are weak in geometry, be it known that in any parallelogram the angle *DAC* will always be equal to its counterpart *ACB*, in this case 72°. The three angles of a triangle when added together make exactly 180°, so that if two are known, the third is easily found. Then $ACD + DAC$, or $68° + 72° = 140°$, which subtracted from 180°, gives the angle *ADC* as 40°, and since according to the definition of a parallelogram the angle *ADC* is equal to its opposite angle *ABC*, the latter must be equal to 40° also.

scale, say a tenth of an inch to the ton; also draw *AB* parallel to *DC*, and *AD* parallel to *BC*. Then by simple proportion of the parts, *DC* will represent the strain on the after pennant = 1·480 inches by scale, or 14·80 tons; and *CB* the strain on the forward pennant = 1·442 inches by scale, or 14·42 tons.

### By Calculation.

| To Find *D.C.* | | To Find *CB.* | |
|---|---|---|---|
| As the sine of 40° .................. | 9·808067 | As the sine of 40° .................. | 9·808067 |
| is to 10 tons .................... | 1·000000 | is to 10 tons .................... | 1·000000 |
| So is the sine of 72° .............. | 9·978206 | so is the sine of 68° .............. | 9·967166 |
| to *DC* = 14·80 tons .............. | 1·170139 | to *CB* = 14·42 tons................ | 1·159099 |

Similarly, having ascertained the strain on the pennants, it is easy by constructing other two parallelograms to calculate the "up and down" or crushing strain on each mast, as well as the bending or exact "fore-and-aft" pull.

In the foregoing example—common enough on board ship—the strain on the two parts of the span is shewn to be something excessive, much more so, indeed, than one would at first sight conceive to be possible, and this, too, without taking into account the additional stress which the span would have to sustain were it required to *lift* the weight instead of merely *suspending* it, as in the diagram.

**Flat Cargo Spans.** This example, though not pertaining to Navigation, is specially introduced because of its exceeding value in putting the sailor on his guard as to the peculiar properties of a span in connection with the dangerous operation of taking heavy weights in or out. The flatter the span, the greater will be the breaking or tensile strain it will have to endure, and the greater also will be the bending or shearing strain upon the masts. Therefore, when practicable, make it a rule to have the parts as much "up and down" as the drift necessary to clear the hatchway and bulwarks will admit of.

We will now try what stress the span would have to bear, supposing the weight still the same, but the angle *DCB* *acute* instead of *obtuse* as before.

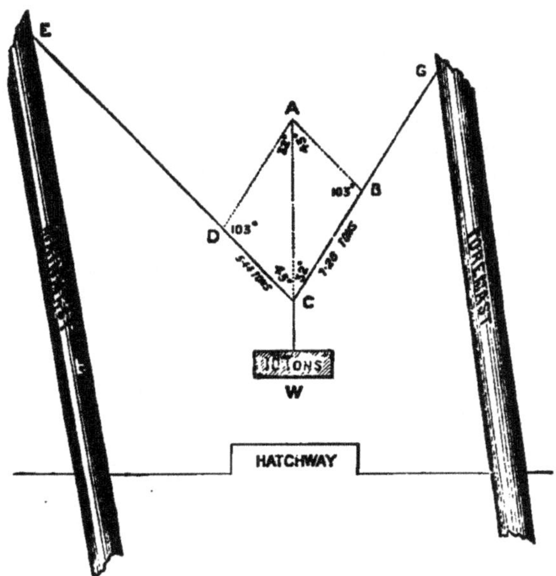


Let the angle $DCB = 77°$, and the angle $ACB = 32°$, then the angle $ACD$ will $= 45°$. The remaining angles are got as already explained.

| To Find *DC*. | |
|---|---|
| As sine of 103° | 9·988724 |
| is to 10 tons | 1·000000 |
| so is sine of 32° | 9·724210 |
| to $DC$ = 5·44 tons | 0·735486 |

| To Find *CB*. | |
|---|---|
| As sine of 103° | 9·988724 |
| is to 10 tons | 1·000000 |
| so is sine of 45° | 9·849485 |
| to $CB$ = 7·26 tons | 0·860761 |

We here see that the strain on the span is positively much *less than half what it was in the first case*, shewing very clearly the impropriety of rigging cargo gear straight across from mast to mast. Through pure ignorance of the danger incurred, this arrangement is quite common, as one may find out for himself by taking the trouble to walk round the docks of any large port. The consequences are seen in loss of life, broken spars, and claims for smashed up cargo. These evidences of grievous ignorance occur more frequently than one would imagine. The writer recollects the case, not so very long ago, of two celebrated steamers belonging to the same owners, where, through this cause, the masts were brought down on deck when taking out their funnels, though the heavier funnel of the two had but the paltry

**Stand from under.**

weight of four tons!!! Yet later, the taking out of a crank-shaft in a certain vessel had a similar result.

As an illustration familiar to every seaman take this one:—When a weak-handed watch can get no more of a rope, (say the lee fore brace) by straight pulling on it, what do they do? Why, make it fast to the pin and "swig it off." By so doing they are unconsciously acting the part of the weight on a straight span. The belaying pin may be taken to represent one mast, the leading block the other, and the part of the brace between these two points as the span. So powerful is the effect that the invariable result is to gain more of the brace after total failure to do so in the ordinary way.

**Disposition of anchors in a gale.**

There is scarcely a limit to the application of this important principle in the science of Forces. It comes into play in a marked manner in the case of a vessel riding to two anchors—one broad on each bow. The proof is easy that when the spread is great, two anchors, so placed, are actually weaker to hold the vessel in a gale than one anchor right ahead. As this question of strains if pursued further would be outside the limits of the present work, the reader is referred for detailed information to that very interesting and useful book, entitled, "*An Enquiry relative to various important points of Seamanship considered as a branch of Practical Science*," by Nicholas Tinmouth, Commander R.N., Master Attendant of Her Majesty's dockyard at Woolwich.

---

## CHAPTER XVII.

### ALGEBRA.

Algebra is usually a great bugbear to sailors, and although in the Practice of Navigation it cannot be considered an *essential*, a knowledge of the first four rules will occasionally be found very useful indeed. And these rules are so simple, that to commit them to memory within an hour or two need not "pawl the capstan" of any one possessing average intelligence. They are here given for reference when wanted.

### ALGEBRAIC ADDITION.

*Positive* quantities added together give a *positive* result.

**EXAMPLE.**

| | |
|---|---|
| | + 2 |
| Added to | + 4 |
| Equal | + 6 |

*Negative* quantities added together give a *negative* result.

**EXAMPLE.**

| | |
|---|---|
| | − 2 |
| Added to | − 4 |
| Equal | − 6 |

To add together *unlike* quantities, take their difference, and prefix the sign of the greater.

**EXAMPLE.**

| | |
|---|---|
| | − 2 |
| Added to | + 4 |
| Equal | + 2 |

### ALGEBRAIC SUBTRACTION.

To subtract one quantity from another, change the sign of the quantity to be subtracted, take their difference, and affix the sign of the greater, *if they are then of opposite names;* but if changing the sign of the subtrahend, make it similar to that of the minuend, then add arithmetically both quantities together, and prefix the same (or common) sign.

EXAMPLES.

| | | | |
|---|---|---|---|
| From . . . . . | − 4 | From . . . . . | − 4 |
| Subtract . . . | − 2 (change the sign). | Subtract . . . | + 2 (change the sign). |
| Remains . . . | − 2 | Remains . . . | − 6 |

### ALGEBRAIC MULTIPLICATION.

*Like* signs give +, and *unlike* signs give −.

EXAMPLES.

| | | | | | | | |
|---|---|---|---|---|---|---|---|
| If . . . . . . | − 4 | If . . . . . . . | + 4 | If . . . . . . . | + 4 | If . . . . . . . | − 4 |
| Be multiplied by | − 2 | Be multiplied by | + 2 | Be multiplied by | − 2 | Be multiplied by | + 2 |
| The product equals | + 8 | The product equals | + 8 | The product equals | − 8 | The product equals | − 8 |

### ALGEBRAIC DIVISION.

When the Divisor and Dividend have *like* signs, the sign of the quotient is plus; and when the signs are *unlike*, that of the quotient is minus.

EXAMPLES.

| | | | |
|---|---|---|---|
| −2) −4 (+2 | +2) +4 (+2 | −2) +4 (−2 | +2) −4 (−2 |
| 4 | 4 | 4 | 4 |
| — | — | — | — |

### DOMINO.

# APPENDIX.

## (A).

*On the method of correcting the rate of a Marine Chronometer.*

When the mean rates which a chronometer has made in the three temperatures, 55°, 70°, and 85°, are known from the Observatory rate sheets, it is necessary to calculate the quantities, C, T, and R, for that watch.

T is the temperature in which the watch attains its maximum gaining rate.

R is the rate at T.

C is a constant factor, which, multiplied by the square of any number of degrees from T, shows the amount of loss for that number of degrees.

It may be here mentioned that C and T have been found by experiment to remain constant for long periods, seldom changing, unless the watch is either cleaned or repaired. R, on the contrary, is liable to change occasionally, and should be verified at every opportunity of obtaining a rate by observation.

Formula for finding C, T, and R.*

Rate in 55° say — 0·72s. ... r
... r — r′ = — 0·45 ... d
" 70° " — 0·27s. ... r′
... r′ — r″ = + 1·08 ... d′
" 85° " — 1·35s. ... r″
d — d′ = — 1·53
d + d′ = + 0·63

To find C

$$C = \frac{2(d - d')}{30^2} = \frac{-3{\cdot}06}{900} = -0{\cdot}0034$$

---

* Sign + indicates fast error, or gaining rate.
" — " slow " or losing

To find T

$$(T - 70°) = \frac{d + d'}{C \times 60} = \frac{+\ 0{\cdot}63}{-\ 0{\cdot}204} = -\ 3{\cdot}1°$$

$$T = 70° - 3{\cdot}1° = 66{\cdot}9°$$

To find R $(T - 70)^2 \times C = 9{\cdot}61 \times 0{\cdot}0034 = 0{\cdot}03^s$

Rate at - 70° = $-\ 0{\cdot}27^s$ losing.

Difference to T = $+\ 0{\cdot}03^s$ faster.

R - - - - - = $-\ 0{\cdot}24^s$ losing.

Let - - N = any number of degrees from T.

Then $C \times N^2$ = amount of loss for N.

The quantities C, T, and R, for any watch, having been found, the rule for finding the rate of the same watch in any given temperature is as follows:—

Take the difference between the given temperature and T (calling this difference N).

Multiply $N^2$ by C, and the result will be the amount by which the watch will go slower at the given temperature than it does at T; and, therefore, by applying the amount thus obtained to R (the rate of the watch at T), the rate in the given temperature will be obtained.

When C, T, and R have been found, the rate which the watch will keep in various temperatures can be found from the Table on page 356.

The Table gives the amount by which a watch will go slower than at T, at any given number of degrees from T. The rule for using the Table is:—

Take the difference between the given temperature and T (that is, N).

Take C to the nearest third decimal place. Enter the Table with C at the head. Enter the column marked N, with N as given to nearest degree, and in the column marked Cor'n will be found the amount by which the watch will go slower for N degrees.

*Example*:—

T 72° C 0·003 R $-\ 0{\cdot}54^s$

Required the rate in 60°.

Difference between T and given temperature = 12° = N.

Enter Table headed C 0·003, and column N, and take 12°

The column headed Cor'n gives $-\ 0{\cdot}43^s$ losing.

R $-\ 0{\cdot}54$ -

Rate in 60° - $-\ 0{\cdot}97^s$

The "thermal error" or correction of the rates for temperature, as carried out at the Bidston Observatory, has led to the discovery by Mr. Hartnup of a small but very systematic difference between the "Sea" and "Shore rates" of chronometers. With very few exceptions, chronometers used in steamships have been found to go somewhat *slower* at sea than on shore—the amount in different instruments ranging from a small fraction of a second to upwards of one second a day. This is probably caused by the motion of the ship, or the magnetic effect of the iron of which she is built. It is small in comparison with the thermal error, and is only capable of being detected in cases where the corrections for change of temperature have been carefully applied at sea during the voyage.

## TABLE OF CORRECTIONS DUE TO CHANGES OF TEMPERATURE.

### C 0·001.

| N. | Cor'n. | N. | Cor'n. | N. | Cor'n. | N. | Cor'n. | N. | Cor'n. |
|---|---|---|---|---|---|---|---|---|---|
| | s. | | s. | | s. | | s. | | s. |
| 1 | 0·00 | 21 | 0·44 | 41 | 1·68 | 61 | 3·72 | 81 | 6·56 |
| 2 | 0·00 | 22 | 0·48 | 42 | 1·76 | 62 | 3·84 | 82 | 6·72 |
| 3 | 0·01 | 23 | 0·53 | 43 | 1·85 | 63 | 3·97 | 83 | 6·89 |
| 4 | 0·02 | 24 | 0·58 | 44 | 1·94 | 64 | 4·10 | 84 | 7·06 |
| 5 | 0·02 | 25 | 0·62 | 45 | 2·02 | 65 | 4·22 | 85 | 7·22 |
| 6 | 0·04 | 26 | 0·68 | 46 | 2·12 | 66 | 4·36 | 86 | 7·40 |
| 7 | 0·05 | 27 | 0·73 | 47 | 2·21 | 67 | 4·49 | 87 | 7·57 |
| 8 | 0·06 | 28 | 0·78 | 48 | 2·30 | 68 | 4·62 | 88 | 7·74 |
| 9 | 0·08 | 29 | 0·84 | 49 | 2·40 | 69 | 4·76 | 89 | 7·92 |
| 10 | 0·10 | 30 | 0·90 | 50 | 2·50 | 70 | 4·90 | 90 | 8·10 |
| 11 | 0·12 | 31 | 0·96 | 51 | 2·60 | 71 | 5·04 | 91 | 8·28 |
| 12 | 0·14 | 32 | 1·02 | 52 | 2·70 | 72 | 5·18 | 92 | 8·46 |
| 13 | 0·17 | 33 | 1·09 | 53 | 2·81 | 73 | 5·33 | 93 | 8·65 |
| 14 | 0·20 | 34 | 1·16 | 54 | 2·92 | 74 | 5·48 | 94 | 8·84 |
| 15 | 0·22 | 35 | 1·22 | 55 | 3·02 | 75 | 5·62 | 95 | 9·02 |
| 16 | 0·26 | 36 | 1·30 | 56 | 3·14 | 76 | 5·78 | 96 | 9·22 |
| 17 | 0·29 | 37 | 1·37 | 57 | 3·25 | 77 | 5·93 | 97 | 9·41 |
| 18 | 0·32 | 38 | 1·44 | 58 | 3·36 | 78 | 6·08 | 98 | 9·60 |
| 19 | 0·36 | 39 | 1·52 | 59 | 3·48 | 79 | 6·24 | 99 | 9·80 |
| 20 | 0·40 | 40 | 1·60 | 60 | 3·60 | 80 | 6·40 | 100 | 10·00 |

### C 0·002.

| N. | Cor'n. | N. | Cor'n. | N. | Cor'n. | N. | Cor'n. | N. | Cor'n. |
|---|---|---|---|---|---|---|---|---|---|
| | s. | | s. | | s. | | s. | | s. |
| 1 | 0·00 | 21 | 0·88 | 41 | 3·36 | 61 | 7·44 | 81 | 13·12 |
| 2 | 0·01 | 22 | 0·97 | 42 | 3·53 | 62 | 7·69 | 82 | 13·45 |
| 3 | 0·02 | 23 | 1·06 | 43 | 3·70 | 63 | 7·94 | 83 | 13·78 |
| 4 | 0·03 | 24 | 1·15 | 44 | 3·87 | 64 | 8·19 | 84 | 14·11 |
| 5 | 0·05 | 25 | 1·25 | 45 | 4·05 | 65 | 8·45 | 85 | 14·45 |
| 6 | 0·07 | 26 | 1·35 | 46 | 4·23 | 66 | 8·71 | 86 | 14·79 |
| 7 | 0·10 | 27 | 1·46 | 47 | 4·42 | 67 | 8·98 | 87 | 15·14 |
| 8 | 0·13 | 28 | 1·57 | 48 | 4·61 | 68 | 9·25 | 88 | 15·49 |
| 9 | 0·16 | 29 | 1·68 | 49 | 4·80 | 69 | 9·52 | 89 | 15·84 |
| 10 | 0·20 | 30 | 1·80 | 50 | 5·00 | 70 | 9·80 | 90 | 16·20 |
| 11 | 0·24 | 31 | 1·92 | 51 | 5·20 | 71 | 10·08 | 91 | 16·56 |
| 12 | 0·29 | 32 | 2·05 | 52 | 5·41 | 72 | 10·37 | 92 | 16·93 |
| 13 | 0·34 | 33 | 2·18 | 53 | 5·62 | 73 | 10·66 | 93 | 17·30 |
| 14 | 0·39 | 34 | 2·31 | 54 | 5·83 | 74 | 10·95 | 94 | 17·67 |
| 15 | 0·45 | 35 | 2·45 | 55 | 6·05 | 75 | 11·25 | 95 | 18·05 |
| 16 | 0·51 | 36 | 2·59 | 56 | 6·27 | 76 | 11·55 | 96 | 18·43 |
| 17 | 0·58 | 37 | 2·74 | 57 | 6·50 | 77 | 11·86 | 97 | 18·82 |
| 18 | 0·65 | 38 | 2·89 | 58 | 6·73 | 78 | 12·17 | 98 | 19·21 |
| 19 | 0·72 | 39 | 3·04 | 59 | 6·96 | 79 | 12·48 | 99 | 19·60 |
| 20 | 0·80 | 40 | 3·20 | 60 | 7·20 | 80 | 12·80 | 100 | 20·00 |

### C 0·003.

| N. | Cor'n. | N. | Cor'n. | N. | Cor'n. | N. | Cor'n. | N. | Cor'n. |
|---|---|---|---|---|---|---|---|---|---|
| | s. | | s. | | s. | | s. | | s. |
| 1 | 0·00 | 21 | 1·32 | 41 | 5·04 | 61 | 11·16 | 81 | 19·68 |
| 2 | 0·01 | 22 | 1·45 | 42 | 5·29 | 62 | 11·53 | 82 | 20·17 |
| 3 | 0·03 | 23 | 1·59 | 43 | 5·55 | 63 | 11·91 | 83 | 20·67 |
| 4 | 0·05 | 24 | 1·73 | 44 | 5·81 | 64 | 12·29 | 84 | 21·17 |
| 5 | 0·08 | 25 | 1·88 | 45 | 6·08 | 65 | 12·68 | 85 | 21·68 |
| 6 | 0·11 | 26 | 2·03 | 46 | 6·35 | 66 | 13·07 | 86 | 22·19 |
| 7 | 0·15 | 27 | 2·19 | 47 | 6·63 | 67 | 13·47 | 87 | 22·71 |
| 8 | 0·19 | 28 | 2·35 | 48 | 6·91 | 68 | 13·87 | 88 | 23·23 |
| 9 | 0·24 | 29 | 2·52 | 49 | 7·20 | 69 | 14·28 | 89 | 23·76 |
| 10 | 0·30 | 30 | 2·70 | 50 | 7·50 | 70 | 14·70 | 90 | 24·30 |
| 11 | 0·36 | 31 | 2·88 | 51 | 7·80 | 71 | 15·12 | 91 | 24·84 |
| 12 | 0·43 | 32 | 3·07 | 52 | 8·11 | 72 | 15·55 | 92 | 25·39 |
| 13 | 0·51 | 33 | 3·27 | 53 | 8·43 | 73 | 15·99 | 93 | 25·95 |
| 14 | 0·59 | 34 | 3·47 | 54 | 8·75 | 74 | 16·43 | 94 | 26·51 |
| 15 | 0·68 | 35 | 3·68 | 55 | 9·08 | 75 | 16·88 | 95 | 27·08 |
| 16 | 0·77 | 36 | 3·89 | 56 | 9·41 | 76 | 17·33 | 96 | 27·65 |
| 17 | 0·87 | 37 | 4·11 | 57 | 9·75 | 77 | 17·79 | 97 | 28·23 |
| 18 | 0·97 | 38 | 4·33 | 58 | 10·09 | 78 | 18·25 | 98 | 28·81 |
| 19 | 1·08 | 39 | 4·56 | 59 | 10·44 | 79 | 18·72 | 99 | 29·40 |
| 20 | 1·20 | 40 | 4·80 | 60 | 10·80 | 80 | 19·20 | 100 | 30·00 |

### C 0·004.

| N. | Cor'n. | N. | Cor'n. | N. | Cor'n. | N. | Cor'n. | N. | Cor'n. |
|---|---|---|---|---|---|---|---|---|---|
| | s. | | s. | | s. | | s. | | s. |
| 1 | 0·00 | 21 | 1·76 | 41 | 6·72 | 61 | 14·88 | 81 | 26·24 |
| 2 | 0·02 | 22 | 1·94 | 42 | 7·06 | 62 | 15·38 | 82 | 26·90 |
| 3 | 0·04 | 23 | 2·12 | 43 | 7·40 | 63 | 15·88 | 83 | 27·56 |
| 4 | 0·06 | 24 | 2·30 | 44 | 7·74 | 64 | 16·38 | 84 | 28·22 |
| 5 | 0·10 | 25 | 2·50 | 45 | 8·10 | 65 | 16·90 | 85 | 28·90 |
| 6 | 0·14 | 26 | 2·70 | 46 | 8·46 | 66 | 17·42 | 86 | 29·58 |
| 7 | 0·20 | 27 | 2·92 | 47 | 8·84 | 67 | 17·96 | 87 | 30·28 |
| 8 | 0·26 | 28 | 3·14 | 48 | 9·22 | 68 | 18·50 | 88 | 30·98 |
| 9 | 0·32 | 29 | 3·36 | 49 | 9·60 | 69 | 19·04 | 89 | 31·68 |
| 10 | 0·40 | 30 | 3·60 | 50 | 10·00 | 70 | 19·60 | 90 | 32·40 |
| 11 | 0·48 | 31 | 3·84 | 51 | 10·46 | 71 | 20·16 | 91 | 33·12 |
| 12 | 0·58 | 32 | 4·10 | 52 | 10·82 | 72 | 20·74 | 92 | 33·86 |
| 13 | 0·68 | 33 | 4·36 | 53 | 11·24 | 73 | 21·32 | 93 | 34·60 |
| 14 | 0·78 | 34 | 4·62 | 54 | 11·66 | 74 | 21·90 | 94 | 35·34 |
| 15 | 0·90 | 35 | 4·90 | 55 | 12·10 | 75 | 22·50 | 95 | 36·10 |
| 16 | 1·02 | 36 | 5·18 | 56 | 12·54 | 76 | 23·10 | 96 | 36·86 |
| 17 | 1·16 | 37 | 5·46 | 57 | 13·00 | 77 | 23·72 | 97 | 37·64 |
| 18 | 1·30 | 38 | 5·74 | 58 | 13·46 | 78 | 24·34 | 98 | 38·42 |
| 19 | 1·44 | 39 | [illegible] | 59 | [illegible] | 79 | [illegible] | 99 | [illegible] |
| 20 | [illegible] | 40 | [illegible] | 60 | [illegible] | 80 | [illegible] | 100 | [illegible] |

### C 0·005.

| N. | Cor'n. | N. | Cor'n. | N. | Cor'n. | N. | Cor'n. | N. | Cor'n. |
|---|---|---|---|---|---|---|---|---|---|
| | s. | | s. | | s. | | s. | | s. |
| 1 | 0·00 | 21 | 2·20 | 41 | 8·40 | 61 | 18·60 | 81 | 32·80 |
| 2 | 0·02 | 22 | 2·42 | 42 | 8·82 | 62 | 19·22 | 82 | 33·62 |
| 3 | 0·04 | 23 | 2·64 | 43 | 9·24 | 63 | 19·84 | 83 | 34·44 |
| 4 | 0·08 | 24 | 2·88 | 44 | 9·68 | 64 | 20·48 | 84 | 35·28 |
| 5 | 0·12 | 25 | 3·12 | 45 | 10·12 | 65 | 21·12 | 85 | 36·12 |
| 6 | 0·18 | 26 | 3·38 | 46 | 10·58 | 66 | 21·78 | 86 | 36·98 |
| 7 | 0·24 | 27 | 3·64 | 47 | 11·04 | 67 | 22·44 | 87 | 37·84 |
| 8 | 0·32 | 28 | 3·92 | 48 | 11·52 | 68 | 23·12 | 88 | 38·72 |
| 9 | 0·40 | 29 | 4·20 | 49 | 12·00 | 69 | 23·80 | 89 | 39·60 |
| 10 | 0·50 | 30 | 4·50 | 50 | 12·50 | 70 | 24·50 | 90 | 40·50 |
| 11 | 0·60 | 31 | 4·80 | 51 | 13·00 | 71 | 25·20 | 91 | 41·40 |
| 12 | 0·72 | 32 | 5·12 | 52 | 13·52 | 72 | 25·92 | 92 | 42·32 |
| 13 | 0·84 | 33 | 5·44 | 53 | 14·04 | 73 | 26·64 | 93 | 43·24 |
| 14 | 0·98 | 34 | 5·78 | 54 | 14·58 | 74 | 27·38 | 94 | 44·18 |
| 15 | 1·12 | 35 | 6·12 | 55 | 15·12 | 75 | 28·12 | 95 | 45·12 |
| 16 | 1·28 | 36 | 6·48 | 56 | 15·68 | 76 | 28·88 | 96 | 46·08 |
| 17 | 1·44 | 37 | 6·84 | 57 | 16·24 | 77 | 29·64 | 97 | 47·04 |
| 18 | 1·62 | 38 | 7·22 | 58 | [illegible] | 78 | 30·42 | 98 | 48·02 |
| 19 | 1·80 | 39 | 7·60 | 59 | 17·40 | 79 | 31·20 | 99 | 49·00 |
| 20 | [illegible] | 40 | [illegible] | 60 | [illegible] | 80 | [illegible] | 100 | [illegible] |

## APPENDIX (B).

It has been considered advisable to give a place to the following correspondence between the author and another, bearing as it does upon a very important consideration in the navigation of iron ships:—

*The Editor, Mercantile Marine Service Association "Reporter."*

### HEELING ERROR.

Sir,—Will any correspondent kindly give the method usually employed at the Board of Trade Examinations for calculating the Heeling Error? Given the heel, the direction of the ship's head by compass, and the Heeling Error observed, to find the approximate Heeling Error, with a greater or less given heel, and with the ship's head on some other named point of the compass, the ship's magnetic latitude being in both cases the same. —Yours faithfully, INGANNO.

*December*, 1877.

---

*The Editor, Mercantile Marine Service Association "Reporter."*

### HEELING ERROR.

Sir,—In answer to "Inganno," in your January number, I submit that the first thing to be done is to determine what is called the *heeling co-efficient.* It is the error on the North or South point *by compass*, caused by *one* degree of heel, and is found by dividing the difference between the deviation, ship upright and ship heeling, by the number of degrees of heel.

For example, given the deviation on North, ship upright, equal to $-21°$; when heeling $12°$ to starboard, equal to $-3°$; this is equivalent to a *plus* change of $18°$, which, divided by $12°$ of heel, gives $+1°{\cdot}5$ as the *heeling co-efficient* for each degree of heel to starboard. From this it will be seen that the heeling error is *directly proportional* to the amount of heel. Now, when the heeling error is given for any other than the North or South points, it is easily reduced to these by simply dividing it by the natural cosine of the number of points from North or South then divide the result by the inclination to starboard or port, as the case may be, and you have the *heeling co-efficient* as before.

For example, the heeling error on W.N.W., with 16° of heel to port, is $-9°{\cdot}19$; divide this by ·383 (the natural cosine of 6 points) and you get 24°; divide this by the heel (16°), and once again we shake hands with our friend the *heeling co-efficient.*

Now it is evident that if we require the heeling error for any other given point, we have merely to *multiply the heeling co-efficient* by the natural cosine of the number of points contained between North *or* South (taking the nearest) and the stated point, multiply the result by the fresh heel, and we have the error required.

For example, the *heeling co-efficient* on North is $+ 1°{\cdot}5$ for each degree of heel to starboard; required the heeling error on N.E. by N. ½ N., heeling 10° to starboard. Multiply $+ 1°{\cdot}5$ by ·882 (the natural cosine of 2½ points): the result is $+ 1°{\cdot}32$; multiply this again by 10° inclination to starboard, and we get $+ 13°{\cdot}23$ as the answer.

I have treated the foregoing solution of the question asked by "Inganno" at considerable length, and in piecemeal fashion, hoping that by so doing it would be rendered clearer. The mathematical expression is very concise, but seamen are more accustomed to regard *weather* signs than to study *algebraic* ones. Before quitting this subject I must warn "Inganno" that if the heeling error has a *plus* sign when heeling to starboard, it will have a *minus* one with a heel in the opposite direction; also, that the signs are reversed when the Northern semicircle of the compass is substituted for the Southern one, or the contrary. For example, if the *heeling co-efficient* on North is $+1°{\cdot}5$ when heeling to starboard, it will be $-1°{\cdot}5$ on South when heeling the same way. In conclusion, the *heeling error* on any given point must not be confounded with the *deviation* on the same point. For example, the *deviation*, ship upright on S.W. is +13°, but when heeling 17° to port it is only +2°, the heeling error is consequently −11°.

Complete Example.—With ship's head S.E. by E., and upright, the deviation is +23°; when heeling 8° to port it is +3°. Required the deviation on N.N.W., when heeling 15° to starboard; the deviation on that point, when upright, being −14°; magnetic latitude the same in each case? Answer, $-76°{\cdot}25$.

Squire T. S. Lecky.

*February 20th*, 1878.

# APPENDIX (C).

## STAR TELESCOPE FOR SEXTANTS.

About the first thing to be seen to on getting a star telescope fitted to one's sextant, is that its collimation adjustment is perfect. If the line of sight of the telescope is at all inclined to the plane of the instrument, instead of being strictly parallel to it, as it should be, all angles measured with it will be too great; and the larger the angle so measured, the greater will be the error. To determine the value of the error corresponding to the various angles or altitudes, which may at any time be observed, proceed as follows:—The sextant being in perfect adjustment, screw in the ordinary direct telescope, and, on a fine clear night, measure carefully the angle between two stars, whose distance apart is between 100° and 110°. Read off and note this angle, but do not move the index; then insert the star telescope, and verify the measure—*taking care to make it in the very centre of the field.* If the line of collimation is correct, the stars will be in contact as before; but if it is not so, the stars will appear to have separated. Bring them again into contact, and, having read off the angle, the difference between it and the first reading is, of course, the error for that particular angle.

To find what it would be for smaller angles, one might proceed as before, by selecting stars at the required distance apart; but it is better to adopt another method, wherein a knowledge of the error of parallelism of the telescope is pre-supposed.

Raper, in his explanation to Table 54, already referred to on page 49, gives a rule for determining the error for any given altitude or angular distance when the error of parallelism of the telescope employed is known; and this same rule, *when worked backwards*, serves of course to find the error of parallelism.

### RULE TO FIND THE ERROR OF PARALLELISM.

From the log. sine of the error belonging to any given angle, measured by sextant, subtract the log. tangent of half the same angle, and the remainder divided by 2 will be the log. sine of the error of collimation.

EXAMPLE.

Let the error at 100° due to defective adjustment of the line of collimation be 8′; required the inclination of the telescope to the plane of the sextant.

| | |
|---|---|
| Log. sine of 8′ .................................. | 7·36682 |
| Log. tangent of half 100° = 50° ........... | 10·07619 |
| 2 | 17·29063 |
| Log. sine 2° 32′ ..................... | 8·64531 |

Now, having ascertained the angular inclination of the telescope to the plane of the sextant, if it be required to know the quantity to be subtracted from any other altitude or distance measured with the same star telescope and sextant, we must employ Raper's rule in its direct form as follows:—

"To twice the log. sine of the error in the parallelism of the telescope, add the log. tangent of *half* the angle measured. The sum will be the log. sine of the required error in the observed angle."

EXAMPLE.

The error of parallelism having been determined as 2° 32′, required to know the quantity to be subtracted from an observed altitude of 40°.

| | |
|---|---|
| 2° 32′ Log. sine 8·64531 × 2 .................. | 7·29062 |
| Half of 40° = 20° Tangent .................. | 9·56107 |
| Quantity to be subtracted 2′ 27″ Sine ...... | 6·85169 |

Having ascertained by *direct measurement* the error at 100° or thereabouts, it is recommended to ascertain, by *calculation* as above, the error for all other altitudes at intervals of say 5°. Having thus made a small table, gum it on the inside of the lid of the sextant case for ready reference. Whether the errors are known or not, don't forget the advice on page 237, to observe stars on *both sides of the zenith*. The diameter of the object glass of the star telescope should not exceed 1⅝ inches clear aperture, unless special provision is made for one of greater size by raising the horizon-glass an additional $\frac{1}{16}$ of an inch or thereabouts above the plane of the instrument. *In using the star telescope be careful to observe as nearly as possible in the exact centre of the field.*

# APPENDIX (D).

## USEFUL NAVIGATIONAL STARS.

| NAMES. | Mag. | Right Ascension. | Declination. |
|---|---|---|---|
| | | H. M. | |
| α Andromedæ (*Alpheratz*) | 1 | 0 2 | 28½ N. |
| γ Pegasi (*Algenib*) | 3.2 | 0 7 | 14½ N. |
| α Cassiopeiæ (*Schedar*) | 2.3 | 0 34 | 56 N. |
| β Ceti (*Deneb-Kaitos*) | 2 | 0 38 | 18½ S. |
| β Andromedæ (*Mirach*) | 2.3 | 1 3 | 35 N. |
| α Ursæ Minoris (*Polaris*) | 2 | 1 16 | 89 N. |
| α Eridani (*Achernar*) | 1 | 1 33 | 58 S. |
| α Arietis (*Hamal*) | 2 | 2 1 | 23 N. |
| α Ceti (*Menkar*) | 2.3 | 2 56 | 4 N. |
| α Persei (*Mirfack*) | 2 | 3 16 | 49½ N. |
| α Tauri (*Aldebaran*) | 1 | 4 29 | 16 N. |
| α Aurigæ (*Capella*) | 1 | 5 8 | 46 N. |
| β Orionis (*Rigel*) | 1 | 5 9 | 8¼ S. |
| β Tauri (*Nath*) | 2 | 5 19 | 28¼ N. |
| δ Orionis | 2 | 5 26 | 0½ S. |
| ε Orionis | 2 | 5 30 | 1¼ S. |
| α Columbæ | 2 | 5 36 | 34 S. |
| κ Orionis | 3.2 | 5 42 | 10 S. |
| α Orionis (*Betelguese*) | 1 | 5 49 | 7½ N. |
| α Argûs (*Canopus*) | 1 | 6 21 | 52½ S. |
| α Canis Majoris (*Sirius*) | 1 | 6 40 | 16½ S. |
| ε Canis Majoris | 2.1 | 6 54 | 29 S. |
| α² Geminor (*Castor*) | 3.1 | 7 27 | 32 N. |
| α Canis Minoris (*Procyon*) | 1 | 7 33 | 5¼ N. |
| β Geminor (*Pollux*) | 1.2 | 7 38 | 28 N. |
| ι Argûs | 2 | 9 14 | 59 S. |
| α Hydræ (*Alphard*) | 2 | 9 22 | 8 S. |
| α Leonis (*Regulus*) | 1.2 | 10 2 | 12½ N. |
| γ¹ Leonis | 2 | 10 14 | 20½ N. |
| α Ursæ Majoris (*Dubhe*) | 2 | 10 57 | 62¼ N. |
| β Leonis (*Denebola*) | 2 | 11 43 | 15 N. |
| γ Ursæ Majoris (*Megrez*) | 2.3 | 11 48 | 54 N. |
| α¹ Crucis | 1 | 12 20 | 62½ S. |
| ε Virginis (*Vindemiatrix*) | 3.2 | 12 56 | 11½ N. |
| α Virginis (*Spica*) | 1 | 13 19 | 10½ S. |
| η Ursæ Majoris (*Benetnasch*) | 2 | 13 43 | 50 N. |
| β Centauri | 1 | 13 56 | 60 S. |
| α Bootis (*Arcturus*) | 1 | 14 10 | 20 N. |
| α² Centauri | 1 | 14 32 | 60 S. |
| α Libræ (*Zubenasch*) | 2.3 | 14 45 | 15½ S. |
| β Ursæ Minoris (*Kochab*) | 2 | 14 51 | 74½ N. |
| β Libræ (*Zubenelg*) | 2 | 15 11 | 9 S. |
| α Coronæ (*Gemma* or *Alphacca*) | 2 | 15 30 | 27 N. |
| α Serpentis (*Unuk*) | 2.3 | 15 39 | 7 N. |
| β¹ Scorpii | 2 | 15 59 | 19½ S. |
| α Scorpii (*Antares*) | 1.2 | 16 22 | 26 S. |
| α Trianguli Australis | 2 | 16 37 | 69 S. |
| ζ Herculis | 3.2 | 16 37 | 32 N. |
| α Ophiuchi (*Ras Alhague*) | 2 | 17 30 | 12½ N. |
| γ Draconis (*Rastaban*) | 2.3 | 17 54 | 51½ N. |
| α Lyræ (*Vega*) | 1 | 18 33 | 39 N. |
| α Aquilæ (*Altair*) | 1.2 | 19 45 | 8½ N. |
| α Pavonis | 2 | 20 17 | 57 S. |
| α Cygni (*Deneb*) | 2.1 | 20 38 | 45 N. |
| α Cephei (*Alderamin*) | 3.2 | 21 16 | 62 N. |
| α Gruis | 2 | 22 1 | 47½ S. |
| α Piscis Australis (*Fomalhaut*) | 1.2 | 22 51 | 30 S. |
| α Pegasi (*Markab*) | 2 | 22 59 | 14½ N. |

# EXTRACTS FROM NAUTICAL ALMANACS

FOR VARIOUS YEARS,

WHICH HAVE REFERENCE TO THE EXAMPLES

GIVEN IN THE BODY OF THIS BOOK.

II. AUGUST, 1875. 143

| AT MEAN NOON. | | | | | | |
|---|---|---|---|---|---|---|
| Day of the Week. | Day of the Month. | THE SUN'S *Apparent* Declination. | THE SUN'S Var. in 1 Hour. | Equation of Time, *to be subtracted from Mean Time.* | Var. in 1 Hour. | Sidereal Time. |
| | | ° ′ ″ | ″ | m s | s | h m s |
| Sat. | 14 | 14 25 49·4 | 46·19 | 4 30·93 | 0·460 | 9 30 0·27 |
| *Sun.* | 15 | 14 7 14·1 | 46·75 | 4 19·63 | 0·483 | 9 33 56·83 |
| Mon. | 16 | 13 48 25·3 | 47·30 | 4 7·78 | 0·505 | 9 37 53·38 |

APPARENT PLACES OF STARS, 1875. 395

| AT UPPER TRANSIT AT GREENWICH. | | | | |
|---|---|---|---|---|
| Month and Day. | α Virginis. (*Spica*). R.A. | α Virginis. (*Spica*). Dec. *South.* | α Piscis Australis. (*Fomalhaut*). R.A. | α Piscis Australis. (*Fomalhaut*). Dec. *South.* |
| | h m 13 18 s | ° ′ 10 30 ″ | h m 22 50 s | ° ′ 30 16 ″ |
| Jan. 1 | 35·84 | 28·0 | 43·49 | 79·1 |
| 11 | 36·19 | 30·1 | 43·41 | 78·6 |
| 21 | 36·52 | 32·2 | 43·35 | 77·9 |
| 31 | 36·84 | 34·2 | 43·32 | 76·9 |
| Feb. 10 | 37·14 | 36·1 | 43·32 | 75·7 |
| 20 | 37·40 | 37·9 | 43·35 | 74·2 |
| Mar. 2 | 37·63 | 39·4 | 43·43 | 72·3 |
| 12 | 37·83 | 40·7 | 43·53 | 70·4 |
| 22 | 37·99 | 41·8 | 43·67 | 68·4 |
| April 1 | 38·11 | 42·7 | 43·86 | 66·2 |
| 11 | 38·20 | 43·4 | 44·08 | 63·9 |
| 21 | 38·26 | 43·8 | 44·33 | 61·6 |
| June 10 | 38·20 | 43·7 | 46·00 | 50·9 |
| 20 | 38·13 | 43·4 | 46·36 | 49·3 |
| 30 | 38·05 | 43·0 | 46·71 | 48·0 |
| July 10 | 37·96 | 42·5 | 47·05 | 47·0 |
| 20 | 37·86 | 41·9 | 47·36 | 46·4 |
| 30 | 37·75 | 41·3 | 47·63 | 46·1 |
| Aug. 9 | 37·65 | 40·8 | 47·86 | 46·1 |
| 19 | 37·55 | 40·2 | 48·04 | 46·5 |
| 29 | 37·46 | 39·7 | 48·17 | 47·2 |

II. 3

## JANUARY, 1880.

| AT MEAN NOON. | | | | | | |
|---|---|---|---|---|---|---|
| Day of the Week. | Day of the Month. | THE SUN'S *Apparent* Declination. | THE SUN'S Var. in 1 hour. | Equation of Time, *to be subtracted from Mean Time.* | Var. in 1 hour. | Sidereal Time. |
| | | ° ′ ″ | ″ | m s | s | h m s |
| Thur. | 15 | S.21 11 6·0 | 27·35 | 9 33·02 | 0·893 | 19 37 18·37 |
| Frid. | 16 | 20 59 57·6 | 28·36 | 9 54·09 | 0·863 | 19 41 14·93 |
| Sat. | 17 | 20 48 25·3 | 29·36 | 10 14·45 | 0·833 | 19 45 11·48 |
| *Sun.* | 18 | 20 36 29·2 | 30·34 | 10 34·09 | 0·803 | 19 49 8·04 |

## FEBRUARY, 1880.

| Day of the Week. | Day of the Month. | Apparent Declination. | Var. in 1 hour. | Equation of Time. | Var. in 1 hour. | Sidereal Time. |
|---|---|---|---|---|---|---|
| Frid. | 20 | S. 11 1 37·9 | 53·72 | 14 0·54 | 0·266 | 21 59 14·38 |
| Sat. | 21 | 10 40 3·5 | 54·13 | 13 53·82 | 0·294 | 22 3 10·93 |
| *Sun.* | 22 | 10 18 19·4 | 54·53 | 13 46·44 | 0·321 | 22 7 7·48 |

## MARCH, 1880.

| Day of the Week. | Day of the Month. | Apparent Declination. | Var. in 1 hour. | Equation of Time. | Var. in 1 hour. | Sidereal Time. |
|---|---|---|---|---|---|---|
| Sat. | 6 | S. 5 23 49·8 | 58·27 | 11 18·95 | 0·600 | 22 58 22·68 |
| *Sun.* | 7 | 5 0 28·9 | 58·45 | 11 4·37 | 0·615 | 23 2 19·23 |
| Mon. | 8 | 4 37 3·9 | 58·61 | 10 49·42 | 0·630 | 23 6 15·79 |

## MAY, 1880.

| AT MEAN NOON. | | | | | | |
|---|---|---|---|---|---|---|
| Day of the Week. | Day of the Month. | THE SUNS *Apparent* Declination. | THE SUNS Var. in 1 hour. | Equation of Time, *to be added to Mean Time.* | Var. in 1 hour. | Sidereal Time. |
| | | ° ′ ″ | ″ | m s | s | h m s |
| Tues. | 18 | N. 19 41 57·7 | 32·44 | 3 44·80 | 0·099 | 3 46 11·13 |
| Wed. | 19 | 19 54 46·1 | 31·59 | 3 42·16 | 0·121 | 3 50 7·69 |
| Thur. | 20 | 20 7 14·1 | 30·74 | 3 38·99 | 0·143 | 3 54 4·24 |

## II. JUNE, 1880. 93

AT MEAN NOON.

| Day of the Week. | Day of the Month. | THE SUN'S Apparent Declination. | | | THE SUN'S Var. in 1 hour. | Equation of Time, *to be added to* / *subt. from Mean Time.* | | Var. in 1 hour. | Sidereal Time. | | |
|---|---|---|---|---|---|---|---|---|---|---|---|
| | | ° | ′ | ″ | ″ | m | s | s | h | m | s |
| Frid. | 4 | N. 22 | 30 | 59·9 | 16·86 | 1 | 52·41 | 0·431 | 4 | 53 | 12·60 |
| Sat. | 5 | 22 | 37 | 32·7 | 15·87 | 1 | 41·88 | 0·446 | 4 | 57 | 9·16 |
| *Sun.* | 6 | 22 | 43 | 41·7 | 14·88 | 1 | 31·02 | 0·459 | 5 | 1 | 5·72 |
| Mon. | 7 | 22 | 49 | 26·8 | 13·88 | 1 | 19·85 | 0·471 | 5 | 5 | 2·28 |
| Tues. | 8 | 22 | 54 | 47·9 | 12·88 | 1 | 8·40 | 0·483 | 5 | 8 | 58·83 |
| Wed. | 9 | 22 | 59 | 44·8 | 11·87 | 0 | 56·69 | 0·493 | 5 | 12 | 55·39 |
| Frid. | 18 | 23 | 25 | 55·8 | 2·65 | 0 | 56·10 | 0·538 | 5 | 48 | 24·41 |
| Sat. | 19 | 23 | 26 | 47·0 | 1·62 | 1 | 9·02 | 0·538 | 5 | 52 | 20·97 |
| *Sun.* | 20 | 23 | 27 | 13·4 | 0·58 | 1 | 21·93 | 0·537 | 5 | 56 | 17·53 |
| Mon. | 21 | 23 | 27 | 15·1 | 0·45 | 1 | 34·82 | 0·536 | 6 | 0 | 14·09 |
| Tues. | 22 | 23 | 26 | 52·0 | 1·48 | 1 | 47·67 | 0·534 | 6 | 4 | 10·65 |
| Wed. | 23 | 23 | 26 | 4·2 | 2·51 | 2 | 0·46 | 0·531 | 6 | 8 | 7·20 |
| Thurs. | 24 | 23 | 24 | 51·7 | 3·54 | 2 | 13·16 | 0·527 | 6 | 12 | 3·76 |
| Frid. | 25 | 23 | 23 | 14·4 | 4·57 | 2 | 25·76 | 0·523 | 6 | 16 | 0·32 |
| Sat. | 26 | 23 | 21 | 12·5 | 5·60 | 2 | 38·25 | 0·517 | 6 | 19 | 56·88 |

## JULY, 1880.

| Day of the Week. | Day of the Month. | Apparent Declination. | | | Var. in 1 hour. | Equation of Time. | | Var. in 1 hour. | Sidereal Time. | | |
|---|---|---|---|---|---|---|---|---|---|---|---|
| Tues. | 6 | N. 22 | 38 | 30·8 | 15·68 | 4 | 31·97 | 0·414 | 6 | 59 | 22·46 |
| Wed. | 7 | 22 | 32 | 2·8 | 16·66 | 4 | 41·73 | 0·399 | 7 | 3 | 19·01 |
| Thur. | 8 | 22 | 25 | 11·4 | 17·63 | 4 | 51·11 | 0·382 | 7 | 7 | 15·57 |

## SEPTEMBER, 1880. 147

AT MEAN NOON.

| Day of the Week. | Day of the Month. | THE SUN'S Apparent Declination. | | | THE SUN'S Var. in 1 hour. | Equation of Time, *to be added to Mean Time.* | | Var. in 1 hour. | Sidereal Time. | | |
|---|---|---|---|---|---|---|---|---|---|---|---|
| | | ° | ′ | ″ | ″ | m | s | s | h | m | s |
| Tues. | 14 | N. 3 | 10 | 10·9 | 57·72 | 4 | 41·13 | 0·883 | 11 | 35 | 21·32 |
| Wed. | 15 | 2 | 47 | 3·5 | 57·86 | 5 | 2·35 | 0·885 | 11 | 39 | 17·88 |
| Thurs. | 16 | 2 | 23 | 52·9 | 57·99 | 5 | 23·61 | 0·886 | 11 | 43 | 14·43 |
| Wed. | 22 | N. 0 | 4 | 0·8 | 58·46 | 7 | 30·62 | 0·871 | 12 | 6 | 53·75 |
| Thur. | 23 | S. 0 | 19 | 23·1 | 58·50 | 7 | 51·46 | 0·865 | 12 | 10 | 50·30 |
| Frid. | 24 | 0 | 42 | 47·7 | 58·51 | 8 | 12·15 | 0·858 | 12 | 14 | 46·85 |
| Sat. | 25 | 1 | 6 | 12·5 | 58·52 | 8 | 32·67 | 0·850 | 12 | 18 | 43·41 |

II. DECEMBER, 1880. 201

| AT MEAN NOON. | | | | | | |
|---|---|---|---|---|---|---|
| Day of the Week. | Day of the Month. | THE SUN'S *Apparent* Declination. | THE SUN'S Var. in 1 hour. | Equation of Time, *to be added to Mean Time.* | Var. in 1 hour. | Sidereal Time. |
| | | ° ′ ″ | ″ | m. s. | s. | h. m. s. |
| Frid. | 17 | S. 23 23 37·9 | 4·63 | 3 23·84 | 1·229 | 17 45 57·50 |
| Sat. | 18 | 23 25 14·9 | 3·45 | 2 54·26 | 1·236 | 17 49 54·06 |
| *Sun.* | 19 | 23 26 23·6 | 2·28 | 2 24·55 | 1·240 | 17 53 50·61 |

## JANUARY, 1880.

| MEAN TIME. | | | | |
|---|---|---|---|---|
| THE MOON'S | | | | |
| Hour. | Right Ascension. | Var. in 10m. | Declination. | Var. in 10m. |
| | SATURDAY, 17. | | | |
| | h m s | s | ° ′ ″ | ″ |
| 0 | 0 16 33·25 | 19·150 | N. 7 29 2·0 | 128·56 |
| 1 | 0 18 28·14 | 19·148 | 7 41 52·0 | 128·10 |
| 2 | 0 20 23·02 | 19·146 | 7 54 39·2 | 127·63 |
| 3 | 0 22 17·89 | 19·145 | 8 7 23·6 | 127·16 |
| 4 | 0 24 12·76 | 19·145 | 8 20 5·1 | 126·68 |
| 5 | 0 26 7·63 | 19·145 | 8 32 43·7 | 126·19 |
| 6 | 0 28 2·50 | 19·145 | 8 45 19·4 | 125·71 |
| 7 | 0 29 57·37 | 19·147 | 8 57 52·2 | 125·21 |
| 8 | 0 31 52·26 | 19·149 | 9 10 21·9 | 124·70 |
| 9 | 0 33 47·16 | 19·152 | 9 22 48·6 | 124·19 |
| 10 | 0 35 42·08 | 19·155 | 9 35 12·2 | 123·07 |
| 11 | 0 37 37·02 | 19·159 | 9 47 32·6 | 123·14 |
| 12 | 0 39 31·99 | 19·164 | 9 59 49·9 | 122·62 |
| 13 | 0 41 26·99 | 19·168 | 10 12 4·0 | 122·08 |
| 14 | 0 43 22·01 | 19·174 | 10 24 14·8 | 121·53 |
| 15 | 0 45 17·08 | 19·181 | 10 36 22·4 | 12[illegible] |
| 16 | 0 47 12·18 | 19·188 | 10 48 26·6 | 120·42 |
| 17 | 0 49 7·33 | 19·195 | 11 0 27·4 | 119·80 |
| 18 | 0 51 2·52 | 19·203 | 11 12 24·9 | 119·29 |
| 19 | 0 52 57·76 | 19·212 | 11 24 18·9 | 118·72 |
| 20 | 0 54 53·06 | 19·221 | 11 36 9·5 | 11[illegible]·13 |
| 21 | 0 56 48·41 | 19·230 | 11 47 56·5 | 117·[illegible] |
| 22 | 0 58 43·82 | 19·240 | 11 59 40·0 | 116·95 |
| 23 | 1 0 39·29 | 19·251 | N. 12 11 19·9 | 116·34 |

# APPARENT PLACES OF STARS, 1880.

AT UPPER TRANSIT AT GREENWICH.

| Month and Day. | | α Andromedæ. R.A. | α Andromedæ. Dec. N. | α Aurigæ. (*Capella*) R.A. | α Aurigæ. (*Capella*) Dec. N. | α Canis Majoris. (*Sirius*) R.A. | α Canis Majoris. (*Sirius*) Dec. S. | α Leonis. (*Regulus*) R.A. | α Leonis. (*Regulus*) Dec. N. |
|---|---|---|---|---|---|---|---|---|---|
| | | h m<br>0 2 | ° ′<br>28 25 | h m<br>5 7 | ° ′<br>45 52 | h m<br>6 39 | ° ′<br>16 33 | h m<br>10 2 | ° ′<br>12 32 |
| | | s | ″ | s | ″ | s | ″ | s | ″ |
| Jan. | 1 | 11·88 | 55·3 | 52·81 | 34·0 | 53·90 | 10·3 | 0·81 | 61·1 |
| | 11 | 11·75 | 54·4 | 52·81 | 35·3 | 53·97 | 12·7 | 1·08 | 59·7 |
| | 21 | 11·62 | 53·2 | 52·74 | 36·5 | 53·98 | 14·9 | 1·31 | 58·5 |
| | 31 | 11·51 | 51·8 | 52·62 | 37·4 | 53·95 | 16·9 | 1·50 | 57·6 |
| Feb. | 10 | 11·42 | 52·2 | 53·45 | 38·1 | 53·87 | 18·6 | 1·63 | 57·0 |
| | 20 | 11·35 | 48·6 | 52·24 | 38·5 | 53·75 | 20·0 | 1·72 | 56·6 |
| Mar. | 1 | 11·32 | 47·0 | 52·00 | 38·7 | 53·60 | 21·2 | 1·76 | 56·4 |
| | 11 | 11·32 | 45·4 | 51·75 | 38·5 | 53·42 | 22·0 | 1·75 | 56·5 |
| | 21 | 11·37 | 44·0 | 51·50 | 38·0 | 53·24 | 22·5 | 1·70 | 56·7 |
| | 31 | 11·46 | 42·8 | 51·27 | 37·2 | 53·05 | 22·6 | 1·62 | 57·1 |
| Apr. | 10 | 11·60 | 42·0 | 51·08 | 36·2 | 52·86 | 22·4 | 1·52 | 57·6 |
| | 20 | 11·79 | 41·5 | 50·92 | 35·0 | 52·69 | 21·9 | 1·40 | 58·1 |
| | 30 | 12·02 | 41·4 | 50·81 | 33·7 | 52·54 | 21·2 | 1·28 | 58·7 |
| May | 10 | 12·28 | 41·7 | 50·76 | 32·3 | 52·42 | 20·1 | 1·15 | 59·2 |
| | 20 | 12·58 | 42·4 | 50·78 | 30·8 | 52·34 | 18·8 | 1·03 | 59·7 |
| | 30 | 12·91 | 43·4 | 50·86 | 29·4 | 52·30 | 17·3 | 0·91 | 60·2 |
| June | 9 | 13·25 | 44·8 | 51·01 | 27·9 | 52·29 | 15·6 | 0·81 | 60·6 |
| | 19 | 13·60 | 46·6 | 51·20 | 26·6 | 52·33 | 13·7 | 0·73 | 61·0 |
| | 29 | 13·95 | 48·6 | 51·45 | 25·5 | 52·40 | 11·8 | 0·67 | 61·3 |
| July | 9 | 14·29 | 50·8 | 51·75 | 24·6 | 52·52 | 9·6 | 0·63 | 61·5 |
| | 19 | 14·61 | 53·2 | 52·08 | 23·9 | 53·66 | 7·6 | 0·61 | 61·6 |
| | 29 | 14·89 | 55·7 | 52·44 | 23·3 | 52·84 | 5·8 | 0·61 | 61·6 |
| Aug. | 8 | 15·16 | 58·2 | 52·83 | 23·0 | 53·05 | 4·1 | 0·64 | 61·4 |
| | 18 | 15·39 | 60·7 | 53·24 | 22·9 | 53·28 | 2·6 | 0·70 | 61·1 |
| | 28 | 15·57 | 63·2 | 53·65 | 22·9 | 53·53 | 1·5 | 0·79 | 60·6 |
| Sept. | 7 | 15·72 | 65·5 | 54·07 | 23·1 | 53·79 | 0·7 | 0·91 | 60·0 |
| | 17 | 15·82 | 67·7 | 54·49 | 23·6 | 54·07 | 0·3 | 1·05 | 59·2 |
| | 27 | 15·89 | 69·8 | 54·89 | 24·1 | 54·36 | 0·3 | 1·23 | 58·1 |
| Oct. | 7 | 15·91 | 71·6 | 55·29 | 24·8 | 54·65 | 0·8 | 1·44 | 56·8 |
| | 17 | 15·90 | 73·1 | 55·67 | 25·7 | 54·95 | 1·7 | 1·69 | 55·4 |
| | 27 | 15·86 | 74·4 | 56·03 | 26·7 | 55·24 | 3·1 | 1·96 | 53·8 |
| Nov. | 6 | 15·79 | 75·4 | 56·36 | 27·8 | 55·52 | 4·8 | 2·25 | 52·0 |
| | 16 | 15·70 | 76·2 | 56·65 | 29·0 | 55·78 | 6·9 | 2·47 | 50·1 |
| | 26 | 15·59 | 76·6 | 56·90 | 30·4 | 56·02 | 9·2 | 2·90 | 48·2 |
| Dec. | 6 | 15·47 | 76·7 | 57·10 | 31·7 | 56·24 | 11·6 | 3·23 | 46·3 |
| | 16 | 15·34 | 76·5 | 57·24 | 33·1 | 56·41 | 14·2 | 3·56 | 44·5 |
| | 26 | 15·20 | 75·9 | 57·33 | 34·5 | 56·54 | 16·8 | 3·87 | 42·8 |
| | 36 | 15·06 | 75·1 | 57·35 | 35·8 | 56·63 | 19·2 | 4·15 | 41·2 |

## APPARENT PLACES OF STARS, 1880. 343

### AT UPPER TRANSIT AT GREENWICH.

| Month and Day. | | α Ursæ Majoris. | | α Virginis. (*Spica*) | | α Ursæ Majoris. | | α Bootis. (*Arcturus*) | |
|---|---|---|---|---|---|---|---|---|---|
| | | R.A. | Dec. N. | R.A. | Dec. S. | R.A. | Dec. S. | R.A. | Dec. N. |
| | | h m<br>10 56 | ° ′<br>62 23 | h m<br>13 18 | ° ′<br>10 32 | h m<br>13 42 | ° ′<br>49 54 | h m<br>14 10 | ° ′<br>19 47 |
| | | s | ″ | s | ″ | s | ″ | s | ″ |
| Jan. | 1 | 21.54 | 30.8 | 53.10 | 9.2 | 49.12 | 21.8 | 11.76 | 74.7 |
| | 11 | 22.07 | 31.1 | 53.44 | 11.2 | 49.55 | 19.9 | 12.09 | 72.4 |
| | 21 | 22.56 | 32.0 | 53.77 | 13.2 | 49.99 | 18.5 | 12.42 | 70.5 |
| | 31 | 22.97 | 33.3 | 54.08 | 15.2 | 50.41 | 17.8 | 12.74 | 68.9 |
| Feb. | 10 | 23.30 | 35.2 | 54.37 | 17.0 | 50.81 | 17.7 | 13.06 | 67.7 |
| | 20 | 23.53 | 37.4 | 54.63 | 18.7 | 51.18 | 18.2 | 13.35 | 67.0 |
| Mar. | 1 | 23.67 | 39.8 | 54.86 | 20.2 | 51.51 | 19.2 | 13.61 | 66.7 |
| | 11 | 23.71 | 42.4 | 55.05 | 21.4 | 51.78 | 20.8 | 13.84 | 66.9 |
| | 21 | 23.66 | 45.0 | 55.20 | 22.4 | 51.99 | 22.8 | 14.04 | 67.5 |
| | 31 | 23.53 | 47.5 | 55.32 | 23.2 | 52.15 | 25.1 | 14.20 | 68.4 |
| Apr. | 10 | 23.33 | 49.9 | 55.41 | 23.8 | 52.25 | 27.7 | 14.32 | 69.5 |
| | 20 | 23.07 | 52.0 | 55.46 | 24.2 | 52.30 | 30.4 | 14.41 | 71.0 |
| | 30 | 22.76 | 53.7 | 55.49 | 24.4 | 52.29 | 33.1 | 14.47 | 72.6 |
| May | 10 | 22.43 | 55.0 | 55.49 | 24.4 | 52.24 | 35.7 | 14.50 | 74.2 |
| | 20 | 22.08 | 55.9 | 55.47 | 24.3 | 52.14 | 38.2 | 14.50 | 75.8 |
| | 30 | 21.72 | 56.4 | 55.43 | 24.1 | 52.00 | 40.5 | 14.47 | 77.4 |
| June | 9 | 21.38 | 56.3 | 55.37 | 23.7 | 51.83 | 42.4 | 14.42 | 78.9 |
| | 19 | 21.06 | 55.8 | 55.30 | 23.3 | 51.64 | 43.9 | 14.35 | 80.2 |
| | 29 | 20.77 | 54.7 | 55.21 | 22.8 | 51.42 | 45.0 | 14.26 | 81.4 |
| July | 9 | 20.51 | 53.2 | 55.11 | 22.2 | 51.19 | 45.7 | 14.14 | 82.3 |
| | 19 | 20.30 | 51.4 | 55.00 | 21.5 | 50.94 | 45.9 | 14.01 | 83.0 |
| | 29 | 20.13 | 49.2 | 54.89 | 20.9 | 50.69 | 45.7 | 13.87 | 83.4 |
| Aug. | 8 | 20.01 | 46.6 | 54.78 | 20.3 | 50.45 | 45.0 | 13.72 | 83.5 |
| | 18 | 19.96 | 43.8 | 54.67 | 19.6 | 50.22 | 43.9 | 13.58 | 83.4 |
| | 28 | 19.96 | 40.8 | 54.58 | 19.0 | 50.00 | 42.3 | 13.44 | 83.0 |
| Sept. | 7 | 20.03 | 37.2 | 54.50 | 18.5 | 49.80 | 40.3 | 13.31 | 82.2 |
| | 17 | 20.17 | 33.9 | 54.45 | 18.0 | 49.64 | 37.9 | 13.20 | 81.2 |
| | 27 | 20.37 | 30.5 | 54.43 | 17.7 | 49.53 | 35.3 | 13.11 | 79.9 |
| Oct. | 7 | 20.64 | 27.2 | 54.45 | 17.7 | 49.46 | 32.3 | 13.06 | 78.3 |
| | 17 | 20.98 | 24.0 | 54.52 | 17.9 | 49.44 | 29.0 | 13.06 | 76.4 |
| | 27 | 21.39 | 20.9 | 54.63 | 18.3 | 49.50 | 25.2 | 13.10 | 74.2 |
| Nov. | 6 | 21.85 | 18.1 | 54.79 | 19.0 | 49.62 | 21.7 | 13.19 | 71.6 |
| | 16 | 22.37 | 15.6 | 54.[illegible]9 | 20.0 | 49.80 | 18.2 | 13.32 | 69.1 |
| | 26 | 22.92 | 13.6 | 55.24 | 21.3 | 50.04 | 14.7 | 13.51 | 66.4 |
| Dec. | 6 | 23.50 | 12.0 | 55.52 | 22.8 | 50.34 | 11.5 | 13.74 | 63.7 |
| | 16 | 24.09 | 10.9 | 55.83 | 24.5 | 50.70 | 8.5 | 14.01 | 61.1 |
| | 26 | 24.68 | 10.3 | 56.16 | 26.4 | 51.10 | 5.9 | 14.31 | 58.5 |
| | 36 | 25.23 | 10.3 | 56.49 | 28.3 | 51.52 | 3.7 | 14.63 | 56.1 |

## APPARENT PLACES OF STARS, 1880. 357

### AT UPPER TRANSIT AT GREENWICH.

| Month and Day. | | α Ophiuchi. R.A. | α Ophiuchi. Dec. N. | α Acquilæ. (*Altair*) R.A. | α Acquilæ. (*Altair*) Dec. N. | α Cygni. R.A. | α Cygni. Dec. N. |
|---|---|---|---|---|---|---|---|
| | | h m<br>17 29 | ° ′<br>12 38 | h m<br>19 44 | ° ′<br>8 33 | h m<br>20 37 | ° ′<br>44 50 |
| | | s | ″ | s | ″ | s | ″ |
| Jan. | 1 | 21.42 | 49.5 | 55.33 | 9.3 | 19.36 | 76.3 |
| | 11 | 21.62 | 47.3 | 55.40 | 7.8 | 19.32 | 73.5 |
| | 21 | 21.85 | 45.3 | 55.52 | 6.2 | 19.32 | 70.7 |
| | 31 | 22.11 | 43.5 | 55.66 | 4.7 | 19.38 | 67.5 |
| Feb. | 10 | 22.38 | 41.9 | 55.83 | 3.4 | 19.49 | 64.6 |
| | 20 | 22.67 | 40.7 | 56.03 | 2.3 | 19.65 | 62.0 |
| Mar. | 1 | 22.97 | 39.9 | 56.26 | 1.5 | 19.85 | 59.7 |
| | 11 | 23.26 | 39.5 | 56.51 | 1.1 | 20.10 | 57.8 |
| | 21 | 23.56 | 39.5 | 56.77 | 1.0 | 20.39 | 56.4 |
| | 31 | 23.85 | 39.9 | 57.05 | 1.3 | 20.72 | 55.5 |
| Apr. | 10 | 24.12 | 40.7 | 57.34 | 1.9 | 21.07 | 55.2 |
| | 20 | 24.38 | 41.9 | 57.64 | 2.9 | 21.43 | 55.5 |
| | 30 | 24.62 | 43.3 | 57.94 | 4.3 | 21.81 | 56.4 |
| May | 10 | 24.84 | 45.0 | 58.24 | 5.9 | 22.19 | 57.8 |
| | 20 | 25.03 | 46.9 | 58.52 | 7.8 | 22.56 | 59.8 |
| | 30 | 25.20 | 48.9 | 58.79 | 9.8 | 22.91 | 62.2 |
| June | 9 | 25.33 | 50.9 | 59.04 | 11.9 | 23.23 | 64.9 |
| | 19 | 25.42 | 52.9 | 59.26 | 14.0 | 23.52 | 67.9 |
| | 29 | 25.48 | 54.9 | 59.44 | 16.2 | 23.77 | 71.2 |
| July | 9 | 25.50 | 56.7 | 59.59 | 18.3 | 23.96 | 74.6 |
| | 19 | 25.47 | 58.3 | 59.69 | 20.2 | 24.10 | 78.0 |
| | 29 | 25.41 | 59.8 | 59.75 | 22.0 | 24.18 | 81.4 |
| Aug. | 8 | 25.32 | 61.1 | 59.76 | 23.6 | 24.20 | 84.7 |
| | 18 | 25.19 | 62.1 | 59.74 | 25.1 | 24.18 | 87.8 |
| | 28 | 25.04 | 62.8 | 59.67 | 26.3 | 24.10 | 90.7 |
| Sept. | 7 | 24.87 | 63.3 | 59.56 | 27.3 | 23.96 | 93.3 |
| | 17 | 24.69 | 63.5 | 59.43 | 28.0 | 23.79 | 95.5 |
| | 27 | 24.51 | 63.4 | 59.28 | 28.5 | 23.58 | 97.4 |
| Oct. | 7 | 24.33 | 63.1 | 59.11 | 28.7 | 23.34 | 98.8 |
| | 17 | 24.17 | 62.5 | 58.94 | 28.7 | 23.08 | 99.8 |
| | 27 | 24.04 | 61.5 | 58.77 | 28.4 | 22.82 | 100.2 |
| Nov. | 6 | 23.94 | 60.3 | 58.62 | 27.9 | 22.56 | 100.2 |
| | 16 | 23.89 | 58.8 | 58.49 | 27.2 | 22.31 | 99.7 |
| | 26 | 23.88 | 57.1 | 58.39 | 26.2 | 22.09 | 98.7 |
| Dec. | 6 | 23.92 | 55.2 | 58.32 | 25.0 | 21.89 | 97.2 |
| | 16 | 24.01 | 52.9 | 58.29 | 23.7 | 21.73 | 95.2 |
| | 26 | 24.15 | 50.7 | 58.30 | 22.3 | 21.61 | 92.9 |
| | 36 | 24.32 | 48.6 | 58.35 | 20.7 | 21.54 | 90.3 |

USED IN DETERMINING THE LATITUDE BY OBSERVATIONS OF THE POLE STAR OUT OF THE MERIDIAN.

TABLE I.

Containing the *First* Correction.

*Argument*:—Sidereal Time of Observation.

| Sidereal Time. | Correction. | Sidereal Time. | Sidereal Time. | Correction. | Sidereal Time. |
|---|---|---|---|---|---|
| h m | ° ′ ″ | h m | h m | ° ′ ″ | h m |
| 0 0 | −1 15 45 + | 12 0 | 6 0 | −0 25 43 + | 18 0 |
| 10 | 1 16 48 | 10 | 10 | 0 22 23 | 10 |
| 20 | 1 17 42 | 20 | 20 | 0 19 1 | 20 |
| 30 | 1 18 28 | 30 | 30 | 0 15 36 | 30 |
| 40 | 1 19 4 | 40 | 40 | 0 12 10 | 40 |
| 50 | 1 19 31 | 50 | 50 | 0 8 43 | 50 |
| 1 0 | 1 19 50 | 13 0 | 7 0 | 0 5 14 | 19 0 |
| 10 | 1 19 59 | 10 | 10 | −0 1 45 + | 10 |
| 20 | 1 19 59 | 20 | 20 | +0 1 45 − | 20 |
| 30 | 1 19 50 | 30 | 30 | 0 5 14 | 30 |
| 40 | 1 19 31 | 40 | 40 | 0 8 43 | 40 |
| 50 | 1 19 4 | 50 | 50 | 0 12 10 | 50 |
| 2 0 | 1 18 28 | 14 0 | 8 0 | 0 15 36 | 20 0 |
| 10 | 1 17 42 | 10 | 10 | 0 19 1 | 10 |
| 20 | 1 16 48 | 20 | 20 | 0 22 23 | 20 |
| 30 | 1 15 45 | 30 | 30 | 0 25 43 | 30 |
| 40 | 1 14 34 | 40 | 40 | 0 29 0 | 40 |
| 50 | 1 13 14 | 50 | 50 | 0 32 13 | 50 |
| 3 0 | 1 11 45 | 15 0 | 9 0 | 0 35 23 | 21 0 |
| 10 | 1 10 8 | 10 | 10 | 0 38 29 | 10 |
| 20 | 1 8 24 | 20 | 20 | 0 41 30 | 20 |
| 30 | 1 6 31 | 30 | 30 | 0 44 27 | 30 |
| 40 | 1 4 31 | 40 | 40 | 0 47 18 | 40 |
| 50 | 1 2 23 | 50 | 50 | 0 50 4 | 50 |
| 4 0 | 1 0 9 | 16 0 | 10 0 | 0 52 45 | 22 0 |
| 10 | 0 57 47 | 10 | 10 | 0 55 19 | 10 |
| 20 | 0 55 19 | 20 | 20 | 0 57 47 | 20 |
| 30 | 0 52 45 | 30 | 30 | 1 0 9 | 30 |
| 40 | 0 50 4 | 40 | 40 | 1 2 23 | 40 |
| 50 | 0 47 18 | 50 | 60 | 1 4 31 | 50 |
| 5 0 | 0 44 27 | 17 0 | 11 0 | 1 6 31 | 23 0 |
| 10 | 0 41 30 | 10 | 10 | 1 8 24 | 10 |
| 20 | 0 38 29 | 20 | 20 | 1 10 8 | 20 |
| 30 | 0 35 23 | 30 | 30 | 1 11 45 | 30 |
| 40 | 0 32 13 | 40 | 40 | 1 13 14 | 40 |
| 50 | 0 29 0 | 50 | 50 | 1 14 34 | 50 |
| 6 0 | −0 25 43 + | 18 0 | 12 0 | +1 15 45 − | 24 0 |

## TABLE II.

Containing the *Second* Correction (*always to be added.*)

*Arguments:*—Sidereal Time and Altitude.

| Sidereal Time. | Altitude. | | | | | | | | Sidereal Time. |
|---|---|---|---|---|---|---|---|---|---|
| | 0° | 5° | 10° | 15° | 20° | 25° | 30° | 35° | |
| h m | ′ ″ | ′ ″ | ′ ″ | ′ ″ | ′ ″ | ′ ″ | ′ ″ | ′ ″ | h m |
| 0 0 | 0 0 | 0 1 | 0 1 | 0 2 | 0 2 | 0 3 | 0 3 | 0 4 | 12 0 |
| 30 | 0 0 | 0 0 | 0 0 | 0 1 | 0 1 | 0 1 | 0 1 | 0 1 | 30 |
| 1 0 | 0 0 | 0 0 | 0 0 | 0 0 | 0 0 | 0 0 | 0 0 | 0 0 | 13 0 |
| 30 | 0 0 | 0 0 | 0 0 | 0 0 | 0 0 | 0 0 | 0 0 | 0 0 | 30 |
| 2 0 | 0 0 | 0 0 | 0 0 | 0 1 | 0 1 | 0 1 | 0 1 | 0 1 | 14 0 |
| 30 | 0 0 | 0 1 | 0 1 | 0 2 | 0 2 | 0 3 | 0 3 | 0 4 | 30 |
| 3 0 | 0 0 | 0 1 | 0 2 | 0 3 | 0 4 | 0 5 | 0 6 | 0 8 | 15 0 |
| 30 | 0 0 | 0 2 | 0 3 | 0 5 | 0 6 | 0 8 | 0 10 | 0 12 | 30 |
| 4 0 | 0 0 | 0 2 | 0 4 | 0 7 | 0 9 | 0 11 | 0 14 | 0 17 | 16 0 |
| 30 | 0 0 | 0 3 | 0 6 | 0 8 | 0 11 | 0 15 | 0 18 | 0 22 | 30 |
| 5 0 | 0 0 | 0 3 | 0 7 | 0·10 | 0 14 | 0 18 | 0 22 | 0 27 | 17 0 |
| 30 | 0 0 | 0 4 | 0 8 | 0 12 | 0 16 | 0 21 | 0 26 | 0 31 | 30 |
| 6 0 | 0 0 | 0 4 | 0 9 | 0 13 | 0 18 | 0 23 | 0 29 | 0 35 | 18 0 |
| 30 | 0 0 | 0 5 | 0 9 | 0 14 | 0 20 | 0 25 | 0 31 | 0 38 | 30 |
| 7 0 | 0 0 | 0 5 | 0 10 | 0 15 | 0 20 | 0 26 | 0 32 | 0 39 | 19 0 |
| 30 | 0 0 | 0 5 | 0 10 | 0 15 | 0 20 | 0 26 | 0 32 | 0 39 | 30 |
| 8 0 | 0 0 | 0 5 | 0 9 | 0 14 | 0 20 | 0 25 | 0 31 | 0 38 | 20 0 |
| 30 | 0 0 | 0 4 | 0 9 | 0 13 | 0 18 | 0 23 | 0 29 | 0 35 | 30 |
| 9 0 | 0 0 | 0 4 | 0 8 | 0 12 | 0 16 | 0 21 | 0 26 | 0 31 | 21 0 |
| 30 | 0 0 | 0 3 | 0 7 | 0 10 | 0 14 | 0 18 | 0 22 | 0 27 | 30 |
| 10 0 | 0 0 | 0 3 | 0 6 | 0 8 | 0 11 | 0 15 | 0 18 | 0 22 | 22 0 |
| 30 | 0 0 | 0 2 | 0 4 | 0 7 | 0 9 | 0 11 | 0 14 | 0 17 | 30 |
| 11 0 | 0 0 | 0 2 | 0 3 | 0 5 | 0 6 | 0 8 | 0 10 | 0 12 | 23 0 |
| 30 | 0 0 | 0 1 | 0 2 | 0 3 | 0 4 | 0 5 | 0 6 | 0 8 | 30 |
| 12 0 | 0 0 | 0 1 | 0 1 | 0 2 | 0 2 | 0 3 | 0 3 | 0 4 | 24 0 |

## TABLE III. (*for* 1880.)

Containing the *Third* Correction (*always to be added.*)

*Arguments:*—Sidereal Time and Date.

| Sidereal Time. | Jan. 1. | Feb. 1. | March 1. | April 1. | May 1. | June 1. | July 1. |
|---|---|---|---|---|---|---|---|
| h | ′ ″ | ′ ″ | ′ ″ | ′ ″ | ′ ″ | ′ ″ | ′ ″ |
| 0 | 1 34 | 1 31 | 1 24 | 1 14 | 1 6 | 1 2 | 1 4 |
| 2 | 1 36 | 1 38 | 1 34 | 1 26 | 1 17 | 1 9 | 1 6 |
| 4 | 1 28 | 1 35 | 1 36 | 1 31 | 1 23 | 1 13 | 1 6 |
| 6 | 1 13 | 1 22 | 1 28 | 1 28 | 1 23 | 1 14 | 1 4 |
| 8 | 0 54 | 1 4 | 1 12 | 1 17 | 1 17 | 1 11 | 1 2 |
| 10 | 0 37 | 0 46 | 0 53 | 1 2 | 1 6 | 1 5 | 0 59 |
| 12 | 0 26 | 0 29 | 0 37 | 0 46 | 0 54 | 0 58 | 0 56 |
| 14 | 0 24 | 0 22 | 0 26 | 0 34 | 0 43 | 0 51 | 0 54 |
| 16 | 0 32 | 0 25 | 0 24 | 0 29 | 0 37 | 0 47 | 0 54 |
| 18 | 0 47 | 0 38 | 0 32 | 0 32 | 0 37 | 0 46 | 0 56 |
| 20 | 1 6 | 0 56 | 0 48 | 0 43 | 0 43 | 0 49 | 0 58 |
| 22 | 1 23 | 1 14 | 1 7 | 0 58 | 0 54 | 0 55 | 1 1 |
| 24 | 1 34 | 1 31 | 1 24 | 1 14 | 1 6 | 1 2 | 1 4 |

TABLE II.

Containing the *Second* Correction (*always to be added.*)

*Arguments*:—Sidereal Time and Altitude.

| Sidereal Time. | Altitude. 35° | 40° | 45° | 50° | 55° | 60° | 65° | 70° | Sidereal Time. |
|---|---|---|---|---|---|---|---|---|---|
| h m | ′ ″ | ′ ″ | ′ ″ | ′ ″ | ′ ″ | ′ ″ | ′ ″ | ′ ″ | h m |
| 0 0 | 0 4 | 0 5 | 0 6 | 0 7 | 0 8 | 0 10 | 0 12 | 0 16 | 12 0 |
| 30 | 0 1 | 0 2 | 0 2 | 0 3 | 0 3 | 0 4 | 0 5 | 0 6 | 30 |
| 1 0 | 0 0 | 0 0 | 0 0 | 0 0 | 0 0 | 0 0 | 0 1 | 0 1 | 13 0 |
| 30 | 0 0 | 0 0 | 0 0 | 0 0 | 0 0 | 0 0 | 0 1 | 0 1 | 30 |
| 2 0 | 0 1 | 0 2 | 0 2 | 0 3 | 0 3 | 0 4 | 0 5 | 0 6 | 14 0 |
| 30 | 0 4 | 0 5 | 0 6 | 0 7 | 0 8 | 0 10 | 0 12 | 0 16 | 30 |
| 3 0 | 0 8 | 0 9 | 0 11 | 0 13 | 0 16 | 0 19 | 0 23 | 0 30 | 15 0 |
| 30 | 0 12 | 0 14 | 0 17 | 0 21 | 0 25 | 0 30 | 0 37 | 0 47 | 30 |
| 4 0 | 0 17 | 0 20 | 0 24 | 0 29 | 0 35 | 0 42 | 0 52 | 1 7 | 16 0 |
| 30 | 0 22 | 0 26 | 0 32 | 0 38 | 0 45 | 0 55 | 1 8 | 1 27 | 30 |
| 5 0 | 0 27 | 0 32 | 0 39 | 0 46 | 0 55 | 1 7 | 1 23 | 1 46 | 17 0 |
| 30 | 0 31 | 0 38 | 0 45 | 0 54 | 1 4 | 1 18 | 1 36 | 2 3 | 30 |
| 6 0 | 0 35 | 0 42 | 0 50 | 1 0 | 1 12 | 1 27 | 1 47 | 2 18 | 18 0 |
| 30 | 0 38 | 0 45 | 0 54 | 1 4 | 1 17 | 1 33 | 1 55 | 2 28 | 30 |
| 7 0 | 0 39 | 0 47 | 0 56 | 1 6 | 1 19 | 1 36 | 1 59 | 2 33 | 19 0 |
| 30 | 0 39 | 0 47 | 0 56 | 1 6 | 1 19 | 1 36 | 1 59 | 2 33 | 30 |
| 8 0 | 0 38 | 0 45 | 0 54 | 1 4 | 1 17 | 1 33 | 1 55 | 2 28 | 20 0 |
| 30 | 0 35 | 0 42 | 0 50 | 1 0 | 1 12 | 1 27 | 1 47 | 2 18 | 30 |
| 9 0 | 0 31 | 0 38 | 0 45 | 0 54 | 1 4 | 1 18 | 1 36 | 2 3 | 21 0 |
| 30 | 0 27 | 0 32 | 0 39 | 0 46 | 0 55 | 1 7 | 1 23 | 1 46 | 30 |
| 10 0 | 0 22 | 0 27 | 0 32 | 0 38 | 0 45 | 0 55 | 1 8 | 1 27 | 22 0 |
| 30 | 0 17 | 0 20 | 0 24 | 0 29 | 0 35 | 0 42 | 0 52 | 1 7 | 30 |
| 11 0 | 0 12 | 0 14 | 0 17 | 0 21 | 0 25 | 0 30 | 0 37 | 0 47 | 23 0 |
| 30 | 0 8 | 0 9 | 0 11 | 0 13 | 0 16 | 0 19 | 0 23 | 0 30 | 30 |
| 12 0 | 0 4 | 0 5 | 0 6 | 0 7 | 0 8 | 0 10 | 0 12 | 0 16 | 24 0 |

TABLE III. (*for* 1880.)

Containing the *Third* Correction (*always to be added.*)

*Arguments*:—Sidereal Time and Date.

| Sidereal Time. | July 1. | Aug. 1. | Sept. 1. | Oct. 1. | Nov. 1. | Dec. 1. | Dec. 31. |
|---|---|---|---|---|---|---|---|
| h | ′ ″ | ′ ″ | ′ ″ | ′ ″ | ′ ″ | ″ | ′ ″ |
| 0 | 1 4 | 1 11 | 1 21 | 1 32 | 1 44 | 1 52 | 1 55 |
| 2 | 1 6 | 1 7 | 1 13 | 1 23 | 1 34 | 1 44 | 1 52 |
| 4 | 1 6 | 1 1 | 1 2 | 1 7 | 1 15 | 1 25 | 1 35 |
| 6 | 1 4 | 0 55 | 0 50 | 0 49 | 0 52 | 1 0 | 1 9 |
| 8 | 1 2 | 0 51 | 0 41 | 0 34 | 0 32 | 0 34 | 0 40 |
| 10 | 0 59 | 0 48 | 0 37 | 0 26 | 0 18 | 0 15 | 0 17 |
| 12 | 0 56 | 0 49 | 0 39 | 0 28 | 0 16 | 0 8 | 0 5 |
| 14 | 0 54 | 0 53 | 0 47 | 0 37 | 0 26 | 0 16 | 0 8 |
| 16 | 0 54 | 0 59 | 0 58 | 0 53 | 0 45 | 0 35 | 0 25 |
| 18 | 0 56 | 1 5 | 1 10 | 1 11 | 1 8 | 1 1 | 0 51 |
| 20 | 0 58 | 1 9 | 1 19 | 1 26 | 1 28 | 1 26 | 1 20 |
| 22 | 1 1 | 1 12 | 1 23 | 1 34 | 1 42 | 1 45 | 1 43 |
| 24 | 1 4 | 1 11 | 1 21 | 1 32 | 1 44 | 1 52 | 1 55 |

II.

## MARCH, 1881.

| AT MEAN NOON. | | | | | | |
|---|---|---|---|---|---|---|
| Day of the Week. | Day of the Month. | THE SUN'S *Apparent* Declination. | THE SUN'S Var. in 1 hour. | Equation of Time, *to be subtracted from Mean Time.* | Var. in 1 hour. | Sidereal Time. |
| | | ° ′ ″ | ″ | m s | s | h m s |
| *Sun.* | 27 | N. 2 45 59·5 | 58·65 | 5 21·64 | 0·765 | 0 20 13·02 |
| Mon. | 28 | 3 9 25·6 | 58·50 | 5 3·29 | 0·764 | 0 24 9·57 |
| Tues. | 29 | 3 32 48·1 | 58·34 | 4 44·98 | 0·761 | 0 28 6·13 |

## AUGUST, 1881.

| Day of the Week. | Day of the Month. | Apparent Declination. | Var. in 1 hour. | Equation of Time. | Var. in 1 hour. | Sidereal Time. |
|---|---|---|---|---|---|---|
| Mon. | 1 | N. 17 56 8·1 | 38·05 | 6 4·48 | 0·154 | 8 40 55·62 |
| Tues. | 2 | 17 40 46·0 | 38·78 | 6 0·47 | 0·180 | 8 44 52·18 |
| Wed. | 3 | 17 25 6·8 | 39·49 | 5 55·84 | 0·206 | 8 48 48·74 |
| Thur. | 4 | 17 9 10·7 | 40·18 | 5 50·59 | 0·231 | 8 52 45·29 |

## OCTOBER, 1881.

| AT MEAN NOON. | | | | | | |
|---|---|---|---|---|---|---|
| Day of the Week. | Day of the Month. | THE SUN'S *Apparent* Declination. | THE SUN'S Var. in 1 Hour. | Equation of Time, *to be added to Mean Time.* | Var. in 1 Hour. | Sidereal Time. |
| | | ° ′ ″ | ″ | m s | s | h m s |
| *Sun.* | 23 | S. 11 33 44·2 | 52·50 | +15 37·21 | 0·324 | 14 8 9·55 |
| Mon. | 24 | 11 54 39·0 | 52·06 | 15 44 61 | 0·294 | 14 12 6·11 |
| Tues. | 25 | 12 15 22·8 | 51·59 | 15 51·31 | 0·264 | 14 16 2·66 |

## NOVEMBER, 1881.

| Day of the Week. | Day of the Month. | Apparent Declination. | Var. in 1 Hour. | Equation of Time. | Var. in 1 Hour. | Sidereal Time. |
|---|---|---|---|---|---|---|
| Thur. | 17 | S. 19 6 19·6 | 36·30 | 14 48·87 | 0·516 | 15 46 43·43 |
| Frid. | 18 | 19 20 40·2 | 35·44 | 14 36·06 | 0·551 | 15 50 39·98 |
| Sat. | 19 | 19 34 39·9 | 34·56 | 14 22·40 | 0·586 | 15 54 36·54 |

## APPARENT PLACES OF STARS, 1881. 345

### AT UPPER TRANSIT AT GREENWICH.

| Month and Day. | | α Ursæ Majoris. | | α Crucis (Mean.) | | α Virginis. (Spica) | |
|---|---|---|---|---|---|---|---|
| | | R.A. | Dec. N. | R.A. | Dec. S. | R.A. | Dec. S. |
| | | h m 10 56 | ° ′ 62 22 | h m 12 20 | ° ′ 62 26 | h m 13 18 | ° ′ 10 32 |
| | | s | ″ | s | ″ | s | ″ |
| Jan. | 1 | 25·02 | 70·3 | 1·25 | 12·2 | 56·36 | 27·5 |
| | 11 | 25·55 | 70·7 | 1·83 | 14·2 | 56·69 | 29·5 |
| | 21 | 26·02 | 71·6 | 2·37 | 16·7 | 57·02 | 31·5 |
| | 31 | 26·42 | 73·0 | 2·86 | 19·5 | 57·33 | 33·4 |
| Feb. | 10 | 26·74 | 74·9 | 3·29 | 22·7 | 57·62 | 35·2 |
| | 20 | 26·96 | 77·1 | 3·64 | 26·0 | 57·87 | 36·9 |
| Mar. | 2 | 27·09 | 79·6 | 3·92 | 29·5 | 58·09 | 38·3 |
| | 12 | 27·12 | 82·2 | 4·13 | 33·0 | 58·27 | 39·5 |
| | 22 | 27·06 | 84·8 | 4·26 | 36·5 | 58·42 | 40·5 |
| Apr. | 1 | 26·92 | 87·4 | 4·32 | 39·9 | 58·53 | 41·3 |
| | 11 | 26·70 | 89·8 | 4·32 | 43·1 | 58·61 | 41·8 |
| | 21 | 26·43 | 91·8 | 4·26 | 46·1 | 58·66 | 42·1 |
| May | 1 | 26·12 | 93·6 | 4·13 | 48·8 | 58·68 | 42·3 |
| | 11 | 25·78 | 94·9 | 3·95 | 51·1 | 58·68 | 42·3 |
| | 21 | 25·43 | 95·8 | 3·74 | 53·1 | 58·66 | 42·1 |
| | 31 | 25·07 | 96·2 | 3·48 | 54·6 | 58·61 | 41·9 |
| June | 10 | 24·73 | 96·1 | 3·19 | 55·6 | 58·55 | 41·5 |
| | 20 | 24·40 | 95·5 | 2·88 | 56·2 | 58·47 | 41·1 |
| | 30 | 24·11 | 94·5 | 2·55 | 56·3 | 58·38 | 40·5 |
| July | 10 | 23·85 | 93·0 | 2·22 | 55·9 | 58·27 | 39·9 |
| | 20 | 23·63 | 91·1 | 1·89 | 55·0 | 58·16 | 39·3 |
| | 30 | 23·46 | 88·9 | 1·58 | 53·6 | 58·04 | 38·6 |
| Aug. | 9 | 23·35 | 86·3 | 1·30 | 51·9 | 57·93 | 37·9 |
| | 19 | 23·29 | 83·5 | 1·06 | 49·8 | 57·82 | 37·2 |
| | 29 | 23·30 | 80·5 | 0·87 | 47·4 | 57·72 | 36·6 |
| Sept. | 8 | 23·37 | 77·0 | 0·74 | 44·8 | 57·64 | 36·1 |
| | 18 | 23·51 | 73·6 | 0·69 | 42·0 | 57·59 | 35·7 |
| | 28 | 23·71 | 70·3 | 0·72 | 39·1 | 57·57 | 35·4 |
| Oct. | 8 | 23·99 | 67·0 | 0·85 | 36·5 | 57·59 | 35·3 |
| | 18 | 24·33 | 63·8 | 1·07 | 34·1 | 57·66 | 35·5 |
| | 28 | 24·73 | 60·8 | 1·38 | 32·1 | 57·77 | 35·9 |
| Nov. | 7 | 25·20 | 58·0 | 1·77 | 30·4 | 57·93 | 36·6 |
| | 17 | 25·72 | 55·6 | 2·24 | 29·3 | 58·13 | 37·6 |
| | 27 | 26·27 | 53·6 | 2·77 | 28·7 | 58·38 | 38·9 |
| Dec. | 7 | 26·85 | 52·0 | 3·34 | 28·7 | 58·66 | 40·4 |
| | 17 | 27·44 | 51·0 | 3·93 | 29·4 | 58·97 | 42·1 |
| | 27 | 28·02 | 50·5 | 4·53 | 30·6 | 59·30 | 43·9 |
| | 37 | 28·57 | 50·6 | 5·12 | 32·3 | 59·63 | 45·9 |

| MARS, 1881. MEAN TIME. | Apparent Declination. Noon. |
|---|---|
| July 3 | 13 4 3·4 |
| 4 | N. 13 18 2·7 |

II. FEBRUARY, 1882.

| AT MEAN NOON. | | | | | | | |
|---|---|---|---|---|---|---|---|
| Day of the Week. | Day of the Month. | THE SUN'S Apparent Declination. | THE SUN'S Var. in 1 hour. | Equation of Time, *to be subtracted from Mean Time.* | Var. in 1 hour. | Sidereal Time. |
| | | ° ′ ″ | ″ | m s | s | h m s |
| *Sun.* | 26 | 8 38 20·1 | 56·14 | 13 4·60 | 0·433 | 22 24 55·61 |
| Mon. | 27 | 8 15 49·0 | 56·44 | 12 53·92 | 0·456 | 22 28 52·16 |
| Tues. | 28 | 7 53 10·8 | 56·73 | 12 42·69 | 0·479 | 22 32 48·71 |

APPARENT PLACES OF STARS, 1882. 333

| AT UPPER TRANSIT OF GREENWICH. | | |
|---|---|---|
| Month and Day | *a* Canis Minoris. (*Procyon*) R.A. | *a* Canis Minoris. (*Procyon*) Dec. N. |
| | h m 7 33 | ° ′ 5 31 |
| | s | ″ |
| Jan. 1 | 9·89 | 24·7 |
| 11 | 10·01 | 23·4 |
| 21 | 10·09 | 22·2 |
| 31 | 10·12 | 21·2 |
| Feb. 10 | 10·10 | 20·4 |
| 20 | 10·03 | 19·8 |
| Mar. 2 | 9·92 | 19·3 |
| 12 | 9·78 | 19·1 |

SATURN, 1882. 259

| MEAN TIME. | | |
|---|---|---|
| Month and Day. | *Apparent* Right Ascension. *Noon.* | *Apparent* Declination. *Noon.* |
| | h m s | ° ′ ″ |
| Feb. 26 | 2 24 45·00 | 12 1 16·2 |
| 27 | 2 25 4·46 | 12 3 7·8 |
| 28 | 2 25 24·22 | N. 12 5 0·6 |

For converting INTERVALS of MEAN SOLAR Time into Equivalent INTERVALS of SIDEREAL Time.

| HOURS. | | | | MINUTES. | | | | | | SECONDS. | | | |
|---|---|---|---|---|---|---|---|---|---|---|---|---|---|
| Hours of Mean Time. | Equivalents in Sidereal Time. | | | Minutes of Mean Time. | Equivalents in Sidereal Time. | | Minutes of Mean Time. | Equivalents in Sidereal Time. | | Seconds of Mean Time. | Equivalents in Sidereal Time. | Seconds of Mean Time. | Equivalents in Sidereal Time. |
| | h | m | s | | m | s | | m | s | | s | | s |
| 1 | 1 | 0 | 9·8565 | 1 | 1 | 0·1643 | 31 | 31 | 5·0925 | 1 | 1·0027 | 31 | 31·0849 |
| 2 | 2 | 0 | 19·7130 | 2 | 2 | 0·3286 | 32 | 32 | 5·2568 | 2 | 2·0055 | 32 | 32·0176 |
| 3 | 3 | 0 | 29·5694 | 3 | 3 | 0·4928 | 33 | 33 | 5·4211 | 3 | 3·0082 | 33 | 33·0904 |
| 4 | 4 | 0 | 39·4259 | 4 | 4 | 0·6571 | 34 | 34 | 5·5853 | 4 | 4·0110 | 34 | 34·0931 |
| 5 | 5 | 0 | 49·2824 | 5 | 5 | 0·8214 | 35 | 35 | 5·7496 | 5 | 5·0137 | 35 | 35·0958 |
| 6 | 6 | 0 | 59·1388 | 6 | 6 | 0·9857 | 36 | 36 | 5·9139 | 6 | 6·0164 | 36 | 36·0986 |
| 7 | 7 | 1 | 8·9953 | 7 | 7 | 1·1499 | 37 | 37 | 6·0782 | 7 | 7·0192 | 37 | 37·1013 |
| 8 | 8 | 1 | 18·8518 | 8 | 8 | 1·3142 | 38 | 38 | 6·2424 | 8 | 8·0219 | 38 | 38·1040 |
| 9 | 9 | 1 | 28·7083 | 9 | 9 | 1·4785 | 39 | 39 | 6·4067 | 9 | 9·0246 | 39 | 39·1068 |
| 10 | 10 | 1 | 38·5647 | 10 | 10 | 1·6428 | 40 | 40 | 6·5710 | 10 | 10·0274 | 40 | 40·1095 |
| 11 | 11 | 1 | 48·4212 | 11 | 11 | 1·8070 | 41 | 41 | 6·7353 | 11 | 11·0301 | 41 | 41·1123 |
| 12 | 12 | 1 | 58·2777 | 12 | 12 | 1·9713 | 42 | 42 | 6·8995 | 12 | 12·0329 | 42 | 42·1150 |
| 13 | 13 | 2 | 8·1342 | 13 | 13 | 2·1356 | 43 | 43 | 7·0638 | 13 | 13·0356 | 43 | 43·1177 |
| 14 | 14 | 2 | 17·9906 | 14 | 14 | 2·2998 | 44 | 44 | 7·2281 | 14 | 14·0383 | 44 | 44·1205 |
| 15 | 15 | 2 | 27·8471 | 15 | 15 | 2·4641 | 45 | 45 | 7·3924 | 15 | 15·0411 | 45 | 45·1232 |
| 16 | 16 | 2 | 37·7036 | 16 | 16 | 2·6284 | 46 | 46 | 7·5566 | 16 | 16·0438 | 46 | 46·1259 |
| 17 | 17 | 2 | 47·5600 | 17 | 17 | 2·7927 | 47 | 47 | 7·7209 | 17 | 17·0465 | 47 | 47·1287 |
| 18 | 18 | 2 | 57·4165 | 18 | 18 | 2·9569 | 48 | 48 | 7·8852 | 18 | 18·0493 | 48 | 48·1314 |
| 19 | 19 | 3 | 7·2730 | 19 | 19 | 3·1212 | 49 | 49 | 8·0495 | 19 | 19·0520 | 49 | 49·1342 |
| 20 | 20 | 3 | 17·1259 | 20 | 20 | 3·2855 | 50 | 50 | 8·2137 | 20 | 20·0548 | 50 | 50·1369 |
| 21 | 21 | 3 | 26·9859 | 21 | 21 | 3·4498 | 51 | 51 | 8·3780 | 21 | 21·0575 | 51 | 51·1396 |
| 22 | 22 | 3 | 36·8424 | 22 | 22 | 3·6140 | 52 | 52 | 8·5423 | 22 | 22·0602 | 52 | 52·1424 |
| 23 | 23 | 3 | 46·6989 | 23 | 23 | 3·7783 | 53 | 53 | 8·7066 | 23 | 23·0630 | 53 | 53·1451 |
| 24 | 24 | 3 | 56·5554 | 24 | 24 | 3·9426 | 54 | 54 | 8·8708 | 24 | 24·0657 | 54 | 54·1479 |
| | | | | 25 | 25 | 4·1069 | 55 | 55 | 9·0351 | 25 | 25·0685 | 55 | 55·1506 |
| | | | | 26 | 26 | 4·2711 | 56 | 56 | 9·1994 | 26 | 26·0712 | 56 | 56·1533 |
| | | | | 27 | 27 | 4·4354 | 57 | 57 | 9·3637 | 27 | 27·0739 | 57 | 57·1561 |
| | | | | 28 | 28 | 4·5997 | 58 | 58 | 9·5279 | 28 | 28·0767 | 58 | 58·1588 |
| | | | | 29 | 29 | 4·7640 | 59 | 59 | 9·6922 | 29 | 29·0794 | 59 | 59·1615 |
| | | | | 30 | 30 | 4·9282 | 60 | 60 | 9·8565 | 30 | 30·0821 | 60 | 60·1643 |

## OPINIONS OF THE PRESS.—*Continued.*

"The author of this work states in his preface that 'the particular aim of the treatise is to furnish seamen with thoroughly *practical* hints, such as are not found in the ordinary works on Navigation,' and he has stuck to his text. The work abounds in excellent and sound advice on every subject and science with which a navigator should be acquainted; and in discussing instruments, books, and methods, though there are no novelties, there is much practical information that will be serviceable alike to old and young."—*Nautical Magazine.*

"The great charm of the work is that the author does not ascend to what some term the scientific; he is never too learned, but has well carried out the task he sets himself in the preface.

"In a pleasant, attractive, and sailor-like style he deals with what Captain Bedford, in the 'Sailor's Pocket Book,' so well terms 'the important simplicities' of navigation. The mariner's compass, the sextant, chronometer, chart, dividers, parallel rulers, log and lead, station pointer, barometer and thermometer, are each in turn treated upon, and valuable 'wrinkles' with regard to their manipulation and individual peculiarities are given to the public.

"These 'wrinkles' are the result of the observations of a sailor who has not only gone to sea with his eyes open, but who also has had the industry to read and weigh the opinions of others.

"The student of 'Wrinkles' will not only derive advantage from the experience of its observant author, but he will also find himself introduced to the best men and works connected with the instruments and subjects treated upon. Numerous examples and illustrations illuminate the ordinary letterpress."—*United Service Gazette.*

"Nautical works are almost as 'plentiful as blackberries,' and it is rather difficult for an author in these days to bring anything before the public in the nautical way which has not already appeared in print. Captain Lecky has, however, proved that there is no rule without an exception, for his 'Wrinkles' in Practical Navigation is quite an exception to the general run of instructive books on navigation, for he takes the sailor from the 'cradle to the grave,' and tells him what to do when he first leaves the former until he finishes his education. The information conveyed in 'Wrinkles' is told in a thoroughly readable way, and put in a form at once concise and intelligible; and however full the seaman's library may be, we are sure that he cannot do better than find space on his book-shelf for 'Wrinkles in Practical Navigation.'"—*Hunt's Yachting Magazine.*

"Captain Lecky's 'Wrinkles' may be accepted with confidence; the vast amount of matter which the work contains is astonishing, but, after a careful perusal, competent readers will, we think, admit that not a single page has been penned in vain.

"The most ancient of mariners can, we believe, obtain from Captain Lecky's work a large supply of useful 'Wrinkles.'"—*Army and Navy Gazette.*

"A valuable addition to the science of practical navigation is the work under the above title by Captain Lecky of the American Steamship Line. Captain Lecky's announced purpose in the preparation of this volume 'is to furnish seamen with thoroughly *practical* hints, such as are not found in the ordinary works on navigation,' and he has accomplished this in a large degree, not the least valuable feature of his production being its numerous illustrations and diagrams, which ought to make their subjects clear to the dullest mind. The appearance of such a work on navigation should be warmly welcomed by seamen, whose arduous vocation generally prevents them from giving much thought or time to investigations other than those which lie near the surface of things.

"But the general public, as well as navigators, have much to learn from Capt. Lecky's '*Wrinkles.*' The author conclusively demolishes the theory that in approaching icebergs thermometric tests of the water can be confidently relied on to reveal through darkness or fog the proximity of these floating dangers. He also throws out some valuable hints on fog navigation, and forcibly overthrows the plea for high speed in fogs, especially when near land, and trusting to that 'stupid old pilot—dead reckoning.' To the general reader his chapter on 'Weatherology' will present peculiar attractions. Captain Lecky has evidently been a keen weather observer at sea, and has informed himself of most that has been advanced by modern meteorologists on the 'law of storms.' It is to be regretted, however, both for science and seamanship, that he seems to underrate the benefits the navigator has derived, or is likely to derive, from concerted meteorological observations on the ocean. 'If,' he says, 'concerted action avails so little, what chance has an isolated individual, such as the commander of a ship, who has nothing to guide him but his own local observations, of satisfying himself as to the weather he may expect for even a single coming day?' Captain Lecky overlooks the fact that, as yet, no 'concerted action' for investigation of ocean meteorology at all commensurate with the magnitude of the marine storm-field has ever been taken; and, unhappily, while giving his nautical brethren minute instructions as to almost everything that concerns them to know or to do, he omits to spur them up to the work of co-operating in the great modern international scheme of marine weather-research, designed to supply the very lack he seemingly deplores. If Captain Lecky and half of the commanders of the merchant marine, who will read his book with eager interest, would enter heartily on this observational work, and contribute their simultaneous ocean weather reports to the signal service, the results deduced from such co-operation might hasten that better day he hopes for, in which the seaman will not have to depend solely upon his own individual weather experience, but will go on his ocean course having his way, so to speak, 'blazed' through the winds and latitudes and longitudes, and will be in possession of knowledge by which he can, in a large degree, forecast to-morrow's 'probabilities.'"—*Public Ledger and Daily Transcript, Philadelphia.*

## OPINIONS OF THE PRESS.—*Continued.*

"A practical and direct help to merchant captains will be found in a work lately published by Messrs. George Philip and Son, of Fleet Street, London. The author, Captain S. T. S. Lecky, R.N.R., is well-known in the mercantile marine as a careful, clever, and scientific navigator, and he has brought a large amount of his knowledge and practical ability to bear upon the present publication. The aim of the author has evidently been to convey, in simple language, thoroughly practical hints, and he has condensed, in a clear succinct style, the teachings of standard works and the results of his own experience into a handy and clever work. The author states in his preface that 'The volume contains but little that is claimed as strictly original; it is based upon life-long observation, matter gleaned from the works of men of repute, and information derived from intercourse with shipmasters and the cloth generally.'—Notwithstanding this modest preface, Captain Lecky has thrown out some valuable hints, and has given his information in a very sensible form. This is particularly applicable to his selection of books necessary for reference and guidance, and his list of indispensable nautical instruments of navigation. The Chapter on the 'Mariner's Compass' contains a large amount of useful information, and will be read with interest by all practical navigators. His remarks on the marine chronometer, the sextant, and the artificial and sea-horizons, form the subjects of three very able chapters, and will well repay careful perusal. This applies also to his observations on the use of instruments, their adjustment, and comparative value, and, although there is little that is novel, his "wrinkles" are given in a sailor-like and concise form. The astronomical portion of the volume is all good and practical, and such as all who have charge of life and property at sea should have a knowledge of. Especially clear and concise are his remarks on "Latitude by meridian altitude," and his "Longitude by chronometer," while those chapters devoted to the subjects of "shaping a course," and "The danger angle and correct determination of distance from land," will commend themselves to all practical and enquiring minds.

"The author has collected some useful notes on tides, currents, waves and breakers, which should be of much service to those interested in such physical phenomena.

"The book is well printed, and contains 70 or 80 illustrations, including some carefully executed physical maps."—*The Englishman, Calcutta.*

"This work is certainly the very best of its class ever emanating from a practical seaman, and to us it was a real source of pleasure to read it through, as we did from preface to appendix. Captain Lecky has written in a charming, off-hand style, and from the start captures his reader and leads him on in deep interest through the thirty-three chapters of his work. He makes the study of navigation a real pleasure, and as attractive as a romance, yet full, practical, and correct. We claim to know something of 'navigation wrinkles,' but Captain Lecky has quickly and tersely taught us how little we really did know. He is not only a keen observer, but has cleverly adapted the good opinions of others, and blended them so adroitly with those of his own, which are ripened with experience, that the work stands without a peer in the literature of things pertaining to the science of navigation. There is no work that we know of that we can so urgently recommend to the practical navigator as this one. It is a library in itself. It is the work of a true sailor, and one whom we must esteem very highly for his superior talents and attainments. No work of its class ever received higher commendation from the British press than 'Wrinkles' has, and deservedly so. It is a work that can be understood by the professional mariner of any grade, and being devoid of the 'wholly too learned,' is suited to all degrees of progress in the study of navigation; and even the oldest master mariner can learn from its pages very much that is valuable, while to the 'youngster' it is invaluable. We hope our shipmasters will secure a copy of this work, and we feel assured that they will thank us for pointing out its existence and merits. Captain Lecky is now in command of one of the American Line steamers, and hence he is well posted in the Atlantic trade, and was in Sir Thomas Brassey's famous yacht *Sunbeam*, in her cruise around the world. We congratulate the captain upon the results of his labours, and he certainly deserves the thanks of his brethren everywhere."—*The Nautical Gazette* (New York).

---

## List of Shipowners who have supplied copies of Captain Lecky's book to their vessels.

PENINSULAR AND ORIENTAL STEAM NAVIGATION CO. (53 copies).

PACIFIC STEAM NAVIGATION CO., LIVERPOOL.
INMAN STEAMSHIP CO. ,,
RATHBONE BROS. ,,
ALFRED BOOTH & CO. ,,
ISMAY, IMRIE & CO. ,,
BRITISH SHIPOWNERS CO. ,,
LAMPORT & HOLT. ,,
G. H. FLETCHER & CO. ,,
AFRICAN ROYAL MAIL STEAMSHIP CO. ,,
TAYLOR, CAMERON & CO. ,,
RICHARDSON, SPENCE & CO. ,,
J. D. NEWTON, ESQ. ,,

DONALD CURRIE & CO. LONDON.
GELLATLY, HANKEY & SEWELL, ,,
GRAY, DAWES & CO. ,,
M'INTYRE BROS. & CO., of NEWCASTLE.
WILSON & SONS, HULL.
RED STAR LINE, NEW YORK and ANTWERP.
ULSTER STEAMSHIP CO., BELFAST.
ROBERT HENDERSON, ESQ., ,,
WILLIAM GRAY & CO., WEST HARTLEPOOL.
AMERICAN STEAMSHIP CO., PHILADELPHIA.
BUREAU OF NAVIGATION, WASHINGTON, FOR UNITED STATES NAVY—50 copies.

## EXTRACTS FROM LETTERS RECEIVED BY THE AUTHOR.

**From Captain Sir Fred. Evans, R.N., F.R.S.**
*Hydrographer to the Admiralty.*

"You deserve success, for your work contains a great deal of useful information, well prepared from sound practical experience."

**From A. C. Johnston, Esq., R.N., M.A.**
*Naval Instructor H.M.S. "Britannia," Training Ship for Naval Cadets.*

"The more I see of your book the better pleased I am with it. It is quite a treasury of nautical knowledge, and contains within its pages an amount of information which could only otherwise be acquired by years of actual practical experience at sea. It is correct in principle, and a safe guide to the seaman; and no one who aspires to become a thoroughly efficient navigator should be without it. I trust that your labours may be rewarded in a manner commensurate with their deserts."

**From Sir William Thomson, F.R.S.**
*The University, Glasgow.*

"I have looked into your book a good deal, and have been greatly pleased with it. I approved thoroughly of everything I saw."

**From Captain Fred. Geo. Bedford, R.N.**
*Captain of the Royal Naval College, Greenwich.*

"It strikes me as being a most useful book, and one that will commend itself from its being so eminently practical, and placing the matter before people in clear, homely language."

**From Clements R. Markham, Esq.**
*Honorary Secretary Royal Geographical Society.*

"I have been reading with much interest your 'Wrinkles in Practical Navigation.' It appears to me to be a most useful and opportune work, and just what is needed by great numbers of people."

**From John Hartnup, Esq.**
*Astronomer to the Mersey Dock and Harbour Estate, Bidston Observatory.*

"In accordance with your desire, I have looked over your book on Navigation. During the past thirty years I have been in the habit of conversing with officers in the mercantile marine on subjects connected with the various methods which have been devised for finding the position of a ship at sea, and I have been strongly impressed with the importance of *short practical rules* for their guidance in all calculations. I have not heretofore met with a work which has appeared to me so well adapted to meet their requirements as 'Wrinkles in Practical Navigation,' and therefore think you have conferred a great benefit on mariners by its publication."

**From Captain Henry Toynbee, F.R.A.S.**
*Superintendent of the Meteorological Office, 116, Victoria Street, London.*

"So far as I can give an opinion, it carries out the idea suggested by its name ('Wrinkles') very well, and does not frighten the sailor by too many algebraical signs. It does, in fact, give a large amount of experience in a chatty form."

**From W. C. Bergen,**
*Teacher of Navigation, and author of several Works on Navigation, Sunderland.*

"I have read your work, entitled 'Wrinkles in Practical Navigation,' with much interest. I think it contains a very great amount of information useful to captains and officers of ships, presented to them in a style which they will thoroughly understand."

EXTRACTS FROM LETTERS.—*Continued.*

**From Captain W. B. Duncan,**
*Teacher of Navigation, South Shields.*

"I like your 'Wrinkles' exceedingly. Owners, for their own interest, should supply a copy as part of the ship's stores."

---

**From Captain John Halder,**
*South Shields.*

"I think the title you have chosen for your work is an admirable one,—they are 'Wrinkles' indeed."

---

**From Captain Henry Morrison,**
*Senior Officer American Steamship Co., United States Mail Steamer "Ohio."*

"To my mind you have conferred a great boon on the profession, as the book meets a want that all familiar with the subject will admit has been long felt."

---

**From Captain Henry F. Watt,**
*Liverpool.*

"You have, it appears to me, done a solid and good piece of work, and it has merit enough to ensure it success."

---

**From H. M. Hozier, Esq.**
*Secretary for Lloyd's, London.*

"The Committee of Lloyd's have ordered a copy of your work entitled 'Wrinkles in Practical Navigation' to be supplied to the Library of this Institution."

---

**From Captain W. W. Kiddle, R.N.**
*Principal Officer of the Board of Trade, Dublin.*

"I have looked over your book with much interest, and must congratulate you on having rendered a great service to seamen in general. My opinion is that it will be translated into foreign languages; for I am not aware of a similar work in any continental marine. The type, engravings, and general get-up, are also good; and you may rest assured that it will be long before there is a rival in the field."

---

**From R. C. Carrington, Esq.**
*Indian Marine Survey Department, Calcutta.*

"Your book contains a vast amount of information, and really useful 'Wrinkles' to a thinking man."

---

**From Captain D. Hume,**
*Superintendent Dock Master, Hull.*

"Such is my opinion of the book, that I think it ought to be supplied to every foreign-going vessel (whether sail or steam), and I shall take every opportunity of pointing this out to shipowners.

"Speaking from my own experience of sea life, I should indeed have been only too glad to have had it myself when afloat. So clearly are some of the difficult problems of navigation explained and illustrated, that, to say the least of it, the thanks of all worthy of the name of seamen are due to Captain Lecky for his valuable publication. I hope it will become a standard work, and take its proper place accordingly."

---

**From Sir Thomas Brassey, K.C.B., M.P.**
*Civil Lord of the Admiralty.*

"I have gone carefully through your book, and think it admirable."

EXTRACTS FROM LETTERS.—*Continued.*

**From Alex. Sinclair, Esq.**
*Manager African Steamship Co.*

"There seems to be but one opinion about it, namely, that it is a very valuable and instructive handbook for masters of ships."

---

**From Archibald T. Miller, R.N.**
*Commanding School Frigate "Conway."*

"It affords me very real pleasure to be able to speak in the highest terms of your most valuable work '*Wrinkles.*' Having heard of its preparation for many years past, I am not surprised to find it containing the ripe fruit of long service at sea, with a very wide experience in all sorts of ships and services. The book is most interesting, as well as instructive; and I have heard a landsman declare that he found it more absorbing than any novel. If sailors do this also, and study closely the chapter on compasses (even if nothing more), we will hear of far fewer disasters from 'suspected currents,' and what not. So much is the value of the book recognized, that it is proposed to give it as a prize on board here; and I may mention that a Liverpool shipowner recently sent us six copies for my lads to study."

---

**From Captain John C. Almond,**
*Nautical Inspector Peninsular and Oriental Steam Navigation Company.*

"I have made the acquaintance of your book, and think very highly of it. The title is well chosen. The 'Wrinkles' cover a pleasant face. A work of this sort was much wanted, and fills a gap that previously existed in every Nautical Library. It is useful as an *aide de memoire* to the old Salt, and a mentor to the young one. A copy will be placed in the chart-room of each of our vessels, and in future will be included in the list of navigational books supplied to every new ship. Captain Angove—our Marine Superintendent—wishes me to say he thoroughly agrees with my estimation of the merits and practical utility of the 'Wrinkles.' If you think it worth while, you are at liberty to make any use of the same."

---

**From Arthur Hill Coates, Esq.**
*Late Honorary Secretary Ulster Royal Yacht Club.*

"I am very glad, but not surprised, to hear your book is getting off so well. To yachtsmen I think it will be of the greatest use, because they have not the same opportunity of learning the 'Wrinkles' from experience that most young merchant officers possess. Amateurs, when they command their own vessels—now not unfrequently the case—have no one to go to when they get into a fog, but must just worry through by themselves. Your book at such times comes to their aid, and gives them the 'short cut,' so to speak."

---

**From Captain John W. King (Ship "Fearnought"),**
*5, Broad Street, Penryn, Cornwall.*

"A word about your 'Wrinkles.' I think it altogether the plainest and most simple book on Navigation I have ever read, and just what we sailors wanted."

---

**From Captain J. G. Walker, U.S.N.**
*Chief of Bureau of Navigation, Washington.*

"I consider that your book 'Wrinkles in Practical Navigation' will be of great service to officers qualifying themselves for examination, and would serve as an excellent work of reference for commanding officers. I have pleasure in sending a copy of a letter received from Rear-Admiral Ammen referring to it."

EXTRACTS FROM LETTERS.—*Continued.*

**From Rear-Admiral Ammen, U.S.N.**

*To Captain J. G. Walker, U.S.N., Chief of Bureau of Navigation.*

"One of my former Naval friends has asked my examination of 'Wrinkles in Practical Navigation,' by Captain Lecky, R.N.R. This I have done attentively, and beg leave to bring it to your notice. It would in general prove an intelligent reminder and guide of procedure in what officers should have learned from text-books, and thus serve a most useful purpose. I appreciate the 40 pages on Deviation and the Correction of compass errors; the more perhaps, as I had aided in the appointment of a gentleman in our Navy of high scientific attainments with an especial view of developing the subject in some such practical form; and although Chief of Bureau at the time, and the gentleman was under my orders, I failed to attain my end. As a reminder, if not an instructor, I consider the book practically of great value."

---

**From Rear-Admiral C. R. P. Rodgers, U.S.N.**

*To Captain Jas. S. Biddle, U.S.N.*

"Captain Lecky's book seems to me an admirable compilation, comprehensive and well arranged, and likely to be very useful to all sea officers, especially to those of the Merchant Service. So far as I have been able to examine it, it has impressed me very favourably, and I quite agree with you in thinking it might well be placed in our ships' libraries."

---

**From Fred. C. Green, Esq.,**

*Woodside Cottage, Breightmet, near Bolton.*

"As an Amateur Navigator I am deriving great benefit from your 'Wrinkles.' It is just the right kind of book to enable one to make the most of one's limited experience, and it is impossible to say which part of it is the most valuable. The 'Horizontal Angle' and 'Danger Angle' were a new idea to me, and I shall certainly practice them. I have never had much to do with Deviation of the Compass, as I have mostly been shipmates with lead ballast and wooden hulls, but your chapter on Compass Correction has cleared up what always appeared very misty to me before. Also the Table of Corrections for Johnson's method is an acquisition: for some time I had worked by the intersectional method, but constantly scoring lines on the charts is objectionable, and caused me to resort to proportional logarithms—which, however, is a long and cumbrous operation. Now that I have your book it is certain that I shall never do so again."

---

**From Campbell M. Hepworth, Esq., F.M.S.**

*Commanding R.M.S. "Danube," Union Steam Packet Co.*

"With regard to your valuable works 'Wrinkles,' and 'The Danger Angle and Off-Shore Distance Tables,' I have recommended them right and left, and in all cases have been considered a benefactor for having done so. For myself, I believe it is impossible to estimate the amount of good they have done already, and are destined to do in years to come. Have they been translated into foreign languages? If not, they should be."

---

**From Captain S. P. H. Atkinson.**

*Late Ship "British Peer."*

"Having read over your work entitled 'Wrinkles in Practical Navigation' several times, I have no hesitation in saying that it is the most useful and comprehensive treatise on the many and various subjects necessary to safe navigation which I have ever met with. I feel sure that it will prove of much practical value to the older members as well as the rising generation of the Mercantile Marine, in tending to eradicate from their minds many prejudices which at present exist in favour of working out problems in navigation by erroneous and non-conclusive methods. It seems to me also that your remarks on Compass Adjustment are the clearest, most easily comprehended, and most instructive of any that I have come across. I had read Towson's before, but, through the want of accompanying diagrams, used to get somewhat confused, and I am very confident that your elucidation of the subject will be much more generally appreciated."

*(Over).*

## OPINIONS OF THE PRESS.

"'The Danger Angle and Off-Shore Distance Tables,' is an excellent little work, from the pen of the Author of 'Wrinkles,' whose name is fast becoming familiar to every Certificated Officer in the British Merchant Service. The unpretentious little volume before us cannot fail to establish its right to a place in the library of all careful navigators.

"It consists of two parts. Part I. containing tables for heights from 50 to 1,000 feet. Distances from the tenth of a mile to five miles. Part II. (*a*) containing tables for heights from 200 to 6,000 feet. Distances from five to seventy miles. Part II. (*b*) Heights from 6,000 to 12,000 feet. Distances from ten to eighty miles. Part II. (*c*) Heights from 12,500 to 18,000 feet. Distances fourteen to one hundred miles. Part I. is explained as only to be used in connection with objects lying *on* or *within* the bounding line of the observer's horizon. Part II. has been calculated for objects *beyond* that boundary.

"The advantages of this little work are evident at a glance. The errors in estimating the distance of vessels from shore too often lead to casualties, for which navigators are sometimes brought up with a round turn by Courts of Inquiry; and while the Author does not champion this method of computing a ship's off-shore distance as superior to all others, he, nevertheless, puts in a compact form a system that the experience of many years has shown to be handy and reliable when used with discretion. The ease and simplicity with which, when coasting, a vessel's position can be fixed; the clue it affords to the detection of faulty steering, compass errors, and currents, together with the sense of security and consequent comfort of mind the painstaking mariner is sure to realize by its use, are all so many arguments in favour of the method.

"The Author's reference to the case of a vessel standing in from seaward, to make her port, and being able to define her *exact* position, and shape a course for it before the coast-line is even visible, and this with scarcely any trouble, is an illustration that navigators will appreciate, and one with which numbers are experimentally familiar, to their intense satisfaction.

"We are half inclined to quote some of the Author's examples, but are persuaded that for the small cost involved, few Masters or Officers will be content to remain unpossessed of this handy book, and will 'read, mark, learn, and inwardly digest' for themselves."—*Mercantile Marine Service Association* ***REPORTER.***

---

"The Merchant Service may be congratulated on being able to number on its muster roll one whose sympathies are so entirely with his brother sailors, that, whilst in the execution of his multifarious duties, he still finds time to compile and prepare for publication works which cannot fail to be appreciated by navigators. It has afforded us pleasure to note the increasing demand for "Wrinkles in Practical Navigation," and to receive from our readers afloat testimony of the value of that work. With the knowledge that the publication is being eagerly sought after, we may predict a similar expression of approval on the part of the painstaking men, who will be pleased to learn that Captain Lecky has made a further contribution to standard nautical works.

"The Danger Angle and Off-shore Distance Tables" has just been issued. It is a work which reflects great credit upon the author, and can only have been completed after very great labour. Casualties befalling ships are frequently found to have arisen from erroneous estimates of their distance from the land. The method of determining this point has hithetto been difficult in practice, owing to the absence of tables to assist the navigator to ascertain by simple reference thereto the vessel's distance from any object of known height. The mariner will now find that the difficulty has been removed, and that by availing himself of the information given in this book, he has gained possession of an additional safeguard to navigation, and one which will recommend itself by its simplicity and easy application.

"Many years' experience and unceasing observation must have been required to test and to compute tables so comprehensive, and in recommending it to our readers we are confident that the work will prove an invaluable friend to the mariner, as it is perfectly sound throughout, and only requires to be known to become universally adopted."—*British Merchant Service Journal.*

Lightning Source UK Ltd.
Milton Keynes UK
UKOW05f0752150616

276268UK00019B/487/P